MW01030589

# The World as an Architectural Project

# The World as an Architectural Project

Hashim Sarkis and Roi Salgueiro Barrio with Gabriel Kozlowski

The MIT Press

Cambridge, Massachusetts

London, England

**The World as an Architectural Project**

Authors: Hashim Sarkis and Roi Salgueiro Barrio with Gabriel Kozlowski

Principal Investigator: Hashim Sarkis

Lead Research and Writing (Entry Numbers):

Roi Salgueiro Barrio (1–6, 8–13, 15–20, 22–26, 29–34, 36–39, 41–45, 47–48, 50)

Gabriel Kozlowski (6–7, 14, 19, 21, 27–29, 35, 36, 40, 46, 49)

Initial Research Collaborators: Daniel Ibáñez and Pablo Pérez-Ramos

Manuscript Editor: Xhulio Binjaku

Copyeditor: Patsy Baudoin

Proofreading: Matthew Abbate and Michael Sims

Illustrators: Milap Dixit and Nitzan Zilberman

Graphic Design and Cover: Gabriel Kozlowski

© 2019 Massachusetts Institute of Technology

All rights reserved. No part of this book may be reproduced in any form by any electronic or mechanical means (including photocopying, recording, or information storage and retrieval) without permission in writing from the publisher.

This book was set in Avenir Next, Avenir Next Condensed, and Adobe Caslon Pro. Printed and bound in Canada.

Library of Congress Cataloging-in-Publication Data is available.

ISBN 978-0-262-04396-0

10 9 8 7 6 5 4 3 2 1

## Acknowledgments

This book stems from "The World According to Architecture," a course and research project initiated at the Harvard Graduate School of Design and further developed and consolidated at the MIT School of Architecture and Planning. Over the past six years, we have benefited from the dialogue with a number of architects and scholars in the conceptual development of the book. Among them, special credit should be given to Peder Anker, Eve Blau, Sibel Bozdogan, Neil Brenner, Adrià Carbonell, Daniel Daou, Daniel Ibáñez, Rania Ghosn, El Hadi Jazairy, Nikos Katsikis, Jarrad Morgan, Erkin Ozay, Pablo Pérez-Ramos, Chris Roach, Dima Srouji, and Brent Sturlaugson. The numerous students who have participated in seminars about this research have also helped us notably to better frame the topic. The research project has generated several outputs, including papers published in a variety of venues and a traveling exhibition that was featured at the Yale School of Architecture, Lisbon Triennale 2016, and the School of Architecture at the University of São Paulo. This book has benefited enormously from these earlier products and their reception.

We would like to thank many of the architects included in the book, as well as many of their heirs and legal representatives, for having generously allowed us to reproduce their work. Our gratitude to Kykah Bernardes, Lonnie van Brummelen, Andrea Branzi, Angelo Bucci, Luc Deleu, Design Earth, Yona Friedman, Siebren de Haan, Renata Hejduk, Joyce Hsiang, Frauke Huber, Regina Khidekel, Uwe H. Martin, Bimal Mendis, Peter Mörtenböck, Helge Mooshammer, Juan Navarro Baldeweg, Franco Purini, Volker Sayn, Carl Steinitz, Urban Theory Lab, Elina Zenetou and Dinos Michalaros, the Arcosanti Archives, the Estate of R. Buckminster Fuller, the Constantinos and Emma Doxiadis Foundation, the Zaha Hadid Foundation, the Het Nieuwe Instituut, the Foundation Le Corbusier, the Mundaneum, the Fondazione Aldo Rossi, the Valparaiso School of Architecture, the Department of Special Collections at Stanford University Libraries, the Frances Loeb Library at Harvard Graduate School of Design, the gta Archives/ ETH Zürich, and the MIT ACT Archives and Special Collections.

The help of several individuals has been essential to obtain information and establish relations with some architects and archives; among them particularly Benjamin Albrecht, Panos Dragonas, Ginés Garrido, Chiara Geroldi, Ignacio Moreno, Melina Philippou, and Silvia Tagliazucchi. The archives that preserve the legacy of architects represented in the book have been very generous in facilitating the publication of their images.

The production of this book would not have been possible without the support of MIT. We would like to thank Melissa Vaughn, who always provided excellent guidance on the shape and content of the book. Peggy Cain, Makeela Searles, Dineen Doucette, Ramona Allen, and Ken Goldsmith all helped in different ways in facilitating the research and production of the book.

On a personal level, Diala Ezzeddine and Dunia Sarkis; Carmen Parga and Alvar Salgueiro Parga; and Michelle Mendlewicz and Maria Kozlowski for championing the different iterations of this project.

We would like to thank Patsy Baudoin for her help in editing the manuscript, and the reviewers MIT Press selected for their valuable comments. Last but not least, our gratitude to Victoria Hindley and Gabriela Bueno Gibbs, as well as Janet Rossi and the production staff of the MIT Press, for their constant support of this project.

## Catalogue List

## Catalogue List

## List of Themes

**Themes.** Architects

9 **Abstraction.** Yves Klein and Claude Parent / Volker Sayn / Fritz Haller / Archizoom Associates / Superstudio / Rem Koolhaas with Madelon Vriesendorp / Zaha Hadid / Franco Purini / Angelo Bucci

3 **Aerial View.** Élisée Reclus and Louis Bonnier / Le Corbusier and Paul Otlet / Rudolf Schwarz

5 **Automation.** Constant Nieuwenhuys / Kiyonori Kikutake / Takis Zenetos / Sergio Bernardes / Fritz Haller

9 **Autonomy.** Lazar Khidekel / Ivan Leonidov / Mikhail Okhitovich and Moisei Ginzburg / Raimund Abraham / Paolo Soleri / Rem Koolhaas with Madelon Vriesendorp / Zaha Hadid / Aldo Rossi / John Hejduk

6 **Circulation.** Arturo Soria y Mata / Georgii Krutikov / Le Corbusier and ASCORAL / Yona Friedman / Volker Sayn / Alan Boutwell and Michael Mitchell

5 **Colonialism.** Herman Sörgel / Rudolf Steiger / Erwin Anton Gutkind / Alberto Cruz, Godofredo Iommi, et al. / T.O.P. Office (Luc Deleu et al.)

5 **Cybernetics.** Alexei Gutnov et al. / Archigram (David Greene with Michael Webb) / Takis Zenetos / Sergio Bernardes / Juan Navarro Baldeweg

7 **Decentralization.** Bruno Taut / Mikhail Okhitovich and Moisei Ginzburg / Le Corbusier and ASCORAL / Rudolf Schwarz / Erwin Anton Gutkind / Alexei Gutnov et al. / Juan Navarro Baldeweg

4 **Ecology.** Alison and Peter Smithson / Sergio Bernardes / Paolo Soleri / Design Earth (Rania Ghosn and El Hadi Jazairy)

5 **Environmental Control.** R. Buckminster Fuller / Herman Sörgel / R. Buckminster Fuller et al. / Yves Klein and Claude Parent / Superstudio

10 **Geography.** Patrick Geddes / Élisée Reclus and Louis Bonnier / Bruno Taut / Lazar Khidekel / Le Corbusier and Paul Otlet / Rudolf Schwarz / Alexei Gutnov et al. / Vittorio Gregotti et al. / Saverio Muratori / Angelo Bucci

7 **Geopolitics.** Bruno Taut / Herman Sörgel / Rudolf Steiger / Alberto Cruz, Godofredo Iommi, et al. / T.O.P Office (Luc Deleu et al.) / Neil Brenner and Urban Theory Lab / Carl Steinitz

13 **Geo-visualization.** Patrick Geddes / Élisée Reclus and Louis Bonnier / Rudolf Steiger / R. Buckminster Fuller et al. / Constantinos Doxiadis / Alberto Cruz, Godofredo Iommi, et al. / Vittorio Gregotti et al. / Saverio Muratori / T.O.P. Office (Luc Deleu et al.) / Neil Brenner and Urban Theory Lab / Carl Steinitz / Design Earth / Plan B (Joyce Hsiang and Bimal Mendis)

5 **Human-Earth System.** Bruno Taut / R. Buckminster Fuller et al. / Saverio Muratori / Paolo Soleri / Design Earth (Rania Ghosn and El Hadi Jazairy)

4 **Human-Nature Split.** Georgii Krutikov / Kiyonori Kikutake / Takis Zenetos / Zaha Hadid

## List of Themes

**Themes.** Architects

4 **Immateriality.** R. Buckminster Fuller / Yves Klein and Claude Parent / Archigram (David Greene with Michael Webb) / Zaha Hadid

7 **Infrastructure.** Lazar Khidekel / Herman Sörgel / Alison and Peter Smithson / Yves Klein and Claude Parent / Yona Friedman / Archizoom Associates / Plan B (Joyce Hsiang and Bimal Mendis)

3 **Interiorization.** Constant Nieuwenhuys / Alan Boutwell and Michael Mitchell / Archizoom Associates

5 **Linearity.** Arturo Soria y Mata / Le Corbusier and ASCORAL / Constantinos Doxiadis / Raimund Abraham / Volker Sayn

3 **Megastructure.** Kiyonori Kikutake / Volker Sayn / Alan Boutwell and Michael Mitchell

8 **Monumentality.** Le Corbusier and Paul Otlet / Viktor Kalmykov / Raimund Abraham / Paolo Soleri / Superstudio / Aldo Rossi / Design Earth (Rania Ghosn and El Hadi Jazairy) / Angelo Bucci

5 **Nomadism.** Mikhail Okhitovich and Moisei Ginzburg / Viktor Kalmykov / Constant Nieuwenhuys / Sergio Bernardes / John Hejduk

9 **Parallelism.** Lazar Khidekel / Georgii Krutikov / Viktor Kalmykov / Alison and Peter Smithson / Constant Nieuwenhuys / Yona Friedman / Archigram (David Greene with Michael Webb) / Takis Zenetos / Alan Boutwell and Michael Mitchell

6 **Place(lessness).** Patrick Geddes / Ivan Leonidov / Yona Friedman / Alberto Cruz, Godofredo Iommi, et al. / Aldo Rossi / Franco Purini

6 **Remoteness.** R. Buckminster Fuller / Georgii Krutikov / Viktor Kalmykov / Kiyonori Kikutake / Raimund Abraham / Angelo Bucci

6 **Taxonomy.** Patrick Geddes / Le Corbusier and Paul Otlet / John Hejduk / T.O.P. Office (Luc Deleu et al.) / Carl Steinitz / Plan B (Joyce Hsiang and Bimal Mendis)

9 **Telecommunications.** R. Buckminster Fuller / Ivan Leonidov / Mikhail Okhitovich and Moisei Ginzburg / R. Buckminster Fuller et al. / Alison and Peter Smithson / Archigram (David Greene with Michael Webb) / Juan Navarro Baldeweg / Superstudio / Franco Purini

4 **Territorial Gestalt.** Le Corbusier and ASCORAL / Constantinos Doxiadis / Vittorio Gregotti et al. / Saverio Muratori

4 **Territorial Intensification.** Rudolf Schwarz / Erwin Anton Gutkind / Vittorio Gregotti et al. / Neil Brenner and Urban Theory Lab

5 **Total Urbanization.** Alexei Gutnov et al. / Archizoom Associates / Rem Koolhaas with Madelon Vriesendorp / Neil Brenner and Urban Theory Lab / Plan B (Joyce Hsiang and Bimal Mendis)

8 **Typology.** Arturo Soria y Mata / Ivan Leonidov / Fritz Haller / Juan Navarro Baldeweg / Rem Koolhaas with Madelon Vriesendorp / Aldo Rossi / John Hejduk / Franco Purini

7 **World Urbanization.** Arturo Soria y Mata / Élisée Reclus and Louis Bonnier / Rudolf Steiger / Erwin Anton Gutkind / Constantinos Doxiadis / Fritz Haller / Carl Steinitz

# Prologue

# Architecture and the World Scale

## History, Geography, and the World

A world does not predate its images. It is shaped by them.

In 1929, on a flight over Buenos Aires with the pilot and writer Antoine de Saint-Exupéry, Swiss architect Le Corbusier confronts a scale that he has not visually encountered before. Writing in *The Four Routes*, he attributes to this flight a moment where he "began to think in terms of *geography* and *world*."[1] Le Corbusier is reacting to the advent of commercial aviation, which is transforming the perception of a new cadre of civilian travelers. It gives them new eyes and a new vantage point. This perspective had been imagined long before but never occupied by ordinary citizens until after World War I. Seeing the earth from the plane, Le Corbusier realizes that modern architecture needs to transcend its context and enable a larger vision. Until then, his architectural imagination stopped at cities. After this momentous flight, he proposes a two-dimensional architecture to be perceived from high above and grafted onto the geography of the earth. True, in his iconic 1922 City of Three Million People, the plane already flies into the city center and its citizens see the city from above; but even from that vantage point, a flat horizon line confines the city's space. After 1929 the surface of the earth replaces the sky as the background of the city, and the scope of his architectural operations expands to regions, territories, and the world at large. In the second postwar Le Corbusier will coin the notion of "geo-architecture" to reflect these scalar possibilities. Yet, he will hardly develop the notion beyond the neologism. It will be muddled with republications of older writings on cities, and the impact of his flight with Saint-Exupéry will be lost. Even though Le Corbusier is the most canonical and exhaustively studied representative of modern architecture, his engagement with the planet constitutes a relatively unknown episode of his career. It has been effectively reduced to a mere footnote in his lifelong involvement in the two truly important realms of action the discipline of architecture has accepted as its areas of expertise: buildings and cities.[2]

1. Le Corbusier, *The Four Routes*, trans. Dorothy Todd (London: D. Dobson, 1947), 104.

2. For a detailed bibliography about Le Corbusier's interest in the planetary scale see projects 8 and 15.

Le Corbusier's geo-architectural works are among this book's fifty projects dealing with the world scale. His enthusiastic, geographic epiphany seems today the product of a bygone era. Today, encounters with the planet are a quotidian phenomenon, dulled by increasing international relations and new means of communication. At the same time, too often we face the globe in darker, more somber ways. Contemporary perceptions of the world are unavoidably associated with critical phenomena that are in themselves the deleterious, unanticipated results of the modernity Le Corbusier embraced: urban expansion across the planet; transcontinental migratory flows; environmental hazards; sea level rise; and global warming. All these changes bring the world scale within our daily experiences and, without a doubt, to the core of our most pressing social concerns.

Architecture's responses to these contemporary, global challenges has mostly favored technical solutions. Architects are addressing environmental questions and global warming through a new ethics of construction supporting hard choices of renewable materials and passive environmental systems. On another front, when mobilized to respond to the problems of refugees, migratory movements, and other humanitarian crises, architects justifiably tend to switch hats and take on the role of relief workers focused on shelter and delivering it quickly. As indispensable as these responses are, they stop short of addressing all the scalar complexities environmental and migratory phenomena present. By addressing problems of a planetary scale with a predominantly problem-solving attitude, architects often stop short of questioning the causes of the problems they are facing. The more recent projects presented in this book suggest a different, complementary mode of operation. That is, to understand the spatial, technological, and social processes that are shaping the planet, in order to define types and scales of architectural intervention that can challenge the ways in which globalization takes place.

The purpose of this book is to reconnect this trend of contemporary architectural inquiry to a broader disciplinary history that has shaped the ways in which we live and think about our present. The book exposes a profound, but still little-known relation between architecture and the global scale, which starts, roughly, in the late nineteenth century. Today, we need to address a planet that has been intensely shaped by the spatial logics of modernity and that continues to be produced through systems of geospatial control and technical rationality that are a direct continuation of them. And yet, we have an insufficient understanding of the many ways in which architectural modernity has addressed the world as a scale of reflection or intervention. In an effort to fill this historiographic gap, this book describes how architects have historically thought and imagined at the world scale well before the advent of contemporary globalization. It unpacks the complex and contested relation architecture maintained with these sociospatial processes; the ways in which the discipline sometimes anticipated, sometimes contributed to, sometimes reacted against the emergence of global systems. It presents how architects embraced and helped formulate globalizing ideologies, at times uncritically accepting or reinforcing associated projects of domination, discrimination, and inequality, while sometimes profoundly challenging them. It shows how some proposals were critical of the inequalities these ideologies might generate, and how some predicted global risks, including the environmental crisis and the morass of urbanization. By extending these histories into the present, the book shows how modern interest in the planetary scale is being recovered as well as reconsidered and challenged today.

Why has this history been suppressed? What forces and voices silenced it? For one, national discourses and ideologies marginalized it by adopting as their instrument of realization a version of modernism devoid of any global ambitions. Associating world-scale projects with communism may have also contributed to its elision. At a practical level, there were no commissions for architects to design worlds, except as the unexamined, broader context of their work. Importantly, the suppression of this dimension of architectural modernism may have to do with the neglect of geography as an influential discipline on architecture. Until recently, histories of modern architecture generally disregarded the role that geography played in shaping architectural thinking and in helping architects situate their work in broader cultural and transregional settings. Countering this tendency, many of the architects featured in this book used geography as a guide to help them apprehend, perceive, and reconfigure the scales and conditions of their interventions. By recovering their legacy, this book lays claim to the importance of a geographical imagination. It posits that the scale and challenges of the world, beyond the city and beyond the nation-state, constitute a vital architectural project—one that needs the same level of disciplinary debate and analysis that it enjoyed in the past.

### "Fill the earth"

Our history of projects begins in the late nineteenth century with the almost contemporaneous works of town planners Arturo Soria y Mata and Patrick Geddes. While we acknowledge the futility of determining a definitive origin of architecture's engagement at this scale, this beginning point is an important part of our undertaking. German historian Jürgen Osterhammel maintains in *The Transformation of the World* that the nineteenth century creates the framework for the global systems that continue until today.[3] Similarly, geographer Giovanni Arrighi dates the beginning of the world-system that dominates the long twentieth century at around 1870. This world-system reinforces the domination of European countries and, especially, the United States over world-economic space and culminates in the phenomenon we term globalization.[4] The first projects in our book coincide with this period, reflecting architecture's early participation in a world that is starting to operate globally.

Indeed, the late nineteenth century witnesses the constitution of the first truly effective forms of globalization and recognizes the strong influence humans have in shaping the planet. As Karl Marx notes in his 1848 *Communist Manifesto*, the international consolidation of capitalism causes a series of social and spatial changes—the rise of cities and domination over the countryside, clearing whole continents for cultivation, and creating networks of global transport—that are instrumental to extend the market across the "whole surface of the globe."[5] Natural sciences detect equivalent scalar phenomena in their field of study. Welsh geologist Thomas Jenkyn proposes the term "anthropozoic" to describe this contemporaneous "human epoch."[6] His suggestion, followed in 1865 by Reverend William Houghton, thus establishes a framework to describe the human modification of the planet that resurfaces insistently after atmospheric chemist Paul Crutzen and biologist Eugene Stoermer introduce the thesis of the Anthropocene in 2000.[7] The promoter of the Arts & Crafts movement, William Morris, expresses a similar awareness of the human influence on the planet in his 1881 lecture "The Prospects of Architecture in Civilisation," when he affirms that architecture must intervene in a process of development that has implied "the molding and altering to human needs of the very face of the earth itself, except in the outermost desert."[8]

From the beginning, our selection responds to this global dimension in very physical, almost literal terms. Taking Ildefons Cerdà's 1848 motto "Fill the earth!" as the basis for his own urban program, Arturo Soria y Mata imagines in 1882 how the planet can be connected through an urban network. One decade later, influenced by his friendship with anarchist geographer Élisée Reclus, author of *The Universal Geography. Earth and Its Inhabitants*, Patrick Geddes conceives his Outlook Tower to make legible the diverse scales of planetary interconnectedness. Although the ambition to represent the cosmos architec-

**3.** Jürgen Osterhammel, *The Transformation of the World: A Global History of the Nineteenth Century* (Princeton: Princeton University Press, 2014).

**4.** Giovanni Arrighi, *The Long Twentieth Century: Money, Power, and the Origins of Our Times* (New York: Verso, 1994). Arrighi develops the world-systems theories that had been developed, among others, by Immanuel Wallerstein in the four volumes of *The Modern World System* (1974–2011).

**5.** Karl Marx, *The Communist Manifesto* (Marxists Internet Archive, 2010 [1848]), 17. Accessed online May 17, 2019: https://www.marxists.org/archive/marx/works/download/pdf/Manifesto.pdf

**6.** Simon Lewis and Mark Maslin, "Defining the Anthropocene," *Nature* 519, no. 7542 (March 12, 2015): 174–175. Quoted in T. J. Demos, *Against the Anthropocene: Visual Culture and the Environment Today* (Berlin: Sternberg Press, 2017), 10.

**7.** Paul J. Crutzen and Eugene F. Stoermer, "The Anthropocene," *Global Change Newsletter* 41 (May 2000): 17–18.

**8.** William Morris, *Hopes and Fears for Art: Five Lectures Delivered in Birmingham, London, and Nottingham, 1878–1881* (New York: Garland, 1979 [1882]), 170–171.

turally certainly predates Geddes's Tower, his work redirects the architectural imagination toward a more precise and material engagement with the order and construction of the earth. This engagement offers a different story of the spatial questions motivating modern architecture and urbanism. Among some of modernism's most prominent precursors—such as Cerdà, author of the *General Theory of Urbanization,* and his follower Soria y Mata; Geddes, who coined the term "conurbation"; and Morris, who so influentially shaped the ethics of modern design—there is already present an emphatic interest in charting a space for action well beyond cities or regional space.

Without a doubt, there are design precedents and intellectual preconditions that support the emergence at this moment of architectural projects dealing with the planetary scale, ranging from the pre-Magellan use of architecture to articulate territorial power, to the imperial and cosmopolitan projects of some French revolutionary architects, to the Saint-Simonian, positivist proposals of territorial ordering.[9] Among these diverse precedents, what for us is more influential is the simultaneous development, during the Enlightenment, of the concepts of aesthetic autonomy and of cosmopolitanism. The separation of the aesthetic realm from other aspects of social life opens spaces of discussion testing hypotheses about modes of perceiving and being that are independent, for the first time, of naturalistic or cosmotheological ideas of predetermined order.[10] This separation, or autonomy, allows artists to speculate about what is possible to do aesthetically and politically. Far from implying the creation of spaces of isolation and exile from actual social space, the movement toward autonomy helps to define new modes of socialization that can be then mobilized to transform actual social space.[11] The interrogation about the possible universal validity of these new, imagined, and acted modes of being helps to initiate, in turn, the cosmopolitan discourse about forms of living together.

The fifty projects included in this book exhibit a vast range of cosmopolitan thinking: from the most naïve to the most sophisticated, from the most politically motivated to the least and from the optimistic to the grim. They also show that the notion of autonomy is a persistent leitmotif among the selected projects—a fact that interestingly counters the common *doxa* that tends to associate tightly ideas of planetary totality with the imposition of totalizing systems, and which suggests the possibility of producing new worlds from interrelated, independent acts.

**9.** Robert David Sack, *Human Territoriality: Its Theory and History* (Cambridge, UK: Cambridge University Press, 1986). Stuart Elden, *Terror and Territory: The Spatial Extent of Sovereignty* (Minneapolis: University of Minnesota Press, 2009). Antoine Picon, *French Architects and Engineers in the Age of the Enlightenment* (Cambridge, UK: Cambridge University Press, 1992). Antoine Picon, *Les Saint-Simoniens: Raison, Imaginaire et Utopie* (Paris: Belin, 2002). Among the diverse approximations to the world as an architectural topic in the architecture of the French eighteenth century see the works of Claude-Nicolas Ledoux (Cemetery for the Ville de Chaux, and House for the Agricultural Guard of Maupertuis, ca. 1785), Étienne-Louis Boullée (Newton Cenotaph, 1784, and Temple of Nature, 1793), Antoine Vaudoyer (House for a Cosmopolitan, 1785), and Jean-Jacques Lequeu (Temple of Equality and Temple of the Earth, 1794).

**10.** Jordi Claramonte, *La República de los fines. Contribución a una crítica de la autonomía del arte* (Murcia: Cendeac, 2013), 35–107.

**11.** Jacques Rancière, *The Politics of Aesthetics: The Distribution of the Sensible* (London: Continuum, 2004).

While at first blush, our emphasis on addressing the planet exposes the biases of modernism, whether colonialist, ideological, or megalomaniacal, we also hope to show that the universalist aspirations of some of these projects (e.g., spatial interventions connecting distant regions) can be separated from the totalizing tendencies of others (e.g., the imposition of a single form of governance worldwide). Inevitably, by juxtaposing these ambitions we hope readers will discern vaster differences in attitude within the modernist project that would otherwise continue to remain unnoticed. At this scale, doctrines and canons acquire complexities that reveal nuances, internal contradictions, or simply additional layers, all of which need to be written back into the normative readings of architectural modernity.

## A Different Vision of Modernism

To affirm the historical correspondence between architecture's attention to the world scale and the rise of modernism may seem almost tautological. After all, the modern movement is also known as the international style, and it is promoted from the start as part of a broader process of economic and social transformation that requires unifying formal languages as well as construction technologies. Moreover, the development of architectural modernity entails the global spread of a series of techniques supporting the advent of urbanization; a fact that historians like Marino Folin and Manfredo Tafuri denounce, the latter famously describing the entire course of modern architecture as an attempt to solve the problems produced by the capitalistic reorganization of the world market.[12]

**12.** Marino Folin, *La Città del capitale: Per una fondazione materialistica dell'architettura* (Bari: De Donato, 1976). Manfredo Tafuri, "Toward a Critique of Architectural Ideology," in *Architecture Theory since 1968*, ed. K. Michael Hays (Cambridge, MA: MIT Press, 1998 [1969]), 32.

Our purpose in this book is to reach beyond these readings of modernity. Surely, the international style quickly settled into a shorthand for what a cosmopolitan aesthetics of architecture could be. Yet, modernity's attention to the world scale was not limited to the definition of a single formal language to be implemented at the architectural scale. Modern architects were also trying to spatialize the cosmopolitan ideal ahead of its realization in politics. Correspondingly, this book focuses on plans for the whole earth, geopolitical proposals, analyses of continental processes, and interventions in them. Projects for cities or buildings are also included, but only if they are explicitly conceived as contributing to the definition of a world system.

To address the discipline's engagement with the planetary requires departing from some well-settled analytical conventions about what architectural design is. Important among them is the privilege of the implementable over the speculative.[13] The scalar ambition of these projects tends to impede actual realization. Often, they lack a direct impact. Acknowledging this fact, our work purposefully conflates utopian and dystopian propositions with feasible ones, futuristic speculations with analytical and realistic studies. The book strategically refuses to differentiate among these contrasting possibilities. It accepts that architecture can operate like other artistic practices that use documentary procedures, analysis, and fiction indistinctly to produce visions of social totalities. The projects included in this book that approach the realm of fiction are analyzed through that intellectual lens. In line with Ernst Cassirer and Suzanne Langer's studies of the symbolic, or most explicitly, with Nelson Goodman's pluralistic theorization of world-making, Fredric Jameson's analysis of the utopian, and Lauren Berlant's understanding of realism not as a genre, but as an effect produced by the possible continuity between proposition and world, we consider the projects for their capacity to represent the whole, and, through that representation, to suggest possible transformations of actual space.[14] The book focuses on designed worlds, not just represented ones. Our preoccupation is with how design can address the world scale—by proposing projects or by contributing with design tools to theory and analysis—rather than presenting only how architects have textually theorized the planet.

The book unfolds as a catalogue of fifty projects, each with an analytical text explaining the proposal, its context, and its relation to other projects. Two symmetrical questions structure those texts, namely: what does architecture do for the world? And, conversely, what does the world do for architecture? While the first question addresses how the planet could be otherwise, that is, how architecture suggests modes of organization and promotes specific spatial, aesthetic, political, and ideological conditions, it also ponders the particular modalities of knowledge architecture produces. In other words, our first question addresses how architects have sought to intervene at the world scale *and* to provide practical and theoretical knowledge about it to complement other disciplines like geography, political science, and ecology. Our second question focuses on the repercussions of this scale on the discipline of architecture. Enlarging the table of the architect to fit the planet requires developing the tools to tackle this scale. The book highlights such changes in architectural language, means of representation, and techniques of construction.

**13.** While important architectural historians such as Kenneth Frampton have produced historical narratives that incorporate speculative architectures, there is still a marked tendency to treat the fictional as a subject in itself, detached from the realm of practice. Significant attempts of mediation appear in the scholarship of Pier Vittorio Aureli, Manuel Orazi, Martin Van Schaik, and Otakar Máčel. See Kenneth Frampton, *Modern Architecture: A Critical History* (London: Thames & Hudson, 2007 [1980]). Pier Vittorio Aureli, "Archizoom, Superstudio and the Critique of Architectural Ideology," in *Architecture and Capitalism: 1845 to the Present*, ed. Peggy Deamer (New York: Routledge, 2014), 132–147. Pier Vittorio Aureli and Manuel Orazi, "The Solitude of the Project," *Log* 7 (2006): 21–32. Martin Van Schaik and Otakar Máčel, eds., *Exit Utopia: Architectural Provocations 1956–76* (Munich: Prestel Verlag, 2005).

**14.** Nelson Goodman, *Ways of Worldmaking* (Hassocks, Sussex: Harvester Press, 1978). Fredric Jameson, *Archaeologies of the Future: The Desire Called Utopia and Other Science Fictions* (London: Verso, 2005). Lauren Berlant, *Cruel Optimism* (Durham: Duke University Press, 2011), 52.

## What Does Architecture Do for the World?

### 1. To spatialize and visualize contrasting conceptions of the world.

The fifty projects in *The World as an Architectural Project* develop numerous, often highly contrasting propositions about structuring the earth. Spatially, they range from the attempt to concentrate the whole of humanity in a dozen huge settlements, to the desire to entirely abolish cities and scatter the population across the countryside. Politically, they move from overtly imperialistic ambitions to counterhegemonic territorial visions. We have avoided making choices based on our personal views in order to better highlight the breadth of architectural thinking that these projects reveal. Their common denominator is the production of a vision of a possible whole. They spatialize and make visible various and varied ideological aspirations, and they anticipate their physical and material dimensions. In so doing, their first contribution is to open social and spatial positions to public scrutiny, turning them into visible, vulnerable objects of contestation and debate.

These visualizations reveal the many occasions in which architecture has favored totalizing agendas. Yet, they also show how many other proposals entail a form of totality, but not a project of totalization. This oscillation, and the consequent possibility of differentiating between totality and totalization, constitutes a central motif of architectural inquiry running throughout our study; one which our question, "what does architecture do for the world?" would like to highlight above all, as it resonates with ongoing debates about the conditions of globalization and about the ways of conceiving alternatives to it.

Since the early 1990s, philosophers such as Jacques Derrida, Jean-Luc Nancy, Michel Serres, and Peter Sloterdijk and anthropologists such as Tim Ingold and Bruno Latour have criticized the assimilation of the planet to the notion of globe, arguing from different positions against the homogenizing tendencies of globalization.[15] The reasons for such a critique have been carefully delineated in Sloterdijk's *Spheres*, a philosophic history of globalization that presents the notion of globe as the conceptual precondition for thinking of the planet as an integrated, unitary totality. The globe and thus its planetary equivalent, the spherical earth, are a geometrically perfect, self-contained object, a seamless surface capable of encompassing everything, and perceived from outside as a

**15.** Jacques Derrida, *Negotiations: Interventions and Interviews, 1971–2001*, trans. Elizabeth Rottenberg (Stanford, CA: Stanford University Press, 2002). Jean-Luc Nancy, *The Creation of the World, or, Globalization* (Albany: State University of New York Press, 2007). Michel Serres, *Atlas* (Paris: Editions Julliard, 1994). Peter Sloterdijk, *Spheres. Volume 2: Globes. Macrospherology* (Pasadena, CA: Semiotext(e), 2014 [1999]). Tim Ingold, "Globes and Spheres: The Topology of Environmentalism," in *Environmentalism: The View from Anthropology*, ed. Kay Milton (London: Routledge, 1993), 31–43. Bruno Latour, *Facing Gaia: Eight Lectures on the New Climatic Regime* (Cambridge, UK: Polity, 2017).

closed unity. This form of conceptualizing the planet constitutes, in Sloterdijk's idealistic vision of history, the fundamental tool for imposing upon the planet any totalizing, unitary views—significantly, those imposed by the capitalist and colonial project. Modernity is, in this view, the summit of the spherical project. In it, the consolidation of circuits of capital and transport definitively transforms the planet's geography into its spherical reference: every location acquires the same valence once it becomes a mere point within a network. Geography becomes geometry.

While this narration fails to notice that globalization simultaneously promotes homogeneity *and* exploits and increases geographical disparities, its argument is nonetheless important. Its corollary is that the contestation of contemporary globalization requires abandoning the spherical model of the planet that modernity culminated, and finding new ways of relating the world to its internal multiplicity. To overcome the idea of globe thus implies finding alternative models for thinking and creating a totality. This challenge remains open. Sloterdijk's pessimistic conclusion is that after breaking with the globe the only possible totality is the planetary sum of immunized isolations, of individual monads protected from the outside.[16] For Latour, the response to the contemporary social and ecological crises can only appear by reformulating or resetting modernity in a manner that ensures the existence of irreducible singularities, (re)positioned at last in particular locations.[17] In Derrida's and Nancy's attempt to reconcile difference and universal commonality, the idea of globalization needs to be replaced with a project of *mondialisation* (world-forming), but the vision of such a totality must incessantly be propelled forward by our imagination, as the cosmopolitan project of a universal democracy always "to come."[18]

By unfolding the many scenarios that architecture developed in order to address the world scale, *The World as an Architectural Project* seeks to disentangle the conception of globes from the imposition of the global, as well as to help to overcome reductionist dichotomies between circulation and location, between global totality and fragmentation, and, as Ernesto Laclau points out, between particularity and universality.[19] Countering the many times in which the discipline has entertained totalizing visions of the globe, architects have also imagined multiple ways to conceive of a common planet while acknowledging and fostering its internal singularities. Examples of this reconciliation abound: conceiving of territorial systems based on the free association of globally connected, autonomous collectives from the 1920s on; designing urban systems

**16.** Sloterdijk, *Spheres. Volume 2: Globes. Macrospherology*, 134.

**17.** Bruno Latour and Christophe Leclercq, eds., *Reset Modernity!* (Karlsruhe, Germany: ZKM Center for Art and Media, 2016).

**18.** Fred Evans, "Cosmopolitanism to Come: Derrida's Response to Globalization," in *A Companion to Derrida*, ed. Zeynep Direk and Leonard Lawlor (London: John Wiley & Sons, 2016), 550–564.

**19.** Ernesto Laclau, "Universalism, Particularism, and the Question of Identity," *October* 61 (1992): 83–90.

that reveal the structuring importance of physical geography in the aftermath of the two world wars; showing the potential of the vertical overlay of contrasting spatial and social logics during the 1950s and 1960s; recognizing that a just social system requires both subverting existing territorial and geopolitical hierarchies and imagining new possibilities of integration that run the gamut from the Soviet disurbanist discourse to the Metabolist designs for a maritime planet, to the South American projects of the 1960s, or to the attempt to globally balance the relation between urbanization and nature that dominates ecological thought.

What is more, this corpus of modern projects and its continuation to the present shows how ideating world systems does not depend on conceiving of and implementing a single global spatial logic or on operating at vast transcontinental scales. The world can be addressed by means that range from designing a building typology to conceiving of new methods of cartographic projection, from defining wearable devices to developing urban models, from constructing ephemeral interventions to producing visual narratives. Through all these means, design is oriented toward the act of building but also, importantly, to intellectual production.

In this sense, architecture's engagement with the global does not simply seek to transform existing conditions, but also to know them. For the architectural criticism of modernity, one of the most problematic consequences of architecture's participation in the generating and influencing of larger systems (be they political or environmental, or be they urban, territorial, or global) is the loss of architecture's function as an instrument of knowledge.[20] Architecture is often instrumentalized for fixing or organizing a specific aspect of the totalities rather than a way to understand and question them. Common among most of the projects in this book is an intended reaction to this loss and a parallel interest in using architecture as a cognitive tool, either by defining spatial devices or by using design to investigate, analyze, and understand world phenomena. From this point of view, *The World as an Architectural Project* expands that the second crucial contribution of architecture to the world is to add to its knowledge.

**20.** Tafuri, "Toward a Critique of Architectural Ideology," 22.

## What Does Architecture Do for the World?

### 2. To help to know and question the existing conditions of the world.

To that end, architecture has developed strategies to link spatial conditions and cognitive goals. Admittedly, categorizing these strategies risks reducing their diversity. Yet, many of the proposals studied in this book share key methods: microcosmic concentration, partiality, (in)visibility, and parallelism.[21] Present from the very first entries of this collection, these four strategies are often deployed as the spatial equivalents of rhetoric and literary mechanisms aimed at facilitating the transition between part and whole.

21. Hashim Sarkis with Roi Salgueiro Barrio and Gabriel Kozlowski, "The World in the Architectural Imaginary," *New Geographies* 08 (2016): 176–194. Roi Salgueiro Barrio, "Micro, Partial, Parallel, (In)visible," *New Geographies* 8 (2016): 194–203.

From Geddes's Outlook Tower to Franco Purini's Equal City, the microcosmic approach constructs buildings that allow their occupants to understand the whole world from a localized spot. Enclosed and dissociated from its immediate context, each microcosm acts like a monad: it creates in its interior a spatial *analogy* of the architect's understanding of world order. Instead of using this *analogical* procedure, partial strategies treat architecture as if it were a *synecdoche*, a part that is capable of representing a larger whole. In this case, the approach is *typological*: partial strategies proceed by classifying the most relevant elements that constitute the world and, based on this classification, by defining prototypes or typologies that represent segments of the broader totality. The section of Soria y Mata's Linear City or the typologies of Fuller's 4D Tower represent this second strategy, as each of their elements acts as a piece of a planetary system it creates. Microcosms and partial strategies thus operate in contrasting manners. While each microcosm can diverge from the others, fostering pluralism and multiple manners of understanding the world, the use of partiality favors sameness and repetition.

The strategy of making (in)visible extends from the well-established dialectic strategy of *revelation* and *negation*. In this third form, architecture seeks to bring to light specific aspects of the globe, for instance, as in Bruno Taut's Alpine Architecture, by selecting key places that could help to structure a planetary system and by defining building and urban forms that highlight geographic factors. Yet, this act of revealing often requires a symmetrical operation: radically eliminating those elements which contradict that reading of the world structure in order to emphasize the preserved aspects. The problematic relation between world-making and world-unmaking is thus laid bare. In literary terms, Jameson describes a similar operation with the concept of world-reduction, which he defines as "a principle of systemic exclusion, a kind of surgical excision of empirical reality, something like a process of ontological attenuation in which the sheer reality of what exists, of what we call reality, is deliberately thinned and weeded out through an operation of radical abstraction and simplification."[22] The world is here reduced to essentials.

22. Jameson, *Archaeologies of the Future*, 270.

The projects often complement all these forms of cognition with the construction of new points of view from which to observe and thus to apprehend the planet. The strategy of parallelism provides the limit-case of this exploration of vision. In the lineage of projects that goes from Lazar Khidekel's Aero-Cities to Takis Zenetos's Electronic Urbanism, the calibration of the vertical separation between buildings and planet allows humans to see the planet from above, creating a disconnection between subject and Earth that paradoxically helps in recognizing the significance of the latter. The capacity to perceive the horizon situates the subject in a particular place, which becomes related to the confines of the visible world. The progressive elevation of the point of view fosters a perception of the planet as an entity that is increasingly independent of humans—as happens in the "overview effect," that cognitive shift astronauts experience when they see the planet from outer space.

While the aforementioned four strategies involve spatial and formal means and take shape as buildings, architecture also engages in the production of knowledge by using design tools that complement and question the information provided by other fields of knowledge. The efforts of French architect Maurice François Rouge immediately after World War II to create a new terrestrial science—geonomy—which he added to architectural curricula, epitomizes this reconsideration of architecture as a discipline concerned first with the analysis and study of the planet and only later with its transformation. The constant investigation throughout this collection of techniques of data visualization and terrestrial representation—both spherical-volumetric and superficial-cartographic—is an essential component of this attempt to generate knowledge. This happens, to begin with, at the purely technical level. Examples such as Élisée Reclus and Louis Bonnier's interest in creating the most precise and comprehensive terrestrial globe; Buckminster Fuller and Shoji Sadao's preoccupation with generating the most accurate method of cartographic projection; or the later development, at Harvard's Graduate School of Design and other schools of architecture, of geographical information systems (GIS) to sustain contemporary digital tools of geovisualization and geolocation reveal how intensely architects sought to construct the very technical means that allow us to define and represent the planet.

But technical innovation is not the only way of generating knowledge. As a discipline fundamentally concerned with construction, form, and spatial order, architecture is well aware of the interplay between technique and ideology, and of the limitations or possibilities that formal conditions impose on cognition. From this perspective, repositioning the architect as a geographer or cartographer exceeds the technical dimension, helping to question well-settled assumptions about the order of the planet. Architectural investigations into different methods of cartographic projection—as in the works of the School of Valparaiso or of Plan B's Joyce Hsiang and Bimal Mendis—show that, rather than being a stable object, the world is a construct that has to be interrogated from a variety of points of view, and serve to counter the power relations that are embedded in the most used cartographic renderings. Exploring diverse techniques of cartographic analysis, in turn, serves to understand the interplay between geography and past and present forms of urbanization—allowing architects such as Saverio Muratori or Constantinos Doxiadis to articulate their hypotheses about territorial organization. The combination of cartography, data visualization, and historical analysis contributes to putting into question early twentieth-century geography's focus on regional studies and the conventional limitation of urbanism to the space of the metropolis, and supports the claim that urban phenomena need to be contemplated from a world perspective—in the works of Rudolf Steiger or Erwin Anton Gutkind. Nowadays it informs the analysis of the planet as a completely urbanized system, as in Neil Brenner's Urban Theory Lab's work. All these explorations help to elaborate concepts and methods that address terrestrial conditions and which can be transmitted to other forms of intellectual inquiry and social practice, including architectural practice itself.

## What Does the World Do for Architecture?

The orientation of architectural practice toward geography already reveals how an interest in the scale of the world helps to transform the discipline—in this case, by broadening the discipline's intellectual activity and the forms of expertise designers developed. Exploring notions of microcosm, partiality, (in)visibility, and parallelism to spatialize architecture's cognitive role shows, in turn, how addressing this scale means investigating specific formal mechanisms. By coupling the question "what does architecture do for the world?" with "what does the world do for architecture?" we intend to foreground the importance of formal inquiry. In order to introduce propositions about the planet, architecture had to reconsider and expand its own methodological store. Because of this, specific spatial and formal strategies, building techniques, and methods of representation were developed or gained particular significance and value. One goal of the book is, thus, to understand how, in addressing this scale, architects have expanded their repertoire as a practice and helped to question and push the discipline's limits.

Two deeply intertwined investigations underlie this aspect of the book, respectively structured around the relations of architecture with infrastructure and physical geography. Ever since the late nineteenth century, architects recognize the power of new modes of communication such as railroads, cars, and airplanes, but also radio and telephone, to enable a world system and explore the relation between architecture and infrastructures. At one extreme of this relation is the reinforcement of the idea of autonomy. In this vision, the consideration that inter-human relations no longer need physical contiguity leads to the production of systems made by autonomous, isolated cities, buildings, and individuals interconnected thanks to telecommunications and other means of transport. Imagining the typologies, functions, and institutions of the resulting forms of human association runs through the work of Ivan Leonidov to some of Le Corbusier's projects and to Yona Friedman's designs for spatial cities, to name but a few. At the other extreme, infrastructure merges with buildings. From Soria y Mata, to Alison and Peter Smithson, and to the megastructures movement, it is possible to detect an increasingly intense assimilation of the infrastructural. The megastructural experiment of creating fully integrated environments to resolve with a single spatial artifact all the necessities life may require is the limit of such investigation—one in which buildings no longer need Earth, whose functions have been completely interiorized. Allan Boutwell and Michael Mitchell's Continuous City is, probably, the most extreme example of this approach.

The opposite of this project of total interiorization fuses architecture with physical geography in order to organize territorial- and Earth-systems. Importantly, the architectural engagement in geography is an exploration of all of the earth's layers. This approach motivates an interest in defining the section of the planet as both a geographical and sociotechnical construct, which starts with Geddes's Valley Section, continues through the work of Fuller, the Smithsons, Juan Navarro Baldeweg, and Plan B, and leads to the definition of artifacts that operate in every geographical space: from under the ground to the atmosphere to outer space.

In their most radical expressions, the investigations of infrastructure and physical geography converge at one point: the disappearance of architecture. If there is a common outcome among these planetary explorations, it is the critique of the discipline of architecture itself. From the elimination of cities in the work of the Soviet disurbanists, to Fuller's investigation of the notion of "ephemerality," to the multiple explorations after World War II of invisible infrastructures of communication and climatic control that can create inhabitable environments without buildings, architecture has investigated and cherished the possibility of its own disappearance. This elimination can be thought of in ecological terms, since the eradication of architecture helps recover a new, pristine nature. But the disappearance of architecture in the face of other technologies of environmental control points above all to a different intention: the suppression of the spatial and ideological constraints that architecture produces. Ultimately, the architectural preoccupation with Earth ends up abolishing architecture itself.

In this way, the investigation of the world scale tests architecture's disciplinary limits—its actual capacity to design and produce a built environment, its power to induce transformation. To question the boundaries in this manner also implicates investigating architecture's means of representation. Showing how projects operate in planetary terms challenges the techniques of orthographic projection and perspectival representation, which the discipline developed to represent buildings and cities. Such conventional forms as plans, sections, and axonometric views continue to be used, but many other means complement them: charts, maps, tables, diagrams, text-accompanied visual narratives, comics, films, installations. Unfurling the many ways to represent the world visually has been one of the most rewarding aspects of this research. This catalogue of projects seeks to present this visual richness and includes a significant number of previously unpublished images. Our selection is not meant to cover all aspects of each project but to bring to light the design and graphic strategies the architects use to communicate their visions and their goals. The graphic dimension is an important aspect of the book in its own right, one that can be appreciated independently from the text.

## One Hundred and Fifty Years of World-making

For *The World as an Architectural Project* we sought out architects who explicitly support their work in notions such as Earth, terrestrial, planet, planetary, world, ecumenes, globe or global—a method that showed that the use of the latter term in architecture predates the emergence of the notion of globalization by decades. This method not only allowed us to immediately detect the most salient and recognized planetary thinkers, such as Fuller, Doxiadis, and Muratori. It also brought to light an important number of designers whose works have not been previously associated with planetary ambitions, but for whom addressing this scale strongly informed their disciplinary positions and design work. Canonical modern figures such as Le Corbusier and the Smithsons belong to this group, together with architects such as Vittorio Gregotti, Franco Purini, and Sergio Bernardes. In all of these cases we sought to clarify what the notion of world (and related terms) meant to them, thus teasing out the conceptual nuances and design possibilities embedded in the terms we use to describe the planet.

The resulting research shows a continuous and transgeographic interest in the planet among architects. *The World as an Architectural Project* presents the work of more than fifty architects, from thirty countries and five continents. Their diverse biographies often register migration and forced relocation across the planet. Unfortunately, they also reflect the imbalances of class, race, and gender that are still pervasive in the profession of architecture. Geographical diversity does not camouflage the fact that most propositions are produced in the Global North, often in the very same countries that benefit from geopolitical power. The presence in our selection of ten women as authors or coauthors does not diminish the fact that most projects are authored by men. These numbers and trends are one of the serious imbalances that our research confirms, and they underscore the necessity to deeply question our world. Yet, we believe that they should not impugn the worldwide ambition of the entries in this collection. They should, instead, lead toward the pressing necessity of multiplying the points of view and geographies from which world projects are thought.

We have organized the works chronologically in order to illustrate the historical relationship between architecture and processes of globalization. In very

23. Interestingly, Koolhaas participated in the exhibition Terra I, organized at the Museum of Architecture, Wrocław in 1975. Curated by Polish architect Stefan Muller, the exhibition gathered, in a last international event devoted to world-making, architects such as Constantinos Doxiadis, Yona Friedman, Oskar Hansen, Alison and Peter Smithson, Superstudio, Minoru Takeyama, and Aldo Rossi. Muller designed the very interesting planetary project Terra X.

broad terms, this historical reading starts with the nineteenth-century investigations of the terrestrial repercussions of urbanization, it continues throughout the first half of the twentieth century with peaks in the aftermath of the two world wars, and it has a very intense moment of planetary speculation in the mid-1960s and early 1970s. By that time, it is entirely clear that modernity had ended up subjecting the world to multiple, global challenges: the risks of total military destruction, unprecedented demographic and urban growth, the diminution of ecological diversity, among others. The symbolic conclusion of this period rests in Rem Koolhaas and Madelon Vriesendorp's City of the Captive Globe, an image that shows that the ultimate consequence of modernity is that the urban condition completely entraps the planet.[23] Its cultural death comes after the late 1970s with the consolidation of a postmodernism that reacts against the architectural profession's involvement with broader societal issues by reorienting design toward the internal conditions of the discipline, history, and the space of the city. The last quarter of the twentieth century thus shows a clear historical break with previous preoccupations with the planet.

Postmodernism, though, does not completely abandon the understanding of the world as the ultimate reference of architectural production. Our analysis of works by Aldo Rossi, John Hejduk, and Zaha Hadid registers the uses and invocations of notions of world and planet in fundamentally metaphoric and sometimes nostalgic ways. Yet, it also shows that the recuperation of precedents and the critique of modern, positivist models of knowledge and territorial organization that happen at this time help elaborate—especially in Hejduk's case—techniques of world-making that will become relevant in the new millennium. The final part of this book precisely addresses a series of works produced after the year 2000. These projects explore topics such as the impact of climate change, the emergence of new modes of citizenship, the urbanization of the planet, and the parallel operationalization of nature. They point, in our view, to a positive resituation of architecture as a practice that fully assumes its social responsibility by critically addressing globalization. More, we believe, will follow.

Chronology generates unexpected, welcome discoveries: the radical transformation of worldviews within a single decade from the still romantic vision of Bruno Taut to the technological visions of Fuller and Leonidov; how advanced South American and Greek projects of the 1960s are in relation to contemporaneous works of Northern and Western countries. Undoubtedly, it also exposes common, generational themes. And yet, as will become evident in the catalogue, architectural thinking about the planet does not follow a linear progression. The capacity of design to visualize the impact of technological advancements or social and spatial trends before they actually take place has allowed architects to test possible transformations of the planet well before they are realized. In this sense, architects advance themes, design motifs, and manifest intellectual preoccupations that are later developed or contested by other designers.

*The World as an Architectural Project* is structured so that every entry can be read separately and treated as a particular vision within a complex web of propositions. In order to unpack the dynamic of suggestion, development, abandonment, and reconsideration of design questions, we associate each project to four main themes. These bring to light the crucial topics architects face as they speculate at the planetary scale and plan to intervene in it. By following their historic unfolding, it is possible to see the persistence of social and political intentions, and of spatial and formal ones. They show how architecture not only reflects upon the world but also, ultimately, upon its own mechanisms of world-making. The "List of Themes" included in the book highlights these interrelations. With a similar intention, each entry bears cross-references to other projects.

By exposing this abundance of themes, *The World as an Architectural Project* demonstrates that for more than a century architects and urbanists never stopped projecting possible organizations and conceptions of the planet. In so doing, they constantly reflected upon the repercussions of diverse aesthetic, social, and political currents, and upon the impact and possible uses of technological and scientific advances. Through these projects, we detect a constant interrogation of the ultimate possibilities, roles, and limits of architecture and urbanism vis-à-vis society. In this sense, rather than indulging in the megalomaniacal cliché of the modern architect-qua-demiurge, this book adopts a position of disciplinary self-reflexivity, in which metageographic and holistic considerations test the limits of ethical and aesthetic positions. Taking architecture to its most ambitious extreme becomes, then, the most demanding form of interrogation. It stretches architectural thinking. Confronting these limits should, no doubt, inform a critique of the methods of intervening in the world our discipline has endorsed. It should also trigger the development of new and more inclusive forms of thinking. By showing what attitudes were and are being exercised at this scale, *The World as an Architectural Project* seeks to inspire architecture's renewed commitment to global issues. By highlighting that the spatial imagination is constitutive of the social imagination, it stresses that spatial thinking can encourage and contribute to other media and other ways of imagining worlds, but also that architecture needs to be complemented by them as well. These, we hope, are steps toward a much needed collective reimagination of the planet.

# La Ciudad Lineal

## The Linear City

**Project:** 1. **Author:** Arturo Soria y Mata (1844–1920). **Date:** 1882–1913. **Themes:** Circulation. Linearity. Typology. World Urbanization.

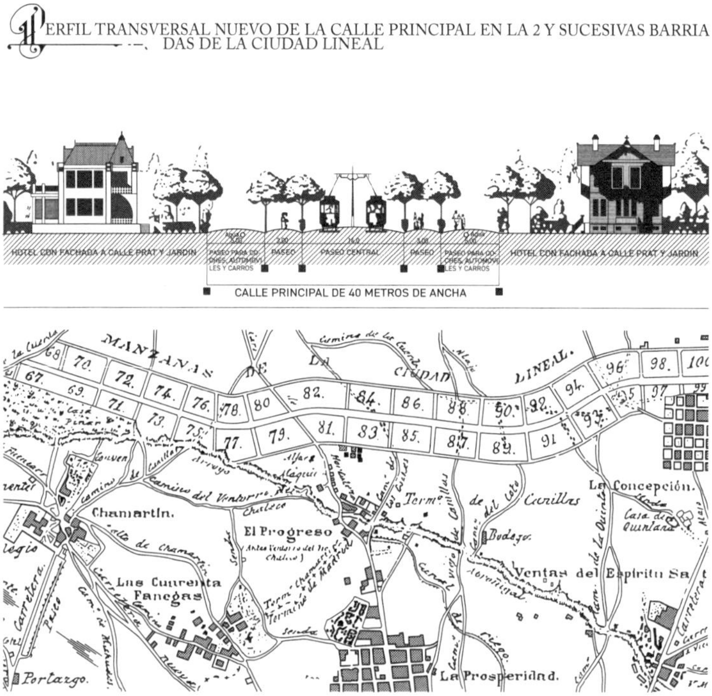


Figure 0. Transverse section and plan of the first neighborhoods of the Linear City. After Arturo Soria y Mata. ca. 1894.

"Ruralize the city . . . urbanize the countryside. Fill the earth! (*Replete terram!*)"[1]

Arturo Soria y Mata choses this motto to promote his "theory of the Linear City."[2] The phrase comes from Ildefons Cerdà's *General Theory of Urbanization* (1867), the text that coins the terms "urban" and "urbanization."[3] Cerdà's biblical reference ("*replete terram*" is the expression the god of the Old Testament uses to exhort Adam, and later Noah, to populate Earth) already expresses the universalist aspirations of the very first theorization of urbanization.[4] After carrying out a survey of models of cities across the world, Cerdà not only establishes a series of standards for city design, he also advances the main conceptual traits that should characterize the urban: association of urban expansion to infrastructural networks of transport, diminution of the differences between city and countryside, and potential "worldwide" dimension.[5] Cerdà gives to the notion of urbanization an ideological content and a scale that predates the actual urbanization of the planet during the twentieth century, but it is Soria y Mata who gives these ideological notions their first spatial formalization by conceiving of a system of linear cities that can cover the whole "surface of the earth."[6]

The transition from Cerdà to Soria y Mata shows how, in just fifteen years, the theorization of urbanization as a force capable of transforming the planet progresses into formal strategies that can make effective that territorial dimension. Cerdà, an engineer immersed in Saint-Simonian positivism and technological optimism, considers that the new means of mechanical transport, such as steam railways and ships, will foster the social and economic development of rural areas and produce a new scale of territorial relations.[7] Cerdà's theory translates this belief in the transformative power of communications to a spatial ideology structured around the notion of "circulation" in which cities cease to be thought of as distinct communal and political structures of collective living in a particular place, in order to become part of the generic spatial substance of a system of interchanges.[8] By replacing the notion of "city" by the term "urban," Cerdà aims to offer a new signifier for the spatial condition that will emerge out of the territorial encounter between circulation and settlement. Such a conceptual operation is not, though, entirely explored in design terms. Cerdà's planning proposals are still centered on the spatial characteristics of the city, and his intention to define schemas for territorial urbanization around water canals and lines of transport remains incomplete at the moment of his death in 1876.[9] Soria y Mata, instead, strictly addresses the territorial implications of urban-

**1.** Arturo Soria y Mata, "La Ciudad Lineal" [04/10/1882], in *Arturo Soria y La Ciudad Lineal*, ed. George Roseborough Collins and Carlos Flores (Madrid: Revista de Occidente, 1968), 171–173.

**2.** Arturo Soria y Mata, *La Cité linéaire: Conception nouvelle pour l'aménagement des villes* (Paris: Centre d'Études et de Recherches Architecturales, 1979), 16.

**3.** The terms Cerdà coins in Spanish are: "*urbe*" and "*urbanización*." Cerdà, who is very interested in etymology, devotes part of his book to justifying the necessity of creating a new term to address settlements, and his reasons for selecting the word "urbe." In particular, he establishes a clear contrast between the Latin notions of *civitas* and *urbs*, and explains his predilection for the second based on the necessity of finding an encompassing term that can refer to every possible type of settlements: "While we understand that there must be a logical reason behind the proper name of every urbs, we have no objection to confessing our inability to understand this reason, to analyze it and to express it." See Ildefons Cerdà, Vicente Guallart, Angela Kay Bunning, Anne Ludlow, Graham Thomson, Institut d'Arquitectura Avançada de Catalunya, *General Theory of Urbanization, 1867* (Barcelona: Actar Publishers, 2018), 65–71 and 443–494.

**4.** We take these observations from George R. Collins, "Introducción," in Collins and Flores, *Arturo Soria y La Ciudad Lineal*, 29.

**5.** As noted, Cerdà is extremely careful about terminology. The word he uses to refer to the planet, or the "worldwide," was in Spanish "orbe," which stems directly from the Latin *orbis*. Compared with the other Latin words that designate the planet (*tellum, terra*) that have informed Spanish language, "orbe" is the one that most directly reflects the spherical condition of the planet, and thus, the possibility of circumscribing the earth. It is also, a word extremely close to "urbe."

ization. His schemes disregard cities as such in order to explore what happens outside, or between, them.

Soria y Mata elaborates his proposal through different texts, which span from its original 1882 formulation in an article published in the newspaper *El Progreso* to the 1913 presentation of the project in the *Premier Congrès International de l'Art de Construire Villes et Organisation de la Vie Municipale* organized in Ghent by the internationalist thinker Paul Otlet **[project 8]**. As is common in late nineteenth-century urban thinking, Soria y Mata's texts begin with a critique of the density, lack of social justice, and deleterious health conditions of emerging industrial metropolises. Yet, he immediately abandons the metropolitan scale in order to propose three models of territorial organization of linear cities. The first one consists of the construction of a linear ring around existing cities. This possibility is not established in the initial description of linear cities in *El Progreso*, but it guides Soria y Mata's partially implemented proposal of a Linear City around Madrid **[figs. 0, 1, and 2]**. The second and third scales are the author's original intentions. The second consists in what Soria y Mata terms "triangulation," connecting existing "point cities" at the national scale through linear cities **[fig. 3]**.[10] The third extends this triangulation to construct transcontinental connections: "A unique street of 500 meters width and of the required length. We must emphasize it: of the required length. This will be the future city, whose extremes can be Cádiz and Saint Petersburg, or Beijing and Brussels."[11]

This latter, most ambitious scale would give a proper functional, social, and formal response to the necessity of covering the earth that Soria y Mata envisages. The linear city treats the distribution of functions as a means of territorial organization that can foster socioeconomic development. In his project, two symmetrical residential bands surround a central axis dedicated to transport, the railroad being the main system that he considers. Agricultural plots are placed further apart, in the periphery of the residential areas. Finally, natural areas remain intact behind the agricultural fields **[fig. 4]**. This elementary division, constant along the linear city, aims to warrant a continuous relation between production and consumption. By extending this system in the territory, the linear city seeks to curtail the abandonment of rural areas and to promote the industrialization of the countryside. At the same time, it facilitates the conditions for two social operations: an egalitarian distribution of the land inspired by the writings of the American political economist Henry George, and an interclassist occupation of space, which Soria y Mata believes is guaranteed

**6.** Arturo Soria y Mata, "Comparación entre las Ciudades Jardines y las Ciudades Lineales," in Collins and Flores, *Arturo Soria y La Ciudad Lineal,* 315.

**7.** Carlos Sambricio, "Arturo Soria y la Ciudad Lineal," *Q,* no. 58 (1982): 22–30. Accessed online September 1, 2018. DOI: http://oa.upm.es/10922/

**8.** Ross Exo Adams, "Natura Urbans, Natura Urbanata: Ecological Urbanism, Circulation, and the Immunization of Nature," *Environment and Planning D: Society and Space* 32, no. 1 (2014): 12–29.

**9.** Cerdà understands that the process of urbanization should be accompanied by a process of "rurización," or ruralized urbanization, but he does not develop a theory of it. See in this respect Arturo Soria y Puig, *Hacia una teoría general de la urbanización: Introducción a la obra teórica de Ildefons Cerdà (1815–1876)* (Madrid: Ediciones Turner, 1979), 195–205.

**10.** Soria y Mata, "La Ciudad Lineal," 171–173.

**11.** Arturo Soria y Mata, "La Cuestión Social y la Ciudad Lineal" [03/05/1883], in Collins and Flores, *Arturo Soria y La Ciudad Lineal,* 191. Our translation.

by minimizing the distance between the borders and the central axis of the linear city.[12] Such social ambitions translate Soria y Mata's reformist attitude to a spatial plan. A member of the Spanish parliament for a time, Soria y Mata believes that urbanization should serve to curtail social unrest.[13] He also understands that, in order to do so, urban expansion should no longer be a means to reinforce the political and economic power of the bourgeoisie thanks to their appropriation of the economic surplus generated by land speculation.[14]

In formal terms, the linear city is a result of its author's interest in geometry, and in finding means to control the form of urban growth. Part of Soria y Mata's work deals strictly with geometry—a topic he treats with almost metaphysical aspirations.[15] His texts praise the straight line for its regularity and rationality, and they describe it as a symbol of cultural progress.[16] Linearity counters the disorder of metropolitan expansion through the perfection of geometry. To limit the width is the tool that allows both the territorial expansion of urbanization and reduces its deleterious spatial effects of uncontrolled land consumption. With that goal, the project advances a mechanism of formal control that will characterize later architectural approaches at the world scale: adopting an infrastructural logic that consists of determining the section in detriment of the design of the plan. By focusing on the section, design is limited to defining just a small part, a segment that can then be repeated. This limitation of formal control is certainly a way to trigger the urban process. Conceptually, it is also a way to ensure that, even if the world project is not complete, a form of totality can be perceived because each fragment is, always, a prefiguration of the whole.

Representations of the linear city evince this oscillation between segment and totality. Soria y Mata uses architectural conventions only to define the sectional template and a detail of the plan. After the definition of these segments, representations jump to the territorial scale, which is rendered with cartographic precision **[fig. 5]**. The overall potential of the design is captured through an aerial view **[fig. 6]**. In it, the project is settled in geographical space, showing a continuous, unlimited city that vanishes over the horizon.

This aerial representation offers a glimpse into Soria y Mata's vision of a world traversed by linear cities. In "La Ciudad Lineal en China" (The Linear City in China) he explicitly explains how his proposal can become an instrument of world "colonization," by accompanying the construction of railroad infrastructures in countries such as China, Siberia, Argentina, or Canada.[17] In the same vein, Soria y Mata also tries to get the political support for building a

**12.** The importance of Henry George is clearly stated in the tenth principle of the linear city, "La justicia en la repartición de la tierra" (Justice in land distribution), included in the article "Nuevas ideas para la construcción de ciudades." In the text, Soria y Mata asserts: "The Linear City is the complement of the doctrine of the American Henry George, the most practical, easy, and conciliatory way to expropriate the current landlords for their own benefit, and for the benefit of all." Our translation. See: Arturo Soria y Mata, "Nuevas Ideas para la Construcción de Ciudades," in Collins and Flores, *Arturo Soria y La Ciudad Lineal,* 306.

**13.** Soria y Mata, "Nuevas Ideas para la Construcción de Ciudades," 300.

**14.** Sambricio, "Arturo Soria y la Ciudad Lineal," 24.

**15.** Collins, "Introduction," 18–19. Collins explains that Soria y Mata's morphological theories consider that under every natural phenomenon there are underlying geometrical figures, and mentions his correspondence, in this respect, with the German biologist Ernst Haeckel.

**16.** Arturo Soria y Mata, "La Línea Recta" [02/27/1882], in Collins and Flores, *Arturo Soria y La Ciudad Lineal,* 163–164.

**17.** Arturo Soria y Mata, "La Ciudad Lineal en China," in Collins and Flores, *Arturo Soria y La Ciudad Lineal,* 307–312. It is important to note that the Spanish word *colonización*, similar to the Italian *colonizzazione*, not only refers to dominating other countries, but also to constructing settlement in order to cultivate the land.

linear city between Ceuta and Tetuán, in Morocco (then a Spanish colony), and suggests constructing other segments of the linear city linking the Mediterranean and Atlantic coasts of that country.[18] The consideration of these territorial possibilities leads him to modulate some of the linear city's spatial conditions: it will consist only in the transportation infrastructures when the city encounters difficult geographical conditions, or crosses national frontiers; it will follow the most convenient topographic levels for railroad construction, only using tunnels when it is unavoidable. These continental visions expose Soria y Mata's Eurocentrism. For him, the cities are a way to integrate colonized countries within the metropolises' commercial and political networks. Yet, the linear schema consciously attempts to coexist with the autochthonous cultures. The linear city appears in addition to, not instead of, each country's settlement structure.[19]

Soria y Mata's internationalist ambition leads him to disseminate the proposal through various media and conferences, where he presents the linear city as an alternative to the nostalgic antiurban promises of Ebenezer Howard's garden city. As a result of this proselytism, the idea becomes the germ of multiple territorial explorations. After Soria y Mata's presentation of the project at the congress of Ghent, the French jurist Georges Benoit-Lévy creates an international association for the promotion of linear cities and publishes Soria y Mata's work in France. Thanks to Benoit-Lévy's advocacy, the linear city project becomes known in the USSR. In 1930 El Lissitzky publishes one of Soria y Mata's diagrams in *Russia: An Architecture for World Revolution,* incorrectly credited as a work of the French economist Charles Gide.[20] In the late 1920s, the notion informs disurbanist thinking in the USSR as well as the propositions of Nikolai Miliutin in *Sotsgorod. The Problem of Building Socialist Cities* **[project 10]**. Le Corbusier, who possesses a copy of Miliutin's work, uses and transforms Soria y Mata's schema in his *Three Human Establishments* **[project 15]**. Constantinos Doxiadis criticizes the rigid formal control of these schemes in order to propose a dynapolis of varying width as the urban basis for generating Ecumenopolis **[project 23]**. Turned into a continuous architecture, linearity supports, among many others, the designs of Raimund Abraham, Alan Boutwell, and Superstudio **[projects 27, 33, and 38]**.

In many ways, Soria y Mata uncritically naturalizes the urban process, failing to perceive it as a contentious realm of spatial and political confrontation. For him, urbanization is an unavoidable and positive phenomenon, capable of solving economic, cultural, and geopolitical tensions, having an innate tendency to

**18.** Arturo Soria y Mata, "La Primera Ciudad Lineal Africana entre Ceuta y Tetuán. Carta abierta al Excmo. Sr. Conde de Romanones," in Collins and Flores, *Arturo Soria y La Ciudad Lineal,* 291–294.

**19.** Soria y Mata, "La Primera Ciudad Lineal Africana entre Ceuta y Tetuán," 291. Interestingly, Le Corbusier also proposes a linear city in his 1933 Plan Obus for Algiers.

**20.** El Lissitzky, *Russia: An Architecture for World Revolution* (Cambridge, MA: MIT Press, 1984), 63.

follow the transportation lines. Despite the naïveté of his analyses, the conceptual persistence of the linear city notion for more than a century derives from its proximity to some of the trends that will affect global urbanization during the twentieth century. Soria y Mata rightly detects the tendency of urbanization to grow along transportation corridors and to occupy coastal plains and valleys; two factors that have led to the proliferation of linear urban systems across the planet. His work takes advantage of those tendencies in order to propose a system that guides urban growth toward the creation of a world system. The design is extremely schematic, but it certainly orients urbanization, for the first time, toward the definition and formalization of territorial relations. Soria y Mata's schema unifies settlement structure, the organization of economic production, and infrastructural networks in a single line that, if implemented across the world, would transform existing cities into the nodes of a continuous urban system. As a result, instead of the unified ruralized urbanity of Cerdà's postulates, Soria y Mata creates a dual system; one where cities maintain their distinct role and spatial singularity while they are being connected through linear networks of communication and exchange.

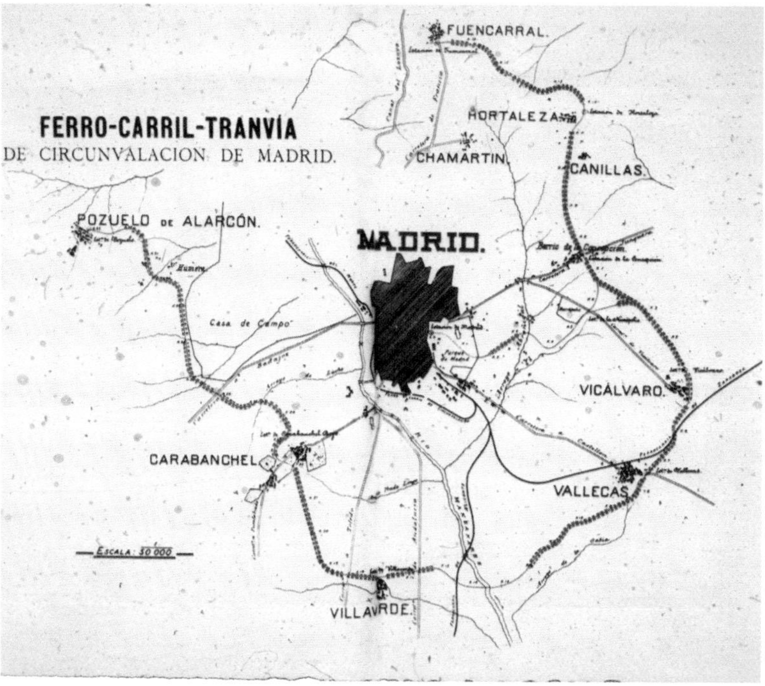


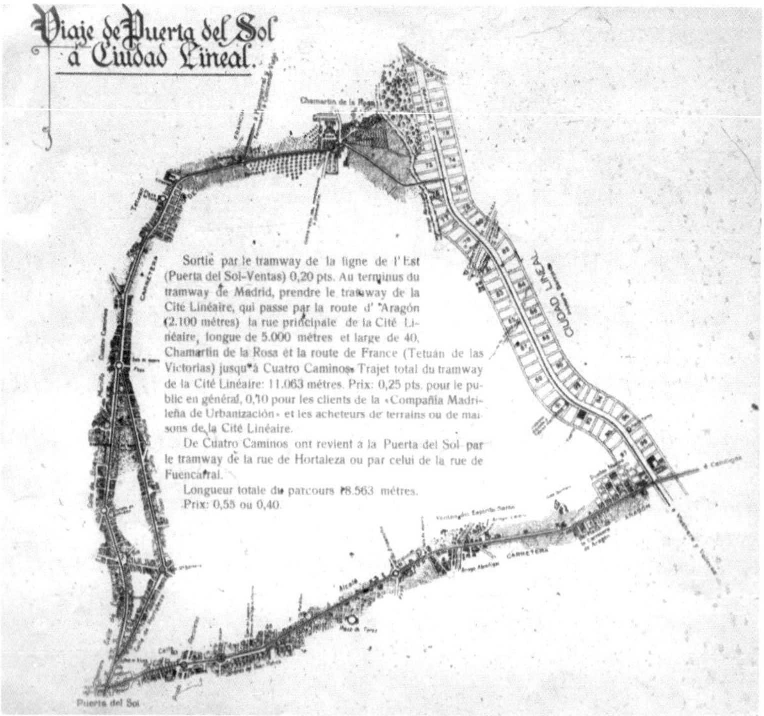


**Figure 1 (Top).** Railway-Tramway ringroad around Madrid. ca. 1892.
**Figure 2 (Bottom).** Travel from Puerta del Sol to the Linear City. Undated.

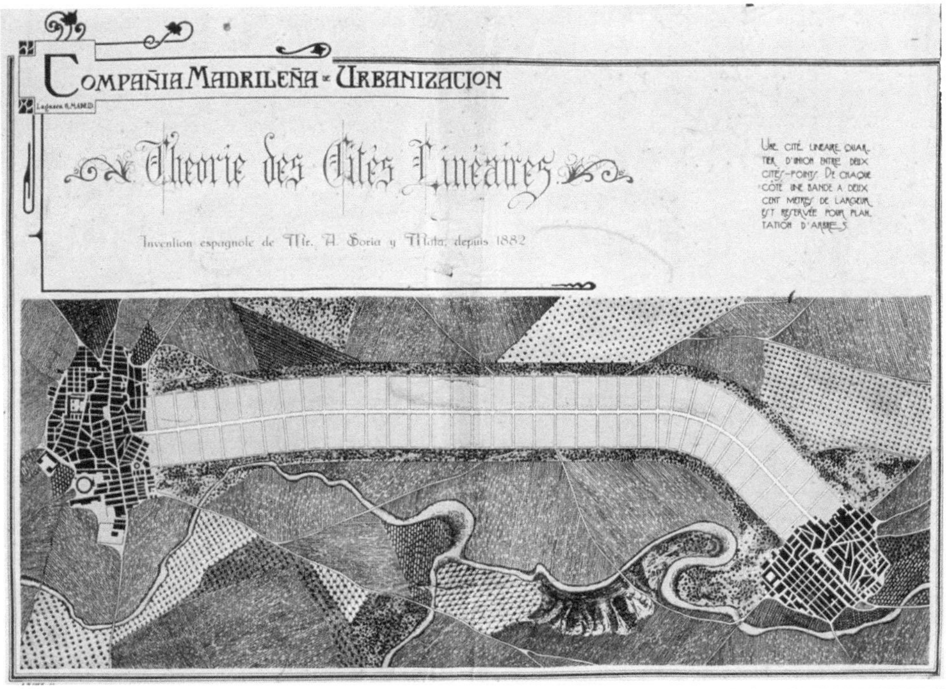


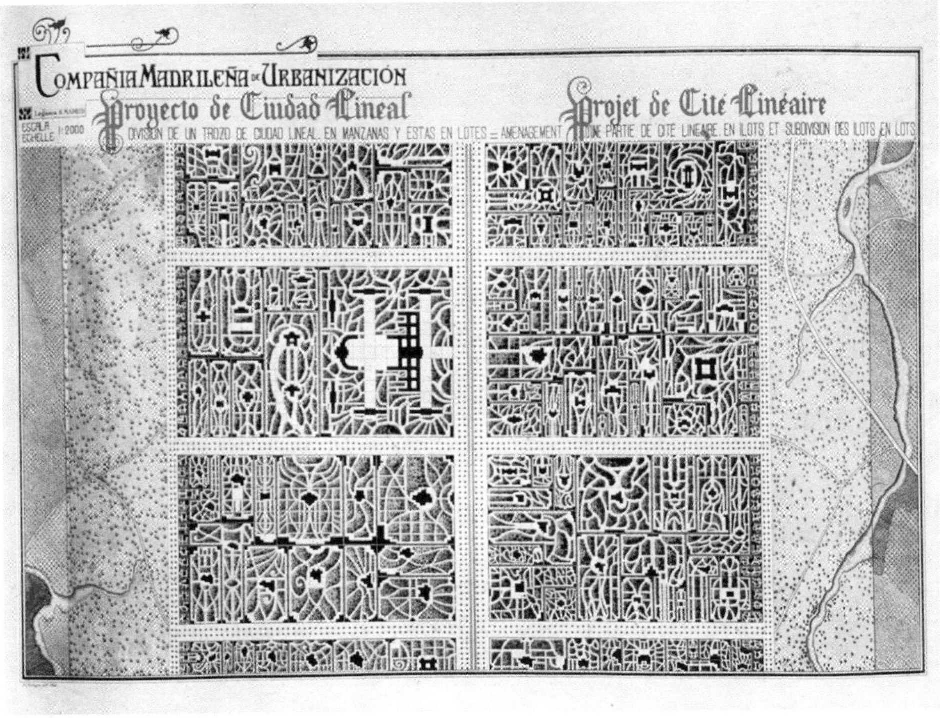


**Figure 3 (Top).** Theory of Linear Cities. ca. 1882.
**Figure 4 (Bottom).** Project of Linear City. ca. 1914.

**Figure 5.** Sketch of Linear City from Ceuta to Tétouan. ca. 1913.

**Figure 6.** Areal view of Linear City. 1926.

# The Outlook Tower

**Project:** 2. **Author:** Patrick Geddes (1854–1932). **Date:** 1892–1906. **Themes:** Geo-visualization. Geography. Taxonomy. Place(lessness).

**Figure 0.** Sketch of the Outlook Tower showing the vision of the world facilitated by the Episcope. After Patrick Geddes. ca. 1890.

The *camera obscura* and the panorama are two visual technologies that represent contrasting epistemological models. In a *camera obscura* light passes through a small hole into an enclosed and dark interior, projecting on the wall opposite the hole a mirror image of the outside world. During the seventeenth and eighteenth centuries this form of projection constituted, as the art critic Jonathan Crary has analyzed, "the most widely used model for explaining human vision, and for representing the relation of a perceiver and the position of a knowing subject to an external world."[1] On one hand, the *camera obscura* seems to replicate the mechanism of retinal vision and thus to demonstrate that the images humans perceive truthfully match reality. On the other, the camera's closed room represents the schism between the interior self and the exterior world, which dominated European ontology at the time. In short, the *camera obscura* was thought of as a visual device that showed both how individuals perceive and where they stand in relation to the world.

A panorama offers a very different model of vision and cognition. Instead of symbolizing the subject's perception of a particular scene, panoramas represent the collective apprehension of a totality. Used for the first time in Robert Barker's *A View of Edinburgh* (1788), panoramas are a drawing technique that allows painters to depict a 360-degree view of an area. The neologism *panorama*—which Barker coined by joining the Greek words *pan* (all) and *horama* (view)—reflects his intention to offer a "comprehensive view" by pictorial means.[2] An extremely popular attraction during the nineteenth century, precisely when the use of *camerae obscurae* starts to decline, panoramas represent a totality from a particular spot. As theorized by the French thinker Bruno Latour, panoramas constitute a metaphor for any comprehensive form of knowledge, and, specifically, for the totalizing philosophical systems that accompany the consolidation of modernity during the nineteenth century.[3]

These two opposing visual devices are central to Patrick Geddes's transformation of Short's Observatory in Edinburgh into the Outlook Tower. Geddes acquires the observatory in 1892, fascinated by two of its features: the building was centrally located in the Old Town promontory, and its terrace housed a cylindrical chamber where a *camera obscura* projected, on top of a circular table, a full panorama of Edinburgh's surroundings. Both conditions eloquently bring together two central theses of Geddes's urban thinking: respectively, the value of city centers as symbolic spaces that condense the meaning of their

1. Jonathan Crary, *Techniques of the Observer* (Cambridge, MA: MIT Press, 1990), 27.

2. "A View of Edinburgh. An Advertisement for Robert Barker's Panorama Exhibited at Leicester Square." National Galleries of Scotland. Accessed February 21, 2019. https://www.nationalgalleries.org/art-and-artists/63244/view-edinburgh-advertisement-robert-barkers-panorama-exhibited-leicester-square.

3. Bruno Latour, *Reassembling the Social: An Introduction to Actor-Network-Theory* (Oxford: Oxford University Press, 2005), 183–190.

surrounding territory, and the consideration of cities as part of broader territorial structures that Geddes terms conurbations.[4] Yet, Geddes's conversion of Short's Observatory into the Outlook Tower also overcomes this grounding of the city merely at a regional scale. His transformation of the Tower turns the building into an instrument to relate a specific physical location and the totality of the world **[fig. 0]**. In order to do so, Geddes's interventions explore how to couple architecture and multiple forms of vision, which constantly negotiate between the positionality of the *camera obscura* and the comprehensiveness of the panorama.

By relating the local to the world, Geddes intends to support the constitution of a universalist epistemology that could serve as the basis of a universalist ethos. Geddes shares this intellectual project with two of his contemporaries: the French anarchist-socialist geographer Élisée Reclus and the Belgian bibliographer Paul Otlet **[projects 3 and 8]**. Similarly interested in the world scale and in the novel importance of urbanization, the three authors consider that Western societies will only be able to understand and question the emergent world system with the help of new means of collective education that go beyond academic conventions and beyond the dominance of the textual.[5] With that purpose, all three resort to combining architectural procedures and different technologies of representation and data visualization. In Geddes's case, these procedures approach both Reclus's interest in the relations between social life and geographical space, and Otlet's idea that a new compendium of global knowledge, a new form of encyclopedia, is necessary to construct the fundamentals of universal citizenship.

These preoccupations motivate the complete reconfiguration of Short's Observatory's original state. Geddes defines his project as an *Index Museum* and an *Encyclopaedia Civica* that presents the human production of increasingly large geographical scales.[6] With that goal, he abandons the sequential organization of the enlightened *encyclopaedia methodica* in order to construct the contrasting and variegated forms of vision of an *encyclopaedia graphica*. The Tower visitor, like the protagonist of Geddes's 1915 treatise *Cities in Evolution*, is a "world citizen" who has to acquire a form of "synoptic" vision, made of multiple points of view, in order to foresee the possibilities of future spatial organization.[7] The best vehicles for such holistic apprehension are aesthetic: "it is so often missed by scientific and philosophic minds that the synthetic vision to which they aspire may be reached more simply from the aesthetic and the emotional side, and thus be visual and concrete."[8] Accordingly, from its very name on, the

**4.** Volker Welter, *Biopolis: Patrick Geddes and the City of Life* (Cambridge, MA: MIT Press, 2002), 60–70.

**5.** Tom Steele, "Élisée Reclus and Patrick Geddes: Geographies of the Mind, the Regional Study in the Global Vision," *Refractions* 4 (1999). Accessed online July 2, 2017: http://www.haussite.net/haus.0/SCRIPT/txt2000/04/reclus_geddes.html. Wouter Van Acker, "Internationalist Utopias of Visual Education: The Graphic and Scenographic Transformation of the Universal Encyclopaedia in the Work of Paul Otlet, Patrick Geddes, and Otto Neurath," *Perspectives on Science* 19, no. 1 (2011): 32–59.

**6.** Patrick Geddes, *Cities in Evolution: An Introduction to the Town Planning Movement and to the Study of Civics* (London: Williams & Norgate, 1915), 320. Alessandra Ponte, "Building the Stair Spiral of Evolution: The Index Museum of Sir Patrick Geddes," *Assemblage* 10 (1989): 52–60.

**7.** Geddes, *Cities in Evolution*, 320.

**8.** Geddes, *Cities in Evolution*, 321.

visual sphere determines the Outlook Tower's organization **[fig. 1]**. Already described by its first commentators as a "temple of vision," the building confronts its public with their visual conventions and trains them to see more.[9] To do that, the interior constantly combines architectural operations and scopic devices, making the visitor aware of the changes, fractures, and possibilities vision contains, as well as how, ultimately, these enable them to understand the world.[10]

The Tower's sectional organization gives spatial form to Geddes's conception of a local–world continuum orchestrated around the individual, visual experience. His project is organized in overlapping, successively up-scaled horizontal strata **[fig. 2]**. At the uppermost level, the *camera obscura* and the terrace show Edinburgh's region. Descending from this level, each floor presents a different territorial scale: Edinburgh, Scotland, the English-speaking countries, Europe, and, finally, the world. Despite its scalar progression, this is a discontinuous path that adopts the disorientation conventions of nineteenth-century panorama buildings.[11] Starting the Tower's itinerary requires abandoning the city and ascending to the top of the building through a closed staircase, and then returning to the city immediately after staying in the world. Between these two scales, the Tower offers multiple and disparate visual experiences.

The *camera obscura* panorama at the top provides the visitor an enclosed, technologically produced simulacrum of omniscience. The camera turns geography into a horizontal stratum, visible from atop, rendering explicit the mechanism of horizontal projection that characterizes the disposition of territorial scales in the remaining floors. After the comprehensive vision of the territory, the next levels fragment and constrain the view. The subjective view of Edinburgh from the terrace has a more limited scope than the one the camera provides. The successive space, called the Meditation Cell, is a chamber without windows. The descent continues alternating close-up views and representations of the distance, enclosure and partial opening, as a way to stress the dialectic between the partiality and specificity of the location and the world at large.[12] The apex of this subject–local–world continuum is, again, a visual device. The Episcope, created by Paul Reclus, Élisée's nephew, and later redesigned by the architect Paul Louis Albert Galeron, attempts to supersede the limitations of the existing representations of the planet **[figs. 3 and 4; and project 3]**.[13] Instead of the convex sphere of conventional terrestrial globes, which unavoidably separates subject and object, the Episcope allows the visitor to see the world from within, in a conical, concave projection. By conflating world geography and perspective

**9.** Bertrand Faure, "Le professeur Geddes et son Outlook Tower," *Le Visiteur* 7 (2001): 77. Reprinted from *Revue Politique et Parlementaire*, April 10, 1910.

**10.** Pierre Chabard, "L'Outlook Tower, anamorphose du monde," *Le Visiteur* 7 (2001): 69.

**11.** Panoramas were usually housed in specific buildings. The access to the panorama required always a transition from the street along a closed passage, and the ascent through a spiral staircase to a circular platform. The public had to stay on that platform to see the panorama.

**12.** Chabard, "L'Outlook Tower, anamorphose du monde," 72. Pierre Chabard, "Towers and Globes: Architectural and Epistemological Differences Between Patrick Geddes's Outlook Tower and Paul Otlet's Mundaneums," in *European Modernism and the Information Society: Informing the Present, Understanding the Past*, ed. Warden Boyd Rayward (Aldershot, UK: Ashgate, 2008), 113.

**13.** Galeron was also the architect of one of the versions of Reclus's terrestrial globe. See project 3.

in a human-scaled apparatus, the Episcope positions the localized subject in the global scale: in it, it is possible to see Earth as it would appear from Edinburgh, if the planet were a transparent sphere.[14] The scalar organization of the Tower seems to reaffirm the structure of the British colonial empire. Culminating the many ways of vision that populate the Tower, the Episcope problematizes that structure by showing that it just corresponds to a partial view of the world; to a vision from a particular locale.

Geddes's insistence on the visual domain situates his work as an intervention in the reconfiguration of perception and subjectivity, which, starting in the mid-nineteenth century, will powerfully affect modernity. In Crary's study of visuality, the abrupt decline in the use of *camerae obscurae* between 1810 and 1840 coincides with the emergence of prephotographic technologies of vision, which, while maintaining the camera's pretenses of objectivity, contribute to further separate the subject from the object of vision. Through these technologies, human visual experience is uprooted and "abstracted from any founding site or referent" in order to be dismantled into exchangeable images that could be massively disseminated within an increasingly globalized capitalist economy.[15] We are, as in Cerdà, in the domain of circulation **[project 1]**. In response to this new condition of the visual, Crary detects the emergence of a new figure, the modern observer, who needs to actively resituate herself in this visual context, while she is also subjected to the same techniques of abstraction and rationalization of the visual domain. Attuned to capital, images and subjects are "never allowed a real world to acquire solidity or permanence."[16]

The Outlook Tower proposes a counterproject to this world of fleeting images and subjects. The visitor of the Tower is certainly an observer who needs to actively reconcile contrasting technologies of vision. She moves between the consolidated, almost bygone, technologies of the *camera obscura* and the panorama and new means of cartographic representation and data visualization. By reconciling these technologies in the building, Geddes explores and questions the status of location. The Tower highlights the capacity of architecture to ground experience and life in a context, but it also shows that the local is just a segment of a broader system of scalar relations. To reunite world and place, Geddes believes that it is necessary to multiply the plurality of individual experiences, but also that these need to be orchestrated in order to form a stable and cohesive whole. While the Tower emphasizes the importance of diversity and local singularity, it defines the world as a system of hierarchically ordered territorial scales whose structure can be intellectually apprehended in the form of the collective and comprehensive picture that the panorama provides. Reassuringly, architecture integrates the fleeting within the order.

**14.** Chabard, "L'Outlook Tower, anamorphose du monde," 72. Georges Guyou, *The Hollow Globe: A New Geographical Apparatus* (Edinburgh: Patrick Geddes and Colleagues, ca. 1902). Reprinted and translated in Chabard, "L'Outlook Tower, anamorphose du monde," 74–75.

**15.** Crary, *Techniques of the Observer,* 14 and 10. Crary associates the emergence of these new visual technologies to the notion of modernization, which he defines, similarly to Marshall Berman's reference to Karl Marx in *All that Is Solid Melts into Air,* as: "the process by which capitalism uproots and makes mobile that which is grounded, clears away or obliterates that which impedes circulation, and makes exchangeable what is singular."

**16.** Crary, *Techniques of the Observer,* 24.

17. Welter, *Biopolis*, 60–80.

In this oscillation between the particular and the comprehensive, the Outlook Tower acts as a microcosm. It is a building that facilitates an overarching apprehension of the world and whose own structure is analogous to its author's understanding of the world structure. The scalar progression of the Tower's floors acts in the same way as Geddes's Valley Section. It is a mental emblem of the world structure and a guide to restore the relations between city and territory.[17] The Tower thus acts as an epistemological device. It seeks to make actions depend on cognition by showing the terrestrial scales where architecture should intervene. Geddes contributes to understanding architecture as a world-building agent by highlighting that, in order to become an instrument of spatial organization, architecture has to be first a means of acquiring knowledge. And for that, the Outlook Tower shows that architecture has to renegotiate its status vis-à-vis the information provided by increasingly powerful technologies of vision and communication. The microcosm is now an apparatus as technological and informational as it is architectural.

**Figure 1.** A First Visit to the Outlook Tower. Booklet cover. 1906.

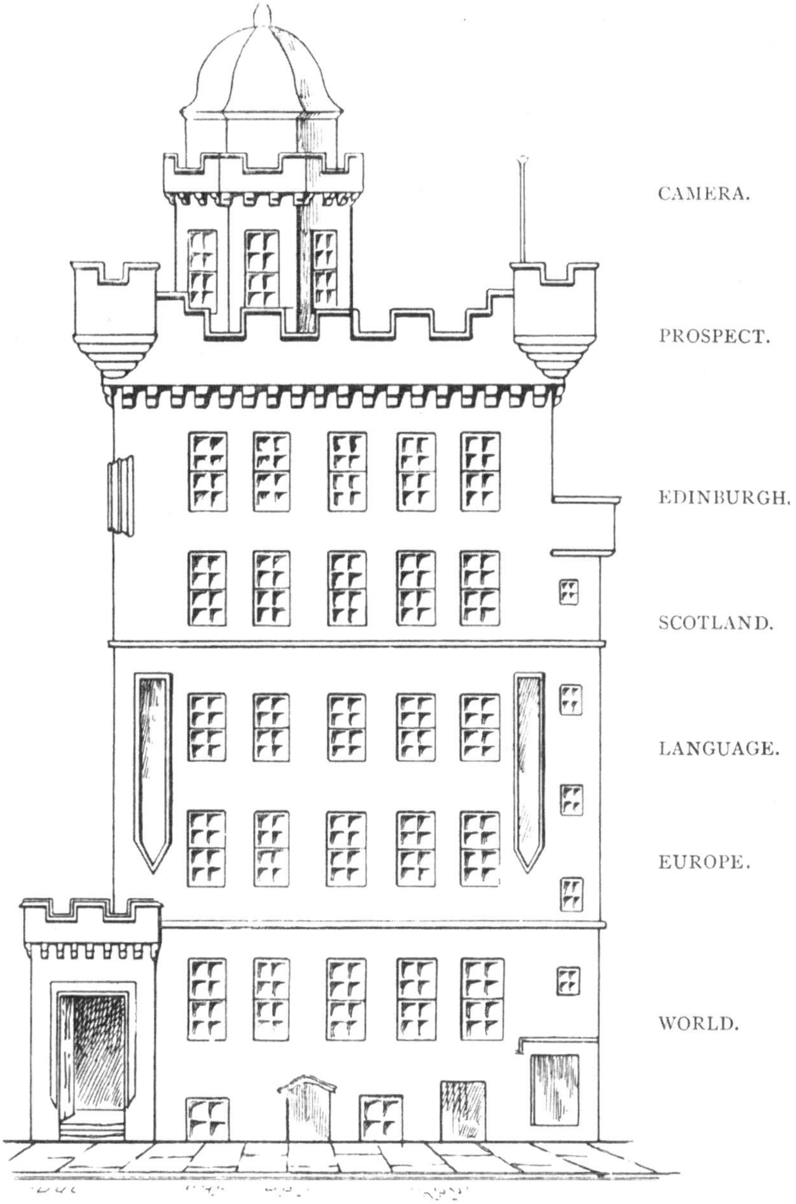


**Figure 2.** Outlook Tower in Diagrammatic Elevation. 1906.

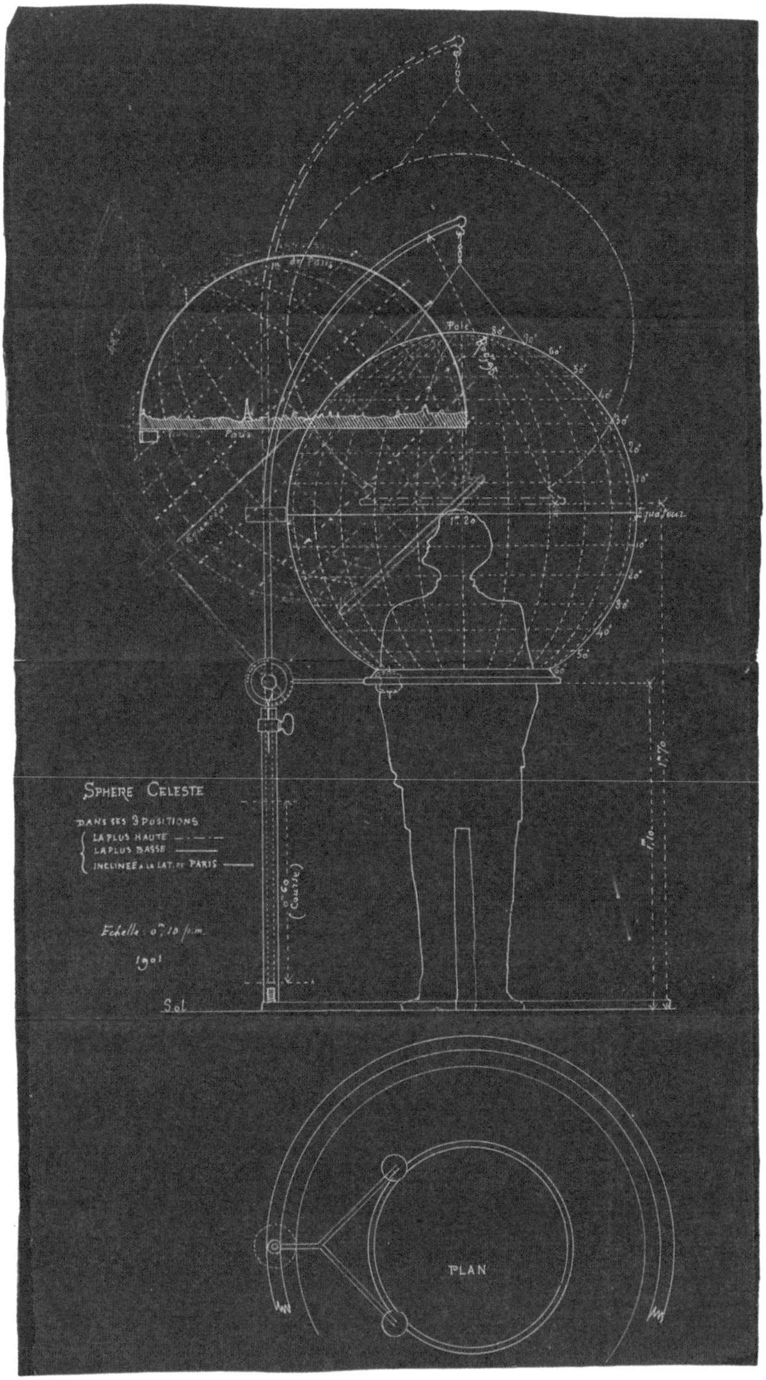


**Figure 3.** "Hollow Celestial Sphere." Paul Louis Albert Galeron. 1901.

**Figure 4 (Following page).** Prototype of the "Hollow Celestial Sphere." Paul Louis Albert Galeron. ca. 1900.

OPHIUCUS
DAUPHIN
SERPENT
AIGLE
ANTINOUS

# Un Globe Terrestre à l'Échelle du 100.000e

## Terrestrial Globe at the Scale 1:100,000

**Project:** 3. **Authors:** Élisée Reclus (1830–1905) and Louis Bonnier (1856–1946). **Date:** 1895–1898. **Themes:** Aerial Vision. Geo-visualization. Geography. World Urbanization.

| Enveloppe au 80,000". | Fers et toles. | Autres matériaux |
|---|---|---|
| Surface vitrée... ... ... ... ... | — | 2,400,000 k. |
| Attaches du vitrage aux fers ... ... | 960,000 | |
| Fers méridiens ... ... ... ... | 800,000 | |
| Fers sulvant les grands cercles verticaux ... | 800,000 | |
| Cointure helicordale externe... ... ... | 850,000 | |
| 〃 〃 interne... ... ... | 620,000 | |
| Poutres principales meridiénnes ... ... | 2,100,000 | |
| Contrefiches, tirants, contreventements ... | 1,200,000 | |
| Poutres des triangles de support ... ... | 840,000 | |
| Fers a planchers ... ... ... ... | 2,120,000 | |
| Gonssets et sabots ... ... ... ... | 910,000 | |
| Gouttieres, escaliers, ascenseure ... ... | 800,000 | |
| Plachers, menuiserie... ... ... ... | — | 2,600,000 |
| Imprevu ... ... ... ... ... | — | 1,000,000 |
| | 12,000,000 k. | 6,000,000 |
| Total ... ... ... ... ... | 18,000 tonnes. | |

| Globe au 100,000"' | | |
|---|---|---|
| Relief en platre, attaches ... ... ... | 300,000 k | 2,000,000 k |
| Pers méridiens et ceinture helicoidale ... | 1,350,000 | |
| Poutres principales méridiennes ... ... | 1,000,000 | |
| Contrefiches, tirants, contreventements ... | 650,000 | |
| Fers a planchers ... ... ... ... | 200,000 | |
| Goussets et sabots ... ... ... ... | 800,000 | |
| Poutres droites du support ... ... ... | 480,000 | |
| Installation mecanique ascenseurs... ... | 720,000 | |
| Armature de la sphere céleste ... ... | 700,000 | |
| Planchers, menniserie, etc ... ... ... | — | 800,000 |
| | 6,200,000 k | 2,800,000 k |
| Total ... ... ... ... ... | 9,000 tonnes. | |

| Prix approximatif. | Globe | Enveloppe |
|---|---|---|
| Fondations ... ... ... ... ... | 500,000 fr. | 100,000 fr. |
| Maconneries ... ... ... ... ... | — | 2,000,000 |
| Construction métallique ... ... ... | 4,500000 | 8,400,000 |
| Planchers, menuiscrie, etc. ... ... ... | 200,000 | 600,000 |
| | 5,200,000 | 12,000,000 |
| Total ... ... ... ... ... | 17,200,000 francs. | |

**Figure 0.** Estimated cost of the Terrestrial Globe at the Scale of 1:100,000. After Élisée Reclus. 1895.

1. Élisée Reclus, "Projet de construction d'un globe terrestre à l'échelle du 100.000e," in *Report of the Sixth International Geographical Congress*, ed. The secretaries (London: John Murray, 1896), 625.

2. Marie-Claire Robic, "Élisée Reclus Visited and Revisited" (paper presented at the Axel Baudoin Homage, Trondheim, Norway, 2006), 8; and Jean-Marc Besse, *Face au monde. Atlas, jardins, géorama* (Paris: Desclée de Brouwer, 2003).

3. Reclus, "Projet de construction d'un globe terrestre à l'échelle du 100.000e," 626. Our translation.

4. Reclus, "Projet de construction d'un globe terrestre à l'échelle du 100.000e," 629.

5. Gary S. Dunbar, "Élisée Reclus and the Great Globe," *Scottish Geographical Magazine* 9, no. 1 (1974): 63.

6. Dunbar, "Élisée Reclus and the Great Globe," 59.

7. Soizic Alavoine-Muller, "Un Globe terrestre pour l'exposition universelle de 1900. L'utopie géographique d'Élisée Reclus," *L'Espace Géographique* 32, no. 2 (2003): 165.

In 1895, at the Sixth International Geographical Congress, the French geographer Élisée Reclus presents an ambitious proposal to construct a terrestrial globe at the scale of 1:100,000. The globe would be the culmination of Reclus's geographical work: the conclusion of his pioneering, nineteen-volume *New Universal Geography* (1876–1894). After finishing this encyclopedic work, Reclus is convinced that texts, and even more critically, maps, are only imperfect, partial approximations to understanding the earth.[1] For the universalist ideology of Reclus, an anarchist-socialist, only a physical globe can visually render the unity of the planet.[2] Yet, not every globe: "A representation of the terrestrial sphere that is worth its name cannot be a simple piece of furniture, but a work of such importance that it becomes a building of its own, of vast dimensions, easily accessible, and permanently at the disposal for the research of scholars."[3] His extremely detailed proposal is thus for a magnificent building, measuring 127.5 meters in diameter and 400 meters of equatorial circumference **[fig. 0]**. This huge object should be more than 30 meters aboveground and placed on a promontory, thus standing above the trees and buildings of the city because it is "indispensable" to see it entirely from afar.[4] In Reclus's more ambitious speculations, such a piece would be built in every major city.[5]

Reclus works intensely on the idea between 1895 and 1898, with the goal of building this globe in the 1900 Paris Universal Exhibition. For a time, he develops the design with architect Paul Louis Albert Galeron. It is the architect who initially contacts the geographer.[6] Galeron had proposed to the Universal Exhibition Commission an idea that he considered close to Reclus's project and that he had named Cosmorama: a globe whose internal surface would deploy the celestial sphere **[fig. 1]**. The collaboration to develop this project, though, does not succeed. What Reclus conceives of as a scientific, educational, and political endeavor is for Galeron simply a visual spectacle.[7] Galeron thus finishes the project on his own—and later designs a reduced version in the proposed Hollow Terrestrial Sphere for Patrick Geddes's Outlook Tower **[project 2]**. Reclus, in turn, contacts architect Louis Bonnier to design a much smaller piece at a scale of 1:500,000 **[figs. 2, 3, and 4]**. Although the geographer and the architect define the building with constructive precision, they abandon the idea in 1898 for lack of funding.

Bonnier's project consists of a double sphere. Following Reclus's indications, the terrestrial globe is encapsulated within an external one. In between these two spheres but detached from them, there is a continuous ramp, which allows the visitors to circumnavigate the earth and to perceive it from an external position. Reclus, heavily influenced by the aerial pictures of his friend Nadar, the balloonist and photographer, considers that the terrestrial globe has to be first experienced through the type of holistic, aerial vision the balloon made possible.[8] Culminating the ramps, two platforms placed at the base and the top of the structure show visitors the external view of the poles. The one situated over the North Pole also offers a view of Paris that closes the circuit by resituating the experience in its urban context. Rooms for a library and an exhibition hall, placed at ground floor, complete the educational purposes of the building.

The reduced scale of Bonnier's two spheres partially diminishes Reclus's original intentions. As the geographer conceives of it, the interior globe should provide an extremely realistic representation of the earth in order to avoid the abstractions and ideological distortions characteristic of planar, cartographic visualizations. For Reclus, the initial 1:100,000 scale is necessary to render topography in three dimensions without vertical magnification, even if the 28 millimeters of maximum altitudinal difference that result are almost imperceptible.[9] At that scale, bathymetry can be also accurately depicted below a thin sheet of glass marking the sea level. Reclus's emphasis on scientific precision is extreme: the 1:100,000 globe is to be built with the real curvature of the spheroid, placed with its real North-South angle, and animated by a constant rotation. The positivist, realist drive is as scientific as it is ideological. Reclus is critical both of cultural Eurocentrism and European imperialism.[10] With his project, Paris, the capital of a colonial empire, would celebrate a Universal Exhibition that revealed the small portion of land Europe actually is.

Accuracy is not the only effect that architecture has to generate. Construction also serves to supplement the conventional experience of the planet. The internal and external spheres provide alternative forms of perception. The situation of the visitors in an aerial position between the two globes allows them only partial visions of the convex surface of the interior globe—promoting movement around geographical regions—while the continents depicted in the con-

8. Dunbar, "Élisée Reclus and the Great Globe," 62. Alavoine-Muller, "Un Globe terrestre pour l'Exposition universelle de 1900," 159.

9. Alavoine-Muller, "Un globe terrestre pour l'exposition universelle de 1900," 160.

10. The relation between Reclus and colonialism has been recently studied in French postcolonial geographic studies. While previous scholarship considered that Reclus's anti-imperialism faded when considering French imperialism, contemporary literature emphasizes his sustained critique of every form of colonial domination. See Federico Ferretti and Philippe Pelletier, "Imperial Science and Heterodox Discourses: Élisée Reclus and French Colonialism," *L'Espace géographique* 43, no. 1 (2013): 1–14.

cave glass surface of the outer sphere can be seen, as in a panorama, at a single glance. The contrast of the duplication is extreme: in the outer shell, the North-South pole is to be placed horizontally, like an equator.

As with Geddes's Outlook Tower, Earth is not to be understood through a unique view, but through oscillating and contrasting perceptions. The Terrestrial Globe incorporates the most advanced means of visualization that the nineteenth century had produced. The visitors are to apprehend the world through a variety of media representing multiple scales. Dioramas, photographic pictures, engravings, and exhibitions on history and geology are to complement the two spheres. In addition, Reclus aims to go beyond Geddes in the dynamism of the project. The interior globe is to be made of replaceable parts, which would be constantly updated and built on-site by the scientific team in charge of the globe. Reclus, a disciple of Friedrich Ratzel, transformed the term the German geographer had created—anthropogeography, or human geography—into "social geography" to emphasize the historical, changing dimension of geographical space. For him, geography is time; space, the result of collective historical processes.[11] The changing parts of the globe incorporate this temporal dimension by literally presenting a world in the making. Rather than a predecessor of the pretenses of real-time global monitoring of current geovisualization technologies, Reclus's emphasis on temporality is a way to visualize that geography is not a given, but a construct: "For geography is not an immutable thing; it makes and remakes itself day by day; it is modified every hour by the action of men."[12]

With this project, Reclus intends to improve previous terrestrial representations. He knew, and had visited, the globe that English cartographer James Wyld had built in London in 1852, in which the continents were deployed in the interior concave surface of a sphere; as well as Théodore Villard and Charles Cotard's Terrestrial Globe for the 1889 Universal Exhibition in Paris.[13] He probably didn't know or neglected, though, the globes that proliferated in France in the aftermath of the 1789 Revolution—the works of Étienne-Louis Boullée and Claude-Nicolas Ledoux, of Jean-Jacques Lequeu, Labadie, or Gay.[14] Understood as a civic monument, Reclus's project embodies the same universalist aspirations of the late eighteenth-century designs, but its scien-

**11.** Élisée Reclus, "The Evolution of Cities," *Contemporary Review* 67 (1895): 258.

**12.** Reclus, "The Evolution of Cities," 258.

**13.** Bernard Marrey, "Un Coquetier métallique de taille internationale," *Archives d'Architecture Moderne* 32 (1986): 77–80. See also Bernard Lightman, "Spectacle in Leicester Square: James Wyld's Great Globe, 1851–61," in *Popular Exhibitions, Science and Showmanship, 1840–1910*, ed. Joe Kember, John Plunkett, and Jill A. Sullivan (Pittsburgh: University of Pittsburgh Press, 2012).

**14.** Jean-Marie Pérouse de Montclos, *Étienne-Louis Boullée. 1728–1799. De l'architecture classique à l'architecture révolutionnaire* (Paris: Arts et Métiers Graphiques, 1969), 82–92.

tific and educational intentions surpass them. Instead of the predominantly symbolic, sublime representations of the planet proper of the Enlightenment, the Terrestrial Globe at scale 1:100,000 highlights the material conditions of Earth. The desire to realistically replicate the planet gives its most literal form to an understanding of architecture as an epistemological instrument. In the project, form and representation coincide in order to present a more comprehensive reality than common perception. In this sense, Reclus's speculation stands in a singular position, joining at once the symbolic drives of the Enlightenment, the comprehensive analytical efforts of Buckminster Fuller's Dymaxion Map, Mini-Earth, and World Resources Inventory **[project 14]**, and the poetics of Rem Koolhaas's De Bol **[project 39]**.

Together with the Outlook Tower, Reclus's Terrestrial Globe reveals the increasing need in the late nineteenth century to understand how architecture can respond to the human transformation of the planet. Geddes addresses this need by building a microcosm of the world; Reclus, by designing a scaled replica of the earth. Despite using different strategies, the two projects share the same objective. They abandon the understanding of architecture as a tool of cosmological representation—a conception that implies the existence of a predefined universal order that architecture's role is to reveal—and show, instead, how humans produce their own, increasingly unified artificial system. Certainly, both projects work strictly at the realm of representation. Yet, they conceptually pave the way for the many projects oriented toward the actual transformation of the planet developed during the twentieth century. Coinciding with his involvement in the Terrestrial Globe project, Reclus writes an opuscule, *The Evolution of Cities* (1895), whose very title explicitly references the work of his friend Geddes. As in Arturo Soria y Mata's writing, Reclus shows a positive attitude toward urban development, which contrasts with emerging antiurban ideologies such as Ebenezer Howard's notion of Garden Cities **[project 1]**. For him, the tendency toward the "indefinite extension of . . . towns," toward the elimination of differences between city and countryside, and toward the emergence of common forms of urban life should be seen as beneficial phenomena.[15] The generation of French geographers that immediately follow Reclus, led by Paul Vidal de la Blache, face this new context by orienting the discipline

**15.** Reclus, "The Evolution of Cities," 246 and 262–264, and Élisée Reclus, "La France," in *Nouvelle Géographie Universelle*, vol. 2 (Paris: Hachette, 1877), 894.

toward the analysis of the regional scale.[16] For Reclus, it is necessary, instead, to understand the whole production of the planet.[17] The extreme detail of the Terrestrial Globe represents the need to preserve geography's utter attention to the physically concrete, but its holistic ambition emphasizes that it is equally necessary to create a comprehensive and synthetic worldview that shows how the entire globe is being spatially produced.

**16.** Guilherme Ribeiro, "Regional Question, National Identity and the Emergence of Urban Industrial World. The Modernity in Paul Vidal's Work," *Annales de Géographie* 699, no. 5 (2014): 1215–1238.

**17.** Robic, "Élisée Reclus Visited and Revisited," 7–8.

Figure 1. Reclus Cosmorama for the Paris Exposition of 1900. Paul Louis Albert Galeron. 1897.

**Figure 2.** Terrestrial Globe Élisée Reclus. Trocadero Square, Paris. Section of the outer shell showing the spiral system of staircases and elevators.1897.

**Figure 3.** Terrestrial Globe Élisée Reclus. Trocadero Square, Paris. Plans. 1897.

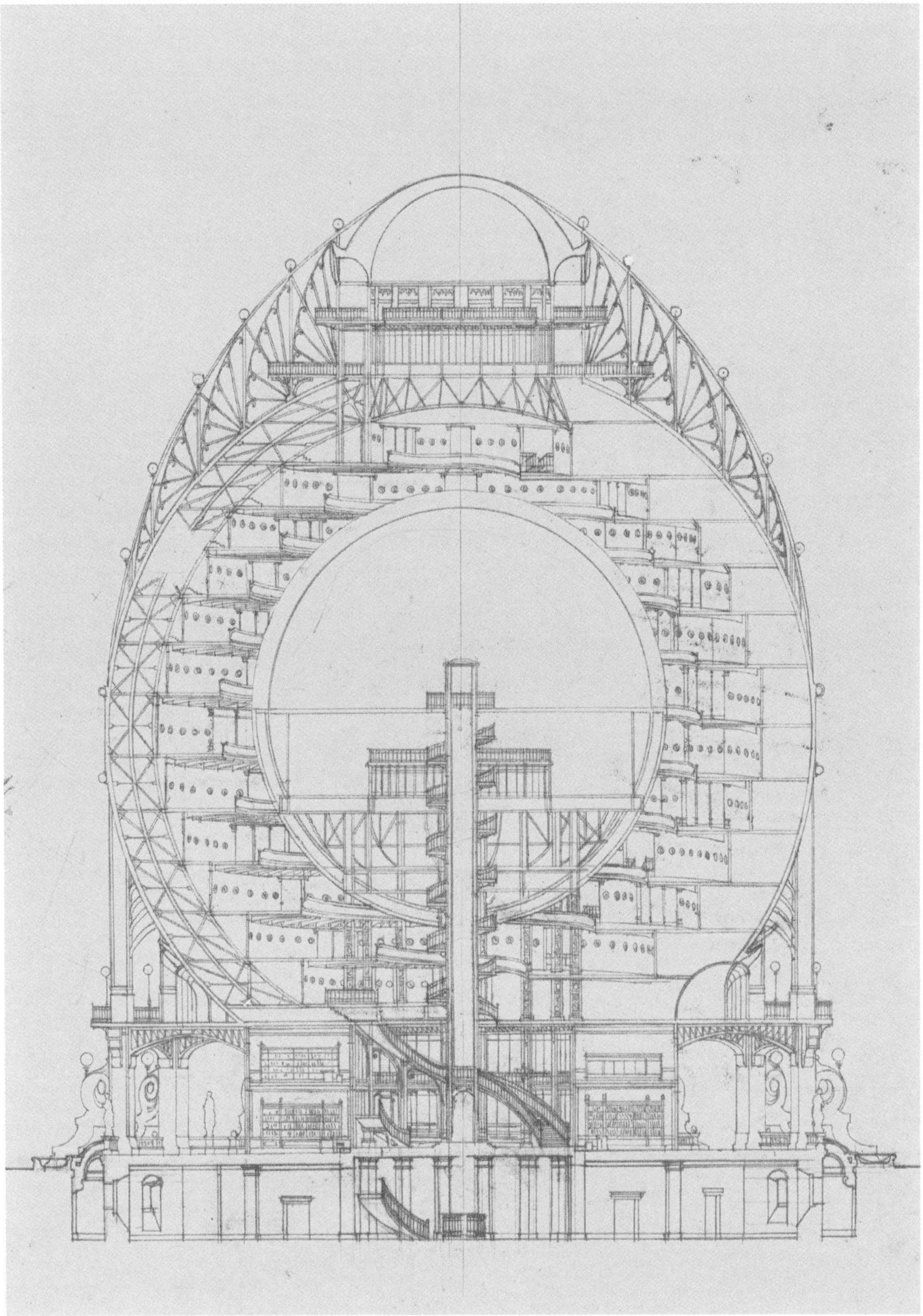

**Figure 4.** Terrestrial Globe Élisée Reclus. Trocadero Square, Paris. Section. 1897.

# Alpine Architektur

## Alpine Architecture

**Project:** 4. **Author:** Bruno Taut (1880–1938). **Date:** 1917–1919. **Themes:** Decentralization. Geography. Geopolitics. Human-Earth System.

**Figure 0.** Part 4: Earth's Crust Building. After Bruno Taut. 1917.

Bruno Taut responds to the unprecedented atrocities of World War I with the pacifist and internationalist utopia of *Alpine Architecture*. In the project, conceived in 1917, when Europe was at the peak of the conflict, Taut turns away from destruction and calls on Europeans to construct a peaceful common environment: "NATIONS OF EUROPE / SHAPE YOUR SACRED ASSETS! – BUILD! / BE A THOUGHT OF YOUR PLANET, EARTH / WHICH WISHES TO ADORN ITSELF – THROUGH YOU!"[1]

For Taut, to build is the path to peace: a huge collective enterprise that represents the common goal of the European population. Their cooperative work would create a symbolic center for Europe—a city crown for the totality of the continent—by placing monumental buildings in isolated locations of the Alps.[2] The primary decision of the project is, thus, geographical. The design intervenes in the space that marks the geographical divisions of Europe—between the northern and Mediterranean countries, between east and west—and that contains the continent's most elevated peaks. The physical attributes of centrality and elevation become symbolic and political ones. The Alps, the geographical link among the powers that constitute the Triple Alliance during the war, are transformed into a symbol of the continent's union.

*Alpine Architecture* is a project in the form of a book. The designs for the Alps that occupy the central portion of the volume are but a sample of the book's broader terrestrial project. As per the title of one of Taut's later publications, *Die Weltbauermeister* (The world-builder, 1919–1920), the task of the architect is that of world-building or world-making.[3] The fourth section of *Alpine Architecture*, "The Earth-Crust Building," explicitly illustrates this ambition. Graphically summarized through a small diagram of the globe, this section extends the Alps projects to other locations around the world **[fig. 0]**. Taut's designs cover the Atlas Mountains and the Caucasus; the area between the Himalayas and Kamchatka; Southeast Asia; and the entire western coast of the American continent. The total figure that these conglomerations create can only be perceived from the air **[fig. 1]**. The image of civilization and the image of Earth coincide. Glittering in the night, Taut's structures celebrate a united world and present it to the universe. Seen globally, they herald the fantasy of a world operating in unison.

The two images of the globe that represent the scope of Taut's planetary project—"Earth: Asiatic Side" and "Earth: American Side"—significantly displace

**1.** Bruno Taut, "Appeal to the Europeans," in *Bruno Taut: Alpine Architektur: Eine Utopie–A Utopia*, by Matthias Schirren and Bruno Taut (Munich: Prestel, 2004), 72.

**2.** Bruno Taut worked on the notion of city crown also in 1919; see Bruno Taut, Paul Scheerbart, Erich Baron, and Adolf Behne, *Die Stadtkrone* (Jena: E. Diedrichs, 1919). However, in *Alpine Architecture*, Taut states that the notion, if understood as dealing only with the city scale, is insufficient: "Yesterday morning it became entirely clear to me: the city crown is obsolete, building beautiful cities and crowning them does not take people much farther–you have to show them the great lonely heights and yoke them to tasks so gigantic that everything is subordinated to these tasks alone. Beauty first and foremost. . . . Just imagine, we–our children–will surely use the aeroplane as a matter of course, as we today use trains or cabs. And then, below them, the radiant, continually growing splendor! . . . If people can then create this greatness, which has begun in rudiments in India, China, Egypt, then their works will appear like a piece of nature which will later speak as profoundly as a tree in the forest." Bruno Taut, "Letter to Wife," in Schirren and Taut, *Bruno Taut: Alpine Architecture*, 120. On the notion of city crown see Iain Boyd Whyte, "The Expressionist Utopia," *Mac Journal* 4 (1999): 81.

**3.** On the notion of *Weltbauen*–world-building or world-making–see Antonio Petrov, "Rescaling Transnational Geographies," *MONU* 22 "Transnational Urbanism" (Spring 2015): 16–17; Iñaki Ábalos, *Atlas Pintoresco*, vol. 2: *Los Viajes* (Barcelona: Gustavo Gili, 2008), 150–174; and Rosemarie Haag, "Global Earthworks," *Art Journal* 42, no. 3 (1982): 222-225.

Europe to the periphery of the world, in consonance with Taut's interest in non-Western cultures.[4] Both drawings are, in any case, the representation of an intermediate scale within Taut's thinking. *Alpine Architecture* is structured as a "symphony" in five parts.[5] It starts with architectural propositions located in unspecified mountainous locations (in the chapter titled "The Crystal Building"). Chapter after chapter, the point of view gradually rises and the scale increases. The second chapter presents the project "above the sea of clouds."[6] The third shows with precision how the project occupies the Alps. The fourth represents the planetary scale, the fifth a cosmological fantasy **[fig. 2]**. The conclusion of this sequence is the void of cosmic space, the "nothingness."[7] Taut's planetary vision is pervaded by broad metaphysical aspirations: nothingness represents a state of personal communion with the universe. The cosmological drawing is a reaction to the theories of the psychophysicist Gustav Theodor Fechner about universal animation.[8] For Fechner, organic and inorganic matter are living entities that need reconciliation. Taut, who shares this position, suggests that it is the task of architecture to produce such a union between the inorganic—the planet—and its organic counterpart—the human.

In addition to the progressive increase of the scales of intervention, Taut's project employs two design procedures that will become an influential means of architectural world-making. The first is the ornamentation of physical geography; the second is visual narration. In *Alpine Architecture*, engaging with the planet equals substantiating Earth's geography. For Taut, the world needs to become "Earth"; a "good home" for humanity.[9] The diagram that represents the idea of earth-crust building depicts that ambition by giving form to the planet's uppermost geographical layer.[10] This attention to geography has different sources. It derives from the romantic appreciation of sublime landscapes, from his reading of Fechner, and is influenced by Eugène Viollet-le-Duc's geographical interpretation of architectural orders and constructions.[11] Yet, distinctively, in Taut's work, natural geography is incomplete and requires architecture to supplement it. *Alpine Architecture* employs an eclectic and transcultural repertoire of crystal pyramids, spires, bridges, and arcs in order to augment the values of the underlying terrain and to create a new human geography out of the physical one. Architecture adds cultural meaning to the landscape. It highlights, connects areas, and reveals geographical features. It challenges the limitations of location by introducing cultural references from disparate traditions.[12] Crucially, it defines different scales of territorial articulation.

**4.** As Matthias Schirren has pointed out, the formula "Nations of Europe/Shape your sacred assets" used in "Appeal to the Europeans" reverses Kaiser Wilhelm II's exhortation to protect Europe from the "Yellow Peril." At a moment when German politicians saw Asia as a potential menace to Europe, Taut vindicates the importance of eastern civilizations. See Schirren and Taut, *Bruno Taut: Alpine Architecture,* 73 and 96.

**5.** Schirren and Taut, *Bruno Taut: Alpine Architecture,* 28.

**6.** Schirren and Taut, *Bruno Taut: Alpine Architecture,* 44.

**7.** Schirren and Taut, *Bruno Taut: Alpine Architecture,* 112.

**8.** Matthias Schirren, "Introduction," in Schirren and Taut, *Bruno Taut: Alpine Architecture,* 18.

**9.** Bruno Taut, "The Earth–A Good Home," *Oppositions* 14 (1978): 84–89, trans. Jane O. Newman and John H. Smith. For Taut, the recovered earth is a feminine entity that can shelter a new form of civilization: "Man possesses his earth again, and need no longer be a mere wanderer on her."

**10.** Taut, "The Earth–A Good Home," 84. The notion of good home or "good dwelling" is also used in *Alpine Architecture.* Bruno Taut, "Preface by the Editor," in Schirren and Taut, *Bruno Taut: Alpine Architecture,* 118.

**11.** Matthias Schirren, "Introduction," in Schirren and Taut, *Bruno Taut: Alpine Architecture,* 15.

**12.** Despite the notable formal differences between their respective works, the attempt to create a transcultural architectural language that reduces the importance of the author, the interest in the capacity of architecture to transform geography, and the understanding of architecture as a force opposed to the urban conceptually connect Bruno Taut and Aldo Rossi [project 41]. For Taut, "architecture and the urban miasma remain insuperable opposites." See Schirren and Taut, *Bruno Taut: Alpine Architecture,* 36.

13. Schirren and Taut, *Bruno Taut: Alpine Architecture*, 76.

14. John A. Stuart, "Unweaving Narrative Fabric: Bruno Taut, Walter Benjamin, and Paul Scheerbart's *The Gray Cloth*," *Journal of Architectural Education* 53, no. 2 (1999): 62. Rosemarie Haag Bletter, "Paul Scheerbart's Architectural Fantasies," *Journal of the Society of Architectural Historians* 34, no. 2 (1975): 90.

15. Bletter, "Paul Scheerbart's Architectural Fantasies," 84.

What the *Alpine Architecture* reader witnesses through the progressive elevation of the point of view is the involvement of architecture in creating novel scalar relations and how these, in turn, generate a new cultural and political landscape. Taut's projects link islands or connect countries before forming a figure out of the entire world **[fig. 3]**. The wide circulation of new visual means such as panoramas, landscape paintings, and atlases since the nineteenth century, which underlay the projects of Patrick Geddes and Élisée Reclus, greatly expanded the geographic imaginary of European city dwellers. In *Alpine Architecture* these visual means are appropriated and altered in order to show that the factual description of natural geography is insufficient to support a collective territorial project. In the plate "The Construction Area," Taut alters one of the published panoramic views of the Monte Rosa chain, exaggerating the geography with architecture **[fig. 4]**.[13] In the "Grotesque Region," he attempts to "paint a non-perspectival picture." The view "From Switzerland" conflates two regions 150 kilometers apart.

The second main strategy of world-building in *Alpine Architecture* is visual narration. Through its narrative form, the project follows a long lineage of fictional utopian speculations. The direct inspiration of Taut's work comes from the texts of the expressionist science-fiction writer Paul Scheerbart, who is credited in *Alpine Architecture*'s unpublished preface as the actual author of the proposal. The two men meet in 1912. Shortly after, they initiate a dialogue about the possibilities of glass architecture: Scheerbart writes the manifesto *Glass Architecture*, and Taut designs the Glass Pavilion for the 1914 Cologne Deutscher Werkbund Exhibition. This collaboration is the sign of a deeper intellectual affinity concerning the political role of artistic creation. Scheerbart's fiction explores, especially after 1905, how new forms of architecture, infrastructure, and means of transportation can expedite the world's unification.[14] What Scheerbart describes are utopias of aesthetics and artistic creation. His texts confer on artifacts, not on politics, the primary role in creating a world system. In *Alpine Architecture*, Taut adopts an equivalent position. Peace and world society emerge through the reorganization of space and the consequent creation of a new sensibility.

Taut shares Scheerbart's thematic and methodology. The visual narrative format allows him to present a planetary totality through fragments. While "epigrammatic brevity" characterizes Scheerbart's prose, Taut works by defining partial interventions that leave open the relations between them.[15] Architectural typologies that can be applied in different locations and broad visions of new settlement systems are the parts of a global system dominated by gaps, or undefined zones. Certainly, geography appears through these gaps. They manifest the importance of preserving nature. At the same time, these gaps are also a recognition that *Alpine Architecture* is not an architectural project in the sense of a technical guide to physical construction. It is rather a means to transmit ideas and possibilities. "The pure idea must be allowed to speak of itself," Taut states.[16] "Ideas are road signs. The image of a distant future must light up the way for our aspirations."[17] When the historian Iain Boyd White assimilates Taut's procedures to the work of the Activists, a contemporary collective of German writers of socialist and internationalist ideology who aimed to move from expressionism toward "neo-enlightenment by elevating psychological revolt to the level of practical and social reform," he clarifies how important it is for the architect to use architecture to advance social transformation, and how this goal implies using media other than mere construction.[18] After *Alpine Architecture*, Taut produces the architectural books *Die Auflösung der Städte* (The dissolution of cities, 1920), *Die Stadtkrone* (The City Crown, 1919), and *Die Weltbauermeister*. Immediately after the war, he founds the *Arbeitsrat für Kunst* (Work Council for the Arts) to further disseminate his ideas and to promote a socialist-oriented reformulation of art practices.

Taut's political intentions become more explicit in these later works and initiatives. They complete the worldview that *Alpine Architecture* starts to delineate, and ground *Alpine Architecture*'s poetics in a precise critical analysis of the urban and social realities of the earlier twentieth century. Taut understands both the processes of capital accumulation that favor the expansion of metropolises to the detriment of the countryside, and the forms of industrial production that, although facilitating dispersion, cause an exploitative relationship with the land.[19] By seeking alternatives to the notion of the city, Taut makes use of spatial means to contradict capitalist social relations and their environmental manifestations. The theoretical underpinnings of Taut's thinking derive from Karl Marx, but his proposals lean toward the anarchistic tradition. His works promote forms of self-sufficiency and *Gemeinschaft* that come from the anarchist writings of Pyotr Alexeyevich Kropotkin and the German thinker Gustav Landauer.[20] Taut's is a "world without cities, without money, without politics."[21] Also, without states.

Socially, Taut's settlements construct a fragmented world of autarchic structures. *Alpine Architecture* balances this fragmentation by proposing a common formal language that points toward the cultural, symbolic, and political union

**16.** Taut, "Preface by the Editor," 118.

**17.** Taut, "The Earth–A Good Home," 88.

**18.** Iain Boyd Whyte, *Bruno Taut and the Architecture of Activism* (Cambridge, UK: Cambridge University Press, 1982), 7.

**19.** Taut, "The Earth–A Good Home," 87.

**20.** Taut directly references Kropotkin: Taut, "The Earth–A Good Home," 87. For Landauer, see Whyte, *Bruno Taut and the Architecture of Activism*, 52–54.

**21.** Ludovico Scarpa, "The Earth–A Good Home," *Oppositions* 14 (1978): 85, and Taut, "The Earth–A Good Home," 87.

of the parts. This common language is architecture. Taut believes architects are the only artists whose creations emanate directly from people's will.[22] The project of a reconciled world is, in this sense, primarily an affirmation of architecture's role. "Yet beyond all politics, the value of this work lies in itself, [its] purifying and resolving [effect] in the fundamental questions of architecture, and thus [in its] being culture itself become form."[23] Taut's ultimate goal is to construct an essential architecture that expresses collective aspirations. The search for a shared formal language then becomes the search for a new form of anonymity. Fittingly, Taut intends to publish *Alpine Architecture* without his name. By manipulating archetypal architectural forms, Taut seeks to establish a repertoire of common transcultural symbols that bridge the world's new settlements. Conceived outside and "against the city," these symbols stand in isolation, facing geography directly, revealing it, seeking a direct relation between individual, geography, and world.[24]

**22.** Whyte, *Bruno Taut and the Architecture of Activism*, 61.

**23.** Taut, "Preface by the Editor," 118.

**24.** Taut, "The Earth–A Good Home," 88.

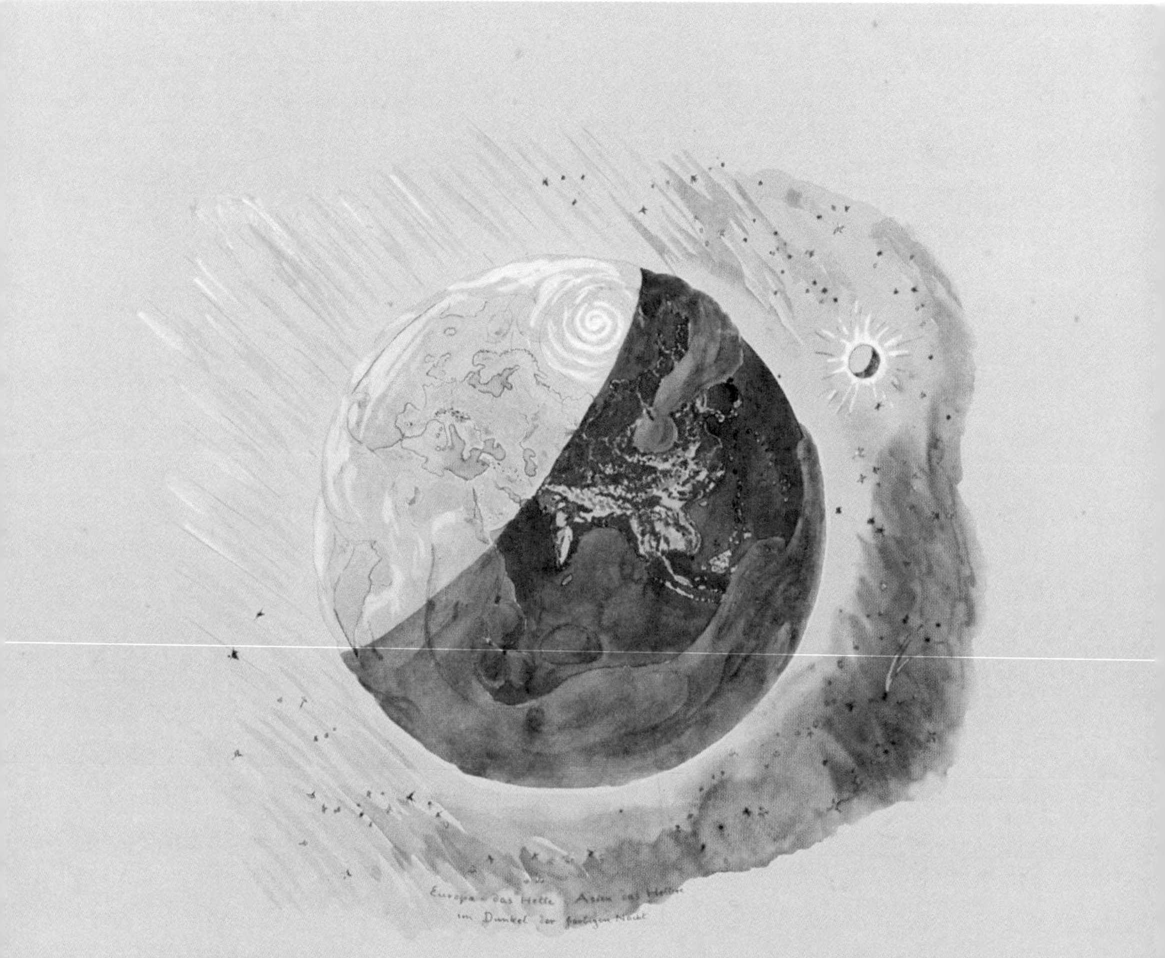


**Figure 1.** Earth, Asiatic Side. 1917.

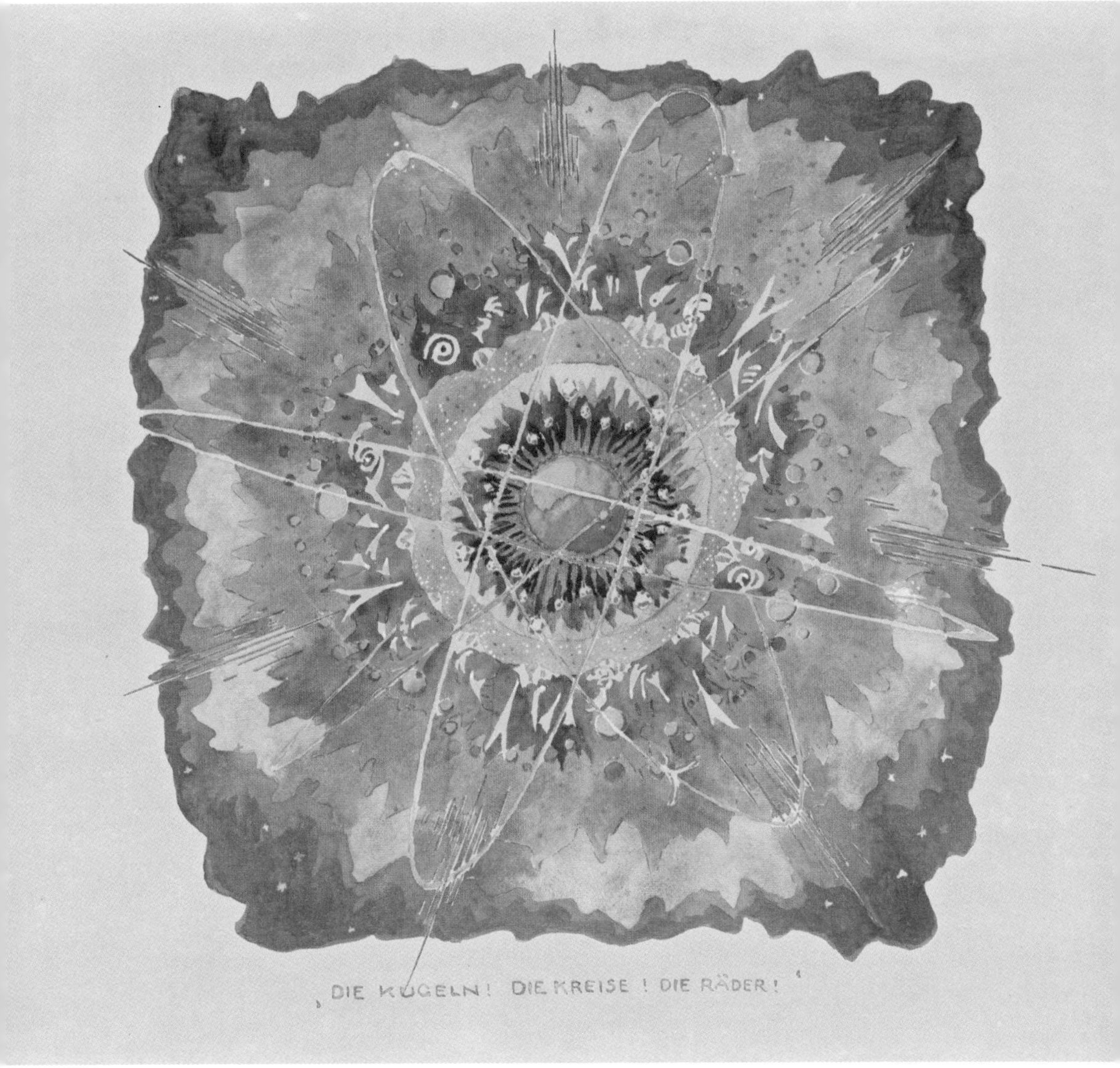


**Figure 2.** Solar System. 1917.

**Figure 3.** The Ralik and Ratak Islands. 1917.

**Figure 4.** The Construction areas. 1917.

# АЭРО Город
## Aero-Cities

**Project:** 5. **Author:** Lazar Khidekel (1904–1986). **Date:** 1925–1930. **Themes:** Autonomy. Geography. Infrastructure. Parallelism.

**Figure 0.** Futuristic City. After Lazar Khidekel. 1929.

Between 1925 and 1930 Russian architect Lazar Khidekel draws several views of cities elevated above Earth's surface, to which he collectively refers as aero-cities. The drawings show an interconnected system of overlaid horizontal bars, which are supported in a few points by enormous prismatic columns. The distances between columns are irregular and vast. Although the drawings lack scale, the supports seem to span between dozens and hundreds of meters. As a result, a strong sense of horizontality prevails in the designs. The buildings suggest a form of life that takes place in constructed horizontal layers that are parallel to Earth: an entirely new aerial space that necessitates only occasional contact with the ground, and whose form of spatial organization is completely independent of the terrain's morphological conditions **[fig. 0]**. The drawings emphasize the independence of the natural and urban systems. The aero-cities always follow a strict orthogonal system, which allows the bars to extend along different perpendicular directions while, below them, the landscape remains unaltered.

This separation is a tool to exacerbate the value of nature and the beauty of Earth. The drawings situate the aero-cities in locations where several natural systems are simultaneously present: waterways, hills, forests, the sky. The role of the buildings is to mediate among these different elements. The bars span from the ground to the water, or they ascend from the top of the trees toward the sky **[fig. 1]**. In fact, Khidekel's descriptions of the cities unfold a sort of protoecological argument. Not only does he justify elevating the aero-cities as a way to break the correlation between the construction of cities and the destruction of nature—since, by raising the cities from the ground, they can be placed in the landscape while preserving nature's original state—but the cities support a holistic project of reconfiguration of the "figural-chaotic world," which reorients industrial civilization toward a new system where machines and nature should mutually reinforce each other to generate a new form of life:[1]

"Construction should not only denote the machine, but also water and wind, living motion, in order to apprehend and explain the opposition and hidden forces of nonmechanical nature, which are forced to operate in a united collective summarizing the figural sensations of the vital dynamic. . . . The construction of future creativity leads to the convergence of all creative spheres of the new life, to the path of economy and a vital dynamic. This should master the whole spatial figural-chaotic world, leading to the unification of life-creating construction."[2]

**1.** Allan Rosenfeld, "Between Suprematist Utopia and Stalinist Reality," in *Lazar Khidekel & Suprematism*, ed. Regina Khidekel and Tatiana V. Goriacheva (New York: Prestel, 2014), 37.

**2.** Lazar Khidekel quoted in Tatiana V. Goriacheva, "'Research in the plane of the Suprematist Field': Lazar Khidekel's Suprematism," in Khidekel and Goriacheva, *Lazar Khidekel & Suprematism*, 18

The diversity of vistas Khidekel employs to represent the project reflects this drive toward the unification of life, artifice, and nature. It is also symptomatic of how his designs situate viewers in a variety of new positions that can allow them to perceive that unity. All of these positions alter the conventional situation of the horizon in conic perspective in order to give a new impression of the position and the extension of the planet. Some drawings depict the aero-city from below, with its many spatial bars framing the view of the sky. In them, the sky ceases to be a mere background and is incorporated as a part of the construction **[fig. 2]**. Other views of the project are axonometric, with the bars only interrupted by the picture frame. The abrupt cut and the lack of a vanishing point characteristic of the axonometric system suggest an unlimited urban system **[fig. 3]**.[3] In a third type, the city is seen from a novel, extraterrestrial point of view. In them, the horizon is the terrain and the city is as an artificial body floating freely above the earth, a structure that lacks any resemblance whatsoever to existing cities **[fig. 4]**.

The radical departure from existing urban forms, the experimentation with new techniques of representation, the search for new forms of visions, the universalism—in all these aspects Khidekel joins central investigations of the postrevolutionary Russian architectural avant-garde. Between 1917 and 1932, when spatial speculation will be condemned as contradictory to the real necessities of construction established in the second Five Year Plan, avant-garde architects focus on elaborating new architectural languages and on defining building types and urban systems that can support an entirely new form of equalitarian, socialist life.[4] Moreover, as architect and theorist El Lissitzky indicates in his book *Russia: Architecture for a World Revolution* (1929), part of the avant-garde follows the early belief in an international revolutionary process by creating models for a world society.[5] Khidekel, who studied with El Lissitzky between 1918 and 1922 and with suprematist painter Kazimir Malevich at the Vitebsk People's Art School, was fully exposed to this intellectual milieu. His work manifests, in fact, the ambiguous project of the Soviet avant-garde, its oscillation between utopianism and the desire to find the means to reformulate the way in which actual space is shaped. On one hand, the aero-cities are completely unrealizable propositions. On the other, they constitute the first attempt to treat as urban questions some of the most utopian planetary aspirations of the Russian artistic avant-garde, especially of the suprematist school in which Khidekel was educated.

**3.** Richard J. Difford, "Proun: An Exercise in the Illusion of Four-Dimensional Space," *Journal of Architecture* 2, no. 2 (1997): 127.

**4.** Anatole Kopp, *Town and Revolution: Soviet Architecture and City Planning, 1917–1935* (New York: G. Braziller, 1970), 101–115.

**5.** Vladimir Shlapentokh, "The World Revolution as a Geopolitical Instrument of the Soviet Leadership," *Russian History/ Histoire Russe* 26, no. 3 (Fall 1999): 315–334.

Malevich defines the notion of suprematism in the period 1913–1915. He proposes the term to refer to a form of pure creation that liberates art from its historical subjection to representation. Suprematism is to be an "object-less" art, autonomous from the ideological mandates that were historically imposed on it. Yet, as the French philosopher Jacques Rancière emphasizes, the search for artistic autonomy was not a form of detachment from reality, but a way to convert art into a means of shaping the world.[6] In Malevich's terms, art has to conquer its own "point of view" and to make it as socially valid as politics or religion.[7]

In this approach to reality, Malevich insists on three questions that art should address, all of which characterize Khidekel's work. The first is the expansion of urbanization. Malevich understands that "new art movements can exist only in a society which has absorbed the tempo of the big city, the metallic quality of industry," and he expects urban culture to shape all space in the immediate future: "the culture of the city will sooner or later embrace all the provinces and subject them to its technology. It is only when this has taken place that futurist art will be able to develop its power and thrive in the provinces as well as in the city."[8] The second one is the novel importance of aerial and extraterrestrial vision in helping humans to understand the planet as a whole and its place within the cosmos. In his photomontage *Analytical Chart No.16: The Relation Between the Painterly Perception and the Environment of the Artist* and, even more clearly, in the chart *The Environment That Motivates Suprematism*, included in his treatise *The Non-Objective World* (1926), Malevich associates suprematism with the view from above.[9] For him, the environment in which suprematism operates "has been produced by the latest achievements of technology, and especially of aviation, so that one could also refer to Suprematism as 'aeronautical.'"[10] The third key aspect is Malevich's argument that art should address the scale of the world, and even the cosmic scale. His criticism of the previous avant-garde movements is that "Futurism and Cubism did not convey, even to the imagination, the presence of world space; its space was limited by the space that divides things from one another on the Earth."[11] Above all, suprematism is a way to present this novel planetary condition.

Malevich understands that these three questions require finding a new artistic language, both pictorial and sculptural. The three-dimensional *Arkitektons* and the series *Planits*—conceived as houses for Earth dwellers—attempt to link

**6.** Jacques Rancière, *Aesthetics and Its Discontents* (Cambridge, UK: Polity Press, 2009), 1–15.

**7.** Kazimir Severinovich Malevich, *The Non-objective World* (Chicago: P. Theobald, 1959 [1926]), 94–98.

**8.** Malevich, *The Non-objective World*, 63.

**9.** Christina Lodder, "Transfiguring Reality: Suprematism and the Aerial View," in *Seeing from Above: The Aerial View in Visual Culture*, ed. Stephen Bann, Mark Dorrian, and Frédéric Pousin (London: I.B. Tauris, 2013), 95–117.

**10.** Malevich, *The Non-objective World*, 61.

**11.** Kazimir Malevich, 1916 letter to Mikhail Matiushin, quoted in Charlotte Douglas, "Aero-Art, The Planetary View: Kazimir Malevich and Lazar Khidekel," in Khidekel and Goriacheva, *Lazar Khidekel & Suprematism*, 29.

the cosmic aspirations of suprematist language to architectural space. Yet, these sculptures and paintings are strict formal explorations, devoid of any consideration of function, construction, or urban structure. What Khidekel does is to connect those formal investigations to precise spatial questions—the role of territory, the importance of infrastructure, the relation between city and nature, the forms that architecture can adopt to operate beyond the urban scale—which link the broader, more speculative project of planetarization to the actual transformations of the urban realm in the early twentieth century. In aero-cities, suprematist forms become a tool to create a nonhierarchical, isotropic, unlimited system in which the infrastructural logic that characterizes the modern city is translated to architectural terms.[12] It is a system that substitutes individual buildings for vast, structural complexes devoid of any signs of functional differentiation or social stratification; for a uniform, exterior frame that can be adapted to any interior use. Khidekel creates machines to extend urbanization across the whole territory. Machines to see Earth and to stay in space, which are no longer buildings but infrastructural frames.

Khidekel's work occupies a transitional position. His designs substantially depend on the pictorial investigations of suprematism—and, consistently, most of his architectural projects are represented as paintings. Yet, as indicated, they also suggest how to relate the suprematist language to the realm of architectural praxis. According to El Lissitzky, one branch of the Russian utopian, planetary imagination seeks to overcome the limitations of the earthbound through the creation of inhabitable aerial structures.[13] This is the terrain of Georgii Krutikov's Flying City and Viktor Kalmykov's Saturn City **[projects 11 and 12]**—the explorations that Manfredo Tafuri condemns as "useless utopias."[14] Through Malevich's influence, Khidekel lays the foundation for this tendency. On another level, he starts redirecting planetary ambitions toward a proper exploration of architectural language and technique. This is the investigation that Ivan Leonidov will fully develop **[project 9]**. In Khidekel's case, the preoccupation with architectural praxis urges him to think beyond the aero-cities and to propose other forms of relating architecture and Earth. Such is the goal of his Floating City, an infrastructural building connecting rivers to ocean, and Garden Cities, a structural frame alternatively occupied by vegetation, systems of transportation, and buildings. Together, the corpus of Khidekel's work presents a vision of an infrastructural architecture that connects the urban to

**12.** Ginés Garrido, "Ciudades aéreas. Visiones de Lazar Khidekel," *Arquitectura Viva* 153 (2013): 58–61.

**13.** El Lissitzky, *Russia: An Architecture for World Revolution* (Cambridge, MA: MIT Press, 1984 [1929]), 64.

**14.** Manfredo Tafuri and Francesco Dal Co, *Modern Architecture*, trans. Robert Erich Wolf (New York: Electa/Rizzoli, 1986), 218.

natural and geographical conditions. The value of such investigation transcends its original 1920s Soviet context. Even if Khidekel's projects remain unknown for decades, similar formal investigations recur between the mid-1950s and the mid-1960s, a period in which abstract frameworks, superimposed structures, and hybrids among architecture, infrastructure, and technical systems become again the tools to rethink the relation among architecture, urban society, and the world scale.

**Figure 1.** Design for a Futuristic City Above Water. 1925.

Figure 2. Sketch for a Futuristic City. 1929.

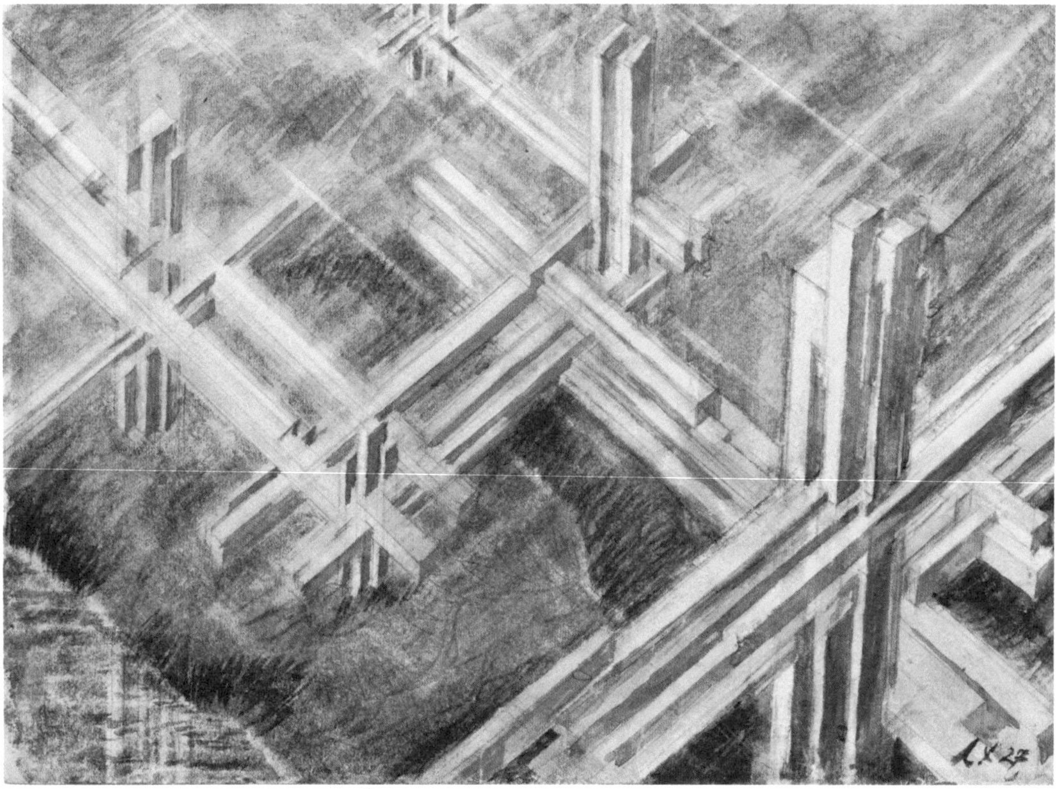

**Figure 3.** Elevated City. 1927.

**Figure 4.** Design for a Flying City. 1926.

# Airocean World Town Plan – 4D Tower

**Project:** 6. **Author:** Richard Buckminster Fuller (1895–1983). **Date:** 1927–1932. **Themes:** Environmental Control. Immateriality. Remoteness. Telecommunications.

**Figure 0.** The Airocean World Town Plan. After Richard Buckminster Fuller. 1927.

Although Buckminster Fuller was a pluralistic inventor, who designed from rowing sculls to whole new structural systems and held patents for twenty-four of his creations, few concepts were enough for him to summarize his ideas. A reductionist by nature, Fuller always broke down complex systems to their fundamental constituents, seeking answers that represented pure syntheses—whether the single central mast solution for housing, the pure-compression/pure-tension of the elements in tensegrity structures, Earth as a spaceship, or the rules of nature and thought responding to the principle of synergy. Expanding progressively, what started as a few ideas under the name *Lightful* evolved into a handful of explorations under *4D* **[fig. 0]**. From *4D*, the few components turned into a plethora of mature, executable inventions like houses or vehicles under *Dymaxion*, and from there the whole universe would be encompassed into *Synergies*.[1]

Initially named Lightful Tower, the 4D Tower is Fuller's answer to the problem of mass housing and to the processes of "world integration" he perceived **[fig. 1]**.[2] Following his characteristic method of reasoning, the Tower is far from being a finite object in itself; it is, rather, an open system designed to respond to the growing challenges of an interconnected world. Fuller disseminates the project through *Shelter*, the journal of architecture he starts editing in 1930 in order to investigate how architectural design can be informed by scientific inquiry and technical innovation.[3] Coherently with the journal's agenda, even if the Tower's purpose is to shelter, it is hardly possible to conceptualize the project as a traditional house. The design can be better understood by analogy with contemporaneous machines and technologies. Instead of being fixed to the ground, the Tower is mobile, like a ship; instead of being heavy and rigid like masonry, it is light and flexible, like steel cables; instead of replicating traditional concepts of ownership and property, it is leased and replaced, like a telephone; instead of being uniquely crafted, it is industrially mass-produced; and instead of being assembled on site, it is delivered complete and fixed in place by a Zeppelin **[figs. 2 and 3]**.

The 4D Tower is one of Fuller's designs for the company 4D, which he founds in 1927 to develop new, light systems of architectural and technical construction.[4] The intellectual basis of the project derives from his design of the 4D Dymaxion House (1927–1931) and from the 1927 article "Universal Requirements of a Dwelling Advantage," where Fuller establishes the "Checklist of

1. K. Michael Hays, "Fuller's Geological Engagements with Architecture," in *Buckminster Fuller: Starting with the Universe*, ed. K. Michael Hays and Dana A. Miller (New York: Whitney Museum of American Art, 2008), 2.

2. R. Buckminster Fuller, "We Call It Earth," in Fuller, *Nine Chains to the Moon* (Philadelphia: J. B. Lippincott Co., 1938), 60.

3. See *Shelter* 2, no. 5 (November 1932): n.p. The magazine also includes articles about "Pan-Continental Service Systems," and other type of "scientific" shelters based on the use of tensile structures.

4. Stanford Libraries, "R. Buckminster Fuller Timeline," https://library.stanford.edu/spc/manuscripts-division/r-buckminster-fuller-timeline. Accessed February 5, 2019.

the / Universal Design Requirements / of a Scientific Dwelling Facility—as a component function / of a new world-encompassing, service industry."[5] The Tower keeps most of the inventions explored in the Dymaxion House, but it transports the idea of shelter from the individual to the collective and expresses the possibility of universal implementation. The design is a featherweight, multistory building supported by a central mast and composed of cutting-edge technologies and high-performance materials (steel, aluminum, plastic, wires, and glass), which can be used anywhere. Each floor is an environmentally controlled unit enclosed in glass. Even if designed with the lightest available materials and touching the ground at a single point, the building is supposed to be guaranteed against every possible natural hazard, doing justice to Fuller's principle of "ephemerization," or doing more with less.[6]

The mast is the project's central piece. It is an organizational device, a load-bearing structure, a crane, and a radio antenna. It allows the Tower to be transported and placed on any terrain. Fuller envisions a system that does not depend on local infrastructure, especially road transportation and communication, but rather replaces these roles by organizing itself as a service station. From Siberia to the Amazon rainforest and from the North to the South Pole, the towers around the globe weave an invisible network of airplane routes and radio signals, acting as receiver and transmitter points for information and people.[7] The drawing of Earth where Fuller depicts the resulting system—titled the Airocean World Town Plan—shows this terrestrial dimension. Not only does the project cover the earth's surface, it also considers the sectional condition of the planet, thus advancing a preoccupation with the world's vertical axis that Fuller will continue to explore throughout his career **[project 14]**. Connected through aerial and maritime infrastructures and means of transportation, the towers generate a four-dimensional network in which the superficial condition of land occupation expands along the atmospheric vertical axis and the temporal dimension of communications. The towers' distribution, no longer tied to cities, depends only on the strategic need for resource extraction and planetary circulation.[8] The quantification of the project is also global: the number of towers responds to the world's need for two billion new homes. Even the perspective from which Earth is represented seeks to be as comprehensive as possible. Fuller chooses a view of the planet that captures where 99.5% of the population lives at the time.[9]

**5.** "Universal Requirements of a Dwelling Advantage," *Shelter Magazine* 1 (1931). The text was first written in 1927 and then revised for its publication in *Shelter*, and later in *Nine Chains to the Moon*. See R. Buckminster Fuller, *The Buckminster Fuller Reader*, ed. James Meller (London: Jonathan Cape, 1970), 242. In the article, Fuller establishes the "Check list of the / Universal Design Requirements / of a Scientific Dwelling Facility–as a component function / of a new world-encompassing, service industry–." Formally, it is possible that Fuller drew inspiration for the project from the housing model developed by the architects Heinz and Bodo Rasch in 1927. See Heinrich Klotz, *Vision der Moderne. Das Prinzip Konstruktion* (Munich: Prestel Verlag, 1986), 224–225.

**6.** R. Buckminster Fuller, "Ephemeralization," in *Nine Chains to the Moon*, 284–288.

**7.** Hays, "Fuller's Geological Engagements with Architecture," 2.

**8.** Fuller's distribution of towers across the earth parallels his understanding of systems of production in global terms: "No teleologic designer, in view of the current world integration, can profess concern with building only within the 'town plan' of Podunk when the materials, structures, and tools he uses are so obviously derived from the entire surface of the earth. . . . We cannot claim that we are doing the most with the least without carefully referring to our cosmic inventory and ascertaining what is now most suitable and available." Fuller, *Nine Chains to the Moon*, 60.

**9.** Fuller, *Nine Chains to the Moon*, 59.

Crucial to this World Town Plan is the integration between architecture, radio communication, and air transportation. In Fuller's view, such relation has the power to rearrange human territories, reconceptualize or even eliminate national borders, and generate a new landscape of dispersed planetary cities.[10] Because the connections between things are no longer material or restricted by geography, the shelter enables new global relations and amplifies each individual's own mind. The shelter establishes a connection between man and the universe; it acts as a linking device that captures and sends waves of information in the same way as the brain communicates with the body.[11] Each individual room becomes a control center with the power to shape the world, connecting one human to every other and beyond, in a regime where sight is no longer a determining factor. The visible horizon ceases to be a threshold when the whole world finds its place in any ordinary room. Interconnected and with no physical limits, "the world [becomes] a world for the first time."[12]

By blending the architecture of shelter with the emerging engineering structures of telecommunication, the 4D Tower denies the isolation of the discipline of architecture. Not only does the project incorporate recently discovered technologies, but it also claims the discipline's own place in the promising path opened by those advancements. In this regard, Fuller continues an exploration of the transformative power of telecommunications that started in the USSR already a decade before, and which spans from Vladimir Tatlin's 1919 Monument to the Third International—a steel tower with a radio communication mast from which Soviet news would be broadcast to the world—to the Vesnin Brothers' 1923 Palace of Labor, to Ivan Leonidov's 1928–1929 Club of a New Social Type and 1929 Columbus Memorial **[project 9]**.[13] Fuller also approaches the ethics of work of his Soviet counterparts, especially the insistence on anonymity and on the organization of individual work within broader intellectual collectives.[14]

For Fuller, dematerialization is the corollary of architecture's transformation into a telecommunication device. The slender frames and the substitution of the more rigid structural elements by weightless wires build a path toward the complete disappearance of the object. Throughout his career, Fuller progressively explores buildings that shift in emphasis from the material to the immaterial. The process of synthesis initiated with the 4D Tower leads to the complete dilution of structure in the postwar Geodesic Domes **[fig. 4]**. The domes abolish solid volumes and replace them with a framework that generates

**10.** Mark Wigley, *Buckminster Fuller Inc.: Architecture in the Age of Radio* (Ennetbaden: Lars Müller Publishers, 2015), 29.

**11.** Wigley, *Buckminster Fuller Inc.*, 49.

**12.** Wigley, *Buckminster Fuller Inc.*, 21.

**13.** Wigley, *Buckminster Fuller Inc.*, 30, and Peter Anders, "Leonidov: Icon of the Future," *Journal of Architectural Education* 37, no. 1 (1983): 20

**14.** Suzanne Strum, *The Ideal of Total Environmental Control: Knud Lönberg-Holm, Buckminster Fuller, and the SSA* (London: Routledge, 2018), 94–99. In particular, Strum analyzes the similarity between Fuller's participation in the collective SSA together with Knud Lönberg-Holm, and Soviet collectives such as OSA or ARU. Interestingly, *Shelter* did often publish news about Soviet architecture.

enclosed spaces solely by defining its edges.[15] These simultaneously become a representation of an architectonic form and a diagram of their structural load path. Thus, the Vitruvian *firmitas* opens space for the destabilization of tectonics, allowing Fuller to work with connections, flows, and paths, and not with fixed objects; with relations instead of matter.

With the 4D Tower, Fuller thus initiates his path toward the progressive dematerialization of architecture. For the 1970 exhibition on antimaterialism at La Jolla Museum of Art, he states: "When successful, tomorrow's architecture will be approximately invisible, not just figuratively speaking, but literally as well. What will count with world man is how well the architecture serves all humanity while sublimating itself spontaneously. Architecture may be accomplished tomorrow with electrical field and other utterly invisible environment controls."[16] The result of architecture's dematerialization is, thus, increasing, potentially total, environmental control **[projects 19 and 22]**.[17] The ultimate stage of this vision is the consideration of Earth as a spaceship, a technically managed entity—a notion Fuller popularizes during the mid-1960s. The seeds of this idea are precisely laid in these early 4D projects. In the book *Nine Chains to the Moon*, where Fuller summarizes his early work, he asserts: "the goal is not 'housing,' but the universal extension of the phantom captain's ship into new areas of environment control, possibly to continuity of survival without the necessity of intermittent 'abandoning ship.'"[18]

In this light, the 4D Tower allows Fuller to test his intention to make architecture disappear at different scales. As a building, it is a multistory construction thinning down to be perceived as a single vertical line as one gains distance and its glass levels disappear against the sky. On a larger scale, the tower is independent of the urban fabric, dissipating the traditional city as it explores previously unoccupied territories and invisibly connects one location to all others. Lastly, the societal structure is the broader scale in which the World Plan of 4D Tower aims to bring the whole "human family" together.[19] In *4D Time Lock*, a book compiling the 4D Tower principles, Fuller discusses how a modern environment achieved with the proper use of new technologies would efface humankind's social and physical defects.[20] By addressing these multiple scales, the project of the tower becomes an open commentary on the way the world is structured, while pointing to the direction toward which life should head. Undoubtedly, Fuller's discourse and methods radically favor a scientific and technocratic vision of world managing. Yet, for him, such an endeavor is

**15.** Alan Colquhoun, "The Modern Movement in Architecture," *British Journal of Aesthetics* 2, no. 1 (1962): 63.

**16.** R. Buckminster Fuller, foreword to *Projections: Anti-Materialism* (La Jolla, CA: La Jolla Museum of Art, 1970), n.p., quoted in Dana Miller, "Thought Patterns: Buckminster Fuller the Science-Artist," in Hays and Miller, *Buckminster Fuller: Starting with the Universe*, 21–44.

**17.** Strum, *The Ideal of Total Environmental Control*, 215–218.

**18.** Fuller, "What Is a House?" in Fuller, *Nine Chains to the Moon*, 43.

**19.** Text included in Buckminster Fuller's "Airocean World-Town Plan" drawing, 1927.

**20.** R. Buckminster Fuller, *4D Time Lock* (Albuquerque: Lama Foundation, 1972), 148, and Antoine Picon, "Fuller's Avatars: A View from the Present," in Hays and Miller, *Buckminster Fuller: Starting with the Universe*, 53.

21. Fuller, "We Call It Earth," 67.

22. Fuller, "We Call It Earth," 67.

also humanistic and poetic. His 4D Tower intends to link architecture and the broader cosmic system. "Scientific shelter design," he believes, "is linked to the stars far more directly than to the earth."[21] It is a form of "star-gazing," of relating humans and universe.[22] The towers foster a total integration between the multiple layers that constitute the systems "people," the "built environment," "Earth," "energy," and the cosmos. With them, Fuller lays his universal principles of "integrity," and enables disappearance to become totality.

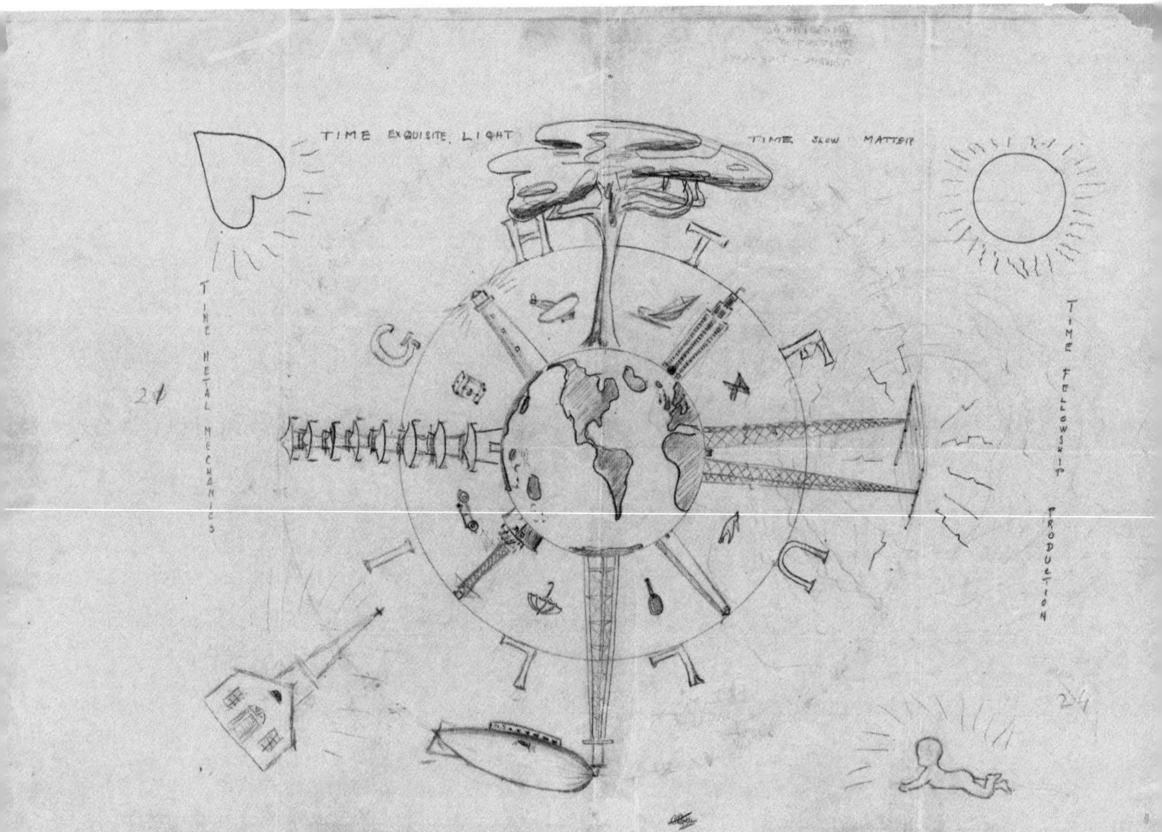


**Figure 1.** Sketch of Lightful Houses "Time Exquisite Light." ca. 1928.

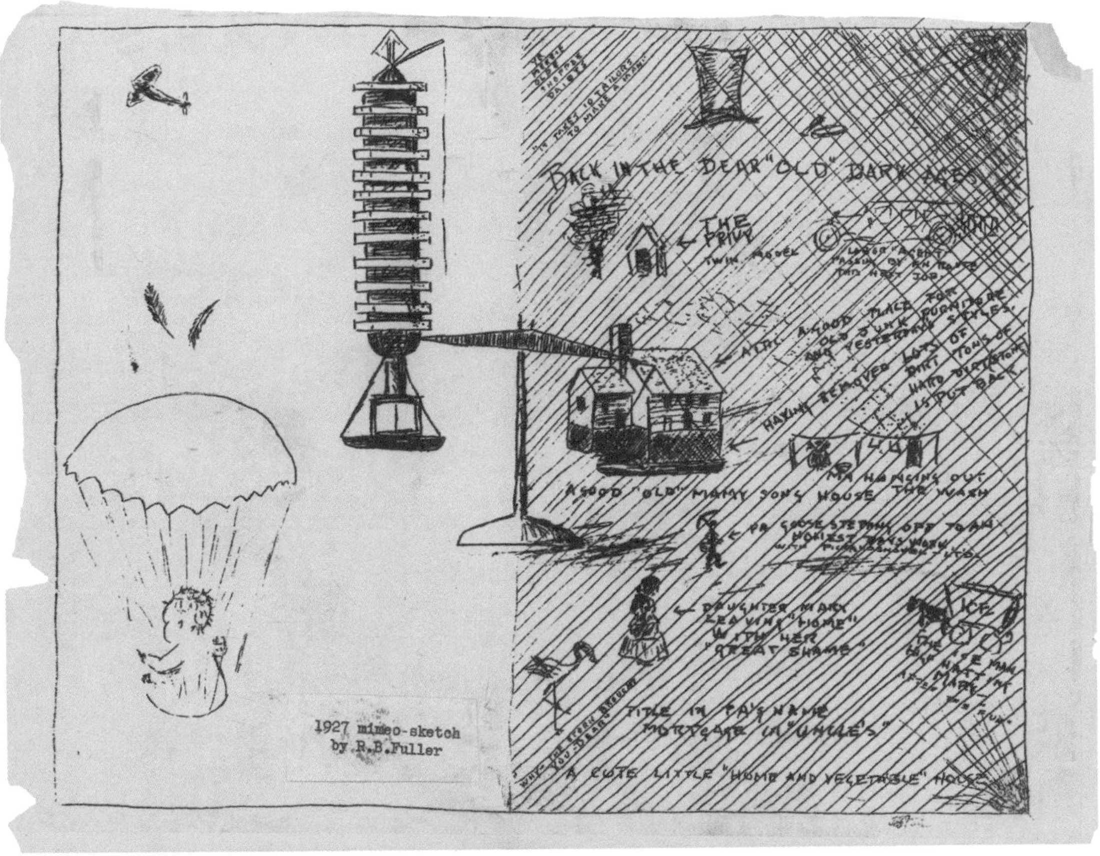


---

**Figure 2.** Comparison of Lightful Tower and traditional home. 1927.

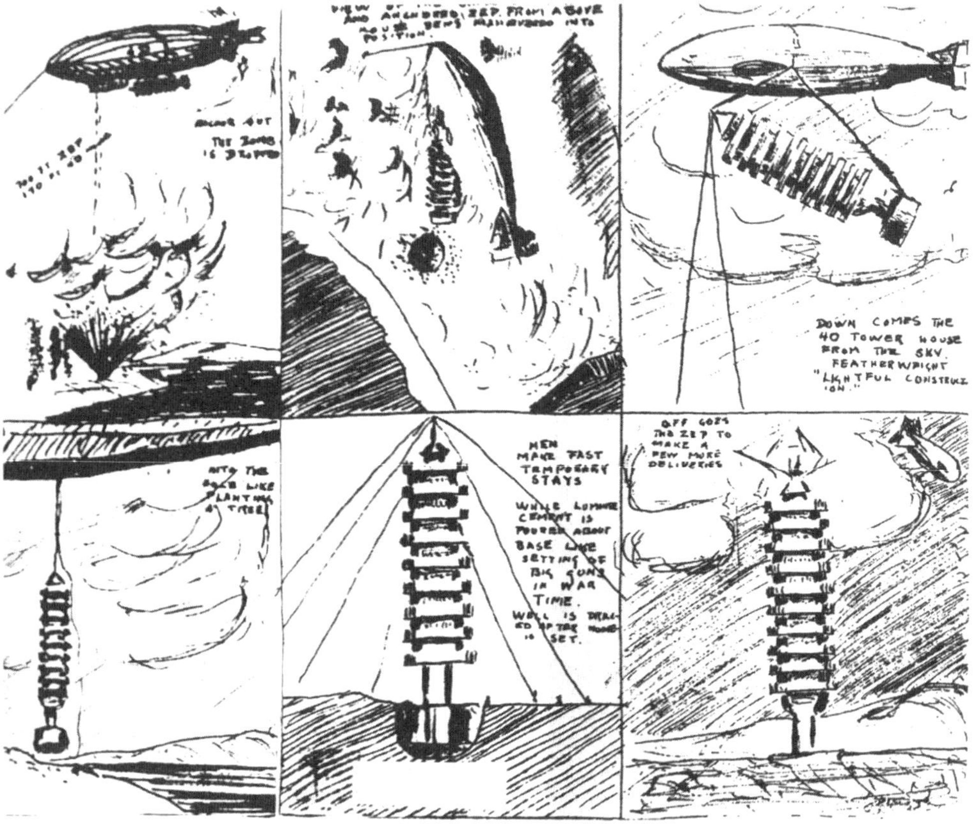


**Figure 3.** Sketch showing installation sequence of a 4D Tower. ca. 1928.

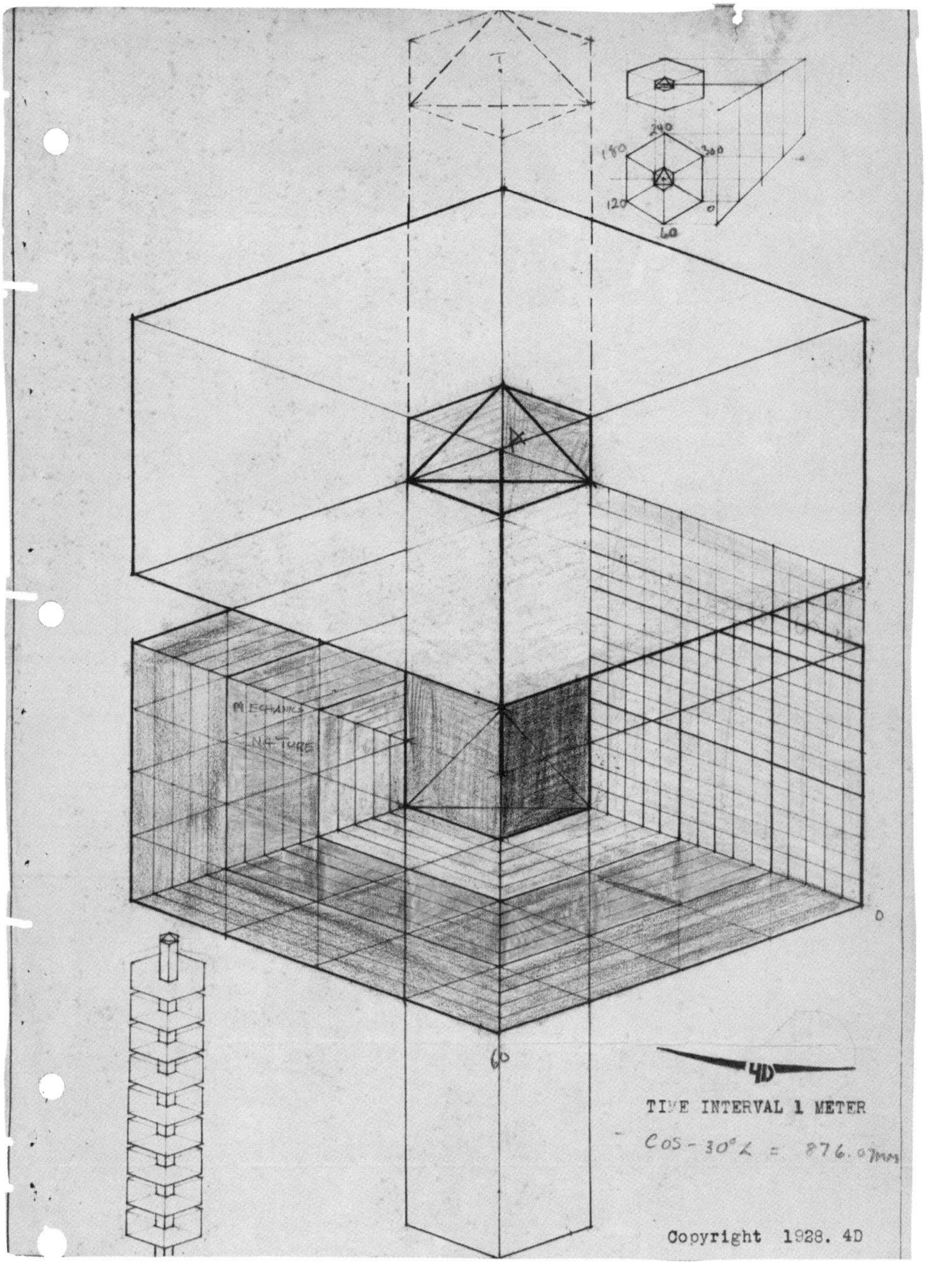


**Figure 4.** 4D Tower: Time Interval 1 Meter. 1928.

# Atlantropa

**Project:** 7. **Author:** Herman Sörgel (1885–1952). **Date:** 1927–1952. **Themes:** Colonialism. Environmental Control. Geopolitics. Infrastructure.

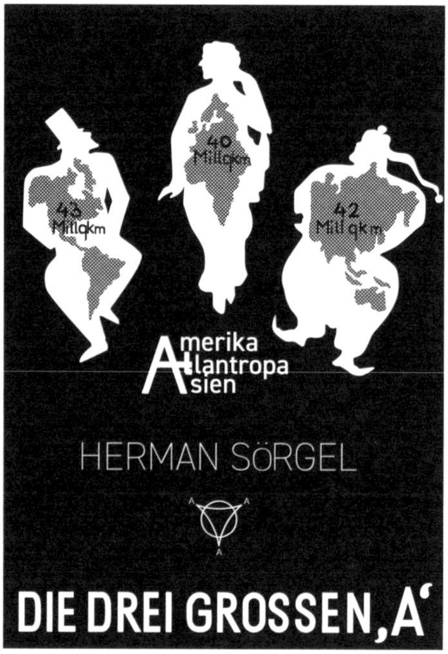


**Figure 0.** The Three Big A's. After Herman Sörgel. 1938.

Herman Sörgel studies architecture in the Technische Universität München during the early 1900s. The school's strong emphasis on civil engineering and Sörgel's personal interest in geography are particularly aligned with the expansionist moment of the German Empire at the time. The Empire's twenty-six constituent territories are going through a massive urbanization process, doubling their population in the thirty years around the turn of the century and achieving the status of the largest European economy. Geographers such as Friedrich Ratzel (1844–1904), the director of the Geographic Institute at the Universität Leipzig, are crucial for building German identity and the country's geopolitical agenda.[1] Ratzel, in fact, coins the notions of *Geopolitik* and *Lebensraum* that naturalized German colonialism.

Sörgel initially conceives Atlantropa as Panropa in 1927. The project's roots go back to 1923 with the foundation of the Pan-European Union and to 1925 when Sörgel visits the Pan American Union Building in Washington, DC, where he is fascinated by the potential for international cooperation.[2] The project's origins also coincide with multiple, large-scale, infrastructural initiatives. The interwar years see a series of proposals for the construction of European power grids aimed at optimizing energy distribution and at facilitating the continent's political integration. In the United States, the New Deal's hydroengineering projects for the Hoover Dam, the Grand Coulee Dam, and the Tennessee Valley Authority interventions mark the 1930s.[3] Germany, in turn, promotes the *Bagdadbahn*: the Berlin–Baghdad Railway (1903–1940). This ambitious 1,600-kilometer connection is designed to provide the country with a direct link to the port of Basra, access to the Mesopotamian oil fields, and the possibility of avoiding the Suez Canal, which is controlled by the British.[4]

Atlantropa is Sörgel's grand vision for this technocratic period of vast infrastructural undertakings **[figs. 0 and 1]**. The project proposes merging the European and African continents into one superpower block. The union between the two forms a continuous landmass, structured through a reconfigured Mediterranean Sea around which flows of capital, products, and people revolve. Physically and functionally integrated, the "new continent" would enable Europe to explore the raw natural resources of Africa and the Middle East, while offering technology and finished goods in return.[5]

To establish this transcontinental connection, the Mediterranean Sea becomes the focus of Atlantropa's main interventions. It is the geographic center where

**1.** Peter Christensen, "Dam Nation: Imaging and Imagining the 'Middle East' in Herman Sörgel's Atlantropa," *International Journal of Islamic Architecture* 1, no. 2 (2012): 327.

**2.** Antonio Petrov, "Rescaling Transnational Geographies," *Monu: Magazine on Urbanism* 22 (2015): 21. Philipp Nicolas Lehmann, "Infinite Power to Change the World: Hydroelectricity and Engineered Climate Change in the Atlantropa Project," *American Historical Review* 121, no. 1 (February 2016): 77.

**3.** Petrov, "Rescaling Transnational Geographies," 73.

**4.** Christensen, "Dam Nation," 328.

**5.** Herman Sörgel, *Atlantropa: Wesenszüge eines Projekts* (Künzelsau: Seemann, 1949).

large energy production infrastructures are to be implemented. For Sörgel, hydropower has the potential to be massively harnessed as a way to escape the economic crisis, scaling unemployment and energy scarcity that coal-reliant Europe experiences at the time. As the plan's most emblematic gestures, Sörgel proposes to dam the Strait of Gibraltar and the Dardanelles with hydroelectric power plants, and to create transcontinental, North-South arteries for the uninterrupted movement of people and materials. With the damming of these two connections to the ocean and to the surrounding seas, Sörgel lowers the Mediterranean's sea level 500 meters. This move would simultaneously allow the newly joint continent to produce enough electricity to supply Europe's energy needs for centuries, and to unveil up to 600,000 square kilometers of fertile agricultural land **[fig. 2]**.[6]

Atlantropa's overall plan consists of lines of movement and stopping points. For each of these points, Sörgel and his collaborators (a numerous team, including architects as sophisticated as Peter Behrens and Erich Mendelsohn) design one specific architectural intervention. Formally, these often flirt with the imaginary of expressionism and futurism, especially with the elongated and dynamic lines of Antonio Sant'Elia. Thus, each of the stops becomes a carefully designed, multipurpose, mega-engineering structure, merging energy production and transportation.

The Strait of Gibraltar dam, a 35-kilometer curved connection topped with seaports on both sides and a massive hydroelectric plant, is the most emblematic of these punctual interventions. It is mirrored at the Dardanelles by a smaller dam that disconnects the Mediterranean from the Marmara and Black seas, and by a two-way incision on land close to Gallipoli, which serves as a thoroughfare for ships, and includes a power plant on the north and a port on its southern end.[7] At the Strait of Sicily and Messina, a highway coming from Germany and cutting across Italy bridges the 66-kilometer-long gap between Europe and Africa through another dam, creating a difference of 100 meters between the East and West Mediterranean Sea. The highway lands on New Tunis, a city imagined by Sörgel, and from there continues into the African continent. The Suez Canal, in turn, is totally reconfigured as an economic node and a transfer station for resources coming from the Middle East, Africa, and Europe **[fig. 3]**. It becomes a complex multimodal facility with airport, seaport, passenger and freight stations, shipyard, and housing for workers.[8] Sörgel complements these main projects with a series of second-tier interventions and some geographical modifications over inland Africa, with the whole accounting for the complete

**6.** Lehmann, "Infinite Power to Change the World," 71. Petrov, "Rescaling Transnational Geographies," 20.

**7.** Christensen, "Dam Nation," 332.

**8.** Christensen, "Dam Nation," 337.

9. Christensen, "Dam Nation," 332.

10. Wolfgang Voigt, *Atlantropa: Weltbauen am Mittelmeer: Ein Architektentraum der Moderne.* (Hamburg: Dölling und Galitz, 1998), 101.

11. Lehmann, "Infinite Power to Change the World," 84.

12. Lehmann, "Infinite Power to Change the World," 84.

13. Christensen, "Dam Nation," 339.

restructuring of the Mediterranean basin and its relation to the surrounding continents.

Together, these spatial interventions define a politically charged vision of Europe, in general, and Germany, in particular. Although Sörgel initially conceives Atlantropa as a "harmonious and bilateral geopolitical construction," far into the interwar years the project's tone changes significantly. The Great Depression, the general escalating of sociopolitical tensions, and the international pressure from the rising powers of Japan and the US demand that Europe reinvents and strengthens its image.[9] Sörgel's proposal addresses these anxieties through an imperialistic logic, where the "conquering" of territory becomes a means of offsetting the old continent's economic decline and its increasing global imbalance. By reconfiguring Europe and Africa into one entity, its sheer landmass compensates for the other continents' geographical presence. The world is stabilized between the 3 A's: America, Asia, and Atlantropa.[10]

Sörgel's imperialistic positions are not limited to land ownership and go far into nationalism and racism. Apart from the many illustrations that depict Atlantropa's dependence on notions of race superiority—such as the image on a 1932 plate in which a partially naked African woman hands out a basket of raw goods to a white man placed on top of the Mediterranean—the architect's discourse reveals the absolute discrimination against African natives. Sörgel constantly refers to Africa as a "vacuum in front of Europe," or to the need of adjusting the continent's climate to make it suitable for the European settlers.[11] When arguing for large landscape operations that can potentially decimate thousands of Africans, Sörgel states that without the project "the Negroes . . . would increase in numbers, until they would finally eat everything the land can produce and not export anything anymore."[12]

These imperialist and racist propositions, which accompany the evolution of the project during the 1930s, link Atlantropa to the rising German National Socialist movement. Even though Sörgel's wife and collaborators such as Mendelsohn are Jewish, Atlantropa gives spatial expression to some of Nazism's most crucial ideological tenets. The consideration of colonialism as a natural national need, the search for a new sense of self for Germany and Europe, and the exaltation of the white race's dominance over other races motivates Sörgel to seek Nazi support for the project. Ultimately, the outcome is the opposite, and Atlantropa ends up being sabotaged and banned from circulation by Hitler's government.[13]

After World War II, Sörgel thoroughly revises Atlantropa. With the aftermath of the war, the discourse on domination has lost its place, and the argument has to shift if the project is to survive in the polarization and economic decay the world is experiencing. Atlantropa is born of the irrefutable belief in technology's capabilities to reorganize society, overcome a financial crisis, and physically mold the environment to suit humanity's needs—and those are the aspects Sörgel is determined to keep. The architect redirects the focus to climate engineering, which is already present since the beginning but not treated as a priority up until that point.[14] Atlantropa starts to be branded as the opportunity to anticipate a future in which microclimates can be designed and atmospheric conditions controlled on a large, global scale.[15]

Correspondingly, Sörgel justifies the interventions in the Mediterranean because of their capacity to remediate the air pollution caused by the intense urbanization and industrialization of the sea shores, and because of their potential to generate surplus energy that can be used to modify the climate of the northern regions of Africa. He explains the damming of Gibraltar as having the added benefit of blocking the cold water current that flows into the Atlantic, which in turn would allow the Gulf of Mexico's warm undercurrents to hit Northern Europe, thereby improving its harsh climate.[16] A similar climatic reasoning motivates the design of artificial lakes in inner Africa and the Sahara. The enlargement of Lake Chad and the damming of the Zambezi and Congo rivers would completely reconfigure Central Africa's arid climate, thanks to the evaporation processes unleashed by the newly created lakes. These are conceived as long-term interventions—the proposed Congo Lake itself would take about 133 years to be filled—but, throughout the process, they would generate electricity on a continental scale and reshape the region's geography **[fig. 4]**.[17]

Despite these shifts in the project's focus, World War II severely impacts Atlantropa. The elevated costs of such a colossal endeavor of environmental modification and its totalizing spirit are incongruent with the delicate moment of reconstruction and negotiation. African pro-independence movements emerge, rightfully rejecting the instrumental visions of the continent that Atlantropa represents. Technologically, Sörgel's emphasis on a hydroelectric matrix is dislodged after the war's display of nuclear power and the intuition of its possible scale of use.[18] The project disintegrates from all sides until its abrupt end in 1952, when Sörgel is struck by a car on his way to a lecture in Munich.

**14.** Lehmann, "Infinite Power to Change the World," 97.

**15.** Lehmann, "Infinite Power to Change the World," 86.

**16.** Lehmann, "Infinite Power to Change the World," 87.

**17.** Lehmann, "Infinite Power to Change the World," 82.

**18.** Christensen, "Dam Nation," 341.

With all its controversies, Atlantropa is a *tour de force* regarding the extent to which humanity can spatially operate at the world scale. Sörgel's three-decade-long project embodies the German notion of *Weltbauen*—meaning "world-building" or "world-making"—which Bruno Taut previously explored with diametrically opposed objectives **[project 4]**.[19] *Weltbauen* expands architecture's agency to include designing territorial relations and reconceptualizing the interplay between artificial and natural geographical systems.[20] For Sörgel, this means treating the world as an inert entity that can be entirely transformed according to the will of Northern and Western powers. The means for such a world transformation is the convergence of architecture, infrastructure, and terraforming into a new type of spatial intervention, which we can now describe as geo-engineering. Through this convergence of techniques, Atlantropa offers foresight into issues of climate control and renewable energy that increasingly dominate current debates, and that in fact propel technocratic visions of the future of Africa as a global provider of energy.[21] It also reveals to what extent spatial interventions can be crucial components of projects of geopolitical domination, and how the vastness of their scale of operations can be the best mirror of the overarching, totalizing ambitions of imperialistic projects. At the same time, contradicting the project's colonial objectives, Atlantropa constitutes an act of geographical imagination that, reuniting Africa and Europe in a single entity, radically reveals the unavoidable interconnectedness between the two continents and, thus, the impossibility of building protective, artificial barriers between them.

**19.** Voigt, *Atlantropa*, 29–33.

**20.** Petrov, "Rescaling Transnational Geographies," 16.

**21.** Lehmann, "Infinite Power to Change the World," 90. Projects such as the 2003 German initiative DESERTEC, promoted by the Club de Rome and the National Energy Research Center Jordan, with the participation of private companies EON, Deutsche Bank, and Siemens, suggests forms of energy harvesting at the Sahara which strongly resemble Atlantropa's theses. Since then, several private companies (like the ones promoted by Italian Tesna, Tunisian STEG, or UK's TuNur), research groups, and engineers have been promoting similar interventions.

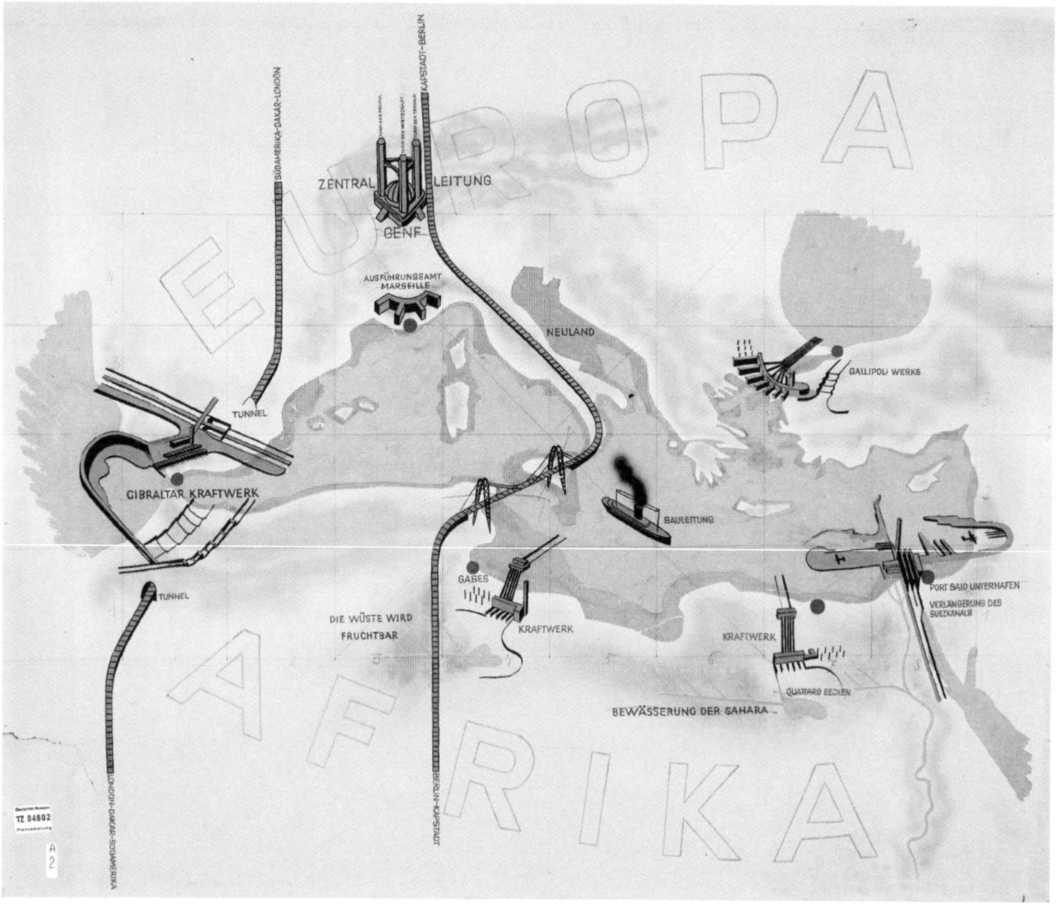


**Figure 1.** New land and energy infrastructures in the Mediterranean. 1932.

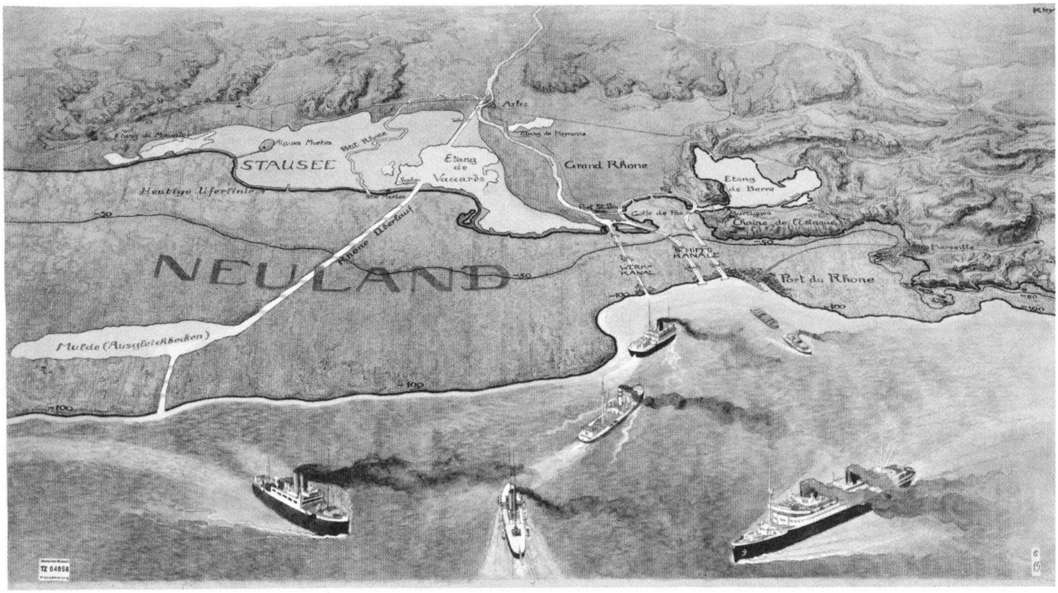


**Figure 2.** New land in southern France. Reservoir and basin around Rhône estuary. 1931.

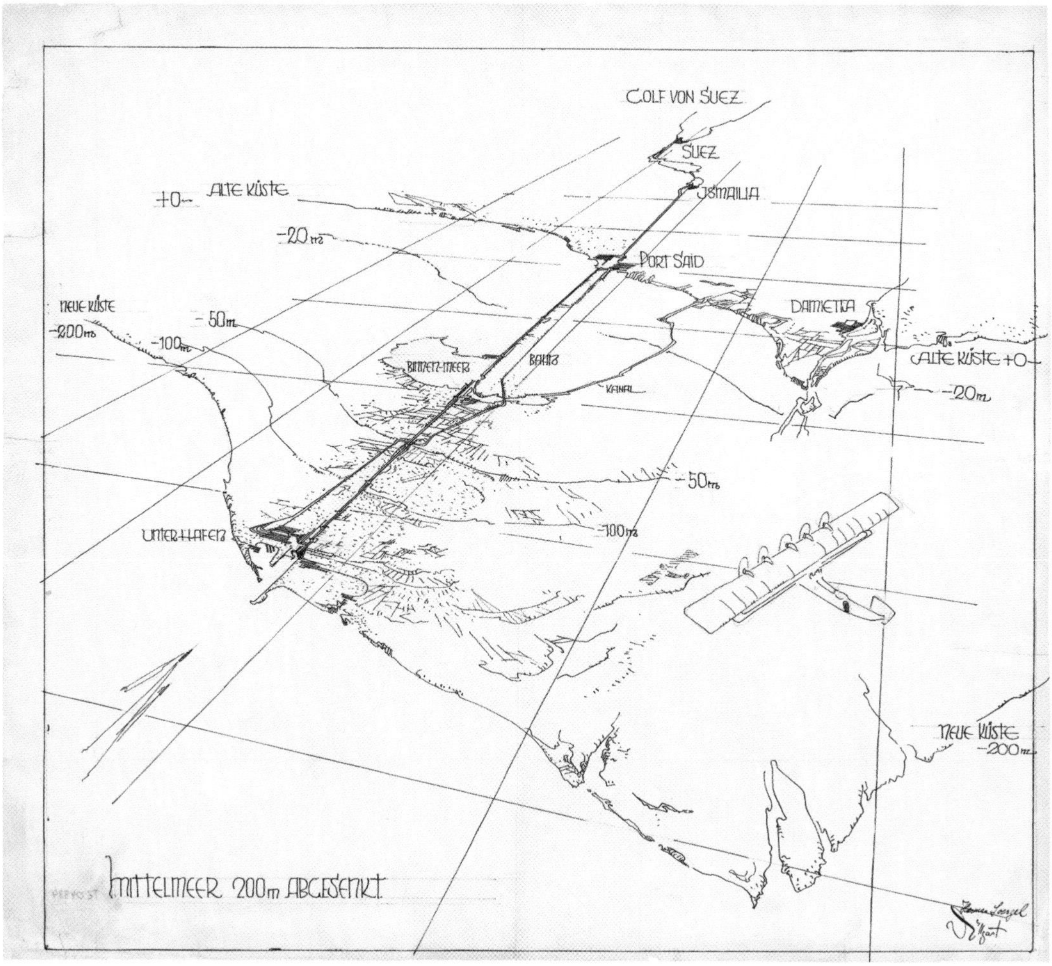


Figure 3. New territory over Egypt with extension of Suez Canal. 1931.

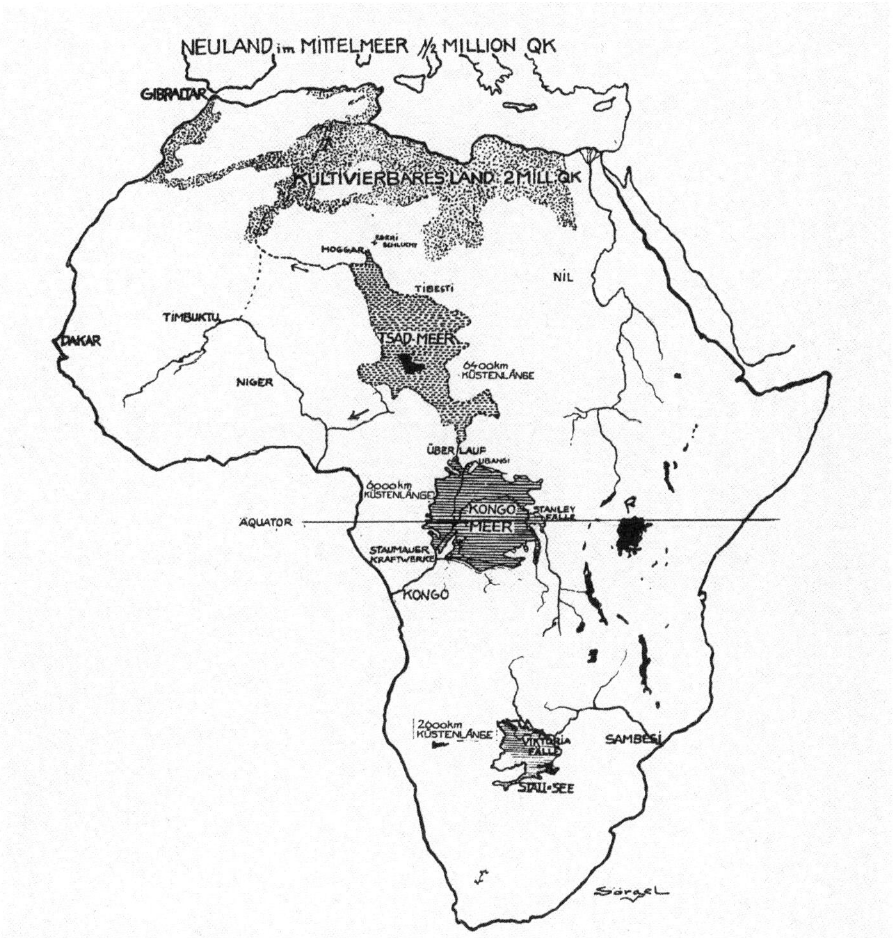


Figure 4. Formation of African inland seas. 1931.

# Le Mundaneum – La Cité Mondiale

The Mundaneum – The World City

**Project:** 8. **Authors:** Le Corbusier (1887–1965) and Paul Otlet (1868–1944). **Date:** 1928–1929. **Themes:** Aerial Vision. Geography. Monumentality. Taxonomy.

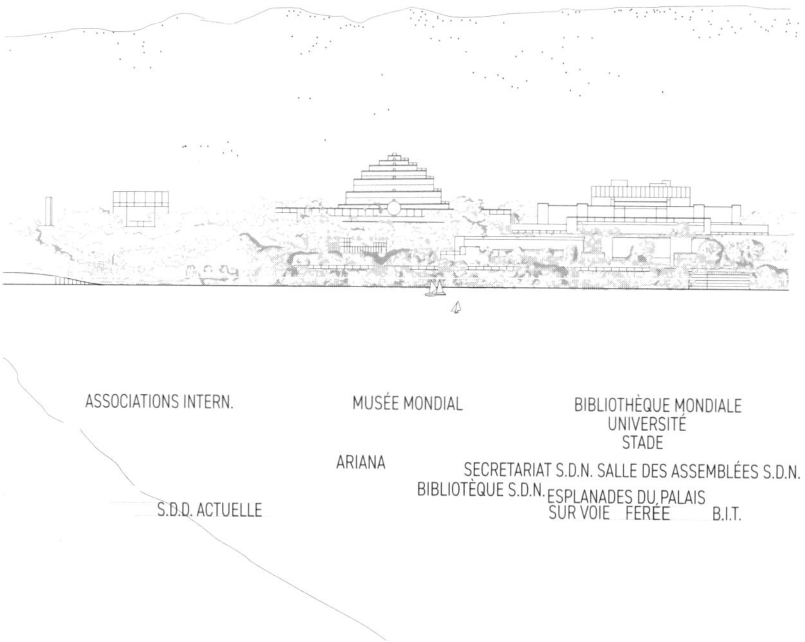


**Figure 0.** Elevation of the World-City. After Le Corbusier. ca. 1929.

**1.** Paul Otlet, quoted in Willy Boesiger and Oscar Stonorov, *Le Corbusier et Pierre Jeanneret: oeuvre complète 1910-1929* (Basel: Birkhäuser, 1995 [1929]), 190. Our translation.

**2.** Wouter Van Acker, "Internationalist Utopias of Visual Education: The Graphic and Scenographic Transformation of the Universal Encyclopaedia in the Work of Paul Otlet, Patrick Geddes, and Otto Neurath," *Perspectives on Science* 19, no. 1 (2011): 33.

**3.** William Whyte, *Ghent Planning Congress 1913: Premier congrès international et exposition comparée des villes* (Abingdon: Taylor and Francis, 2013), vi.

**4.** The institution was, it must be noted, a derivative of the Université Nouvelle that had been created as a result of Élisée Reclus's expulsion from the Université Libre of Brussels.

"Mundaneum: an intellectual Center of union, relation, cooperation, coordination; a representation of the World and what it contains; mirror and survey; a synthetic expression of universal life and a comparator of civilizations; a symbol of the Intellectual Unity of the World and of Humanity: an image of the Community of Nations; the Headquarters of International Associations; a free forum for the discussion and orientation of major interests common to all countries; a way to make People know one another and to get them to collaborate; an assistant to international Administration; an emporium of the works of the spirit; an instrument of documentation, information and studies for the Workers; the Center of a network of local, regional, national, international, connected stations for the intellectual work and the development of world relations.

The desire is: that at one point of the Globe, the total image and meaning of the World can be perceived and understood . . ."[1]

Le Corbusier uses these words of Belgian thinker Paul Otlet, promoter of the Mundaneum, to introduce the project in his *Complete Works*. Otlet considers the Mundaneum the apex of his lifelong commitment to universalism. His initiatives in that respect are unceasing. In 1893, he founds, with lawyer Henri La Fontaine, the *Office International de Bibliographie et d'Informations Sociologiques*, and works with him until 1904 on a global standard of bibliographic classification. In 1907, the couple constitutes the *Office International des Associations Internationales*, which becomes the Union of International Associations in 1910.[2] In 1913, Otlet, politician Emile Vinck (1870–1950), and architect Paul Saintenoy (1862–1952) organize the very first international conference on town planning, the *Premier Congrès International de l'Art de Construire Villes et Organisation de la Vie Municipale*—in which Arturo Soria y Mata and Otlet's friend Patrick Geddes participate **[projects 1 and 2]**. As a result of the congress, they create the first international association for the analysis of urban questions, the *Union Internationale des Villes*.[3] World War I does not diminish Otlet's belief in international cooperation. In 1919, he starts lecturing on the topic "L'Universalisme, doctrine philosophique et économie mondiale" at the Institut des Hautes Études de Bruxelles.[4] In 1925, he starts working on the Mundaneum.

The Mundaneum stems from Otlet's dissatisfaction with how governments attempt to reconstruct international relations after World War I. In 1919 he attends the Paris Peace Conference, which leads to the constitution of the League of Nations.[5] The strictly political purpose assigned to the League contrasts with Otlet's understanding of internationalization as a comprehensive task requiring social and cultural integration. This leads him to approach Le Corbusier in 1927 to request his participation in the Mundaneum project. Otlet intends to place this new institution in Geneva, the city elected as the seat for the League of Nations, and to create there a huge center to document global knowledge that would provide intellectual support for the League's activities and help to elaborate plans for the transformation of the world **[fig. 0]**.[6] The complex would collect all of Otlet's obsessions: an International Museum; buildings for the International Associations, for an International University, and for an International Library; and centers for exhibitions of the continents, countries, and cities—all of them connected to dependent institutions across the world.

Le Corbusier, who meets Otlet in 1922, is sympathetic to these plans.[7] In 1927, he designs his entry for the League of Nations competition—a renowned fiasco that propels the creation of the International Congress of Modern Architecture (CIAM) in 1928.[8] Previously, in 1922, he conceives the Contemporary City of 3,000,000 people as a model unit for a system of interconnected world cities. Thus, for Le Corbusier, Otlet's goals have to be approached both as architectural and urban questions.

Otlet conceives of the Mundaneum as an "idearium" that can provide "a picture of the thoughts that are hidden under facts."[9] Its centerpiece would be the International Museum, a building that would not contain a conventional collection of unique art works, but a comprehensive compilation of reproductions of cultural documents, organized according to their location, time, and kind. Instead of being a space for contemplation, the Museum would be a documentary instrument to relate and compare civilizations. Because of this classificatory spirit, Otlet displaces spiritual, symbolic, and aesthetic values from the collected objects to the Museum itself. In his initial sketches, the complex creates a constellation: the Museum is a dome or a terrestrial globe surrounded by pavilions devoted to the continents.[10]

Le Corbusier's design turns Otlet's abstract ideas into a direct engagement with the surrounding geography. Instead of a globe or dome, Le Corbusier designs the Museum as a stepped pyramid **[figs. 1, 2 and 3]**. The form solves Otlet's museographic program, and it references the Alpine mountains surrounding the complex. The pyramid is accessed from its very top, after walking

**5.** Mariana Siracusa, "Paul Otlet's Theory of Everything," *AA Files* 73 (2016): 50.

**6.** Karel Teige, "Mundaneum," *Oppositions* 4 (October 1974): 588 and 595. Originally published in *Stavba* 7 (1929).

**7.** Van Acker, "Internationalist Utopias of Visual Education," 56.

**8.** George Baird, "Architecture and Politics: A Polemical Dispute. A Critical Introduction to Karel Teige's 'Mundaneum,' 1929 and Le Corbusier's 'In Defense of Architecture,' 1933," *Oppositions* 4 (October 1974): 586.

**9.** Teige, "Mundaneum," 592.

**10.** María Cecilia O'Byrne, "El Museo del Mundaneum: Génesis de un prototipo," *Massilia: Anuario de Estudios Le Corbusierianos* 18 (2004): 115. Pierre Chabard, "Towers and Globes: Architectural and Epistemological Differences between Patrick Geddes's Outlook Tower and Paul Otlet's Mundaneum," in *European Modernism and the Information Society: Informing the Present, Understanding the Past*, ed. William Boyd Rayward (Aldershot, UK: Ashgate, 2008), 111.

up a 2.5-kilometer ramp that offers visitors a "survey of the countryside," and allows them to "have the territory to [themselves]."[11] After this experience, the Museum interior operates as a temporal sequence. The collection starts with the small superior section devoted to prehistory and, as visitors go down and approach the contemporary world, the collection progressively unfolds into increasingly larger areas. That is, the Museum structure starts with humanity's common origins and presents its evolution into increasingly diverse and complex civilizations, which are nonetheless connected in many ways. Additionally, the internal spiral organizes Otlet's division of knowledge into three parallel naves for the objects, their time, and their place to be seen simultaneously. Otlet's comparison of civilizations is material, historical, and geographical.

Le Corbusier also transforms Otlet's preliminary urban scheme in order to create what he terms the World City. To reinforce the project's relation to the world, he cherishes the isolation of the complex from Geneva and its extraterritorial status.[12] For him, the project is an acropolis, detached from everyday city life and placed at the end of a processional axis leading to Geneva. The main buildings he adds are meant to support the Mundaneum's worldwide operations: skyscrapers for the Economic and Financial cities—including an international bank to supervise global debt—huge antennas for radio retransmission, a stadium and a building for the Olympics association, and airport and railway connections. The design thus privileges two spatial themes: its specific geographic surroundings and the wider system of world relations. The project's representations, mostly panoramic and bird's-eye views, always stress the geographic context; the program, in turn, emphasizes the Mundaneum's role at the world scale.

In his virulent analysis of the project, the Czech artist and writer Karel Teige dismisses the Mundaneum as an inconsistent utopia, and Le Corbusier's monumental use of the pyramid as contradictory to the modern movement's attempts at an international architectural vocabulary. Yet, it is precisely in the Mundaneum that Le Corbusier envisages some of the aspects that will inform his later work and his understanding of the relations between modern architecture and the world. From an architectural point of view, the pyramid establishes the model for his 1947 design for the United Nations Museum as well as the centrifugal schema of the museums of unlimited growth.[13] From an urban and geographic point of view, the repercussions run even deeper. In his 1929 response to Teige, Le Corbusier not only justifies the monumental character of his proposal. He indicates that the aerial view that he privileges

11. Le Corbusier, "In Defense of Architecture," *Oppositions* 4 (October 1974): 610.

12. Boesiger and Stonorov, *Le Corbusier et Pierre Jeanneret: oeuvre complète 1910–1929*, 196–197, and Teige, "Mundaneum," 591. Teige, in particular, explains how, in Otlet and Le Corbusier's plans, "The territory of the Mundaneum, an international city, of course has to be international," and how Switzerland should give its inhabitants permanent extraterritoriality.

13. O'Byrne, "El Museo del Mundaneum," 112–135.

when conceiving the Mundaneum, and the understanding of the project in geographical terms, respond to the possibilities offered by the popularization of air flights: it serves to investigate the "possible impact of regulating lines on horizontal space."[14]

This theme is the central leitmotif of Le Corbusier's South American trip later that year and it structures his post–World War II approach to territorial articulation. Similarly, the separation between the World City and Geneva establishes the basis for the detached financial city that he conceives for Buenos Aires during that trip: a new island, projected at the Rio de la Plata, acting as a sign for travelers arriving by sea and air. This vision of urban centers as key actors in the organization of international life characterizes his South American lectures, which he compiles in the book *Precisions*.[15] Conceived immediately after the trip, the 1930 Radiant City prototype transforms the strategies developed for the World City into a model for the construction of new cities. Instead of the center placed in the middle of the Contemporary City, the Radiant City adopts the Mundaneum model and situates the center separated from the settlement, as if it were its head. Starting in the 1930s, Le Corbusier will use this organization in his urban plans until his final implementation in 1951 in Chandigarh, where the Capitol and government centers crown the overall configuration.[16]

For his part, Otlet continues working on the Mundaneum until his death in 1944.[17] In 1935, he summarizes his thinking in the book *Monde: Essai d'Universalisme* (World: an essay on universalism) and develops a series of atlases for the incomplete *Encyclopedia Universalis Mundaneum* **[figs. 4 and 5]**.[18] In them, Le Corbusier's stepped pyramid represents his idea of the organization of universal knowledge. Otlet's *Traité de Documentation* (Treatise on documentation, 1935) furthers this work and posits the idea that all kinds of documents should be broken down into bits of information that can be easily disseminated and reconfigured to create new knowledge—a thesis for which he is credited as one of the forebears of the information society.[19]

The Mundaneum reflects architecture's early engagement with the emerging system of world-governance institutions. Le Corbusier and Otlet's work shares the intellectual ethos and pitfalls of early internationalism. Their project depends upon a positivist belief in the possibility of systematizing all world knowledge and stems from an elitist confidence in the regulation of international relations from a single world center. At the same time, the Mundaneum

**14.** Le Corbusier, "In Defense of Architecture," 608.

**15.** Le Corbusier, *Precisions on the Present State of Architecture and City Planning: With an American Prologue, a Brazilian Corollary Followed by the Temperature of Paris and the Atmosphere of Moscow*, trans. Edith Schreiber Aujame (Cambridge, MA: MIT Press, 1991), 215–231.

**16.** Xavier Monteys, *La Gran Máquina: La Ciudad en Le Corbusier* (Barcelona: Demarcación de Barcelona del Colegio de Arquitectos de Cataluña: Ediciones del Serbal, 1996), 42–48.

**17.** Wouter Van Acker, "Architectural Metaphors of Knowledge: The Mundaneum Designs of Maurice Heymans, Paul Otlet, and Le Corbusier," *Library Trends* 61, no. 2 (2012): 371–396.

**18.** Van Acker, "Internationalist Utopias of Visual Education," 70–71.

**19.** Charles Van den Heuvel, "Building Society, Constructing Knowledge, Weaving the Web: Otlet's Visualizations of a Global Information Society and His Concept of a Universal Civilization," in *European Modernism and the Information Society*, 132.

shows how its authors believe that the construction of a unified world system exceeds political action. It needs to embrace all aspects of social life, and it has to be spatially articulated. These are the aspects that Le Corbusier will elevate to an influential architectural agenda. In his "battle-plan" for the 1928 CIAM inaugural conference, he asserts that the architectural response to world-governance institutions is the elaboration of a universal technical language: "The League of Nations should be approached with a view to making the teaching of a universal technical language compulsory throughout the world; the effect of this, moreover, would be to make all international contacts possible and easy. And this would mean tremendous contribution to the pacification of the world."[20] The same year, the Mundaneum offers a complementary way to develop this intellectual and architectural program. On one hand, the project emphasizes the need to create the centers, institutions, and systems of interconnected cities that can generate the world system. On the other, Le Corbusier posits that these elements should be designed as contextually specific interventions at the geographic scale.

**20.** Le Corbusier, *The Radiant City*, trans. P. Knight, E. Leview, and D. Coltman (New York: Orion Press, 1964 [1933]), 23. See also in this respect Sarah Deyong, "Planetary Habitat: The Origins of a Phantom Movement," *Journal of Architecture* 6, no. 2 (2001): 115.

From the Mundaneum on, geography and world will be inseparable design objectives for Le Corbusier. This architecture–geography–world link is enabled, the architect thinks, by the view from above. Geddes's and Reclus's previous world projects had already explored this point of view as a means of coming to know the planet **[projects 2 and 3]**. Geddes used elevation to show that any vision of the world is geographically grounded, and thus it is also particular in a way. Reclus, instead, linked elevation to scientific accuracy and objectivity in a manner that diminished Europe's relative position in the world. The panoramic path to the Mundaneum's access, and its exhibition program of relating civilizations on equal grounds, expand both Geddes's and Reclus's goals. Yet, for Le Corbusier the view from above has, fundamentally, consequences in the realm of design. The initial design consequences imply the geographical grounding of architecture and the emphasis on the international role of urban centers. In the following years he will understand that the knowledge provided by aerial vision implies designing not only buildings and cities, but the new forms of territorial organization that characterize his post–World War II work **[project 15]**.

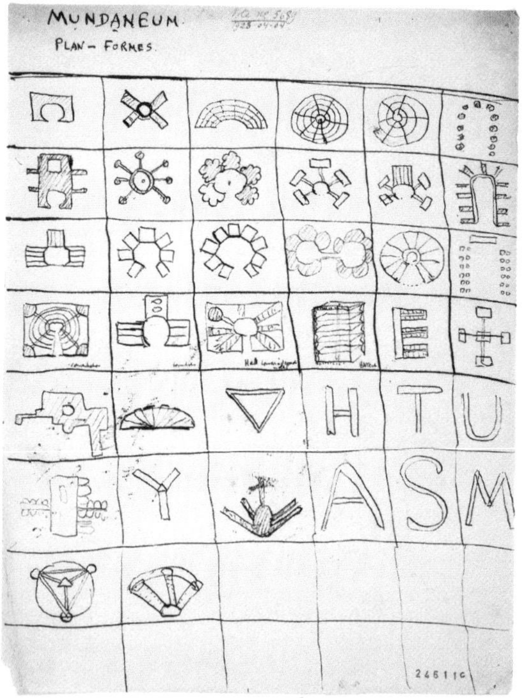


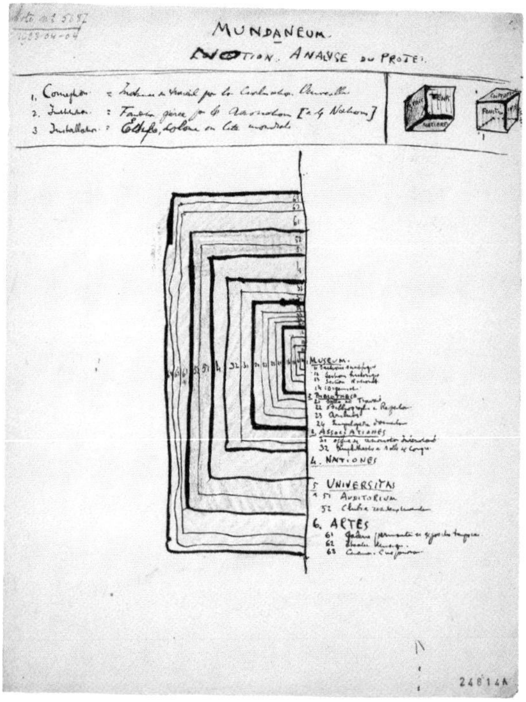


**Figure 1 (Left).** Mundaneum. Plan-Forms. Le Corbusier. ca. 1927.
**Figure 2 (Right).** Mundaneum. Notion: Analysis of the Project. Le Corbusier. ca. 1927.

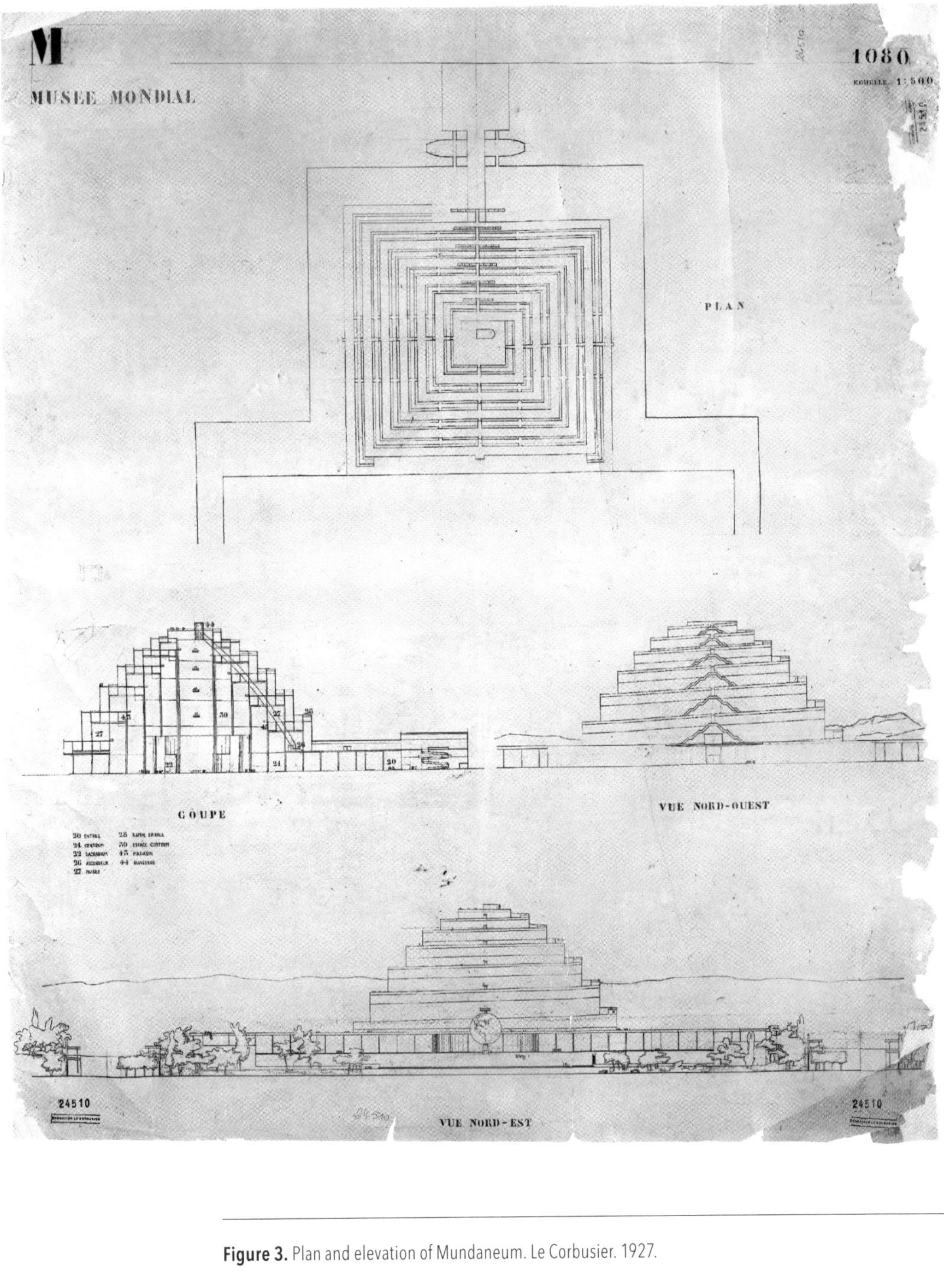


**Figure 3.** Plan and elevation of Mundaneum. Le Corbusier. 1927.

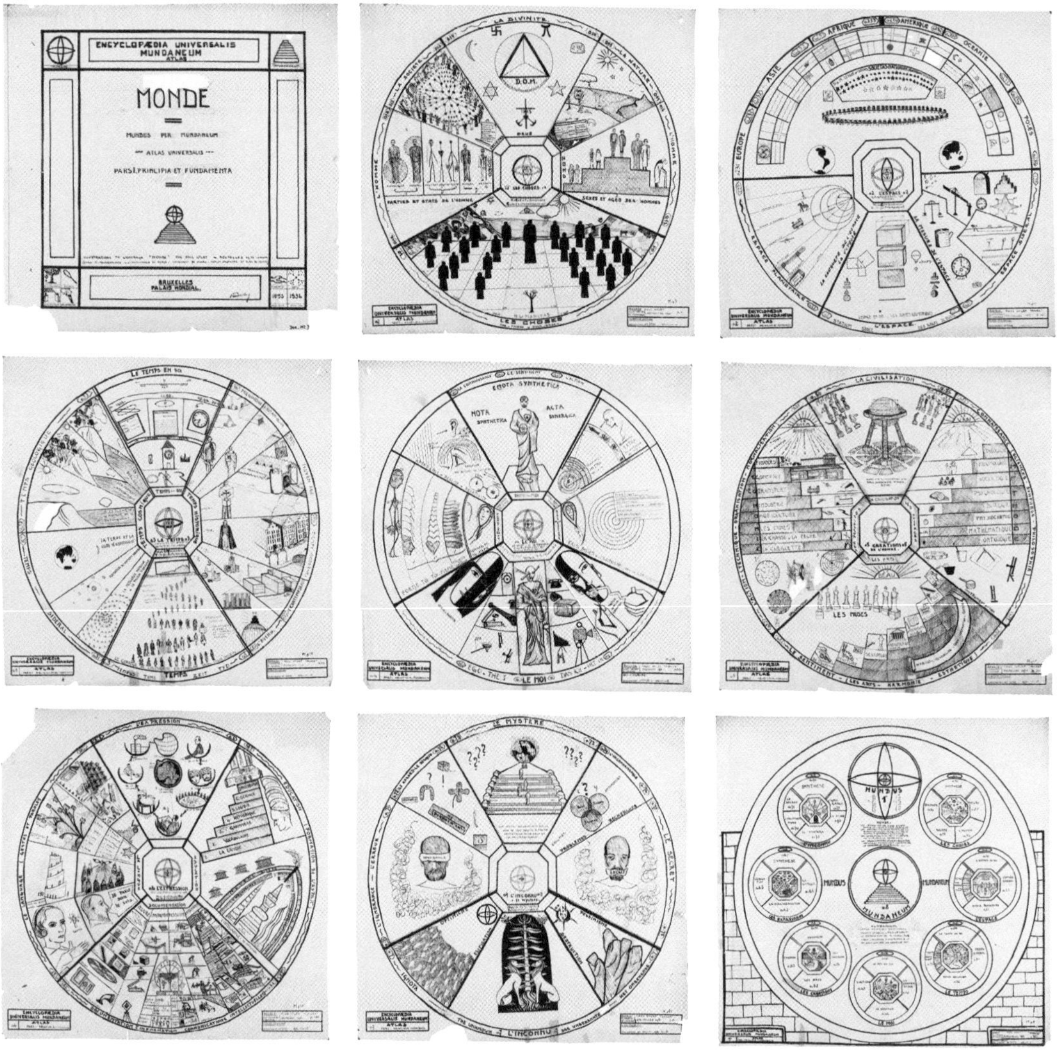


Figure 4. *Encyclopedia Universalis Mundaneum*. Paul Otlet.1935.

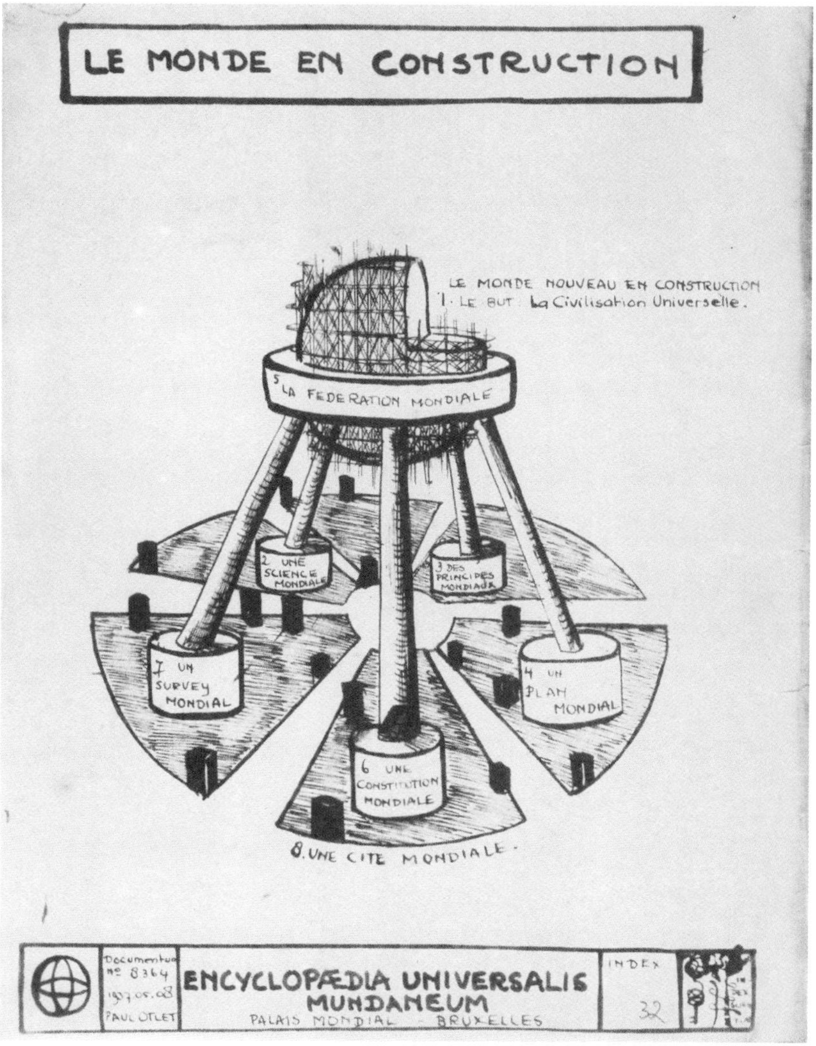


**Figure 5.** The World under Construction. Paul Otlet.1937.

# Проект Клуба Нового Социального Типа
# Club of a New Social Type

**Project:** 9. **Author:** Ivan Leonidov (1902–1959). **Date:** 1928–1929. **Themes:** Autonomy. Place(lessness). Telecommunications. Typology.

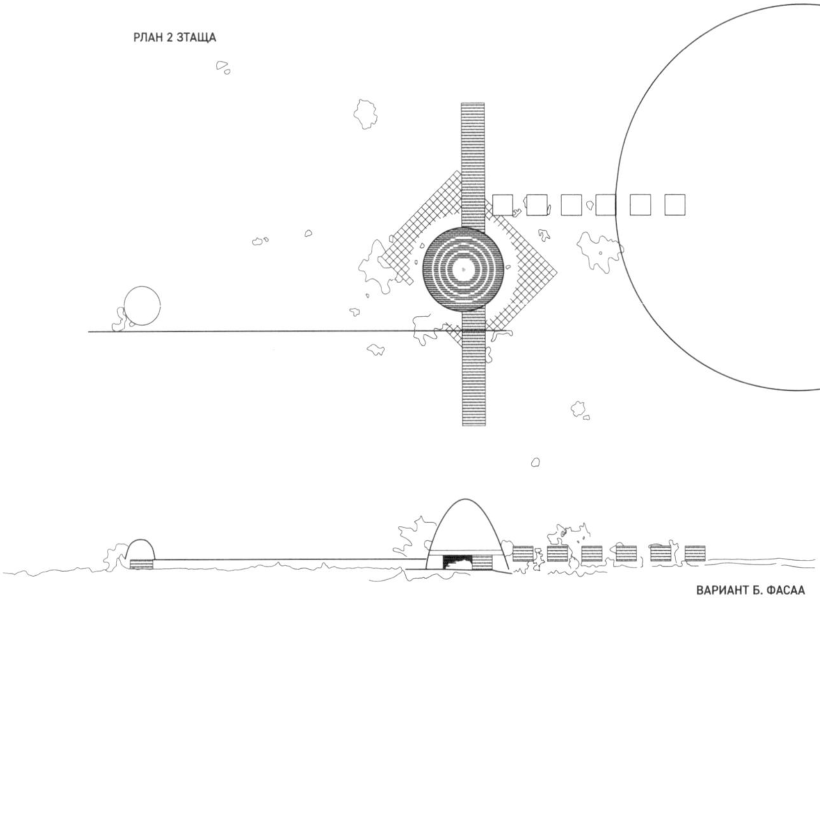


**Figure 0.** Second-floor plan and façade of Club of a New Social Type: Variant B. After Leonidov. 1928.

1. About telecommunications see Richard Anderson, "A Screen That Receives Images by Radio," *AA Files* 67 (2013): 3–15, and Anatole Kopp, *Town and Revolution: Soviet Architecture and City Planning, 1917–1935* (New York: G. Braziller, 1970), 200.

2. Kopp, *Town and Revolution*, 189.

3. Richard Anderson, "Montage and the Mediation of Constructivist Architecture," in *Before Publication: Montage in Art, Architecture, and Book Design*, ed. Nanni Baltzer, Martino Stierli, and Richard Anderson (Zurich: Park Books, 2016), 37.

4. El Lissitzky, *Russia: An Architecture for World Revolution* (Cambridge, MA: MIT Press, 1970), 43–45.

5. Vieri Quilici, "Introduction," in *Ivan Leonidov* (New York: Institute for Architecture and Urban Studies, 1981), 6.

Among the work of his Russian contemporaries, Ivan Leonidov's projects stand out for addressing the world scale only through a strict attention to the architectural object and to the spatial relations between objects. For him, the articulation of a world spatial system and of a universal society fundamentally requires developing a new architectural vocabulary and a new spatial syntax. His is a poetics of microcosms, characterized by an extreme tension between encapsulated objects and their planetary referent. Counterintuitively, the autonomy, and even the isolation of the architectural piece, are his tools to initiate a universal spatial system. In it, sparse architectural units are the cells of a world society interconnected through aerial transport and telecommunications. That is, through means that are then emerging or which—as television—are still unavailable.[1]

Leonidov pursues this research through a succession of projects designed at the very beginning of his career. The Lenin Institute (1927), the Club of a New Social Type (1928–1929), the Columbus Memorial (1929), and the Palace of Culture (1930) constitute a family of designs sharing the same conceptual intentions.[2] In them, Leonidov tests a unique set of formal procedures in different programs and contexts in order to show its universal applicability. The typological ambition of the projects reinforces his repetition of formal strategies. All of the projects aim to be models that can be replicated anywhere or extended infinitely.[3] The design procedures used in the Club of a New Social Type are, thus, common to the other projects. The club's singularity is not formal, but programmatic and strategic. With it Leonidov reveals how a crucial typology for the construction of communist society can serve to organize the world scale.

After the October Revolution, workers' clubs are considered key elements for articulating the new Soviet state.[4] Ideally, they should exist in every city in order to facilitate the social life of workers, to visualize their collective identity, and to encourage the emergence of a collective class consciousness.[5] Leonidov's prototype—presented with great polemic at the first Congress of the Organization of Contemporary Architects (OSA), the group of constructivist architects to which Leonidov belongs—shares these political ambitions while it rejects the formal, programmatic, and urban conventions that characterized the clubs so far. After supporting his critique with images of aerial transport, scientific work, and space exploration, Leonidov shows a design that completely contradicts existing club typologies. Instead of a single building, Leonidov proposes to create a group of isolated pieces—paraboloids, prisms, and cubes—surrounded by open space, and to disseminate the club's activities outside the limits of the complex **[fig. 0]**. Instead of placing this group in an urban location, he advocates for situating it in the countryside.[6] Instead of organizing the activities of the club around a theater, as was customary, he chooses as symbolic centers of the complex a planetarium, a cinema for receiving information and retransmitting the club's activities, and research laboratories.[7]

By adding a radio system to these programs, Leonidov makes communications, information, and the knowledge of the world the core activities of the club. This use of a building as a cognitive tool is instrumental in legitimizing Leonidov's vision of the way architecture can intervene at the scale of the world. The planetarium and related functions enable the workers to comprehend and see the global scale Leonidov attempts to construct. Despite being isolated from the city, the complex would be immersed in a constant process of reception and emission of information, acting as a node within a potentially global system of interconnected centers. These interchanges would extend to the planetary scale the spirit of the 1917 revolution and its communications tactics. The creation of proletarian cells, such as industry committees, and soviets, operating in different geographic regions, precede the October Revolution. Telegraph, telephone, and radio are fundamental to overcoming these groups' separation. Communications technologies make it possible for them to share their actions and activities and spread the social discontent that results in the end of the Tsars' autarchy.[8] Leonidov recuperates these very same technologies to articulate the club's internal and external relations, emphasizing now their overarching scope and, thus, their capacity to effect a planetary change.

This form of relation through telecommunications allows Leonidov to create a novel, trans-scalar system of spatial organization. All of the club's pieces are thoroughly isolated from each other. Their interrelation happens through distance and separation. The effect of this system characterizes the "Scheme of the Spatial Organization of Cultural Services," a drawing that reveals how Leonidov conceives of the club as the trigger of a broader project of territorial articulation **[fig. 1]**.[9] Abstract and scaleless, the plan represents a constellation of clubs that affect an indeterminate area. From one club, concentric orbits emanate that depict its more direct ambit of influence. Other orbits, coming from other clubs that do not appear in the image, intersect with them. By not representing any physical connections, the drawing suggests the abandonment of material infrastructure as the means of spatial organization. Instead,

**6.** In Leonidov's words: "In order to involve those strata of workers who are not so far being properly served, it is essential that CULTURAL WORK SHOULD NOT BE CONFINED WITHIN THE FRAMEWORK OF THE CLUBS, but be developed within the enterprises themselves, the workshops, worker's barracks and hostels, and worker' settlements. Cultural education work must be set up in the countryside in those places where industrial workers and seasonal workers are concentrated, and all this must be closely linked with the whole mass political and propagandist work of the party." Quoted in Andrei Gozak and Andrei Leonidov, *Ivan Leonidov: The Complete Works* (New York: Rizzoli, 1988), 61. Originally published in *Sovremnnaya Arkhitektura* 3 (1929): 103–110.

**7.** Leonidov substitutes the theater, conceived as a space of pure leisure, by a place for the transmission of information; an operation that is followed by his assertion that "it is essential not to restrict cultural work within the framework of the clubs, but to develop it within the enterprises themselves." Leonidov's statement suggests the intention to conflate work, intellectual production, and cultural life that characterizes both constructivism and the Proletkult movement. Sergei Tret'iakov, one of the thinkers of the latter movement, affirms, for instance, that theater is a means "to fill up the leisure time of the proletariat," and that it is necessary to substitute it with initiatives oriented "toward a rhythmically coordinated construction of life." See Ivan Leonidov, "The Socially New Type of Club," in S. O. Khan-Magomedov, *Pioneers of Soviet Architecture: The Search for New Solutions in the 1920s and 1930s* (New York: Rizzoli, 1987), 554, and Sergei Tret'iakov, "Art in the Revolution and the Revolution in Art (Aesthetic Consumption and Production)," *October* 118 (Fall 2006): 17 and 18.

telecommunications and aerial transport create a new, discontinuous regime of spatial relations; one that does not require a predetermined form, and that works strictly through the immaterial connections between units. Leonidov proves this possibility by designing two variants of the club, in which the same architectural pieces are arranged in different manners, without altering the intentions of the project **[figs. 2 and 3]**.

In the resulting spatial system, there is a vast, unbounded space between the buildings. The architectural pieces do not act as agents of spatial delimitation. They stand, isolated, on an undefined and limitless space, which Leonidov characterizes as a mere fragment of the common ground of the world. The terrain's representation in black—a characteristic of his drawings of the period—presents the ground as an abstract void bare of singularities, like cosmic space. In order to emphasize the club's direct link to the world, Leonidov suppresses any contextual particularity. Deterritorialized and placeless, his objects are situated in the universal space they contribute to creating.

Leonidov's spatial system does not only deny the singularity of the place. The direct transition from the object to the world also disrupts all the intermediate scales between them. It particularly negates the conventions and values of the urban scale. Some of Leonidov's contemporaries, architects and critics such as El Lissitzky and Moisei Ginzburg, immediately recognize that his architectural projects contain, *in nuce*, a novel program for reconfiguring the totality of the city **[project 10]**.[10] This reconfiguration is, in fact, a rebuttal. Leonidov titles his doctoral dissertation proposal *Architecture and Design of Inhabited Areas in the Conditions of Contemporary Society Using the Most Advanced Technical Possibilities*, thus making the organization of settlements the lens through which his architectural production has to be understood, but thereby also avoiding defining inhabited areas as cities.[11] Consequently, in the club and his other early projects, the city seemingly disappears **[fig. 4]**. The project shows an ascetic system of dispersed objects, whose interrelation creates a world system where the categorical distinctions and the territorial and political logics associated with the city cease to exist. There are no boundaries, no differentiations between city and landscape, no centers and peripheries. There are just interrelated, autonomous entities that have a similar valence: nodes within an isotropic network.

The territorial scale is constituted by autonomous clubs. Each club is, in turn, made of autonomous buildings. Leonidov's architectural vision results in a project of spatial separations and self-determining pieces. At a formal level, the

**8.** Paul Mason, *Postcapitalism: A Guide to Our Future* (New York: Farrar, Straus and Giroux), 192–196.

**9.** According to El Lissitzky, Leonidov conceives the club as the center of a new settlement system. Lissitzky, *Russia: An Architecture for World Revolution*, 44. For a critical contemporary view of Leonidov's ambitions see R. Khiger, "Masters of the Young Architecture," in Gozak and Leonidov, *Ivan Leonidov*, 104 (translated from *Architecture USSR*, 1934): "Their general argument went something like this: life is taking gigantic steps forward in social and technological progress. The achievements of science conquer nature, space and time. Aviation, radio and television open up hitherto unknown horizons. Physics, chemistry and biology are changing the face of the earth. Meanwhile architecture potters around with task that are as old as the world, in most cases solving them with the antique handicraft techniques. We must therefore bring 'the cultural organisation of life' into architecture, too; that bold spirit of 'daring' which characterises the scientific and technical progress of today."

**10.** See in this respect S. O. Khan-Magomedov, "Ivan Leonidov, un architetto sovietico," in *Ivan Leonidov, 1902–1959*, ed. Alessandro De Magistris and Irina Korob'ina (Milan: Electa Architettura, 2009), 24; and Lissitzky, *Russia: An Architecture for World Revolution*.

**11.** Ekaterina A. Barabanova "Igarka, la costruzione di una città nell'estremo nord dell'Unione Sovietica," in De Magistris and Korob'ina, *Ivan Leonidov, 1902–1959*, 73.

system implies overcoming the aesthetic procedures of early constructivism. The complex aggregation of conflicting geometries in a single building that characterizes early constructivism is substituted by a vocabulary of elementary platonic forms whose linguistic essentialism searches universal applicability.[12] Pyramids, prisms, spheres, and lines are the units of Leonidov's system of formal differences. The vast separation among these elements highlights the importance of the space among them. The constant presence of this space makes evident its role as an element of cohesion, while its abstract neutrality warrants its condition as enabler of a system of independent, differentiated constituents.

Leonidov's contemporaries criticize him for this constant use of a limited number of platonic bodies. In his view, this accusation denotes a backward stylistic preoccupation with "outer" form, while, for him, the architect's task is "organizing."[13] Form is, he states, just "the corollary of the organization and functional interdependence of the workers."[14] As a result, the club is, fundamentally, an instrument for the "general organization of human consciousness."[15] The systematic contrast of platonic forms and the insistence on perceiving the space that surrounds them by different means and from multiple observation points are, in this sense, a way of transmitting a political proposition: the political organism is made by multiple and different aterritorial entities, all sharing the common space of the world. The club promotes a social vision whose ideology, following Vieri Quilici, can be defined as the combination of autonomy and universalism and which Leonidov eloquently expresses with his plan of a "Scheme of Spatial Organization," which takes shape thanks to the relations between territorially dispersed, independent entities.[16] This system believes in the cohesion of the world scale through telecommunications, but it simultaneously understands that the constitution of that scale has to result from architectural operations. Autonomy is the architect's crucial tool in this respect, as it liberates architecture from external and contextual constraints, facilitates the repetition of formal strategies, and allows the constitution of internal, independent microworlds.

The crucial consequence of Leonidov's architectural operations is the transformation of the notion of autonomy into a "relational" or "modal" concept.[17] Instead of a modern understanding of autonomy as a space of negative critique to social conventions, autonomy is for Leonidov a tool to link architecture to the production of new forms of relations and socialization.[18] The goal of Leonidov's project of architectural autonomy is thus social. It promotes, in the architect's words, "the initiative and self-determination of workers," and their interrela-

12. Khan-Magomedov, *Pioneers of Soviet Architecture*, 234; and Quilici, "Introduction," 4.

13. Ivan Leonidov, "Extracts from Leonidov's answers to questions put to him about his lecture devoted to 'A Socially New Type of Club' at the First OSA Congress, 1929," in Khan-Magomedov, *Pioneers of Soviet Architecture*, 555.

14. Leonidov, "Extracts from Leonidov's answers," 555.

15. Leonidov, "Extracts from Leonidov's answers," 555.

16. Quilici, "Introduction," 5 and 8. "As far as he [Leonidov] was concerned, it was preferable to organize into small collectives in which the individual personality does not get lost but has the possibility to develop itself to the maximum degree and to communicate with everyone, by moving progressively from the smallest collective to the largest."

17. We take the notion of "modal" autonomy, and the analysis of its incidence in constructivism, from Jordi Claramonte, *La República de los fines. Contribución a una crítica de la autonomía del arte* (Murcia: Cendeac, 2013), 173–199.

18. For the visions of autonomy during Enlightenment and modernity see also Claramonte, *La República de los fines.*

tion in a global collective.[19] It helps to spatialize the Marxist understanding of working class as the universal subject of world historic transformation.[20] The designs define the architectural typologies that can support such a project and in so doing they consummate, in the production of a new formal system, the initial ideological preoccupations of constructivism. The OSA collective, to which Leonidov belongs, is equally committed to the notion of relational autonomy. The group's adoption of disurbanism in the period 1929–1931 will show, in the following catalogue entry, how this understanding of autonomy serves to expand Leonidov's abandonment of the city into a full project of territorial design, and how such a project relies upon the notions of "organization," communication, and information that Leonidov explores.

**19.** Ivan Leonidov, "Extract from the explanatory note attached to the design for a Palace of Culture, 1930," in Khan-Magomedov, *Pioneers of Soviet Architecture*, 556.

**20.** Ernesto Laclau, "Universalism, Particularism, and the Question of Identity," *October* 61 (Summer 1992): 86.

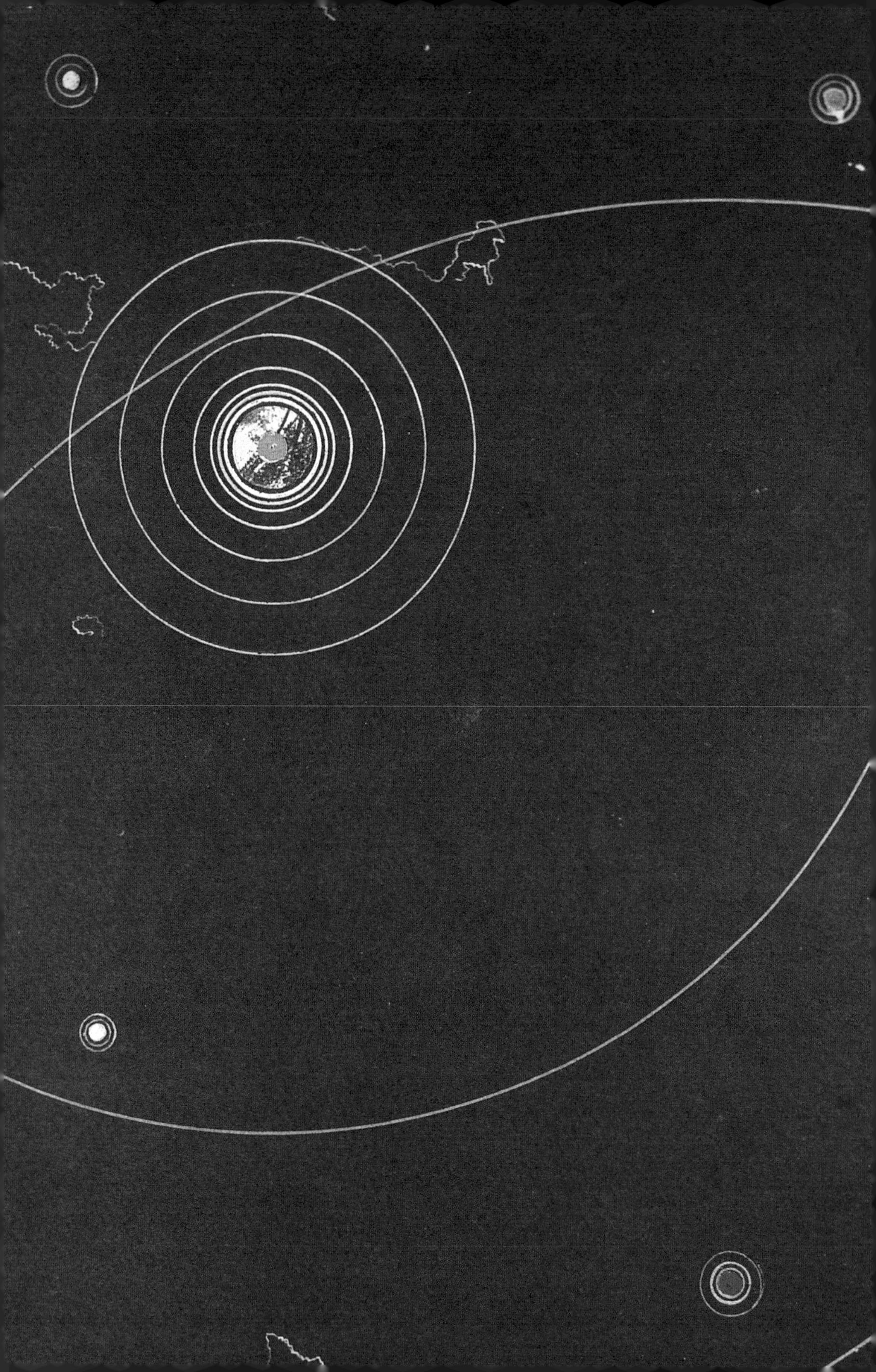

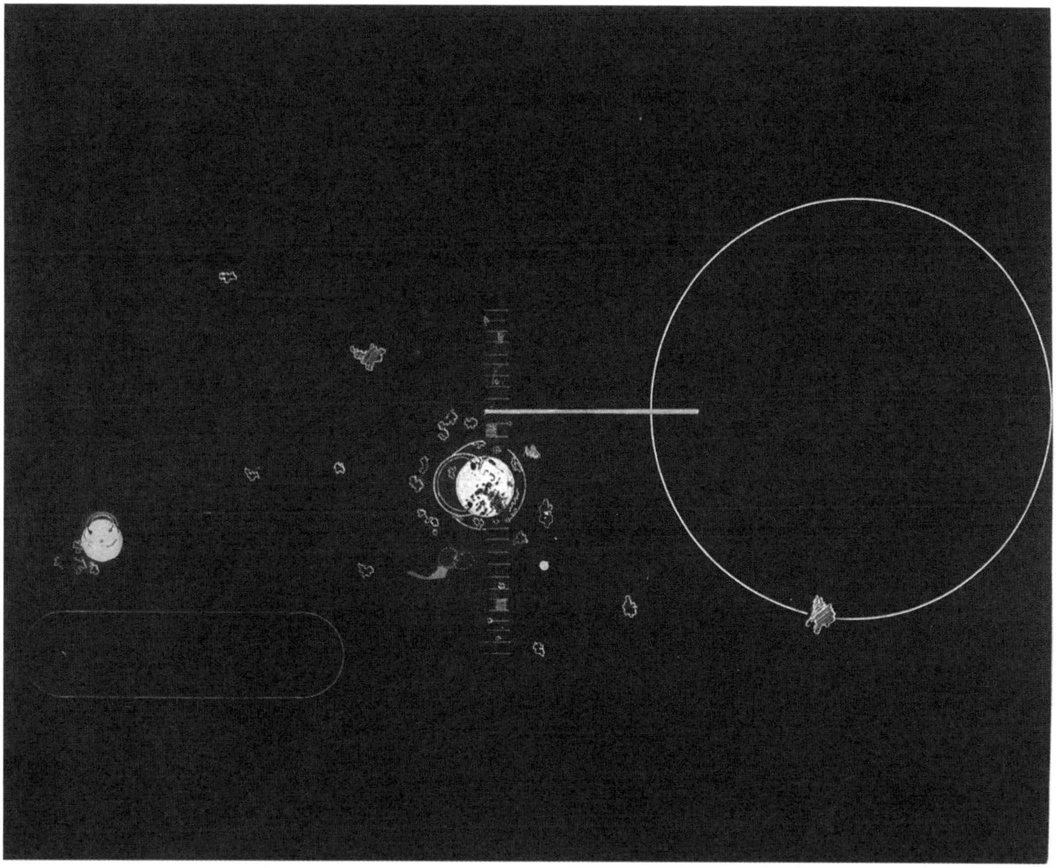

**Figure 1 (Opposite page).** Scheme of the Spatial Organization of Cultural Services. 1928.
**Figure 2.** Plan of the Club of a New Social Type: Variant B. 1928.

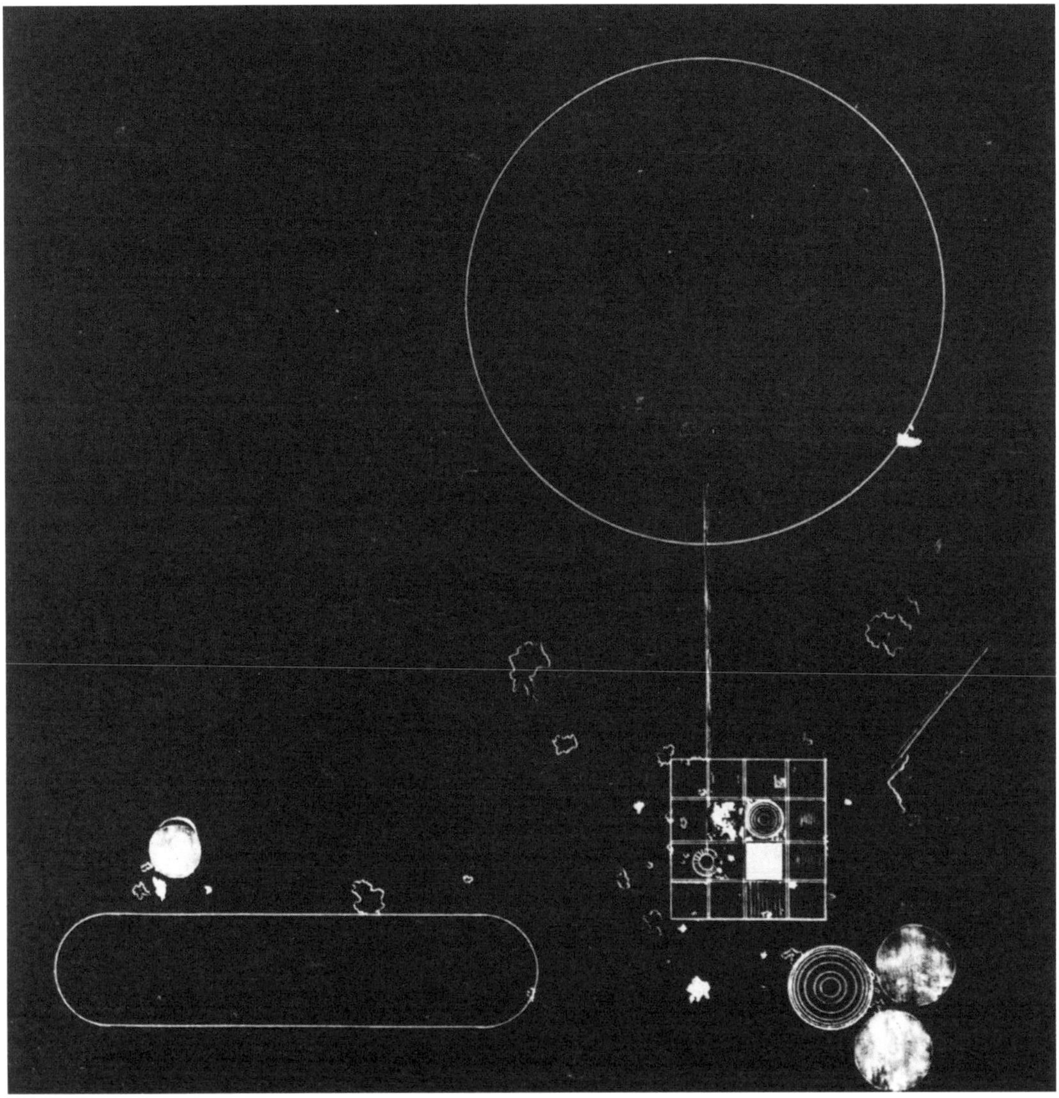

**Figure 3.** Plan of the Club of a New Social Type: Variant A. 1928.

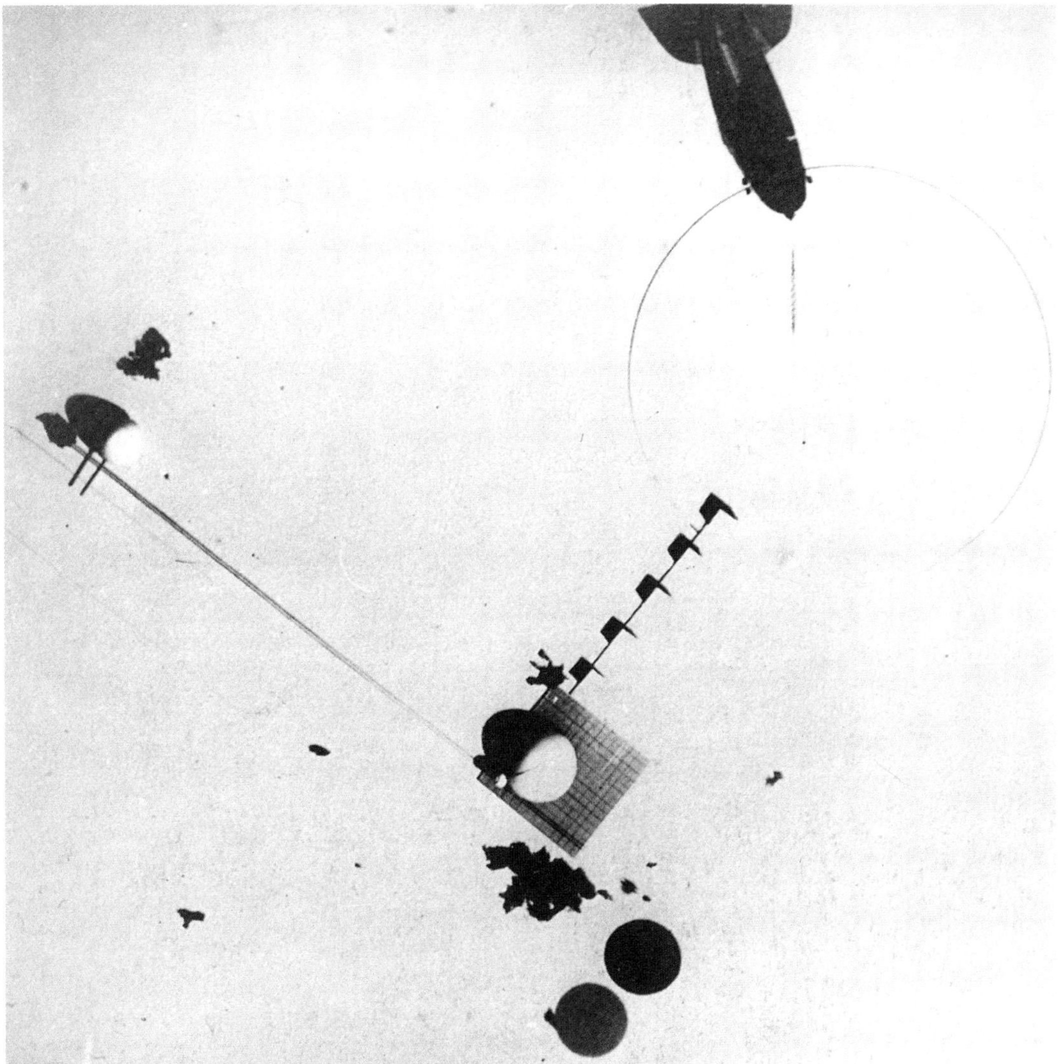

**Figure 4.** Model of the Club of a New Social Type: Variant A. 1928.

# Дезурбанизма

## Disurbanism

**Project:** 10. **Authors:** Mikhail Okhitovich (1896–1937) and Moisei Ginzburg (1892–1946). **Date:** 1929–1930.
**Themes:** Autonomy. Decentralization. Nomadism. Telecommunications.

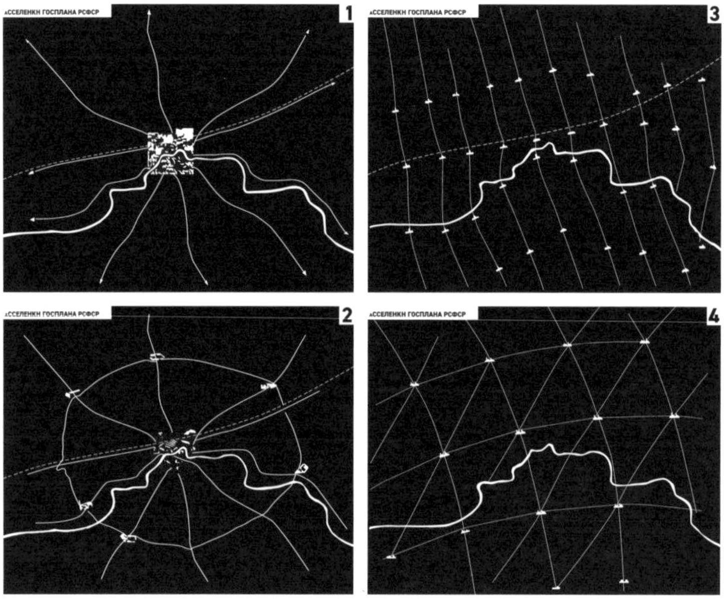


**Figure 0.** Section for socialist settlement according to the USSR state plan. 1920.
Settlement scheme 1: Disurbanize
Settlement scheme 2: Decentralize
Settlement scheme 3: Acentric
Settlement scheme 4: Dispersive

With the implementation of the first Five Year Plan, the authorities of the USSR aim to leave behind the long decade of turmoil that follows the October Revolution. The plan sets the foundation for the consolidation of socialism by determining the objectives of mass collectivization and State-led economic development that are to be accomplished in the period 1928–1932. Crucial among these objectives is the transformation of the USSR into an urban country. The document establishes goals for the construction of towns at a scale hitherto unimaginable: two hundred new industrial towns and around one thousand agricultural towns have to be built during the validity of the plan.[1]

The theories and projects of disurbanism emerge in this context of deep transformation. They constitute an influential contribution to the efforts of urbanization and State-building, but also a harsh critique of their rationale.[2] Disurbanism negates the division of agricultural and industrial cities prescribed in the Plan. It provides, instead, a territorial and political model aimed at entirely abolishing the dichotomy between city and countryside through a process of progressive decentralization, which, oblivious to national boundaries, was to transform the whole Earth.

The main theoretician of disurbanism is a sociologist turned urbanist: Mikhail Okhitovich. In a series of papers published between 1929 and 1930 in *Sovremennaia Arkhitektura* (SA), the journal of the constructivist collective OSA (Organization of Contemporary Architects), Okhitovich argues that socialism has to supersede the notion of city as a spatially bounded, discrete unit, itself an instrumental concept of the capitalist mode of production.[3] Under socialism, instead, cities have to be understood as "a specific socially, not territorially, determined human entity"; that is, as a conglomerate of relations unconstrained by any particular spatial form.[4] The main facilitators of this change are emerging forms of transportation, energy production, and communication, which socialism can utilize to foster a process of dispersal based on the "principles of maximum freedom, ease and speed of communication."[5] This dispersal, termed "disurbanism," has to be conceived of with the same scalar ambitions as the planning of industrial conglomerates operating at the world scale.[6] Okhitovich's description of the resulting world system as the "Red City of the planet of communism" is only a deliberate, symbolic concession to the old, spatial terminology. Disurbanism would not produce a city, but a "single organizational complex" for the "resettlement of mankind."[7]

1. Hugh D. Hudson, Jr., *Blueprints and Blood: The Stalinization of Soviet Architecture, 1917–1937* (Princeton: Princeton University Press, 2015), 62.

2. Through the work of constructivist architects, Okhitovich's theories inform the discussions of the Socialist Settlement Section of Gosplan (the State Planning Commission). Disurbanist work is also supported by the State Institute for the Planning of Cities (Gigopror). See S. O. Khan-Magomedov, *Pioneers of Soviet Architecture: The Search for New Solutions in the 1920s and 1930s* (New York: Rizzoli, 1987), 335; S. O. Khan-Magomedov, *Mikhail Okhitovich* (Moscow: Russkii Avangard, 2009), 103–125; S. Frederick Starr, "Visionary Town Planning during the Cultural Revolution," in *Cultural Revolution in Russia, 1928–1931*, ed. Sheila Fitzpatrick (Bloomington: Indiana University Press, 1978): 224.

3. Mikhail Okhitovich, "On the Problem of the City," *Sovremennaia Arkhitektura* (SA) 4 (1929): 130–134; and "Notes on the Theory of Resettlement," *Sovremennaia Arkhitektura* (SA) 1–2 (1930): 7–13. A whole transcript of the first article appears also in Khan-Magomedov, *Mikhail Okhitovich*, 46–70. There is a partial English translation in Catherine Cooke, *Russian Avant-garde: Theories of Art, Architecture and the City* (London: Academy Editions, 1995), 199. The second article is partially translated in Anatole Kopp, *Town and Revolution: Soviet Architecture and City Planning 1917–1935* (New York: George Braziller, 1970), 248–250, under the title "Editorial Favoring Urbanization." For Okhitovich's critique of the city, see the Russian urbanist's quote in Hudson, *Blueprints and Blood*, 64: "The city must perish in the ruins of the capitalist mode of production, for the city was a requirement of trade-capitalist society. When these requirements vanish, so will the city, their product. The city is the form, the condition, of the social relations of capitalist society."

Disurbanism is, for Okhitovich, not a stage but a process; open-ended and variable. Its emergence depends, however, upon the adoption of some specific spatial guidelines. The general spatial model of disurbanism—a template to be applied worldwide—consists of a triangular grid **[fig. 1]**. The sides of the triangles are infrastructures carrying "raw materials, fuel, semifinished and finished products, and labor."[8] Areas of agriculture or resource extraction occupy the interior of the triangles, while the vortexes house production plants. Dwellings and communal facilities are mere dots dispersed in parklands along the triangle's sides, without forming any agglomeration **[fig. 2]**. The core of the project is hence infrastructural. Its primary operation is to substitute the disposition of transport and energy networks in radial configurations, emanating from cities or places of energy production, with the isotropic triangular network.[9] With this operation, Okhitovich believes, industries can be built directly where resources are, without having to centralize production—and, consequently, the population—in cities **[fig. 0]**.[10] The organizational complex is, therefore, conceived of mainly as a productive complex.[11] But the reorganization of production, in turn, enables the redistribution of population and the rise of new social and political configurations.

Okhitovich elaborates most of the disurbanists' proposals together with Moisei Ginzburg, OSA's intellectual leader, and with other members of that group. Although the constructivist architects initially favor urban concentration, after Ginzburg's meeting with Okhitovich, disurbanism becomes OSA's ideology of the city, and as such it is repeatedly tested in projects and competitions such as the Moscow Green City or the plan for the new town of Magnitogorsk (both 1930) **[fig. 3]**.[12] The total acceptance of disurbanism reveals how much the group's previous reliance on conventional metropolitan models was impeding them from fully spatializing their ideological aspirations, as Ivan Leonidov was already proving **[project 9]**. Disurbanism enables OSA architects to define a territorial model that matches the alternative vision of socialism the collective pursed, one that favors decentralization and internationalism, in contrast to the project of State construction and political centralization Stalinism was promoting. This ideological project is hugely controversial. The 1931 Central Committee plenum not only censures disurbanism as counter-revolutionary, in 1935, Okhitovich is also arrested and condemned to a camp, where he dies. He is accused of Bukharinism and Trotskyism—in other words, of combating forced collectivization and favoring the doctrine of continuous world revolu-

**4.** Mikhail Okhitovich, "On the Problem of the City," in Cooke, *Russian Avant-Garde,* 199. Okhitovich also describes the city as "a knot of communication: a knot of roads and rivers." See Starr, "Visionary Town Planning during the Cultural Revolution," 212.

**5.** Okhitovich, "On the Problem of the City," in Cooke, *Russian Avant-garde,* 199.

**6.** Okhitovich, "On the Problem of the City," in Cooke, *Russian Avant-garde,* 199.

**7.** Okhitovich, "On the Problem of the City," in Cooke, *Russian Avant-garde,* 199, and Mikhail Okhitovich, "Editorial Favoring Deurbanization," in Kopp, *Town and Revolution,* 250.

**8.** Khan-Magomedov, *Pioneers of Soviet Architecture,* 335.

**9.** Hudson, *Blueprints and Blood,* 64.

**10.** Hudson, *Blueprints and Blood,* 65.

**11.** Importantly, for Okhitovich, disurbanism is motivated by modifications in the means of production. This requires a transformation of the figure of the architect into a designer of the social relations of production. Architectural knowledge is not limited, in this sense, to the specific boundaries of the discipline, and thus, the architect has to be involved in different forms of innovation. See Okhitovich, "On the Problem of the City," in Khan-Magomedov, *Mikhail Okhitovich,* 60–65.

**12.** The conversion of Ginzburg, and by extension of the other constructivists, to disurbanism implies a clear break with the hegemonic urban discourse of the early modern movement, which favored concentration. This separation motivates a strong written polemic between Ginzburg and Le Corbusier [projects 8 and 15]. See Le Corbusier and Moisei Ginzburg, "Le Corbusier-Ginzburg Correspondence (1930)," in Kopp, *Town and Revolution,* 252–253.

tion, against Stalin's theory of socialism in just one country.[13] A similar destiny awaits other OSA members. The architect Aleksei Gan, author of the foundational *Constructivism* manifesto (1922), presumably also dies in a camp. And Leonidov is forbidden to teach.

The constructivist commitment to internationalism and decentralization substantially derives from the Proletkult movement and from the thinking of its founder, Alexander Bogdanov (1873–1928).[14] Also a founder of the Bolshevik party, Bogdanov is a multifaceted personality whom Lenin expelled from the party because of his alternative theories about the construction of socialism. Two concepts are central to the foundation of his alternative vision. The first challenges the Marxist understanding of culture as superstructure. For him, socialism cannot result only from the modification of property relations. It also requires cultural and ideological transformation, the creation of an autonomous proletarian culture.[15] The second cornerstone of his thinking is that socialism requires subverting the capitalist relations of production, abolishing the differentiation between organizers and organized.[16] This position motivates Bogdanov's main intellectual endeavor: the elaboration of a "Universal Organizational Science," which he calls tektology.[17] Currently credited as a precedent of cybernetics and systems theory, tektology posits that "organization" is the main principle of social and natural processes. Using this thesis, Bogdanov challenges another central Marxist tenet. Tektology is antidialectical. It is a "monist" philosophy that equates human and natural processes and treats them both as "organizational complexes."[18] Okhitovich's terminology and his projected convergence of cities and countryside in a single entity are, in this sense, deeply close to Bogdanov's monism.

Bogdanov's tektology requires treating every manufacturing process, social formation, or technological product as a form of encapsulating and organizing a certain type of information.[19] Assimilating social and productive processes to knowledge creates a conceptual framework that aims to suppress the class stratifications derived from existing forms of division of labor. Tektology considers, in a novel manner, the manufacturing work of the proletariat as a form of knowledge, and the activity of intellectuals and artists as "intellectual production." Art, Bogdanov explains, is just one form of production: "Creation of all kinds (technological, socioeconomic, everyday, scientific, artistic) represents a variety of different forms of labor, and similarly consists of organizing (or disorganizing) human activity. There is not and cannot be any strict division between creation and basic labor."[20]

**13.** Hudson, *Blueprints and Blood*, 158–160.

**14.** About Bogdanov's influence on constructivism, see Anatole Senkevitch, "Trends in Soviet Architectural Thought, 1917–1932. The Growth and Decline of the Constructivist and Rationalist Movements" (PhD diss., Cornell University, 1974), 129–296. Charlotte Douglas, "A Lost Paradigm of Abstraction: Alexander Bogdanov and the Russian Avant-Garde," in *The Russian Avant-Garde: Representation and Interpretation*, ed. E. A. Petrova (St. Petersburg: Palace Editions, 2001), 203–211; Charlotte Douglas, "Energetic Abstraction: Ostwald, Bogdanov, and Russian Post-Revolutionary Art," in *From Energy to Information: Representation in Science and Technology, Art, and Literature*, ed. Bruce Clarke and Linda Dalrymple Henderson (Stanford, CA: Stanford University Press, 2002), 76–94 and 383–387; Maria Chehonadskih, "The Stofflichkeit of the Universe: Alexander Bogdanov and the Soviet Avant-Garde," *e-flux* 88 (February 2018), unpaged, accessed September 10, 2018, https://www.e-flux.com/journal/88/174279/the-stofflichkeit-of-the-universe-alexander-bogdanov-and-the-soviet-avant-garde/

**15.** Arran Gare, "Aleksandr Bogdanov and Systems Theory," *Democracy & Nature* 6, no. 3 (2000): 346.

**16.** Gare, "Aleksandr Bogdanov and Systems Theory," 342.

**17.** About Tektology see also George Gorelik, "Bogdanov's Tektology: Its Nature, Development and Influence," *Studies in Soviet Thought* 26, no. 1 (1983): 39–57.

**18.** Gorelik, "Bogdanov's Tektology," 40 and 46–52. In the author's description: "Bogdanov is essentially a monist, the world is itself one unified system whose parts, in turn, can be viewed as systems in their own right: individual systems exhibit their own special laws of organization: specialized sciences have been developed to identify and study these laws. . . . The world consists,

Based on this reconsideration of labor, Bogdanov treats social and economic relations as highly dynamic, emergent processes, comprising alternative phases of organization and disorganization.[21] The capacity to understand and manage these dynamic processes depends on the establishment of mechanisms of relation and communication—of forms of transmission of knowledge—between autonomous social and productive agents, and not from any centralized form of decision-making.

With the Proletkult movement, Bogdanov seeks to translate these theories to practice. In the Proletkult clubs, artists and proletarians work together in order to foster the emergence of a new subjectivity. To achieve this goal, the Proletkult theoretician Sergei Tret'iakov states that art has to become an "organizational" and "constructive" task, one oriented to the formation of autonomous subjects who can contribute to the "construction of the world commune of workers."[22] Aleksei Gan, a contributor with Tret'iakov to the journal *LEF*, bases the conceptual foundations of constructivism on these positions. His *Constructivism* manifesto refers extensively to Bogdanov's *Nauka ob Obshchestvennom Soznanii* (*Science of social consciousness*, 1914) in order to define the movement as "the first culture of organized labor and intellect."[23] This form of organization is possible by breaking down artistic processes into three elements: Tectonics, Faktura, and Construction, which represent different moments of the "manipulation," "organization," and "exploitation," of matter.[24] Beyond the possible relation between the notions of tectonics and tektology, this framework allows Gan to define constructivism in Proletkult's terms, as an autonomous movement that works with "all the productive centers and main bodies of unified Soviet mechanism that realize the communist forms of life in practice."[25] Thought through in terms of organization, constructivist art practices equal political or economic determinations in importance, and thus they cannot be subject to governmental control.[26] The idea of autonomy, already present in the suprematist discourse, becomes the central tenet of the constructivists, for whom art has to operate as an autonomous form of political and social action.

The constructivist architects adopt all these principles. For OSA, architecture is a tool to organize new forms of life. This requires rejecting State interference in architectural production and looking for ways to facilitate the emergence of self-determined relations between individuals. Their belief is that "through a process of interaction within a properly engineered built environment men and women would arrive at a consciousness of interdependence."[27] These new forms of interdependence would not rely on dialectical tensions. On the contrary,

then, of a hierarchy of systems, the apex being of course the world system. . . . The aim of tektology is to identify and study the general laws of organization of any given system." For the roots of Bogdanov's monism, see Douglas "Energetic Abstraction," 76–79.

**19.** Gare, "Aleksandr Bogdanov and Systems Theory," 343.

**20.** Aleksandr Bogdanov, "Puti proletarskogo tvorchestva," *O proletarskoi kul'ture 1904–1924* (Moscow: Kniga, 1924), 192. Translated and quoted in the editorial introduction to Sergei Tret'iakov, "Art in the Revolution and the Revolution in Art (Aesthetic Consumption and Production)," *October* 118 (2006): 11–12.

**21.** Paul Mason, *Postcapitalism: A Guide to Our Future* (New York: Farrar, Straus and Giroux, 2016), 218–221. To explain the implementation of tektological principles of organization, Mason describes Bogdanov's utopian description of a Martian communist civilization in his novel *Red Star*. In the book, production is completely controlled by machines similar to a computer that register in real time the relations between all the industries of the planet, and organize production correspondingly. Workers can move at will and participate in the activities they prefer.

**22.** Tret'iakov, "Art in the Revolution and the Revolution in Art," 14.

**23.** Christina Lodder, *Russian Constructivism* (New Haven: Yale University Press, 1983), 98. For Gan's book see Alexander Gan, *Constructivism* (Barcelona: Tenov, 2014 [1922]).

**24.** Willem G. Weststeijn, "Aleksei Gan's Constructivism and Its Aftermath," *Avant Garde Critical Studies* 29, no. 1 (2013): 380–381.

**25.** For the relation tektology-tectonics, see Chehonadskih, "The Stofflichkeit of the Universe," note 21. The author references: Kristin Romberg, "Alexei Gan: vvedenie v tektoniky" (Alexei Gan: Introduction to tectonics), in *Formal'nyi metod: Antologiia*

constructivism is philosophically monist. As Ginzburg indicates, dialectics is valid to explain the historical processes of urban evolution but not to guide the definition of socialist architectural and social practices.[28] Additionally, these are thought to be part of a world transformation. Following Proletkult's internationalism, constructivism always questions the limitation of architectural production within national boundaries.

Ivan Leonidov's clubs had already defined a system of globally connected autonomous cells that merged knowledge and production. The disurbanist projects take this investigation one step further. They define a territorial scheme that materializes goals of internalization, open-ended organization, and autonomy derived from Bogdanov and Proletkult. As profoundly monist propositions, they seek to overcome the division between city and countryside, and between peasant and worker in order to create a new social space for a new type of subject, a worker that is also a manager of knowledge, not a mere producer of it.[29] To relate these new subjects, disurbanism defines only tenuous forms of spatial organization. The architects limit their role to defining the infrastructure for open-ended relations between individual entities. The diagrammatic triangular grids and ribbons that configure the territorial scale are in reality loose arrangements of isolated elements. In them, all the social and productive institutions are distanced from each other. The houses—mostly single houses for almost nomadic individuals—are equally separated **[fig. 4]**.[30] The whole social body is broken up into discrete spatial units, into elements that can be disassembled and reorganized in different configurations.[31] Without form, the collective emerges only through communications. "Community," as Okhitovich explains, "is now a function of separatedness."[32]

As a result of this separatedness, the notion of form becomes a purely relational notion, variable in time, defined by the "connections among elements."[33] The planetary project of disurbanism aims to abolish, in this way, any fixed spatial configuration in order to become pure process. In so doing, disurbanism offers the first schema for a society of interrelated individuals who are at once extremely connected and extremely disaggregated. It envisages a planet governed by communications and distant relations, in which the reduction to the minimum of spatial determinations is a tool—to use Bogdanov's terms—for the changing organization and disorganization of social relations.

*russkogo modernizma,* vol. 1, *Systems,* ed. S. Oushakine, (Moscow: Kabinetny unchenyi, 2016), 851–852. For Gan's quote see Senkevitch, "Trends in Soviet Architectural Thought," 141.

**26.** Senkevitch, "Trends in Soviet Architectural Thought," 144.

**27.** Hudson, *Blueprints and Blood,* 76. Gan was particularly explicit in this respect. "In its planning and development by Constructivists," he wrote, "the communist city represents the first attempt to organize human consciousness," and "to establish a clear notion of public property among the citizenry." See Senkevitch, "Trends in Soviet Architectural Thought," 148.

**28.** For the ideological criticism to constructivism derived from the group's monist positions, and Ginzburg's statements, see Hudson, *Blueprints and Blood,* 80–81. In this respect, the architects follow Gan, who had already advocated for the introduction of monist principles in constructivism. See Lodder, *Russian Constructivism,* 94.

**29.** It must be noted that a crucial piece of the disurbanist diagram of organization is a technical institute for the education of peasants and industrial workers.

**30.** About the transformation of housing into a mobile element, see Okhitovich, "On the Problem of the City," in Khan-Magomedov, *Mikhail Okhitovich,* 67.

**31.** Okhitovich, "Editorial Favoring Deurbanization," 250.

**32.** Okhitovich, "On the Problem of the City," in Cooke, *Russian Avant-garde,*199.

**33.** In a reflection close to Okhitovich's understanding of the articulation of the urban condition, Bogdanov saw that "a change in form can only consist either in the destruction of any former connections or in the appearance of new connections or in both." See Gare, "Aleksandr Bogdanov and Systems Theory," 351.

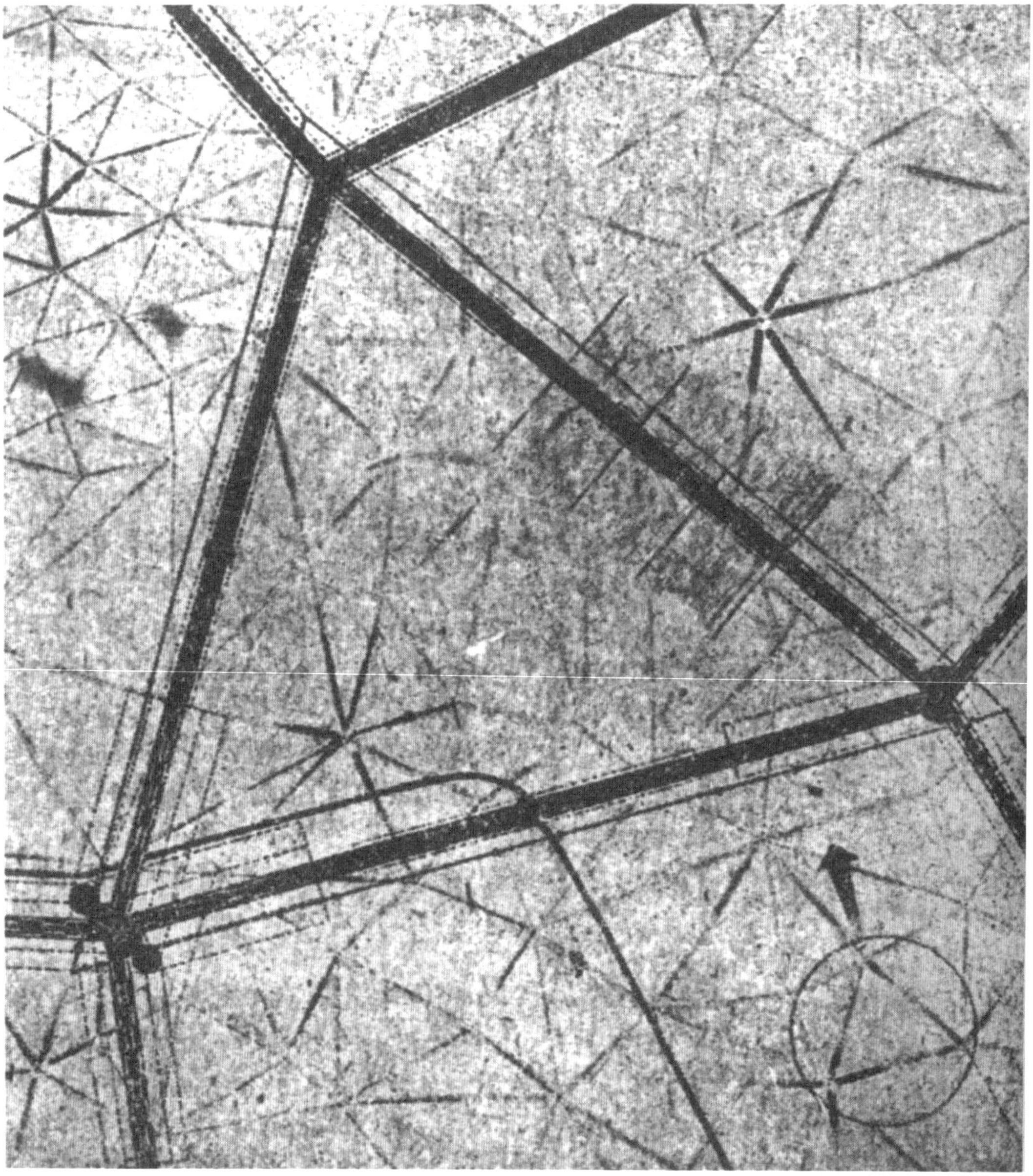

**Figure 1.** General Settlement Scheme. 1930.

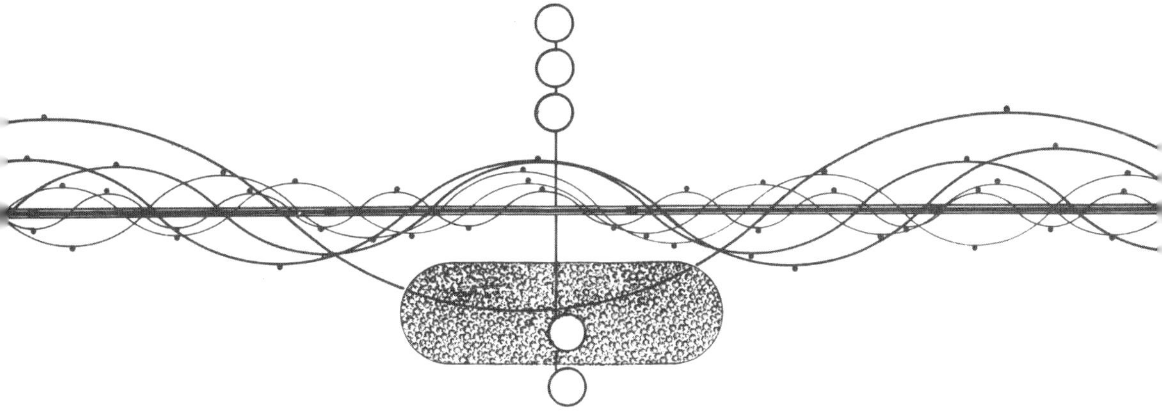

**Figure 2.** Scheme of public service networks. 1930.

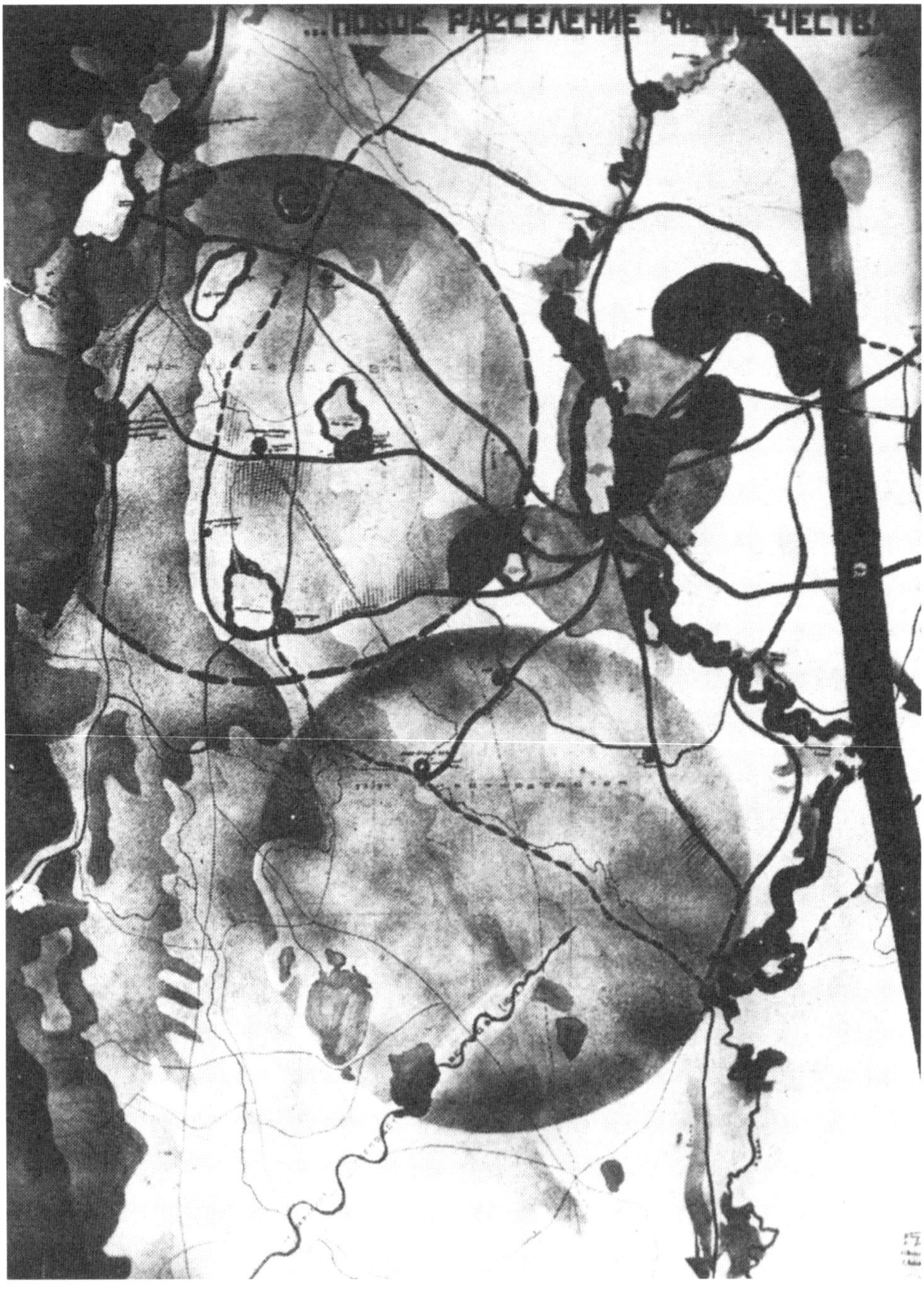


**Figure 3.** General plan for Magnitogorsk competition. Okhitovich with M. Bartsch, N. Vladimirov, and N. Sokolov. 1930.

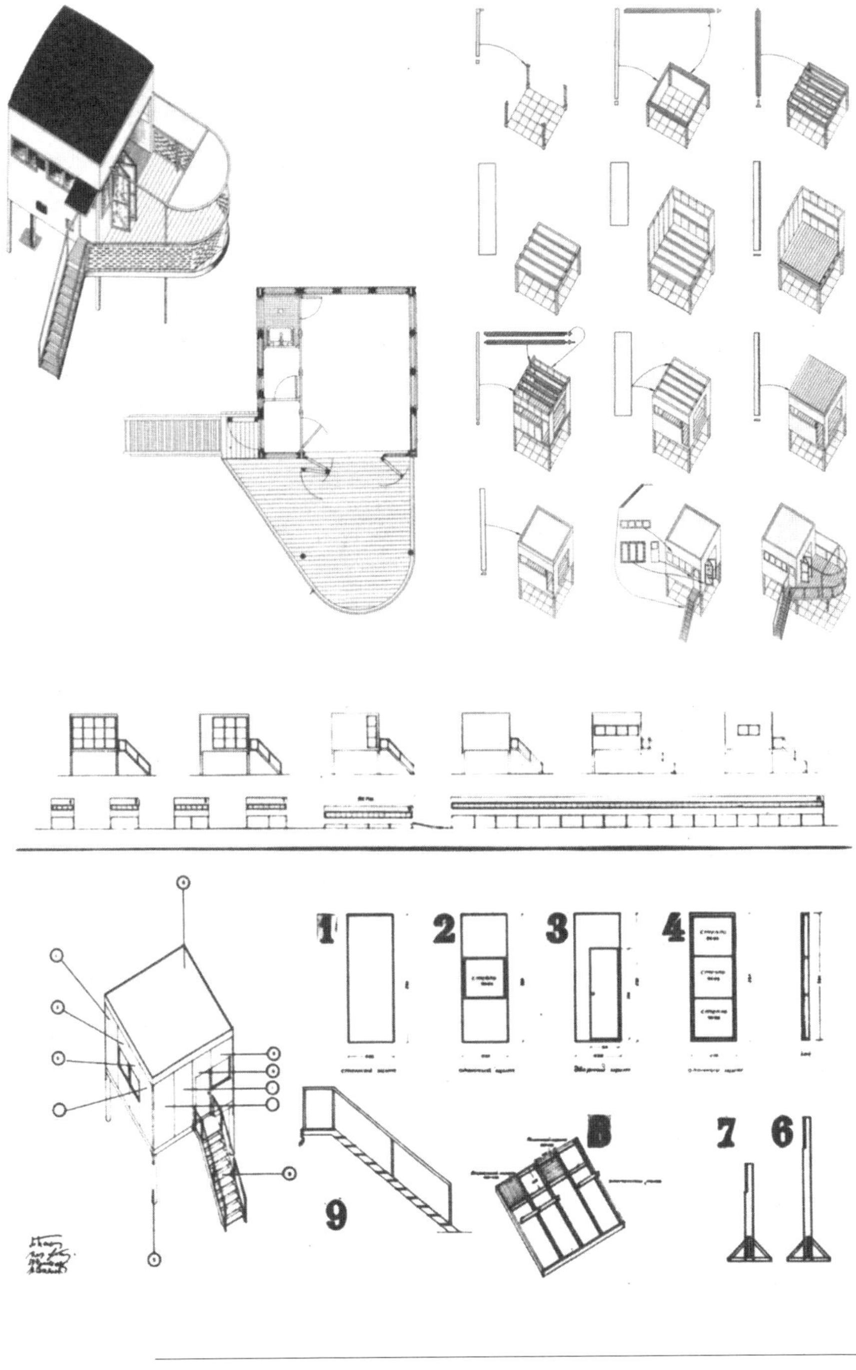


**Figure 4.** Magnitogorsk. Living cell for one person.
Okhitovich with M. Bartsch, N. Vladimirov, and N. Sokolov. 1930.

# Летающий Город

## The City of the Future

**Project:** 11. **Author:** Georgii Krutikov (1899–1958). **Date:** 1928. **Themes:** Circulation. Human-Nature Split. Parallelism. Remoteness.

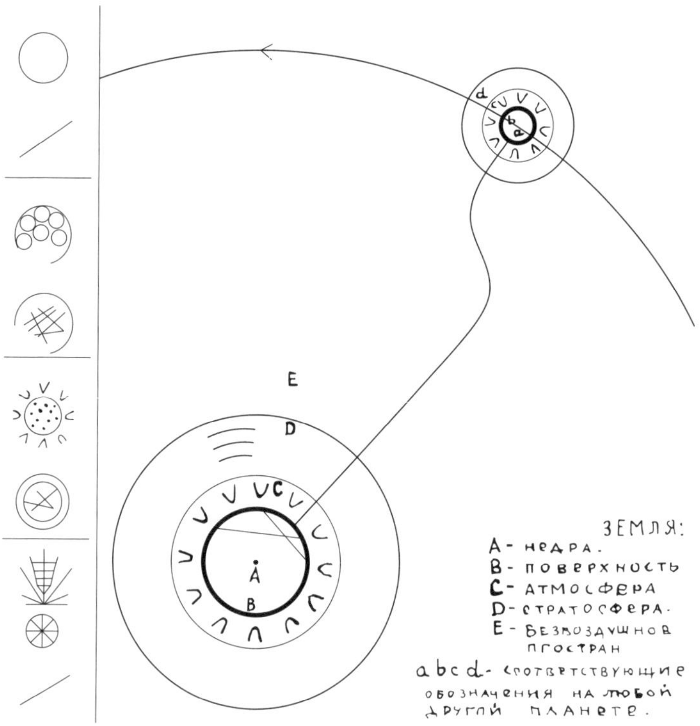


**Figure 0.** The City of the Future. Planetary scheme. After Georgii Krutikov. 1928.

Without a doubt, the most radical proposition in Georgii Krutikov's The City of the Future is the abandonment of planet Earth. In his scheme, the planet becomes completely depopulated. Its function is limited to support industrial production, provide material resources, and offer an occasional space for recreational visits and leisure amid a recovered nature. Permanent human residence, and the elements that used to constitute cities, are located in the atmosphere, in clusters of buildings suspended above the many industrial centers that punctuate the terrestrial surface. Only individual travel capsules link Earth and the aerial settlements, revealing that the design is not only about the stable structures of industry and residence, but also about the movement between the aerial and terrestrial layers. The project is thus characterized by an absolute dissociation between humanity and nature. Krutikov takes to the extreme the idea that architecture and settlements are artificial environments that protect humans from nature. As a way to supplant Earth, ultimately, these artificial domains can altogether do without the planet's spatial support. The buildings of the City of the Future are aerial structures, closed and protected, propelled by their own atomic motors. Being independent from Earth, they can be used to colonize other planets **[fig. 0]**.

The City of the Future is Krutikov's highly polemical diploma project at the VKhUTEIN, the avant-garde Higher Artistic and Technical Institute in Moscow.[1] To defend the project, Krutikov establishes a series of theses, grouped under the headings "social," "architectural," and "technical." As is common among Soviet avant-garde architects, the social ones link the project to the construction of a communist society. Yet, instead of using architecture to imagine the spatial form of communist social relations, as happens in the works of Ivan Leonidov, Mikhail Okhitovich, and Moisei Ginzburg, Krutikov uses socialism as the precondition for a possible future planetary project **[projects 9 and 10]**:

"1. Social Aspects.

The international nature of the mobile capsule. Expanding horizons. The disappearance of the state. Communist society.

A higher level of spatial organisation, corresponding to a higher level of social organisation.

Instead of linear chaos on the chaotic surface of the Earth there is a graceful organisation in the freedom of three-dimensional space. Linear chaos and

1. S. O. Khan-Magomedov, *Viktor Kalmykov* (Moscow: Russkii Avangard, 2011), 35.

the perfection of the circle as spatial contrast, corresponding respectively to: firstly, the anarchistic and individualistic world of capitalism and second to socialism.

Nevertheless, the system of spatial perfection and co-ordination allows the possibility for future free growth and development, conducted in the areas of planetary organisation, the creation of distinct social settlements, the organisation of residential buildings (worker's communes), and separate housing for individuals.

The rational economic organisation for the Earth's sphere and the rational use of the Earth's space.

The principle of flexible planning (planning that can adjust to changes in the way that the living social organism inhabits the city).

The expansion of the architect's outlook beyond the limits of a narrow class context. The broad connection between architectural questions and all the problems stimulating scientific thought."[2]

While some of the questions Krutikov enumerates in the "Social Aspects," such as the dissatisfaction with the "chaotic surface of the Earth," and the interest in the free organization of "three-dimensional space," echo Lazar Khidekel's previous observations, his project pursues a formal vocabulary that is no longer tied to the suprematist legacy **[project 5]**. New means of architectural operation correspond to Krutikov's organization of the terrestrial and atmospheric space. His "architectural" theses describe the formal and experiential conditions derived from his project of planetarization. They associate the occupation of aerial space with an "architecture of mobile structures" that expresses dynamism in formal terms, creates new points of view, and produces an "expansion of architectural horizons."[3] They also relate this expansion to a new scale of perception and to the organization of an "architecture of large spaces."[4] The "technical" theses affirm, in turn, the necessity of using lightweight construction and finding ways to move, indistinctly, among different terrestrial, aerial, and liquid media.[5]

These theses are further developed through the sixteen analytical tables that accompany the project for the City of the Future **[figs. 1 and 2]**. The tables are a crucial part of the work.[6] In them, cutouts from diverse printed media are displayed to illustrate different topics. The procedure is similar to the one Malevich uses in his *Analytical Chart No.16: The Relation Between the Painterly*

**2.** S. O. Khan-Magomedov, *Georgii Krutikov: The Flying City and Beyond*, trans. Christina Lodder (Barcelona: Tenov, 2015), 85–86.

**3.** Khan-Magomedov, *Georgii Krutikov: The Flying City and Beyond*, 86.

**4.** Khan-Magomedov, *Georgii Krutikov: The Flying City and Beyond*, 86.

**5.** Khan-Magomedov, *Georgii Krutikov: The Flying City and Beyond*, 86.

**6.** Khan-Magomedov, *Georgii Krutikov: The Flying City and Beyond*, 14. According to the author, Krutikov devoted most of his efforts to elaborating the tables, while the design itself was produced rapidly and with collaborators.

*Perception and the Environment of the Artist,* and later in *The Environment That Motivates Suprematism* **[project 5]**. Both authors use graphic material as evidence that justifies a radically new disciplinary position based on existing social and spatial conditions. Yet, methodologically, Krutikov is more ambitious than the painter. His charts exemplify the system that his professor, the avant-garde architect and pedagogue Nikolai Ladovskii (1888–1941), proposed in order to grant a solid theoretical basis to architectural production. Ladovskii demanded a selective compilation of the past, "what has been done," of the present, "what we are doing," and an indication of the future, "what must be done."[7] By using this form of historic compilation, Krutikov presents his work as inevitable. The tables support his proposal to abandon the planet with data about the use of Earth's resources, population growth, and city development, and sustain the resource to an aerial architecture by presenting the convergent developments of transportation, energetic production, and construction.[8] They reveal the emergence of a new mobile subject and of a new physical culture by showing the increasing intermingling between mobility and residence in camps, boats, or caravans.[9] Finally, the tables visualize humanity's permanent attempt to inhabit the most elevated places and depict outer space and submarine exploration as a continuation of our species' irresistible urge to move and conquer "new horizons."[10] The exploratory spirit of humans implies a constant movement from the imagined to the real—a transit that turns past utopias into present realities, as the last table reflects.

Together, Krutikov's theses and tables advance the two central formal motifs explored in the design: the big scale and mobility. The theses state that planetary organization requires an architecture of large spaces. The demand is addressed by clustering the aerial buildings and the terrestrial industries in paraboloids and spirals, respectively. In accordance with Ladovskii's teaching, the individual architectures are thus integrated within clear and simple shapes that can be recognized from afar.[11] Krutikov deals with the distant visual relations between Earth and space, simplifying the overall formal structures in order to create a clear gestalt. His is a system in which an increase in the distance between point of view and regarded object implies a further formal reduction: together, the paraboloids form a ring around the Earth, a single planetary figure to be seen from an extraterrestrial position. Additionally, the spiral and the paraboloid are shapes expressive of movement and dynamic expansion that suggest unlimited growth.[12] Moreover, in the project they are not proper constructions but the mere result of grouping visually the buildings and the paths of movement between them.

**7.** Nikolai Ladovskii, "The Working Group of Architects in Inkhuk," in *Architectural Design* 47, *The Avant-Garde. Russian Architecture in the Twenties*, ed. Catherine Cooke (1983): 25.

**8.** The tables are partially published in Catherine Cooke et al., *Architectural Drawings of the Russian Avant-garde* (New York: Museum of Modern Art, 1990), 98–99.

**9.** See in this respect the table "The Evolution of the Mobile Home," in Cooke et al., *Architectural Drawings of the Russian Avant-garde,* 99.

**10.** See in this respect the table "Mastery of the Cosmic Atmosphere Surrounding the Earth," in Cooke et al., *Architectural Drawings of the Russian Avant-garde,* 99.

**11.** S. O. Khan-Magomedov, *Pioneers of Soviet Architecture: The Search for New Solutions in the 1920s and 1930s* (New York: Rizzoli, 1987), 107.

**12.** Regarding this point, the settlement form Krutikov defines resembles the paraboloid model of settlement of unlimited growth his professor Ladovskii had previously proposed. See in this respect Khan-Magomedov, *Pioneers of Soviet Architecture,* 327 and 331.

In this sense, the forms that result from these agglomerations are more important for the planetary system than their own specific architectures. Krutikov designs three types of aerial housing complexes: a living quarter in which six floating towers are interconnected by an inferior ring with common facilities, a tower that floats individually, and a vertical hotel **[figs. 3 and 4]**. All are organized along a vertical axis surrounded by a circular plan. The circular forms allow a complete panoramic vision from the housing cells and for the arrival to the buildings of travel capsules coming from all directions. In fact, the three structures are mostly temporary stops for the capsules. These are, significantly, the only element internally defined. Krutikov bases his design on the work of Konstantin Tsiolkovsky, the first theorist of rocket and satellite science, to whom he sends his ideas.[13] The capsules are "universal vehicles" for aerial, terrestrial, and water and underwater travels, and also small individual homes. They allow their passengers to live in them for several days, during which the inhabitants of Krutikov's project would indulge in exploring the many layers of the world and its surrounding outer space.

The City of the Future thus defines a spatial system tensed between two scalar and formal poles: the big scale of the rigidly defined terrestrial and aerial nodes, and the unpredictable free movement of the individual capsules **[fig. 5 and 6]**. In so doing, the project suggests a possible reconciliation of the contrasting extremes of a global social organization and maximum individual mobility—much as the Soviet disurbanists attempt to do at the surface of the earth **[project 10]**.[14] Ultimately, Krutikov is interested both in the preservation of the planet as well as in the individual exploratory movement across Earth and space granted by the separation of the planet from the orbiting human settlements—the overall title of his research at Ladovskii's studio, "On the path to a mobile architecture," corroborates for this position.[15] The retreat from Earth is not a dystopian consideration, but a means of liberating the globe from private pressures and "to use the land effectively in the interests of society as a whole." It creates the conditions to continue the long history of human exploration of the planet. This is the idea Krutikov's last project about the planetary scale conveys. In the competition entry for the Columbus Monument in Santo Domingo (1929), the architect proposes to construct two interrelated spheres. The bigger, terrestrial one is connected to a superior, distant smaller sphere by a seemingly invisible column, covered by a mirror; so that the superior one appears suspended as a new planet. The Columbian discoveries and the circumnavigation of the earth propelled the first phase of globalization.[16] For

**13.** Khan-Magomedov, *Georgii Krutikov: The Flying City and Beyond*, 26

**14.** Alla Vornskaya, "Two Utopias of Georgii Krutikov's 'City of the Future,'" in *Writing Cities. Working Papers Volume 2. Distance and Cities: Where Do We Stand?* (London: London School of Economics and Political Science, 2012): 46–56.

**15.** Khan-Magomedov, *Georgii Krutikov: The Flying City and Beyond*, 37.

**16.** Peter Sloterdijk, *In the World Interior of Capital: For a Philosophical Theory of Globalization*, trans. Wieland Hoban (Cambridge, UK: Polity Press, 2014), 40–47.

Krutikov, that phase is over, and it is time for extra-terrestrial exploration and to consider what form and what role the planet should play in its entirety.

During the early twentieth century, space exploration and the possible relations between planetary and interplanetary space are powerful topics of discussion in Russia. From one side, the formal language of suprematism is directly related to the possibility of inhabiting outer space—attested by Malevich's interest in constructing satellites. From the other, a group of scientists and thinkers, among them, Tsiolkovsky and the philosopher Nikolai Fedorov, creates Cosmism, an intellectual movement entirely devoted to understanding how the cosmos can solve earthly and human concerns. The City of the Future summarizes, at the architectural level, both strands of artistic practice and thought. In his 1904 article "Astronomy and Architecture," cosmist Fedorov states that, in the same way that astronomy unifies all the sciences in a "world knowledge," architecture can be transformed into a "world order."[17] Architecture's goal should be to apply the discoveries of astronomy at the planetary scale, the exact task that Krutikov's combination of interplanetary travel and world organization tries to achieve.

**17.** Nikolai Fedorov, "Astronomy and Architecture," in *Russian Cosmism*, ed. Boris Groys (Cambridge, MA: MIT Press, 2018), 55.

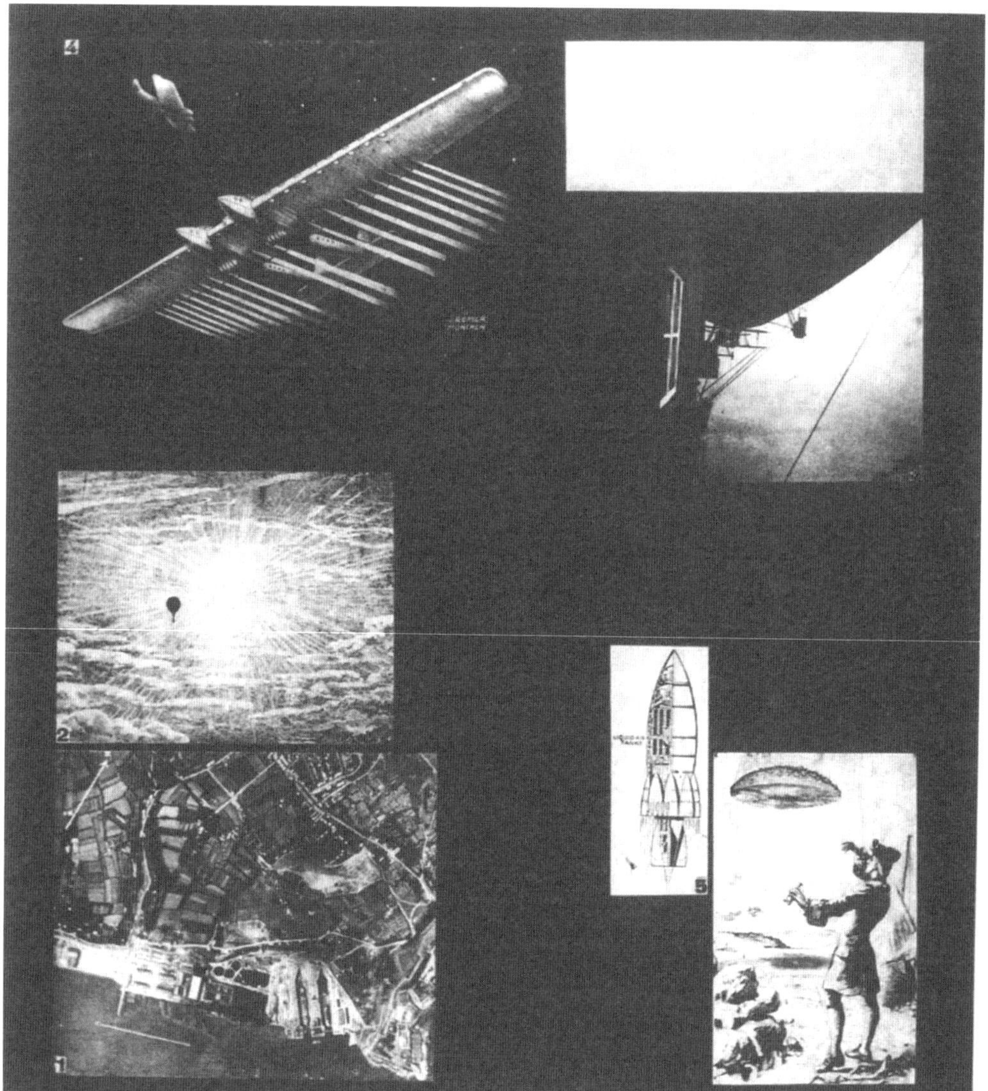

**Figure 1.** A Study of Moving Form. Table 14: The Conquest of New Spaces and New Horizons. 1928.

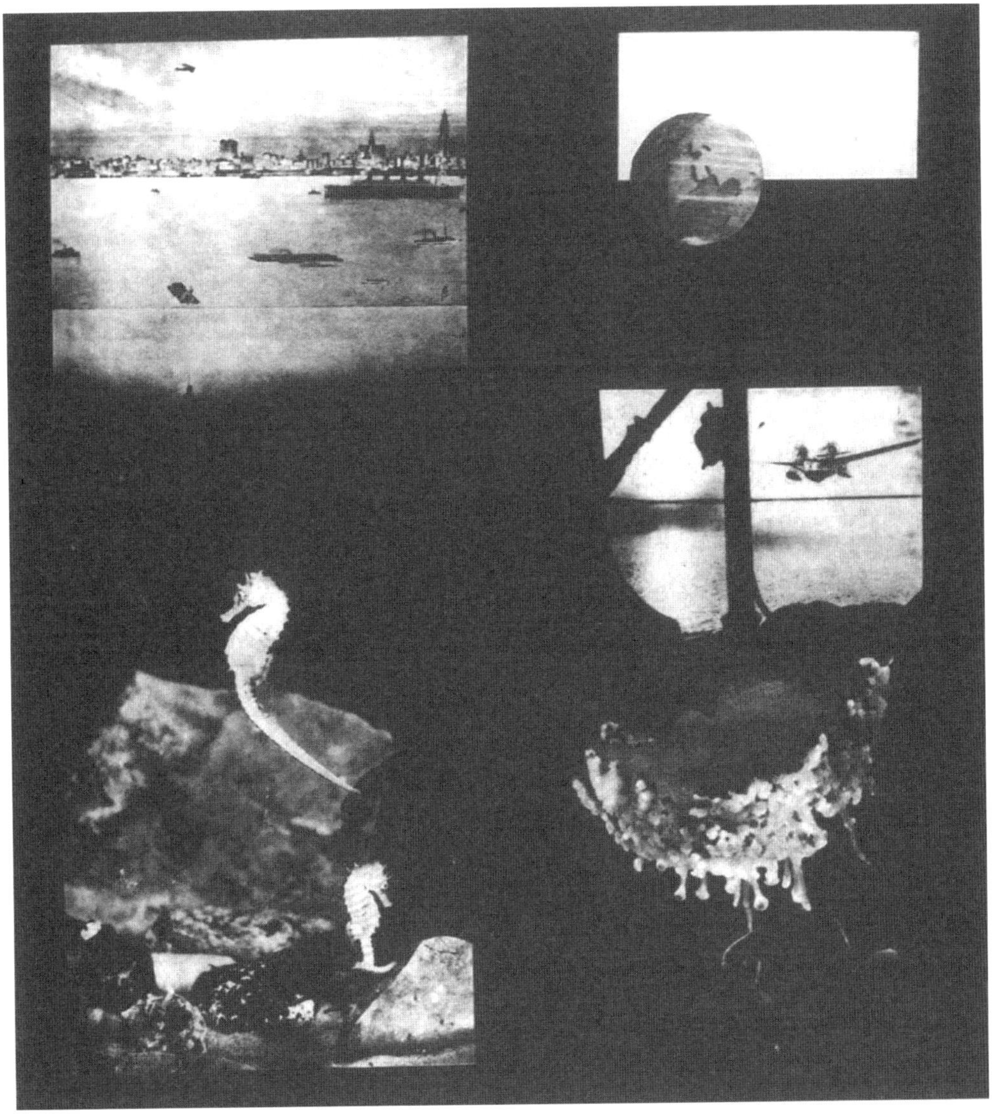

**Figure 2.** A Study of Moving Form. Table 13: Man's Aspirations to Extend His Horizons (Expanding His Perceptions of the Earth and the Universe). 1928.

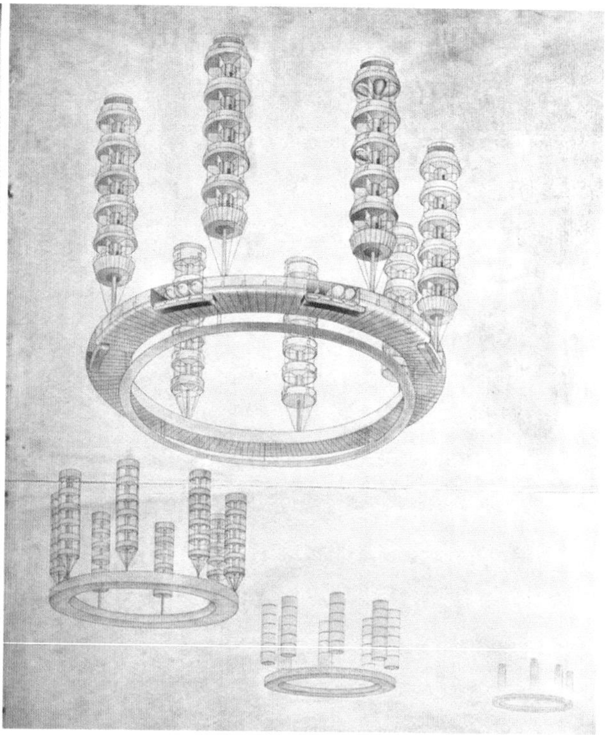

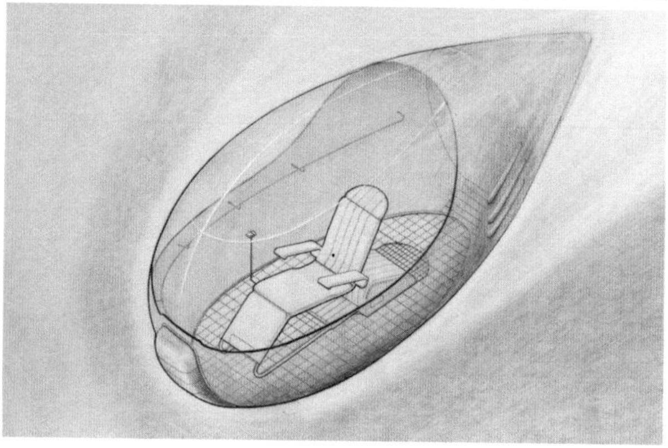

**Figure 3 (Left).** The City of the Future. Apartment-house commune. 1928.
**Figure 4 (Top right).** The City of the Future. Apartment complex. 1928.
**Figure 5 (Bottom right).** The cockpit is the universal vehicle for the City of the Future. 1928.
**Figure 6 (Opposite page).** The City of the Future. 1928.

# Сатурий

## Saturnia

**Project:** 12. **Author:** Viktor Petrovich Kalmykov (1908–1981) **Date:** 1929. **Themes:** Monumentality. Nomadism. Parallelism. Remoteness.

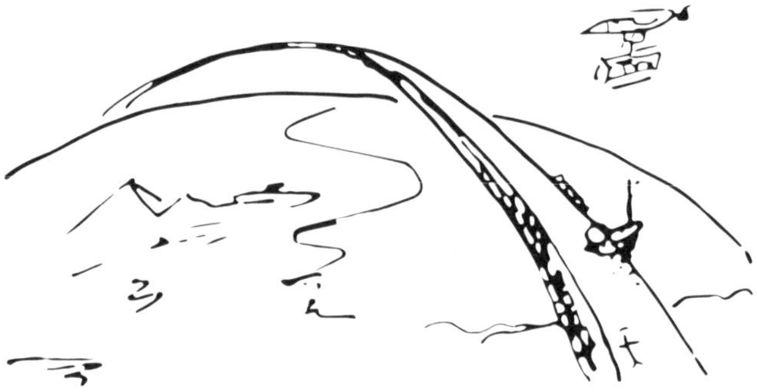

**Figure 0.** Saturnia. After Viktor Kalmykov. 1929.

The presentation of Georgii Krutikov's The City of the Future generates a strong polemic at VKhUTEIN about the limits of architectural education **[project 11]**. Krutikov's exploration of aerial settlements seduces some students. Yet, most of the school faculty discredits it because of its detachment from existing problems and its absolute disregard of realistic implementation. The increasing difficulty of developing such a project becomes evident with Viktor Kalmykov's Saturnia. As a last-year student of VKhUTEIN, Kalmykov asks his unit master, Nikolai Ladovskii (1888–1941), if he can design a planetary, extraterrestrial city for his diploma thesis.[1] Even though Ladovskii consents, Kalmykov ends up abandoning the topic, afraid of the criticism the thesis could raise.[2] The few drawings that represent the project are thus done without academic support. They are simple freehand, ink sketches; a series of vignettes that preliminarily show the central idea the author wants to develop in the project: the creation of an extraterrestrial, inhabited ring surrounding Earth **[figs. 0 and 1]**. By adding this ring, Kalmykov seeks to transform our planet into a new entity: Saturnia. The project's title and its visual language associate his work to science-fiction and thus to the goals and conventions of a literary genre often used in the first years of the USSR to suggest new forms of social articulation.[3]

The simplicity of Saturnia's representations does not hinder the expressivity and capacity for communication of the project. Saturnia's ring, placed above the Equator, provides a powerful symbol of humanity's integration as well as Earth's transformation into a single society that reflects socialism's internationalist political ambition. The drawings show both the planetary dimension of this new entity as seen from outer space and the ways in which it is perceived from Earth. When seen from the ground, the ring creates a new visual horizon; a sort of artificial Milky Way that expands the perception of the reach of human civilization **[fig. 2]**. Rotating with the same speed as Earth, Saturnia creates a permanent link between terrestrial and extraterrestrial spaces, enabled by the use of rockets and huge elevators. In this way, human life takes place indistinctly on the ground and in the air; alternating between public and residential uses equally distributed between the two layers. The key difference between Earth and ring is hence not functional, but organizational. Whereas the ground admits a plurality of urban forms, the aerial band is uniform across the planet in order to emphasize the unity of civilization. Saturnia acts as an inhabited monument. Its possible supplementation with a second ring—placed in some of Kalmykov's sketches along a meridian—would only reinforce that monumental condition **[fig. 3]**.

**1.** Avant-garde education in architecture in Moscow takes place, since 1923, in the Higher Artistic-Technical Studios (VKhUTEMAS), which is rebranded as Higher Artistic-Technical Institute (VKhUTEIN) in 1927. The center closes in 1930. See Elena Ovsyannikova and Vladimir Shukhov, "Phenomenon of the Russian Avant-Garde. Moscow Architectural School of the 1920s," *Docomomo Journal* 49 (2013): 23.

**2.** S. O. Khan-Magomedov, *Viktor Kalmykov* (Moscow: Russkii Avangard, 2011), 35.

**3.** Important members of the Bolshevik party or active socialist ideologies use science-fiction to depict their political views. Such is the case of Anatoly Lunacharsky (who was in charge of the People's Commissariat for Education) and of the founder of the Proletkult movement, Alexander Bogdanov. Lenin himself titles his key political pamphlet *What Is to Be Done?* after Nikolai Chernyshevsky's eponymous utopian and science-fiction text. Cosmist thinkers such as the scientist Konstantin Eduardovich Tsiolkovsky also cultivate the genre.

Saturnia's monumental aspirations extrapolate to the planetary scale the pedagogical and architectural preoccupations of Ladovskii's teaching at VKhUTEIN. An important member of the avant-garde, Ladovskii believes that the crucial step for the emergence of a new type of Soviet architect is modifying the methods of teaching design. The key goal of his agenda is to find a "universalist" architectural methodology that can parallel the internationalist and scientific ethos characteristic of socialist thinking and technological modernity.[4] With this intention, he pursues the constitution of an objective, or "rational," method of architectural design, which would allow the production of what he calls *ratsio-arkhitektura* (ratio-architecture).[5] Saturnia completely embodies the ratio-architecture principles—its utter unfeasibility and its fantastic character notwithstanding.

Ladovskii develops his scientific method in confrontation with the constructivists' attempts to create an architectural syntax based on the assembly of materials and the organization of constructive relations.[6] For him, the scientific method should not be sought, in the constructivist manner, by exploring the internal properties of the materials. Instead it requires analyzing the interrelation of the individual subject and the architectural form. This interrelation sets Ladovskii's research focus on the conditions of human perception, which he studies in order to determine which architectural forms can be more clearly perceived and understood. Ladovskii's objective is to scientifically define the laws of human perception and thus to transform individual appreciations into elements of a universal system. Once this is achieved, the idea is to create an architectural grammar based on the forms that result in more perceptively efficient and communicative expression. He names this procedure the "psycho-analytical" method and tests it with the help of his collaborators Nikolai Dokuchaev and Vladimir Krinsky, first in the VKhUTEMAS, and then in VKhUTEIN.[7] The team's "psycho-analytical" pursuit of ratio-architecture comprises both design exercises with students and experimental tests in a Psychotechnical Laboratory to measure and quantify human reactions to different spatial forms.[8] Additionally, ASNOVA, the group of architects Ladovskii creates and leads, aims to translate the principles of ratio-architecture into the actual practice of building.[9]

Ladovskii's interest in perceptual efficiency leads him to privilege simple platonic forms such as prisms, cubes, pyramids, or parabolas (his own design for an urban system of unlimited growth is, for example, a parabola).[10] In design courses, he encourages students to work with this repertoire of simple forms.

**4.** Anna Bokov, "Teaching Architecture to the Masses: Vkhutemas and the Pedagogy of Space, 1920–1930" (PhD diss., Yale University, 2017), abstract.

**5.** S. O. Khan-Magomedov, *Pioneers of Soviet Architecture: The Search for New Solutions in the 1920s and 1930s* (New York: Rizzoli, 1987), 107; and Anna Bokov, "Space: The Pedagogy of Nikolay Ladovsky," in Walker Art Center's What is an Art School Series. https://walkerart.org/magazine/space-the-pedagogy-of-nikolay-ladovsky. Accessed October 8, 2018.

**6.** For the early confrontation between Ladovskii and the constructivists, see Alla G. Vronskaya, "Composing Form, Constructing the Unconscious: Empiriocriticism and Nikolai Ladovskii's 'Psycho-analytical Method' of Architecture at VKhUTEMAS," in *Architecture and the Unconscious*, ed. John Shannon Hendrix and Lorens Eyan Holm (Farnham, UK: Ashgate Publishing Limited, 2016), 84.

**7.** Ovsyannikova and Shukhov, "Phenomenon of the Russian Avant-Garde," 23.

**8.** Ovsyannikova and Shukhov, "Phenomenon of the Russian Avant-Garde," 23.

**9.** For the emergence of ASNOVA, and the conflicts between ASNOVA and the constructivists OSA, see Hugh D. Hudson, Jr., "Students and the Architectural Wars," in *Blueprints and Blood: The Stalinization of Soviet Architecture, 1917–1937* (Princeton: Princeton University Press, 2015), 101–118.

**10.** Interestingly, parabolic growth is also the method chosen by Constantinos Doxiadis in his attempt to overcome the linear city model in Dynapolis [project 23].

11. Khan-Magomedov, *Pioneers of Soviet Architecture,* 107.

12. Vronskaya, "Composing Form, Constructing the Unconscious," 89.

13. Ovsyannikova and Shukhov, "Phenomenon of the Russian Avant-Garde," 24. VKhUTEMAS and VKhUTEIN are schools of design, not only of architecture. The other sections are Volume, Graphic Arts, and Color.

14. Vronskaya, "Composing Form, Constructing the Unconscious," 84.

15. Ovsyannikov and Shukhov, "Phenomenon of the Russian Avant-Garde," 23.

He asks that they understand how the forms are perceived and the meanings that can be associated with them. In this sense, rather than asking students to address primarily the internal or functional necessities of any architectural piece, Ladovskii and his colleagues encourage them to define an "image"—a concept that for them means the creation of an intelligible form that can stimulate the spectator's imagination.[11] As the historian Alla G. Vronskaya explains, this interest in defining clearly readable forms derives from Adolf von Hildebrand's aesthetic system, according to which a good work of art requires being perceived and understood at first glance.[12] Yet, for Ladovskii and his peers, the necessity of comprehension is not limited to the object itself, but has to include the environment that surrounds it. At VKhUTEMAS and VKHUTEIN, Ladovskii coordinates the teaching of the section "Space," a notion that for him represents the core of architectural production.[13] Ladovskii's assistant Dokuchaev summarizes this conceptual core and defines the goal of the course Foundations of the Art of Architecture as: "a study of (compositional and constructive) means of organisation of architectural form into a system, which gives the maximum of expressivity [*vyrazitel'nost'*] to form and *provides the viewer with an opportunity to orientate in space.*"[14]

Clarity of form, according to Ladovskii's psychoanalytical method, leads to perceiving the object and the environment with a similar degree of clarity. Formal simplicity allows, in addition, the clear appreciation and consideration of the object's symbolic character. Only after this attention to the necessities of the object's image can architecture descend to the realm of function. Ladovskii's pedagogy is, in this sense, extremely rigorous. The students follow a linear procedure. The first stages of their work comprise only formal explorations, without any consideration of scale, site, or program. After this "abstract" exercise, they proceed to "production" assignments, in which they test the reaction of their design against different programmatic requirements.[15]

The requirements of simplicity, symbolic power, and spatial orientation of Ladovskii's pedagogy directly inform Saturnia. The extraterrestrial ring is a synthetic symbol of planetary unity and an instrument of measurement that enables humans to orient themselves in relation to the totality of terrestrial space. Its principal formal operation—the duplication of Earth's circumference with an aerial ring—intends to make visible the shape and scale of an entity, the world, that exceeds human perception. A similar operation was proposed for the urban scale when El Lissitzky—himself, a disseminator of ASNOVA's thinking—suggests placing a ring of horizontal skyscrapers, which he calls "cloud irons," around Moscow (1923).[16] Seven years later, with Kalmykov's project, it is the entire world that can be circumscribed and articulated as a single spatial unit.

16. Khan-Magomedov, *Pioneers of Soviet Architecture*, 141.

17. Khan-Magomedov, *Viktor Kalmykov*, 97–111, and 152.

18. Khan-Magomedov, *Viktor Kalmykov*, 251.

Under the ring, on Earth, Kalmykov also uses the ratio-architecture repertoire of platonic, symbolic forms, now in order to define individual buildings. The terrestrial system is a collection of different monumental artifacts. In his later work, the architect perseveres in the use of this formal language. During the early 1930s, Kalmykov designs settlement and housing models for the Soviet republics of central Asia. Inspired by the simple structure of the nomads' tents of the region, he defines different types of homes with hemispheric, parabolic, and pyramidal forms, conceived both for nomadic and sedentary populations, and groups them in clear and symbolic planar arrangements that can only be entirely perceived from the air **[fig. 4 and 5]**.[17] The definition of the houses and the settlements as symbolic images prevails over any other considerations. In another iteration of this formal project, he later reproposes the housing projects for other geographic locations, including Moscow. Between 1930 and 1935, Kalmykov's forms thus move from outer space to distant territories and lastly to the city itself, consistently preserving in this trajectory an overall conceptual goal which, as the historian of Soviet architecture Selim Omarovich Khan-Magomedov describes, can be qualified as "cosmist."[18]

Kalmykov's cosmism constitutes an original contribution to the diverse explorations of the world scale that Soviet avant-garde architects undertake in the late 1920s. These planetary works respond both to the universalist ideology of socialism and to the increasingly vast and variegated spatial effects of civilization. Despite their notable differences, the works of Lazar Khidekel, Ivan Leonidov, the disurbanists, or Georgii Krutikov recognize that, in order to confront the planetary scale, the discipline of architecture has to be transformed **[projects 5, 9, 10, and 11]**. It not only has to address settlements but also areas of production. It has to define not only the material conditions of buildings but also the tangible and intangible networks of transportation and communication that traverse ground and air. Additionally, architecture not only has to articulate the city, but also the territory. Saturnia does not develop any of those explorations further. What Kalmykov's cosmist architecture does is to focus on the symbolization of planetary civilization and on the use of architecture as a tool of global orientation. Critically considered, Saturnia concludes the planetary explorations of the Soviet avant-garde with a simplistic assimilation of the planetary scale to the realm of fantasy. Seen through a positive lens, the project supplements the avant-garde agenda by emphasizing the importance of architecture's symbolic role. Read as a ratio-architecture design, Saturnia is an image, a symbolic artifact, a monument that aspires to allow humans to perceive and understand their position in the world and the unity of civilization.

Figure 1. Saturnia. 1929.

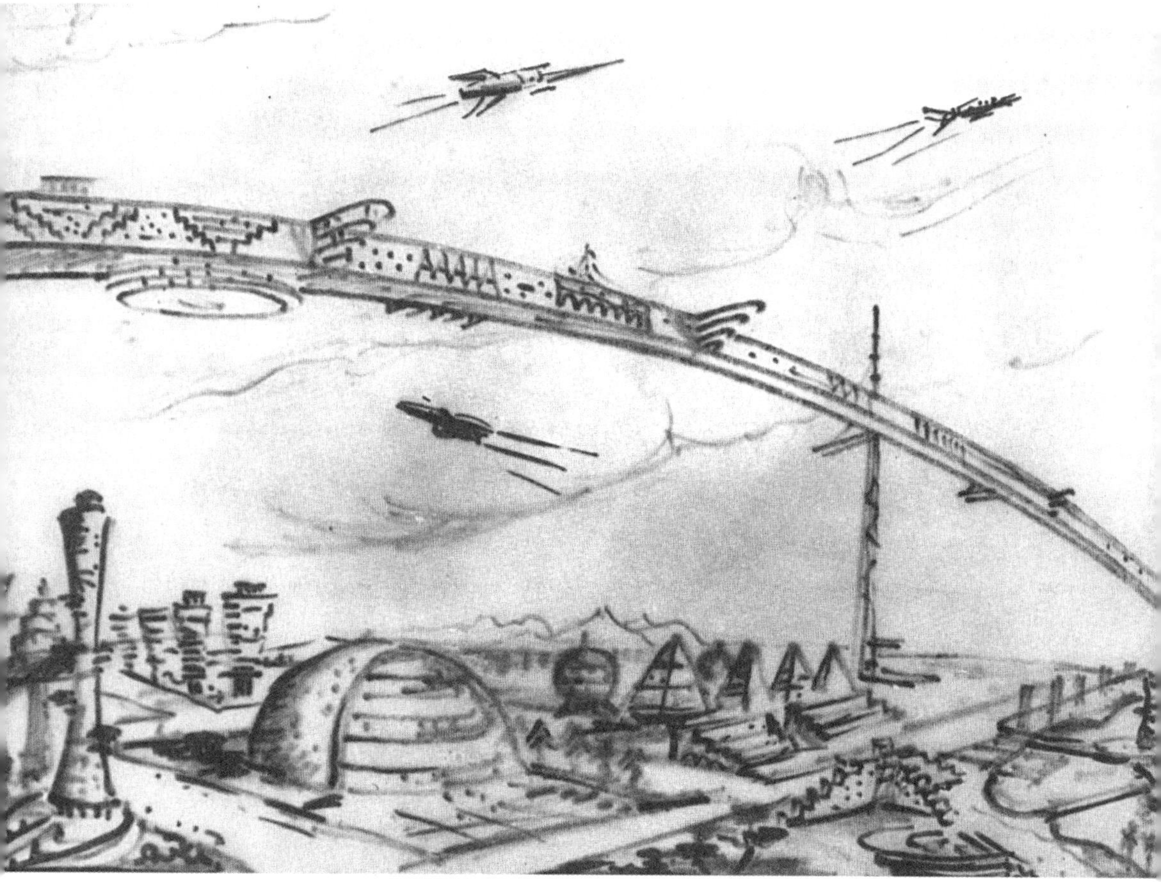

**Figure 2.** Saturnia. Ring City. 1929.

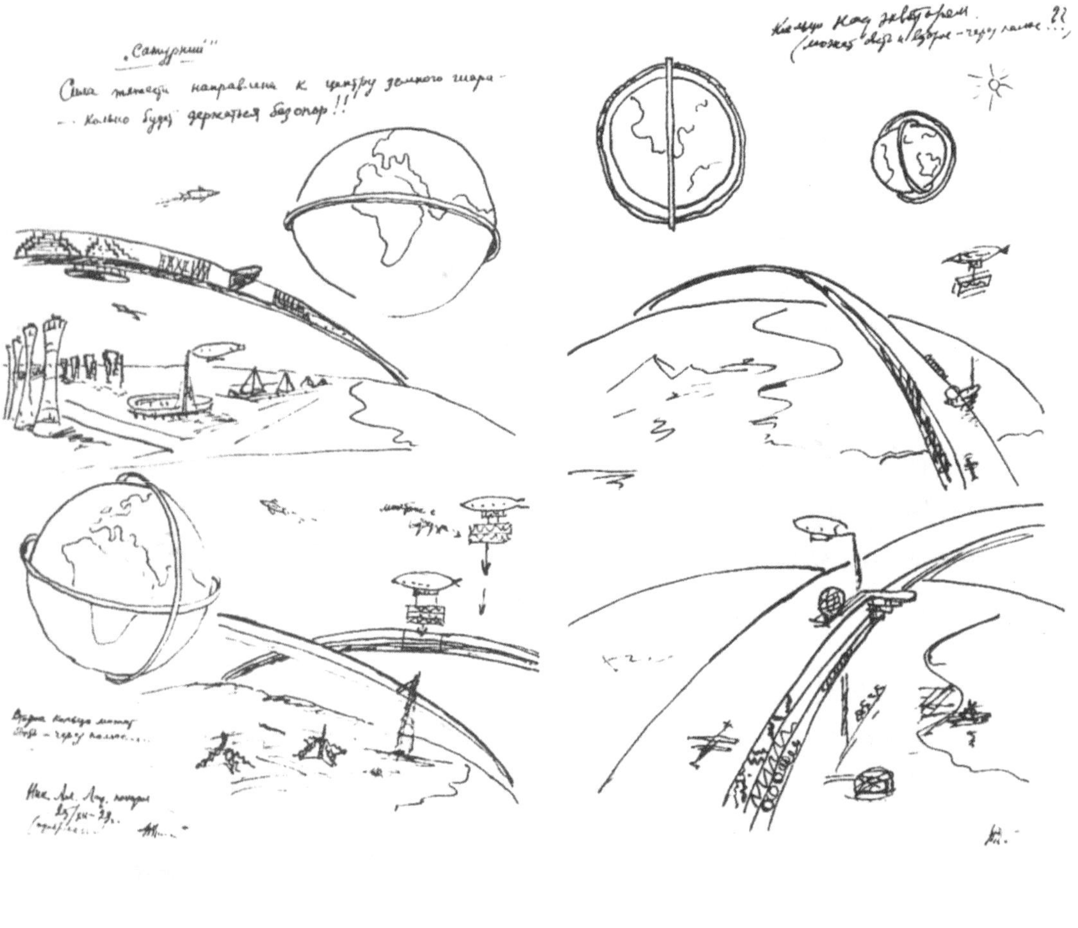


**Figure 3.** Saturnia. Second Ring City. 1929.

**Figure 4 (Top and center).** Kalmykov's photographs of nomadic yurts of Central Asia. 1929.
**Figure 5 (Bottom).** Settlement Schemes. 1933.

# Historical Chart of Urbanism

**Project:** 13. **Authors:** Rudolf Steiger (1900–1982), Wilhelm Hess (1906–1982), and Georg Schmidt (1896–1965).
**Date:** 1934–1935. **Themes:** Colonialism. Geo-visualization. Geopolitics. World Urbanization.

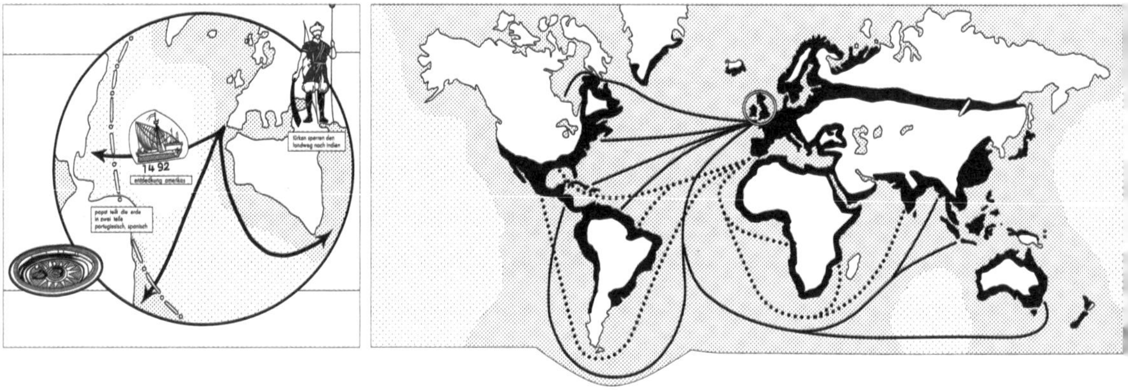


**Figure 0.** Fragment of Historical Chart of Urbanism. Transoceanic transportation of goods and development of colonial coastal cities. After Steiger, Hess, and Schmidt. 1934.

The Historical Chart of Urbanism is a five-meter-long visualization that analyzes the historical and geographical expansion of cities and of the terrestrial systems of organization associated with them **[figs. 0 and 1]**. The Chart is structured as a grid. The horizontal axis is a timeline, each of whose segments represents a historical period, from prehistory until 1934, when the table is drawn. The vertical axis is thematic. The rows present six topics, most of them usually disregarded in urban studies at the time. With this display, the authors seek to produce a materialist analysis of urban processes. To this end, they add to conventional elements of urban analyses, such as form of settlement and means of transport, four other factors: social structure, weapons, exploitation of geographic resources, and forms of production. The authors also employ a variety of graphic mechanisms to explain each cell and the relations among them. Again, few were common in contemporary urban studies. Photographs, aerial views, photomontages, global and continental maps, data charts, texts, arrows indicating relations, and icons predominate in the urban plans.

One of the Chart's main effects is to create a system of violent juxtapositions, which provides a critical understanding of urbanization. In the Chart, architectural, urban, and territorial systems are both the result and the generators of conflicts, forms of production, and social relations. A vertical reading of the last column, for instance, shows the "Commercial Metropolis" as an urban form. The metropolis sits upon a skyscraper—the Empire State Building—representing a finance corporation, around which some building typologies orbit, which are related to industrial production and resource extraction. War submarines and aerial bombs, ocean liners, and railroads support these buildings. Below them, a world map shows how the earth is divided among five great geographic powers and the areas in which they have economic interests, while a pictorial chart represents the regions from which these geographic powers get their material resources. The bottom row shows, through two photographs, that the base of the urban and territorial system is both the result of industrialized production and of semi-slave manual work.

The other crucial message of the chart is that urban forms are inseparable from territorial systems operating at the world scale. These territorial systems link cities and areas of production by means of transportation. The chart shows how the initial system of human settlements evolved through the influence of commercial interchanges and processes of colonization. It depicts, progressively, the development of cities in the interior of Europe, of coastal areas associated with maritime trade, of colonial hinterlands exploited for resource extraction, and so on, and how all these processes generate specific urban forms and architectural typologies. The final message the table transmits is that urbanization unevenly affects the world. As explained by Swiss architect Rudolf Steiger, one of the Chart's authors, the document ultimately shows how modern cities dominate "the world economy through organized finance capitalism."[1]

Steiger designs the Chart with Wilhelm Hess, a Bauhaus graduate, and art historian Georg Schmidt, to summarize the conclusions of the 1933 CIAM 4, which is devoted to the topic "The Functional City."[2] They present a first version of the visualization at the 1934 London meeting of the CIRPAC (International Committee to Address the Problems of Contemporary Architecture), and the definitive version as part of "The Functional City" exhibition held in Amsterdam in 1935.[3] The CIRPAC is, with the HCIEAES (High International Commission for the Extension of Architecture to Economics and Sociology), one of CIAM's branches, as Le Corbusier proposes in the first CIAM meeting in 1928 in order to grant the congress international influence.[4] As previously noted, one of the key factors leading to the creation of CIAM is the dismissal of modern architecture from the 1927 competition for the League of Nations **[project 8]**. In 1928, Le Corbusier and his colleagues intend to overcome that rejection by situating themselves as global actors. The three-tiered organizational framework seeks to facilitate relations between architects and international official clients, such as the League of Nations itself. This collaboration with international agencies is meant to ensure the intervention of architects at the territorial scale, since, according to Le Corbusier, the current socioeconomic situation has put "national territories within the entire scope of urbanism."[5]

"The Functional City" congress is a clear demonstration of CIAM's global ambitions, both in its contents and methods. The congress's purpose is to establish urban solutions that can be applied worldwide. For CIAM's head, Cornelius Van Eesteren, the "Functional City" agenda is "rooted in the universal understanding of the world, which is very much connected to the development of architecture today."[6] For such a comprehensive worldview, it is crucial to establish common criteria of analysis that can enable understanding world urbanization. With that goal, Van Eesteren establishes a common legend of land uses and urban fabrics that is to be used to represent thirty-two metropolises and urban regions at scales of 1:10,000 and 1:50,000. The resulting standardized maps, presented in Athens, constitute for Van Eesteren a unified form of analysis that

1. Rudolf Steiger, quoted in Nader Vossoughian, "Mapping the Modern City: Otto Neurath, the International Congress of Modern Architecture (CIAM), and the Politics of Information Design," *Design Issues* 22, no. 3 (Summer 2006): 63.

2. Steiger received the commission through the Dutch constructivist architect Mart Stam. Wilhelm Hess had been a student of Ludwig Hilberseimer. Georg Schmidt was, like his brother, the architect Hans Schmidt, a committed socialist. The team, thus, represented the more left-oriented side of CIAM.

3. Eric Mumford, *The CIAM Discourse on Urbanism, 1928–1960* (Cambridge, MA: MIT Press, 2000), 94. Nader Vossoughian, *Otto Neurath: The Language of the Global Polis* (Rotterdam: Nai Publishers, 2008), 135.

4. For these observations about CIAM's ambitions of international influence see Mumford, *The CIAM Discourse on Urbanism*, 22–24.

5. Le Corbusier, quoted in Mumford, *The CIAM Discourse on Urbanism*, 15.

6. Cornelis Van Eesteren, "Prospekt für die Funktionelle Stadt," Papers of Cornelis Van Eesteren, Netherlands Architecture Institute. Quoted in Vossoughian, *Otto Neurath: The Language of the Global Polis*, 116.

should support the interventions in settlements around the world according to common criteria.[7] Importantly, the congress's conclusions help to define the crucial topics of the Athens Chart, which will guide the CIAM thinking during the following decade.

With the Historical Chart of Urbanization, Steiger, Schmidt, and Hess decidedly adopt CIAM's universalist agenda in order to go beyond the mere focus on cities and urban regions of "The Functional City" maps, as well as to advance a materialist reading of urbanization. The commission the team receives from CIAM is to summarize the findings of the thirty-two maps for their presentation in Amsterdam. Yet, their work expands its analysis of the urban phenomenon from the metropolitan to the planetary. The visualization situates cities and their architecture within broader circuits of territorial production and treats the whole planet as a spatial construct: the Chart depicts agricultural and oil fields, railroad infrastructures, seas traversed by ships, and power stations. When they first present the document in London, the work receives unanimous approbation.[8] In Amsterdam, the reception is, however, extremely critical. The CIAM authorities, led by Walter Gropius, request the withdrawal of the Chart for its strongly materialist reading of urbanization in relation to socioeconomic conditions.[9]

Essential to Steiger, Schmidt, and Hess's analysis of world urbanization is their critical and exploratory use of forms of visualization. The Chart disregards the cartographic conventions employed in urbanism that characterize Van Eesteren's reliance on metropolitan maps and embraces a variety of representational tools. To be sure, determining which forms of visual communication can facilitate CIAM's universalizing discourse is already a major topic of debate during the preparation of the congress. As historian Enrico Chapel indicates, Van Eesteren's "replacement of analogical by conventional signs testified to the adoption of social facts and human activities as the determinants of urban space."[10] To further develop this visual agenda, the CIAM seeks out the collaboration of Austrian political scientist, activist, and philosopher Otto Neurath, a key proselytizer of the value of visual communication through his position as director of the Museum of Society and Economy in Vienna and of the Vienna Mundaneum—a derivative of Paul Otlet's initiative **[project 8]**. During the 1920s, Neurath and his team elaborated a method of graphic representation through figurative icons that was oriented to politicize the Viennese working class by facilitating the understanding of social questions.[11] The system, named the Vienna Method of Pictorial Statistics, graphically depicts data and quan-

**7.** Vossoughian, "Mapping the Modern City," 50–51.

**8.** Mumford, *The CIAM Discourse on Urbanism*, 94.

**9.** Martin Steinman, ed., *CIAM (Congrès Internationaux d'Architecture Moderne), Dokumente 1928–1939* (Basel: Birkhäuser, 1979), 170.

**10.** Enrico Chapel, "Otto Neurath and the CIAM–The International Pictorial Language as a Notational System of Town Planning," in *Encyclopedia and Utopia. The Life and Work of Otto Neurath (1882–1945)*, ed. Elisabeth Nemeth and Friedrich Stadler (Dordrecht: Kluwer Academic Publishers, 1996), 167.

**11.** Sybilla Nikolow, "*Gesellschaft und Wirtschaft*: An Encyclopedia in Otto Neurath's Pictorial Statistics from 1930," in *European Modernism and the Information Society: Informing the Present, Understanding the Past*, ed. William Boyd Rayward (Aldershot, UK: Ashgate, 2008), 259 and 261.

titative information, in order to offer a materialist vision of the social order of the world.[12] After meeting Otlet in 1929, Neurath became interested in collaborating with the Belgian thinker in creating the Mundaneum in Geneva, and in transforming his graphic work into a tool of universal communication and global knowledge **[fig. 2]**.[13] Accordingly, in 1935, Otlet renames the Vienna Method ISOTYPE, for International System of Typographic Picture Education, and proposes it as a sort of graphic Esperanto.[14] By inviting Neurath to collaborate in their graphic efforts, the organizers of CIAM 4 intend to benefit from this graphic internationalism and to link global intervention and global communication **[fig. 3]**. The adoption of Neurath's graphic methods will serve the CIAM to promote, as Nader Vossoughian explains, "the first systematic attempt at standardizing the language of urban planning on a transnational basis."[15]

In his intervention at the CIAM 4, Neurath—who is very interested in spatial planning and in cartography—claims that urban analyses should use pictorial statistics, and thus pictograms and data, instead of merely maps; that his pictographic method should be standardized and adopted globally; and that it should be clear and figurative in order to facilitate the participation of the public at large in urban debates.[16] Van Eesteren and most of CIAM members consider Neurath's proposal extremely reductive, and consequently his graphic criteria are not implemented. The congress' organizers ask him, however, to supervise the revision of the thirty-two maps presented at the congress as well as the visual summary that Steiger and his team are preparing. It is in the latter that his role is most significant.

If Neurath's collaboration in the elaboration of Van Eesteren's maps is problematic—and ultimately unfruitful—his dialogue with Steiger, Hess, and Schmidt is extremely productive.[17] Van Eesteren fundamentally sees Neurath's graphic system as a support for the technical approaches to urbanization CIAM is starting to develop. In contrast, Steiger and his team see it as a critical instrument of representation and analysis. Not only do they make punctual use of Neurath's pictograms, they also adopt the Austrian thinker's attitude toward representation in order to elaborate a materialist vision of world urbanization very much aligned with Neurath's own goals of social transformation.[18] The Chart's contribution to urban studies is, in this sense, twofold. On one hand, it highlights that urbanization is a multilayered terrestrial process that needs to be analyzed together with the social and material networks that support it. On the other, it shows that, in order to properly intervene in such a complex phe-

**12.** Nikolow, *"Gesellschaft und Wirtschaft,"* 261.

**13.** For the collaboration between Otlet and Neurath see Wouter Van Acker, "Internationalist Utopias of Visual Education: The Graphic and Scenographic Transformation of the Universal Encyclopaedia in the Work of Paul Otlet, Patrick Geddes, and Otto Neurath," *Perspectives on Science* 19, no. 1 (2011): 63. See also Vossoughian, *Otto Neurath: The Language of the Global Polis*, 110.

**14.** Otto Neurath, "L'Urbanisme et le lotissement du sol en représentation optique d'après la méthode viennoise," *Technika Chronika* (15 October–15 November 1933), 1040. Quoted in Kostas Tsiambaos, "Isotype Diagrams from Neurath to Doxiadis," *Architectural Research Quarterly* 16, no. 1 (2012): 49. See also: Nikolow, *"Gesellschaft und Wirtschaft,"* 259–260. Also see project 23.

**15.** Vossoughian, "Mapping the Modern City," 49.

**16.** For Neurath's interest in planning see Antonia Soulez, "Otto Neurath or The Will to Plan," in *Encyclopedia and Utopia. The Life and Work of Otto Neurath (1882–1945)*, 227–228. Neurath, for example, participated directly in Vienna's planning during Karl Seitz's tenure as Social-Democratic major. For Neurath's position at CIAM see Chapel, "Otto Neurath and the CIAM," 169–171.

**17.** Vossoughian, "Mapping the Modern City," 62.

**18.** For an analysis of the use of Neurath's methods of representation in urban studies, see Tsiambaos, "Isotype Diagrams from Neurath to Doxiadis," 49–50.

nomenon, architects and urbanists need to develop forms of visualization that provide more knowledge than mere planimetric projection. The gridded structure of information, the inclusion of a multitude of figurative graphics, and of notations of geographic, historic, and socioeconomic interrelations stand as evidence that Steiger, Hess, and Schmidt are aware of the insufficiencies of cartographic representations and interested in questioning the images upon which conceptions of the world rely.[19] In a moment in which urban and geographic studies are fundamentally concerned with understanding the emerging forms of organization of metropolises and regions, the team emphasizes the necessity of treating those scales as part of broader processes of world structuring. The Chart thus questions the modernist discourse about urban form through a materialist attention to social processes. It also translates this intellectual and political attitude into a visual exploration that addresses the world both as an object of analysis and as an emerging social scale that requires the elaboration of new, shared languages of visual communication.

**19.** For an analysis of Neurath's cartographic methods see Nikolow, "*Gesellschaft und Wirtschaft*," 265–273.

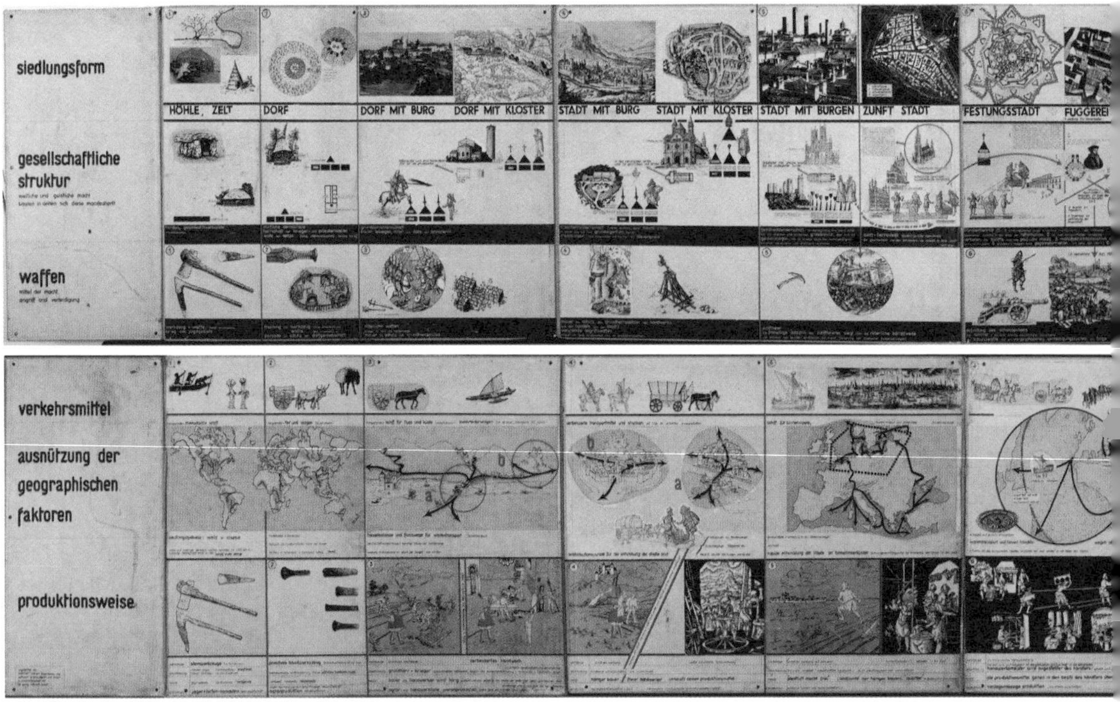


**Figure 1.** Historical Chart of Urbanism. 1934.

LANDESHAUPTSTADT
STADTTEILE
STADTTEILE
VERKEHR
INDUSTRIEQUARTIER
HANDELS METROPOLE
WOHNEN
INDUSTRIE
WOHNEN
siedlungsform
gesellschaftliche
struktur
waffen
verkehrsmittel
ausnützung der
geographischen
faktoren
produktionsweise

**Figure 2.** *Encyclopedia Universalis Mundaneum*. Life Has Become International. Otto Neurath. 1930.

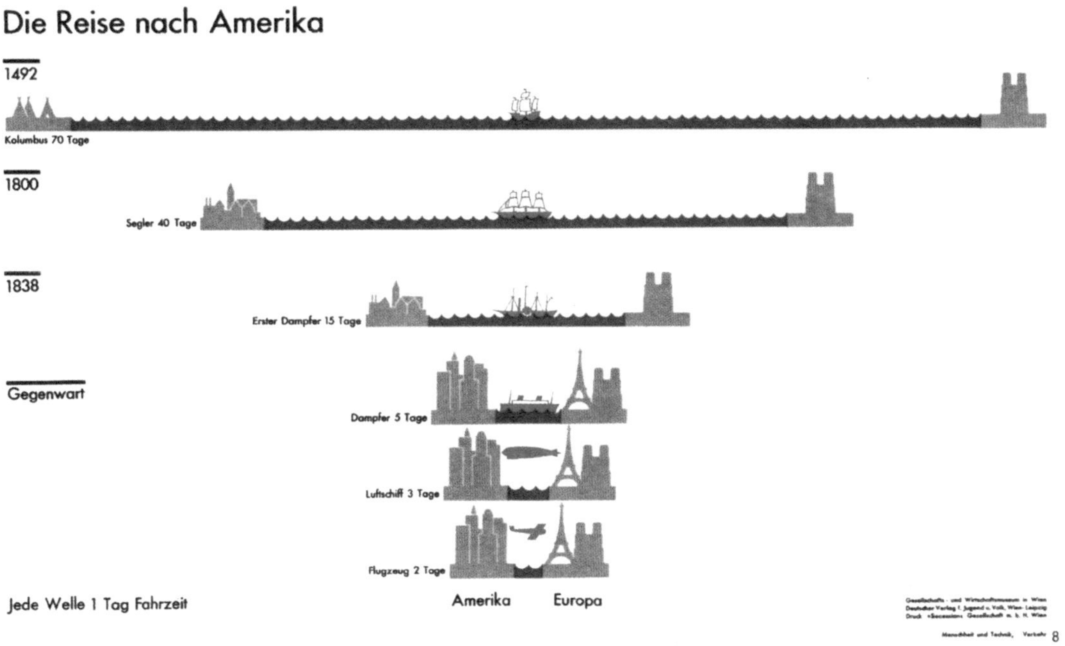


**Figure 3.** The Trip to America, in *Technology and Humanity*. Otto Neurath. 1932.

# Airocean World Map and Geoscope

**Project:** 14. **Author:** Richard Buckminster Fuller (1895–1983), Shoji Sadao (1927), and John McHale (1922–1978). **Date:** 1943–1965. **Themes:** Environmental Control. Geo-visualization. Human-Earth System. Telecommunications.

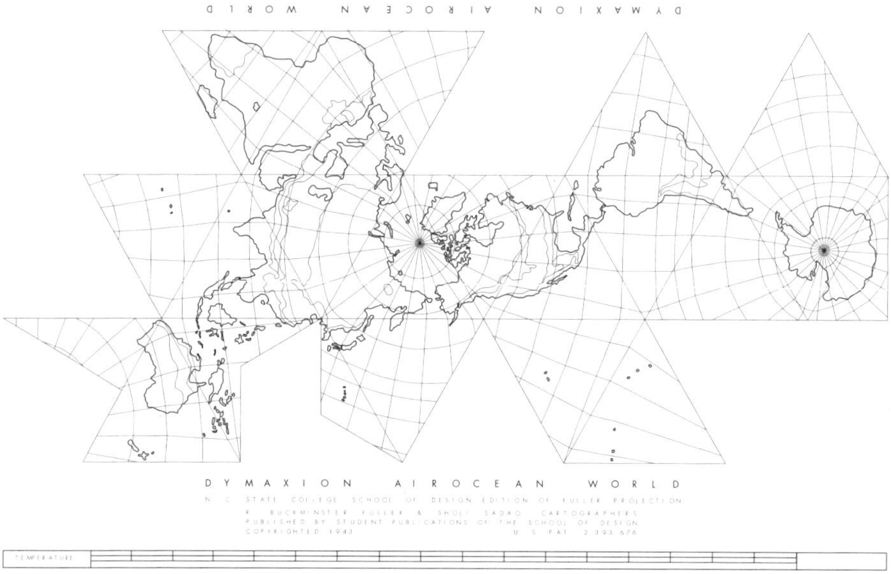


**Figure 0.** Dymaxion Airocean World Map. After Richard Buckminster Fuller and Shoji Sadao. 1943.

At the beginning of the fifteenth century, Ptolemy's *Geography*, a 150 AD treatise on cartography that compiled the Roman Empire's geographical knowledge, is reintroduced to Western Europe. The treatise describes the technique of mapping territorial points with mathematical projections by geometrically locating them through the celestial coordinate system of latitude and longitude. Before this, city-states were mainly depicted through bird's-eye views, and flags imprecisely marked off stretches and areas of land. New representational tools subsequently change the politics of geographical location, the constitution of states' sovereignty, and the international system. Ptolemy's work inaugurates an era in which geographical space is translated into geometry.[1]

Five centuries later, Buckminster Fuller elaborates a process to project a sphere on a plane while preserving the former's geometric properties and relations.[2] Cartographically, it is an answer to the problem that only one fourth of a globe can be seen at a time and that planar representations employ large distortions and wield political biases. For example, the 1569 Mercator map, still the most commonly used projection to date, is only true to scale at the Equator. This is a map whose production heavily relies on political hierarchies and navigation purposes. It subdivides the planet into three oceans and depicts colonizing countries north "above" the rest of the world, in a size that substantially magnifies their actual dimension.

Fuller's Airocean World Map, later rebranded as Dymaxion Map, breaks with these divisions and geographic exaggerations. The twenty-faced, icosahedron-derived map reinterprets the world as one-continent surrounded by one-world-ocean **[fig. 0]**.[3] When Fuller designs the map, his vision is undoubtedly politically charged. Fuller publishes the first version of the map in 1943, when the Allies' victory over the Axis powers starts to be seen as the outcome of World War II.[4] A substantial part of Fuller's argument to develop the map is his belief in the necessity of creating documents that support a "dynamic world citizenry" after the war, but also, and more politically, documents that impede future attitudes in favor of "isolationism."[5] The argument in favor of Dymaxion thus contains a critique of the United States' reluctance and late engagement in the two World Wars. The unfolding of the continents around the North Pole in the first version of the map shows how isolationism is impossible when most of the planet's population lives on an almost continuous landmass.[6] In addition, Fuller's projection creates the technical support to connect this population by revealing the geometric efficiency of the polar hemispheres for air

1. Jordan Branch, *The Cartographic State: Maps, Territory and the Origins of Sovereignty* (Cambridge, UK: Cambridge University Press, 2014), 6.

2. R. Buckminster Fuller, *World Game Series–Document One: The World Game: Integrative Resource Utilization Planning Tool* (Carbondale: World Resources Inventory, Southern Illinois University, 1971), 75.

3. Fuller, *World Game Series,* 75.

4. The first publication of the Airocean map is in *Life*, March 1, 1943.

5. R. Buckminster Fuller, "Fluid Geography," in Fuller, *The Buckminster Fuller Reader*, ed. James Meller (London: Jonathan Cape, 1970), 141–142.

6. While Fuller's Dymaxion Projection is usually credited for mapping the world as a continuous landmass, it is predated by architect Bernard Cahill in his Butterfly Projection in the early 1900's. See Xhulio Binjaku, "The Issue of Geography," *Log* 43 (2018): 35–39.

traffic routes.[7] Still in 1943, curator Monroe Wheeler and designer Herbert Bayer, in collaboration with Fuller, exhibit "Airways to Peace: An Exhibition of Geography for the Future." The exhibition begins with a critique of the insufficiencies of the Mercator projection to sustain postwar world order because it offers a "dangerously misleading [conception of the world] in this air-age."[8] The curators affirm that for postmaritime, aerial forms of communication, the "course over the top of the world is now clearly the shortest way to friend and enemy alike." The team closes its introductory statement claiming: "Man must redraw this world." This is what Fuller wants to achieve by engaging in, from the Dymaxion map on, cartographic production and data visualization.

Fuller, an enthusiast of all types of information gathering and a person who compulsively registers all his activities, is a precursor of data visualization. His Chronofile is a catalogue including sketches, drawings, letters, bills, newspaper clippings, and transactions.[9] The Dymaxion Map constitutes a logical step toward expanding this mentality: the possibility of generating a holistic "transcript" of the planet by plotting in its promiscuously open surface all its imaginable parameters, such as energy consumption or population indexes **[fig. 1]**.

The Dymaxion is neither the first nor the last of Fuller's cartographic experiments. The map's original name, Airocean, reveals its association with the 1927 Airocean World Plan, where Fuller conceives his first world visualization showing the potential of aerial communication **[project 6]**. Shortly after, in 1934, he designs his first one-continent map employing a polar projection.[10] Additionally, within the scope of the Dymaxion House, Fuller designs the "Go-Ahead-With-Life room." Not an object but a space, a room packed with maps, charts, globes, books, and communications devices fulfills the task of convening knowledge in a single place and, from there, broadcasting it to the world.[11]

The evolution of the Dymaxion Map moves back again toward the interior space. Although the map results from transferring sphere to polyhedron and polyhedron to plan, it allows Fuller to think through this sequence backward **[fig. 2]**. By mastering the transformation, Fuller learns to translate information from a flat surface into a globe and to create spherical forms out of linear members. The hinges of a flattened earth become the structure of an inhabitable, representational space, a path that inaugurates Fuller's Geodesic developments.[12] Through them, the Dymaxion Map's intellectual propositions literally fold themselves inward, generating in this process Fuller's most ambitious information-display endeavor.

**7.** Thomas W. Leslie, "Energetic Geometries: The Dymaxion Map and the Skin/Structure Fusion of Buckminster Fuller's Geodesics," *Architectural Research Quarterly* 5, no. 2 (2001): 163.

**8.** Wendell L. Willkie, "Airways to Peace. An Exhibition of Geography for the Future," *The Bulletin of The Museum of Modern Art* 1, vol. 11 (August 1943), 4. Accessed online December 10, 2019: www.moma.org/calendar/exhibitions/3138

**9.** R. Buckminster Fuller, "Buckminster Fuller Chronofile," in *The Buckminster Fuller Reader*, 13.

**10.** R. Buckminster Fuller, *Nine Chains to the Moon* (Philadelphia: J. B. Lippincott Company, 1938), 52–53.

**11.** Dana Miller, "Thought Patterns: Buckminster Fuller, the Science-Artist," in *Buckminster Fuller: Starting with the Universe*, ed. K. Michael Hays and Dana Miller (New York: Whitney Museum of American Art, 2008), 24.

**12.** Leslie, "Energetic Geometries," 164.

In the early 1950s, Fuller starts experimenting with what will later be known as the Geoscope. He conceives of the Geoscope as a transparent 60-meter geodesic sphere, representing a facsimile image of the world. It would be comprised of 10 million small, computer-controlled light bulbs that would allow visitors to "identify [their] own home grounds and even [their] house, which would be a 1/100$^{th}$-of-an-inch speck—the smallest speck seen by human eye."[13] The surface would act as a technologically advanced and inhabitable TV broadcasting a live reflection of the world. It would display the planet's natural and built inventory, while also making complex patterns visible and intelligible.

Between 1948 and 1965, Fuller collaborates with students from several universities and with the artist John McHale to test a series of small-scale prototypes around the idea of the Geoscope.[14] McHale, a former member of the Independent Group, alongside, among others, Reyner Banham and Alison and Peter Smithson **[project 18]**, is an enthusiast of Fuller's universalist discourse. Together, the two men not only work fabricating the Geoscope structures, but also on the means of gathering the enormous amount of data necessary to be displayed. In 1963, McHale starts directing the World Resources Inventory at Southern Illinois University, an exceedingly ambitious enterprise to compile all necessary information about the world's material, economic, and ecological conditions in order to support a "world retooling design" **[fig. 3]**.[15] Fuller and McHale gather the Institute's work in six documents entitled *World Design Science Decade 1965–1975*, which they present to the International Union of Architects (UIA).[16] The documents provide a roadmap on how to make sense of and use the world's resources to serve the whole world population, and call for the engagement of architecture schools to work on a "Ten Year Program" to tackle this issue.[17] The Geoscope is a part of that enterprise.

Throughout the seventeen years of the Geoscope experiment, key propositions mark the project's evolution and history. The first prototype of a miniaturized Earth, developed in 1952 at Cornell University under the mentorship of Fuller and Japanese-American architect Shoji Sadao, consists of a 6 meter-wide blue geodesic sphere made out of wood struts and a bronze-colored screen for the continents.[18] Three years later, Fuller begins research on the "Minni-Earth," which culminates in a formal proposal for the United Nations. In 1961, Fuller presents the concept of a 48 meters spherical electronic display to be elevated above Manhattan's East River, in front of the UN headquarters **[fig. 4]**. The project would remind all nations of the world's "integrating patterns" and its configuration as one large city.[19]

**13.** R. Buckminster Fuller, *Critical Path* (New York: St. Martin's Press, 1981), 175.

**14.** Starting with the first and failed attempt of a dome at the Black Mountain College until the last Geoscope exhibition in the Tuileries Garden.

**15.** Every document is introduced by the sentence: "Five Two Year Phases of a World Retooling Design proposed to the International Union of Architects for Adoption by World Architectural Schools."

**16.** The volumes are Document 1 (1963): *Inventory of World Resources, Human Trends and Needs*. Document 2 (1963): *The Design Initiative*. Document 3 (1965): *Comprehensive Thinking*. Document 4 (1965): *The Ten Year Program*. Documents 5 (1967): *Comprehensive Design Strategy*. Document 6 (1967): *The Ecological Context: Energy and Materials*.

**17.** See in this respect Document 2 (1963): *The Design Initiative*, and Document 4 (1965): *The Ten Year Program*.

**18.** Mark Wigley, *Buckminster Fuller Inc.: Architecture in the Age of Radio* (Ennetbaden: Lars Müller Publishers, 2015), 245.

**19.** Wigley, *Buckminster Fuller Inc.*, 240.

The name Geoscope first appears in 1960 at Princeton University, replacing the term Minni-Earth from then on. The Princeton model is a printed world map wrapped around a 2 meters long plastic sphere on an aluminum exterior frame. In 1964, following this model's repercussion, McHale leads a team of students from the University of Colorado to produce the highest achievement among the Geoscope's prototypes. Although small in scale (less than 2 meters in diameter), the resulting icosahedron is built out of multiple stratum of information, with the land-masses and the ocean occupying two distinct layers of rigid transparent glass between which printed Mylar sheets with specific visualizations are inserted. The "globe" is suspended from the floor on thin steel rods to allow a person to enter the structure and be immersed within the experience of reading the data.[20]

The lineage of built Geoscopes concludes with the 1965 UIA congress and exhibition in the Tuileries Gardens in Paris.[21] There, the Colorado piece is exhibited alongside a 6m-wide translucent Geoscope from the University of Nottingham, produced in 1962 and the largest ever built for public demonstration and the one that most broadly disseminates Fuller's view on the importance of visualizing world data **[fig. 5]**.[22] For many more years, Fuller and McHale work intensely on creating the possible conditions to produce the utmost 60 meters dreamed version—a highly technologically and financially challenging enterprise—but, after multiple failed negotiation attempts, the project's ambitions finally dilute into other organizational forms.

In *Globes*, Peter Sloterdijk's study of the modes and techniques of globalization, the German philosopher contrasts two possible forms of world knowledge.[23] One is represented by the development of cartography since the fifteenth century, and later—and more pronouncedly—by the production of terrestrial globes since the mid-nineteenth century. For the philosopher, all this cartographic enterprise represents the emergence of geographers, seafarers, and conquerors, as producers of world knowledge in substitution of philosophers. It also represents the consolidation of a vision of the planet as a closed entity, only fully comprehensible for a being situated outside it. Such a form of vision allows humans to subject the planet to "polytechnical dreams of control."[24] In its modern stages, such a form of thinking depends upon the "development of a physical-technical, aero-, and astronautical imagination," which Fuller systematically endorsed.[25] The opposite of this form of vision is, for Sloterdijk, philosophical, panoramic circumspection. This is an "all-collecting awareness" that allows humans to perceive the totality of the world from within, as if it

**20.** Wigley, *Buckminster Fuller Inc.*, 249.

**21.** For a complete description of the Geoscope, see John McHale, "Appendix A: The Geoscope Concept," in *World Design Science Decade, 1965–1975: Five Two Year Phases of a World Retooling Design Proposed to the International Union of Architects for Adoption by World Architectural Schools. Phase 1 (1965) Document 4. The Ten Year Program* (Carbondale, IL: World Resources Inventory, 1963), 30–39.

**22.** Wigley, *Buckminster Fuller Inc.*, 250.

**23.** Peter Sloterdijk, *Spheres. Volume 2: Globes. Macrospherology* (Pasadena, CA: Semiotext(e), 2014), 70–91.

**24.** Sloterdijk, *Spheres. Volume 2*, 79.

**25.** Sloterdijk, *Spheres. Volume 2*, 79.

were displayed within a dome. The lineage that goes from Paul Reclus's Episcope, to Élisée Reclus and Louis Bonnier's globe, to Fuller's Geoscope, investigates how to reconcile those two possibilities **[projects 2 and 3]**. The Episcope emphasizes the subject–world relation from a particular location. Reclus and Bonnier's globe increases the kinetic character of this relation, displacing the subjects from the location where they are to other geographies. In Fuller's case, the experience is again static and also, somehow, ecstatic. Fuller's goal is to create a simulacrum of omniscient experience. He is simultaneously interested in compiling all world knowledge, in showing how the constant modifications and dynamism of that knowledge produces a "fluid geography," as well as in situating the individual experience within the globe. In his work, the path from map to sphere is the path of building analogous worlds that can narrate different stories about humanity's home. At the core of this operation there is a profoundly anthropocentric cosmology. When entering the Geoscope, one's point of view is displaced to the center of the world. From there, the universe is perceived from inside out, transporting individualism into collectivism in a Copernican-like move, but instead of the center of the universe shifting from the Earth to the Sun, it shifts from the Earth to one's own mind. What starts in the Renaissance with Ptolemy's book finally finds an alternative formulation in modernity with Fuller's polyhedral worlds, through which "One goes inside to go outside one's self / and into the center of the Earth / and there outward to the stars in seconds."[26]

**26.** R. Buckminster Fuller, *Earth, Inc.* (Garden City, NY: Anchor Press, 1973), 152.

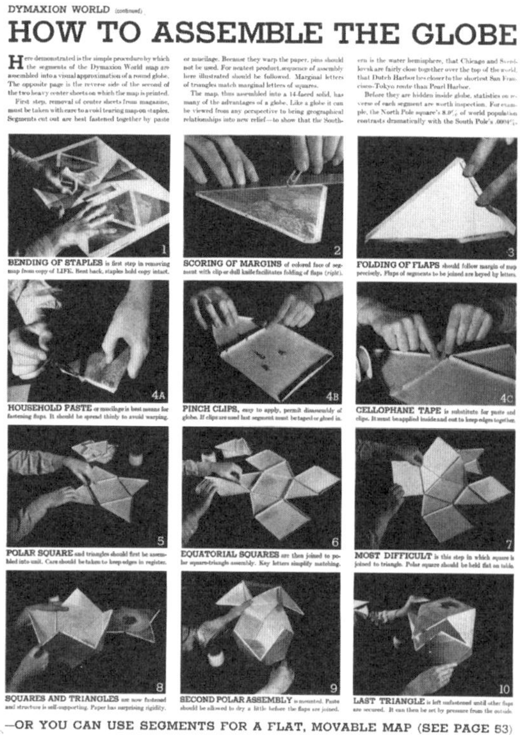

DYMAXION WORLD (continued)

HOW TO ASSEMBLE THE GLOBE

Here demonstrated is the simple procedure by which the segments of the Dymaxion World map are assembled into a visual approximation of a round globe. The opposite page is the reverse side of the second of the two heavy center sheets on which the map is printed.

First step, removal of center sheets from magazine, must be taken with care to avoid tearing map on staples. Segments cut out are best fastened together by paste or mucilage. Because they warp the paper, pins should not be used. For neatest product, sequence of assembly here illustrated should be followed. Marginal letters of triangles match marginal letters of squares.

The map, thus assembled into a 14-faced solid, has many of the advantages of a globe. Like a globe it can be viewed from any perspective to bring geographical relationships into new relief—to show that the Southern is the water hemisphere, that Chicago and Sverdlovsk are fairly close together over the top of the world, that Dutch Harbor lies closer to the shortest San Francisco-Tokyo route than Pearl Harbor.

Before they are hidden inside globe, statistics on reverse of each segment are worth inspection. For example, the North Pole square's 8.0% of world population contrasts dramatically with the South Pole's .0004%.

1 **BENDING OF STAPLES** is first step in removing map from copy of LIFE. Bent back, staples hold copy intact.

2 **SCORING OF MARGINS** of colored face of segment with clip or dull knife facilitates folding of flaps (*right*).

3 **FOLDING OF FLAPS** should follow margin of map precisely. Flaps of segments to be joined are keyed by letters.

4A **HOUSEHOLD PASTE** or mucilage is best means for fastening flaps. It should be spread thinly to avoid warping.

4B **PINCH CLIPS,** *easy to apply, permit disassembly of globe. If clips are used last segment must be taped or glued in.*

4C **CELLOPHANE TAPE** is substitute for paste and clips. It must be applied inside and out to keep edges together.

5 **POLAR SQUARE** and triangles should first be assembled into unit. Care should be taken to keep edges in register.

6 **EQUATORIAL SQUARES** are then joined to polar square-triangle assembly. Key letters simplify matching.

7 **MOST DIFFICULT** is this step in which square is joined to triangle. Polar square should be held flat on table.

8 **SQUARES AND TRIANGLES** are now fastened and structure is self-supporting. Paper has surprising rigidity.

9 **SECOND POLAR ASSEMBLY** is mounted. Paste should be allowed to dry a little before the flaps are joined.

10 **LAST TRIANGLE** is left unfastened until other flaps are secured. It can then be set by pressure from the outside.

—OR YOU CAN USE SEGMENTS FOR A FLAT, MOVABLE MAP (SEE PAGE 53)

**Figure 1 (Left).** Fuller in front of various Dymaxion Map projections. ca. 1945.
**Figure 2 (Right).** How to Assemble the Globe. 1943.

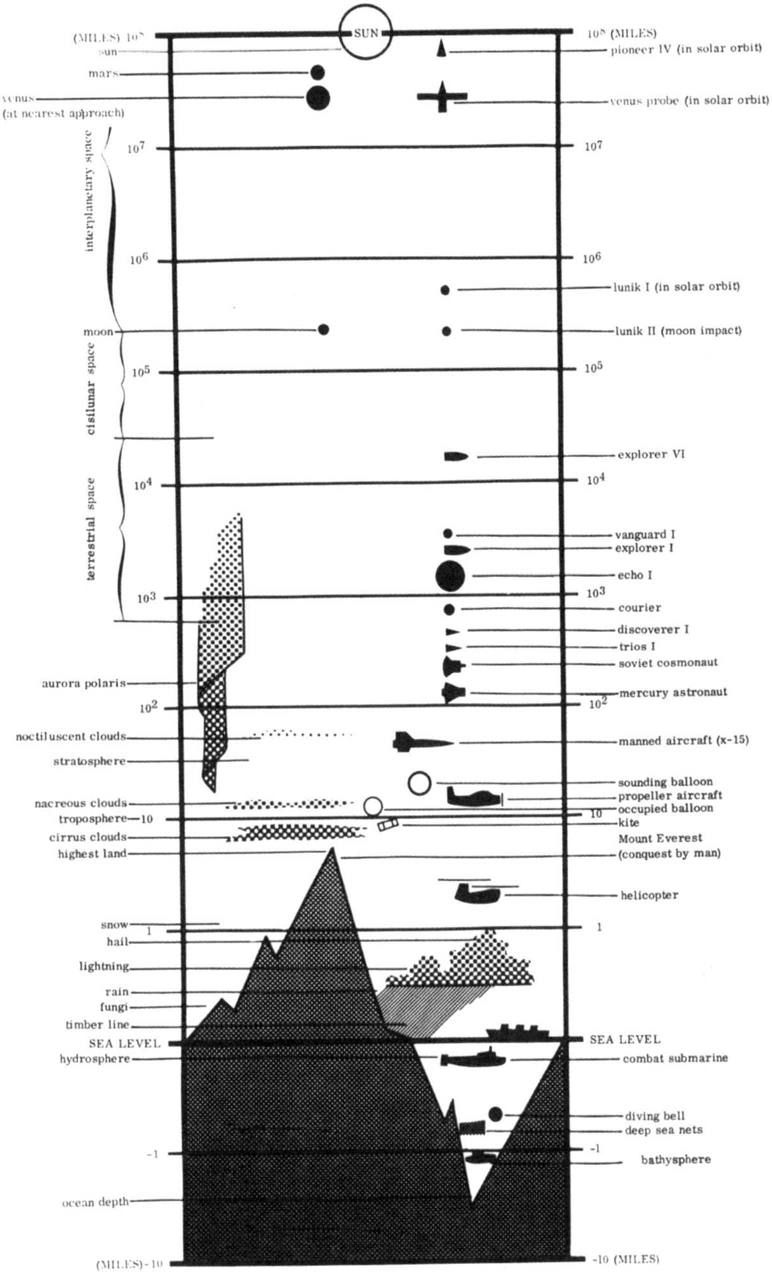


**Figure 3.** Man's Increasing Vertical Mobility. 1963.

Figure 4. Minni Earth Location at UN Building NY. 1956.

**Figure 5.** Geoscope prototype at Nottingham School of Architecture, England. ca. 1962.

# Les Trois Établissements Humains

## The Three Human Establishments

**Project:** 15. **Authors:** Le Corbusier (1887–1965) and ASCORAL. **Date:** 1943–1945. **Themes:** Circulation. Decentralization. Linearity. Territorial Gestalt.

**Figure 0.** Natural Occupation of the Territory. The Map of Europe by Ascoral. After Le Corbusier. 1943.

Stimulated by the design of the Mundancum and by his South American travel in 1929, Le Corbusier says "[I] began to think in terms of *geography* and *world*."[1] The architect's confession appears in the *Four Routes* (1943), the text where he starts pondering how to reconstruct Europe after the Second World War. In the book's conclusions, the large scale reappears as an architectural leitmotif: "we can only divine a scale, the proportion of things to come, a dimension for to-morrow . . . immense, spread to the farthest horizons, universal."[2] The treatise *The Three Human Establishments* (1945) continues this concept and demands architects "to make human geography and geo-architecture"[3] **[fig. 0]**. One year later, Le Corbusier accompanies his claim of the universality of techniques with a world map reflecting the links among major world cities and asks himself to create "the history and the geography . . . that have yet to come" **[fig. 1]**.[4] The war and immediate postwar period constitute the moment of sedimentation of Le Corbusier's thinking about the world scale. Even if his proposals of the period are conceived for France or Europe, the architect's vocabulary constantly refers to broader scales: "earth," "world," "geography," "cosmos," "totality," are the terms through which Le Corbusier deploys his postwar discourse.

The consolidation of his thinking about terrestrial organization leads Le Corbusier to expand his previous strategies of spatial production. A sectional representation of South America exemplifies his prewar, 1929 declaration about the discovery of the world and geography as architectural themes **[fig. 3]**. The section concludes with two operations—the Buenos Aires city of affairs and airport—which serve to extend the continent and to connect it to the Atlantic Ocean and the sky: two spaces of transportation and interchange. The drawing's thematic is twofold: it reflects Le Corbusier's conception of the head of the city as a node within a global circuit of international relations, as well as his reliance on architecture as a tool to measure physical geography and to calibrate our relation to the horizon.[5] The discourse he elaborates during the war abandons the sole focus on architecture and the city. He is increasingly concerned with infrastructures of communication and with the organization of a territorial gestalt that goes beyond mere intercity relations. To do so, instead of the section, it privileges horizontality and planar representation.[6] These two strategies are not irreconcilable. Both are preserved in the author's late thinking, but they tend to be used for different purposes. In *Looking at City Planning* (1946), architecture serves Le Corbusier to visualize intercity linkages while

1. Le Corbusier, *The Four Routes*, trans. Dorothy Todd (London: D. Dobson, 1947), 104.

2. Le Corbusier, *The Four Routes*, 204.

3. Le Corbusier, *The Three Human Establishments* (Chandigarh: Punjab Government, Department of Town & Country Planning, 1979 [1945]), 77.

4. Le Corbusier, *Looking at City Planning*, trans. Eleanor Levieux (New York: Grossman Publishers, 1971 [1946]), 114. For the image with the connections between cities see Le Corbusier, *Concerning Town Planning*, trans. Clive Entwistle (New Haven: Yale University Press, 1948 [1946]), 97.

5. Hashim Sarkis, "Geo-architecture: A Prehistory for an Emerging Aesthetic," *Harvard Design Magazine* 37 (2014): 126.

6. Jean Pierre Giordani, "Territoire," in *Le Corbusier, une encyclopédie*, ed. Jacques Lucan (Paris: Centre Georges Pompidou, Collection Monographie, 1987), 404. Le Corbusier, *The Three Human Establishments*, 154.

communications infrastructures help to define the territorial form **[fig. 2]**. The *Poem of the Right Angle* (1955) will finally summarize an architectural poetic that goes from the two-dimensional, organic, infrastructural systems and geographical components of the territorial milieu to the precision, artificiality, and volume of architecture.

Le Corbusier condenses his discourse on territorial two-dimensionality and transportation infrastructures in *The Four Routes*. In this text, high roads, railroads, waterways, and airways constitute the armature of postwar territorial order. Their continuity is the sign of a world without frontiers and the basis of a new, second stage of "machinist civilization."[7] The high roads and the airways are particularly relevant. The high roads intensify the use of territory. They supersede the discrete system of stops of railroad lines and create, instead, a continuous network where "the earth is accessible as a whole."[8] The airways establish, in turn, unprecedented world relations. Together, the four routes show how territorial form depends upon underlying geographical conditions. The first three networks are substantially determined by preexisting geographical factors. The fourth—the airways—breaks with any geographic limitations, but it requires at ground level airports connected to the other transportation systems. The routes, thus, have to operate totally in coordination with physical geography.

*The Three Human Establishments* defines a comprehensive territorial order based on the relation between this infrastructural system and three settlement types. The "units of agricultural exploitation," the "linear industrial cities," and the "radio-concentric cities of exchange" result from joining formal systems to predominant land uses. Pentagons reflecting Walter Christaller's model of settlement distribution surround the agricultural units.[9] Arturo Soria y Mata's notion of linear city is delinked from its original, mostly residential, finality in order to define the distribution of industry **[project 1]**. Finally, the historical, radial form appears only in the cities for the tertiary sector. Combined, the three settlements create a system that expands to the territorial scale the main preoccupations of Le Corbusier's early urban schemes. Functions, social groups, and typologies are separated and treated distinctly, settlements are defined as formally and dimensionally contained units, and voids act as instruments of separation. As he had done since the 1920s, Le Corbusier continues to praise emptiness as a value to be preserved and highlighted.[10] A green belt that updates the "zone of protection" of the Contemporary City surrounds the radio-concentric cities, impeding their growth. The linear city avoids the

**7.** Le Corbusier, *Concerning Town Planning*, 45; and Le Corbusier, *The Four Routes*, 17.

**8.** Le Corbusier, *The Four Routes*, 31.

**9.** Walter Christaller, *Central Places in Southern Germany*, trans. Carlisle W. Baskin (Englewood Cliffs, NJ: Prentice-Hall, 1966 [1933]).

**10.** Le Corbusier, *The Three Human Establishments*, 145.

expansion of industry toward the countryside and creates vacant, "pure peasant reserves."[11] The association settlement–infrastructure warrants this system of functional and formal differentiations and separations. The industrial city runs strictly along axes where railroads, waterways, and high roads converge. These three routes create a triangular grid with the peasant reserves among them and with the radio-concentric cities at the intersections between infrastructural lines **[fig. 4]**.

Le Corbusier originally proposes this territorial scheme, conceived with the collective of architects and geographers ASCORAL, as a guide to structure the reconstruction of France after the war.[12] Yet, in his writings, he points toward a territorial "totality" alien to any national particularity.[13] His drawings are emphatically abstract. They depict a generalizable, acontextual situation, which can be explained through diagrams. In this general condition, the merging of transport and settlement inverts the historic hierarchies of territorial organization. *The Three Human Establishments* no longer depicts a system dominated by cities but by territorial lines of circulation and production. In this system, radial cities are reconceptualized as merely the intersections of transportation lines.[14] The emergence of a new form of urban development around the industrial lines counters this decline of radial cities. The result is not a map of France, but of Europe, laying out a continental settlement system linked through aerial and terrestrial communications **[fig. 05]**. Le Corbusier takes to its extreme the vision of territory as fundamentally a space of circulation that Ildefons Cerdà and Soria y Mata had started to elaborate in spatial terms.

The architectural historian Mary McLeod explains that, during the 1930s, Le Corbusier searches how his internationalist agenda can be promoted without necessarily relying on global institutions, as was his original intention.[15] Through his participation in the collectives *Plan* and *Preludes* at the time, Le Corbusier joins a group of right-wing intellectuals interested in finding the basis for an international order that can supersede the paralysis of the liberal state's political life and avoid the interstate conflicts that had caused World War I. For both groups, planning and elite intellectual guidance, not liberal politics, are the tools to implement a new international order. This order is to be based on concrete parameters, and not on all-encompassing abstract notions of universality. They believe that by linking areas of cultural influence, geographical conditions, and zones of production, new regions can be created to substitute existing national states, and that these new regions can then be federated into broader complexes. In their proposals, Europe becomes a federation of five regions: the Baltic, the Mediterranean, West Europe, the Danube, and Germany.[16]

**11.** Le Corbusier, *The Three Human Establishments,* 112.

**12.** Patrice Noviant, "Les Trois établissements humains," in Lucan, *Le Corbusier, une encyclopédie,* 414.

**13.** Le Corbusier, *The Three Human Establishments,* 74.

**14.** Le Corbusier, *The Three Human Establishments,* 145; and Noviant, "Les Trois établissements humains," 416. For a broader reflection upon the disappearance of the notion of location because of its integration within circulation networks see Peter Sloterdijk, *Spheres. Volume 2: Globes. Macrospherology,* trans. Wieland Hoban (Pasadena, CA: Semiotext(e), 2014), 783–794.

**15.** Mary McLeod, "Urbanism and Utopia: Le Corbusier from Regional Syndicalism to Vichy" (PhD diss., Princeton University, 1985), 123.

**16.** McLeod, "Urbanism and Utopia," 123.

*The Three Human Establishments* partakes of the extrapolitical attitude of *Plans* and *Preludes*, while it points to a different vision of a future territorial order. Le Corbusier understands that the world system will appear not as a result of political agreements, but through the intermingling of industrial production and communication: "The world is spread over the entire surface of the earth, from one pole to the other, including these poles themselves, a world made of quarries and mines, of gigantic powers of production, of gigantic means of circulation and of transportation."[17] The architect's task is to intensify this logic and to indicate how it modifies the structure of settlements and the notion of national space. In the same way that cities are reconceptualized as nodes within a network of communications, France is understood as "a fragment of production, passage and exchange;" an area between the immense material resources of the East and the transcontinental connections via the Atlantic Ocean.[18] Not only does the individuality of France disappear in the midst of global networks, but also does Le Corbusier's map of Europe not depict the regions envisaged by the *Plans* group. His map represents a territory unified by linear corridors linking ports and hinterlands, all of which are placed along geographically determined areas of passage.

17. Le Corbusier, *The Three Human Establishments*, 148.

18. Le Corbusier, *The Three Human Establishments*, 152.

Le Corbusier's postwar vision of the world grounds production, circulation, and settlements in the specificities of geographical space. What emerges from the formula "contact-information-penetration," which for him characterizes the second machine age, are lines that define a territorial gestalt. Transportation lines join the Atlantic Ocean to the Urals, the Baltic Sea to the Mediterranean Sea. A linear channel connects the Atlantic and the Black Sea. A line along a "planisphere" reaches East Asia.[19] Lines that challenge the latitudinal order with a longitudinal one connect Paris, Algiers, and central Africa, defining relations that for Le Corbusier are as colonial as they are cultural **[fig. 6]**. Lines that link cities structure the world map and create continental ensembles: "the Americas, Europe, Eurasia, Eurafrica."[20]

19. Le Corbusier, *The Three Human Establishments*, 152.

20. Le Corbusier, *The Three Human Establishments*, 154.

The rationality Le Corbusier applies to his territorial proposal derives from revealing the consequences of a global framework on inferior scales. He understands that territorial ordering consists in correctly adapting the realities of world production to the inevitable and determinant conditions of geography in order to restore an equilibrium with nature. In his view, both geographic factors and economic processes are objective and determinant conditions. The acceptance of these factors gives his proposal a tone of inevitability: "The transformation will be gradual and without violence, in the peaceful acceptance of things that must be."[21] The result presented in the map of Europe is not a proposal, but "the natural occupation of territory."

The reactions to *The Three Human Establishments* deem it neither natural nor inevitable, but chimerical and simplistic. In France, urbanists and architects, such as Marcel Lods or Urbain Cassan, and geographers who promote decentralization, such as Jean-François Gravier, criticize the text.[22] When Le Corbusier presents it as a model for rural development in Italy, it causes a similarly negative reaction in the young Aldo Rossi and Silvano Tintori **[project 41]**.[23] In all these cases, Le Corbusier's system is rightly perceived as oblivious to the contextual realities of territorial structures and to their extremely variegated processes of urban and social development. Certainly, Le Corbusier disregards singularities. Instead he limits his work to understanding how globalized economic processes disrupt existing territorial structures and can generate new ones. In so doing, he not only addresses the real emergence of almost continental, linear, urban formations. Importantly, he also imagines how these can be shaped in order to create a more equitable model of territorial development. This model is, for sure, reductionist and insists, as many others of Le Corbusier's works, on isolating social groups and economic sectors. Yet, it also pursues turning economically driven processes of spatial transformation into a system of territorial cohesion, one that can provide a shared and comprehensible formal structure of relations between humans and geography. This attempt to perfectly match economy and territory into a stable spatial structure was, however, doomed to fail. Not for not recognizing contextual singularities—which, after all, postwar, industrial capitalism was not considering either—but because of the contradiction between Le Corbusier's static spatial system and the dynamic restructuring of economic and social relations that will increasingly characterize the second post-war.

**21.** Le Corbusier, "Towards a Synthesis," in *Oeuvre complète. Volume 4: 1938–46*, ed. Willy Boesiger, Oscar Stonorov, Pierre Jeanneret, and Max Bill (Zurich: Les Editions d'Architecture, 1991), 70–71.

**22.** Noviant, "Les Trois établissements humains," 415–417.

**23.** Aldo Rossi and Silvano Tintori, "Aspetti urbanistici del problema delle zone arretrate in Italia e in Europa," in Giovanni Demaria et al., *Problemi sullo sviluppo delle aree arretrate* (Bologna: Il Mulino, 1960), 248–249.

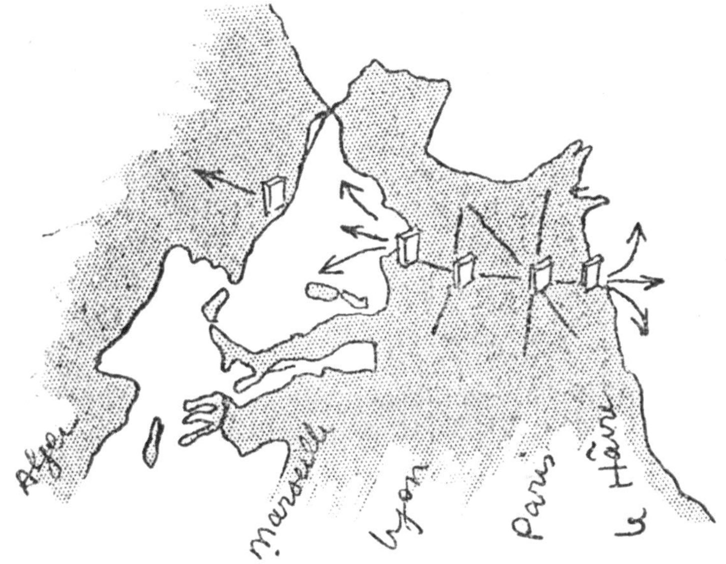


**Figure 1 (Top).** Links between major world cities. 1946.
**Figure 2 (Bottom).** The Hague; Paris; Lyon; Marseille; Algiers. 1946.

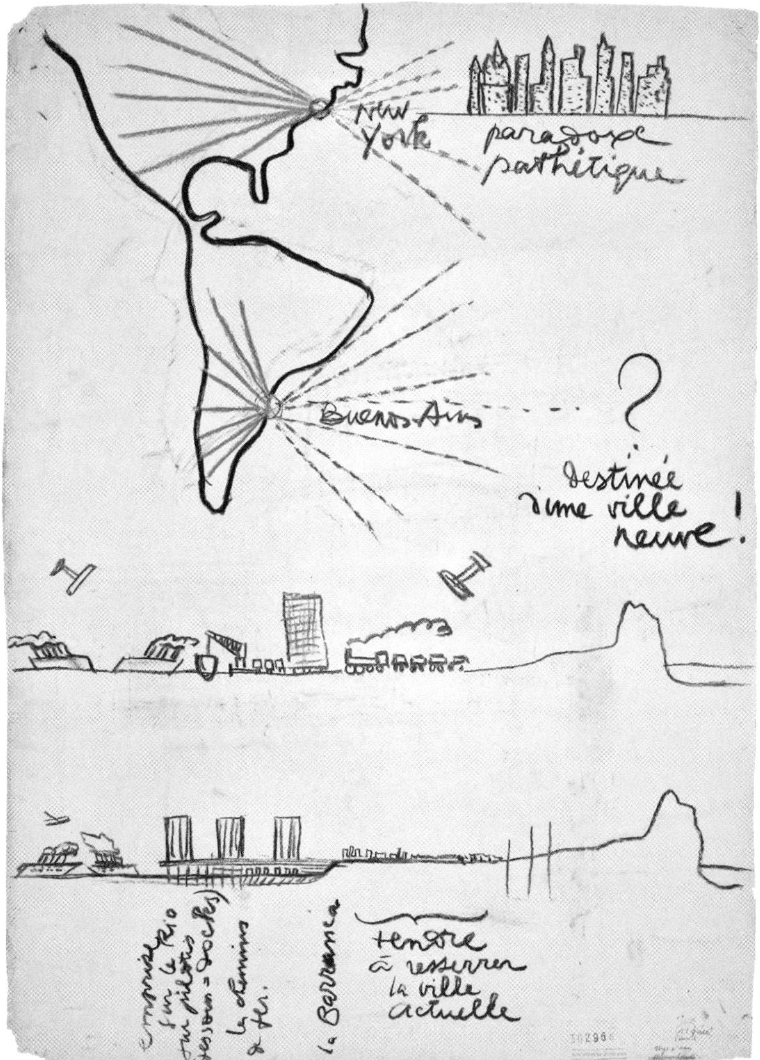


**Figure 3.** Buenos Aires: Destiny of a New City? New York: Pitiful Paradox. 1929.

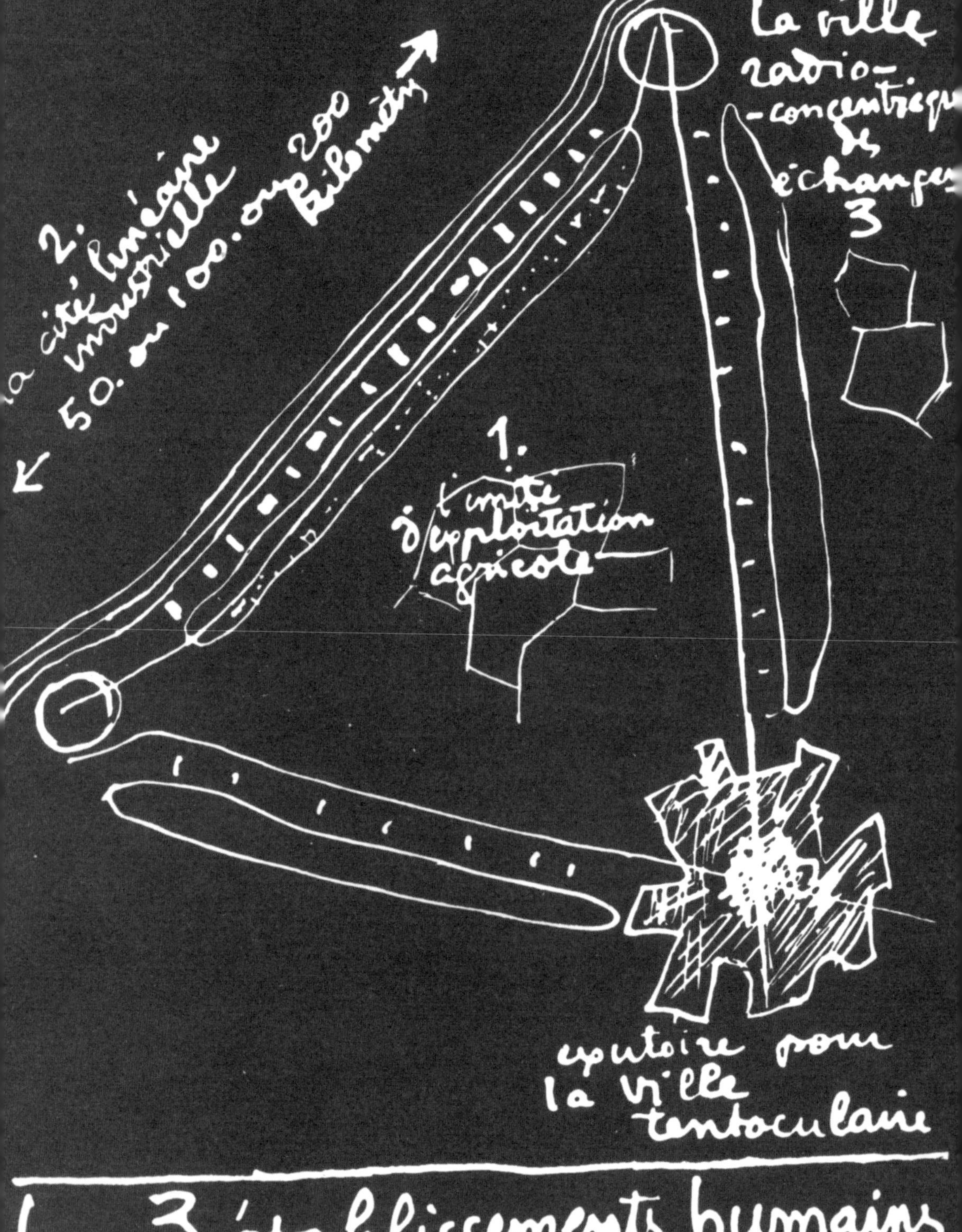


Les 3 établissements humains

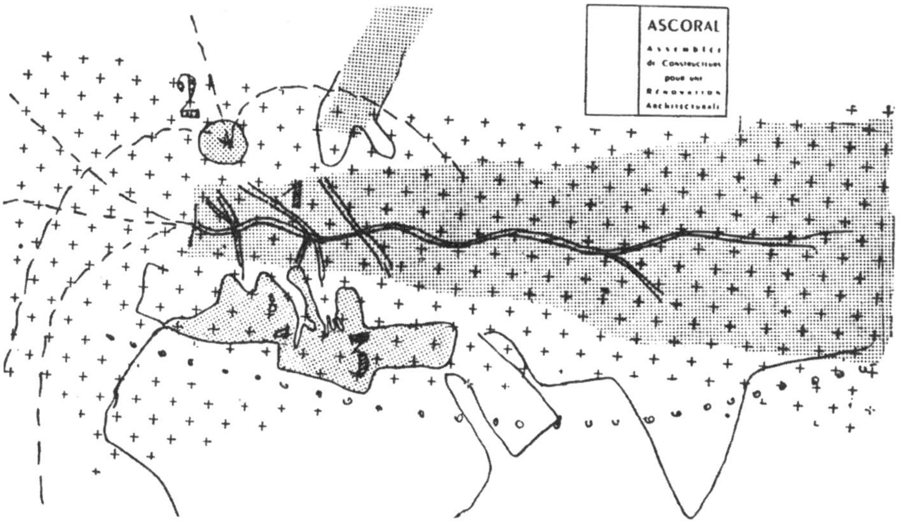


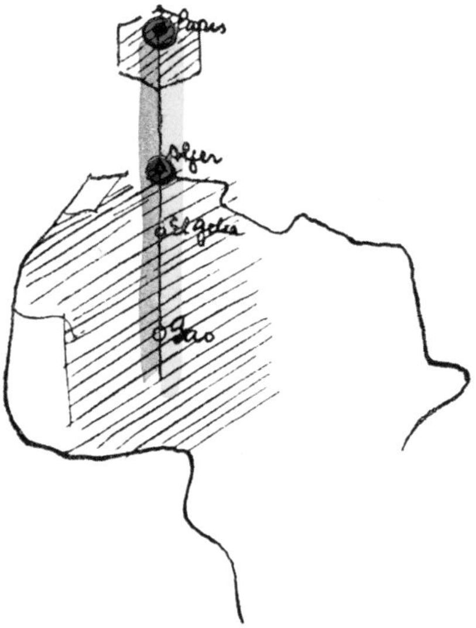


**QUALIFICATION D'ALGER,**
**CAPITALE DE L'AFRIQUE FRANÇAISE :**

*Rôle de la ville, désignation des tâches imparties à la population, limitation sage, jugulant l'envahissement par les activités parasitaires.*

94

**Figure 4 (Opposite page).** The Three Human Establishments. 1945.
**Figure 5 (Top).** From the Ocean to the Ural Mountains. 1945.
**Figure 6 (Bottom).** Qualification of Algiers: Capital of French Africa. 1946.

# Von der Bebauung der Erde

## The Cultivation of the Earth

**Project:** 16. **Author:** Rudolf Schwarz (1897–1961). **Date:** 1943–1945. **Themes:** Aerial View. Decentralization. Geography. Territorial Intensification.

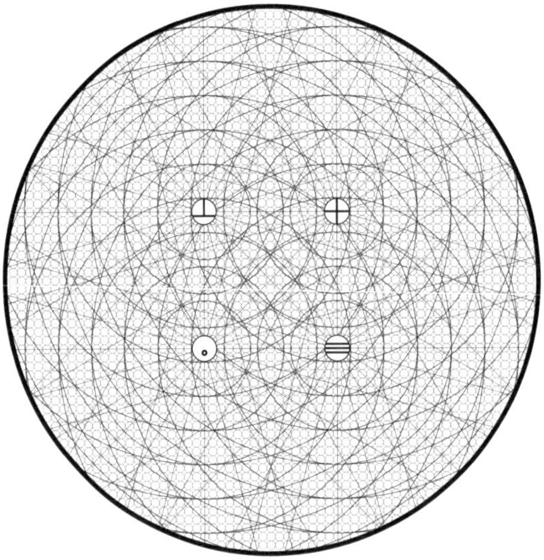

**Figure 0.** The four powers of society: Sovereignty, Education, Worship, and Economy. After Rudolf Schwarz. 1949.

Modernity is, for Martin Heidegger, the historical epoch that reduces the world to a representation. As the philosopher explains in the 1938 lecture "The Age of the World Picture," the key features of the modern age—the domination of scientific research over any other forms of knowledge, the planning and rationalization of human activities, the subjection of all world phenomena to mathematical calculation—are enabled by a previous, metaphysical, operation.[1] This operation consists in transforming the world into an entity that can be accessed only indirectly, through its image, and it consequently disregards all conditions that cannot be reduced to that representation. This conversion of the world into a picture severs modernity from the previous medieval and classical ages. Heidegger's philosophical program, structured around the existential recuperation of an unmediated sense of being-in-the world (*Dasein*), is a reaction to this epochal fracture.

"The Age of the World Picture" reacts to the existential tensions that result from early twentieth-century modernization by establishing a conceptual opposition between scientific and nonscientific understandings of the world. Even if Heidegger himself considers that the recuperation of *Dasein* should operate within the conditions modern science imposes, the text emphasizes that scientific calculation and existential apprehension are, initially, opposed possibilities, and claims that it is necessary to think the world beyond the parameters mere calculation imposes.[2] This confrontation between world picture and being-in-the-world will become spatially articulated immediately after World War II by urban theory. Two contemporary and contrasting treatises represent the different poles of Heidegger's analysis. Maurice François Rouge's *La* géonomie; ou, L'*organisation de l'espace* (Geonomy, or the organization of space, 1947) supports a scientific view of world planning. Rudolf Schwarz's *Von der Bebauung der Erde* (The cultivation of the earth, 1949), which is the main object of this article, conceives in turn a world project outside the scientific episteme, conceptually close to Heideggerian postulates **[fig. 0]**.[3]

Rouge creates the neologism *geonomy* by merging the Greek terms *ge* (earth), and *nomos* (law).[4] His intention is to denominate a new spatial science, aimed at complementing the existing geosciences of geography, geology, or geometry.[5] Contrary to the mostly descriptive goals of those disciplines, the new science would be an operative instrument devoted to "organizing" terrestrial space.[6] Geonomy's scope matches the totality of human "biome."[7] The science aims

**1.** Martin Heidegger, "The Age of the World Picture," in *The Question Concerning Technology, and Other Essays*, trans. William Lovitt (New York: Harper & Row, 1977), 129–130.

**2.** Heidegger, "The Age of the World Picture," 136.

**3.** Panos Mantziaras, "Rudolf Schwarz and the Concept of *Stadtlandschaft*," *Planning Perspectives* 18, no. 2 (2003): 163.

**4.** Maurice François Rouge, *La géonomie; ou, L'organisation de l'espace* (Paris: Librairie Générale de Droit et de Jurisprudence, 1947), 2. Rouge's selection of terms coincides–although with a completely different meaning–to Carl Schmitt's selection in his 1950 book on geopolitical theory, *The Nomos of the Earth* (New York: Telos Press, 2006).

**5.** Jean Gohier, "Un cours à l'E.P.H.E., la géonomie de Maurice François Rouge," *Les Annales de la recherche urbaine* 37 (1988): 94. Accessed online June 7, 2018: doi: https: //doi.rog/10.3406/ aru.1988.1353.

**6.** Rouge, *La géonomie*, 156.

**7.** Rouge, *La géonomie*, 48.

to cover the spatial organization of ground and water surfaces, of the underground, and the atmosphere, and seeks to organize in those realms the necessities of humans and nonhuman species.[8]

Geonomy is to go beyond urbanism, a discipline that Rouge considers dependent upon artistic procedures, by deploying a rigorous and holistic analytical method.[9] Rouge teaches this methodology between 1953 and 1964 in his courses at the Section VI of the École Pratique des Hautes Études, in Paris, which is devoted to the Economic and Social Sciences. The section, founded shortly after the war by historians Lucien Febvre (1878–1956) and Fernand Braudel (1902–1985), offers institutional support for the second generation of the Annales School of historians and for developing structuralist thinking. Geonomy shares the comprehensive ambitions of these two schools of thought, and employs, for its purposes, the forms of vision and analysis of the world through aerial photography initiated in Jean Brunhes's documentary work for the Archives de la Planète (1912–1918), and later developed in Chombart de Lauwe's *La Découverte aérienne du monde* (The aerial discovery of the world, 1948).[10] This form of explaining the world through its picture is oriented in Rouge's work toward the rationalization and intensification of the productive processes of the planet. As is the case in Erwin Anton Gutkind's work, the rationalization of global economy is for Rouge the inevitable outcome of the scientific discovery and political articulation of the totality of the world **[project 17]**. Whereas in the past, the world offered the space for the political and economic expansion of countries, in modernity, the planet has become a completely structured space, in which economic growth can only result from increasing productivity and the global orchestration of synergetic, complementary relations between states.[11] In this relational context, the world space can no longer be the arena for political and war confrontation. It has to be, instead, a realm for technical and spatial organization.[12] Geonomy is the holistic science charged with that task. It can be applied on the national scale, as a preliminary stage toward its implementation worldwide.

*Von der Bebauung der Erde* is the antithesis of Rouge's work. This difference, and Schwarz's proximity to Heideggerian postulates, is already explicit in the title of the German work. Schwarz abandons his original, tentative title, *Von Bau der Welt* (On the building of the world) in favor of *Von der Bebauung der Erde*—a careful choice of words, in which the notions of cultivation and Earth of the second title denote the intention to care, not to transform, the planet; the attention to its tectonics and materiality, not to its representation; and a scalar

**8.** Rouge, *La géonomie*, 4–11 and 48–49.

**9.** Gohier, "Un cours à l'E.P.H.E.," 94.

**10.** Paul Henry Chombart de Lauwe, *La découverte aérienne du monde* (Paris: Horizons de France, 1948), and Jeanne Haffner, "Modeling the Social and the Spatial: 'Social Space' in Postwar French Social-Scientific Research," in *The View from Above: The Science of Social Space* (Cambridge, MA: MIT Press, 2013), 81–107.

**11.** In this regard, Rouge quotes extensively Lucien Febvre's analysis of the successive and complete transformations of Sri Lanka's agriculture and landscape according to the consumption necessities of the West, to portray how productive relations were already structured at the world scale, and the huge spatial consequences this world ordering entailed.

**12.** Rouge, *La géonomie*, 16. In fact, for Rouge the main hindrance to the full implementation of geonomy was not technical, but political. The partition of the world into states limited global coordination.

oscillation between considering the planet as a whole and the specificity of the local terrains.[13] From its title on, Schwarz's treatise is a sustained critique of mere rationalization. While geonomy proposes to structure global productive relations, *Von der Bebauung der Erde* privileges operating at the regional scale in order to reassess the cultural and historical complexity of geographical space. The work wants to counteract urbanization—seen as the uncontrolled expanse of the urban fabric—by reaffirming the relation between settlements and their geographical support. In this integrated schema, production cannot cause—as Rouge suggests—the creation of purely operational landscapes, detached from places of consumption. Economy is, instead, a factor to be understood with the other aspects of social life.[14]

The tone of Schwarz's work is metaphysical. Its goal is to create a conceptual apparatus, not operative tools. Schwarz argues that it is necessary to create a discipline of "spatial planning" to prepare "a new state of the earth."[15] This Earth project will respond to the disappearance, in modernity, of the organic, spontaneous order of relations between humans and environment by enabling the recuperation, and intensification of Earth's values.[16] Thanks to spatial planning, humans will allow the planet to develop its full potential. "The earth," Schwarz asserts, "is full of possibilities and everywhere pregnant with the germ of a new, more real existence. Yet, it will not come into this other being by itself. For this, the earth needs human beings, who must create it anew, as it were."[17]

In a statement very indebted to Heidegger's vocabulary, Schwarz further qualifies the task of planning as: "the restoration of things, so that, reincarnated in their finiteness, they can recover their thingness."[18] The first step toward this restoration consists of revealing the earth's materiality and physical geography **[fig. 1]**. Negating the concept of space as a "mathematical abstract," *Von der Bebauung der Erde* treats space as a physical, tectonic entity.[19] In fact, Earth, history, and construction are all for Schwarz an expression of geological forces.[20] Following in this vein, the text redefines buildings as vertical sedimentations of matter, and settlements as landscapes, while the different conditions of the urban are further described using landscape metaphors such as "mountains," "fields," and "veins and foliage." Schwarz complements this tectonic approach to construction by establishing a second step toward the restoration of thingness. In this case, the intention is not to address the terrestrial object, but the subjects that inhabit it. *Von der Bebauung der Erde* treats settlement systems as the spatial manifestation of the notions of sovereignty, education, worship, and economy **[fig. 2]**. In other words, the text portrays settlements as organic

**13.** Sonja Hildebrand and Matteo Trentini, "The Tectonic of the Ruins: Rudolf Schwarz *Von der Bebauung der Erde*," *Documents of the Università della Svizzera Italiana* USI (Mendrisio: Accademia di Architettura di Mendrisio, 2014), unpaged.

**14.** Rudolf Schwarz, *Von der Bebauung der Erde* (Heidelberg: L. Schneider, 1949, 11 and ff. In this page, Schwarz asserts: "We begin to suspect again that all culture is an ordering of earth, agriculture: that every act must be rooted in earth and spring from earth, cultivated on the field of history, lowered into the depths, grown, and that which is not in the world-ground is aborted. In all our actions, the earth opens the eye and becomes the face, the landscape, and becomes the ground on which we stand, the earth of the home. The economy rediscovers its landscaping." Our translation.

**15.** Schwarz, *Von der Bebauung der Erde*, 7. Our translation.

**16.** Schwarz, *Von der Bebauung der Erde*, 7.

**17.** Schwarz, *Von der Bebauung der Erde*, 213. Our translation.

**18.** Schwarz, *Von der Bebauung der Erde*, 9. Our translation. Heidegger summarizes his thinking about "thingness" in a 1950 lecture titled "The Thing." See Martin Heidegger, *What Is a Thing?* trans. W. B. Barton, Jr., and Vera Deutsch (Chicago: H. Regnery, 1967).

**19.** Schwarz, *Von der Bebauung der Erde*, 24.

**20.** Schwarz, *Von der Bebauung der Erde*, 22, and 27. According to Schwarz: "History is not anything but geological construction, stratified Earth." Our translation.

wholes that integrate economic relations within broader structures of political articulation (sovereignty), cultural formation (education), and metaphysical aspirations (worship). Each of these factors constitutes its own "landscape," so that settlements unite actual geographical landscapes and built, human ones.

*Von der Bebauung der Erde* contains several graphic schemas explaining how Schwarz envisions the convergence of physical and human factors. Despite their pretensions of universality, these diagrams reveal how much the work is related to the conditions of German urbanization and landscape.[21] The main schema defines the organization of a linear settlement system limited by two major urban poles at its extremes, one of them containing the central functions of sovereignty, education, and worship. Despite the schematic character of the drawing, there is in it an implicit geographical condition: the main road between the two poles is to occupy a valley, and the smaller settlements that emanate transversally from the road are placed in the hills surrounding it. These smaller settlements, in turn, connect to other subcenters, again containing the three aforementioned functions. The schema operates quasifractally, replicating at nested scales a unique form of spatial organization, and hence generating a structure that Schwarz names constellation or Milky Way **[fig. 3]**. This structure makes up a singular entity—and not a segment of an expandable system—which synthesizes what Schwarz considers the earlier predominant forms of spatial organization: the enclosed premodern city, and the linear, potentially infinite, urban schema of modern industrial society **[fig. 4; and projects 1, 10, 15, and 23]**.

The resulting finite structure is the embryo of a broader form of territorial organization. Thanks to its formal clarity and finitude, the settlement schema intends to shape the communal aspirations of a particular social whole.[22] In this way, each settlement system would operate as a tool for individuals to access suprapersonal forms of community. In turn, the successive levels of association of different settlement groups would permit them to structure a common world, which Schwarz calls "the earth of all earths."[23] The merging of each of these settlement structures produces, then, an "anticlassicist order of the world."[24] That is, not a hierarchically ordered planet, but a congregation of multiple, geographically inflected, local structures.

*Von der Bebauung der Erde* concludes with Schwarz expressing his fears of a future of total planning and rationalization of the planet.[25] His main antidote against such a "geonomic" possibility is to reduce the process of urbanization

**21.** See in this respect the analysis of Schwarz's position in relation to the German debates about the notion of *Stadtlandschaft* (city-landscape) in Mantziaras, "Rudolf Schwarz and the Concept of *Stadtlandschaft*," 147–176.

**22.** Schwarz, *Von der Bebauung der Erde*, 10 and 64.

**23.** Schwarz, *Von der Bebauung der Erde*, 12. Our translation.

**24.** Schwarz, *Von der Bebauung der Erde*, 12.

**25.** Mantziaras, "Rudolf Schwarz and the Concept of *Stadtlandschaft*," 168.

to the creation of small urban clusters fused with their surrounding landscape. This idea is complemented, in the last chapter of the book, with a proposition that reiterates the proximity of Schwarz's thinking to Heidegger's analyses. "The Age of the World Picture" closes with the assertion that, under the hegemonic conditions of global, technical rationalization, the only space of freedom for the human subject lies in the uncontrollable.[26] Schwarz proposes, with the same ambition, the idea of "unplanned."[27] The metaphysical tone of his prose and the schematic character of his designs are, in this way, a tool to emphasize that his work does not seek to prescribe any detailed urban forms, but to create a philosophical base for design: a universal conceptual framework meant to reconnect urbanization and earth.

**26.** Heidegger, "The Age of the World Picture," 135–136.

**27.** The notion is the title of the last chapter of Schwarz's book. See Schwarz, *Von der Bebauung der Erde*, 225–244.

**Figure 1.** The Mountains. 1949.

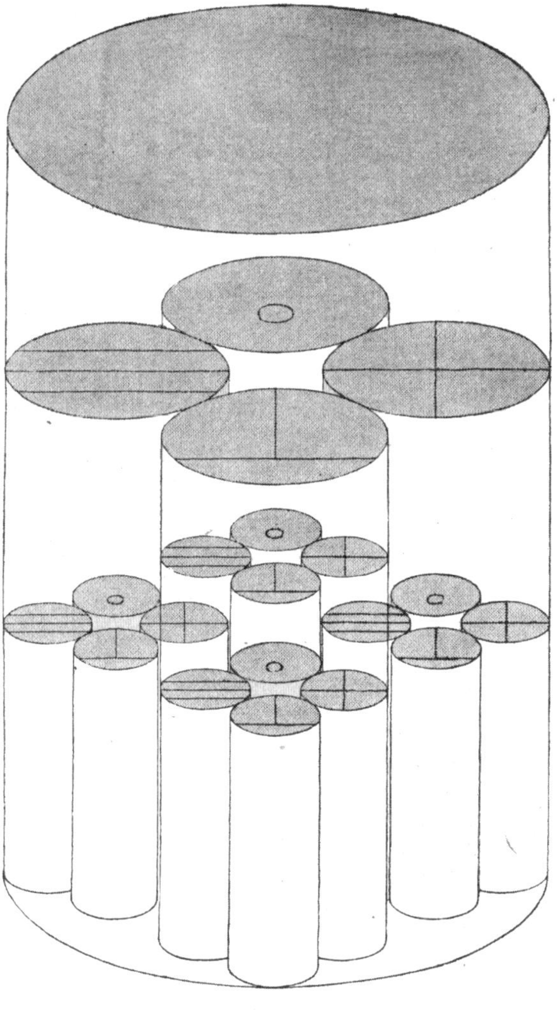

**Figure 2.** The City. The four powers of Sovereignty, Education, Worship, and Economy. 1949.

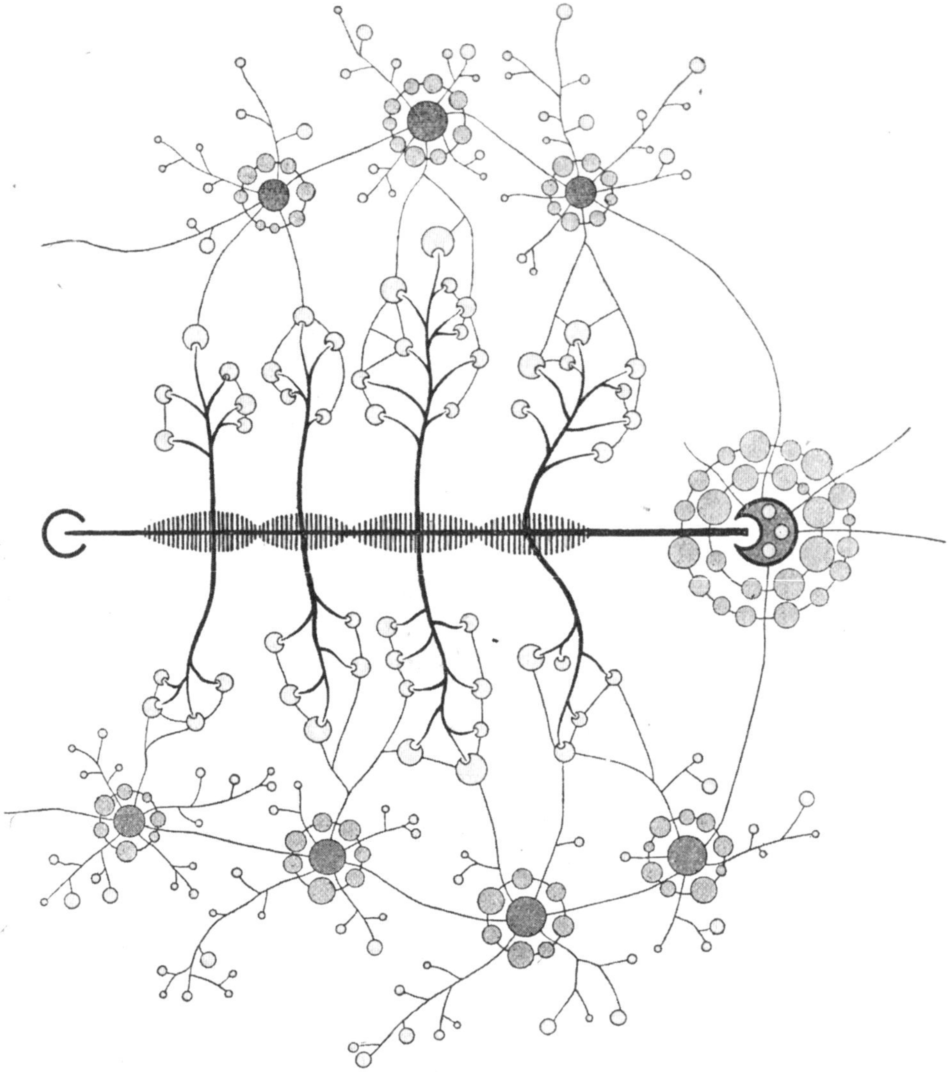

**Figure 3.** The city-landscape as a "Milky Way." 1949.

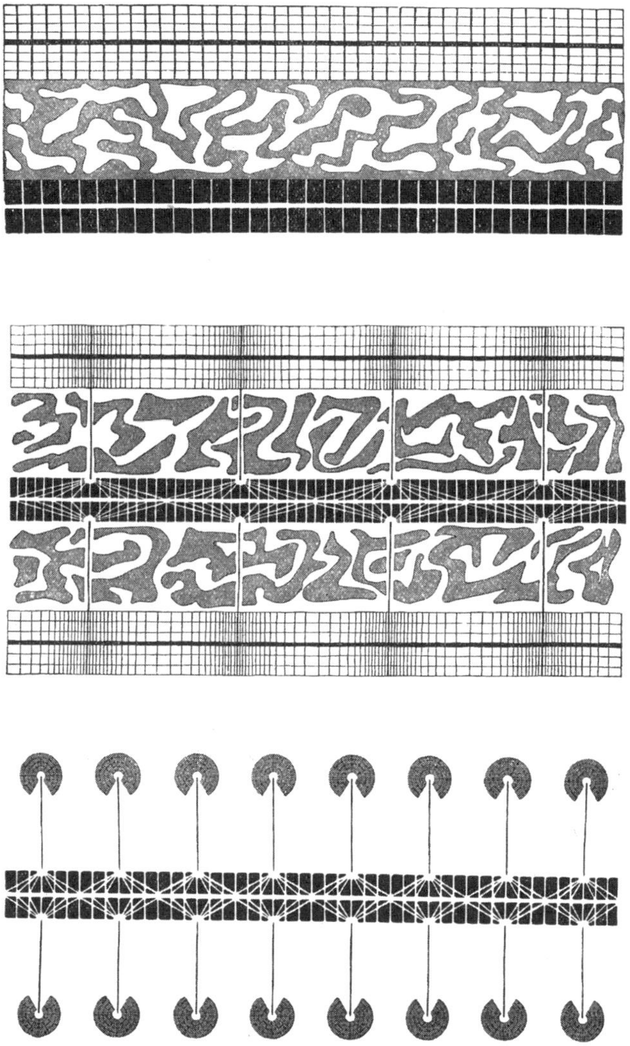

**Figure 4.** The linear city of industrial society. 1949.

# The Expanding Environment

**Project:** 17. **Author:** Erwin Anton Gutkind (1886–1968). **Date:** 1951–1953. **Themes:** Colonialism. Decentralization. Territorial Intensification. World Urbanization.

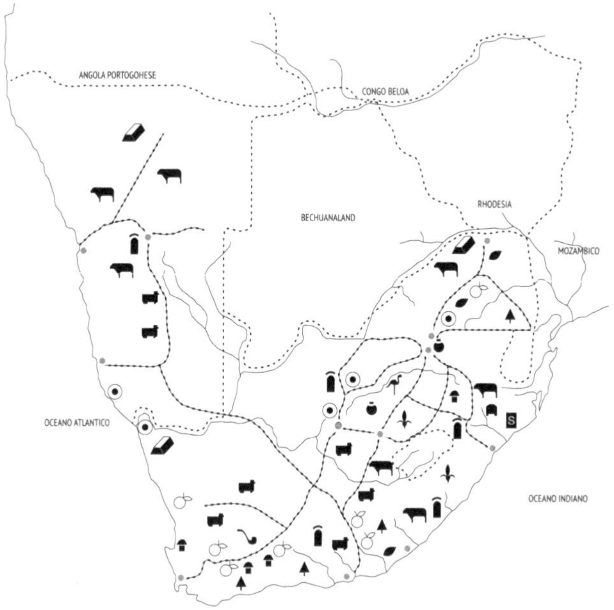


**Figure 0.** Schematic map for the union of South Africa indicating the main mineral and natural resources. After Erwin Anton Gutkind. 1952.

In 1936, German architect Erwin Anton Gutkind publishes a short journal article, almost a manifesto, titled "Universal Planning." At the time he is an expatriate from Nazi Germany for racial and ideological reasons. Yet, his text completely ignores the political convulsions that will soon lead to World War II, instead claiming that the pressing conditions to which architects should respond are none other than world integration: "A proper town-planning specialist labours never for one or even two generations ahead: the result of his work shows itself only after a much longer period. Then let us have no 'town-planning,' nor even 'regional-planning,' but *universal* planning."[1] A variety of factors produce this imperative to work at the universal scale. Gutkind believes that demographic growth is leading to the total utilization of all the world's resources, and that the increase of communications and commercial linkages is fostering a synthesis of civilizations. These factors conspire against the partition of the earth into national "cells." It behooves architects and planners to organize the trans-scalar, spatial consequences this world unification entails. In fact, some signs of the phenomenon can already be perceived and have to be addressed. Power and economic relations are being rebalanced, fostering the development of hitherto economically disadvantaged countries and the loss of relevance of Western powers. The differences between town and countryside are tending to disappear. New settlements are appearing to facilitate interchanges along transportation corridors, seaports, and national frontiers.[2]

"Universal Planning" sets Gutkind's conceptual agenda for the following two decades. During the war, he directs the United Kingdom's Demographic Survey and Plan.[3] As a result of this experience, in 1943 he publishes the book *Creative Demobilisation: Principles of National Planning*. The text focuses on national planning and considers this scale nothing less than a piece within a broader strategy of world planning, one in which a "shrinking world" is "administered as one coherent unit."[4] Gutkind's subsequent works directly address this global scale, both through research and theoretical and design speculations. The two examples this article analyzes, his studies about colonization and the book *The Expanding Environment: The End of Cities, the Rise of Communities*, epitomize, respectively, each of these intellectual quests.

Gutkind publishes the studies "La colonizzazione del Nord America," "La colonizzazione dell'Africa," and "La colonizzazione dell'Australia" (The col-

1. Erwin Anton Gutkind, "Universal Planning," *Building* (UK) 11, no. 2 (February 1936): 70.

2. Gutkind, "Universal Planning," 70.

3. Stephen Grabow, "The Outsider in Retrospect: E. A. Gutkind," *Journal of the American Institute of Planners* 41, no. 3 (1975): 201.

4. Erwin Anton Gutkind, *Creative Demobilisation* (London: K. Paul, Trench, Trubner & Co., 1943), ix.

onization of North America, The colonization of Africa, and The colonization of Australia, respectively) in the Italian journal *Urbanistica* in 1951 and 1952. Together, they form a consistent investigation of Gutkind's concept of a shrinking world. By studying the evolution of the forms of territorial organization of these continents from the moment of their colonization by Europeans, Gutkind explores to what extent their progressive integration within global economic circuits has led to the complete utilization of their territory. As stated in the African case, the research stops in the 1950s, when the whole continent "can be considered as discovered, and the weight of occidental civilization can be felt along the vast expanses of its entire territory."[5] The articles study global commercial relations, city development, and the productive use of the territory as correlated phenomena, which eventually lead to a situation of maximum territorial integration. In this latter stage, so-called expansion is no longer possible, because there isn't any undiscovered territory to explore. The only possible actuation is spatial intensification.[6]

This move from expansion to intensification is the very aim that planning should pursue. Gutkind criticizes the historic, colonialist processes of world integration. He understands that these processes are initiated in Europe, and that they strictly pursue the interests of the Western world. Yet, his intention is to show that the spatial effects of colonization make possible internal regional development through the intensification of territorial uses via planning. Africa, a continent where the process of decolonization has yet to start, is the most eloquent example of this approach. For Gutkind, colonial development has created the conditions to take the continent definitely out from the "myopia" of the European interests that still dominate Africa in 1950.[7] Colonization has intentionally created a territorial structure in which "singular territories are still relatively isolated and independent between themselves, because of a lack of a systematic integration in vaster units."[8] To reverse this situation, what Africa needs is an internal, "coherent effort for the elaboration of a systematic long-term plan that takes the whole continent as an organic unit."[9] The path to decolonization is African integration.

In the studies on colonization, Gutkind employs three main research tools—historical analysis, cartography, and aerial imagery. Together they constitute the basis for the integrative plan that this architect envisages. In his writings, the notion of colonization encompasses the complex of territorial transformations

5. Erwin Anton Gutkind, "La colonizzazione dell'Africa," *Urbanistica* 9 (1952): 5.

6. Erwin Anton Gutkind, "Pianificazione nazionale in un mondo che si restringe," *Urbanistica* 4 (1950): 10.

7. Gutkind, "La colonizzazione dell'Africa," 34.

8. Gutkind, "La colonizzazione dell'Africa," 34.

9. Gutkind, "La colonizzazione dell'Africa," 34.

that affect the continents, while urbanization refers strictly to town development. The cartographic analyses show the intermingling of these two terms by presenting the spatial conditions their co-evolution generate: the growth of urban footprint and transportation infrastructures, the distribution of the primary and secondary economic sectors, the expansion of agricultural land, and the process of deforestation are studied simultaneously. Such maps support Gutkind's analysis of the successive structures of territorial organization, as well as his observations about the continents' possible spatial restructuring **[figs. 0, 1, and 2]**. The aerial imagery complements these analyses by revealing how the marks of territorial structures are visible across all of the continental surface. Gutkind later emphasizes this human influence on a global scale in his 1952 work *The World from the Air*, a book that joins Paul-Henri Chombart de Lauwe's *La Découverte aérienne du monde* (1948), and the MoMA exhibition *Airways to Peace* (1943) in a post–World War II epochal consideration of aviation as a means of territorial analysis and global integration **[projects 16 and 14]**.[10]

The book *The Expanding Environment* summarizes two articles written for *Urbanistica*: "Pianificazione nazionale in un mondo che si restringe" (National planning in a shrinking world,) and "Comunità in un mondo senza stati" (Community in a world without states.)[11] Gutkind explains in the book which should be the spatial conditions of a world that has become unified. One central question structures his argument: both the State and the city need to disappear. Both are incapable of playing any significant role between the two poles that have to be reconciled in this new situation of world integration: the individual and the totality. For Gutkind, the individual needs to organize significant life environments, but the State and the city hinder this possibility, as their scale is too big, fixed, and abstract. They are "anachronisms" derived from extinct socioeconomic conditions.[12] To substitute them, he proposes a radically decentralized urban structure of small communities. His model is not the garden city or similar forms of urban deconcentration, which preserve existing urban hierarchies. Gutkind completely abolishes cities. The whole territory is occupied throughout by small communities associated with each other in a single, interconnected entity; a sort of literal preconfiguration of Marshall McLuhan's notion of global village.[13]

**10.** Paul Henry Chombart de Lauwe, *La découverte aérienne du monde* (Paris: Horizons de France, 1948), and Wendell L. Willkie, "Airways to Peace," *Bulletin of the Museum of Modern Art* 11, no. 1 (1943): 3–21.

**11.** Gutkind, "Pianificazione nazionale in un mondo che si restringe," 18–33, and "Comunità in un mondo senza stati," *Urbanistica* 6 (1950): 18–32.

**12.** Erwin Anton Gutkind, *The Expanding Environment; the End of Cities, the Rise of Communities* (London: Freedom Press, 1953), 14.

**13.** Grabow, "The Outsider in Retrospect," 210.

Gutkind's theory has a strong cosmological component. The title of his book references "The Expanding Universe," a text where the English astronomer Arthur Edington explains the theory of cosmic expansion.[14] In an argument similar to the one Rudolf Schwarz develops in *Von der Bebauung der Erde* (The cultivation of the earth), Gutkind understands that existing urban systems of metropolis and satellite cities mirror a Copernican conception of the world, and that they do not correspond to our life in a center-less universe **[project 16]**. To assume this cosmic condition implies realizing that "all regional delimitations are artificial," and that the scale of the urban systems should be generated, and constantly reconfigured, through the association of communities, and not be imposed by pre-established territorial or political boundaries.[15] Consequently, Gutkind insists that it is not possible to draw a plan of his proposal, and he only offers graphic glimpses of how it would modify our existing world **[figs. 3 to 6]**.[16] Lacking a design, he focuses on defining the main principles guiding a possible new spatial organization. The principle of "New Scale" refers to the transition from communities to world, the "dissemination of new seeds all over the country" to create a system "totally different from any form and structure of settlement which we know from the past."[17] The "New Mobility" requires abandoning thinking of "the structure of settlement as consisting of innumerable fixed points," and imagining instead a changing "network of distances" that supports the movement of "men, immaterial and material goods."[18] The "New Purpose" is an ecological principle that substitutes the exploitation and control of nature by human adaptation to it.[19] Lastly, the "New Oneness" is the result of the previous three principles: the synthesis of communities and nature in a new entity that includes the entire territory.[20] Seen together, Gutkind's system of thinking appears as an attempt to reconcile the dialectical poles of Maurice François Rouge's rationality and Schwarz's geophysical poetics.

Despite his reluctance to offer a plan and his criticism of the State, Gutkind is, above all, a supporter of planning. The German sociologist Karl Mannheim publishes Gutkind's *Creative Demobilisation*, and the text fully embraces the notion of "planning for freedom" that Mannheim had previously proposed.[21] As Manheim does, Gutkind maintains that *laissez-faire* politics have to be counteracted by expanding the powers of centralized planning. Yet, in Gutkind's view, the plan has to focus strictly on spatial organization in order to create a framework for individual freedom.[22] The critical reception of these ideas is fundamentally limited to the two countries where Gutkind publish-

**14.** Gutkind, *The Expanding Environment*, 36.

**15.** Gutkind, *The Expanding Environment*, 38.

**16.** Gutkind, *The Expanding Environment*, 61.

**17.** Gutkind, *The Expanding Environment*, 38.

**18.** Gutkind, *The Expanding Environment*, 39–40.

**19.** Gutkind, *The Expanding Environment*, 55.

**20.** Gutkind, *The Expanding Environment*, 58–60.

**21.** Karl Mannheim, *Man and Society in an Age of Reconstruction* (London: Kegan Paul, Trench, Trubner & Co., 1940).

**22.** Gutkind, "Pianificazione nazionale in un mondo che si restringe," 10, and Herbert Read, in Gutkind, *Creative Demobilisation*, x.

23. Aldo Rossi, "Nuovi Problemi," in *Scritti scelti sull'architettura e la città 1956–1972*, ed. Aldo Rossi and Rosado Bonicalzi (Milan: Clup, 1989 [1975]), 190. Vittorio Gregotti, *Il Territorio dell'architettura* (Milan: Feltrinelli, 2008 [1966]), 63 and 96.

es his work—namely, Italy and the UK—and it revolves around his praise of planning, decentralization, and the human occupation of landscape. In Italy, his theories are severely dismissed by Aldo Rossi, when considering which can be the urban structures that respond to the expansion of urbanization, and partly by Vittorio Gregotti, when reflecting upon the tools and the ideologies through which architects can visualize the landscape.[23] In the United Kingdom, his work is more positively engaged, as it lies behind the discussions about the man-made landscape that pervade the English architectural debate during the early 1950s, and which help to investigate the architectural responses to a situation of complete urbanization **[project 18]**.

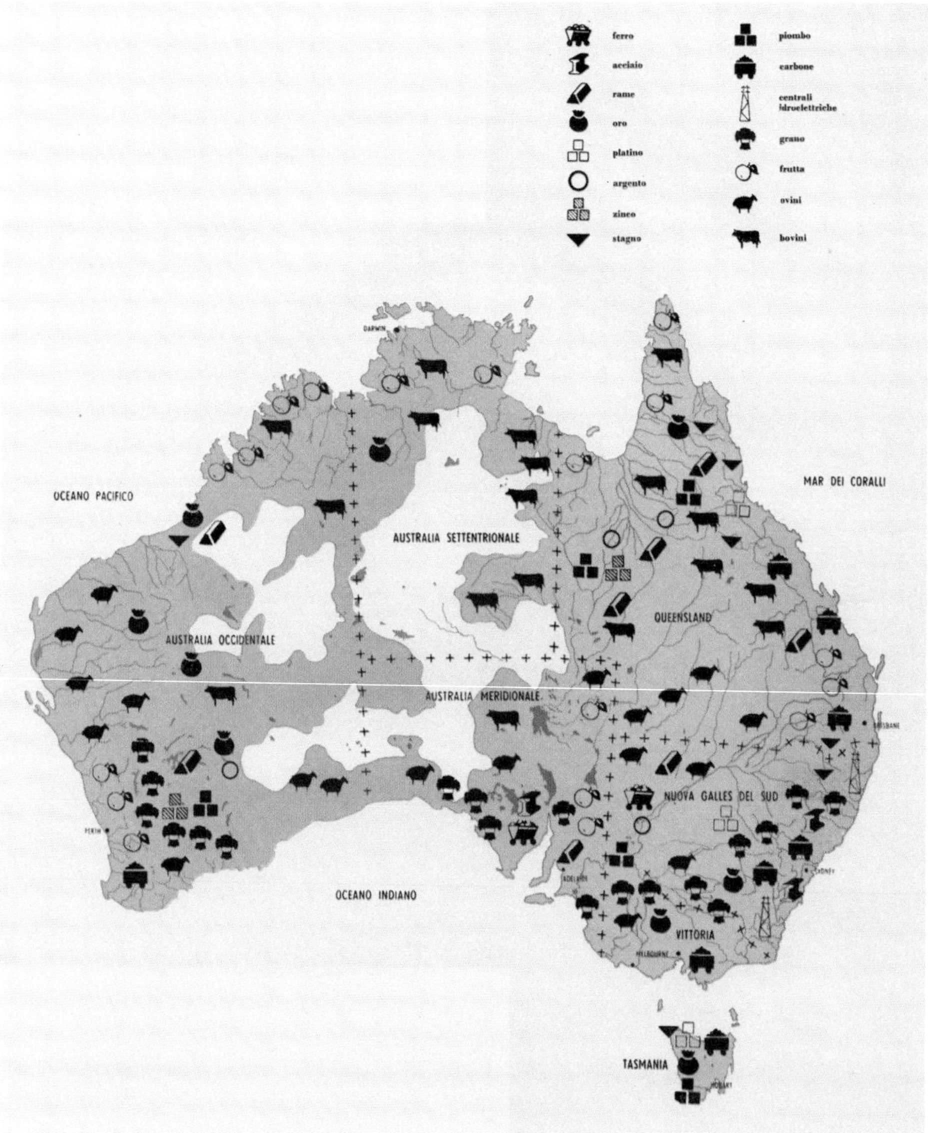


**Figure 1.** Distribution of natural resources and main centers of production in Australia. 1952.

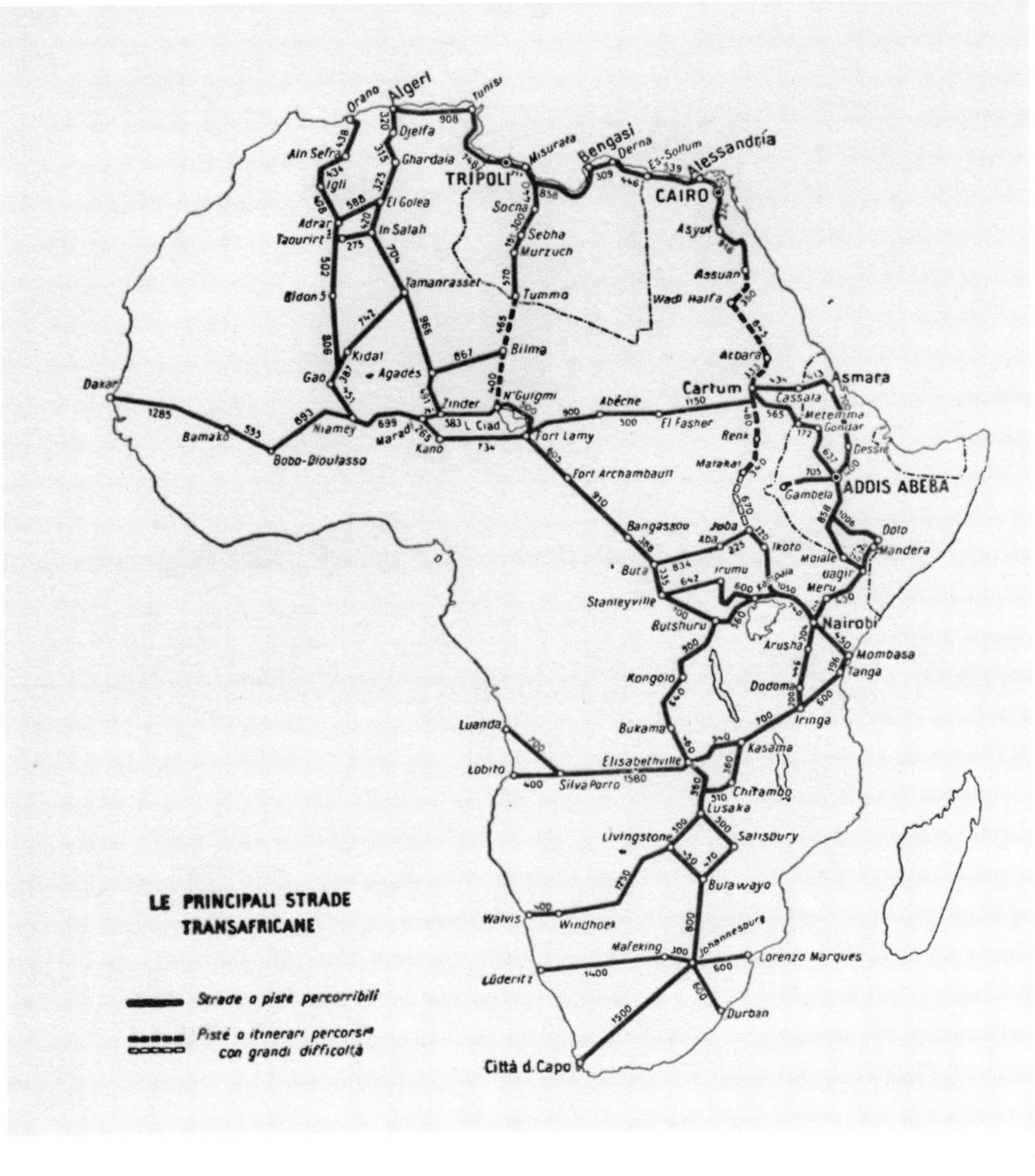


Figure 2. The principal trans-African roads. 1952.

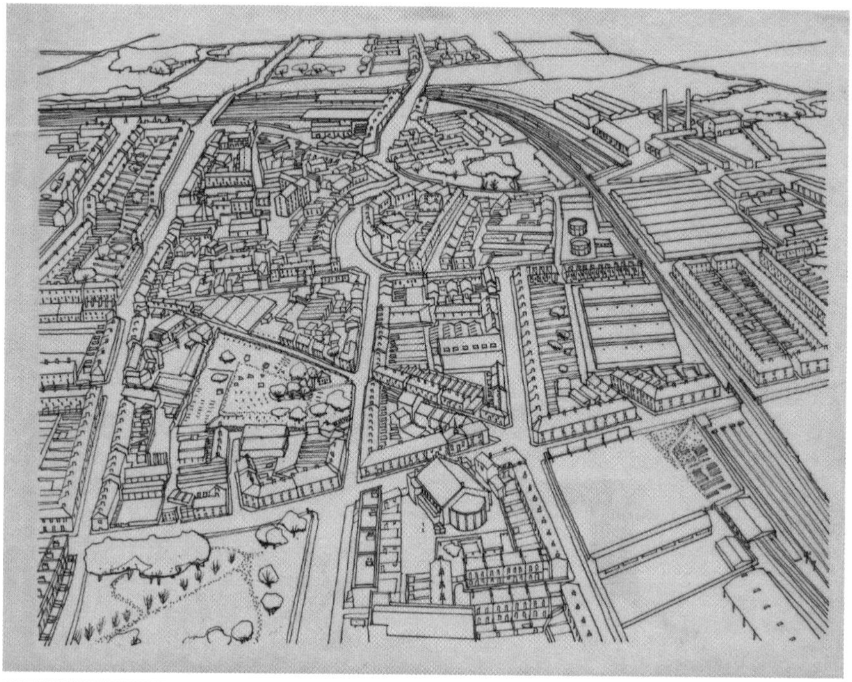

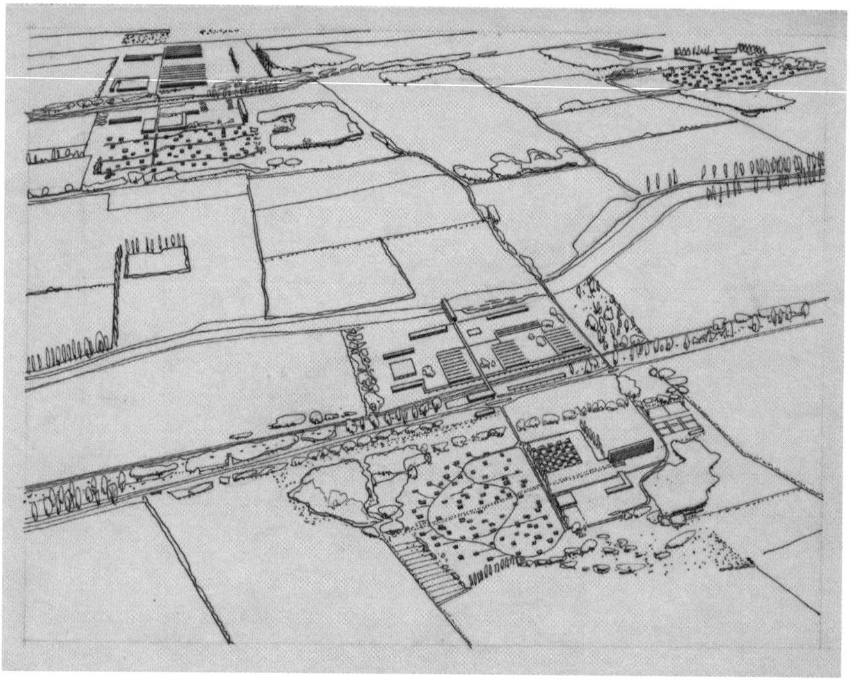

**Figure 3 (Top).** Large fragments. Contracting environment. Rigidity and regimentation. 1953.
**Figure 4 (Bottom).** Small units. Expanding environment. Vitality and openness. Unity by diversity. The continuous park. Social center. Re-creation. Social awareness. Industry and agriculture. Culture: the whole environment. 1953.

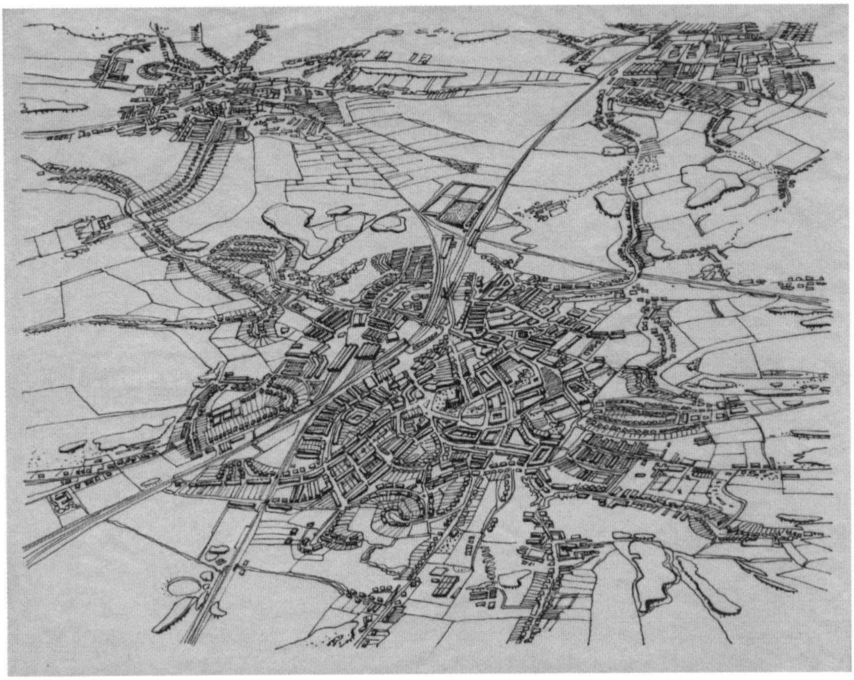

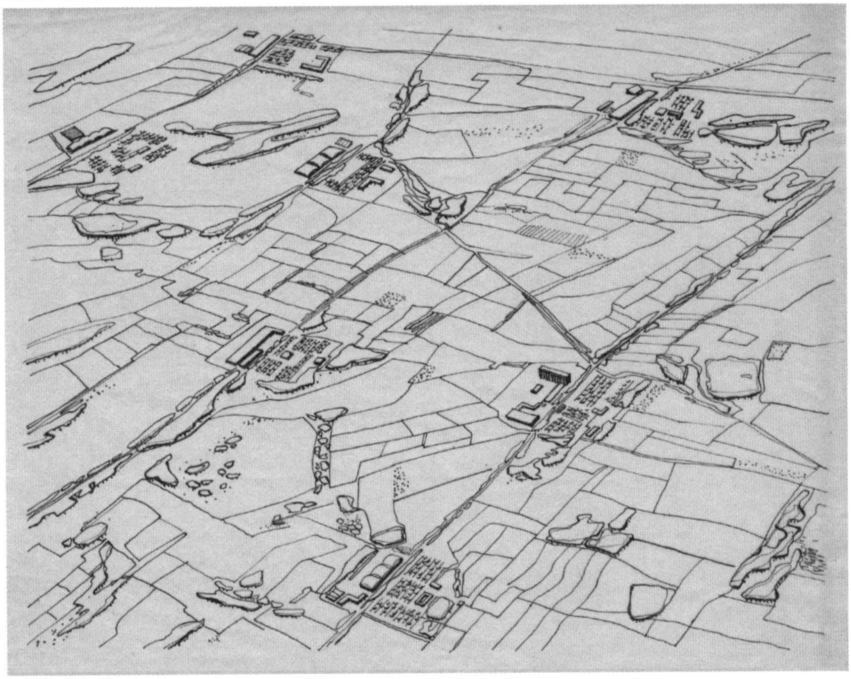

**Figure 5 (Top).** Antagonism of town and country. Landscape tolerated. Imperfect decentralization. Hierarchy of localities. The monster with tentacles. Social stratification. 1953.
**Figure 6 (Bottom).** One living area. Landscape omnipresent. Perfect dispersal. Equality of communities. The loose cluster. Social affinity. Cultural ubiquitousness. Industrial isolation. Rural integration. 1953.

# Berlin Hauptstadt – Ecological Table

**Project:** 18. **Authors:** Alison Smithson (1928–1993) and Peter Smithson (1923–2003). **Date:** 1957. **Themes:** Ecology. Parallelism. Infrastructures. Telecommunications.

**Figure 0.** Berlin Hauptstadt, Spree river and railroad. After Alison and Peter Smithson. 1957.

**1.** Alison and Peter Smithson, *Urban Re-Identification*, in *Ordinariness and Light: Urban Theories 1952-1960 and Their Application in a Building Project 1963-1970* (London: Faber, 1970), 21.

**2.** Smithson and Smithson, *Urban Re-Identification*, 58.

**3.** Already at this point, the Smithsons start to be interested in understanding local patterns, and thus in particularization. See Peter Smithson, "The Slow Growth of Another Sensibility. Architecture as Town Building," in *A Continuing Experiment: Learning and Teaching at the Architectural Association*, ed. James Gowan (London: Architectural Association, 1975), 58.

**4.** See Aneurin Bevan's quote in Smithson and Smithson, *Urban Re-Identification*, 19.

**5.** Kingsley Davis, "The Origin and Growth of Urbanization in the World," *American Journal of Sociology* 5 (1955): 429-437.

**6.** Ian Nairn, ed., "Outrage," *Architectural Review* 117 (1955) and "Outrage 2," *Architectural Review* 120 (1956); Erwin Anton Gutkind, *The Expanding Environment; the End of Cities, the Rise of Communities* (London: Freedom Press, 1953), and Erwin Anton Gutkind, *Our World from the Air: An International Survey of Man and His Environment* (Garden City, NY: Doubleday, 1952).

The 1957 competition entry for Berlin Hauptstadt caps the research that Alison and Peter Smithson initiate with their designs for the Golden Lane building and the Golden Lane Study (1952–1953). In this five-year period, the architects seek a new formal system, "ordered, but not geometric," to serve as a radical alternative to the forms of architecture, urbanism, and territorial order of early modernity.[1] They relate the formal attributes of this new system to contemporary developments in art. In their early manifesto, *Urban Re-Identification* (1953), the description of Jackson Pollock's work—"It is more like a natural phenomenon, a manifestation rather than an artifact; complex, timeless, n-dimensional and multi-evocative"—is a declaration of the qualities that the Smithsons are trying to achieve: the conflation of artifice and nature, the overlay of contrasting forms, complexity.[2] By exploring these formal conditions, the couple does not intend to generate a single world project. Without a doubt, the architects would harshly condemn any ambitions to design or plan the globe.[3] What the Smithsons do is to explore the repercussions that the ongoing consolidation of the world scale might have on architecture and urbanism and to investigate how to express this scale. Berlin Hauptstadt is the most accomplished representation of this search [**figs. 0 and 1**].

The key conceptual questions the Smithsons address in Berlin Hauptstadt are initially formulated in *Urban Re-Identification*. Supporting their argument with lengthy quotes from *In Place of Fear* (1952) by Labour Party politician Aneurin Bevan, the Smithsons claim that architecture has to intervene in a historic situation where humanity ceases to be a "product" of nature in order to become a result of urban society.[4] Bevan is not alone in detecting this epochal change. The intensification of urbanization at the world scale that demographer Kingsley Davis starts to chart in 1955 is a central concern of the intellectual milieu that surrounds the Smithsons.[5] In 1950, Canadian architect Christopher Tunnard publishes in the British journal *Architectural Review* his first analyses of the total urbanization of the United States, a work that will eventually lead to the writing of *Man-Made America*, and which influences the 1955 issue of *Architectural Review* devoted to the urbanization of the UK, edited by Ian Nairn.[6] Some of the images included in *Urban Re-Identification* are taken from *Our World from the Air: An International Survey of Man and His Environment* by Erwin Anton Gutkind, who at the time is initiating his studies about continental territorial structures and divulging his credo of worldwide urban decentralization [**project 17**]. The Smithsons adopt a singular perspective toward these ideas of generalized urbanization. On one hand, they treat the urbanization of society and the emergence of the world scale as converging phenomena, both resulting from *longue-durée* processes of transformation initiated with the Industrial Revolution. On the other, they consider positively the new scalar relations between architecture, city, territory, and world that this situation can produce: "We are faced with scale changes consonant with the internal combustion engine, with road and air transport. The internal combustion engine has created the world city and the world city scale. We are in truth being asked to make human a new vastness! . . . Railways and canals cutting uncompromisingly through countryside and town follow their own laws and extend our sense of location beyond the region to whole continents. Today the international airlines tracking high over our heads on invisible roads locate us in a network of world relationships."[7]

These claims are entirely coincidental with the vision of territorial order that Le Corbusier exposes in *The Four Routes* **[project 15]**. Yet, for the Smithsons, the postwar regime of trans-scalar relations requires abandoning the search for spatial isolation and architectural autonomy that the Swiss architect had influentially preconized. For them, the work of Le Corbusier, epitomized in his Unité d'Habitation, represents a monastic ideal of isolated life, happening in buildings distinctively separated from their physical contexts, which the postwar context of generalized infrastructural connectivity has definitively rendered obsolete. In their view, intervening territorially implies abolishing the separation of architecture from the other elements that articulate the territory, and questioning the distinction between natural and artificial. Their work consequently seeks to express the novel importance of communications and to hybridize architecture with infrastructures and physical geography in order to build an architectural equivalent to the physicality of the land.[8]

The aesthetic sensibility through which the Smithsons approach the idea of generalized urbanization aligns in all these ways with the discourse of the Independent Group, the collective they participated in with critics Reyner Banham and Lawrence Alloway, and artists Nigel Henderson, Eduardo Paolozzi, Richard Hamilton, and John McHale, Fuller's collaborator since 1963 **[project 14]**. While the Independent Group is mostly acknowledged for its early interest in pop culture and mass media, its members' works are, more ambitiously, articulated around the sociospatial consequences of technology. *On Growth and Form,* an exhibition Hamilton and Henderson organized in 1951 that marks the beginning of the activities of the group, advances the Smithsons' interest

**7.** Smithson and Smithson, *Urban Re-Identification*, 63.

**8.** Smithson and Smithson, *Urban Re-Identification*, 68.

in the amalgam of natural and artificial by proposing a "socio-biological synthesis."[9] The exhibition, named after the eponymous book of Scottish biologist D'Arcy Wentworth Thompson, resignifies nature as the driver of artistic production, but, rejecting any romanticism, advocates for an approach to nature constructed through the mechanisms of vision and reproduction of science and technology.[10] Another exhibition, *Man, Machine, Motion*, takes to an extreme the Smithsons' interest in communications by depicting how the world is totally circumscribed by means of transportation **[fig. 2]**.[11] Here, curator Richard Hamilton displays pictures of terrestrial, oceanic, aerial, and interplanetary infrastructures and vehicles on the floor, walls, and ceilings of the exhibition room, revealing the three-dimensional, vertical articulation of the world environment that the architects depict in their "Ecological Table" and in Berlin Hauptstadt.

The "Ecological Table" is a small diagram that guides the Smithsons' approach toward world communications and the hybridization of nature and culture **[fig. 3]**. The notion of "ecology" appears in the Smithsons' work as a result of their active and polemical participation in the 1950s CIAM debates, which famously result in the dissolution of the organization in 1956 after its tenth congress, and in the consolidation of Team X.[12] These CIAM debates are already a clear attempt to reposition the discipline vis-à-vis the territorial expansion of the urban. Le Corbusier proposes to articulate CIAM 9 and 10 around the notion of "habitat" with the intention of establishing a new vocabulary for the spatial organization of the world after the Second World War. In this moment, he observes, the word "urbanism," which he used as the title of his first book, has lost its operative value.[13] The Smithsons respond to this challenge by rearticulating their discourse around the notion of "ecology," a term that reflects their desire to treat simultaneously urbanization and nature. Yet, in interrogating what ecology could mean for architects, the Smithsons detect two divergent paths, which they will try to reconcile. One of them is captured by their notion of "ecological field" and by the redrawing of Patrick Geddes's Valley Section that Peter Smithson traces to illustrate it **[project 2]**.[14] "Ecology" is here used as a tool to particularize geographic areas, and thus to guide design toward the construction of local singularities. In opposition to this notion, the Smithsons reconceptualize as an "Ecological Table" the schema of the vertical stratification, from ground to sky, of infrastructures, land uses, and facilities, which they had initially elaborated in *Urban Re-identification*. This table is the Smithsons' global template. It serves as the generic basis for designing a territorial model

**9.** Victoria Walsh, "Seahorses, Grids and Calypso: Richard Hamilton's Exhibition Making in the 1950s," in *Richard Hamilton*, ed. Vicente Todoli (London: Tate Publishing, 2014), 61–75.

**10.** D'Arcy Wentworth Thompson, *On Growth and Form* (Cambridge, UK: Cambridge University Press, 1917).

**11.** The exhibition was organized in 1955 by Banham and Hamilton. See Anne Massey, *The Independent Group: Modernism and Mass Culture in Britain, 1945–59* (Manchester: Manchester University Press, 1995), 81–84.

**12.** There was a CIAM 11 in Otterlo, Netherlands, organized without the contribution of the organization's founding members.

**13.** Le Corbusier's first treatise about urbanism, titled in English *The City of To-morrow and Its Planning*, is originally simply *Urbanisme*. For Le Corbusier's observations about the lack of relevance of the term urbanism after World War II, see Eric Mumford, *The CIAM Discourse on Urbanism, 1928–1960* (Cambridge, MA: MIT Press, 2000), 218.

**14.** Alison and Peter Smithson, *The Emergence of Team 10 out of C.I.A.M.: Documents* (London: Architectural Association, 1983).

that expresses and makes operative a sense of connectedness to the world at large. As a textual grid, the table does not prescribe forms. Instead, it synthesizes the world structure into a system of relations. Considered as an instrument of world-making, the table establishes a nonformal guideline, which has to be expressed and grounded through the particular operations of the architectural project in each location.[15]

Berlin Hauptstadt represents how to implement the Ecological Table. It is a project that creates a system of sectional relations between ground, land uses, and means of transport, and which results in the transformation of architecture into a piece of geography and infrastructure. The project operates as a landform, formally and dimensionally equated to the Spree River, the highways, and the railroad lines. The irregular grid of elevated, pedestrian platforms that occupies the historic center of Berlin adopts the elevation of the Friedrichstrasse railroad station and links the latter to the Anhalter railroad station and the heliport designed for Mehringplatz. Below this platform, creating punctual, intermodal points of connection, runs a system of regional highways. The core of the project is thus a network of local, regional, and transnational connections. The communications are not only physical. At the head of the project, the Smithsons place a center of communications for radio, press, and television, making explicit their understanding that global society is also constructed by mass media.[16] Finally, by treating the city as part of a broader territorial system, Berlin Hauptstadt inverts the modern understanding of urban centrality. The "Chinese Wall of Offices and Wholesale Houses," which they propose to surround the project, preserves the center of Berlin as an empty void. The ground is maintained free as a landscape. Instead of a dense, and inhabited center, Berlin Hauptstadt is a space of transits, punctuated by commercial and office buildings used only temporally.

The center of Berlin thus becomes a place that one always approaches from outside it, only to be redirected again toward the outside of the city. The section that defines the entire project emphasizes this fact by limiting visual directions to just two possibilities. The opaque handrail that delimits the pedestrian platforms has fenestrations that direct the view from this elevated level to the circulation of vehicles in the highways below. The top edge of the handrail, at eye level, situates, in turn, the flat landscape of Berlin region as the constant horizon of the project **[fig. 4]**. The Smithsons' approach to territoriality concludes by subverting the ideals of interiority and seclusion that, in their view, prewar modernity pursued. The subjects who access Berlin Hauptstadt are al-

**15.** See for instance: "People know about things more, therefore is more the feeling of connectedness rather than the feeling of being in villages which is self-contained, and which as you know perfectly well, ideas are communicated by press, television, radio and so on, advertising, which knits practically the whole world into a net of relationship where people understand each other, and in this sort of situation it seems to me that to think of the image of the city as being a series of self-contained communities, or the new town being a self-contained self-generating entity is that this net of communications we know exists must find expression in the architecture. The word 'expression' is a key one, but one tends to fight shy of it. We are interested in expressing not ourselves, but what is going on and building which denies what is going on is just the opposite of brutalism . . ." Peter Smithson, "Conversation on Brutalism," *Zodiac* 4 (1959): 76.

**16.** Ben Highmore, "Streets in the Air: Alison and Peter Smithson's Doorstep Philosophy," in *Neo-Avant-Garde and Postmodern: Postwar Architecture in Britain and Beyond*, ed. Mark Crinson and Claire Zimmerman (New Haven: Yale Center for British Art, 2010), 79–100.

17. Reyner Banham, *Megastructure: Urban Futures of the Recent Past* (New York: Harper and Row, 1976), 44.

ways outside, placed against geography, amid flows of transport, as fleeting as the messages mass media transmit.

With Berlin Hauptstadt, the Smithsons show how to construct an artificial, sectional ecology that, merging architecture, geography, and infrastructures, expresses a new scale of global relations. From 1957 on, the architects will relegate the central themes of this research in favor of exploring the contextual particularities of the "ecological fields." Certainly, part of the preoccupation that characterizes the Smithsons' initial work will continue in the megastructural movement **[project 35]**.[17] Yet, the power of Berlin Hauptstadt and the "Ecological Table" lies in their condition of counter-model to the megastructural desire to integrate every possible system in a unitary artifact. Contrary to this megastructural dream, the "Ecological Table" individuates and distinguishes the elements that can construct a world system. Berlin Hauptstadt formalizes the relations between these elements *and* preserves their singularity. It is an "n-dimensional," layered project characterized by mismatches and displacements, where multiple scales and systems converge, each with its unique formal expression. Similarly, the project contradicts the interest in absolute interiority that characterizes the megastructural movement. Berlin Hauptstadt's emphasis on formal complexity and exteriority reflects the Smithsons' critical understanding of modern urbanism as a system incapable of treating the urban as a multi-layered world system made by infrastructures, telecommunications, nature, and buildings. While the architects abandoned this research about the world scale, the effects of their critique remained. After the dissolution of CIAM, the Greek Constantinos Doxiadis decides to create a new international conference, the Delos Symposia, strictly concerned with the urbanization of the world **[project 23]**.

**Figure 1.** Berlin Hauptstadt perspective, competition entry. 1957.

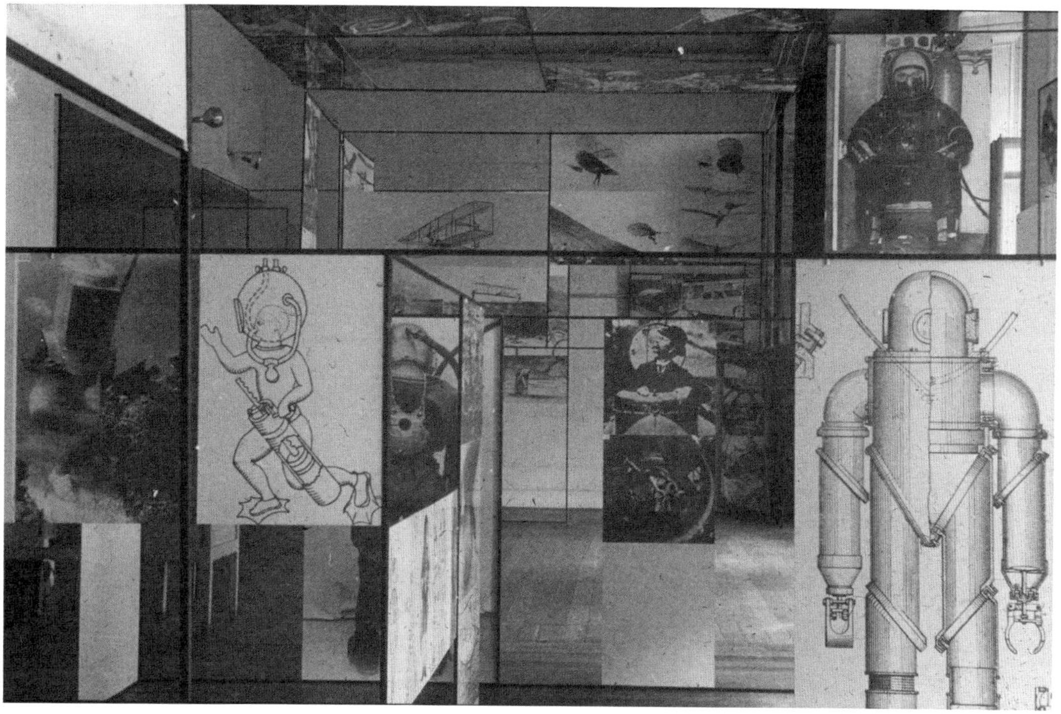

**Figure 2.** Man, Machine, Motion Exhibition, Hatton Gallery. Richard Hamilton. 1955.

## ECOLOGICAL TABLE

| GROUND | | SPACE | |
|---|---|---|---|
| Parks, green, and market gardens<br><br>Horizontal industry<br><br>Places of assembly and ceremonia<br>Shopping | | Those things that are necessary to the life of the street:---<br>Workshops<br>Offices<br>Hotels<br>Public terraces | |
| Road | interchanges<br>service stations<br>transit storage stations | Street | parking<br>all pedestrians<br>hand vehicles |
| Rail | sidings<br>goods yards | Space | new lifts |
| Air | major airfields | Air | helicopters<br>hoppycopters |
| Water | rivers<br>canals<br>estuaries, docks | | |

**Figure 3.** Ecological Table. 1952–1967.

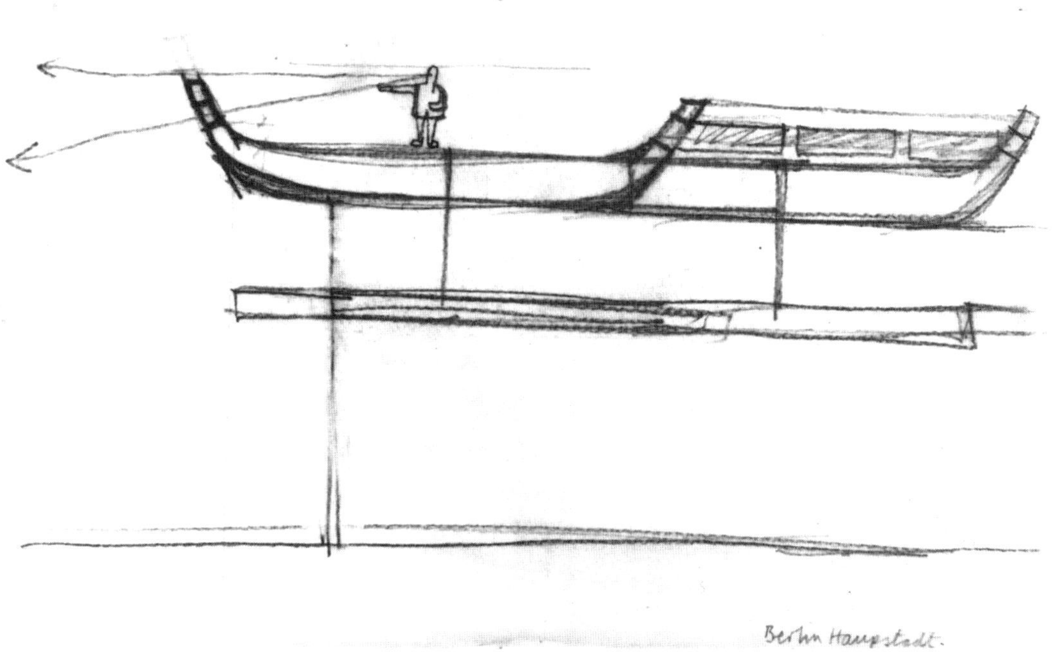


**Figure 4.** Berlin Hauptstadt section. 1957.

# New Babylon

**Project:** 19. **Author:** Constant Nieuwenhuys (1920–2005). **Date:** 1957–1974. **Themes:** Automation. Interiorization. Nomadism. Parallelism.

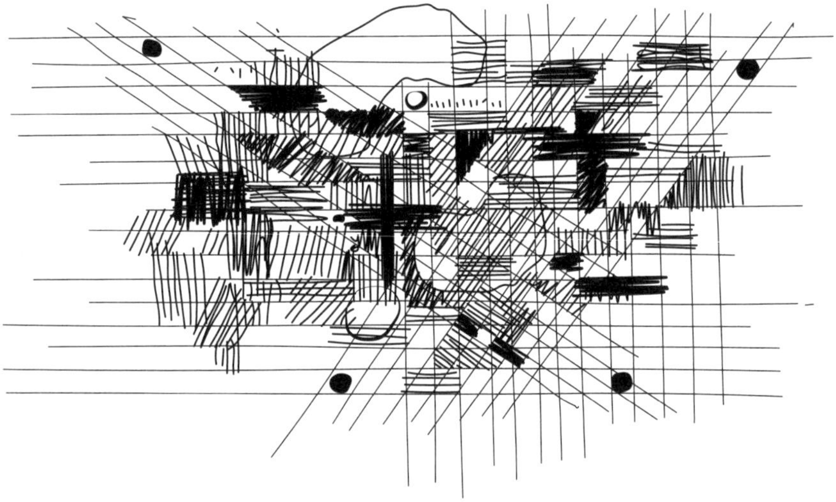

**Figure 0.** Principle of a covered city. After Constant. 1959.

According to Constant Nieuwenhuys, New Babylon continues and reformulates the technological and political ethos of early twentieth-century constructivism **[projects 9 and 10]**. Like the Soviet constructivists, Constant believes that it is possible to create a universal formal language based on the logics of technology **[fig. 0]**.[1] Yet, he also criticizes the privilege of work as the driving force for reorganizing social relations and artistic production, which he believes characterized constructivism, and proposes to replace it with the ideas of human play and creativity derived from sociologist Johan Huizinga's concept of *homo ludens*.[2] Famously described by its architect as "a camp for nomads in a planetary scale," New Babylon acts as the armature for a society of extremely mobile individuals who no longer need to work thanks to radical advances in automation and cybernetics.[3] The liberation from work generates a surplus of time, which allows humans to dedicate their entire lives to social interchange and creative enterprises free of utilitarian concerns. The result is a society in perpetual change whose physical manifestation consists in the incessant production of new and different spaces.

Constant's descriptions present the project as a paroxysm of creation. Nothing in New Babylon is fixed. The activities and words of individuals produce chain reactions among other subjects. Changes in the form of space and in the forms of inhabiting it follow one another with vertiginous speed.[4] The project's most palpable paradox lies in the contradiction between these ideas of change and Constant's necessity to formalize the project as a framework for imagining humanity's future. While he works on the project for more than fifteen years, defining many, almost obsessive, variations of a fixed set of spatial leitmotifs, his texts insist on the tentative character of the work. Every image of New Babylon is a snapshot of a potential, still unknown sociospatial transformation: "New Babylon is the world of the New Babylonians alone, the product of their culture. For us, it is only a model of reflection and play."[5] New Babylon's multiple visualizations are thus an enactment of the creative form of life the project proposes, more than its actual physical form.

As a result, the process of reflection Constant seeks to trigger does not depend so much on the specific conditions of each of the countless visualizations of the project—including hundreds of paintings, architectural models, photographs, maps, sketches, and some technical drawings—as on their overwhelming multiplicity and their organization. There are three structuring levels in Constant's

**1.** About Constant's position toward constructivism, see Constant, "About the Meaning of Construction" [1966], in Mark Wigley, *Constant's New Babylon: The Hyper-Architecture of Desire* (Rotterdam: 010 Publishers, 1998), 174. He also sustains political positions about earth structuring that are close to constructivism. See Constant, "A Few Propositions Concerning the Concepts 'Face of The Earth,' 'Urban Development,' And 'Art'" [1971], in Wigley, *Constant's New Babylon*, 209. His whole movement from painting to architecture is related to an appreciation of the technical dimension of society that he borrows from Sigfried Giedion's *Mechanization Takes Command: A Contribution to Anonymous History* (1948). See Constant, "From Collaboration to Absolute Unity among the Plastic Arts" [1955], in Wigley, *Constant's New Babylon*, 75.

**2.** Interestingly, Constant also emphasizes that the inhabitants of New Babylon will not distinguish between art and non-art. A similar belief structured also the Proletkult ideology that informed 1920s Soviet constructivism [projects 9 and 10].

**3.** Constant, "New Babylon, een schets voor een cultuur," in *New Babylon*, ed. Hans Locher (The Hague: Haags Gemeentemuseum, 1974). Quoted in Wigley, *Constant's New Babylon*, 13.

**4.** Constant, "New Babylon. Outline of a Culture" [1960–1965], in Wigley, *Constant's New Babylon*, 160.

**5.** Constant, "New Babylon. Outline of a Culture," 165.

work, each of them referring to a certain scalar condition. First, there are representations of the project's interior, mostly in paintings **[fig. 1]**. These show vaguely defined spaces with imprecise contours, which reflect the absolute substitution of nature for an internal, completely artificial environment.[6] Second, there are representations of individual buildings, denominated "sectors." These constitute New Babylon's primordial cell, its "micro-scale." Constant predominantly presents them through technical models that are then photographed in close-up views, giving a very fragmentary vision of the project **[fig. 2]**. New Babylon is never shown as a complete entity, thus creating the impression that it constitutes a complex reality that can never be fully grasped and totalized. Finally, New Babylon's "macro-scale" consists of the aggregation of sectors. While each sector constitutes an autonomous unit elevated over the existing ground, "as independent as possible from the viewpoint of their construction," its connection to others generates a potentially planetary network.[7] This possibility appears in maps that overlay New Babylon on top of European cities and regions: Amsterdam, Paris, Barcelona, the Ruhr Region. On all of them, New Babylon is interrupted by the limits of the map. We see only a part of a system that can be extended worldwide, although it emanates from Europe **[fig. 3]**.

In fact, New Babylon is extremely connected to the debates about urban society affecting European architectural discourse in the postwar era. Thanks to his friend the architect Aldo Van Eyck, Constant is familiar with the Team X's work, whose influence is evident in New Babylon's elevation from the ground and in the project's insistence on the ideas of network, growth, and change **[project 18]**.[8] Similarly, Constant is for a time in contact with Yona Friedman and participates in the *Groupe d'Études d'Architecture Mobile*, which Friedman promotes **[project 24]**. Yet, among these intellectual relations, the crucial influence on New Babylon comes from Constant's relation, both personal and intellectual, with Guy Debord, the leading figure of the Situationist International (SI), and with the philosopher Henri Lefebvre.

Constant starts New Babylon after meeting Debord. In 1956 he attends the First Congress of Free Artists organized by The International Movement for an Imaginist Bauhaus. At this Congress he establishes contact with Debord's collective of the moment, the Lettrist International, and becomes interested in the notion of "unitary urbanism" that the group is proposing. Shortly after, Debord promotes the creation of the SI, and Constant joins the group. From that moment on, the idea of unitary urbanism will become crucial in Constant's thought. The concept of unitary urbanism is a critical tool for the SI.

**6.** Constant, "Lecture at the Institute of Contemporary Arts, London (1963)," in Laura Stamps et al., *Constant: New Babylon: To Us, Liberty* (Ostfildern: Hatje Cantz, 2016), 212.

**7.** Constant, "New Babylon. Outline of a Culture," 165.

**8.** For the relations between Constant and other contemporary architects see Wigley, *Constant's New Babylon*, 28–48.

9. Ken Knabb, *Situationist International Anthology* (Berkeley, CA: Bureau of Public Secrets, 1995), 50, "Unitary Urbanism at the End of the 1950s," *Internationale Situationniste* 3 (December 1959).

10. Laura Stamps, "Constant's New Babylon: Pushing the Zeitgeist to Its Limits," in Stamps et al., *Constant: New Babylon. To Us, Liberty*, 15.

11. Henri Lefebvre, *The Production of Space* (Oxford: Blackwell, 1991 [1974]).

12. Benjamin Buchloch and Constant, "A Conversation with Constant," in *The Activist Drawing: Retracing Situationist Architectures from Constant's New Babylon to Beyond*, ed. M. Catherine de Zegher and Mark Wigley (New York: Drawing Center, 2001), 25. Łukasz Stanek, *Henri Lefebvre on Space: Architecture, Urban Research, and the Production of Theory* (Minneapolis: University of Minnesota Press, 2011), 229.

13. Constant, "New Babylon–Ten Years On" [1980], in Wigley, *Constant's New Babylon*. Quoted in Stanek, *Henri Lefebvre on Space*, 222.

It offers an alternative to modern urban planning, itself condemned by the SI as a fundamental arm of the system of social coercion modern capitalism imposes. Strongly resonating with Constant's vision of architecture as an art integrating other types of creation, unitary urbanism promotes producing total ambiances that are thought of as enabling interactive processes where new spatial configurations transform existing codes of behavior, which in turn, transform space. To substantiate unitary urbanism, the SI promotes acting on physical space through drifts (*dérives*) across a city devoid of particular purposes besides that of permitting oneself disoriented encounters with the urban conditions along the way. By drifting, individuals become active agents of production and transformation of space, not passive receptors of conditions defined by the architectural status quo.[9] When Debord suggests the name New Babylon to Constant, it is because the project accurately reflects the group's aims to challenge the modes of living and using space that dominate the West. "New Babylon," Debord thinks, is "loaded with suggestions of human recklessness, non-Christian morals, unprecedented prosperity, and fantastic forms of life . . ."[10]

While Constant terminates his relation with the SI in 1961, considering individuals as agents of spatial production will continue determining New Babylon. In fact, the other theorist in contact with Constant, Henri Lefebvre, praises the project precisely for being a utopian vision of a new type of urban process, in which inhabitants are active creators of the space they live in. The dialogue with Lefebvre also brings other spatial concepts that support Constant's evolution from the SI's postulates. Lefebvre's theorization of "social space," that is, the idea that space is not fixed but constantly influenced by other spheres of social action, is crucial for New Babylon. Similarly, Lefebvre's desire to produce a "differential space" that can recover the unity of lived, conceived, and perceived space against the fragmentation of these spheres produced by modern capital also resonates with Constant's goals.[11] Finally, as historian Łukasz Stanek observes, the major difference between Constant and Situationist thinking—New Babylon's intervention in the territorial scale—announces Lefebvre's theorization of scale.[12] "Unlike other Situationists," Constant claims, "New Babylon proposes not to limit unitary urbanism to the production of 'micro-scales' or 'ambiances'" because these alone cannot alter the existing "macro-structure."[13] What is thus necessary, as Lefebvre asserts in his mid-1970s writings, is to challenge the understanding of scale as a predetermined condition and to imagine new scalar territorial configurations that replace the existing ones.

Constant's interest in constructing a macro-structure is thus a step toward suggesting a broader sociospatial alternative to capitalism than the one Situationist spatial strategies can articulate.[14] Following Stanek's analysis, New Babylon's three-tiered scalar organization enables Constant to think how new scalar relations can be produced, while acknowledging the fractures and tensions there may be between them.[15] The sectors are socially and spatially autonomous entities, which can be built independently. Their articulation in bigger ensembles superimposed on the European geography shows the level of precision with which Constant thought about the project, and the new conditions it creates. The organization of the network responds to specific contextual constraints: the contour of rivers and infrastructures, the free spaces between cities, the places where agglomerations are denser.[16] While the dramatic geometric contrast between the elevated project and the underlying cities and landscapes points to a radical critique of existing space, the accuracy of New Babylon's maps make evident that Constant is seeking a transformation that responds to the actual physical conditions of the spaces in which the project intervenes. Conceived at a moment when a rapid process of spatial reconstruction and transformation is altering European cities, New Babylon suggests a new type of urbanity. It links disparate neighborhoods and different social classes. It inverts the relationships between center and periphery, creating a vaster urban scale. It generates original territorial formations by organizing regional ensembles. It points to a transnational spatial structure where multiple cities are brought together through a single network that entirely abolishes the existing hierarchies among countries.

The structure of the envisioned transnational network is rhizomatic, although New Babylon predates Gilles Deleuze and Félix Guattari's introduction of this concept.[17] Constant is extremely attuned to the idea of emergent phenomena that characterizes Deleuze and Guattari's thinking. His descriptions of chains of spatial transformations suggest the unfolding of a series of events, one after another with immense celerity, thanks to the power of new means of communication. New Babylon is the spatial parallel of a society entirely transformed by cybernetics and communications, always mutating, where interpersonal interchanges play a paramount role. In it, social hierarchies disappear because of a more egalitarian, socialist-oriented, economic system, but also because the absence of work produces a new social mass, where the individuality of its nomad subjects is inseparable, maybe indistinguishable, from broader phenomena of collective communication. Constant sees this as a utopian planetary prom-

**14.** Constant is very explicit about his goals of social transformation: "Let us be consciously imaginary architects, since we know well that only social transformation and radical political transformation can create the basis for actual work . . . for revolution." Buchloh and Constant, "A Conversation with Constant," 25.

**15.** Stanek, *Henri Lefebvre on Space*, 224.

**16.** Stanek, *Henri Lefebvre on Space*, 228.

**17.** Gilles Deleuze and Félix Guattari, *A Thousand Plateaus: Capitalism and Schizophrenia* (Minneapolis: University of Minnesota Press, 1984 [1980]).

ise. Today, it suggests conditions of mobile, deterritorialized existence that are becoming more and more palpable. Devoid of utopian character, the emergence of these often precarious forms of life is currently compatible with the preservation of the territorial power of the nation-state. Constant challenges this reconciliation between new forms of subjectivity and existing social forms. For him, new conditions of life should transform our political and territorial structures. Correspondingly, New Babylon marks a potentially global horizon that completely abolishes national frontiers. The drawings recognize that such a possibility depends on technological conditions that, when the project is conceived, only exist in the West. As a rhizomatic project that suggests a possible model in evolution, and not a fixed state, Constant's maps represent New Babylon where he thought the project could emerge and most polemically operate: in technologically advanced Europe. From there it would spread, creating the conditions of a world society still to come. His position thus follows a line of thinking that, from Karl Marx to Antonio Gramsci and to Lefebvre, sustains that social transformation can only emanate from a reappropriation and subversion of the very modes of production that it needs to overcome.[18]

Unsurprisingly, the utopian promise starts vanishing after 1969—one year after the events of May '68 in France. From then on Constant returns to painting. The same scenes that he once pictured with hope or joy, now become themes of aggression and despair, as in *Massacre* **[fig. 4]**.[19] Nude bodies in blood, marks of violence, and destruction fill the atmosphere of the technological labyrinth in which people were supposed to play and enjoy getting lost. Nomadism is no longer safe nor positive.[20] New Babylon is washed away by the rough persistence of a society that resituates the changes of modes of existence within the spatial and political structures of the past, and where architecture, Constant realizes, "can neither dictate nor design . . . playful or inventive behavior."[21]

**18.** Stanek, *Henri Lefebvre on Space*, 166.

**19.** Mark Wigley, "Extreme Hospitality," in Stamps et al., *Constant: New Babylon. To Us, Liberty*, 39.

**20.** Laura Stamps, "New Babylon–Destruction and Confusion," in Stamps et al., *Constant: New Babylon. To Us, Liberty*, 190.

**21.** Constant, "New Babylon–Ten Years On," 224.

**Figure 1.** The Blue Daredevil. 1969.

**Figure 2.** Model of New Babylon. Detail Yellow sector. 1961.

**Figure 3.** Symbolic Representation of New Babylon. 1969.

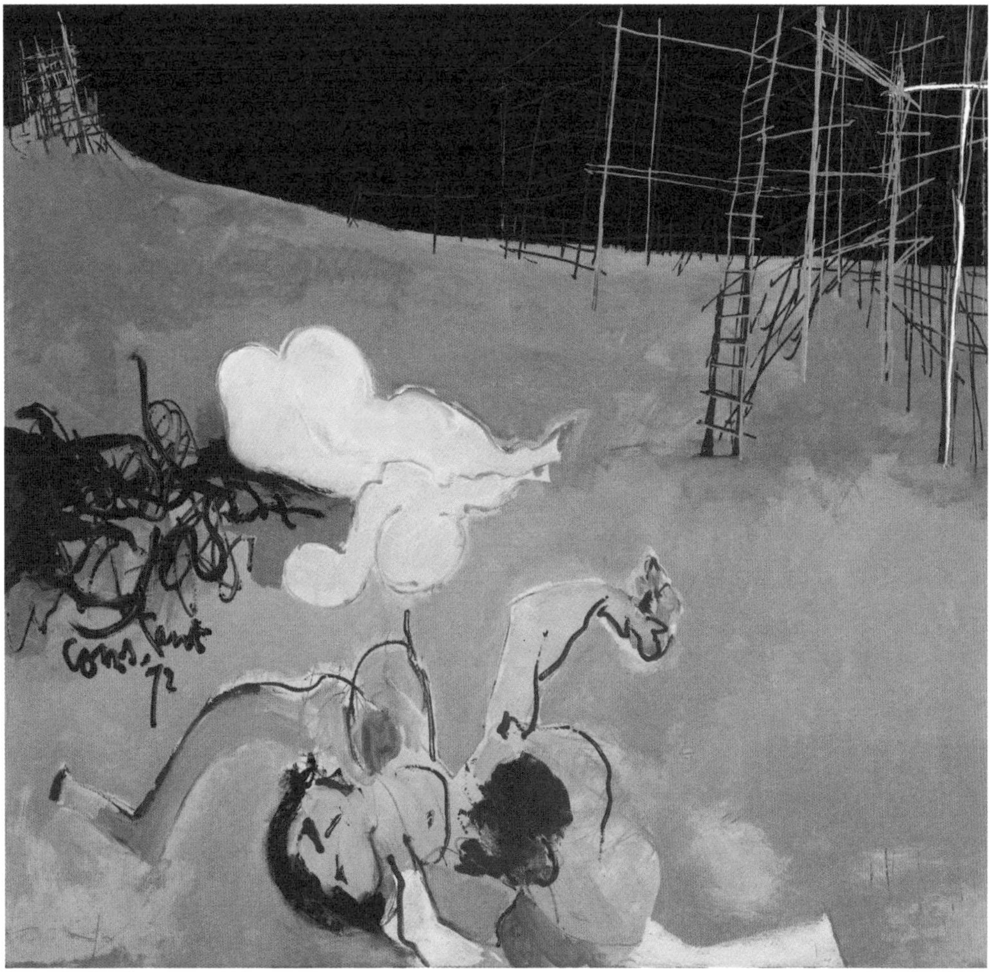

**Figure 4.** Massacre of My Laij. 1972.

# Новый элемент расселения (НЭР)
## The New Unit of Settlement (NUS)

**Project:** 20. **Authors:** Alexei Gutnov (1937–1986), A. Baburov, G. Djumenton, S. Kharitonova, I. Lezava, and S. Sadovskij.
**Date:** 1957–1968. **Themes:** Cybernetics. Decentralization. Geography. Total Urbanization.

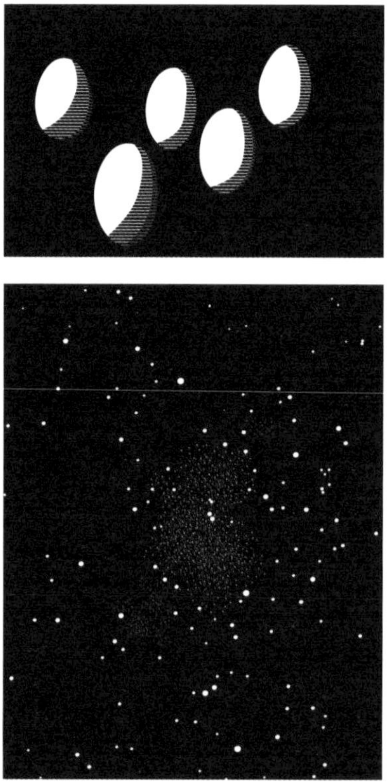

**Figure 0.** Continuity and discontinuity: two contradictory features linked indissolubly together, and found generally in natural, social, and mental phenomena. After Alexei Gutnov et al. 1966.

The New Unit of Settlement (NUS), or *Novyj Ėlement Rasselenija* (NER) in Russian, is the central piece of the urban system designed by a team of young Russian architects, led by Alexei Gutnov, from 1957 to 1968.[1] Originally part of their common diploma thesis at the Moscow Institute of Architecture, the group's research on urban systems expands until the publication in 1966 of the book *NER: Po sledam goroda budushchego* (NER, Tracing the Future City), which portrays how to create a regional urban system by linking autonomous and independent cells, each dedicated to specific uses **[fig. 0 and 1]**. Later translated into Italian (1968), and into English (1971) as *The Ideal Communist City*, the work of Gutnov and his team seeks to define an ideal urban schema.[2] Profiting from the climate of intellectual and ideological debate that follows Joseph Stalin's death in 1953, the NUS team wants to define an alternative to the forms of urban planning that had become hegemonic in the USSR during his three decade long presidency.[3] In fact, the team's critique of the urban *status quo* goes hand in hand with a desire to recuperate the avant-garde tradition of speculative thinking about architecture and urbanism that disappeared in the 1930s.[4] As the 1920s avant-garde projects did, the NUS also establishes a new model for urbanization to eventually replace the existing ones altogether. As the authors state: "The goal is to transform the whole planet into a unified sociological environment."[5] For them, "NUS represents an attempt to involve the thought and imagination of the architect on a global scale, outside of which the search for the new is impossible."[6]

In his preface to the Italian edition of the book, Giancarlo de Carlo avers that the NUS proposal encourages "world-wide urbanization," and thus abandons the naturalistic ideologies of assimilation of the city to the countryside that had dominated urban planning since the nineteenth century.[7] Certainly, the architects understand the emergence in the postwar era of "gigantic urban centers" as the preamble to an even bigger wave of urbanization, and support their proposal with demographic projections that estimate a 75 percent increase in urban population by the year 2000.[8] The proposal is then an anticipatory mechanism to address this immense level of urbanization and the technical and social transformations that will accompany it. Substantively, the authors envision the technological improvement of productive systems and a corresponding trend toward automatization, and they conclude from these trends that it is necessary to conceive unified urban environments that are able to rationalize the "interdependence of the different environmental elements."[9] The authors

**1.** The activities of the NER collective expand, though, until 1977. See Program of the International Scientific Symposium "Tracing the Future City," Graduate School of Urbanism of the Faculty of Urban and Regional Development, Moscow. December 20–22, 2018. Unpaged. Accessed online January 24, 2019: https://urban.hse.ru/en/ner_programme/

**2.** Alexei Gutnov et al., *Idee per la città comunista* (Milan: Il Saggiatore, 1968); and Alexei Gutnov et al., *The Ideal Communist City*, trans. Renee Neu Watkins (New York: George Braziller, 1971), respectively.

**3.** Masha Panteleyeva, "Alexei Gutnov, the NER Group ('New Element of Settlement') and Giancarlo De Carlo." Accessed online May 17, 2018: http://radical-pedagogies.com/search-cases/e06-moscow-institute-architecture-triennale-milano/.

**4.** In fact, the authors even recuperate some of the typological elements that were at the core of the Soviet avant-garde proposals, such as the workers' club, which, as in Ivan Leonidov's design, is also a club for "Cultural and Scientific Projects" [project 9]. See Gutnov et al., *The Ideal Communist City*, 90–94.

**5.** Gutnov et al., *The Ideal Communist City*, 101.

**6.** Gutnov et al., *The Ideal Communist City*, 166.

**7.** Giancarlo de Carlo, "Preface," in Gutnov et al., *The Ideal Communist City*, ix. For a contemporary Italian critique of the naturalist ideologies of the city see Antonio Monestiroli, "La città come avventura della conoscenza. Architettura e teoria dell'architettura nella città dell'Illuminismo," in *L'Architettura della realtà* (Turin: Umberto Allemani & Co., 1979), 139–175.

**8.** Gutnov et al., *The Ideal Communist City*, 7–8.

**9.** Gutnov et al., *The Ideal Communist City*, 105.

seek to translate this rationalization of space into their design methods: they see social and productive relations as translatable material into information and data, which must support, through cybernetic analysis, the process of design. This appeal to scientific, data-driven methodology, which the authors actually do not take up in their design process, is in any case strictly oriented toward the rationalization of space. For the team, systematization is the precondition of an opposing trend toward personal freedom and creativity, where individuals can engage in new forms of creative work and benefit from abundant leisure time.[10]

As it corresponds to a project for an essentially urban world, agriculture is a sector that lacks structuring importance in the proposal. For the architects, the expected improvement of cultivation techniques makes agriculture independent of geographic conditions, and thus a productive activity that can be undertaken anywhere. The urban system they conceive operates then as a functionally integrated regional complex that joins housing and the full cycle of material production: from material extraction, to manufacturing, to investigation, as well as to spaces for agriculture. This attention to the spatial requirements of production, which derives from the authors' Marxist understanding that the organization of the environment results from considering the "sum of productive forces and relations of production," is mirrored by the definition of the spaces for social reproduction **[fig. 2]**.[11] In fact, the term "NUS" itself refers to the latter function. Within the overall regional system, the NUS is predominantly a residential sector conceived as the "quantum" of urbanization. Each is a cell of limited size, for a population of between one hundred and two hundred thousand people, organized in linear or concentric form—although, without a doubt, the authors consider that the latter is easier to apply worldwide.[12] The value of this cell is to maintain a settlement size that permits intense forms of collective relations. The NUS gives rise to a form of urban organization in which cells appear progressively, according to the new demographic and functional needs, located without a pre-established overall order. In this sense, the schema maintains a dialectical relation with the overall regional urban system. The whole is thought of integrally in order to systematize productive relations. The NUS, on the other hand, acts as an independent and autonomous element; one that admits evolutionary processes of appearance or extinction. The constant repetition of its units allows one to maintain the formal cohesion of all of the urban system but without defining, a priori, how it must be globally structured.

**10.** For a contemporary treatment of the same topics, see the proposals of Constant, and of Yves Klein with Claude Parent, in this book [projects 19 and 22].

**11.** Gutnov et al., *The Ideal Communist City*, 23.

**12.** Gutnov et al., *The Ideal Communist City*, 23.

As a result, Gutnov and his team generate a flexible regional urban system. They create a polynuclear, "dynamic," "web-like" framework that integrates the full metabolism of material production on a regional scale.[13] In a first sense, the mechanism through which this proposal may operate at the world scale is replication, although the limitation of the formal decisions to the dimension and shape in plan of each NUS unit would lead, eventually, to multiple, variable forms of regional organization. In this manner, the NUS is more a method of settlement than a form. This idea of a method of settlement consisting of the construction of autonomous, self-sustainable units is presented as a strategic form of infiltration in, and modification of, the existing conditions of urbanization around the world. By indicating how the NUS can be implemented in large metropolitan regions, small cities, and agricultural areas, the architects aim to demonstrate the capacity of their system to progressively modify the whole environmental spectrum, gradually substituting existing conditions for the new ones **[fig. 3]**.[14]

With this logic, the NUS addresses the world scale through the definition of regional relations and systems. This position has two main corollaries. The first is that, instead of a disurbanist idea of total occupation of territory, the NUS organizes limited, regional complexes as unified urban systems **[project 10]**.[15] The second is that the authors do not consider any type of scalar relations that may go beyond the regional scale—there is no metalevel of global conditions that affect the urban system in any way. This lack of attention to the world at a functional level is replaced by a consideration of physical geography as a reference for architectural design. As Giancarlo de Carlo observes, the project creates a productive dialectical tension between nature and settlements. In it, the limitation in size and form of each unit is a way to put them in direct contact with the natural landscape. Every unit is seen as a unique architectural complex, with a dimension of formal definition that dialogues with the scale of geography **[fig. 4]**. Gutnov and his team approach not only the rhetoric about flexible and dynamic urban systems that is being developed simultaneously in the West, but also the interest in a new, geographic scale of architectural formalization **[projects 18 and 19]**.[16] This consideration of each unit as a formal entity is to situate architecture as the hinge between the world scale and the organization of regions, albeit this is an intuited, but unresolved, trans-scalar relation: "Whereas a single building was once perceived as a unique spatial composition, we are now ready to conceive a unified spatial field, which includes the entire community. The new tone and speed of life are forcing us to

**13.** Gutnov et al., *The Ideal Communist City*, 107.

**14.** Gutnov et al., *The Ideal Communist City*, 109–110.

**15.** In this sense, their proposal critically reacts to the work of contemporary Soviet geographers such as B. Khorev, G. Lappo, and P. Polyan who advocate for the organization of a network of large settlements areas, closer to megacities. See Program of the International Scientific Symposium "Tracing the Future City."

**16.** In addition to the speculation about a new scale of architectural production, the authors also consider other architectural possibilities contemplated in Europe and the US at the same time, such as environmental climatic control and the covering of cities with vast domes.

extend our concepts of unified space to a global scale. On that scale we visualize the nuclear configurations of NUS in organizing geographic and economic regions."[17]

The NUS team presents the project at the 1968 Triennale de Milano at the invitation of Giancarlo de Carlo. Broadly focused around "The Great Number," the Triennale contains sections devoted to the "macro-transformations of territory," and "the new visual perception of the urban environment." It includes the work of emerging architectural groups such as Archigram and the Japanese Metabolists **[projects 21 and 25]**. Two years later, the project is included in the Osaka Expo '70, an event that represents the apex of influence of the Metabolist group and which serves to congregate international architects concerned with globalization, territorial transformations, and the societal changes associated with urbanization, but who are approaching these themes with strategies that differ completely from the diagrammatic schemas of the NUS.[18]

A more pertinent comparison to the NUS is with the Pan-Urban Land Use System (or PLUS), which Colombian American architect Jorge Arango proposes in *The Urbanization of the Earth* (1970). Arango's text, published one year before the English translation of Gutnov's work, registers a similar preoccupation with the global trend toward urbanization and an equivalent questioning of the spatial repercussions of this phenomenon. For the author, the city is a residue of agrarian societies—and, thus, of a mode of production close to extinction—which will be superseded by the emergence of huge urban systems.[19] Just as the NUS, Arango presents the PLUS as a way to channel this process and to control its scalar consequences.[20] We see again the proposal of a monofunctional unit of limited size—in this case two square miles—conceived to preserve a sense of collectivity within the new urban space **[fig. 5]**. But here the similarities end. Arango's schema is conceived, explicitly, to be developed within the logics of competitive free markets, and it is in fact presented as the North American contribution to a new urban world.[21] Interestingly, the spatial translation of this position is an up-scaling of the speculative grid that constitutes the historic basis of the North American metropolis: in the PLUS, the overall urban system is nothing more than the unlimited repetition of this grid.[22] Moreover, Arango obliterates geography and environmental materiality, at every level. The proposal treats any form of material or agricultural production as external and entirely alienated from the urban system. Designed three years before the publication of Daniel Bell's influential *The Coming of Post-Industrial Society*, PLUS is an urban system exclusively conceived for the tertia-

**17.** Gutnov et al., *The Ideal Communist City*, 164.

**18.** Reyner Banham, *Megastructure: Urban Futures of the Recent Past* (London: Thames and Hudson, 1976), 102–103.

**19.** Arango sustains his project in a simplistic historical narrative, linearly developed, in which societies progressively abandon previous historical stages. In this conceptual schema, agriculture disappears, overcome by the coming of technological and scientific civilization. Jorge Arango, *The Urbanization of the Earth* (Boston: Beacon Press, 1970), vii–ix.

**20.** The PLUS is also, like the Soviet project, an instrument to substitute the existing urban conditions. Arango even estimates how much it would cost to replace existing cities with the PLUS. Arango, *The Urbanization of the Earth*, 159.

**21.** Arango, *The Urbanization of the Earth*, 175.

**22.** Manfredo Tafuri, *Architecture and Utopia: Design and Capitalist Development* (Cambridge, MA: MIT Press, 1976), 37–40.

ry sector. In this sense, despite the schematic development of both proposals, they do represent contrasting imaginaries of an urban world. The PLUS portrays a purely urban realm, understood as an entirely distinct stage compared to previous forms of production and environmental organization. The urban, the agricultural, and the natural are drastically divided spatial conditions, in a schema that subjects nature to the same operations of rationalization and spatial distribution that characterize the gridded urban system in the United States **[fig. 6]**.[23] The integral consideration of cycles of production in the NUS informs, instead, a vision that considers the natural environment as a part of the urban that has its own characteristics—a vision in which the natural is both a functional element integrated within the system and the geographical referent that reveals the very artificiality of the NUS.

**23.** The book contains a strong critique of conventional ecological thought for its anti-artificiality. The anti-naturalism that Giancarlo de Carlo detects in Gutnov is here extreme. For Arango, "the urban problems of today are not going to be solved by imitating the wilderness." In this sense, Arango argues for a total rationalization of nature within the PLUS. Arango, *The Urbanization of the Earth*, 93–95 and 159.

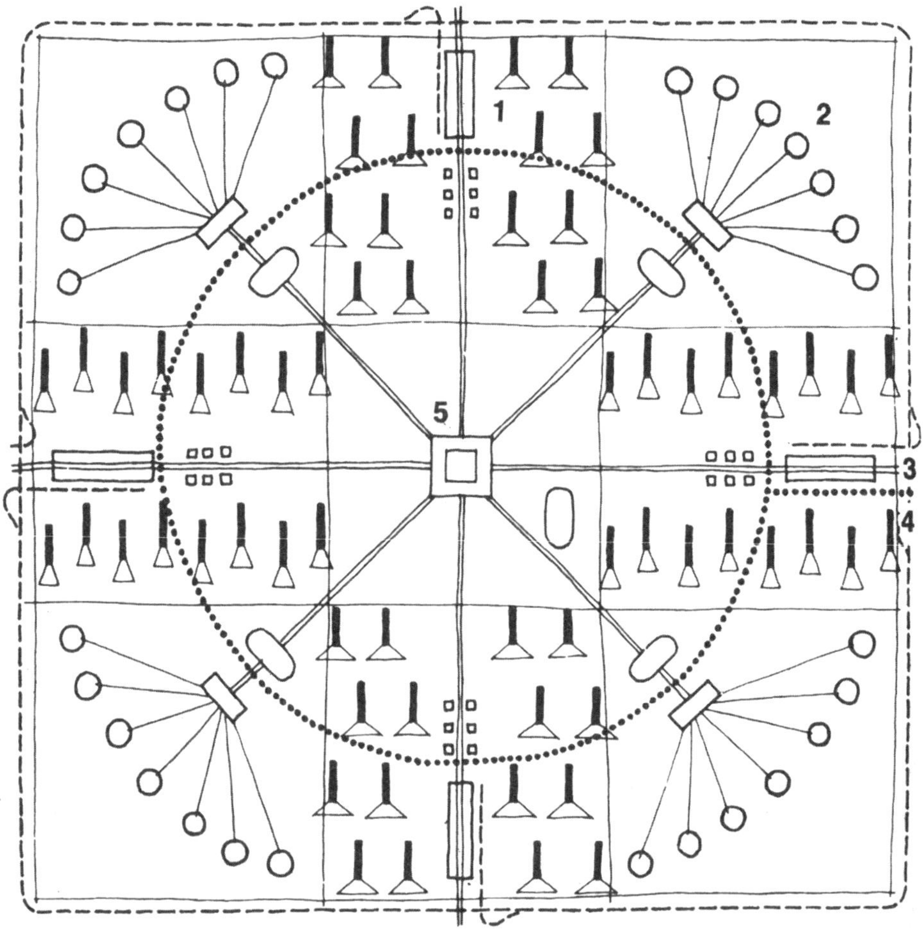


**Figure 1.** Diagram of NUS. 1: Residential units; 2: School and sports area; 3: Rapid transport above pedestrian level; 4: Highway; 5: Community center of NUS. 1966.

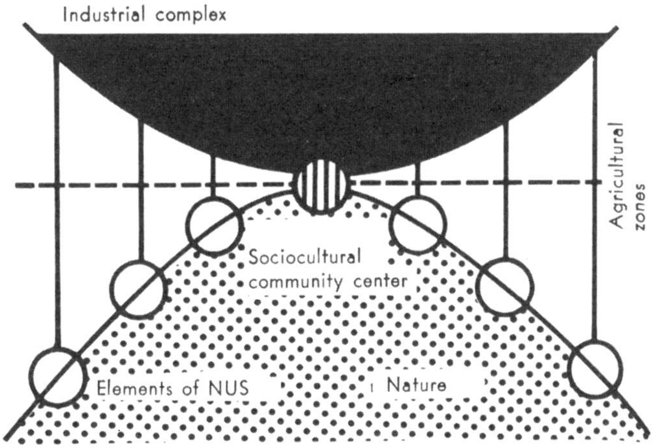


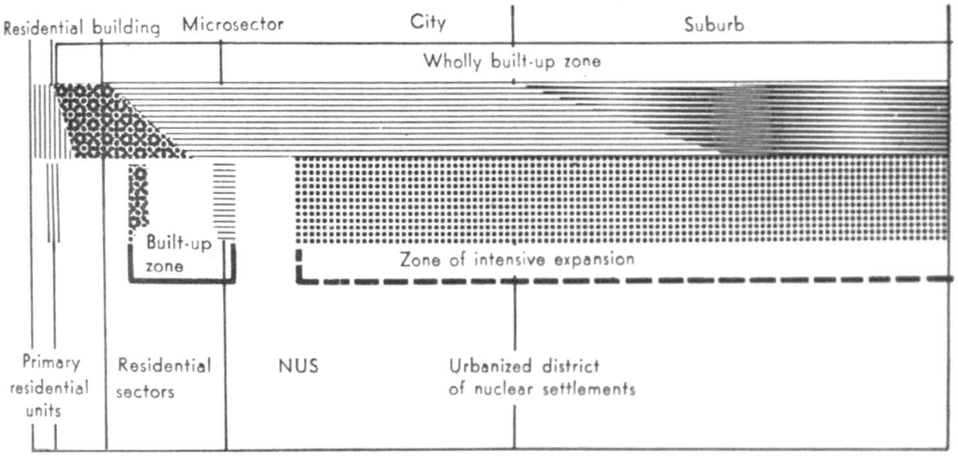


**Figure 2 (Top).** Diagram of group distribution in the urban environment. 1966.
**Figure 3 (Bottom).** Present and future structure of the urban environment. 1966.

**Figure 4.** The physical unity of the NUS. 1966.

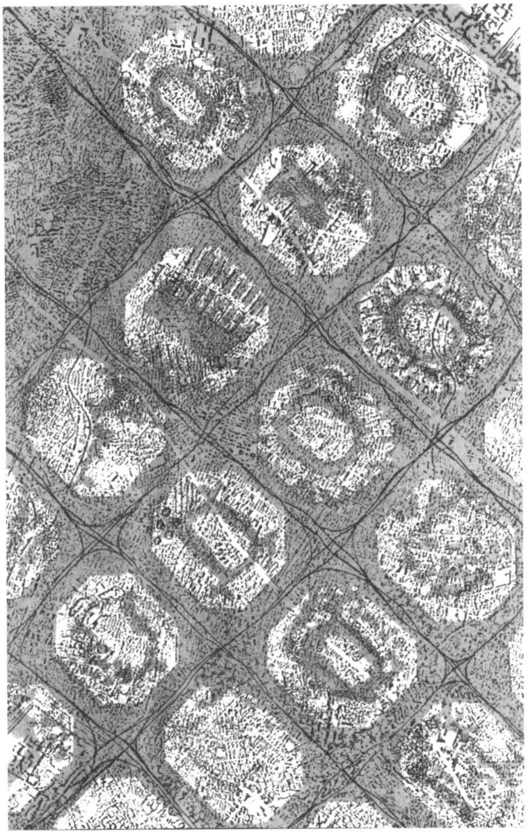

**Figure 5 (Left).** PLUS: Pan-Urban Land Use System. Plan. Jorge Arango. 1970.
**Figure 6 (Right).** View from a PLUS urban unit. Jorge Arango. 1970.

# 海上都市
# Marine Cities

**Project:** 21. **Author:** Kiyonori Kikutake (1928–2011). **Date:** 1958–1975. **Themes:** Automation. Human-Nature Split. Megastructure. Remoteness.

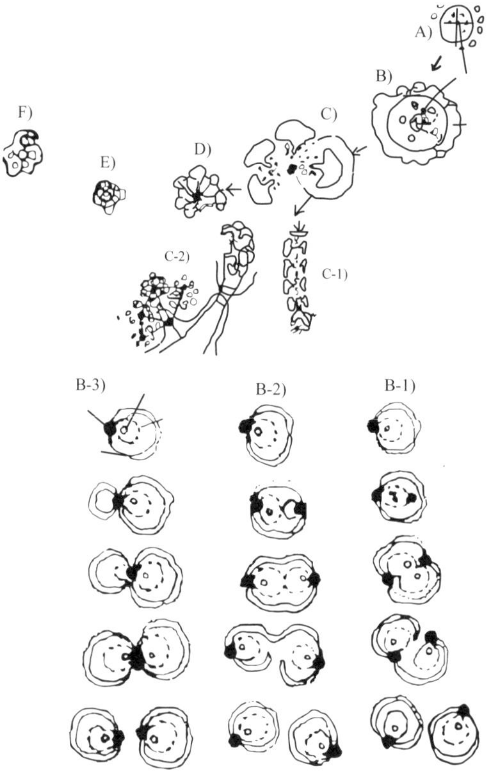


**Figure 0.** Interrelations among Marine City towers. After Kiyonori Kikutake. 1978.

"I want to be a bacterium. . . . In the future, man will fill the whole earth, and fly into the sky. I am a cell of bacteria that is in constant propagation. . . . There is no more individual consciousness, only the will of mankind as a whole."[1]

In 1960, architectural critic and theorist Noboru Kawazoe, alongside architect Kenzo Tange, brings together a group of young Japanese architects to speculate on designs for a possible coming future and inquire about the "unique qualities and ideas Japan could bring to the world."[2] Under the name Metabolism, the group, including architects Kiyonori Kikutake, Kisho Kurokawa, Masato Otaka, and Fumihiko Maki, and designers Kenji Ekuan and Kiyoshi Awazu, proposes that human society should be understood as a process of continuous development intrinsically dependent on, and resulting from, the progress of design and technology, which, in turn, emulates a biological logic of life, death, and constant renewal **[fig. 0]**. "From atom to nebula," both micro- and macrocosms are thought of as one single unit integrating man and its artificial built environment with nature.[3]

As the atom-to-nebula image illustrates, for the Metabolists it is crucial to address trans-scalar phenomena **[fig. 1]**. The relation between the local and the global and between the domesticity of Japan and its position in the world are at the center of their concerns. In the aftermath of WWII and during the American occupation, Japan is strictly closed, with restrictions ranging from external commerce to travel and mobility outside the country.[4] Reacting against this context, the team feels the need to own a place in the discourse of international architecture that can broaden and facilitate the movement of ideas between the West and Japan, if not an immediate physical displacement. In this sense, Metabolism, with Team X, can be seen within the history of architecture as one of the last cohesive movements seeking to address global development. It can also be seen as the first non-Western architectural movement truly impacting the international architectural scene.[5] For Kawazoe, it is a "theory originating from Japan but applicable to the world in general."[6]

Congruent with this understanding of the group's goals, from the very beginning the Metabolists participate in international architectural associations and conferences. The very first, albeit indirect and unofficial, exposure of the Metabolists' ideas takes place at the CIAM meeting at Otterlo (1959), led by Team X **[project 18]**. In the following decade, Tange and Maki occasionally attend the Delos symposia, which Constantinos Doxiadis organized **[project 23]**.[7]

1. Noboru Kawazoe, "Material and Man," in Noboru Kawazoe et al., *Metabolism: The Proposals for New Urbanism* (Tokyo: Bijutsu Shuppansha, 1960), 51.

2. Kiyonori Kikutake interviewed by Rem Koolhaas and Hans Ulrich Obrist, in Rem Koolhaas, Hans Ulrich Obrist, et al., *Project Japan: Metabolism Talks* (Cologne: Taschen, 2011), 135.

3. Kawazoe et al., *Metabolism: The Proposals for New Urbanism*, 3.

4. Meike Schalk, "Inventing a Culture of Resilience," *Arts* 3, no. 2 (2014): 283.

5. Arata Isozaki, "Foreword," in Zhongjie Lin, *Kenzo Tange and the Metabolist Movement: Urban Utopias of Modern Japan* (New York: Routledge, 2010), xiv.

6. Lin, *Kenzo Tange and the Metabolist Movement*, 20.

7. The presentation of two of Kikutake's projects preceded the group's formation. Tange, who was not a direct member of the group, presents the projects. James Steele, *Contemporary Japanese Architecture* (Abingdon: Routledge, 2017), 106. Yuriko Furuhata, "Architecture as Atmospheric Media: Tange Lab and Cybernetics," in *Media Theory in Japan*, ed. Marc Steinberg and Alexander Zahlten (Durham, NC: Duke University Press, 2017), 52-79.

Moreover, the formation of the Metabolist group itself takes place in the context of one of these international events: the World Design Conference (WoDeCo), which Japan hosts in 1960. Tange, recently back from a visiting professorship at MIT, sits in the organizing committee of this event.

The WoDeCo is a milestone for Japanese design as it creates a bridge between Japan and the world at large, which Japanese industries are eager to support as a way to reach Western markets. The conference signals a promise to unify professions in Japanese trade to "give them a single style and coordination identifiable to the outside world."[8] With the theme "Total Image for the 20th Century," Japanese designers and their international counterparts from twenty-six countries gather in Tokyo to envision what the second half of the twentieth century could look like and discuss the state of the newest technologies in industrial and graphic design, architecture, education, and broader environmental concerns. The conference helps launch Japanese design onto the world stage as does the short pamphlet *Metabolism 1960: The Proposals for New Urbanism* that circulates among the attendees and which expresses the theoretical formulations and architectural designs of what becomes the Metabolist group.[9] Furthermore, reinforcing the Metabolist attitude toward global positioning, Kurokawa's conference presentation, titled "Character in Design Stems from the Universality of New Quality," advocates for Japanese design's inherent "universal validity."[10] The incredibly successful WoDeCo facilitates international recognition of the group's work, which is broadcast around the world in the following years, including on MoMA's "Visionary Architecture" exhibition (1960) and the journals *Architectural Review* (1962) and *Architectural Design* (1964).[11]

The Metabolists' ambition to influence the world rests on their belief that the strong processes of modernization and urbanization that are affecting Japan made of the country a living laboratory for humanity's immediate future. The group understands that advanced technologies of construction, infrastructural systems, and cybernetics can inflect architectural investigation, and that Japan can start implementing them. One of the clearest arenas in which the country can show the path to the rest of the world is in the orchestration of urbanization. While Western forms of planning focus on the permanence of built form, these notions are alien to Japanese culture, regardless of the country's strong tradition of large-scale and national planning, which became particularly important as part of its colonial occupation of Manchuria.[12] The Metabolists combine this tradition of large-scale planning with their own flexible

**8.** Charles Jencks, "Preface," in Kisho Kurokawa, *Metabolism in Architecture* (London: Studio Vista, 1977), 9.

**9.** Kawazoe et al., *Metabolism: The Proposals for New Urbanism.*

**10.** Kurokawa, *Metabolism in Architecture*, 27.

**11.** Schalk, "Inventing a Culture of Resilience," 293. Within architectural theory, Metabolists would be featured in Tafuri and Dal Co's *Architettura contemporanea* and Reyner Banham's *Megastructure*, both from 1976, as integral contributions to architecture's global landscape. See Lin, *Kenzo Tange and the Metabolist Movement*, 9.

**12.** Schalk, "Inventing a Culture of Resilience," 284–285. Notably, the Western concept of planning had to be put in Japanese as "the will to plan," as indicated by J.M. Richards, editor of the *Architecture Review*, or as "a product of the power of relationships," as Tange observed. For the Japanese spatial interventions in Manchuria, see Furuhata, "Architecture as Atmospheric Media," 57–59.

understanding of spatial organization. According to Kawazoe, planning should admit the relation between order and disorder: the master plan should give way to a continuous programming or a *master program*. Kurokawa's participation in 1962 in the Comprehensive National Development Plan, followed later by designs of infrastructural plans for the country with the Institute of Social Engineering in 1969, shows how such flexible spatial principles could structure a completely urbanized society **[fig. 2]**. The total urbanization that for Doxiadis would dominate the planet in 2100 would already be, for Kurokawa, Japan's reality as early as 2000. While his plans envisage the construction of a totally integrated urban system at the national scale, they also challenge the conventional understanding of urbanization by offering a vision of a "dematerialized-discontinuous city, linked through the air."[13]

A corollary of this idea of total urbanization is the Metabolists' treatment of every geographical site as potentially subject to processes of settlement. Kurokawa's own Agricultural City, and the many Metabolists' marine schemes, like Tokyo's Marine City Plan (Otaka), the many proposals for Tokyo Bay (Tange and others), and Helix City (Kurokawa again), attest to this possibility. Kikutake's water cities, one of the foundational Metabolist projects, however, represents the clearest vision of a different path. His Marine City, Tower-shaped City, and Ocean City *Unabara* do not seek to complement existing cities but to substitute them **[figs. 3 and 4]**. Based on the possibility of using the "two-thirds of the surface of the Earth . . . making a residential environment upon the splendor of the sea," Kikutake's projects offer an alternative vision of urbanization and, through it, a project for the reorganization of world society and political relations.[14]

Conceived in 1958, Marine City and Tower-shaped City mark the symbolic beginning of Metabolism. The projects are showcased at Otterlo's CIAM and inspire Kawazoe's naming the group Metabolists, in English on purpose to "emphasize the concept's universality."[15] These two works, together with Kikutake's 1960 Ocean City, also set the stage for concepts that the group will further elaborate, such as *artificial land* and *major/minor structure*, while filling a disproportional thirty-five of the eighty-seven pages of the 1960 Metabolist manifesto.[16] Kikutake believes it is just a matter of time for civilization to transcend their need of land—origins for him of all human afflictions—by inhabiting the sea.[17]

**13.** Koolhaas, Obrist, et al., *Project Japan*, 585.

**14.** Kiyonori Kikutake, "Ocean Urbanism 1856–1975," in *Kiyonori Kikutake: Between Land and Sea*, ed. Ken Tadashi Oshima (Cambridge, MA: Harvard University, Graduate School of Design, 2016), 183.

**15.** Lin, *Kenzo Tange and the Metabolist Movement*, 22.

**16.** Lin, *Kenzo Tange and the Metabolist Movement*, 25.

**17.** Kiyonori Kikutake, "Marine City," in Oshima, *Kiyonori Kikutake: Between Land and Sea*, 93.

Marine City goes through a handful of different iterations and parallel designs, which present alternative versions of the *vertical community + floating platform* configuration. In the diagrammatic chart of 1958, which first presents the project accompanied by analogies of sea creatures, Kikutake suggests five possible variations, including one rendered with inverted towers that descend into the water while acting as buoys. Overall, each configuration creates a system of floating islands that can be anchored as needed in locations across the globe, ultimately eliminating their bonds to any particular place. The floating formations act as a living organism with its own life cycle; once obsolete, they will drift to the middle of the ocean and sink themselves, becoming a home for coral reefs and fish beds.[18] Based on these first ideas, Kikutake plans in detail a version of Marine City (1971) for the coast of Hawaii. Later, in 1975, a simplified and miniaturized variant of the scheme, named *Aquapolis*, is actually built on the occasion of the Okinawa Ocean Expo '75 **[fig. 5]**.[19]

Kikutake drafts the most elaborated of his floating vertical community in the 1958 Tower-shaped City, and later applies it to Marine City in 1963. There, the residential towers are concrete cylinders fifty meters large and three hundred meters high. On the outer surface, prefabricated steel capsules will be plugged into the main structure progressively as the population of those communities increases. On the inner space, a factory will be installed to fabricate and assemble the units on site, which later will be fixed in their final position by a crane, also self-contained in the tower's core.[20] This same logic of auto-construction is then expanded to entire islands. In Ocean City *Unabara*, for example, the residential towers are inserted onto a larger industrial complex, organized in concentric belts, that self-expand into a bigger and more populous city until arriving at a dimensional threshold where the city splits through a process similar to a cellular mitosis, generating two smaller, more manageable configurations.[21]

In the end, all Kikutake's marine projects share a desire to liberate land and create a new society as they do so. Ownership and sovereignty over land are to be completely re-evaluated, if not altogether dismantled. Instead of the private sector, land will be put under the agency of the public initiative. Constraints on mobility will be eliminated as boundaries between cities are abolished and nation-states are no longer necessary.[22] The elimination of the ties between people and place is followed by a refounding of civil society based on equality and the flattening of resource imbalances among individuals. Once the dependence on continental land is erased, so are the complications derived by it—from large-scale issues such as wars, to more localized problems such as housing

**18.** Kiyonori Kikutake, "Marine City," in Kawazoe et al., *Metabolism: The Proposals for New Urbanism*, 23.

**19.** Koolhaas, Obrist, et al., *Project Japan*, 358. The size of a city-block of 100 m$^2$, *Aquapolis* was built as the Japanese Pavilion to celebrate the return of the Okinawa Islands from the US to Japan.

**20.** Noboru Kawazoe, "The City of the Future" (1960), translated by Ignacio Adriasola, *Review of Japanese Culture and Society* 28 (December 2016): 160

**21.** For a detailed account of each Marine City variant, see Agnes Nyilas, "On the Formal Characteristics of Kiyonori Kikutake's 'Marine City' Projects Published at the Turn of the 50's and 60's," *Architecture Research* 6, no. 4 (2016): 104.

**22.** Zhongjie Lin, "Metabolist Utopias and Their Global Influence: Three Paradigms of Urbanism," *Journal of Urban History* 42, no. 3 (2016): 608.

**23.** Kawazoe, "The City of the Future," 166.

**24.** Kawazoe, "Material and Man," 51.

shortages and unplanned sprawl. For Kikutake, building on water should not be confused with an attempt to produce more ground on which to replicate the same archaic land logics. It is, rather, the opportunity to democratize individual access to society's commons while fostering freedom of mobility and spatial relationships instead of fixed settling patterns.

New modes of human organization on water are to replace the old decaying continental agglomerations, a process that will eventually liberate Earth from traditional predatory occupational models toward a return to a natural state. Humanity will make way for nature to reestablish the balance between the two. Over the seas, a new civilization will flourish on artificial grounds allowing man to find an alternative way to live without competing with nature or being bound to a particular geography, whereas "on the mainland, the last of the human megalopolises will become a ruin that tells the story of a bygone era."[23] Ultimately, the term "metabolism" describes two interrelated global forms, a ubiquitous biological process and an artificial socio-spatial manifestation; thus, both bacteria and man will always propagate, "the only difference will be man's capacity to dream a magnificent dream."[24]

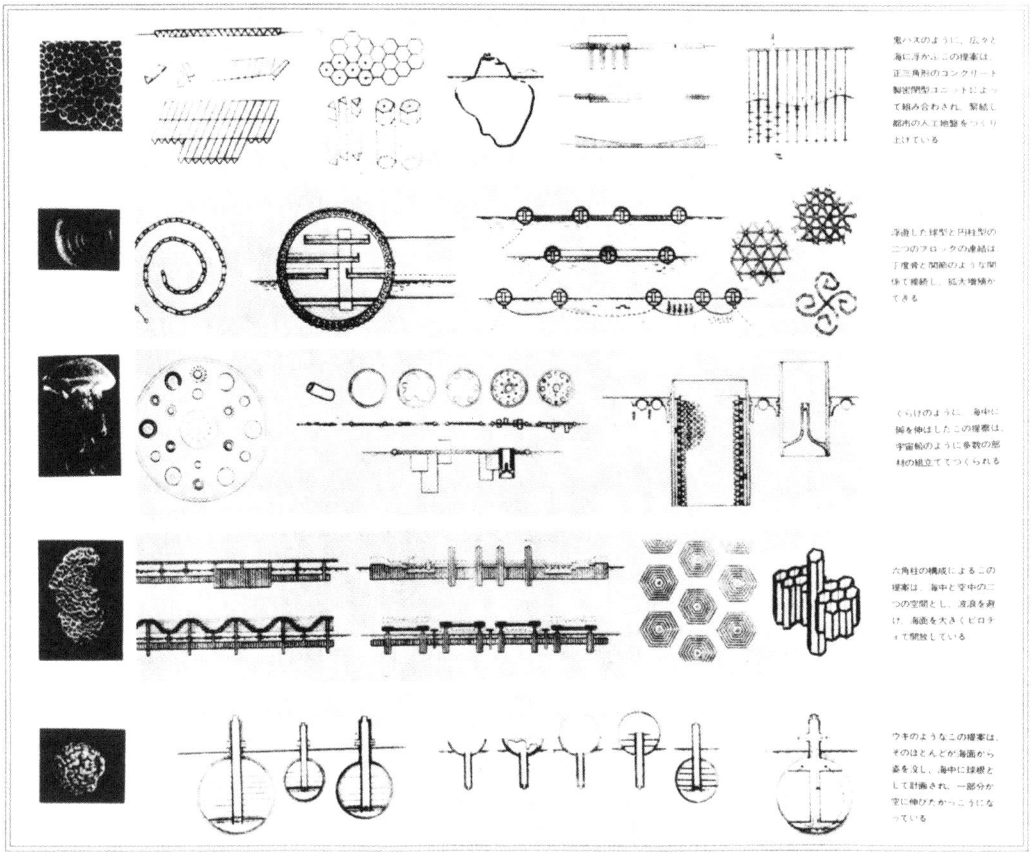

**Figure 1.** Basic types of space formations for Marine City: i) Like a water lily; ii) Like a sea plant; iii) Like a jellyfish; iv) Hexagonal columns to defend against the waves; v) Like a buoy. 1959.

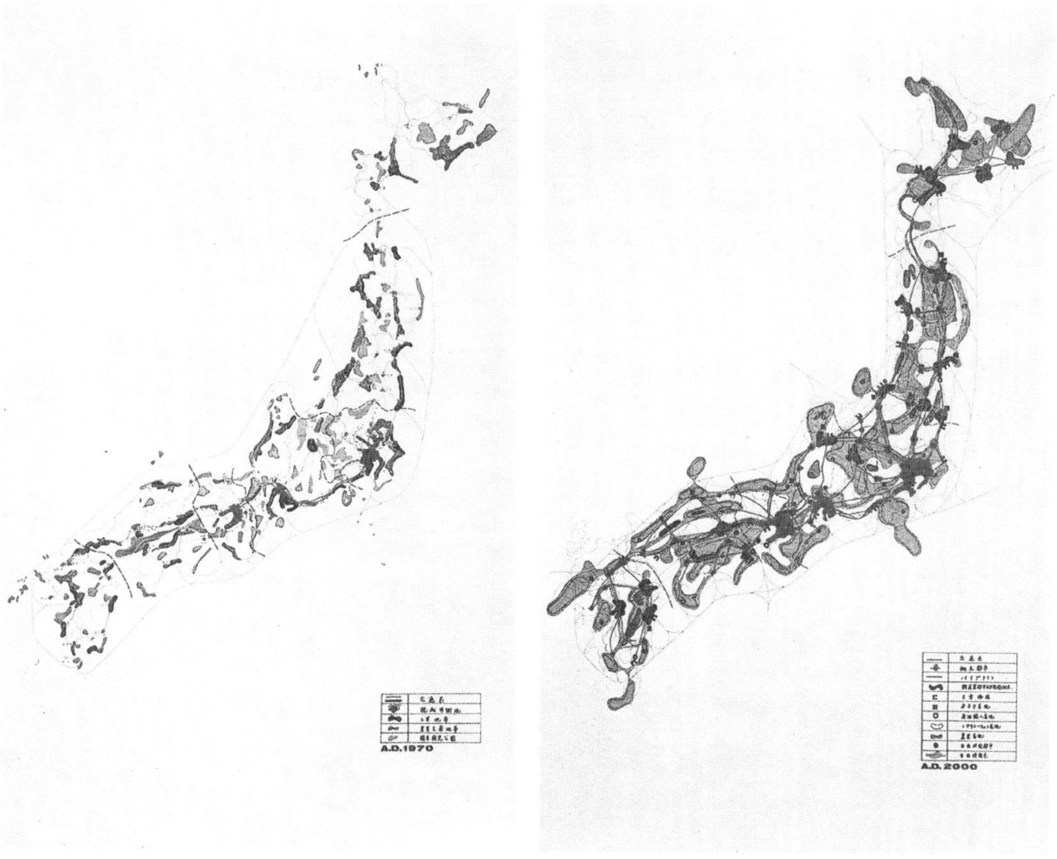


**Figure 2.** Research on the Role of V/STOL Aircraft in City-to-City Transportation.
From 1970 City Constellation to projected 2000 City Constellation. Kisho Kurokawa. 1969.

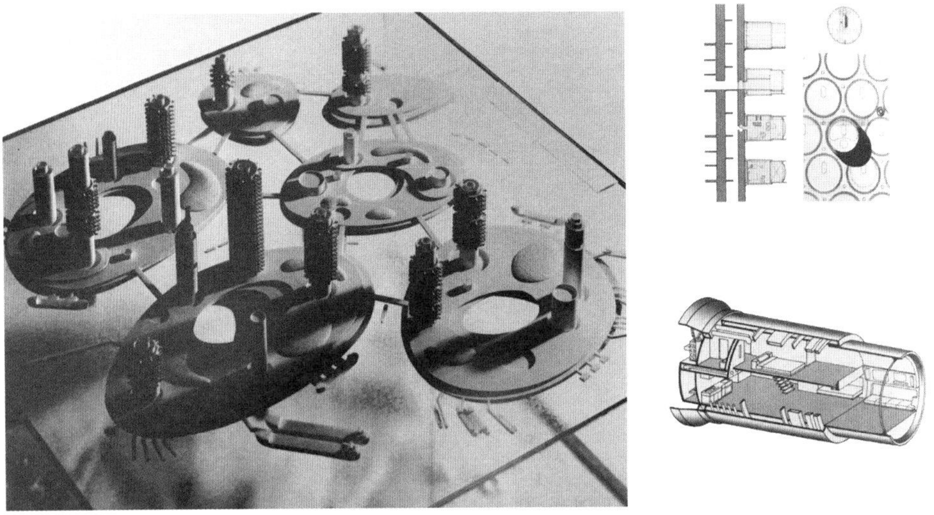

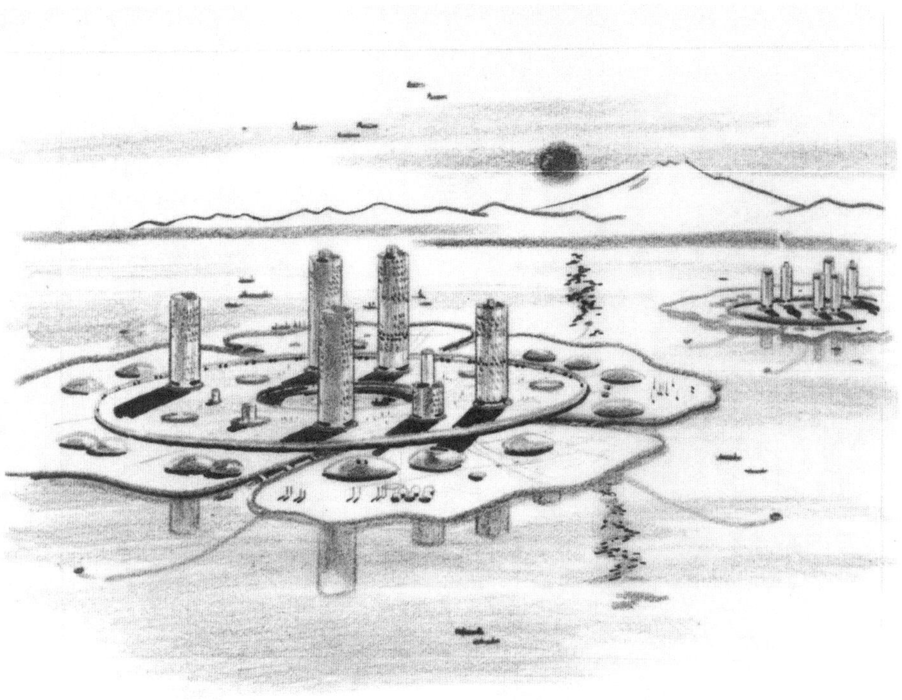

**Figure 3 (Top).** Marine City. Model and elevation, section and isometric of housing unit. 1963.
**Figure 4 (Bottom).** Marine City. Sketch. 1963.

**Figure 5.** Aquapolis. Delivery of pavilion by tow ships.1971–1975.

# Architecture de l'Air

## Air Architecture

**Project:** 22. **Authors:** Yves Klein (1928–1962) and Claude Parent (1923–2016). **Date:** 1959–1962. **Themes:** Abstraction. Environmental Control. Immateriality. Infrastructure.

**Figure 0.** Air Architecture: Climate-controlled city (roof of air, beds of air, and walls of fire). After Yves Klein and Claude Parent. ca. 1961.

The air-conditioning of large urban spaces is a constant theme of architectural exploration during the mid-1950s and early 1960s. Projects as diverse as Frei Otto's pioneering Arctic cities, Yona Friedman's Spatial City (1956), or Buckminster Fuller and Shoji Sadao's Manhattan Dome (1960) share the conviction that the overall climatic control of settlements is necessary to create more efficient and sustainable urban environments **[projects 14 and 24]**. Air Architecture is the extreme case of this exploration. The project, which Yves Klein develops first in collaboration with German architect Werner Ruhnau, himself in contact with Otto and Friedman, and later with Claude Parent, is at once part of Klein's artistic work and a radical incursion into the central architectural and urban debates of the time.[1] By 1961 Klein declares himself the inventor of the architecture and urbanism of air, and proclaims that this new conception "transcends the traditional meaning of the terms 'architecture' and 'urbanism.'"[2] The declaration, although grandiloquent, is not unjustified. Air Architecture uses air-conditioning to create a novel, extremely abstract type of environment: a flat, unlimited void, undisturbed by any kind of construction **[figs. 0 and 1]**. The elimination of architecture in favor of the void is the central piece through which the project articulates three interrelated themes: the sociospatial conditions of the emerging society of mass consumption; the intensification of modern urban spatiality in the postwar era; and the expansion of the urban condition to the world scale. Instead of using air-conditioning to control the climate of discrete settlements—à la Otto, Friedman, or Buckminster Fuller—Air Architecture uses this technology to turn the whole Earth into an urban system. As Klein states: "Air Architecture is at the surface of our globe. The technical and scientific conclusion of our civilization is buried in the depths of the earth and ensures the absolute control of the climate on the surface of all continents, which have become vast communal living rooms" **[fig. 3]**.[3]

Air Architecture operates at a predominantly discursive level. Klein and Parent inaugurate a way of addressing the world scale in which architectural design ceases to be an instrument to define a new spatial system in order to become an intellectual tool to reflect upon ongoing social conditions. In this case generalized, worldwide urbanization. For developing their intellectual proposition, Klein and Parent use a logic that is more retroactive than projective.[4] Air Architecture faces the consolidation of global urbanization, which informs the works of Alison and Peter Smithson, Constant, or Friedman through a strategy that contradicts, in general terms, the work of those architects **[projects 18, 19,**

1. For a complete description of the project see Peter Noever and François Perrin, eds., *Air Architecture: Yves Klein* (Ostfildern: Hatje Cantz, 2004); Dominique Rouillard, *Superarchitecture: Le Futur de l'architecture, 1950–1970* (Paris: Editions de la Villette, 2004); Larry Busbea, *Topologies: The Urban Utopia in France, 1960–1970* (Cambridge, MA: MIT Press, 2007); and Roi Salgueiro Barrio, "Birds Must Be Eliminated: Air Architecture and the Planetary Reenactment of the Modern Void," *Journal of Architectural Education* 70, no. 2 (2016): 311–323.

2. Yves Klein, "Chelsea Hotel Manifesto," in *Overcoming the Problematics of Art: The Writings of Yves Klein*, ed. Klaus Ottman (Putnam, CO: Spring Publications, 2007), 192.

3. Text contained in Yves Klein's 1961 painting *Architecture de l'air*.

4. Benjamin Buchloch, "Plenty or Nothing: From Yves Klein's *Le Vide* to Arman's *Le Plein*," in *Premises: Invested Spaces in Visual Arts, Architecture and Design from France, 1958–1998*, ed. Blistene Bernard (New York: Guggenheim, 1998), 86–99.

**and 24]**. Instead of seeking alternatives to the formal systems developed during the prewar era, Air Architecture's global environment results from intensifying one key spatial feature of the modern urban project—namely, void space. This idea of void is then opportunistically used to understand how central notions of the modern project, such as spatial abstraction, the control of nature, technological positivism, or the importance of infrastructural space, are still essential to understanding the postwar period.

It is Le Corbusier's foundational *The City of To-morrow and its Planning* (concisely titled in French *Urbanisme*) that states that the construction of the modern city orbits around managing the void. In this foundational text, Le Corbusier uses the term void (*vide*) to explain the central purposes of his early understanding of what urbanism should be. The meaning of the term is broad and multifarious. First and foremost, it reflects a condition of spatial indeterminacy that matches the self-acknowledged nihilism of Le Corbusier's early project and the novel and free conditions of modern subjectivity—the void is, in his words, an expression of the "modern feeling."[5] It is also a spatial tool to counteract the overcrowding and confusion of the nineteenth-century metropolis. Le Corbusier describes in a novel manner the central project of his book, the Contemporary City for Three Million Inhabitants, as a city of "solids and voids," in which the latter serve to distance and isolate the different types of buildings, functions, and users of the city. The void is, finally, the crucial tool to counteract urban expansion. The Contemporary City is a confined city, surrounded by a huge void, the "*zone asservie*," which separates the built fabric from nature **[project 15]**. This zone, which has been translated into English as "zone of protection," is, in a more literal translation, the "enslaved" zone. It is an area where nature is subjugated in order to highlight the distinctiveness of the urban realm and its radical alienation from nature. The void is, thus, an instrument of environmental control that grants the very existence of the urban.

The conditions of modern urban space are a central concern of the New Realists, the collective of artists to which Klein belongs.[6] The group shares with the contemporaneous Situationist International the desire to address the emerging conditions of generalized urbanization and mass consumption. Yet, instead of the critical, Marxist-oriented perspective of the Situationists, the New Realists maintain an ambivalent position in relation to the new social and spatial conditions, their attitude a mixture of criticism and fascination. Their work often appropriates the new materials that industry or mass media generates as a way to reveal the values of the existing environment.[7] The group's spokesman,

**5.** See in this respect the image titled "Left blank for a work expressing modern feeling" at the end of the chapter "Sensibility Comes into Play," in Le Corbusier, *The City of To-morrow and Its Planning* (London: Architectural Press, 1971 [1929]). For an analysis of Le Corbusier's relation to the void see Manfredo Tafuri, "Machine et Mémoire: The City in the Work of Le Corbusier," in *Le Corbusier*, ed. Allen Brooks (Princeton: Princeton Architectural Press, 1987), 203-218.

**6.** In addition to Klein, the group includes the painters and sculptors Arman, Martial Raysse, Jean Tinguely, and Daniel Spoerri, together with the Ultra-Lettrists François Dufrêne, Raymond Hains, and Jacques de la Villeglé.

**7.** Kaira M. Cabañas, "Yves Klein's Performative Realism," *Grey Room* 31 (Spring 2008): 6-31; and Hal Foster, Yve-Alain Bois, Rosalind Krauss, and Benjamin Buchloh, "1957" in *Art since 1900: Modernism, Antimodernism, Postmodernism* (London: Thames and Hudson, 2011), 429–435.

Pierre Restany, summarizes their position and concerns: "The urban phenomenon plays an increasingly important role. Industrial sociology and advertising sociology have deeply modified the landscape of our cities. What the New Realists are attempting to do is *to make this contemporary reality visible* through the specific images it arouses."[8]

Restany's analysis distances Klein's work from the urban preoccupations of his colleagues.[9] Certainly, Klein describes Air Architecture as an absolute refutation of the built urban environment. It is an "Eden," a return to nature.[10] Yet, in most ways, the project points in an opposite direction. The dissolution of architecture and the conversion of the planet to an air-conditioned void is not a negation of the city, but the most radical representation of the expansion of the urban to the world scale. In Le Corbusier, the void is both the central spatial condition of the city and the means to delimit it. In Air Architecture, the void is again treated as the paradigmatic space of urban modernity. Its lack of confinement is a tool to extend the effects of the urban worldwide.

The resulting planetary system merges the central themes of prewar, modern urbanism with the emerging conditions of postwar urban society. The project adopts, nominally, the division in functional areas for residence, work, transportation, and leisure established in the 1933 CIAM Athens Charter **[project 13]**.[11] Yet, the design conflates them in two single layers: leisure and infrastructure. According to the project descriptions, a central highway divides the city in areas of residence and work.[12] Yet, in Air Architecture there are no visible signs of any of the two last functions. What Parent's and his assistant Sarcologo's drawings show is an empty, vast space where some subjects move freely, unconstrained by any architectural obstacle. The only physical structure built above ground is the elevated highway, a technical infrastructure that also supports the air-conditioning machinery and links the city to airports.

The lack of architecture signals powerfully the disappearance of any sense of social collectivity. Klein's texts refer only to "individuals," indicating a condition of subjective isolation that is exacerbated by the anemic, shadowy figures that populate the most laconic of the project's representations **[fig. 2]**. These individuals inhabit a social regime that only superficially resembles 1950s prospects of an emerging ludic society. Here, leisure becomes labor, an "occupation," and subjectivity is reduced to an act of representation.[13] In Air Architecture, Klein affirms, the "official theatre is 'to be', and 'I am.'"[14] Correspondingly, the project's conditions of absolute transparency generate an environment without

**8.** Pierre Restany, *Les Nouveaux réalistes* (Paris: Editions Planète, 1968), 46. Our translation. Our emphasis.

**9.** Restany, *Les Nouveaux réalistes*, 46.

**10.** Klein persistently used the term Eden in his descriptions of Air Architecture. See for instance his painting *Architecture de l'air (ANT 102)*, 1961.

**11.** Yves Klein, "Air Architecture," *ZERO* 3 (1961). Reprinted in Otto Piene et al., *ZERO* (Cologne: DuMont Schauberg, 1973), n.p.

**12.** Klein, "Air Architecture," n.p.

**13.** Yves Klein, *Architecture de l'air (ANT 102)*, 1961.

**14.** Yves Klein, "Dimanche," in Klein, *Overcoming the Problematics of Art*, 102.

privacy, where every individual thought and action must be a representation immediately accessible to others.[15] For the artist's contemporaries the central conditions of postwar urban society are representation, or spectacle, and the emergence of the *homo ludens* as a new type of subject devoted to leisure (the Situationists), and mass communication and extended mobility (the Smithsons and the Independent Group).[16] Air Architecture assumes these same conditions but with a skeptical tone of disbelief, and posits that the spatial expression of the resulting urban society and of the forms of subjectivity that it creates should be a radical, global version of the modern void.

This air-conditioned void has to be produced and reproduced through the same technologies that support urban society and urban space. Air Architecture's Eden is nature after being abstracted and artificialized. In 1958, Klein responds to a questionnaire of the art journal *ZERO* titled "Does Contemporary Painting Influence the Shape of the World?"[17] There he argues that artistic operations should operate at the scale of the atomic bomb, that of the "ultimate abstraction imaginable."[18] Certainly, the scalar progression that can be observed in the evolution of the project—from the original small-scale, technical investigations with Ruhnau, to the global project with Parent—is accompanied by Klein's design of machines of destruction and by his proclamations declaring the necessity of turning the earth into an abstract plane **[fig. 4]**.[19] Air-conditioning appears after this act of global leveling. The resulting Eden is repeatedly described, in the texts, as a "desert."[20] The primeval garden is now a controlled nature that extends Le Corbusier's *zone asservie* to the planetary scale as a global *tabula rasa*. For Klein, modern world-making is above all world-unmaking.

The exaggeration of some of modernity's most critical aspects notwithstanding—from emptiness and abstraction, to transparency and surveillance—Klein presents Air Architecture positively, as a utopia. Only the artist's death in 1962 interrupts three years of passionate work on the project. Parent does not continue it, although his later works, *Colère, ou La Nécessite de détruire* (Anger, or the need to destroy, 1982) and *Demain, la Terre . . .* (Tomorrow, the earth . . . , 2009), pick up Air Architecture's concern with the scale of the world.[21] While Air Architecture lacks a direct continuation, its methods and themes will heavily resonate during the decade to come. The Italian studios Archizoom and Superstudio consolidate the use of design as an instrument of reflection, and explore, in their projects, the same abstract, superficial, air-conditioned, infrastructurally produced environments that Klein and Parent foresee **[projects 36 and 38]**. Despite Klein's assertions, Air Architecture is more heterotopian than

**15.** Klein, "Dimanche," 102.

**16.** Foster, Bois, Krauss, and Buchloh, "1957," 429–435.

**17.** The journal was edited by the eponymous art collective. The ZERO group had been promoted in 1958 by the two German artists Otto Piene and Heinz Mack. Klein was loosely affiliated with the group.

**18.** Yves Klein, "My Position in the Battle between Line and Color," in Piene et al., *ZERO*, 34.

**19.** See Yves Klein's statement in the short piece: *Je raserai tout. . . .* Div. sn. 613. Yves Klein's Archives, Paris.

**20.** Klein, "It is by staying in one's place that one can be anywhere," in Noever and Perrin, *Air Architecture: Yves Klein*, 30. Klein's use of the term "desert" is once again a reference to prewar modernity. The notion of "desert" was crucial for the suprematist painter Kazimir Malevich, who thought it was represented by his white abstract paintings. The term conveyed for him the idea of transcendence and journey. Klein, who often portrayed himself as a continuator of Malevich, associated the term to its literal conditions of absence, elimination, and violence.

**21.** Claude Parent, *Colères, ou, La Nécessité de détruire* (Marseille: M. Schefer Editions, 1982), and Claude Parent, *Demain, La Terre . . .* (Paris: Manuella Editions, 2009).

utopian. It presents a planet populated by naked, isolated individuals who reject all traditional social ties—again, a 1960s aspiration, captured in Superstudio's Supersurface or in Archigram's LAWUN **[project 25]**. The value of Air Architecture derives from advancing all the ambivalence implicit in such a project of subjective liberation, showing that it depends on the same technologies that support the existing social order and the environmental management of the world. Klein and Parent intuit that the prospect of an urban society equals an increasing technical administration of Earth. For them the void is a metaphor for the modes of existence in urban society. It is also the most literal representation of modernity's approach to nature. The void is no longer the open space for novel, nonregulated forms of life, but the emblem of a system of technological domination that runs from the body to the world.

Figure 1. Air Architecture: Climate-controlled City. 1961.

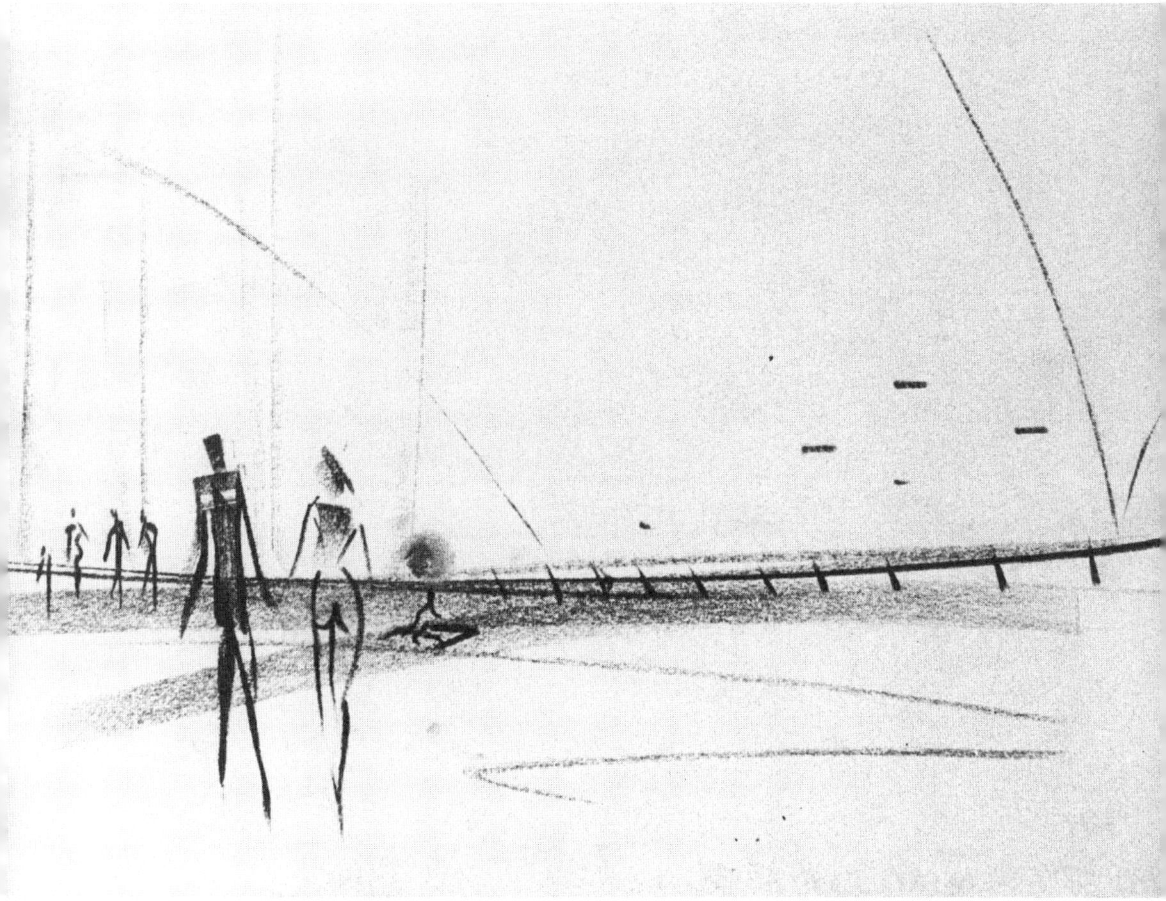

**Figure 2.** Air Architecture: Project for a City. ca. 1960.

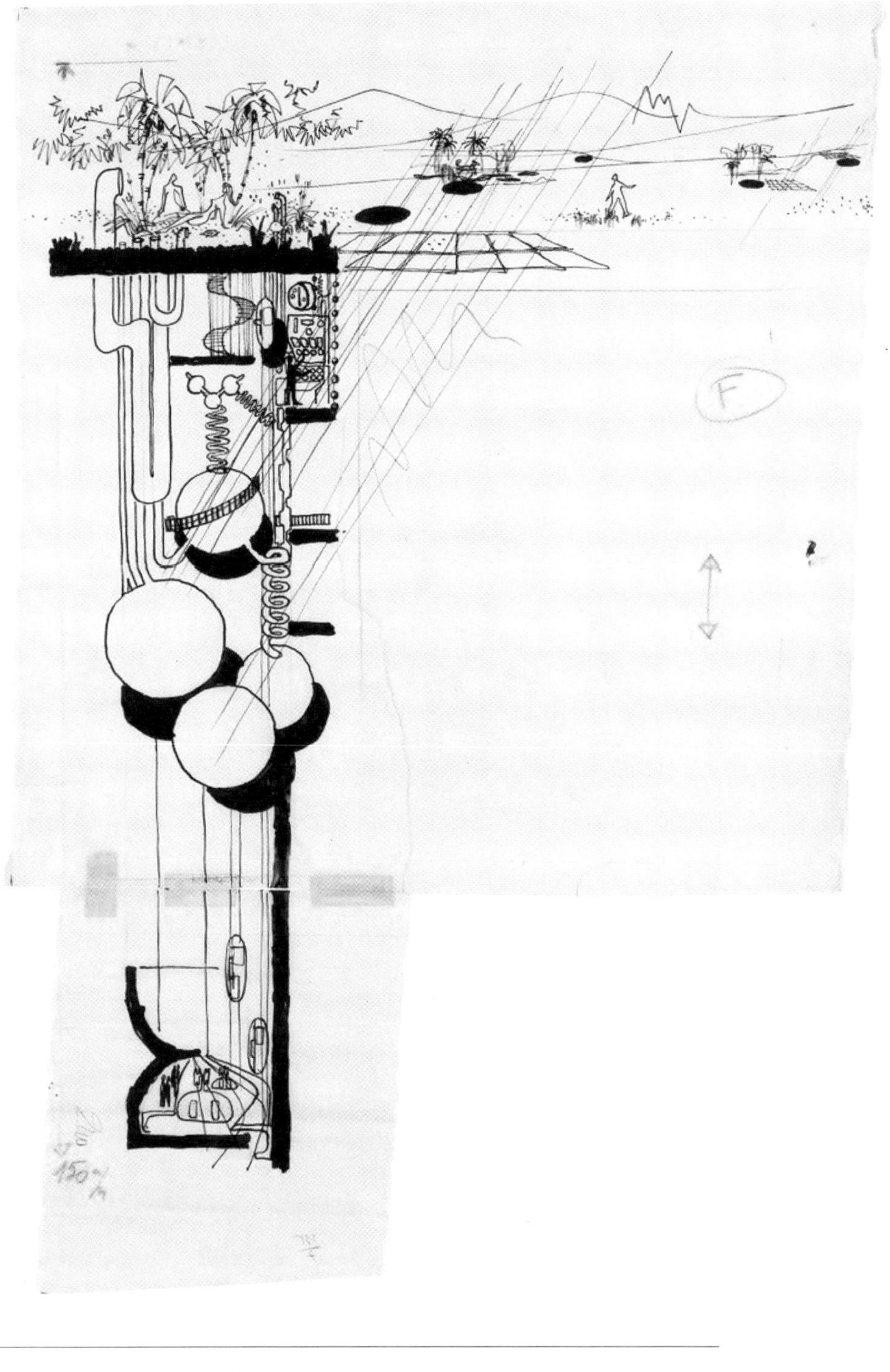

Figure 3. Air Architecture: Underground Area of a Climate-controlled City, "Climate Control of Space." ca. 1959.

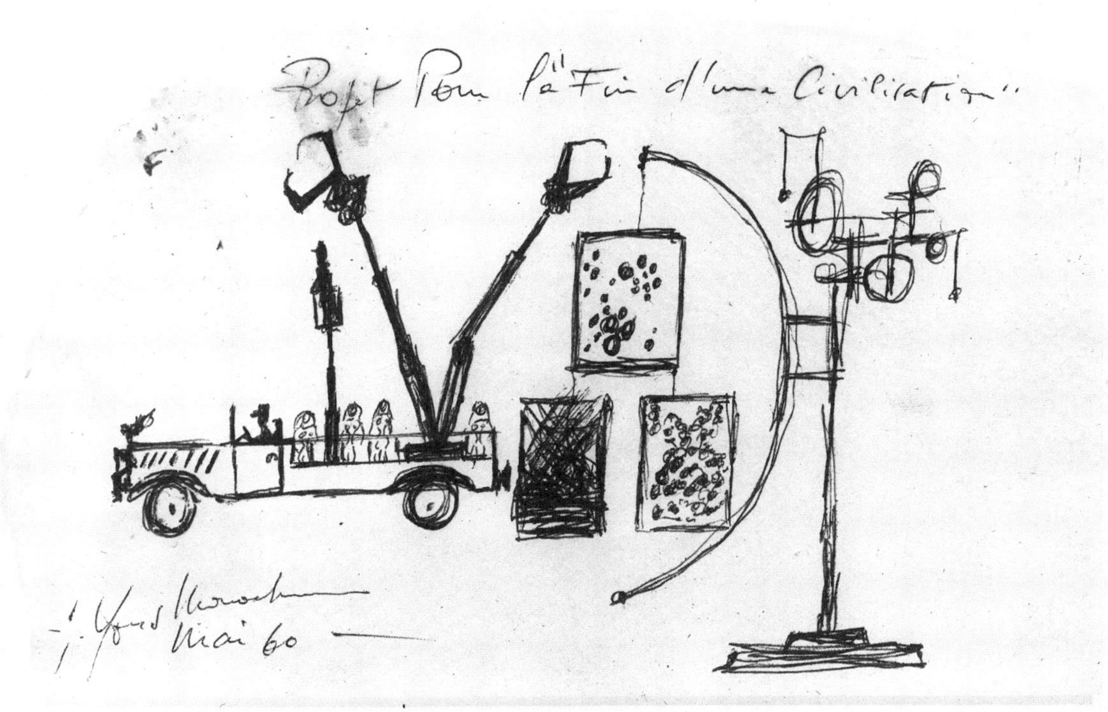


**Figure 4.** Project for the End of a Civilization. Yves Klein. 1960.

# Οικουμενόπολη
## Ecumenopolis

**Project:** 23. **Author:** Constantinos Apostolou Doxiadis (1913–1975). **Date:** ca. 1962–1975. **Themes:** Geo-visualization. Linearity. Territorial Gestalt. World Urbanization.

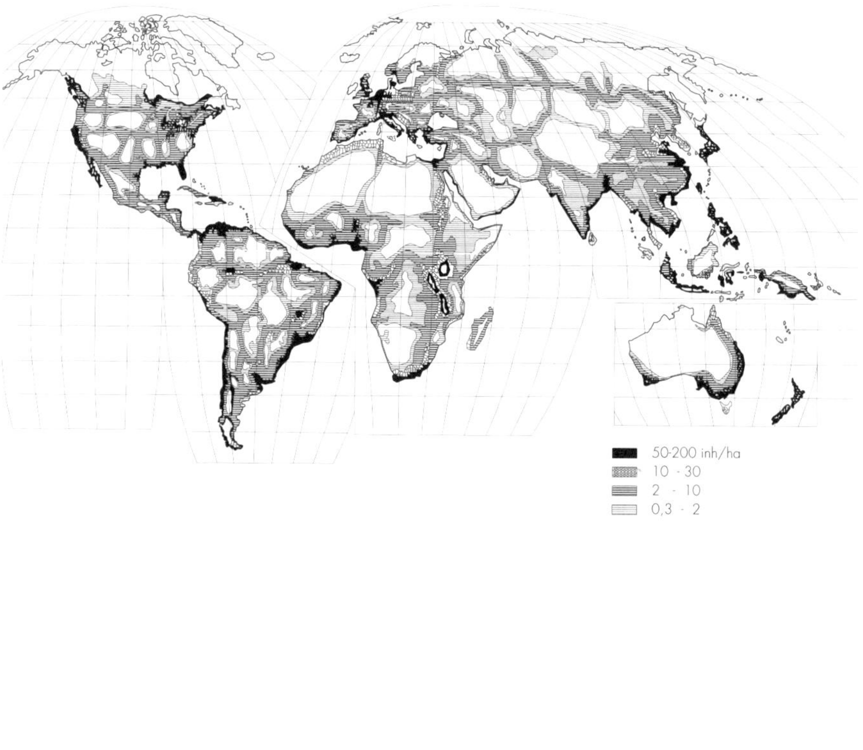


**Figure 0.** Ecumenopolis at the end of the 21st century. After Constantinos Doxiadis. 1970.

Ecumenopolis is the "inevitable city of the future" **[fig. 0]**.[1] We see here the world in the year 2100. After the period of crises and transitions of the twentieth and twenty-first centuries during which cities grew from metropolises, to megalopolises, to eperopolises (cities-continents), the world's settlements have finally merged into a single, continuous, planetary city. Ecumenopolis, or the Universal Human Settlement, thus represents a culminating moment, a final stage where urbanization, population growth, and the natural resources of the planet have found a successful equilibrium. Its mirrors and counterparts are Ecumenokepos, the planetary garden of food production that puts Ecumenopolis into permanent contact with nature, and Ecumenohydor, which supplies this global system with water **[fig. 1]**.[2] Together, the city, the garden, and the water constitute the three broad categories through which Constantinos Doxiadis conceives the totality of Anthropocosmos—the human terrestrial space—and thus the main spatial conditions that humanity will have to manage and protect **[fig. 2]**.

Total world management is the corollary of Doxiadis's vision of an urban planet.[3] Ecumenopolis abolishes all distance and all externalities. All parts of the city-world are contiguous and face the necessity of controlling the earth's resources in order to warrant the stability of the global system and, conversely, to avoid a general catastrophe.[4] The need for world management implies the complete mobilization of nature for human purposes and an absolute confidence in scientific control: land apportionment, geoengineering, and even climate control are its tools **[fig. 3]**.[5] Yet, the technocratic utopia that Doxiadis summarizes in the Anthropocosmos model is only part of a broader political and socio-ontological eschatology. All the dynamics that lead to Ecumenopolis are described as evolutionary and natural **[fig. 4]**.[6] As a result of this natural logic, Ecumenopolis will necessarily secrete its own political structure: a world democratic federation. The city-world will also end up constituting a sort of organism, a unified body. Its population of twenty billion people will coincide, Doxiadis points out, with the number of cells of the human brain.[7] The world will be a huge, collective thinking entity.

**1.** The first published mention of the notion of Ecumenopolis appears in Constantinos Apostolou Doxiadis, "Ecumenopolis: Toward a Universal City," *Ekistics* 13, no. 75 (1962): 3–18. The author will devote many articles and lectures to the topic, until the publication in 1974 of a monograph about the question. See Constantinos Apostolou Doxiadis, John Papaiōannou, and Athēnaïko Kentro Oikistikēs, *Ecumenopolis: The Inevitable City of the Future* (New York: Norton, 1974).

**2.** Panayiota Ioanni Pyla, "Ekistics, Architecture, and Environmental Politics, 1945–1976: A Prehistory of Sustainable Development" (PhD diss., MIT, 2003), 121–151; and Panayiota Ioanni Pyla, "Planetary Home and Garden: Ekistics and Environmental-Developmental Politics," *Grey Room* 36 (2009): 10 and 17.

**3.** Constantinos Apostolou Doxiadis, *Ecology and Ekistics* (Boulder: Westview Press, 1977), 7; and Nikos Katsikis, "Two Approaches to 'World Management': C.A. Doxiadis, and R.B. Fuller," in *Implosions/Explosions*, ed. Neil Brenner (Berlin: Jovis Verlag, 2014), 482–489. *Ecology and Ekistics* is a posthumous publication, edited by Gerald Dix from Doxiadis's draft. About the uses of nature in Doxiadis see also Gerald Dix, "Ekistics, Ecumenopolis and the Wilderness," *Land Use Policy* 2, no. 1 (1985): 41–53. For more on Fuller, see projects 6 and 14.

**4.** Doxiadis, *Ecology and Ekistics,* 9 and 50–51.

**5.** John Papaioannou, "Geography and the Future of Human Settlements," *Ekistics* 24, no. 145 (1967): 452.

**6.** Constantinos Apostolou Doxiadis, *Ekistics: An Introduction to the Science of Human Settlements* (New York: Oxford University Press, 1968), 200–264. See also in this respect Doxiadis's criticism of previous model of linear cities,

Ecumenopolis is the unit number 15 of the ekistic territorial scale, a quasilogarithmic system that classifies human environments from Anthropos (number 1) to the Biosphere (number 18). Doxiadis starts using the term *ekistics* in 1942 in order to designate the "science of human settlements," although the total system of such a science is not completed until the publication in 1968 of *Ekistics: An Introduction to the Science of Human Settlements* and *Ecology and Ekistics* in 1977.[8] Through these texts and the constant research that motivated them, Doxiadis seeks to establish an objective discipline that allows urbanists to move from deduction to induction. Statistics, maps, data, and charts are continuously elaborated and analyzed by the team Doxiadis employs at the Athens Technological Institute, which he created in 1958.[9] This accumulation of evidence supports the notion of Ecumenopolis, but only after it is synthesized through the theoretical work of concept creation. As Doxiadis recognizes, the creation of a "theory" is the milestone of his work.[10] This theory defines the laws of the evolution of settlements and establishes a new conceptual vocabulary—reflected, as in a philosophical system, in an entire lexicon of neologisms—that allows the architect to name and understand the result of those laws.[11] The notion of Ecumenopolis appears in this sense as the result of a process of logical induction, as a consequence of the laws of development, internal balance, and formal organization of settlements that Doxiadis defined.

Doxiadis's theory has two central aspects that challenge previous urban theories. The first one concerns the very definition of settlement. The second addresses the relation between that notion and time. Etymologically, *ekistics* derives from *oikos*, the Greek term for home, and it thus shares the same root as economy and ecology. As it happens in those two terms, the notion of *ekistics* describes systems of organization. The term is oriented to overcoming the limitations, the conceptual traps, of linking settlements to built-up space: "The result of this limitation," Doxiadis states, "is confusion concerning the concept of the geographic extension of a human settlement."[12] To avoid this error, Doxiadis's notion of settlement incorporates all those man-made elements—e.g., transportation infrastructure and areas of production—which already affect the entire earth.[13] At the same time, settlements are seen as an amalgam of relations. Their structure results from the variable combination of five *ekistic* elements: Nature, Man, Society, Shells, and Networks.[14]

such as Arturo Soria y Mata's and Le Corbusier's, for being rigid and not allowing evolution, in: Constantinos Apostolou Doxiadis, "On Linear Cities," *Town Planning Review* 38 (1967): 35–42. See projects 1 and 15.

**7.** Doxiadis, *Ekistics*, 377.

**8.** John Papaioannou, "C.A. Doxiadis' Early Career and the Birth of Ekistics," *Ekistics* 72, no. 430–435 (2005): 13–17.

**9.** Mark Wigley, "Network Fever," *Grey Room* 4 (2001): 98. Among other things, Wigley references the intensity of this process of compilation, in which participated three shifts of workers, twenty-four hours a day.

**10.** "Theory" is the title of book three of *Ekistics*, which describes the concept of Ecumenopolis. Using similar terms, Doxiadis also aims to construct models. See Constantinos Apostolou Doxiadis, "Anthropocosmos Model," *Ekistics* 72, no. 430–435 (2005): 70–77.

**11.** Doxiadis, *Ekistics*, 287–317.

**12.** Doxiadis, *Ekistics*, 25.

**13.** Doxiadis, *Ekistics*, 25. Consequently, in *Ecology and Ekistics*, Doxiadis indicates that settlements are made of *anthropareas*, where anthropos lives, and *industrareas*, where resources are transformed, but also of *cultivareas*, where nature is cultivated, and *naturareas* where *anthropos* is an occasional visitor.

**14.** Doxiadis, *Ekistics*, 35.

"Shells" correspond to the static, built structures. "Networks," in turn, include all sorts of systems of functional relations. Doxiadis credits the CIAM zoning principles for the discovery of functions as the central constituent of the urban.[15] Yet, he concedes to the notion of network a primacy that exceeds CIAM's conceptions. Dynamic functional relations produce the disruptive transition from the enclosed and static historical city to the constantly expanding urban systems that form the contemporary world. As a consequence, what Doxiadis finds important is to reconceptualize cities as "cities in transition," or "dynapolises," that is, as complex and evolving organisms where shells and infrastructures constantly react to the forces of demographics, economy, geography, climate, nature, and communications.[16] What for CIAM and especially for Le Corbusier was anathema—surrendering control of the city to unchecked urban expansion—is the basis of the system Doxiadis proffers and the primordial condition from which Ecumenopolis emanates.

While Doxiadis heavily criticizes prewar CIAM urban models, his overall reliance on modernist principles shapes his decision to use the CIAM model of organization to promote the notion of Ecumenopolis.[17] Between 1963 and 1974, Doxiadis organizes a series of Symposia in Delos with the collaboration of Jacqueline Tyrwhitt. Tyrwhitt, who had been the secretary of CIAM's council from 1948 to the CIAM X of 1956 and editor of the journal *Ekistics* since 1955, helps to situate Delos as a continuation of the defunct CIAM by bringing Siegfried Giedion to the first *symposion*.[18] Yet, instead of bringing together mainly architects and urbanists, Delos groups a diverse array of professionals, scientists, thinkers, and bureaucrats. Geographers (Walter Christaller, Jean Gottmann), media theorists (Marshall McLuhan), biologists (Conrad Waddington), and sociologists (Edward T. Hall) join cybernetic urban planners such as Richard Louis Meier, architects such as Buckminster Fuller and Kenzo Tange, and public opinion leaders such as Margaret Mead and Barbara Ward. This network is meant to influence a broader institutional environment. Doxiadis and the society of *Ekistics* participate repeatedly in UN conferences and forums, from the 1963 Committee on Housing, Building, and Planning of the Economic and Social Council to the 1972 Human Environment Conference in Stockholm and the 1976 UN Conference on Settlements—to the point that the latter is eventually dedicated to Doxiadis.[19]

**15.** Pyla, "Planetary Home and Garden," 18.

**16.** Constantinos Apostolou Doxiadis, *Architecture in Transition* (New York: Oxford University Press, 1963).

**17.** While Doxiadis is critical of early modernism, he approaches in his work some of the topics that restructured CIAM after the war, from the notion of habitat to the revision of the scale of the city, to Le Corbusier's interest in infrastructure and the four routes, which directly parallels Doxiadis's desire to join terrestrial, water, and aerial transportation in a unified *lanwair* system [project 15]. For the notion of lanwair see Doxiadis, *Ecology and Ekistics*, xxiv.

**18.** Wigley, "Network Fever," 95.

**19.** Pyla, "Planetary Home and Garden," 10–24.

His involvement in the efforts of international coordination at the United Nations can be seen as the logical culmination of Doxiadis's work. His postwar concern with settlements is triggered by his participation in the Marshall Plan for Greece and his consequent familiarization with national scale planning.[20] The global range of the plans Doxiadis Associates designs since 1952 (Baghdad, Beirut, Karachi, Khartoum, Islamabad, and Rio de Janeiro, among others) covers a good number of postcolonial states that embraced the post–Bretton Woods belief in progressive development.[21] In this context, Doxiadis's design and theoretical work tries to situate planning as an objective science. This alleged scientific neutrality warrants planning the status of an extrapolitical technique of growth management consonant with the camouflaging of political decisions under a developmentalist ideology characteristic of global institutions.

To this managerial view of Doxiadis's urbanism, structured around his technocratic thinking and around the notions of circulation, growth, and exchange that networks facilitate, it is possible to counter a reading of Ecumenopolis as a tool to define the ideal urban and territorial form. It is not growth that interests Doxiadis, but stasis. By defining a stable future scenario, Ecumenopolis is a means to exorcise the uncertainty of change. Prior to *ekistics*, Doxiadis coined the term *chorotaxia*: "bringing order (*taxis*) to space (*choros*)."[22] The whole Ecumenopolis appears as a gigantic effort to achieve this goal. The classification and division of land into 12 zones, the organization of Ecumenopolis through structural axes defined as figures against the background of the urban fabric, the definition of a planetary regime of built areas and voids, all extend to the world scale consolidated, even conservative, formal strategies of urban design. The world becomes an architectural object.[23] All the attention to the changing nature of Dynapolis is the mere analytical precondition that allows Doxiadis to shape a future stage, and to preserve, in it, the existing social and formal attributes of the city. The expansion of Dynapolis toward bigger urban scales is paralleled by the growth of its center, so that residential areas can maintain a close relation to the urban core **[fig. 5]**. The resulting cities "need" to be organized through "static cells," whose dimensions are determined in order to maintain civic cohesion and the overall legibility of the urban form.[24] The interlocking of urban and ecogrids keeps a balanced relation between city and nature.[25] The planetary vision of Ecumenopolis, then, justifies a logic of design that seeks

**20.** Papaioannou, "C.A. Doxiadis' Early Career and the Birth of Ekistics," 13–17.

**21.** Ahmed Zaib Khan Mahsud, "Rethinking Doxiadis' Ekistical Urbanism," *Positions* 1 (2010): 6–39.

**22.** Papaioannou, "C.A. Doxiadis' Early Career and the Birth of Ekistics," 14. For Doxiadis's interest in the visual organization of space, see Kostas Tsiambaos, "The Creative Gaze: Doxiadis' Discovery," *Journal of Architecture* 14, no. 2 (2009): 255–275.

**23.** For a summary of the debates in Delos, see Wigley, "Network Fever," 87–92 and 96–99.

**24.** Doxiadis, *Ekistics*, 355–363.

**25.** Mahsud, "Rethinking Doxiadis' Ekistical Urbanism," 33.

conservation, equilibrium, and balance. Ecumenopolis emerges, at every scale, through successive measures that abandon all the prewar ambitions of radical urban transformation. For Doxiadis, urbanization is not a factor of social and spatial disruption, but a process to be managed. Neither is it a utopia for the future, but a static *entopia*; a real, "practicable place" for the everlasting present.[26]

**26.** Pyla, "Planetary Home and Garden," 6; and Ahmed Zaib Khan Mahsud, "Doxiadis' Legacy of Urban Design: Adjusting and Amending the Modern," *Ekistics* 73, no. 436–441 (2006): 241–264.

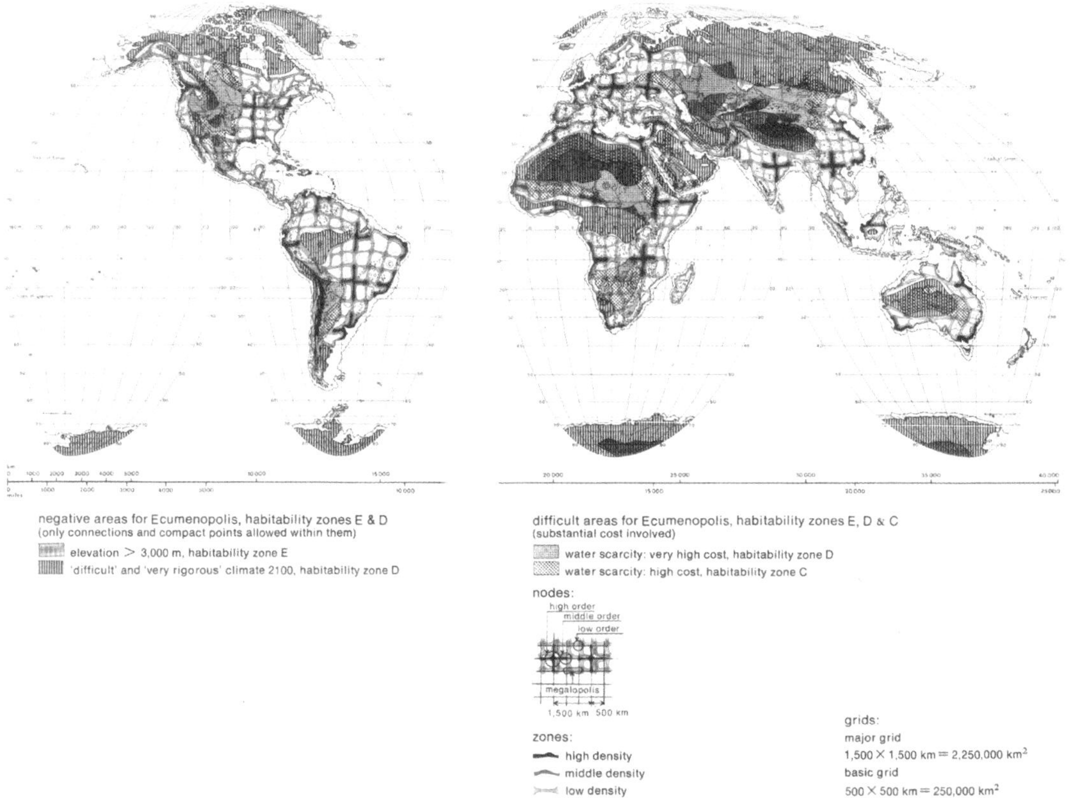


**Figure 1.** Ecumenopolis. Theoretical configuration of global axes and centers adjusted for distorting factors. ca. 1974.

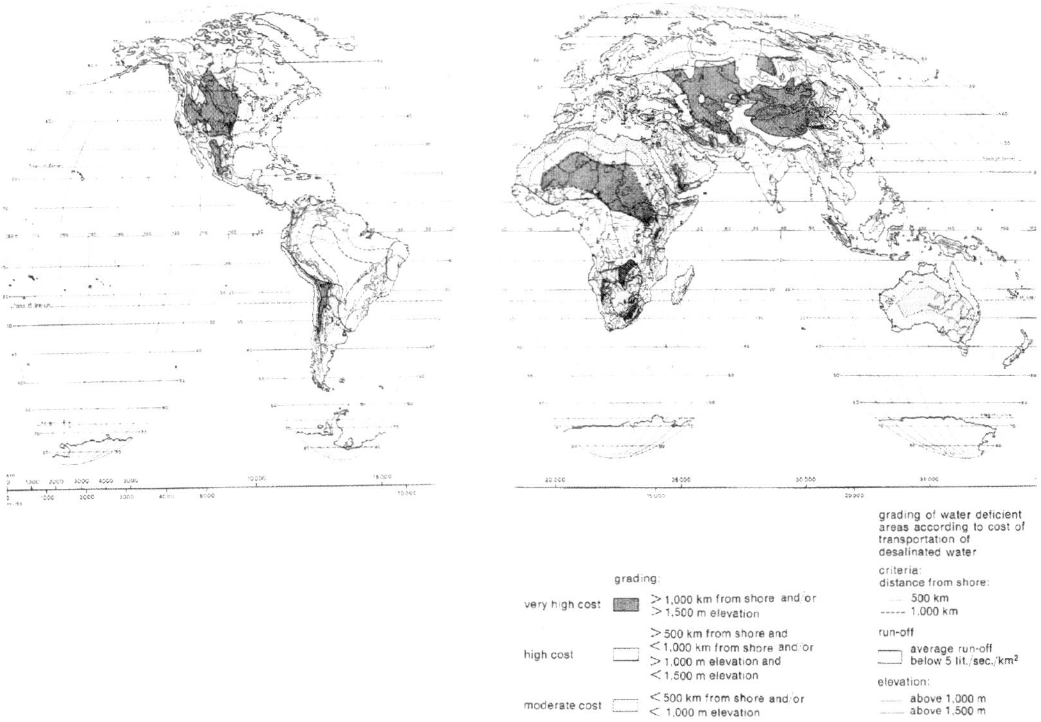


**Figure 2.** Habitability of the globe in 2100 according to water supply. ca. 1974.

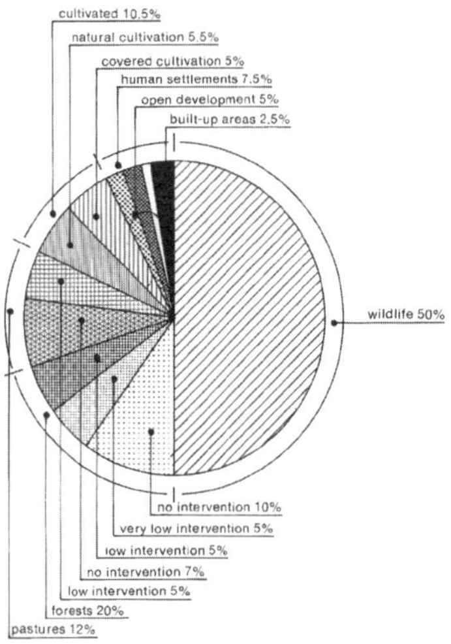


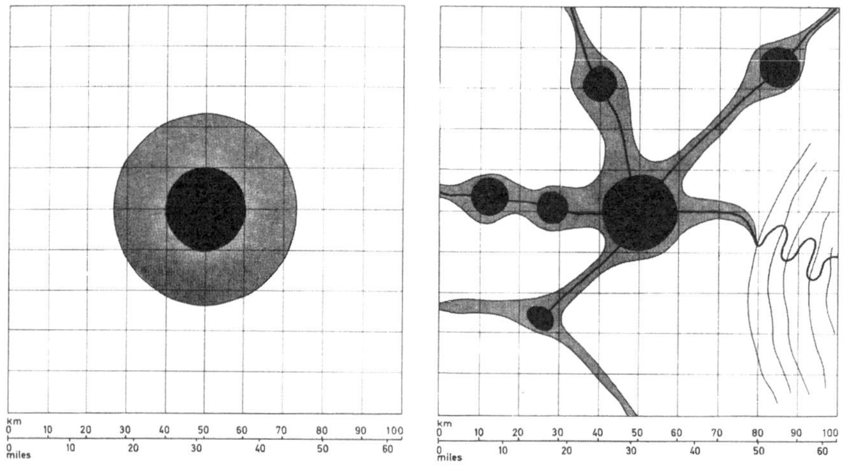


**Figure 3 (Top).** Ecumenopolis. Chart of the 12 global land uses. ca. 1973.
**Figure 4 (Bottom).** Growth of a contemporary human settlement. Concentric to linear. ca. 1978.

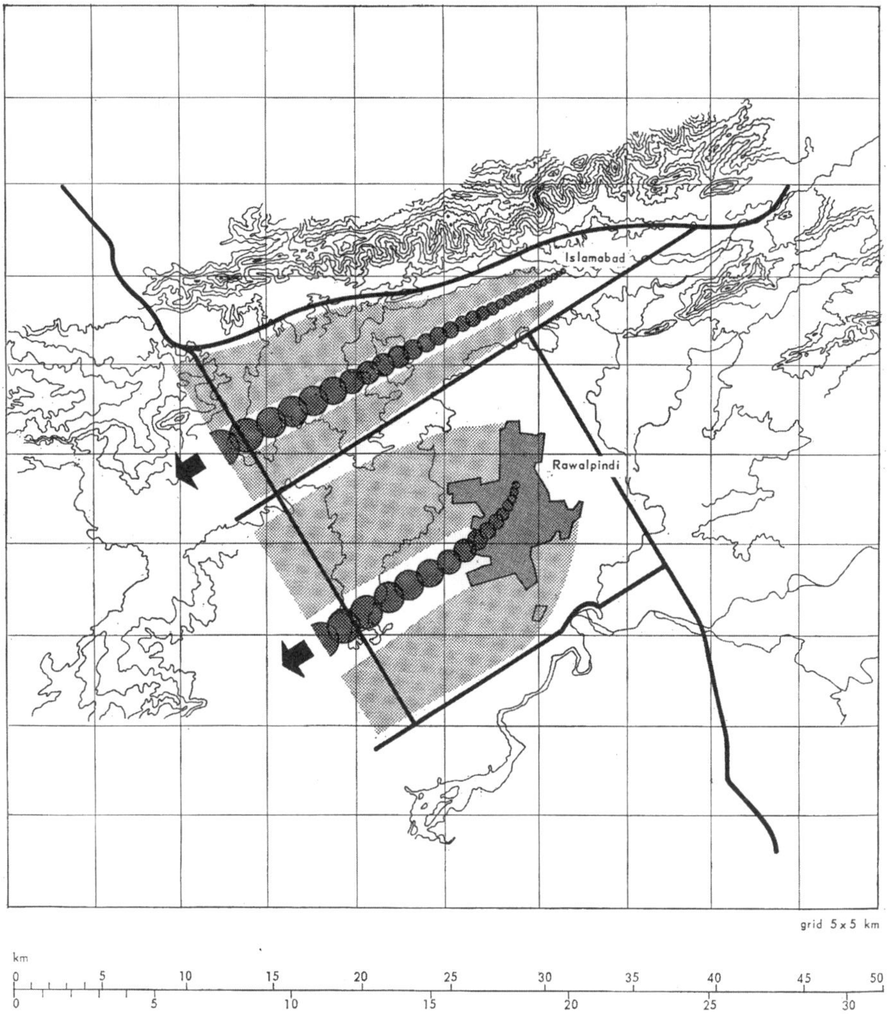


**Figure 5.** Dynamically growing Dynametropolis Islamabad, Pakistan. 1960.

# Seven Bridge Cities to Link Four Continents

**Project:** 24. **Author:** Yona Friedman (1923). **Date:** 1963. **Themes:** Circulation. Infrastructure. Parallelism. Place(lessness).

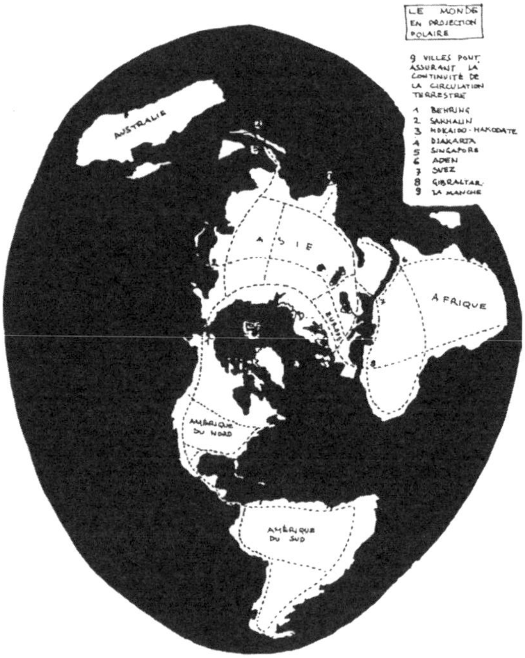


**Figure 0.** The World in Polar Projection . 9 bridge cities assure continuous terrestrial circulation. After Yona Friedman. 1963.

The Seven Bridge Cities unite the world's continents, creating a new form of Pangea. The project begins by displacing the conventional point of view through which we tend to picture Earth **[fig. 0]**. Since the sixteenth century, post-Mercator cartographic representations have depicted a maritime planet oriented from North to South. These maps represent sea distances with dimensional accuracy, reflecting the maritime routes that connect a Eurocentric world system.[1] Yona Friedman's project employs, in turn, a polar projection that shows the continents *almost* as a single landmass—as Buckminster Fuller had already suggested **[project 14]**. The Seven Bridge Cities are strategic interventions in this map: a supplement to existing natural conditions that take advantage of the fact that, in the most distant cases, fewer than 150 km separate the continental shores.

On a first level, the bridges play an infrastructural role, facilitating the construction of a continuous, global system of land transportation. They are, even if Friedman is unaware of it, the ultimate manifestation of two nineteenth-century dreams of infrastructural connectivity: the idea of building a railroad bridge at the Bering Strait, and William Gilpin's 1890 proposal for a Cosmopolitan Railway "compacting and fusing together all the world's continents," which engineer Joseph Baerman Strauss formalized in his 1892 design **[fig. 1]**.[2] Yet, the power of these interventions is also symbolic. For Friedman, bridges have always been "artificial continents" that establish terrestrial links where water imposes a natural barrier, thereby generating new relationships between disparate parts and creating moments of intensified activities.[3] Taking this logic to the scale of the planet, Friedman's Bridge Cities create nodal points of world union that symbolize the interrelations of the human collective. Their explicit models are Florence's Ponte Vecchio, Paris's Pont-Neuf, and Venice's Rialto: bridges that are inhabited and occupied.[4] Converted into actors at the world scale, these historic, inhabited bridges, formerly parts of a city, become cities in themselves that integrate infrastructural, productive, and residential uses **[fig. 2]**.

Although Friedman indicates that the construction techniques and the functional conditions of the Bridge Cities will vary according to their location, the drawings repeatedly present them as an implementation of the principles he had previously defined for Mobile Architecture (1956–1959). The Bridge Cities adopt the major formal characteristics of that project—they are discrete and elevated urban units conceived using a systematic logic that is infrastructural, not architectural—and culminate its conceptual goals. For Friedman, Mobile

**1.** Peter Sloterdijk, "Waterworld: On the Change of the Central Element in the Modern Age," in *In the World Interior of Capital: For a Philosophical Theory of Globalization*, trans. Wieland Hoban (Cambridge, UK: Polity Press, 2014).

**2.** William Gilpin, *The Cosmopolitan Railway: Compacting and Fusing Together All the World's Continents* (San Francisco: The History Company, 1890). Quoted in Marc Shell, *Islandology: Geography, Rhetoric, Politics* (Stanford, CA: Stanford University Press, 2014), 78 and 276 (note 117). Shell explains that Gilpin initially formulates his proposal in 1860, and that its design materialization by Strauss is a sign of the Hegelian thinking that dominated University of Cincinnati at the time.

**3.** Yona Friedman, "Une Architecture pour des milliards d'hommes," in *Les Visionnaires de l'architecture*, ed. Jean Balladur (Paris: R. Laffont, 1965), 73.

**4.** Friedman, "Une Architecture pour des milliards d'hommes," 73. It must be noted that bridges are a constant reference in the imaginary of the megastructural movement, as Reyner Banham explains. Reyner Banham, *Megastructure: Urban Futures of the Recent Past* (New York: Harper and Row, 1976), 13–15.

Architecture is a way to respond to the emergence of a global urban society in which 80 percent of the world population will live in cities.[5] Instead of accepting, as Constantinos Doxiadis does, that this trend will inevitably lead to superficial urban expansion, Friedman proposes a model of urban intensification and concentration consisting of the conversion of existing cities into Spatial Cities by deploying a spatial grid on top of them **[project 23]**.[6] Such a grid's role is twofold: it serves the quantitative necessities of new inhabitants by adding a new vertical layer to the built fabric, and it constrains the superficial growth of the city. This strategy, conceived originally only for the city scale, not only seeks to enable new mobile and ephemeral ways of life, but also fosters a process of world-restructuring. Through a progressive elevation of the point of view that concludes in the world map representing the Bridge Cities, Friedman's drawings reveal the emergence of a new structure of world urbanization. The initial perspectives showing spatial cities are designed for specific locations, which they frame and contain, converting each city into a delimited unit. The diagrams of *Mobile Architecture: 10 Principles of Spatial Urbanism* (1959) depict these urban units as the tool to redraw the whole map of Europe, now turned into a constellation of 120 interrelated cities of three million inhabitants **[fig. 3]**. In "Une Architecture pour des milliards d'hommes" (An Architecture for billions of men) China is imagined as a country of two hundred cities and the world as a planet of one thousand cities.[7] The Seven Bridge Cities are thus the key symbolic pieces of a broader project of world-making, whose main traits are the construction of a territorial system of discrete but connected urban units, the privileging of infrastructural space over architecture, and the vertical separation between project and terrain.

The Bridges, just as the Spatial City, are elevated, aerial structures. In operational terms, this vertical separation between project and terrain—what we term parallelism—allows architectural projects since Khidekel's in the 1920s to treat proposition and Earth as dialectical opposites: since the project does not have to respond to contextual constraints, it can be thought of, entirely, as an independent world **[project 5]**. The elevation is also a way to link vision and cognition. In its more direct, phenomenal use, distance grants a wider visual comprehension of the surroundings and thereby opens the horizon of any particular intervention. In more conceptual terms, the vertical split has a more primordial cognitive dimension: removing the subject from the surface of the earth emphasizes that the world is already an entity in itself, an object distinct from the observer.

5. Friedman, "Une Architecture pour des milliards d'hommes," 72.

6. In this regard, Friedman appropriates Konrad Wachsmann's structural system for urban purposes. See Manuel Orazi, "Konrad Wachsmann's Technological Utopia," in Yona Friedman and Manuel Orazi, *Yona Friedman: The Dilution of Architecture* (Zurich: Park Books, 2015).

7. Friedman, "Une Architecture pour des milliards d'hommes," 72.

Friedman's insistence on parallelism between the mid-1950s and the mid-1960s informs a very singular and constant exploration of the aforementioned tensions between project and world as well as between viewing and acting subject and terrestrial object. Still, the titles of two of the author's more recent texts, "Seen From Outside," and "Architecture and Urban Design From a Particular Point of View," reflect the persistence of those pairs of dialectic confrontations in Friedman's thinking, and reiterate his way of linking cognition to visual positions.[8] The idea of detached vision, or vision from outside, refers to Friedman's privileging the production of generic models and so-called scientific theories over applied knowledge and ad-hoc solutions—an attitude which, in Mobile Architecture, leads him to define the rules of a unitary, gridded infrastructural system that can be applied worldwide.[9] With the idea of particularity, as architectural historian Manuel Orazi maintains, Friedman facilitates the emergence of "a strictly subjective point of view."[10] Not only do Mobile Architecture's elevated structures deny the definition of the city by a single authority, and allow, instead, a multitude of individual occupations, they also allow citizens to see the resulting ensemble from a plurality of points of view. Instead of architectures, the grids are neutral infrastructural supports, which situate individuals as the nuclei of the construction process and present urban society as a visual spectacle comprising a sum of individual acts. Friedman's early parallelism is thus the instrument to reconcile these two scales and visual positions: the detached view of a global logic of intervention and the subjective dimension of individual participation. The neutral and abstract character of the matrix is the basis for an open process of individual appropriation. The separation from Earth, in turn, allows the architect to intervene across the world with a single design procedure, while respecting contextual conditions. Elevation allows citizens to perceive Earth as an entity, the urban units that constitute the planet, and the individual efforts toward their construction **[fig. 4]**.

During the late 1960s and early 1970s, Friedman becomes increasingly skeptical about the possibilities of implementing the single form of global intervention he had initially envisaged. Although his insistence on parallelism as a universal formal strategy diminishes accordingly, he reinforces the main postulates of his early work; including his understanding of the earth as a unified entity that the Bridge Cities aim to make intelligible. *Utopies Réalisables* (Feasible utopias, 1975), Friedman's most ambitious treatise, consolidates his

**8.** Yona Friedman, "Architecture and Urban Design from a Particular Point of View," and "Seen From Outside," in *Arquitectura con la gente, por la gente, para la gente = Architecture with the People, by the People, for the People: Yona Friedman*, ed. María Inés Rodríguez (Barcelona: Actar, 2011), 54–62 and 92–100, respectively.

**9.** Yona Friedman, *Utopies réalisables* (Paris: Union Générale d'Editions, 1976), 299. The possibility of a scientific architecture is key for Friedman, who devotes to this topic his book *Pour une architecture scientifique* (Paris: P. Belfond, 1971).

**10.** Manuel Orazi, "The Erratic Universe of Yona Friedman," in Rodríguez, *Arquitectura con la gente, por la gente, para la gente*, 110. See also Yona Friedman, "Mobile Architecture: 10 Principles of Spatial Urbanism," in Friedman and Orazi, *Yona Friedman: The Dilution of Architecture*, 214–219.

thinking, and presents a nonuniversalist, incremental, theoretical model of world transformation in which the global scale results from the infrastructural link of discrete, differentiated urban units. The text entirely rejects universalist utopias of the global State, the attempt to "organize" the entire world's social and physical space, for being based on an unattainable ideal of transparent, universal communication.[11] The single universal project is deemed as a totalizing impossibility. Instead, he praises cities—which he retheorizes in association with his notion of "critical groups," meaning, the maximum number of people that can pursue effective collective actions—as a form of real utopia.[12] In this schema, each city is an independent social and spatial collective project. It is, in this sense, an "environment," a term Friedman prefers to "society" because it emphasizes that human collectives are inseparable from the spaces they build and the objects they produce. The global scale appears through the weak communication of these delimited, urban communities.[13] In a social sense, global space is then a collection of fragments, but physically, it is unitary. In fact, says Friedman, the unity already exists, although the real "global infrastructure" has remained beyond our attention. It is Earth itself, whose unity and linkages have only to be made visible and reinforced.[14]

Ultimately, Friedman envisions a globe in tension between the already existing unity of the earth and the plurality of forms that can inhabit it. In his approach to the world scale, the dreams of "global organization" are finally replaced by processes of construction that allow internal differences to proliferate within a system of global linkages.[15] At the beginning of his career, Friedman is intensely engaged in the multiple debates concerning the emergence of a global urban society and the architectural response to the world scale, which characterize the late 1950s. The Smithsons and Constant also explore parallelism[16] **[projects 18 and 19]**. Friedman's structures derive from Konrad Wachsmann's and establish a dialogue with the work of Frei Otto. Different types of spatial structures are investigated by the members of the Group d'Études d'Architecture Mobile (GEAM), which Friedman creates in 1958. Two of this group's members, Werner Ruhnau and Eckhard Schulze-Fielitz—Friedman's collaborator on the Bridge City for the English Channel (1962–63)—insist on the idea of occupying the air **[fig. 5]**.[17] Climate control of the urban space, one of the characteristics of Mobile Architecture, is also a generational trope **[project 22]**. Friedman's elaboration of all these themes ends up informing a distinc-

11. Friedman, *Utopies réalisables*, 71, 244, 262, and 278.

12. Friedman, *Utopies réalisables*, 230.

13. Friedman, *Utopies réalisables*, 230.

14. Friedman, *Utopies réalisables*, 235.

15. Friedman, *Utopies réalisables*, 269. In fact, Friedman asserts that this organization is starting to emerge. See also in this respect: Pier Vittorio Aureli and Manuel Orazi, "The Solitude of the Project," *Log* 7 (2006): 21–32.

16. For a detailed analysis of the differences between the Smithsons and Friedman see Friedman and Orazi, *Yona Friedman: The Dilution of Architecture*, 385–394.

17. Friedman and Orazi, *Yona Friedman: The Dilution of Architecture*, 416; and Wolfgang Fiel, *Eckhard Schulze-Fielitz: Metasprache des Raumes = Metalanguage of Space* (Vienna: Springer, 2010), 216–221.

tive understanding of the world as the integral of multiple spatial collectives, each shaped by the direct action of mobile individuals. As a Hungarian who migrated to Israel after World War II and then abandoned the Zionist project in 1957 in order to live in Paris, Friedman thinks about a world system that conflates the participatory dimension of the kibbutz and the stateless condition of the migrant.[18] The Bridge Cities—spaces of transit built with the flexible structures of Mobile Architecture—epitomize, symbolically, the place where the agent of globalization and the inhabitant/builder of the city coincide in the figure-in-transit of a stateless individual.

**18.** Friedman, *Utopies réalisables,* 262–269.

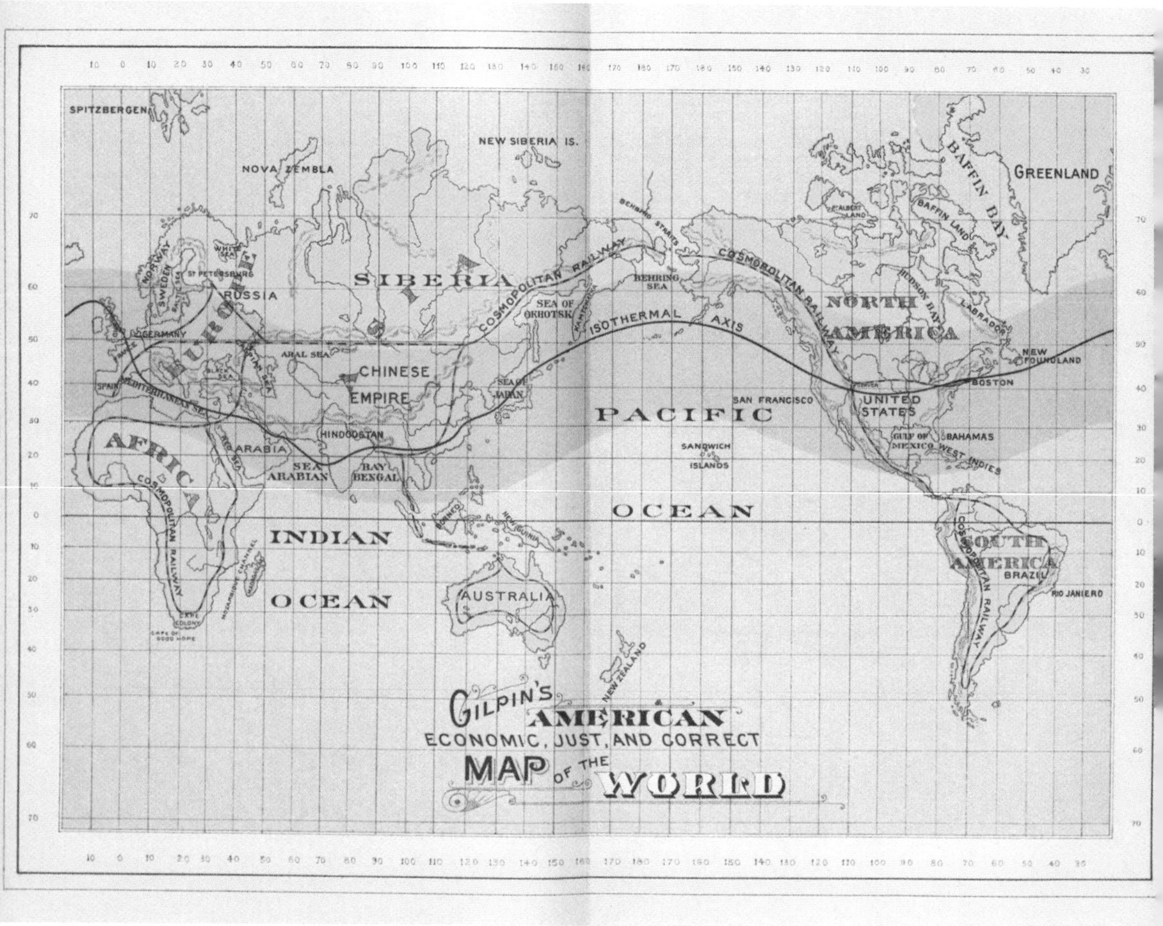


Figure 1. Cosmopolitan Railway map. William Gilpin. 1890–1892.

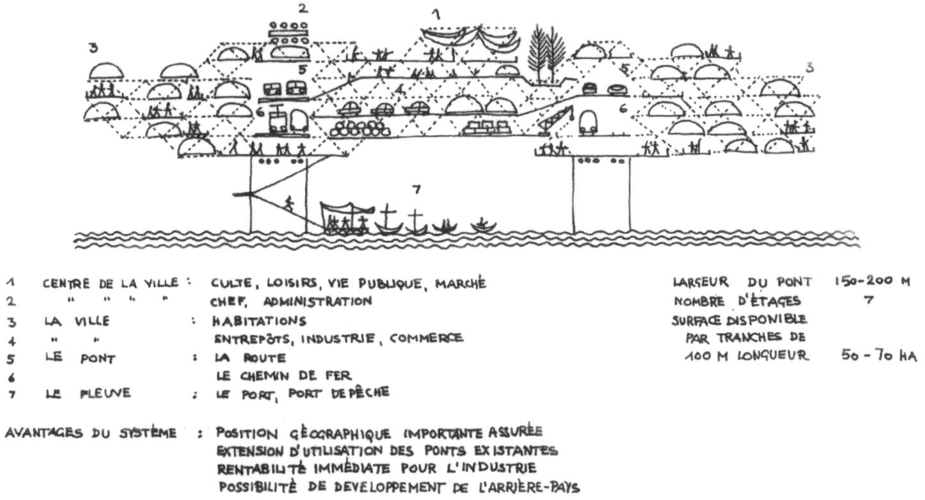

**Figure 2 (Top).** Section of an African Bridge City. ca. 1962.
**Figure 3 (Bottom).** All European Population Divided in 120 Cities of 3 Million People. 10 Principles of Spatial Urbanism: Principle number 10. 1959.

**Figure 4.** The Bridge-Town at Gibraltar. ca. 1962.

**Figure 5.** Bridge City over the English Channel. Model. Yona Friedman with Eckhard Schultze-Fielitz. 1963.

# Dream City

**Project:** 25. **Authors:** Archigram: David Greene (1937) with Michael Webb (1937). **Date:** 1963. **Themes:** Cybernetics. Immateriality. Parallelism. Telecommunication.

**Figure 0.** Dream City. Fragment *Story of the Thing*. After David Greene and Michael Webb. 1963.

Dream City is one of the segments of the Living City Exhibition (1963), the show that brings together for the first time all the members of Archigram: Warren Chalk, Peter Cook, Dennis Crompton, David Greene, Ron Herron, and Michael Webb **[fig. 0]**.[1] Both chronologically and conceptually, the project is, thus, part of one of the group's seminal works, as the Living City introduces some of the major themes that will inform Archigram's later production. Starting with the claim that the city must be considered a "unique organism" and with severe criticism as to the uniformity and dullness of suburbia, the Living City explores how design can contribute to intensifying the urban experience.[2] The exhibition presents the urban environment as a domain shaped by two contrasting and yet deeply intertwined social conditions: a newly acquired capacity for subjective expression and the omnipresent, technologically produced, mass forms of communication and consumption. To respond to this situation, Archigram proposes, it is necessary to situate architecture anew, rescaling it as just one among the many material and social constituents of the urban, and to embrace the transience that increasingly pervades Western societies. Instead of being designed as static elements, oblivious to the changes of social life, architecture and the city should be conceived with the same level of dynamism that characterizes social and individual life.

The Living City advances Archigram's interest in the design of spatial systems that admit change, that can respond to individual desires and grant subjective gratification; and reveals an intellectual attitude that is consonant with Karl Popper's theorization of the "open society" and with emerging critiques of spatial planning.[3] Dream City can be partially understood as the extrapolation of these ideas to the scale of the world. The project proposes building an extremely light aerial net, covering the earth, which acts as a scaffold for individual appropriation and as the basis for extending the urban environment to the whole planet. At the same time, Dream City is, explicitly, a fantasy—and arguably a dark one. The image that summarizes the project uses a symmetrical disposition reminiscent of the Rorschach tests employed to reveal unconscious psychological conditions and mental disorders **[fig. 1]**. The urban world of Dream City, hovering above a derelict rural landscape, is the projection of our social desires. It is a condition that still doesn't exist, an unconscious social project, at once desired and feared. It is a world occupied by dismembered, technologized bodies that enjoy occupying the sky while they lack an Earth to rest on **[figs. 2]**. It is a fragmentary space, made of explosions and violent juxtapositions **[fig. 3 and 4]**.

1. Cook, Greene, and Webb start editing the magazine *Archigram* in 1961. The collective thus takes the name from the magazine, to which Chalk, Crompton, and Herron contributed starting with the third issue, "Expendability: Towards Throwaway Architecture," also edited in 1963.

2. From the presentation of the exhibition. See Living City Exhibition. Archigram Archival project. Accessed online at The Archigram Archival Project, March 6, 2018: http://archigram.westminster.ac.uk/project.php?id=36

3. Hadas A. Steiner, "Bathrooms, Bubbles and Systems: Archigram and the Landscapes of Transience" (PhD diss., MIT, 2001), 134.

Dream City is characterized, in this sense, by an ambivalence, even a negativity, that challenges the optimistic tone for which Archigram is recognized.

The Archigram members elaborate a world vision through their 1960s designs that is generally read as an optimistic, apolitical project, reliant on an uncritical faith on technological progress.[4] Seduced by Marshall McLuhan's idea that the interchange of information and cybernetics can create a new global domain, "an all-at-once world," the group wants, in Hadas Steiner's words, to define the image "of the architectural global village."[5] With that purpose, the collective adopts the Independent Group's attention to mass media, mobility, and communications; Buckminster Fuller's technologically driven vision of a global system; and an understanding of architecture as a means of fostering individual agency as put forward by Cedric Price or Yona Friedman, as the initial ingredients for its own architectural explorations of the global domain **[projects 6, 14, 18, and 24]**.[6] The resulting designs, although fascinated with the technologization of architecture, are more interested in the rhetoric expression of technology as the aesthetic basis of a new type of environmental organization than in its rational implementation. In fact, Archigram's work deliberately collapses the fantastical and the feasible, in projects that combine incipient technological possibilities with the imaginaries of science fiction, B-series films, and comic books.[7] Disregarding any consideration about feasibility, Archigram presents their work as part of a collective urge to "predict the patterns of the future" and to conceive a new kind of global environment in which technology supports a project of personal liberation.[8]

Archigram's vision of the global village sublimates technologies and social conditions that in the 1960s are in early developmental stages in the most economically developed countries only, extending them to the whole world. The result tends to appear like a visual apotheosis of the fashions of 1960s London: a pop planet. Yet, the extension of local conditions—but globally hegemonic—to the world often anticipates some aspects of the coming globalization. The Walking City (1964), a series of mobile cities that take their inhabitants across the globe, presents Earth as a space to be colonized by a new form of nomad citizenship, which operates throughout the planet while remaining entirely detached from it. The mobile, temporal infrastructures that constitute the Instant City (1968) indicate a new status of the urban—dissociated from the notion of metropolitan agglomeration—and an understanding of geographical space as a commodity devoid of any inherent value and subjected to temporary cycles of consumption and abandonment. The Soft Scene Monitor (1968) turns domes-

**4.** Simon Sadler, "The Living City: Pop Urbanism circa 1963," in *Archigram: Architecture Without Architecture* (Cambridge, MA: MIT Press, 2005), 53–89. Steve Parnell, "The Collision of Scarcity and Expendability in Architectural Culture of the 1960s and 1970s," *Architectural Design* 82, no. 4 (July 2012): 130–135. The Italian architectural collectives Superstudio and Archizoom will develop their projects precisely as a criticism of Archigram's social optimism. See projects 36 and 38.

**5.** Steiner, "Bathrooms, Bubbles and Systems," 11. For Archigram's interest in Marshall McLuhan and the idea of an all-at-once world, see Warren Chalk, "Hardware of a New World," *Forum* (October 1966). Accessed at The Archigram Archival Project, March 8, 2018: http://archigram.westminster.ac.uk/essay.php?id=291

**6.** Sadler, *Archigram: Architecture without Architecture*, 95–124. Steiner, "Bathrooms, Bubbles and Systems," 17 and 56.

**7.** Luis Miguel Lus Arana, "BUILDING A UTOPIE AUTRE [AMAZING ARCHIGRAM! – 50 YEARS OF ZOOM!/ ZZZZRRTT!/ THUD!/ BLAAM!" *Revista Proyecto, Progreso, Arquitectura* 11 (November 2014): 90–103.

**8.** The collective ambition of Archigram is constantly present in the pages of the magazine, which tried to articulate an international network of architects dedicated to "experimental architecture." Gathered under that rubric, the magazine presents the works of architects such as Friedman, Eckhard Schulze-Fielitz, Constant, the Japanese Metabolists, and the French group Utopie. In 1966, Archigram organized the Folkstone Conference in order to gather and exhibit the work of this international network.

tic space into a mere receptacle of flows of communication oriented to individual consumption. Additionally, the consideration of technology as the main driver of architectural design forces Archigram to portray a world in which architecture is increasingly less relevant. Borrowing the emerging vocabulary of computer science, the collective divides its work in two successive stages: a phase of hardware followed by a phase of software. Archigram's evolution thus seemingly follows a linear path toward dematerialization, in which the collective successively explores forms of construction through prefabricated capsules, inflatables, and mobile systems, to conclude with the very absence of architecture.[9]

Dream City questions some aspects of this linear sequence toward dematerialization and introduces a discordant, less optimistic, note in the group's global project **[fig. 1]**. The project is conceived by David Greene, the member of Archigram who is most critical of the group's lack of political commitment.[10] Despite being one of the founding members of the collective, Greene participates in Archigram only intermittently: in 1965 he leaves England to teach in the United States and does not return until 1969. This absence is indicative of a number of differences between Greene and his colleagues. Especially during his stay in the United States, Greene becomes interested in conceptual art, an experience that helps him understand that the transformation that Archigram is seeking also requires a modification of the role of the architect as knowledge producer.[11] A symptom of this attitude is that the graphic exuberance characteristic of Archigram's drawings is replaced in his case by visual vagueness and indeterminacy and by an emphasis on the textual content of the work. Dream City prefigures the decoupling of words and images that will resurface constantly in Greene's work. The project is an exercise in concision: it suggests a world in just four pages of images, and less than one hundred words. A poetic text addresses the project and its relation to the world, while the accompanying photomontages maintain an elliptical relation to the words, thus opening a gap in the project's significance. Such questioning of the precise architectural definition of the project is also a distinctive mark of Greene's persistent commitment to dematerialization. The aerial net of Dream City already points to the possibility of an immaterial architecture, which Greene's later works will carry to its ultimate consequences. The project forms a triad about the absence of architecture in a global world with the Dream City House (1964)—in which he exhorts architects to consider "total world problems"—and the LAWUN (Locally Available World Unseen Networks, 1969).[12] This last project, a vision

**9.** We take the distinction of these two phases from Hadas Steiner's dissertation.

**10.** David Greene, "A Prologue. Concerning Archigram," in *Concerning Archigram*, ed. Dennis Crompton (London: Archigram Archives, 2002), 1.

**11.** Greene, "A Prologue. Concerning Archigram," 2. Ross K. Elfline, "The Dematerialization of Architecture: Toward a Taxonomy of Conceptual Practice," *Journal of the Society of Architectural Historians* 75, no. 2 (June 2016): 201–223.

**12.** David Greene, "C.S.8.634," *Zoom: Archigram Magazine* 4 (1964). Accessed at The Archigram Archival Project, March 8, 2018. http://archigram.westminster.ac.uk/project.php?id=215

of a planetary garden devoid of architecture, which is included in *Archigram* 9, the very last issue of the magazine the collective edited, appears in the context of the group's production as a new stage of a progressive sequence toward dematerialization.[13] Seen as part of Greene's work, it is, instead, the last iteration of an ongoing quest for immateriality, absence, and the planetary scale that already guides the author's first works.

Dream City is also called The Story of the Thing. The imprecision of the term "thing" casts doubts about the nature of a project that is unclassifiable as architecture. Additionally, the term refers to the alien of Christian Nyby's science fiction horror film *The Thing From Another World* (1951). Popularly known as *The Thing,* the film narrates the story of an extraterrestrial invasion by an organism that, although seemingly animal, is in reality vegetal and can spread by disseminating seeds through the air. The final, global alarm of the film: "Tell the world. Tell this to everybody. Wherever they are. Watch the skies everywhere. Keep looking. Keep watching the skies," sets the tone of Greene's project.[14] Dream City portrays "a change of space into urbanism" through a viral process of expansion: "this thing could be a vast net encircling the earth / or it could be the molecular structure of a virus."[15] Greene's fragmentary visual and textual narrative, jumping across different scales and media—from the microscopic representation of viruses to the aerial depiction of terrain—does not leave space for hope. The images of zeppelins, spaceships, and astronauts that cross the project conclude in a double image of the net and an aerial explosion, threaded by the words: "IT CAME FROM OUTER SPACE / BATTLE IN OUTER SPACE / BATTLE IN OUTER SPACE/ rescue of the world! / cosmic fortress."[16]

Greene's text relates the advent of Dream City to the failure of the project for a "Europe city" spanning the English Channel—the same idea Yona Friedman had suggested—because of the absence of an adequate political framework. Facing this situation, Dream City imagines the emergence of a global system by other means than international political coordination. These other means are predominantly the technologies of communication, which Green believes can cause a radical disruption / explosion of existing conditions. When Green recovers the themes of Dream City in 1969 with the Locally Available World Unseen Networks (LAWUN)—described, in premonitory terms, as a preparation for an "invisible network in the air"—the elimination of architecture is total, and the world is turned into a hyperconnected planetary garden.[17] Greene's polemical goal is to foster this conversion and to portray the consequences:

**13.** We refer here to *Fruitiest Yet: Archigram Magazine* 9 (1970). There is also *Archigram Magazine* 9½, which the collective does not recognize as a full magazine.

**14.** *The Thing from Another World*, directed by Christian Nyby (1951; Burbank, CA: Warner Home Video, 2003), DVD.

**15.** David Greene, "Story of the Thing: for Boys at Heart." Accessed at The Archigram Archival Project, March 4, 2018: http://archigram.westminster.ac.uk/project.php?id=41

**16.** Greene, "Story of the Thing: for Boys at Heart."

**17.** David Greene, quoting Jack Burnham, in *Archigram,* ed. Peter Cook (Basel: Birkhäuser Verlag, 1991), 110. Greene's reference is in Steiner, "Bathrooms, Bubbles and Systems," 159.

the LAWUN is "the world's last hardware event."[18] Together with this project, *Archigram* 9 contains a packet with seeds, so that readers can make their own, individual contributions to the transformation of the world environment. At this point, Greene's work develops, by different means, the same concerns that Yves Klein and Claude Parent pursued in Air Architecture **[project 22]**. As it happened in that project, the consummation of Greene's planetary garden implies the absolute insertion of nature within technological circuits. The world without architecture is a world where technology reigns supreme; a "fully serviced natural landscape."[19] In the last stages of Greene's world-project, this becoming artificial exceeds Klein and Parent's speculation. Both nonhumans and humans become new, hybrid technological entities for whom "the organic birth-death-life-earth-heaven is no longer valid."[20] By planting the seeds included in the magazine, readers of *Archigram* 9 symbolically promote the coming of the Dream City world where architecture ceases to be the main form of organization of the environment, and embrace—either joyfully or resigned—their future conversion into cyborgs, dreaming, perhaps, with electric sheep.

**18.** David Greene, "LAWUN project number one: BOTTERY," in Crompton, *Concerning Archigram*, 144.

**19.** Greene, "LAWUN project number one: BOTTERY," 144.

**20.** David Greene, "Popular Park," *Archigram Magazine* 8 (1968): n.p. See also Todd Gannon, "Return of the Living Dead: Archigram and Architecture's Monstrous Media," *Log* 13/14 (2008): 171–180.

## Dream City

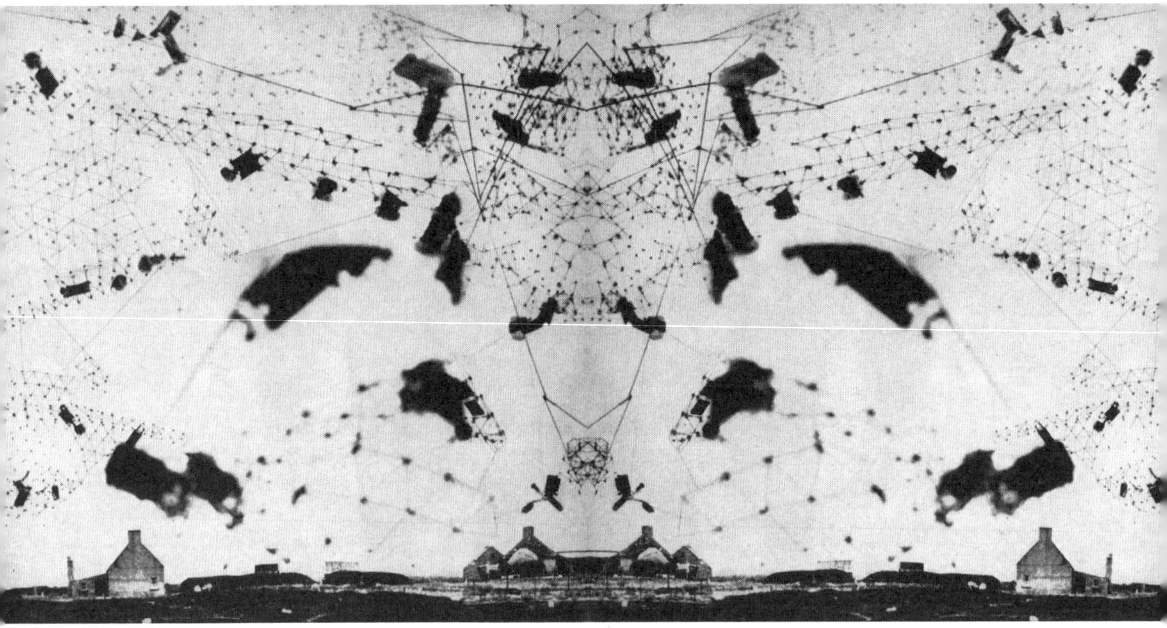

**Figure 1.** Dream City. Speculative proposal for "city" suspended on tension system, expanding to cover the earth. 1963.

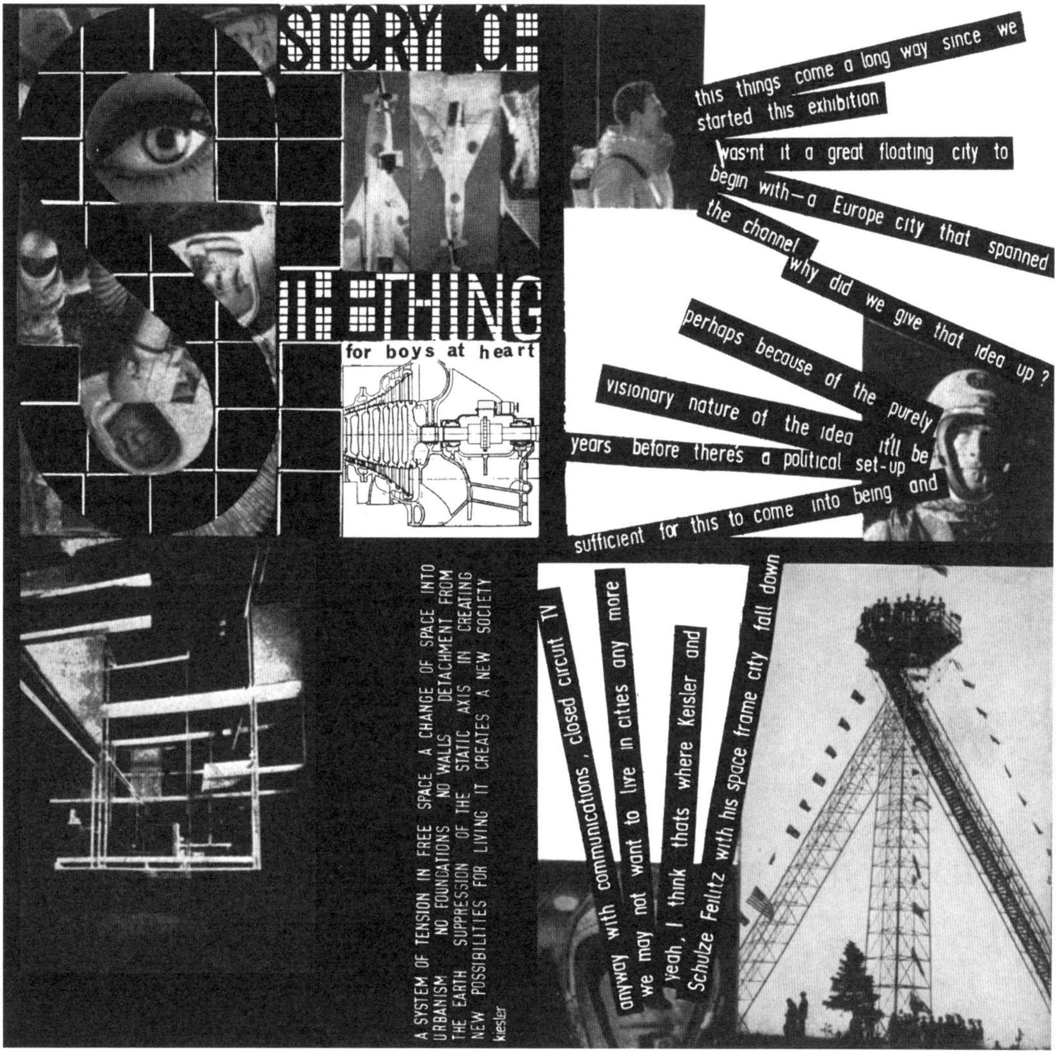


**Figure 2.** Dream City. Left hand panel. 1963.

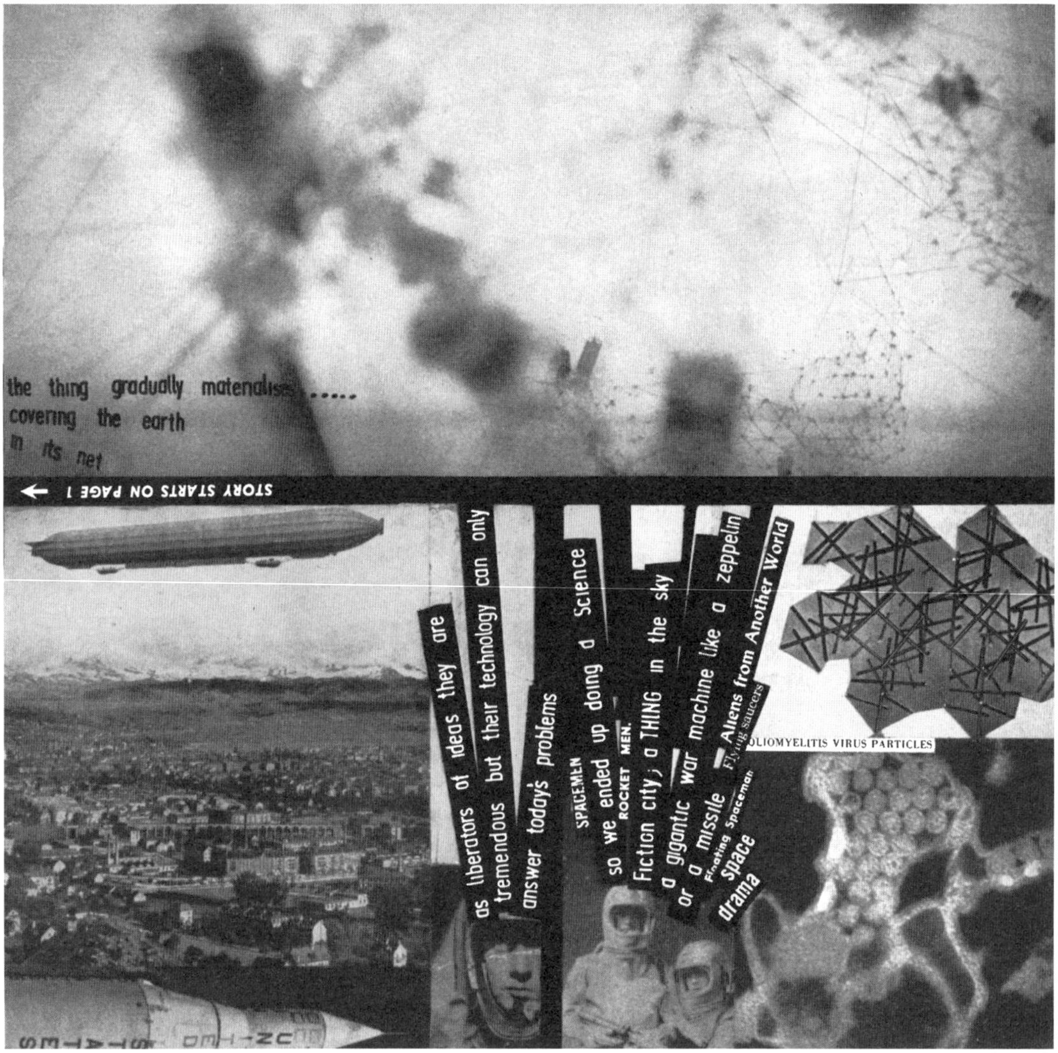


**Figure 3.** Dream City. Central panel. 1963.

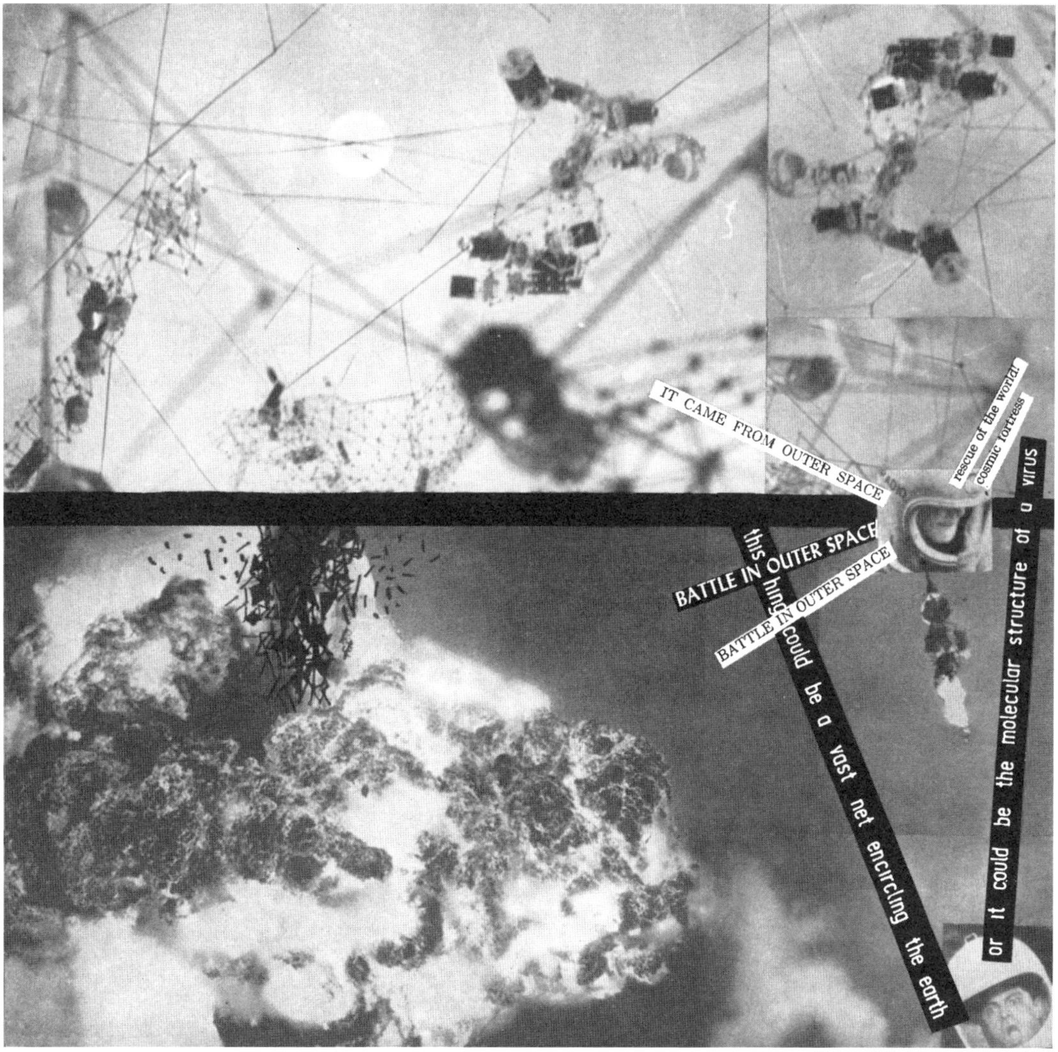


**Figure 4.** Dream City. Right hand panel. 1963.

# Ἠλεκτρονικὴ Πολεοδομια
## Electronic Urbanism

**Project:** 26. **Author:** Takis Zenetos (1926–1977). **Date:** 1962–1974. **Themes:** Automation. Cybernetics. Human-Nature Split. Parallelism.

**Figure 0.** A: Satellite-towns. B: Satellite-continents (articulate spherical surfaces). After Takis Zenetos. 1963.

Greek architect Takis Zenetos explicitly articulates his planetary project Electronic Urbanism around the notion of parallelism, the definition of a settlement system in layers above Earth. The project's initial title (1963) is "Town and Dwelling in the Future. Town Planning in Space," but between 1969 and 1974, Zenetos denominates the work with variations of the title of his book *Electronic Urbanism—City Planning and Electronics, Parallel Structures* (1969).[1] Humanity's future, electronics, and parallelism are thus the interlinked themes of the project throughout its decade long elaboration. Zenetos argues that a series of global problems—intense urbanization, population growth, environmental degradation, and lack of food resources—can be solved if humans "exploit all the altitude of the atmosphere."[2] For him, the development of ongoing trends in construction and digital technologies should facilitate the construction of a planetary network of elevated buildings, rising as high as one thousand floors, and the consequent recuperation of most of the earth's surface for nature and agriculture **[fig. 0]**. No doubt, this is a utopian vision, imagined for the distant future. Yet, Zenetos believes that the construction of such a system could begin as early as 1980, once the technologies that make it possible become widely available.[3] Hence Zenetos's project oscillates between determining actions to implement it in the short-term and a vision of a condition to be achieved in the long run. In this final stage, Electronic Urbanism would restructure the earth as an all-encompassing, collective construction visible from outer space **[fig. 1]**.

Technical rationality drives the futuristic character of Zenetos's world project.[4] A member of many scientific societies, Zenetos supports any design decision based on factual considerations: lists of inventions, research, and patents justify the technologies that appear in the project and the architect's claims about the plausibility of absolute automation and digitization of communications and experiences. Parallelism is also technically justified. Electronic Urbanism radically investigates structural suspension as a way to minimize the use of material. Only widely separated supports, containing vertical communications, work in compression, while tensioned cables suspend the rest of the vertical and horizontal forces **[fig. 2]**. Zenetos's representations emphasize this technical rigor. Structures are carefully detailed **[fig. 3]**.[5] So are the utilities, the partitions, and even the furniture; all of them presented as elements of a technical catalogue that can be implemented, by any individual, in a variety of ways **[fig. 4]**. The society of Electronic Urbanism is also entirely shaped by technological systems. On the project, information and communications flow through digital chan-

1. For a complete description of the project see Takis Zenetos, "Town and Dwelling in the Future. Town Planning in Space. A study, 1962," *Architektoniki* 41 (1963): 48–55; and Takis Zenetos, *Electronic Urbanism–City Planning and Electronics, Parallel Structures* (Athens: Architecture in Greece Press, 1969). The study was subsequently expanded in Takis Zenetos, "Electronic Urbanism, City Planning and Electronics," *Architecture in Greece* 3 (1969): 112–119; Takis Zenetos, "Electronic Urbanism, Town Planning and Electronics," *Architecture in Greece* 7 (1973): 112–119; and Takis Zenetos, "Electronic Urbanism, Town Planning and Electronics," *Architecture in Greece* 8 (1974): 122–135. Zenetos dates the first version of the project in 1962, when he presents it at the Annual Exhibition of the Organization of the Model Home. In this text we use the date 1963 to refer to the first version of the project, published that year.

2. Zenetos, "Town and Dwelling in the Future," not numbered. This is for Zenetos, in any case, a stage previous to the human occupation of other planets.

3. Zenetos, "Electronic Urbanism, City Planning and Electronics" (1969), 117.

4. Zenetos summarized his technical credo in three main points: "1) minimise structural loads; 2) make the least possible use of earth surface; 3) take into account technologies." See Zenetos, "Electronic Urbanism, City Planning and Electronics" (1969), 117.

5. It must be noted that, despite the detail, Zenetos suggests that his system could be replaced in the future by a completely tensile system, where all the buildings would hang from floating columns.

nels. Individuals work and socialize using digital networks, which eliminate the need for actual, physical displacement and undermine the very notion of place. "In there," Zenetos writes, the inhabitant of Electronic Urbanism "will be everywhere or nowhere."[6]

Zenetos's technologically driven approach to the world scale participates of the constant interchange of ideas and borrowing of spatial strategies that characterize most world projects of the time. He uses tensile structures to minimize the consumption of building materials, as Buckminster Fuller did, all the while explicitly disregarding the American architect's investigations of urban-scale domes and climatic control of the environment[7] **[projects 6 and 14]**. Constantinos Doxiadis's technocratic approach to the urbanization process and land-management supports Zenetos's way of thinking about urban systems, even if the two authors propose radically divergent spatial concepts **[project 23]**. Importantly, elevated structures are a recurrent generational trope, which Zenetos pushes to the utmost spatial and technical limits **[projects 18, 19, 24, and 25]**. There is nothing in his work of the speculative character of, for instance, Archigram's aerial Dream City. Electronic Urbanism entirely rejects the idea of intellectual provocation. It is a project seeking actual implementation. All of Zenetos's forms of visual and textual argumentation point in that direction. Addressing the world scale is for him an opportunity to resituate architecture within the path of radical technical speculation and rigor. The definition of the project begins at the scale of the world, with planetary representations. Progressively, the level of detail increases, until he reaches the domestic sphere. Numerically ordered vignettes explain the different systems of construction. The extremely synthetic, textual apparatus only provides factual and technical information. The project appears as a series of ordered propositions that can be explained with the most conventional mechanisms of architectural representation. Electronic Urbanism requires only diagrams, models, plans, and sections—all technical documents that explain the construction process.

Through these forms of representation, Zenetos moves from the world-scale to the precise definition of buildings, interior spaces, and internal equipment, unfolding a constant process of zooming-in. The chronological evolution of the project between 1963 and 1974 reflects the patient evolution in the scales of definition. This sequence determines one specific way of understanding the role of the world project. The first, 1963 version is the one that represents with more

**6.** Zenetos, "Electronic Urbanism, Town Planning and Electronics" (1974), 123.

**7.** Zenetos, "Electronic Urbanism, Town Planning and Electronics" (1973), thesis 28, 118. Additionally, the use of cables to stabilize a tent-like structure and the overall biomorphism of the system are related to the structural works of Frei Otto, with whom Zenetos maintained correspondence. See in this respect Dimitris Papalexopoulos and Helene Kalaphate, *Takis Zenetos: visioni digitali, architetture costruite* (Rome: Edilstampa, 2006), 28.

ambition the planetary scale of the project and that settles its rationality. It offers a general conceptual and spatial framework that remains constant in the different iterations of the project. After setting this global framework, Zenetos addresses the detail of the project to respond to specific contextual conditions and actual material opportunities. The consideration of local, small-scale conditions then allows the architect a reconsideration of the general template. The initial process of zooming-in is reversed now by an inverse movement of zooming-out.

The clearest example of these modifications of the global scheme is the 1969 proposal to implement Electronic Urbanism in Greece. This plan for the totality of the country is explicitly a counterproposal to the absolute continuity of Doxiadis's notion of linear city. Consequently, Zenetos abandons the idea of building a continuous aerial network of the 1963 planetary representations and suggests defining several elevated urban nodes, interconnected through telecommunications. The detail for Athens reiterates the fragmentation of Electronic Urbanism in different sets of buildings, and explains the gradual replacement of the city fabric with new aerial structures, the recuperation of nature between those structures, and the construction in the ground of tertiary facilities. A similar willingness to modify the planetary framework for contextual reasons presides over Zenetos's diagrams for implementing Electronic Urbanism in developing countries, in different geographic conditions, or for its complementation with floating structures. It also characterizes the variations of the building's interior from the initial versions to the final design. In sum, Electronic Urbanism does not fix a single, universal model. The preservation of the overall aerial frame allows the architect to respond to local conditions and temporal variation, while seeking global unity. It acts as a system that can be permanently enriched with new and variable inputs.

The implementation of Electronic Urbanism would be a gradual process in time. And yet, Zenetos says, as "a revolutionary innovation, like all changes, it will have to be brought about by the working class."[8] Mostly conceived when Greece is under the fascist dictatorship of the Regime of the Colonels (1967–1974), Zenetos's statement affirms the project as a politically charged countermodel to existing social relations. His proposal for Greece suggests, thus, not only a spatial but also a political change. After this revolutionary cry, Zenetos refrains from encouraging any particular political system—the project becomes, "applicable to any and all political regimes"—and disregards defining any space for political action.[9] This lack of definition, however, is only partial:

**8.** Takis Zenetos, *Takis Ch. Zenetos 1926–1977* (Athens: Architecture in Greece Press, 1978), 6.

**9.** Zenetos, *Takis Ch. Zenetos 1926–1977*, 6.

there are three ways in which the project suggests the organization of a specific kind of political structure and social system. The first is the articulation of the urban system as a series of discrete, dense cities of limited size, which points to the reorganization of the nation-state as a conglomerate of city-states. The second is Zenetos's insistence on the use of the atmosphere to abolish land-property, and to liberate the earth surface for common use **[project 21]**.[10] The third is the reorientation of public administration toward the cyclical management of resources. Zenetos only specifies two organisms to regulate the project: the ODCG (Organization for the Distribution of Consumer Goods) and the ORRM (Organization for the Restitution of Raw Materials).[11] The main objective of the project, the cause of the insistence on architectural dematerialization and parallelism, is thereby to avoid exploiting the planet's resources. Zenetos's political objectives are environmental. The partial liberation from work that automation makes easier is a tool to redirect individual action from the use of the earth to its care. The first causes of ethical human self-esteem in Electronic Urbanism are "the very act of improving and preserving the natural environment," and the knowledge of the "historical past by the preservation of existing cities and historic monuments."[12]

Electronic Urbanism's social objectives are thus associated with a transformation of individual life. A constant in the various iterations of the project is the speculation about the new conditions of its subjects. The separation of the city from the earth requires a "corresponding adaptation of human constitution," a physical transformation that allows humans to live in the air: in the last drawings of the project, the inhabitants float inside capsules, seemingly unaffected by gravitation **[fig. 5]**.[13] Automation and a new relation to work also produce new forms of existence, among them the expansion of human capacities by technological means.[14] Paradoxically, they also enable humans to return to the species' social origins. Familiar and sexual relations are no longer confined to the private sphere. In Electronic Urbanism, "Man will do away with all his acquired inhibitions and will be living in the manner of ancient societies, specimens of which have been preserved to our day (Eskimos, Indians, African Tribes.)."[15]

In light of the previous statement, it is possible to interpret Electronic Urbanism in two ways. On one hand, the emphasis on the residential domain (all the project's details concern the domestic sphere) matches the orientation of Zenetos's work toward the exploration of new forms of individual subjectivity. Its spaces conflate individual and family life, work, social interaction, commu-

**10.** Zenetos, "Town and Dwelling in the Future," n.p.

**11.** Zenetos, "Electronic Urbanism, Town Planning and Electronics" (1974), 123.

**12.** Zenetos, "Electronic Urbanism, Town Planning and Electronics" (1974), 125. In addition to these factors, Zenetos considers: the infinite potential of humans, thanks to technological improvement, the possibility of creating "instant monuments," and the improvement in arts and social relations.

**13.** Zenetos, "Town and Dwelling in the Future," n.p.

**14.** Zenetos, "Town and Dwelling in the Future," n.p.

**15.** Zenetos, "Electronic Urbanism, Town Planning and Electronics" (1974), 125.

nications, and travel; every function orbit around the house. In this reading, the project appears as a technologically advanced housing monument, which expresses at the scale of the world Zenetos's belief that residence should be "society's most luxurious product" and not an existential minimum.[16] On the other hand, Electronic Urbanism appears as a way to construct a new, but ancient, society by recovering a lost relation to nature. The unceasing replication of the earth's crust into multiple and parallel levels is the most evident sign of the author's will to extend nature. All the project's design decisions are justified as oriented toward naturalization, or, in Zenetos's words, toward the creation of a "non-architecture."[17] The elevated floors are new artificial grounds for trees. The project's skin filters the incidence of sunlight and weather. The form, structure, and assembly of the buildings express the potential to overcome forces of earthquakes and wind and respond to topographical conditions. Speaking about his built work, Zenetos states: "my own effort has been to integrate architecture with the environment."[18] Electronic Urbanism's extreme artificiality is for Zenetos the ultimate, and paradoxical, means toward that integration, required once we think on the world scale. Only technique can enable the recuperation of Earth's nature by facilitating the occupation of aerial space, an investigation of which the project constitutes the last, and most rigorous, exploration.

**16.** Zenetos, *Takis Ch. Zenetos 1926–1977*, 6.

**17.** Zenetos, *Takis Ch. Zenetos 1926–1977*, 6.

**18.** Zenetos, *Takis Ch. Zenetos 1926–1977*, 6.

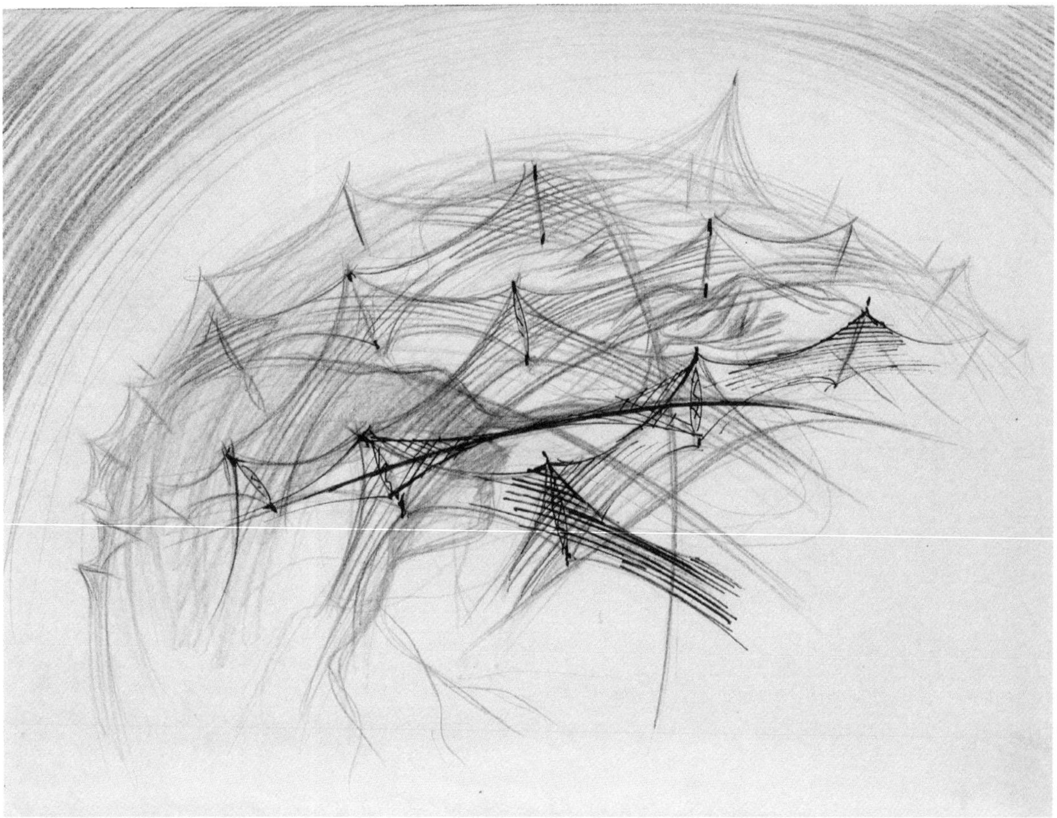

Figure 1. Electronic Urbanism's spider web surrounding Earth. 1962.

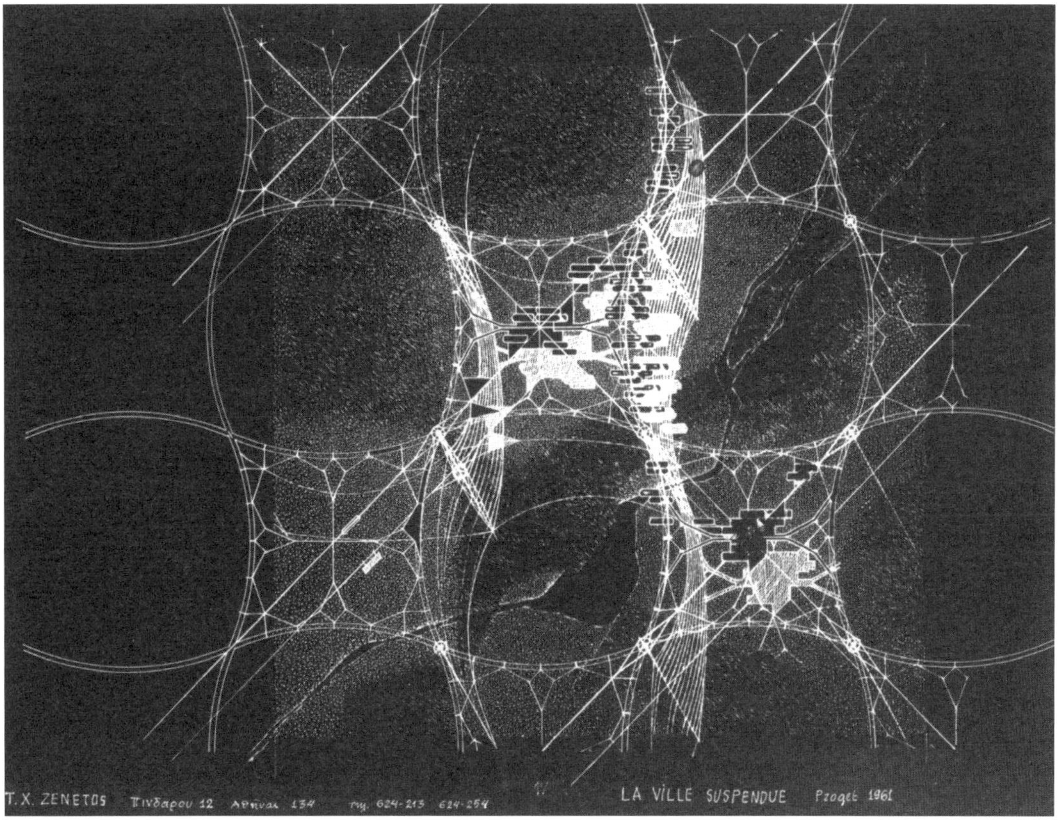


**Figure 2.** The Suspended City. 1961.

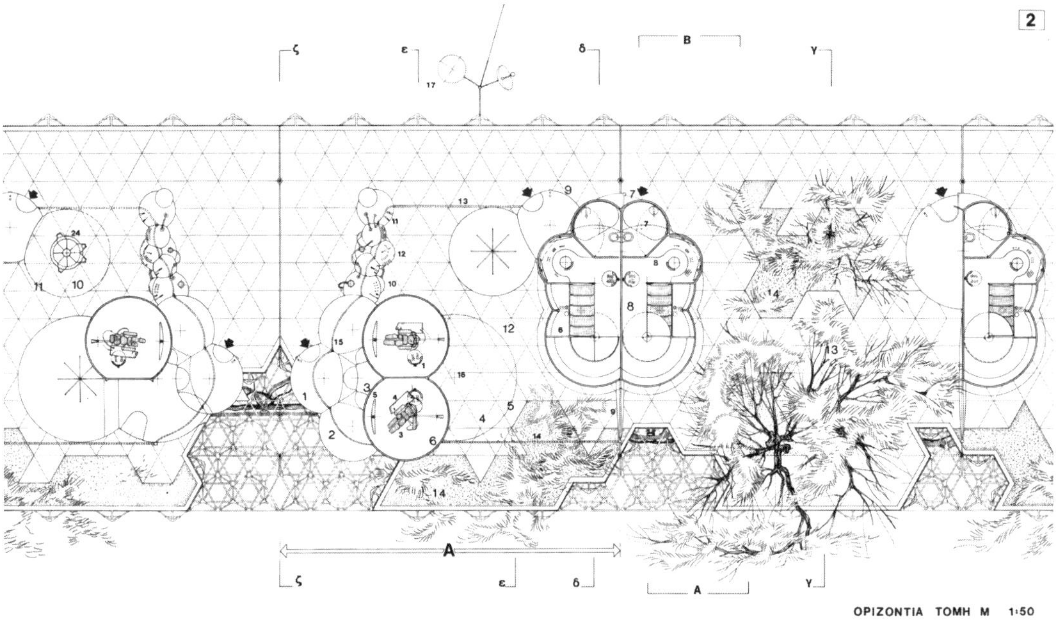


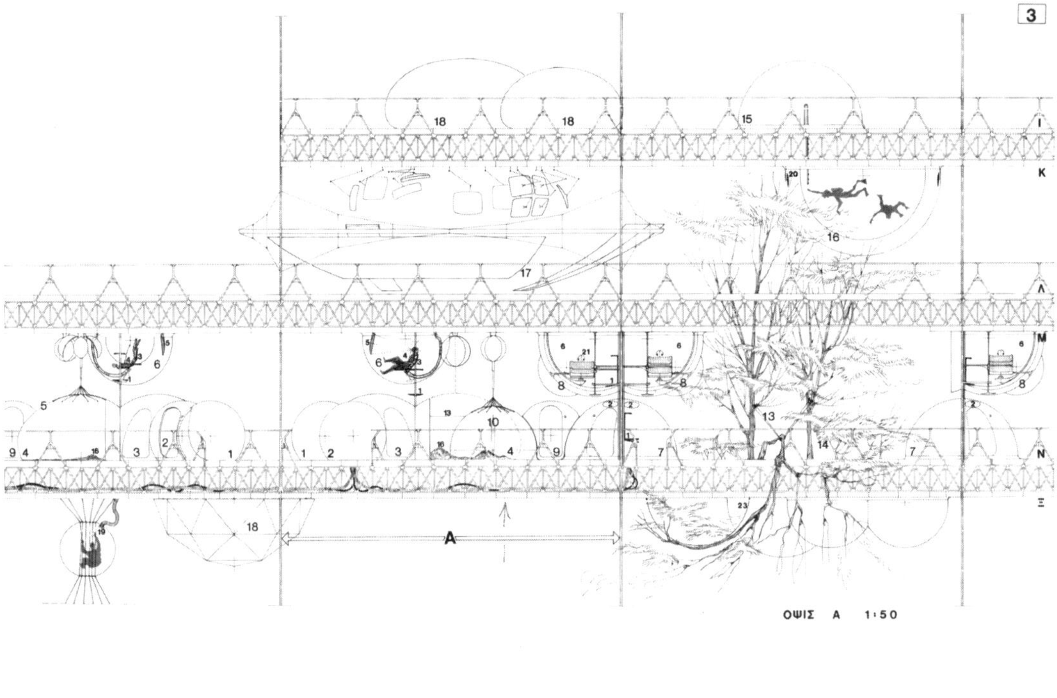


**Figure 3 (Top).** Plan at roof level showing dwelling units for four people and for individuals. 1971.
**Figure 4 (Bottom).** Section of the urban space grid showing dwelling units for four people and for individuals. 1971.

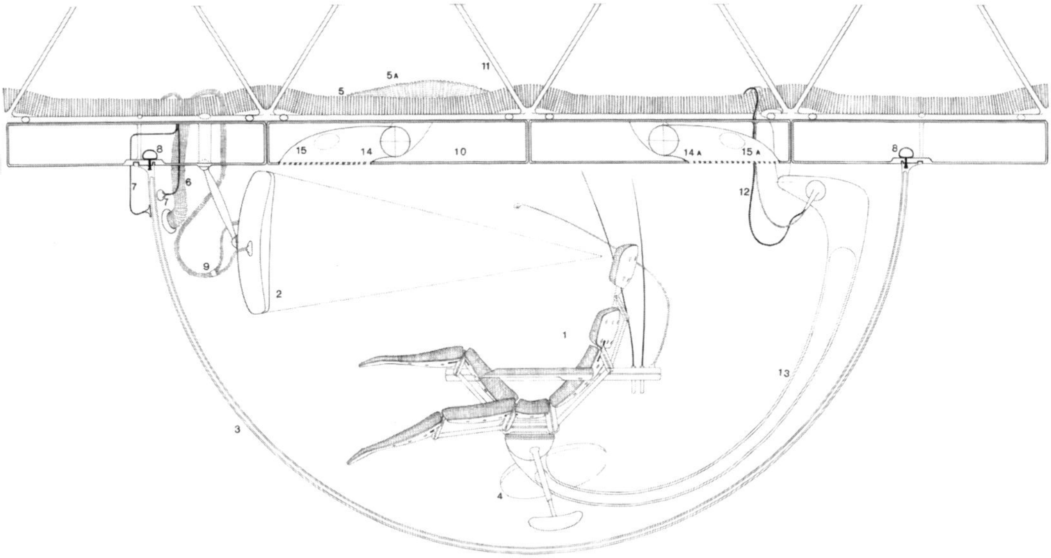


**Figure 5.** Tele-processing cell with mobile "body-carrier." 1971.

# Imaginary Cities

**Project:** 27. **Author:** Raimund Abraham (1933–2010). **Date**: 1961–1967. **Themes:** Autonomy. Linearity. Monumentality. Remoteness.

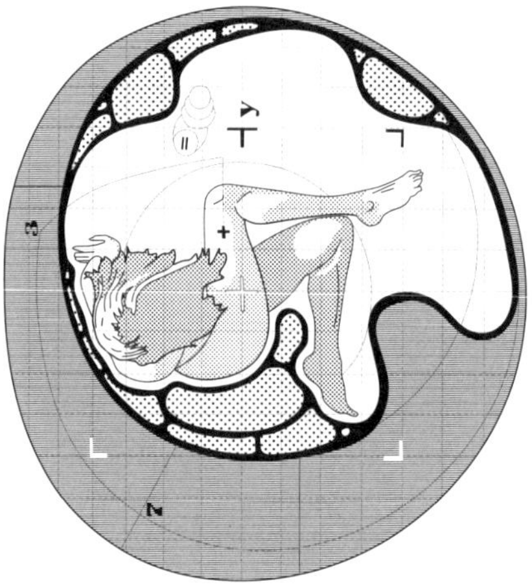

**Figure 0.** Air Ocean City. Living capsule. After Raimund Abraham. 1966.

"Raimund was a cosmologist. I have really no word for what I thought he was looking for."[1]

In cosmology the formation of theories and hypotheses about the formation of the universe derives from mathematics and physics; Raimund Abraham believes one expresses such hypotheses through drawings. As long as architecture is not built, drawing is inevitably the predominant means through which one conveys meaning. Abraham's work takes this fact to the extreme and stretches the practice of drawing to the point of divorcing it from its secondary, functional role, until it acquires its own, autonomous status. Drawing, then, is no longer attached to a necessary representation of an anticipated reality, but it is a reality of its own.[2] When displaced from process to end, drawings become the mechanism to conceive other worlds that, through dissimilitude, comment on the one we live in. Abraham uses this method not only to reflect on society, but also to attack the profession of architecture, which he criticizes for being too centered on the act of building. In his view, investing drawing with autonomy is a step of resistance against "the ignorant self-confidence displayed by the building architects . . . victims of their own compulsion to build."[3] Abraham's desire is to imagine architecture **[fig. 0]**.[4]

The relation between architecture and architectural drawing starts with a collision. That is the basis of Abraham's view regarding the ontological grounds of the discipline. An idea violates a silence; a drawing cuts a space onto which it places an idea; thoughts collide with matter. Only then does design surface to reconcile the original encounter. Design is a secondary act. The collision, however, is primary and manifests in architecture in different forms: from denying function to emancipating objects from gravity. Architecture happens in that moment of contact, which Abraham refers back to the archetypal image of the horizon, the site where Earth touches sky.[5]

The horizon is the line that holds maximal tension. It holds the suspension and anticipation of the meeting between "the uppermost surface of the earth" and "the undermost surface of the sky." Commenting on this exact moment prior to the touching of the surfaces, John Hejduk mentions how emblematically that represents Abraham's work for it involves mystery, grace, and creation.[6] The horizon does not belong to either of the two sides that create it. As a result, it concentrates all its potential between the two, reducing "the whole world to a line where two dimensions collide." It is like the contraction of language to its

1. Eric Owen Moss, "The Presence of Absence," in *In the Absence of Raimund Abraham: Vienna Architecture Conference 2010*, ed. Peter Noever and Wolf D. Prix (Vienna: MAK, 2011), 53.

2. Carlos Brillembourg and Raimund Abraham, "Raimund Abraham," *BOMB* 77 (2001): 60.

3. Norbert Miller, "Imagination and the Calculus of Reality," in *Raimund Abraham (Un)Built*, ed. Brigitte Groihofer (New York: Springer, 1996), 11.

4. Raimund Abraham, "The Enigma of the Muses," in Groihofer, *Raimund Abraham (Un)Built*, 124.

5. Raimund Abraham, "In Anticipation of Architecture," in Groihofer, *Raimund Abraham (Un)Built*, 114.

6. John Hejduk, "Raimund Abraham, Architect," in Groihofer, *Raimund Abraham (Un)Built*, 214. On this point, Hejduk recalls the image of Leonardo da Vinci's *Annunciation*, whose angel gently touches Earth after descending from the sky.

point of genesis, its zero state.[7] Abraham's obsession, a view of architecture as language, consists of a similar contraction, seeking the possibility of arriving at, or extending beyond, the discipline's limits.

The search for architecture's limits leads Abraham to conceive, throughout the 1960s, a series of *Imaginary Cities*. Understanding that architecture will always be confined to the horizon as its initial state, he sees that architectural solutions will necessarily either reach up to the sky or dig down into the earth.[8] Either way, some sort of violence—a destruction of its counterpart—lies hidden in the choice of the one or the other. "While you build the wall / you shall destroy the stones / while your eyes long for the window / you shall destroy the wall . . . / while you reach for the sky / you shall destroy the earth."[9] Thus, Abraham's fantastic explorations—as framed in 1967 at the MoMA exhibit "Architectural Fantasies"—set out to experiment with the extreme consequences of these two propositions on the city scale.[10] These projects challenge the concept of the "city" by offering new readings on its formal structure, organizational models, and social role.[11]

The twenty cities Abraham imagines during this six-year-period fall into three categories: Compact Cities, Linear Cities, and Space Cities, the last two of which engage more directly with the world scale. Linear Cities deal both with naked land and the existing city, although the relationship with the latter is one of contrast, dissociation, or even denial. The representation of these cities is emblematic and uniform and takes the form of perspectival cross-sections against which Abraham highlights specific aspects of the site: trees, mountains, or the ocean. Some insertions into realistic contexts through minimal photomontages complement the technical character of these drawings. These are moments when scale can be assessed.

As the name suggests, Linear Cities grow only along one axis **[fig. 1]**. Their configurations resemble what Reyner Banham would later call megastructure. Abraham uses linearity as an ordering device to compose a formal and organizational macrosystem where smaller units can be arranged and multiplied. In between the living units, a complex of tubes of varied diameters runs throughout the entire city, building an infrastructural backbone to supply the used space with water, energy, sewer, public transportation, etc. This almost visceral, artery-like longitudinal core reflects Abraham's image of the city as "altars of mechanical intestines."[12] In his representations, such altars are at times drawn as finite configurations, suggesting a module of potential systematic growth; at

**7.** Brillembourg and Abraham, "Raimund Abraham," 64. Abraham compares the horizon to Kazimir Malevich's white square over white canvas or Stéphane Mallarmé's blank voids of the white page.

**8.** Raimund Abraham, "The Reality of the Unbuilt," in Groihofer, *Raimund Abraham (Un)Built*, 129.

**9.** Abraham, "In Anticipation of Architecture," 115.

**10.** The exhibition, curated by Arthur Drexler, presents the work of Abraham, and two other avant-garde Austrian architects of his circle: Walter Pichler and Hans Hollein.

**11.** Abraham, "The Reality of the Unbuilt," 130.

**12.** Groihofer, *Raimund Abraham (Un)Built*, 26.

others, they are stretched until touching and merging with the horizon, suggesting the project's infinite expansion. "In my early works I was obsessed with the conquest of site, the theories of universal cities where either the site itself would aspire to the formal structure of the city, or where the city as an artificial man-made structure would conquer the entire site of the globe."[13]

Two of the Linear Cities, in particular, openly speculate on this conquering of the globe. In Glacier City (1963–1964), a Cartesian, seemingly homogeneous surface extends over a valley, underneath of which the tubular, infrastructural gut runs. Although in this case the city does not reach the vanishing point, the section again leaves open the question of the city's physical limits, which, nonetheless, allows for the possibility of noninterruption. The second case is Universal City (1966), where the city's width is confined to that of Manhattan's Central Park but its length extends until it reaches the edges of the drawing **[figs. 2 and 3]**. The city is dug in the ground, inside a channel that is sometimes placed inside existing cities. In all cases, the city functions as if it was conventionally placed over a clear landscape, suggesting that its "universal" character lies in the structure it offers to be applied on whichever site, rather than offering any social or formal adaptation to the specificities of its contexts.[14]

For Raimund Abraham, architecture starts with the conquest of a site, the initial manipulation of the topographical surface.[15] Such a transformation of the earth to create the very possibility of architecture is an essential part of Abraham's imaginary; he is fascinated with the metaphysics of the subterranean world.[16] He sees graves as the utmost symbolic origins of architecture. They signify the presence of an absence, a room that romantically extends existence to the eternal.[17] Thus, when the actual prospects of global destruction—owing to the escalating tensions of the Cold World and the Cuban Missile Crisis—reveal the potential total installment of a complete state of absence, the architect begins to imagine how site transformations and architecture itself can happen outside Earth.[18] There the series on Space Cities begins.

Abraham's cities for other planets take the duality of either "digging down into the earth or rising up to the sky" to the extreme as they dwell in the form of new settlements under completely controlled environments. Moon-Crater City (1967) is directed downward **[fig. 4]**. A massive crater is covered to house an underground urban society. Large shafts on the covering surface become launching stations for space rockets connecting this city to any other possible reachable locations on the galaxy. On the other hand, in Air Ocean City

**13.** Raimund Abraham, "Essay by Raimund Abraham," *Design Quarterly Site: The Meaning of Place in Art and Architecture* 122 (1983): 14.

**14.** Raimund Abraham, "Elementary Architecture," in Groihofer, *Raimund Abraham (Un)built*, 134.

**15.** Abraham, "Essay by Raimund Abraham," 14.

**16.** Miller, "Imagination and the Calculus of Reality," 13.

**17.** Abraham, "The Reality of the Unbuilt," 129.

**18.** *Raimund Abraham, Collisions: Exhibition* (New Haven: Yale School of Architecture, 1981), 5.

(1966)—possibly a reference to Buckminster Fuller's 1929 Airocean Town Plan—the direction is the opposite **[fig. 5; and project 14]**. The city ascends from inside a crater toward the sky, until completely releasing itself from the land. Here, a transparent giant orb, attached to a depression on the ground, incubates spherical capsules of different sizes, for individuals or collectives. The proliferation of these capsules allows the city to develop and grow until reaching a maximal community size, limited by the orb's volume. The planet's surface then releases fully formed cities to free float on the atmosphere.

For Kenneth Frampton "the imaginary works by Abraham insist on a simultaneous assertion and denial of the possibility of dwelling."[19] Abraham's Imaginary Cities exist in this gray zone, where we do not clearly know if those environments can actually be able to sustain life or if, instead, they are thought of from the beginning as pure plastic expressions to touch the limits of alternative ideas about living together as society. Not by chance, this (programmed) uncertainty is recurrently accompanied by the representation of the underground, the place where image is never fully revealed and objects are occult. The English etymology of "dwell" refers to the meaning "to hide within," and the Greek one "to go astray in the dark."[20] Abraham's projects always avoid revealing themselves completely. The images hide their own characteristics by the way they are drawn or even by the lack of drawings, gradually yielding the other-world they create, "obscured to us, but visible to his very eyes."[21]

Arriving in the 1970s, Raimund Abraham's work shifts in scale and translates his preoccupation with the universal down to the housing unit. The project Universal House (1967) establishes the transition. Universal House and his subsequent explorations on the theme are attempts to investigate the program of the house in relation to its universal form. In this project, the architect recycled his Air Ocean's transparent orb but miniaturized it to the size of a house. In its interior, a central core supports a series of kinetic circular plates that form a system of vertically organized rooms.

In Abraham, the search for a universal form also reflects a need to achieve an ideal geometry, eternal and infinite. The clash between geometry and the body, idea and matter, also reproduces the external process of collision that marks his architecture—the collision that forms the horizon and the first contact of the architectural object with the topography. The solidity and eternity of the one compensates for the fragility and temporality of the other.[22] From cities suspended in the outer space to houses grounded on the earth, Abraham sees architecture purely as language and poetry, and his projects are his means to

**19.** Kenneth Frampton, "Fragmentary Notes," in Groihofer, *Raimund Abraham (Un)Built*, 215.

**20.** Adams Sitney, "Dwelling-Place and Universe," in Groihofer, *Raimund Abraham (Un)Built*, 221.

**21.** Adams Sitney, "Utopia Before One's Very Eyes," in Groihofer, *Raimund Abraham (Un)Built*, 228.

**22.** Raimund Abraham, "Negation and Reconciliation," *Perspecta* 19 (1982): 7.

not compromise such language while seeking to achieve a form of radical clarity capable of commenting on the physical world as well as on the role of the discipline. He understands that architecture's universality demands interpretation through a system of metaphors.[23] A city represented by a perfect sphere, a city stretched endlessly throughout the globe, and a city buried beneath the ground are such metaphors. The same way that for Abraham the grave is the nonsite that symbolically alludes to pure architecture, in the end, the architect's sole mission is to "find uniquely, and idiosyncratically how to make nowhere, somewhere."[24]

**23.** Abraham, "In Anticipation of Architecture," 113.

**24.** Eric Owen Moss, "The Presence of Absence," in Noever and Prix, *In the Absence of Raimund Abraham*, 53.

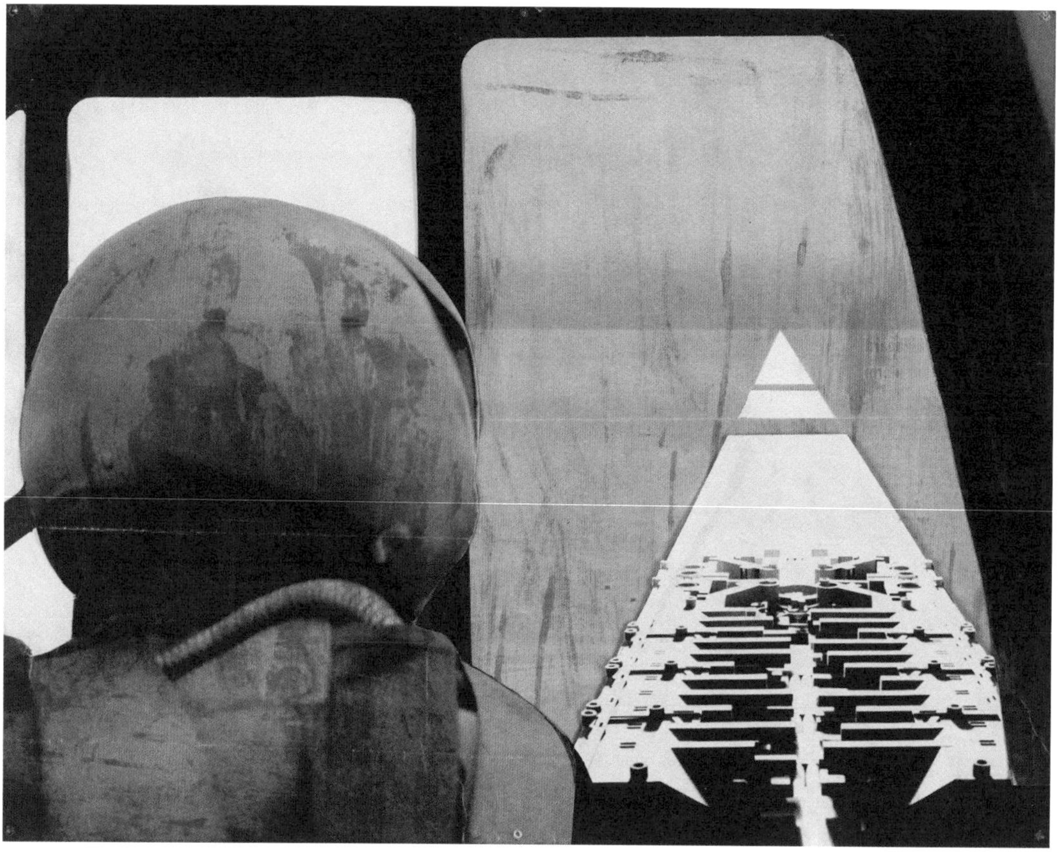

Figure 1. Universal City. Perspective view. 1966.

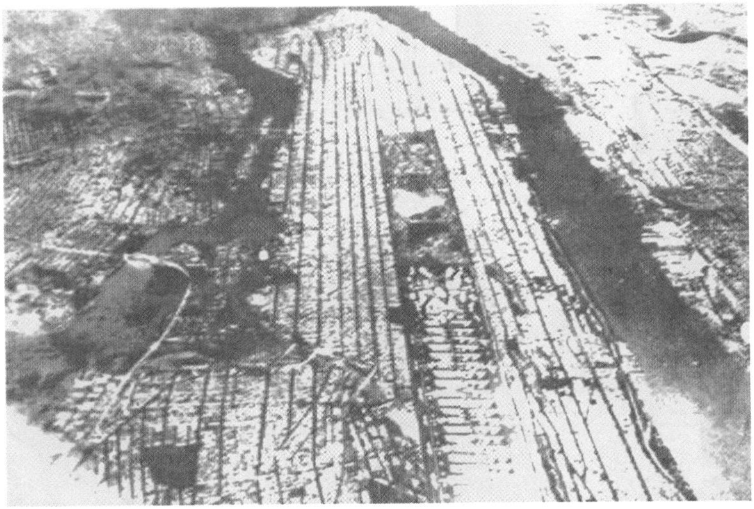

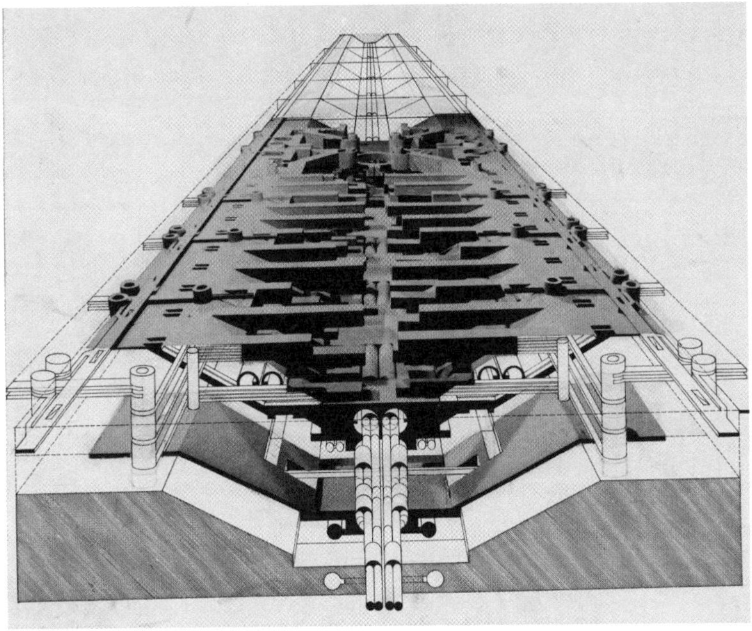

**Figure 2 (Top).** Universal City. Aerial view, extending from Central Park. 1966.
**Figure 3 (Bottom).** Universal City. Perspective section. 1966.

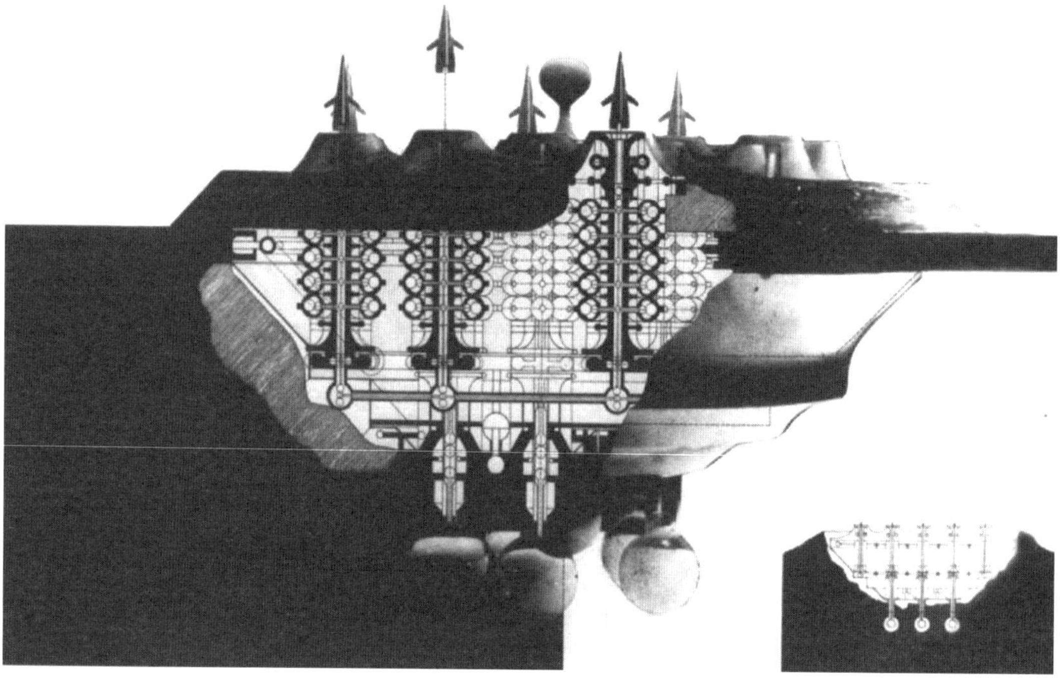

**Figure 4.** Moon-Crater City. Sectional elevation. 1967.
**Figure 5 (Opposite page).** Air Ocean City. Perspective. 1966.

62

# O Mundo na Idade da Cibernética
## The World in the Cybernetics Era

**Project:** 28. **Author:** Sergio Bernardes (1919–2002). **Date:** 1965. **Themes:** Automation. Cybernetics. Ecology. Nomadism.

**Figure 0.** The Sun Never Sets for the Man of the Future. After Sergio Bernardes. 1965.

One of the most important and controversial figures of Brazil's late modernism is Rio de Janeiro–born architect Sergio Bernardes. If it weren't for his disdain for the word "revolution," it would not be an overstatement to call Bernardes a revolutionary. The architect prefers thinking about his work as "evolutionary" for, in his terms, evolution is a natural human process, whereas revolution is an unnatural rupture to be avoided.[1] Bernardes's work can be read, though, through each of those lenses. On one hand, Bernardes situates even his most radical visions on the fringe of the sequence of events that build up the present. On the other hand, his work and thought are neither confined to nor limited by established conventions and the *status quo*, but rather addresses wide-reaching organizational changes on the existing spatial and social structures.

Evolution to Bernardes also means that humans should look beyond established conventions. Coherently, the architect develops a radical ethics of work. Bernardes avoids looking back at past projects, to the point that he plans to burn his whole archive more than once. Similarly, at the peak of his professional career, he secretly leaves for New York, disappearing and leaving everything behind.[2] Later, in a letter, he states that he needed to dedicate his life solely to his work to be able to properly engage with the scale at which the world should be addressed. A scale that is so large that it makes any of his personal affairs insignificantly small and ultimately forces him to deny that the past can play a role in the present.[3] Evolution is thus for Bernardes relentless change, rather than continuity.

In the early 1960s, Brazil is going through a strong process of modernization. Juscelino Kubitschek's controversial presidency (1956–1961) politically and economically stabilizes the country. In this context, the construction of Brasília, which the president starts promoting in 1957, not only acts as the sign of the country's territorial consolidation, but also as the symbol of its integration within international political and economic circuits. Additionally, Brasília consolidates the recognition of such prominent architects as Lucio Costa and Oscar Niemeyer as well as Brazil's position as a global agent with its own cultural voice and a distinct way of addressing modernity.

Bernardes distances himself from this context of architectural production and seeks the references for his own vision of internationalization outside Brazil. In 1965, MoMA's *Visionary Architecture* is exhibited at the VIII São Paulo Architecture Biennale, helping Bernardes to align his intellectual concerns with

1. Sergio Bernardes, "Revolução," in *Módulo Especial: Sergio Bernardes* (Rio de Janeiro, 1983), 3.

2. *Bernardes*, directed by Gustavo Gama Rodrigues and Paulo de Barros (6D Filmes e Rinoceronte Produções, 2014), DVD.

3. Sergio Bernardes, "Letter to Clarice Bernardes" [November 2, 1968], referenced in Rodrigues and Barros, *Bernardes*.

the work of other architects in the world. The show displays the designs of thirty architects, among them contemporary figures such as Paolo Soleri, Kisho Kurokawa, Kiyonori Kikutake, William Katabolos, Michael Webb, and Buckminster Fuller—for whom architecture offers the means of coupling "vision and reality" to reimagine society's future **[projects 21, 25 and 35]**.[4] In the following year, Bernardes connects to the one he identifies as his equal: Fuller. The two men share a passion and boldness for thinking about the world–human system holistically, and a desire to use cutting-edge technologies to make their projects possible. This coincidence leads to their collaboration in designing a couple of geodesic domes in Brazil and even to contemplating opening an office together. It also supports Bernardes's belief that architects need to address "global problems" as well as his later redefinition of his professional position from architect to "social inventor."[5]

In 1965, Bernardes translates his interest in visionary thinking and in the scale of the world to a project that addresses the planning of Rio de Janeiro for the year 2000 and the city's future status within an increasingly integrated planet. The resulting project, Rio in the Cybernetics Era, establishes an alternative to the two most salient projects of urban planning in Brazil at the time: Costa's design for Brasília (1957) and Constantinos Doxiadis's plan for Rio (1965). While Costa conceives of the form of the capital as a permanent, static symbol representing the country's new political status, Doxiadis's plan, a highly criticized governmental commission, uses a gridded system, driven by data and socioeconomic analysis, in order to treat Rio as a fragment of his idea of a continuously expandable Ecumenopolis **[project 23]**.[6] Bernardes's work adopts, in turn, an almost megastructural logic, in which architecture takes on the task of organizing the territory through prototypical solutions that respond to different systems and areas of the city, e.g., prototypes for vertical incremental neighborhoods, hotel-bridges, interconnected floating harbors, cellular commercial centers, multimodel transportation rings, etc. These architectural interventions are, in addition, part of a broader project of sociospatial restructuring that takes into consideration the position Rio should occupy in the world, the reorganization of productive systems, and the impacts of technological change and new forms of communication in our forms of life.

*Manchete*, the most influential national magazine at the time, commissions the Rio project. It chooses to precede Bernardes's work with the summary of an article that *Time* magazine publishes the same week, "The Age of Cybernetics," and presents Bernardes's design as a proposal for a world governed by digi-

**4.** For a description of the exhibition and the relation of participants see Arthur Drexler and Museum of Modern Art, "Visionary Architecture," Press Release 108 (September 29, 1960). Accessed online, September 6, 2018: https://www.moma.org/documents/moma_press-release_326200.pdf

**5.** Sergio Bernardes, "Considerações de base," in *Sergio Bernardes*, ed. Kykah Bernardes and Lauro Calvacanti (São Paulo: ARTVIVA Editora, 2010), 141; and Guilherme Wisnik, "A Civilização tropical e seu contrário," in Bernardes and Calvacanti, *Sergio Bernardes*, 126. English translations on pages 276 and 284.

**6.** On the occasion of the selection of Doxiadis's office for the planning of a Brazilian city, the Institute of Architects of Brazil repudiates the decision, stating that it goes against the current state of technical progress of Brazilian culture. In the same line, Lucio Costa calls Doxiadis a presumptuous comedian whose office is no more than a "contractor firm to explore urban plans of underdeveloped countries." Lucio Costa, "O contrato com a Doxiadis Internacional Associados," in *Correio da Manhã* (Rio de Janeiro, February 4, 1964), quoted in Ana Luiza de Souza Nobre, "Fios Cortantes: projeto e produto, arquitetura e design no Rio de Janeiro (1950–70)" (PhD diss., Pontifícia Universidade Católica do Rio de Janeiro, 2008), 107. For Bernardes's critique of Brasilia see Sergio Bernardes, "Entrevista 1976," in Bernardes and Calvacanti, *Sergio Bernardes*, 210.

tal technologies. In reality, following his evolutionary philosophy, Bernardes treats cybernetics as one element within a series of encompassing, sociotechnical transformations with geographical impact—a fact that he represents by reinterpreting Patrick Geddes's Valley Section as a technical and temporal diagram, whose apex is the automation of production **[fig. 3]**. In this sense, the processes of automation that cybernetics enables joins forces with supersonic flight and with satellite communications, helping altogether to "intensify universal interchange."[7]

Thanks to the convergence of these elements, Rio should become one nodal point within a world system of cities interconnected by supersonic airplanes—an idea depicted in a world map reminiscent of the world system Le Corbusier defined in *Looking at City Planning* **[project 15]**. Geographically, Bernardes's world map levels the importance of the global South to that of the North and Western powers: the nodes of the network are Los Angeles, New York, Zurich, Hong Kong, and Darwin, but also Rio, Lima, Dakar, Cairo, Johannesburg, and Mumbai **[fig. 2]**. In political and economic terms, the proposal joins seemingly opposing trends. Each city in the world network constitutes a Universal Node of Free Trade. It is the point through which economic actors operating at the world scale can access the productive activity of vast hinterlands surrounding each city. While this possibility presupposes the consolidation of capitalism around the world (something evinced by the absence of Soviet or Chinese controlled cities in the map), Bernardes aims to unlink production from the interference of the state ("state capitalism") or individuals ("private capitalism").[8] For him, national and continental production should be "coordinated to respond to universal necessities." Cybernetics is instrumental to that purpose, as it supports the dream of an entirely automatic coordination between world production and consumption, unaffected by any particular interest. The resulting absence of economic or political conflict leads to universal, temporal migratory movements, through which the populations of the planet's North and South meet in the Equatorial zone **[fig. 0]**.

Rio in the Cybernetics Era integrates the global South within a world system that is still based on a citycentric logic. Bernardes's world map is, above all, a network of metropolitan centers. During the following years, his interest in tackling spatial questions from a global perspective will lead him to question this citycentric view and the very disciplinary status of urban design. Through his writings of the mid-1970s such as *Cidade: A sobrevivência do poder* (City: the survival of power, 1975), and through the activities of the Laboratory of

**7.** Sergio Bernardes, "O Rio do futuro," *Manchete* 678 (April 17, 1965): 50.

**8.** Bernardes, "O Rio do futuro," 46; and Sergio Bernardes, "Terrismo: Uma ideologia" [1975], in Bernardes and Calvacanti, *Sergio Bernardes*, 215. English translation on page 293.

Conceptual Investigations (LIC) that he founds in 1979, Bernardes starts envisioning the transformation of urbanism from being an applied discipline that follows the dictates of state power, to becoming an independent intellectual activity operating in the realm of biological sciences. This transformation means abandoning the very idea of urbanism in favor of notions of "ecology" and "urbecology."[9] Only through this disciplinary transformation, Bernardes believes, it will be possible to make "human life viable on Earth," and to preserve the existence of other species. Bernardes's most ambitious theoretical proposition derives from those ecological notions. Through the idea of "earthism" (*terrismo*) that he formulates in 1975, he advocates for the total merging of "Man" and "Earth" systems in a new entity: "Homogeofusion" (*homogeofusao*) **[fig. 1]**.[10] Earthism takes to its logical extreme Bernardes's evolutionary credo, as it replaces any possible dialectic analysis of conflicts by a reading of social process based on the constant overcoming of the irrationalities and difficulties regarding the use of resources. The biological understanding of human processes impedes their consideration from a social or economic perspective.[11]

This new, ecologic, and symbiotic lens leads Bernardes to substitute his interest in the metropolis for a broader concern with physical geography and territorial organization. His Brazil Project, labeled also A Planetary Model for the Organization of Brazilian space, proposes a homogeofusion of all the waterways of the vast Amazon basin, human settlements, and productive systems **[fig. 4]**. Such a strategy allows the comprehensive exploitation of Brazilian resources and, in Bernardes's view, a more socially equitable development of the whole territory. It also generates a new territorial model that reconciles the valuation of nature as a vital resource and its rationalization for productive purposes. For Bernardes, such a reconciliation supports a broader geopolitical project. If Rio in the Cybernetic Era demonstrates the possibility of integrating the Northern and Southern hemispheres, the Brazil Project shows, Bernardes believes, the territorial structure of an emerging "Tropical Civilization" and its potential as a planetary model for development.

To be sure, Bernardes's approach to ecology is anthropocentric. For him, "man has the right to receive all the products derived from the transformation of the earth until achieving the total fusion of the two (man and Earth) systems." While this vision of ecology does support the exploitation of natural resources that has characterized the history of colonization, Bernardes's work tends, more broadly, to challenge the predominant forms of world organization. His project of a planet of interconnected but geographically distributed world cities and

**9.** Sergio Bernardes, "Filosofia urbana," in Bernardes and Calvacanti, *Sergio Bernardes*, 170–175. English translation on pages 286–290. Originally published in Sergio Bernardes, *Cidade. A sobrevivência do poder* (Rio de Janeiro: Guavira Editores, 1975).

**10.** Bernardes, "Terrismo: Uma ideologia," 215 and 293.

**11.** Bernardes's thought is, in this sense, close to Manuel DeLanda's. See Manuel DeLanda, *A Thousand Years of Nonlinear History* (New York: Zone Books, 1997). For an analysis of Bernardes's position in this respect see Wisnik, "A Civilização tropical e seu contrário," 120–129 and 276–279.

his Brazil Project's vision of a country integrally developed have in common the idea of a more equitable and just territorial development. His optimistic, cybernetic considerations about the abandonment of the logic of the market in the organization of production does point in a similar direction, as its objective is to adjust production to universal needs. His ecological thinking, despite its anthropocentric tone, takes into consideration the necessity of rationalizing productive systems in order to find a more equilibrated symbiosis between humans and Earth. At a moment in which Brazilian architectural culture is fascinated with the poetics of the object, Bernardes challenges the social role of the profession by emphasizing the need to question the discipline's scalar and intellectual boundaries. For him, the imperative to think at the world scale is also the imperative to reconsider the role of the architect, linking the emphasis on built forms to the invention of social and environmental forms of relations.

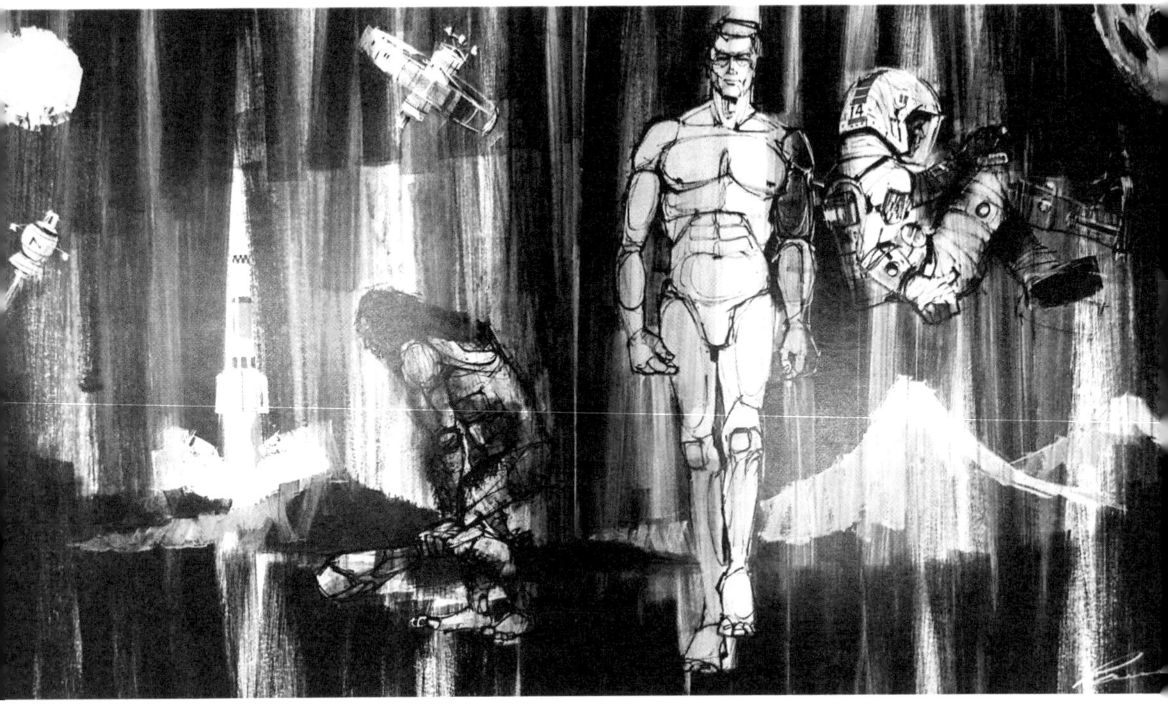

**Figure 1.** Man in the Universe. 1965.

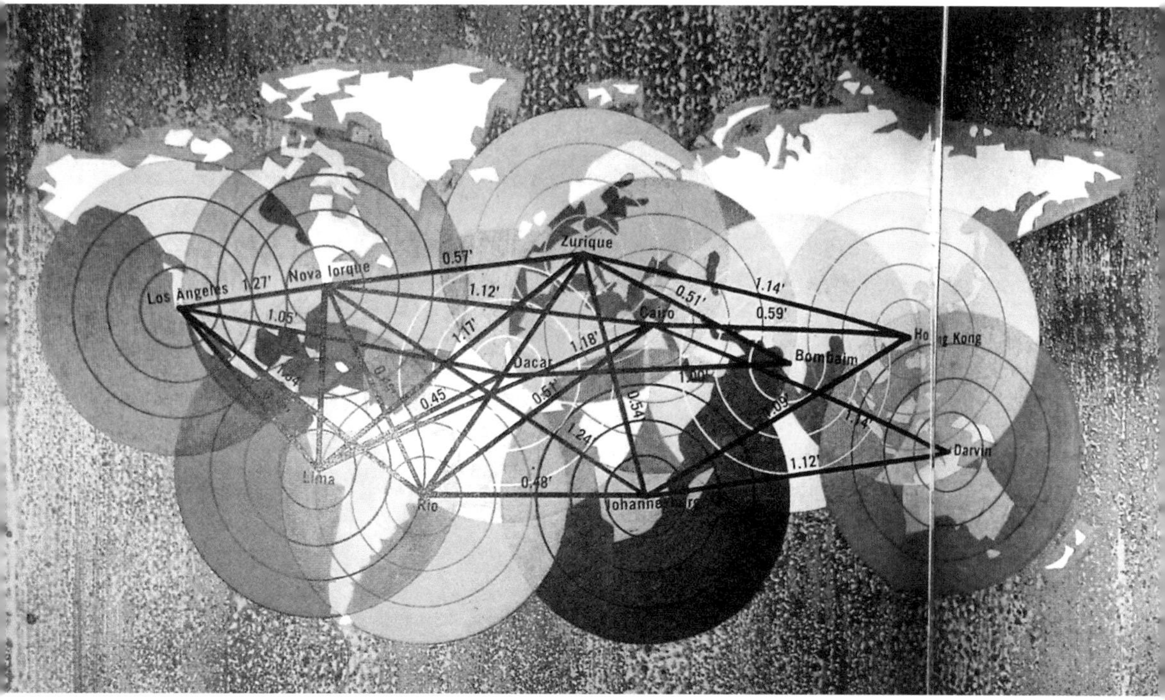


**Figure 2.** Universal Free Trade Points. 1965.

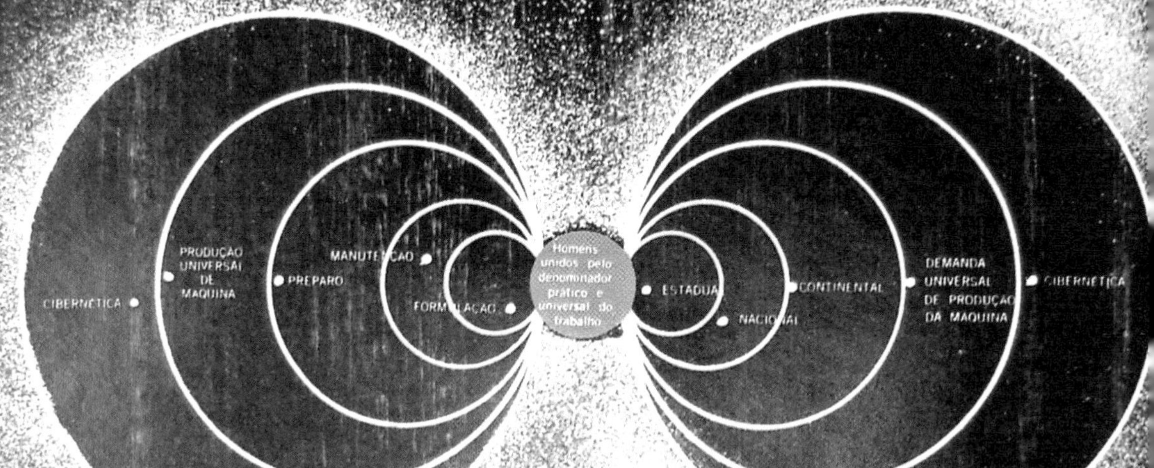


A CIBERNÉTICA A SERVIÇO DO HOMEM • O homem formula, mantém e prepara a máquina, partindo de um processo em que as demandas estadual, nacional e continental sòmente se justificam em função de uma produção mundial coordenada para atender a necessidades universais. Assim, admitindo-se que proprietário é aquêle que decide do uso, não terá sentido que a máquina automática — com capacidade de produção acima da demanda local — seja propriedade de grupos nem do Estado. Pertencerá aos homens unidos pelo denominador prático e universal do trabalho, nos diferentes níveis científicos e técnicos — da formulação e manutenção à preparação e programação. Todo o processo da demanda e produção, nessa escala universal — mas respeitando a pessoa e os níveis culturais de cada povo — sòmente poderá ser controlado pela Cibernética, que é a ciência da análise e comando dos processos através da informação e da comunicação. Entendemos a Cibernética em sua função específica a serviço do homem e não como instrumento de subordinação do homem a uma tecnocracia, que seria novamente um grupo ou um Estado.

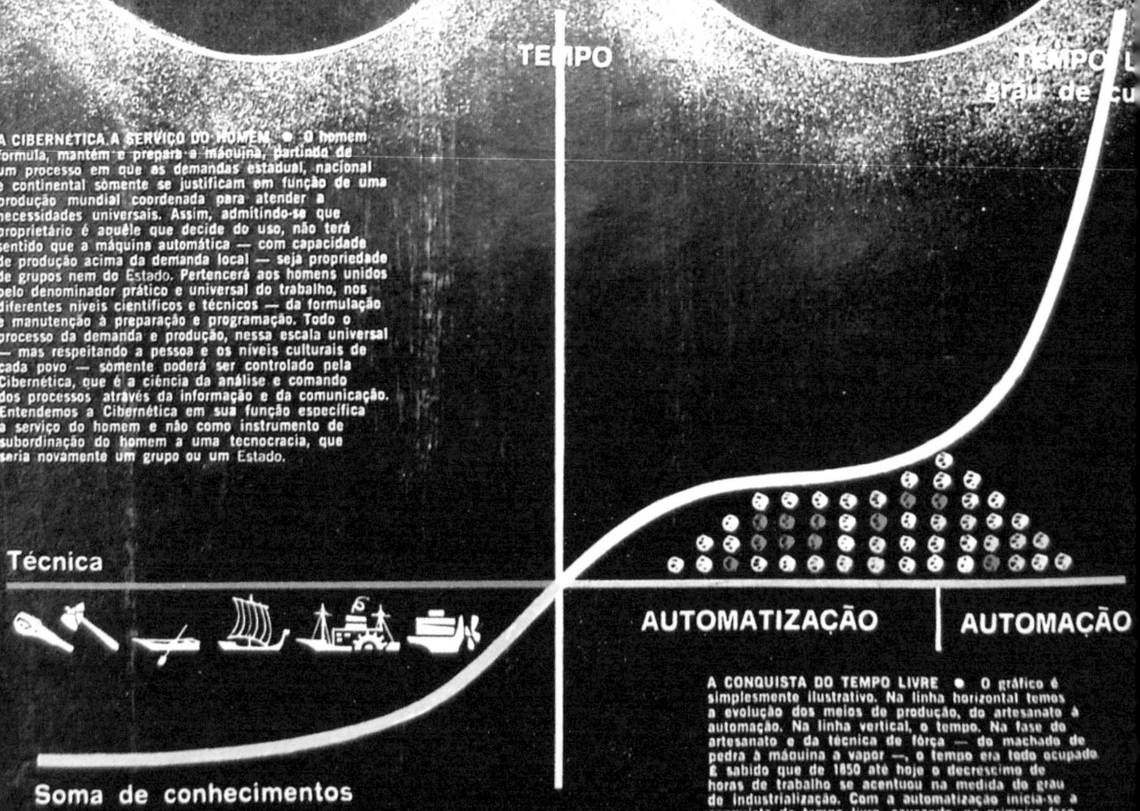


A CONQUISTA DO TEMPO LIVRE • O gráfico é simplesmente ilustrativo. Na linha horizontal temos a evolução dos meios de produção, do artesanato à automação. Na linha vertical, o tempo. Na fase do artesanato e da técnica de fôrça — do machado de pedra à máquina a vapor —, o tempo era todo ocupado. É sabido que de 1850 até hoje o decréscimo de horas de trabalho se acentuou na medida do grau de industrialização. Com a automatização inicia-se a conquista do tempo livre, causando, na primeira fase, fenômenos de desemprêgo para, a seguir, gerar novos tipos de emprêgo.

A automação simplifica, ainda mais, as operações, cria mais ocupações informativas, tende a liberar progressivamente o homem, permitindo-lhe mais horas de lazer, diversão e cultura. Cada nova conquista técnica afasta o produto do homem, impossibilitando o cálculo de seu custo em têrmos de tempo aplicado. A capacidade profissional passa a medir-se pela responsabilidade e pela aptidão mental em informar à máquina, colhêr e interpretar suas informações em

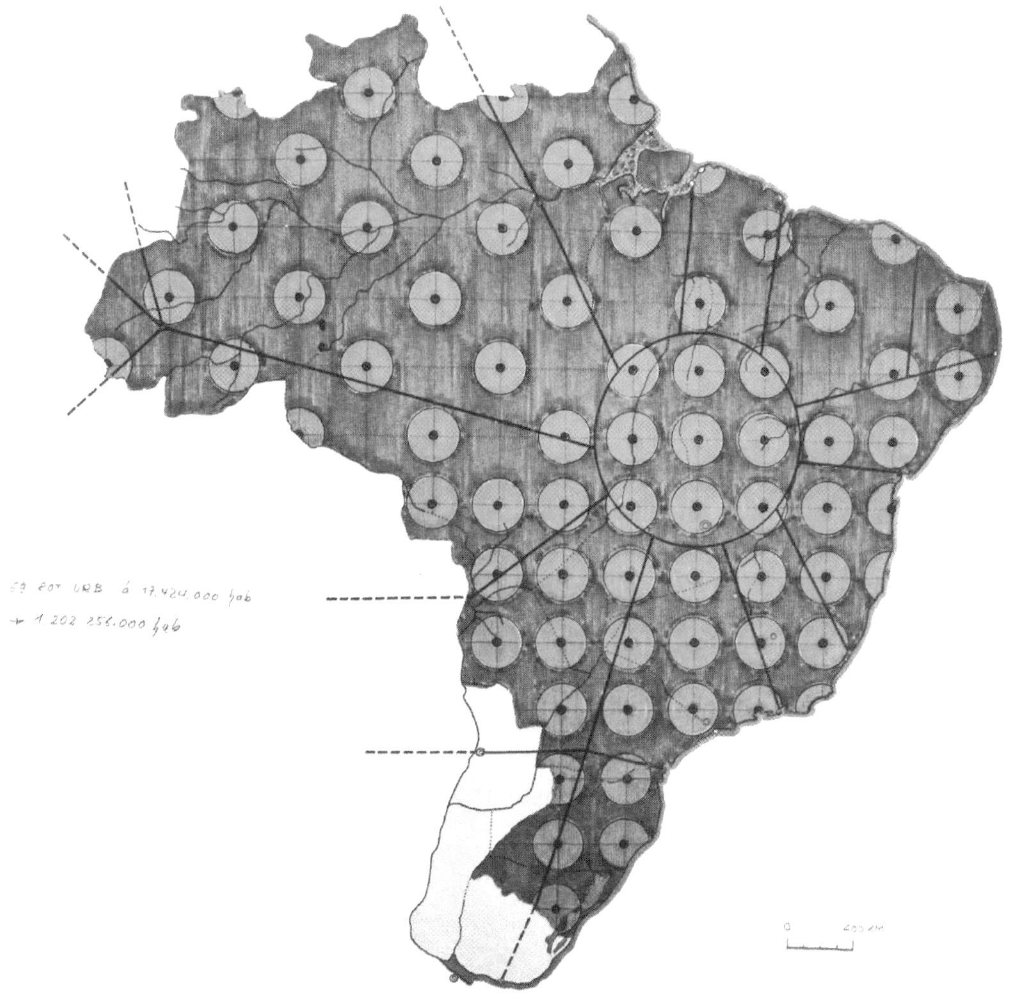


**Figure 3. (Opposite page)** Cybernetics at the Service of Man. 1965.
**Figure 4.** Project Brazil. 1991.

# Amereida and Travesías

**Project:** 29. **Authors:** Alberto Cruz (1917–2013), Godofredo Iommi (1917–2001), et al. **Date:** 1966–. **Themes:** Colonialism. Geo-visualization. Geopolitics. Place(lessness).

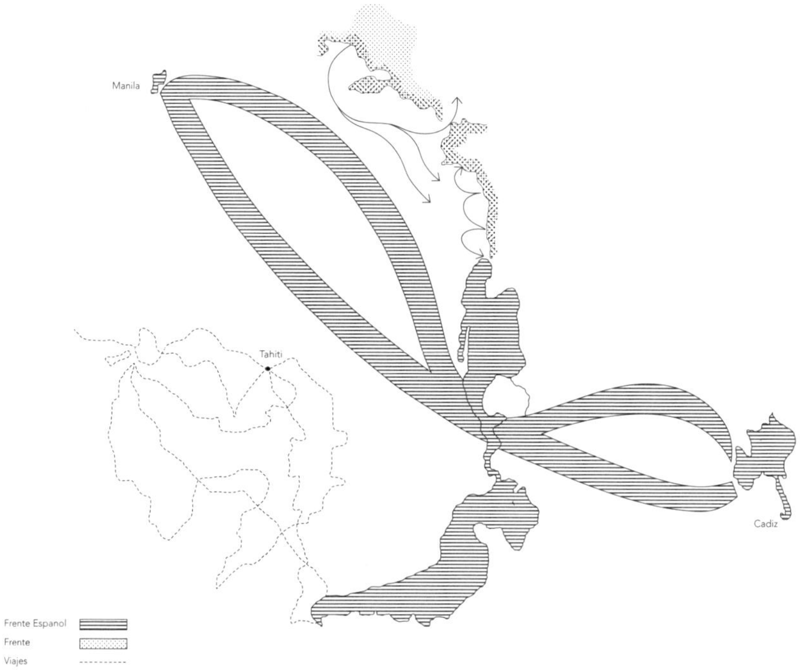


**Figure 0.** The Americas between the Pacific and Atlantic Oceans. After Oscar Butazzoni et al. 1970.

How can the merging of architecture and poetry contribute to uniting the South American continent? How can it produce a collective idea of the continent that situates South America once again within the global imaginary and global political relations **[fig. 0]**? Chilean architect Alberto Cruz, Argentinian poet Godofredo Iommi, and the collective of architects who join them in the early 1950s to launch the Valparaiso School of Architecture anew, turn these questions into a leitmotif for architectural education and for the practice of building. As the School's founders and most influential faculty members, Cruz, Iommi, and their colleagues shape the pedagogical methods and objectives of the institution. Originally, the group seeks to reveal that architecture is a collective, poetic enterprise. With that goal, they promote the writing of collective poems called *phalenes* to define the School's common objectives.[1] The most significant of those poems, *Amereida*, expresses their collective vision of South America and becomes the milestone for all the school's activities for years. Not only are there two later versions expanding the original text, but for five decades now, the School has developed a range of activities extending the purpose of *Amereida* into different domains of action. Initiatives as diverse as creating a legal document for the reform of university education in 1968, the self-constructed Valparaiso Open City, and, especially, the series of journeys and architectural interventions across South America referred to as *Travesías* (journeys) are all conceived as continuations of *Amereida*'s continental project by other means.[2]

*Amereida* results, in fact, from a voyage that anticipates the *Travesías*. In 1965, Cruz, Iommi, and a group of architects, philosophers, and poets travel from Cape Horn to Bolivia, following an almost straight path from South to North. The end of the journey, in Santa Cruz de la Sierra, reveals this city as South America's symbolic and geometrical core. The poem, written immediately after the trip, presents similar revelations about South America's structure and conditions, establishing them as the foundations for the collective construction of a united continent. *Amereida*'s title makes that foundational intention explicit by referencing the *Aeneid*, Virgil's poem about Rome's mythical origins. In so doing, the title also highlights that South America is united through Latin culture and not only through its indigenous origins.

*Amereida*'s theoretical underpinnings derive from the writings of Edmundo O'Gorman (1906–1995), a Mexican historian and thinker who devoted his work to understanding what the notion of America means as a spatial and

1. Fernando Pérez Oyarzun, "The Valparaiso School," in *Valparaíso School: Open City Group*, ed. Raúl Rispa, Rodrigo Pérez de Arce, and Fernando Pérez Oyarzun (Montreal: MQUP, 2003), 8.

2. Oscar Buttazoni, Manuel Casanueva, Alberto Cruz, Claudio Díaz, Godofredo Iommi, Jorge Sánchez, and Juan Verchueren, *Para una Situación de América Latina en el Pacífico.* Work presented to the Centro de Estudios del Pacífico for the Conferencia del Pacífico (September 27 to October 3, 1970), 2. Accessed online October 10, 2018: https://wiki.ead.pucv.cl/Para_una_Situación_de_América_Latina_en_el_Pac%C3%ADfico. See also "Claves de Amereida son presentadas en la 13 Bienal de Venecia," https://www.ead.pucv.cl/2012/bienal-venecia/. Accessed October 15, 2018.

ideological concept. Importantly, O'Gorman's inquiry is both historical and philosophical. In his seminal article "Do the Americans Have a Common History?" (1941), the author criticizes the construction of the idea of America in European philosophy, and especially in Hegel, as a mere projection of European desires, which impedes any of the continent's efforts to self-theorize.[3] The first step to supersede such Eurocentric models consists of abandoning the idea of America as the space of the "future," because this vision implies a teleological understanding of progress based on the assumption of Western models and technologies, and the framing of Latin America as an underdeveloped region according to European standards. This analysis informs O'Gorman's critique of early twentieth-century, pan-American discourse, which promoted a project of continental integration based on the intensification of economic relations as well as on the construction of continental infrastructures of communication and transportation. O'Gorman considers that such a project produces relations without content, while continental integration has to be achieved by cultural means, through the creation of a collective idea of America. Two subsequent texts, *La Idea del descubrimiento de América* (The idea of American discovery), from 1951, and *The Invention of America: An Inquiry into the Historical Nature of the New World and the Meaning of Its History* (1958) develop precisely such a thesis, again in philosophical and historical terms. In them, O'Gorman sustains his understanding of America as a cultural project in a critique of the notion of continental discovery. The two books posit that Columbus did not discover America, not only because he was not looking for the continent, but also because, lacking a concept, there was not at that moment any continent to be found. For O'Gorman, America is not a preexisting, objective entity. Its existence begins with Amerigo Vespucci's naming of the continent, which for the first time conceptualizes an otherwise unrecognized, and thus inexistent, geographical entity. O'Gorman advocates continuing this operation of continental conceptualization, supplementing its purely geographical content with a vision of America's cultural specificity.

The first pages of *Amereida* explicitly reference O'Gorman's postulates. The poem begins by negating the 1492 discovery ("Columbus / never came to America / he was looking for India / In the middle of his effort / this land / appeared as a gift"), and continues by presenting the continent as a message or sign that has to be poetically interrogated in order to be understood ("We can poetically interrogate / the sign's internal development / we can try to discern it").[4] In

3. Edmundo O'Gorman, "Do the Americans Have a Common History?" *Points of View* 3 (December 1941): 1–10, and Edwin C. Rozwenc, "Edmundo O'Gorman and the Idea of America," *American Quarterly* 10, no. 2 (1958): 102–104.

4. *Amereida Volumen Primero* (Santiago de Chile: Editorial Cooperativa Lambda, Colección Poesia, 1967), 5 and 7. Our translation.

*Amereida* this process of poetic interrogation proceeds through the elaboration of geographical concepts or "theses," which its authors describe textually and cartographically.[5] The first of these concepts, the "Thesis of our Own North," establishes that Latin America's main geographical reference is the polar South, not the North. The thesis's representation, which will become the standard of most *Amereida* maps, subverts the conventional cartographic depiction of the planet by situating the South at the top of the page **[fig. 1]**. The second key concept is the "Thesis of the Internal Sea," according to which South American settlements border a vast internal sea, delimited by the Pampas and the Amazon Forest, which acts as the common patrimony of the continent. As a result, the settlements create a peripheral, transitional, built ribbon, placed between the Atlantic and Pacific oceans and this Internal Sea. The thesis presents South America as a maritime continent, whose internal structure can be revealed by projecting on the land the cardinal points and the constellations that help navigate it **[fig. 2]**.

Cartographic depiction is the tool *Amereida* uses to create and visualize geographic concepts, and thus to constitute a geographic imaginary. The maps portray South America as a formally intelligible geographic figure, a single entity whose internal structure can be strengthened by spatial interventions. Defining the continent's structure in this manner is not just a tool to act on South America's internal conditions, but also an instrument to recast the continent in geopolitical terms. The "Thesis of our Own North" adopts the combination of universalism and Americanism that Uruguayan painter Joaquín Torres Garcia theorized in his drawing "Because of this we turn the map" (1935), which also inverts the position of the poles. Torres Garcia, who in 1944 collects his writing under the title *Universalismo Constructivo: Contribución a la unificación del arte y la cultura de América* (Constructive universalism: contribution towards the unification of American art and culture), seeks to define a universal project that recognizes the singularity of each continental entity. To subvert the order of cartographic representation is a crucial part of that project. The inverted map expresses South America's cultural and political liberation from European domination and the continent's emergence as an agent capable of promoting a new type of global relations: "We can only define the North in opposition to our South. We draw the map upside-down in order to have a fair idea of our position, and not one imposed by the rest of the world."[6] The maritime vision of South America established with the "Thesis of the Internal Sea" similarly

5. See in this respect Rodrigo Pérez de Arce, "So Far Yet So Near: The Open City and the Travesías," in Rispa, Pérez de Arce, and Pérez Oyarzun, *Valparaíso School: Open City Group*, 14–16.

6. Joaquín Torres-García, *Universalismo Constructivo; Contribución a la Unificación del Arte y la Cultura de América* (Buenos Aires: Editorial Poseidón, 1944). Our translation.

aims to delink the continent from its Western colonizers by revealing how the continent's settlements relate to each other. With similar ambitions, one of the key books extending *Amereida*, titled *Para una Situación de América Latina en el Pacífico* (In order to situate Latin America in the Pacific, 1971), explores through texts and maps how South America's relation with the Pacific Ocean has been obliterated in order to favor Atlantic relations with the European metropolises.[7] The "lack" or "absence" of the Pacific historically served to undermine South America's "continentality," and global significance.[8] To situate the continent anew geopolitically requires understanding and enhancing its transitional role between East and West **[figs. 3 and 4]**.

This understanding of South America as a space of transit is a crucial component of the *Travesías*, which are the School's activities that most explicitly translate *Amereida* into architectural design. Through the *Travesías*, the practice of traveling becomes the very cornerstone of architecture. In them, geopolitics becomes geopoetics. Each is an individual enterprise, consisting of a journey across the continent and an architectural intervention. The journey serves to recognize the American territory, to document it in maps, pictures, and drawings, and to select the site for the interventions. These, in turn, reveal the physical and poetic values of territory and the importance of its land and geography.[9] While they are not necessarily ephemeral, they emphasize the provisional character of architecture when measured against the landscape. They are always fragile and elemental constructions, built with materials that are available at hand. Programmatically, they support the process and the experience of travelling or are in themselves instruments for moving across the continent and its internal and external seas **[figs. 5 and 6]**.[10]

The *Travesías* form a cumulative project. Since 1984 the School has undertaken six *Travesías* every year. Together, they constitute a body of almost two hundred projects that attest to the School's unceasing effort to tackle and to articulate the continental scale. By continuing *Amereida* with the *Travesías*, the architects of the Valparaiso School promote a system of teaching and creation in which writing, mapping, travelling, and designing are all activities that contribute to reimagining South America's social and spatial articulation as well as the continent's insertion in the world. The continuous combination and merging of those activities suggests that the core of such a project of reimagination consists in an ethics of collective investigation, work, and design. Instead of determining a unique project, the Valparaiso School's continental vision promotes de-

7. Buttazoni et al., *Para una Situación de América Latina en el Pacífico*, 25–45.

8. Buttazoni et al., *Para una Situación de América Latina en el Pacífico*, 25–45.

9. Iván Ivelic in "Claves de Amereida son presentadas en la 13 Bienal de Venecia," https://www.ead.pucv.cl/2012/bienal-venecia/. Accessed October 15, 2018. According to Ivelic, current director of the Valparaiso School, "The transformation of the ground is the essence of architectural work, and the materialization of an interior, a frame, an axis, or an architectural envelope is the culmination of that ground. For us, the ground lifts the work as the pedestal lifts a statue." Our translation.

10. Boris Ivelic and Escuela de Arquitectura y Diseño Pontificia Universidad Católica de Valparaíso, *Embarcación Amereida y la Épica de Fundar el Mar Patagónico* (Valparaíso, Chile: Escuela de Arquitectura y Diseño, Pontificia Universidad Católica de Valparaíso, 2005).

veloping a creative process that needs to be constantly enacted in practice. The temporal unfolding of such a process for more than forty years and the contribution of multiple individuals are a way of stating that a project considering the continental scale not only must be a collective effort, but also can constitute, in itself, a tool toward the creation of a social collective. *Amereida's* objective is to proliferate. The measure of its success lies in the incorporation of objects, texts, documents, designs, and persons that contribute to embodying the project's dream of continental integration.

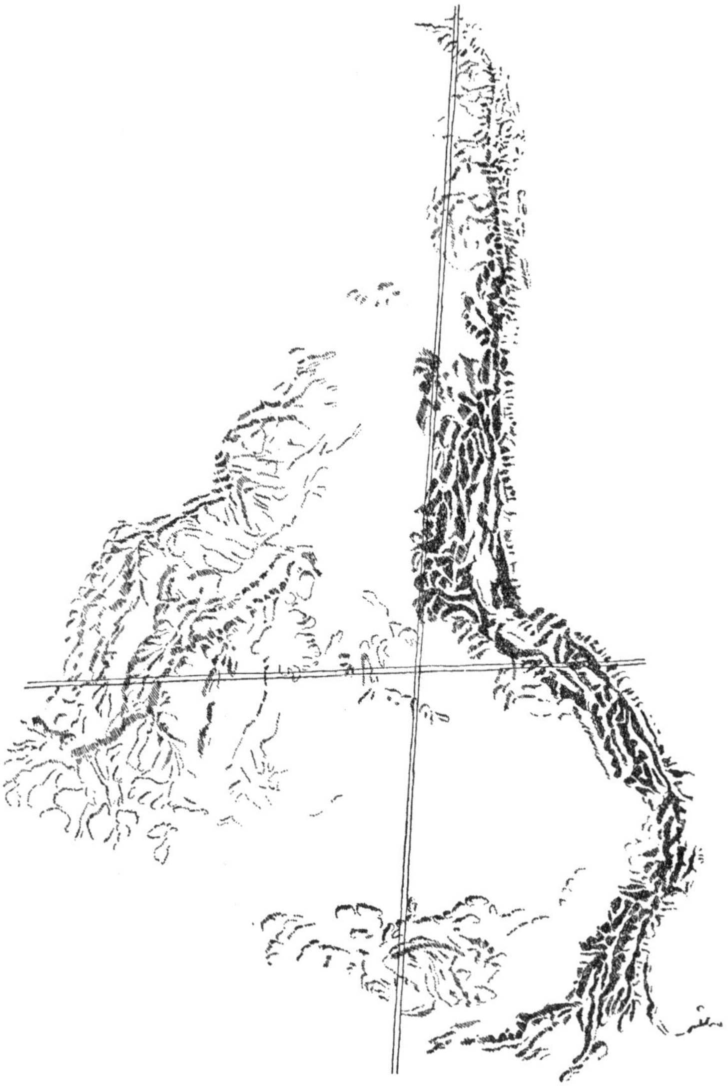

Figure 1. South America inverted with the Southern Cross constellation mapped on top. 1967.

**Figure 2.** South America's inland seas with air and land travels as constellations. 1970.

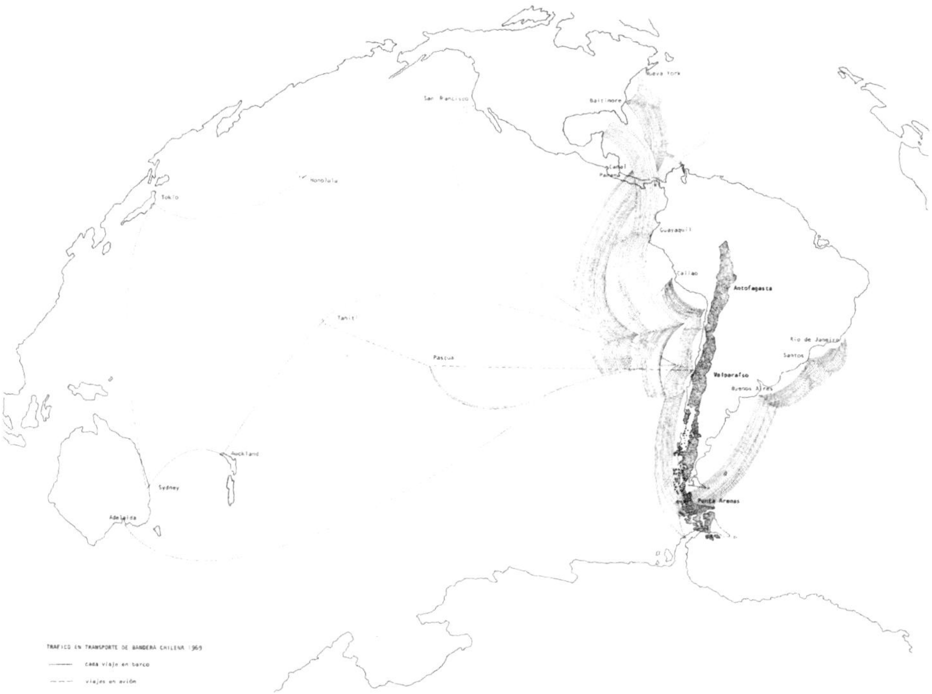


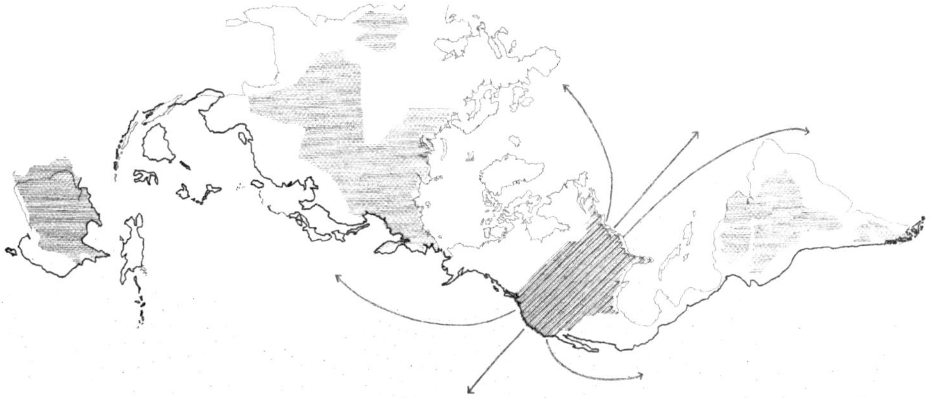

**Figure 3 (Top).** Chilean flag transport traffic. 1970.
**Figure 4 (Bottom).** The interior seas of the United States, Asia, and South America. 1970.

**Figure 5 (Top).** Edros. José Vial Armstrong. Undated.
**Figure 6 (Bottom).** Windroller (Eolo). José Vial Armstrong. Undated.

# La Forma del Territorio

## Form of Territory

**Project:** 30. **Authors:** Vittorio Gregotti (1927) with Emilio Battisti, Dario Borradori, Paolo Caruso, Pierluigi Crosta, Sergio Crotti, Roberto Orefice, Cesare Pellegrini. **Date:** 1966. **Themes:** Geo-visualization. Geography. Territorial Gestalt. Territorial Intensification.

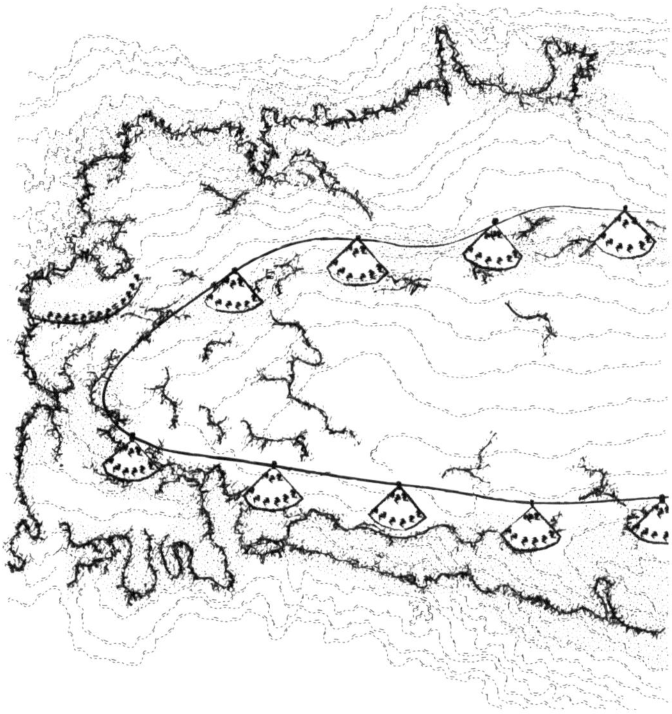

**Figure 0.** Scheme of an urban development on a hilly terrain. After Giorgio Piccinato. 1965.

Tens of aerial pictures of agricultural fields and productive landscapes, from millenary terraced hills in Israel, to large states of industrialized cereal cultivation in Napa, California. Photographs and technical drawings of dams, highways, and infrastructures. Underground tanks. Fragments of villages, towns, cities, metropolises. Natural landscapes—mountains, deserts, rivers, oceans—affected by different degrees of human occupation. Cultivated fields in the Sahara. Photographs of lunar relief. Cartographies of lunar relief. Archaeological sites. Still inhabited prehistoric settlements. Medieval cities. New York skyscrapers. Hiroshima devastated in 1945. Volcanic eruptions. Different forms of monumental symbolization of geography: the Carnac menhirs, Fischer von Erlach's imaginary reconstruction of Mount Athos, Mount Rushmore. The list may continue. *La Forma del territorio* (The form of territory), a special issue of *Edilizia Moderna* that Vittorio Gregotti edited in 1966, presents the world in all its exuberance through constant conceptual, scalar, and temporal superpositions **[figs. 0 and 1]**. The graphic organization of the journal is in itself the visual expression of a world project. The journal's proposition about how the world should be seen—extremely concrete, physical, fragmented, multifarious, nonhierarchical, synchronic—is a statement about how it must be built: these very properties pervade the essays through which Gregotti and the other contributors to *Edilizia Moderna* explain their worldview and the role architecture plays in building it.

To resituate the discipline of architecture as an agent of territorial construction is, for Gregotti and his peers, the key step toward that new form of world project. Admittedly, their use of the concept of territory is a malleable one: it integrates, in an indistinct manner, notions as diverse as geography, landscape (*paesaggio*), or surroundings (*circomdante*)[1]. The open character of the term, even its imprecision, is nonetheless indicative of the group's determined attempt to change the ways in which contemporary Italian architecture and culture is considering the topic, and of their ambition to use the term as to invoke and address a new set of themes. From the late 1950s to the mid-1960s, the idea of territory in Italy is mostly associated with the expansion of the city—in debates about the "*città-territorio*" and "*la nuova dimensione*"—or with ideas of regional planning.[2] For Gregotti, it is in turn a way to address global conditions of sociospatial structuring which exceed the regional and urban limits:

> "In five years we can build polders or colonize a desert; a hydro-electric dam transforms the entire configuration of a valley in a few years; it is possible

1. Significantly, the English translation of Gregotti's editorial included in *Edilizia Moderna* is titled "The Shape of Landscape," and not "Form of Territory," as it was later more literally translated (see Vittorio Gregotti, "Form of Territory," *OASE* 80 (2009): 7–22). The translation highlights not only the limited diffusion that the notion of territory had in the 1960s in English-language architectural discourse, but also the strong intermingling between the notions of landscape and territory in the discourse of the authors. Paolo Caruso, Emilio Battisti, Sergio Crotti, and Cesare Pellegrini use the word *paesaggio* (landscape) in the titles of their essays. Assimilating the two concepts, which Gregotti acknowledges in his editorial, derives in many ways from the geographic literature that the authors privilege. See especially in this respect Emilio Battisti and Sergio Crotti, "Note sulla lettura del paesaggio antropogeografico," *Edilizia Moderna* 87–88 (1966): 53–59.

2. Arturo Lanzani, *Immagini del territorio e idee di piano, 1943–1963: dagli approcci generalizzanti all'interpretazione dei contesti locali* (Milan: F. Angeli, 1996).

> to create an artificial isthmus in months; to carry energy everywhere; it is reasonable to suppose that, in the future, systems of climate control will allow even faster transformations.
>
> . . .
>
> We detect a progressive reduction of nature into culture that is oriented to its functional and productive exploitation and a consequential universalization of the values associated to nature, which is considered only as a resource to put to profit. The technologization of landscape makes the notion of 'place' less important within our systems of collective values, that is, the idea of place loses its operative value as it becomes dependent of supralocal economies. We also witness an increase of the anthropogeographic surface, which is produced by the concentration of settlement systems and by the diminution of free space. We need to address the formal consequences of these phenomena on the landscape, of which the changes of the urban environment are only one aspect."[3]

Gregotti orients architectural design toward a space shaped by vast environmental modifications and by a parallel process of universal technological and cultural integration, one which produces what he calls a "total environment."[4] But the position of the group toward this condition is a critical one, seeking to find an alternative for the totalizing approach to the process of universalization. It is necessary, Gregotti will later say, to counteract Buckminster Fuller's neopositivist games of world-structuring.[5] With that goal, the notion of territory is mobilized mainly in a twofold manner. It designates a new scale of architectural intervention, a reorientation of practice toward a series of geographic topics that the focus on urban problems had neglected. At the same time, territory is claimed as a physical, material, concrete space that contradicts any attempts to reduce the world to a single condition. Its formalization is a way to cultivate the multiplicity of the world. According to the authors, both thoughts imply a necessary reorientation of architectural practice, and a modification of the techniques and *modus operandi* of the discipline.

The intersection of architecture with the procedures of geography constitutes the core of that disciplinary modification. Certainly, geographical theory had been very present in the work of Italian architects and urbanists since the 1950s.[6] Authors as varied as Giuseppe Samonà, Aldo Rossi, and Ludovico Quaroni support their arguments with the teachings of geographers or historian-geographers, mostly from the French school of human and urban ge-

**3.** Vittorio Gregotti, *Il Territorio dell'architettura* (Milan: Feltrinelli Editore, 2008 [1966]), 72–73. Our translation. The text in Il *Territorio dell'architettura* slightly modifies Gregotti's original article in Vittorio Gregotti, "La Forma del territorio," *Edilizia Moderna* 87–88 (1966): 2 and 6. English translation of the latter in *Edilizia Moderna*, 149.

**4.** Vittorio Gregotti, "L'Ambiente totale," in *Il Territorio dell'architettura*, 46–48.

**5.** Vittorio Gregotti, "Il Filo rosso del razionalismo italiano," *Casabella* 42, no. 440–441 (October-November 1978): 31–34.

**6.** Lanzani, *Immagini del territorio e idee di piano, 1943–1963.*

ography (Vidal de la Blache, Maximilien Sorre, Jean Brunhes), the Annales School (Ferdinand Braudel, Lucien Febvre), or the theorists of active geography (Pierre George) **[project 41]**.[7] *La Forma del territorio* is a collective endeavor. As a part of it Gregotti's editorial connects articles that his research team produced for the 1965 X Convegno dell'Istituto Nazionale di Urbanistica or as part of previous academic investigations, and some external contributions. Despite the intellectual discrepancies such variety occasionally produces, the group's efforts to merge the techniques of geographic visualization with those of architectural design distances their work from other Italian attempts to link architecture and geography. The authors privilege a very physical and visual understanding of geography that sustains their interest in multiplicity and particularization.[8] Instead of appealing to the French geographers, they situate architectural work under Friedrich Ratzel's idea of anthropogeography and recover the postulates of early twentieth-century geographers, such as the Finn Johannes Gabriel Granö and Germans Siegfried Passarge and Ewald Banse, who produce typological classifications of regions by linking patterns of settlement and geographical conditions **[fig. 2]**.[9] The investigation of new forms of planning, extracting formal guides for urban development from the geographical vectors, which appear in *Edilizia Moderna*, result from this physicalist understanding, as it is Gregotti's own demand to create a cartography of the formal values of territory that can help to make coincident the "environment of a region with its linguistic body."[10]

This mention of linguistics points to one of the most ambitious aspects of the group's attempt to rethink the discipline from a territorial prism. Various borrowings from semiotics, structuralism, and theories of cognition, including Kevin Lynch's ideas of "imageability," inform their efforts to think about how architecture can intervene in the total environment. They also trigger a reconsideration of the concepts that the discipline uses and a questioning of its inherited vocabulary. "The architect as a privileged manager of the future global form of the world can be recovered and accepted by us," says Dario Borradori in "Parametri scalari e strutturazione formale negli insiemi a dimensione territoriale" (Scalar parameters and formal structure of groups of territorial dimension), "as long as we are able to clarify some of its boundary conditions."[11] The exploration of notions such as field, ensemble, relational structure, quasi-object, architectural matter, or dimension becomes in this sense instrumental to recalibrate the position of the architect as a global agent. Borradori and Gregotti argue that, beyond a certain scale, it is impossible to understand a thing or an

**7.** Giuseppe Samonà, *L'urbanistica e l'avvenire della città negli stati Europei* (Bari: Editori Laterza, 1960). Aldo Rossi, *The Architecture of the City*, trans. Diane Ghirardo and Joan Ockman (Cambridge, MA: MIT Press, 1982 [1966]), 48–55 and 100–112.

**8.** This position is especially developed in Gregotti's editorial and in Emilio Battisti and Sergio Crotti's article. These two authors argue against the socially oriented vision of geography of the Italian geographer Lucio Gambi who, interestingly, would later be Vittorio Gregotti's collaborator on his project for the University of Calabria. Emilio Battisti and Sergio Crotti, "Note sulla lettura del paessagio antropogeografico," *Edilizia Moderna* 87–88 (1966): 53–59.

**9.** Johannes Gabriel Granö, *Pure Geography*, ed. Olavi Granö and Anssi Paasi; trans. Malcolm Hicks (Baltimore: Johns Hopkins University Press, 1997).

**10.** Gregotti, "Una interpretazione semiologica," in *Il Territorio dell'architettura*, 70–72.

**11.** Dario Borradori, "Parametri scalari e strutturazione formale negli insiemi a dimensione territoriale," *Edilizia Moderna* 87–88 (1966): 88–95.

environment as an object. The territorial scale is, in this sense, not an object, but an amalgam of heterogeneous conditions, disorganized "collections" of elements. In order to understand how architects can intervene at this level, it is thus necessary to go beyond the discipline's understanding of what objects are. Not only should objects be rethought as "connections, relational knots," instead of as "resistant, opaque materials," but architecture should assemble the disconnected, heterogeneous materials that populate territory into multiple "quasi-objects" that solidify and allow one to read, at least for a given time, a set of relations.[12] Quasi-objects are in this sense, aggregates, compounds of the many elements that can now be taken as architectural "matter"—buildings, infrastructures, productive landscapes, social formations; the already existing fabric of territory—which they integrate, as in a language, within a relational structure.[13]

The creation of quasi-objects adds a strong level of indeterminacy and variability to the procedures of regional delimitation that the group had derived from Granö. Quasi-objects produce potential "fields" or "ensembles," rather than regions. They are a construct, produced by linking existing spatial conditions through architectural interventions, rather than a preexisting fixed reality **[fig. 3]**. Their scale and limits are thus variable; the result of attending to the different relations between the elements they bring together. They reflect the fact that the world comprises overlapping relations at multiple scales, which it is neither possible nor desirable to assimilate. Borradori affirms: "total environment is the central objective of disciplinary reflection."[14] Gregotti reiterates the idea, and yet clarifies: "The constitution of a figure for the total environment is impossible."[15] The production of figures, of formal complexes, is only possible for dimensional levels that are below that of the world. This is what quasi-objects do. They translate territorial relations into figurative organizations. They produce provisional configurations, reunions of heterogeneous and conflicting materials, fragments; "open forms," which neither intend nor allow one to totalize the world into a single image, but permit one, instead, to understand through concrete, partial formations the total environmental processes of organization **[fig. 4]**.[16]

Above all, the texts and projects of *La Forma del territorio* claim the power of form to create intelligible and meaningful environments and emphasize that to produce forms is, precisely, the very task of architecture. The disciplinary boundaries that the collective seeks to demarcate limit architecture to an activity almost strictly devoted to formalization: "[the architectural discipline]

**12.** Borradori, "Parametri scalari," 91. See also: Vittorio Gregotti, "Architettura e metodo scientifico," in *Il Territorio dell'architettura*, 14–18.

**13.** Both for Borradori and for Gregotti, architectural matter can be composed of radically heterogeneous elements, which can be manipulated and made homogeneous through the act of design.

**14.** Borradori, "Parametri scalari," 88. Our translation.

**15.** Gregotti, "L'Ambiente totale," 46. Our translation.

**16.** Gregotti takes the notion of open form from Umberto Eco's notion of open work. See Umberto Eco, *The Open Work* (Cambridge, MA: Harvard University Press, 1989 [1962]).

17. Borradori, "Parametri scalari," 90. Our translation.

18. Borradori, "Parametri scalari," 90.

proposes itself to us, who want to participate in it, as the tradition of a type of relationship to the world that wants to be, let's say, 'architectural' (and nothing else), and therefore acts as a discipline that introduces a peculiar experience of the form."[17] The role of architecture is to help the world give itself to us as a form.[18] As interventions in an intellectual environment which is severely questioning the legacy of modernity, the contributions to *Edilizia Moderna* disregard the belief in spatial planning as an all-embracing activity. Instead, they conceive of the architect as an agent whose role is, strictly, to spatialize the programmatic and territorial requests previously defined by different social and economic sectors. The architect's task is to structure relations, facilitate the understanding of territorial organizations, create a cohesive, even if provisional, ensemble out of disparate objects—but not to define their content. By entirely refraining from intervening in the programmatic dimensions of geographic space, these authors seek a re-engagement with the world that is also, paradoxically, a notable retreat from architectural engagement in the production of the world's social, economic, or political conditions. One that prefigures in many ways the 1980s postmodern approach to the world as a theme that can be addressed only at the scale of architectural expression.

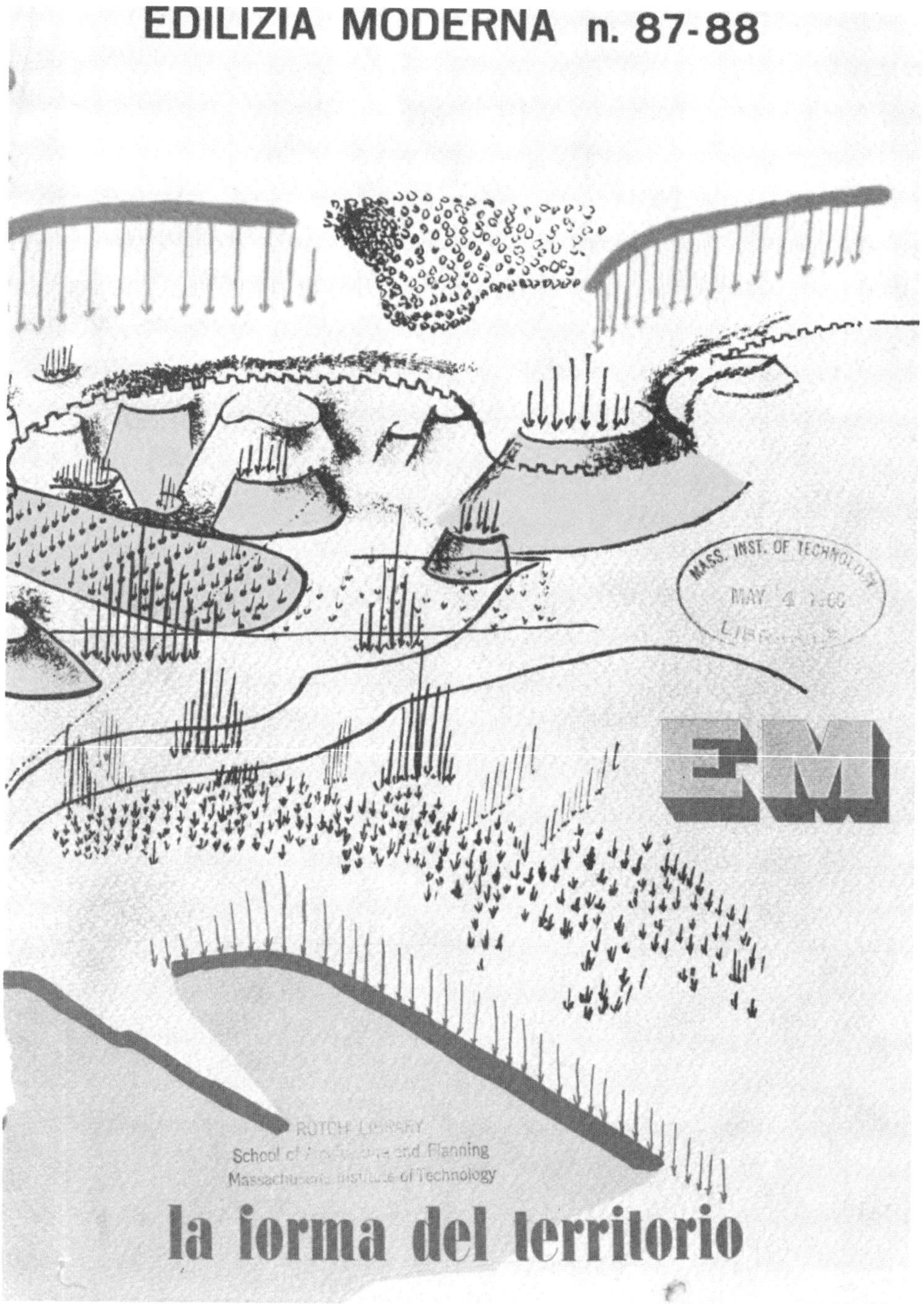


**Figure 1.** *Edilizia Moderna* 87–88. Cover. 1965.

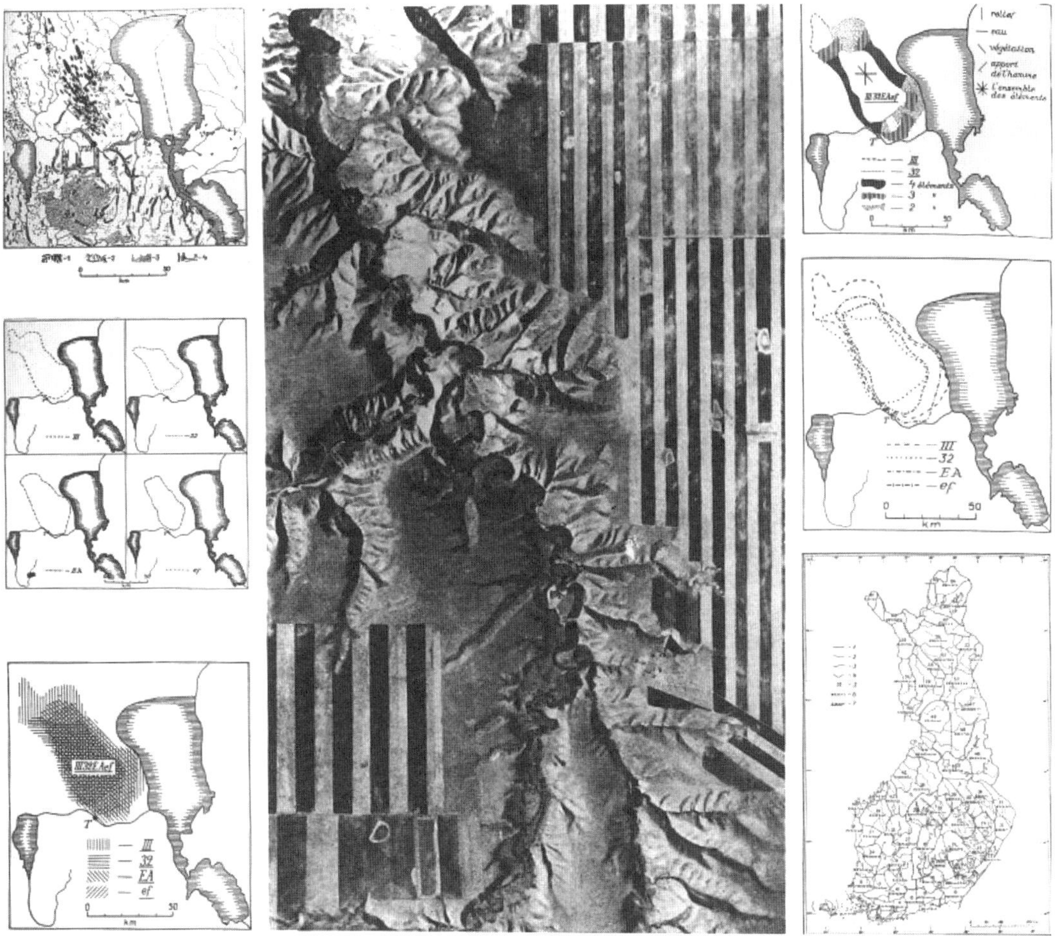


**Figure 2.** Analysis of cultivation destroyed by erosion in Great Plains of Northern Montana, and J. G. Granö's cartographic analysis of East Estonia. *Edilizia Moderna* 87–88. 1965.

**Figure 3.** Figural characteristics of the territory for groups of homogeneous presences, Milan. Valerio di Battista. 1965.

Figure 4. Proposal for a territorial sequence, Milan-Adda. Cesare Pellegrini. 1965.

# Studi per una Operante Storia del Territorio

## Study for an Operational History of Territory

**Project:** 31. **Author:** Saverio Muratori (1910–1973). **Date:** 1967–1973. **Themes:** Geo-visualization. Geography. Human-Earth System. Territorial Gestalt.

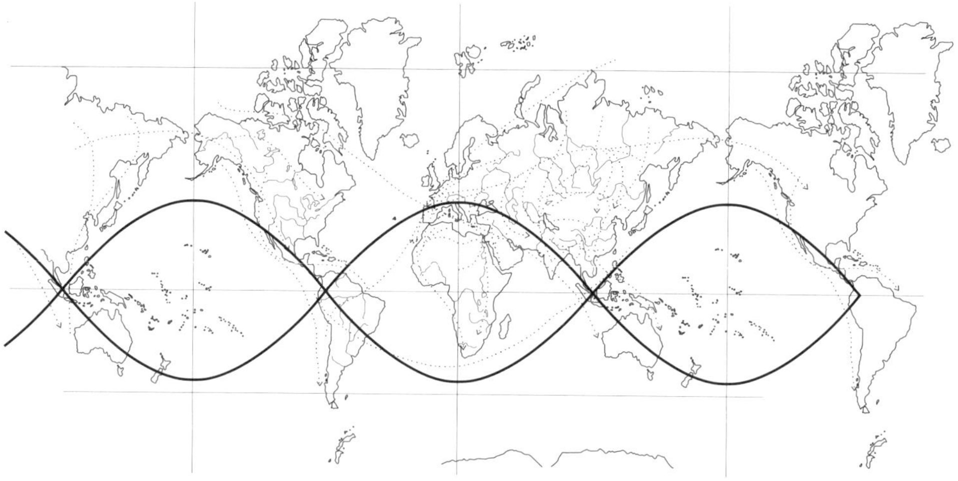

**Figure 0.** Lines of propagation and seasonal migration. After Saverio Muratori. ca. 1969.

It is only at a late, conclusive moment in his career that Saverio Muratori becomes preoccupied with the territorial articulation of the "ecumene" and the "world" (*mondo*). He publishes his theoretical treatise on this topic, *Civiltà e territorio* (Civilization and territory) in 1967 at the age of fifty-seven. The accompanying, unfinished cartographic project *Studi per una operante storia del territorio* (Study for an operative history of territory) is interrupted by the author's death in 1973. Until then Muratori had sought to formulate an alternative to what he understood as the modern "ideologies of crisis"—in which the relentless drive toward social and spatial transformation disrupted environmental equilibriums—by investigating a nonmodern form of intervening at the architectural and urban scales.[1] With that goal his seminal research *Studi per una operante storia de Venezia* (Study for an operative history of Venice, 1959) established the notion of operative history and the methodological fundamentals of typomorphological analysis and design. The procedures of historic reconstruction by cartographic means developed in that study show the historic processes of construction of the city and reveal how these rely on a series of recurrent architectural types. In Muratori's view, it is the recognition of these types, their recuperation as the primary mechanism of urban design, which can set the base for anticritical forms of urban development that preserve the continuity of history. Conceived as an operational-oriented form of making history, cartographic reconstruction is then a tool of design. His works on territory share the goal of finding alternatives to the ideologies of crisis and cartographic procedures of his studies on cities, but Muratori now understands that solutions to crises can only come after a reflection about the spatial articulation of the world scale.

*Civiltà e territorio* sets the theoretical basis of *Studi per una operante storia del territorio*. The book's explicit theme, the "planning of the world," reflects Muratori's attempt to find the conceptual and methodological support to intervene in a situation where civilization—his term for humanity's social and spatial organization—has found its dimensional limits.[2] Formerly an expanding phenomenon that affected only parts of the earth, civilization now constitutes a dimensionally fixed system: the "ecumene" covers the entire surface of the globe, "remaining always identical to itself."[3] This situation, which only permits internal growth, requires for Muratori finding a "relatively stable way of putting into orbit the system man-Earth" by determining the laws that can govern the spatial organization of humanity.[4] It is at this point where the notion of

1. Saverio Muratori, *Civiltà e territorio* (Rome: Centro studi di storia urbanistica, 1963), 28–30. Additionally, the notion of crisis is the central object of the book Muratori wrote immediately before *Civiltà e territorio*. See Saverio Muratori, *Architettura e civiltà in crisi* (Rome: Centro studi di storia urbanistica, 1963). All the translations are by the author.

2. Muratori, *Civiltà e territorio*, 491.

3. Muratori, *Civiltà e territorio*, 491.

4. Muratori, *Civiltà e territorio*, 28.

territory becomes for the architect the crucial operational category. The architectural and urban scales are insufficient to address world spatial organization. Territory, by contrast, refers precisely to the spatial intermingling between geography and culture that contemporary civilization needs to assume as a global condition.[5] In territory, "the world becomes architecture, humanized space."[6] Its formalization is the way to articulate the world beyond the limitations of the urban logic.[7] Muratori's goal is then to construct the notion of territory as a conceptually autonomous spatial category, and, based on it, to define the procedures of a "territorial technology."[8] *Civiltà e territorio* does this by studying how the forms of historical constitution of territory give concrete material expression to the social spheres of logic, economy, ethics, and aesthetics. This multilayered, historical analysis of the territory lays out global ways of occupying the ground as well as their rationale, and it posits that these forms of symbiosis between geography and culture constitute the spatial framework for every new, possible, future system. The maps of *Studi per una operante storia del territorio* present this spatial framework, from the scale of a region to that of a continent. They are, in this sense, the visual foundation of a new approach to global spatial articulation and the key agents of the territorial technology that Muratori ventures to define.

One maxim presides Muratori's cartographic project: to do is to read, and to read is to do.[9] His position inaugurates an understanding of cartography as an act where territorial hermeneutics and territorial project collide.[10] For him, world-making results from cartographic production. Subjected to the logics of selection, composition, and ordering of aesthetic thinking, the maps treat design as a way to render territorial reality visible and knowledgeable. As cognitive tools, they are not a project as such, but the foundations for a way of designing that preserves the correct rapport between civilization and Earth. Explicitly, they do not establish a global plan. Their potential effect resides in the modification of human knowledge they may produce; in how they increase the cultural "self-awareness" that society must acquire.[11] To this self-awareness, the maps contribute various propositions. Territory is a palimpsest; the spatial overlap of progressive historical stages and forms of territorial occupation that follow similar logics across the world. Its physical form is the result of universal processes determined by the movements of populations and the necessities of using the ground **[fig. 0]**. These processes are global, but their formation always remains specific. The combinations of road structure, land division, geographic relief, and settlements create different "territorial types" or "territorial

5. Muratori, *Civiltà e territorio,* 198.

6. Muratori, *Civiltà e territorio,* 487.

7. See in this respect Carlo Ravagnati, *L'Invenzione del territorio: L'Atlante inedito di Saverio Muratori* (Milan: F. Angeli, 2012), 64.

8. "Tecnologia territoriale" is the title of *Civiltà e territorio*'s last chapter. Regarding the elaboration of territory as an autonomous concept, at once different from the city and the landscape, see in particular Saverio Muratori, *Civiltà e territorio*, 531–532. Territory is additionally defined as a space of materialization of processes in a "concrete, homogeneous, and continuous field," and as "the only instrument we have to submit to methodical inquiry the operating forces, not only of nature, but also of society." Muratori, *Civiltà e territorio*, 195–196.

9. Muratori, *Civiltà e territorio,* 494.

10. Manuel de Solà-Morales, "La Forma d'un pais," *Quaderns d'Arquitectura i Urbanisme,* special issue (1981): 4–13, and Manuel de Solà-Morales, "The Culture of Description," *Perspecta* 25 (1989): 16–25.

11. Muratori, *Civiltà e territorio,* 497.

individuals" **[fig. 1]**.[12] As a result, Muratori tenses the spatial structure of the world between the two scalar poles that dominate his cartographic representations: regional formations and continental structures **[figs. 2 and 3]**. Global processes are visible only through the action of local territorial individuals; the world is made through the relation of geographically bounded concrete units. As scholar Carlo Ravagnati accurately points out, for Muratori the planet has the structure of a puzzle.[13]

By depicting the world as a complete system made of overlapping, successive historical stages, Muratori's maps define a spatial structure that combines temporal change and stasis. Philosophically influenced by Friedrich Hegel's *The Phenomenology of the Spirit* and by Benedetto Croce's idealist theories (from whom he takes the categorical division of human activities in logics, economics, ethics, and aesthetics), Muratori sees the occupation of the world in terms that echo Hegel's universal unfolding of the spirit, but that also question the idea of dialectical succession.[14] His conception of humans as the apex of evolutionary development determines his understanding of human territorial structure as "the representative of all superficial terrestrial phenomenology, of which it determines an evolution more homogeneous and compact."[15] The creation of territorial forms is, in this light, the way in which humans reveal an otherwise imperceptible geographic structure. At the same time, his definition of historic territorial forms establishes a structuralist spatial framework in which notions of permanence and cyclical alternation replace the idea of dialectical succession. For Muratori civilization has been constituted in three stages: first occupying mountains with ridge-settlements and ridge-roads; later inhabiting hillsides; and finally organizing valleys. Civilization creates, throughout this process ecumenic systems of continental or maritime relations, which, in turn, generate four types of territorial structures: occasional, systemic, organized, and hierarchical, which represent the structural possibilities of a Greimasian semiotic square.[16] But the transitions between these modes are not temporally unidirectional. History shows the recurrent use of previous modes of territorial occupation. For Muratori, the possible collapse of our contemporary valley and maritime civilization may imply a return to interior, mountainous territorial structures.[17] The cartographic project is then both a method to bring to light the form of the earth as a human structure and an instrument to assist on how to use and recover the historic forms of territorial organization that constitute the "stable patrimony of civilization."[18]

**12.** These are the terms that appear in the legends of the research *Studi per una operante storia del territorio*.

**13.** Ravagnati, *L'Invenzione del territorio*, 66–72.

**14.** For a review of Muratori's idealism see Giancarlo Cataldi, "From Muratori to Caniggia: The Origins and Development of the Italian School of Design Typology," *Urban Morphology* 7, no. 1 (2003): 19–34.

**15.** Muratori, *Civiltà e territorio*, 39. It must be noted here also that Muratori limits the occupation of the earth to the use of its surface. Using oceans, the subsoil, or the atmosphere is outside his considerations. His reliance on maps is completely consequential with these considerations. A superficial understanding on territory is also depicted two-dimensionally.

**16.** The Lithuanian linguist Algirdas Greimas defines the semiotic square in his work *Sémantique structurale*, published one year before *Civiltà e territorio*. The square synthesizes a system of oppositions and contradictions that exhaust all possible developments of a given concept. In general, Muratori's thinking is organized not in dialectical triads, but in matrices of four concepts, as happens in Greimas's schema.

**17.** Muratori, *Civiltà e territorio*, 529.

**18.** Muratori, *Civiltà e territorio*, 491.

Muratori's thinking informs a whole school of morphological analysis, which is mainly influential in Italy.[19] Gianfranco Cannigia, Gian Luigi Maffei, and Giancarlo Cataldi develop Muratori's thesis in works devoid of the global ambitions of the original project.[20] From this point of view, instead of dialoguing with its more direct continuations, the ideas of *Studi per una operante storia del territorio* find their paradoxical counterpart on the opposite side of the ideological spectrum. The proximity between Muratori and Constantinos Doxiadis—the ultimate representative of the activist, transformative ideology of the crisis that the Italian despises—goes beyond their common interest in the notion of ecumene. As Doxiadis does when elaborating the notion of *ekistics*, Muratori understands that any speculation about the role architecture can play at the scale of the world needs to be framed by a previous phase of theoretical production **[project 23]**. As a result, both authors end up establishing a trans-scalar system that goes—linearly, consistently—from architecture, to territory, to world. The all-encompassing ambition of both projects finds common methodological tools in the elaboration of diagrams, systems of classification, and graphic grids—what Muratori called *tabellone*. If Doxiadis thinks of *ekistics* as a new science of settlements, Muratori develops his system as a substitute for existing geographic theories. His reference to existing geographical knowledge is limited to the use of previous cartographies to elaborate his own maps, while his classification of global territorial types and forms of historical occupation of territory refutes the idiosyncratic, regionalist tradition of the French school of human geography as well as the domineering, postwar theories of "volitional geography" or "active geography" that see territory as an empty canvas waiting for human transformation and economic development.[21]

The result of this critique of activism is a eulogy of limits and constants. For Muratori, geography imposes limits to growth and marks directions for territorial formations. He thinks that the territorial types that result from the interaction between humans and Earth are transcendental and universal—relying on Immanuel Kant to define types as "a priori synthesis." His cyclical understanding of historical processes is not transformative, but restorative. The objections to his typomorphological thinking have noted that it limits the future to the assumption of forms established in the past and that it reads the relations between geography and civilization through an entirely determinist prism.[22] The intellectual rigor that Manfredo Tafuri appreciated in Muratori appears, for the latter's critics, as *rigor mortis*.[23] The most beautiful aspects of his project derive, however, from his attempt to overcome some of these limitations. His under-

**19.** Pierre Gauthier and Jason Gilliland, "Mapping Urban Morphology: A Classification Scheme for Interpreting Contributions to the Study of Urban Form," *Urban Morphology* 10, no. 1 (2006): 41–50; Giancarlo Cataldi, Gian Luigi Maffei, and Paola Vaccaro, "Saverio Muratori and the Italian School of Planning Typology," *Urban Morphology* 6, no. 1 (2002): 3–14.

**20.** See for instance: Gianfranco Caniggia and Gian Luigi Maffei, *Architectural Composition and Building Typology: Interpreting Basic Building* (Florence: Alinea, 2001), and Giancarlo Cataldi, *Per una scienza del territorio: studi e note* (Florence: Uniedit, 1977).

**21.** For the cartographic sources used by Saverio Muratori see Silvia Tagliazucchi, "Studi per una operante storia del territorio. Il libro incompiuto di Saverio Muratori" (PhD diss., Università di Bologna, 2015), 54. Although Muratori's bibliography of geographical references is vast, at a theoretical level he elaborates his own geographical system. The notion of "active geography" is especially elaborated in Pierre George, R. Cugliemo, B. Kaiser and Y. Lacoste, *La Géographie Active* (Paris: Presses Universitaires de France, 1964). The notion of "volitional geography" is used for similar purposes. See in this respect Kenny Cupers, "*Géographie Volontaire* and the Territorial Logic of Architecture," *Architectural Histories* 4, no. 1 (2016): 1–13.

**22.** Arturo Lanzani, *Immagini del territorio e idee di piano, 1943–1963: dagli approcci generalizzanti all'interpretazione dei contesti locali* (Milan: Franco Angeli, 1986), 50–53. Manuel de Solà-Morales, *Las Formas de crecimiento urbano* (Barcelona: UPC, 1997), 13–17.

**23.** Manfredo Tafuri, *History of Italian Architecture, 1944–1985* (Cambridge, MA: MIT Press. 1989), 61.

standing of human action as an autonomous sphere accompanies an emphasis on the world as a concrete object that predefines directions, forms, limits.[24] For Muratori, humanity and Earth maintain a dialogue. He presents the history of the formation of territorial types as a register of creative acts. Each territory is a form of terrestrial "interpretation"; each has triggered a process of symbolization and integration of geography and Earth.[25] Muratori sees his cartography of the ecumene as a way to gain new freedom in this process of interpretation, a freedom that for him emanates from grounding the actions of civilization in real knowledge of the concrete, material, terrestrial object that humans inhabit and not in ideological abstractions or economically driven plans of territorial control.[26]

**24.** Muratori, *Civiltà e territorio,* 28.

**25.** Muratori, *Civiltà e territorio,* 535–536.

**26.** Muratori, *Civiltà e territorio,* 43 and 52.

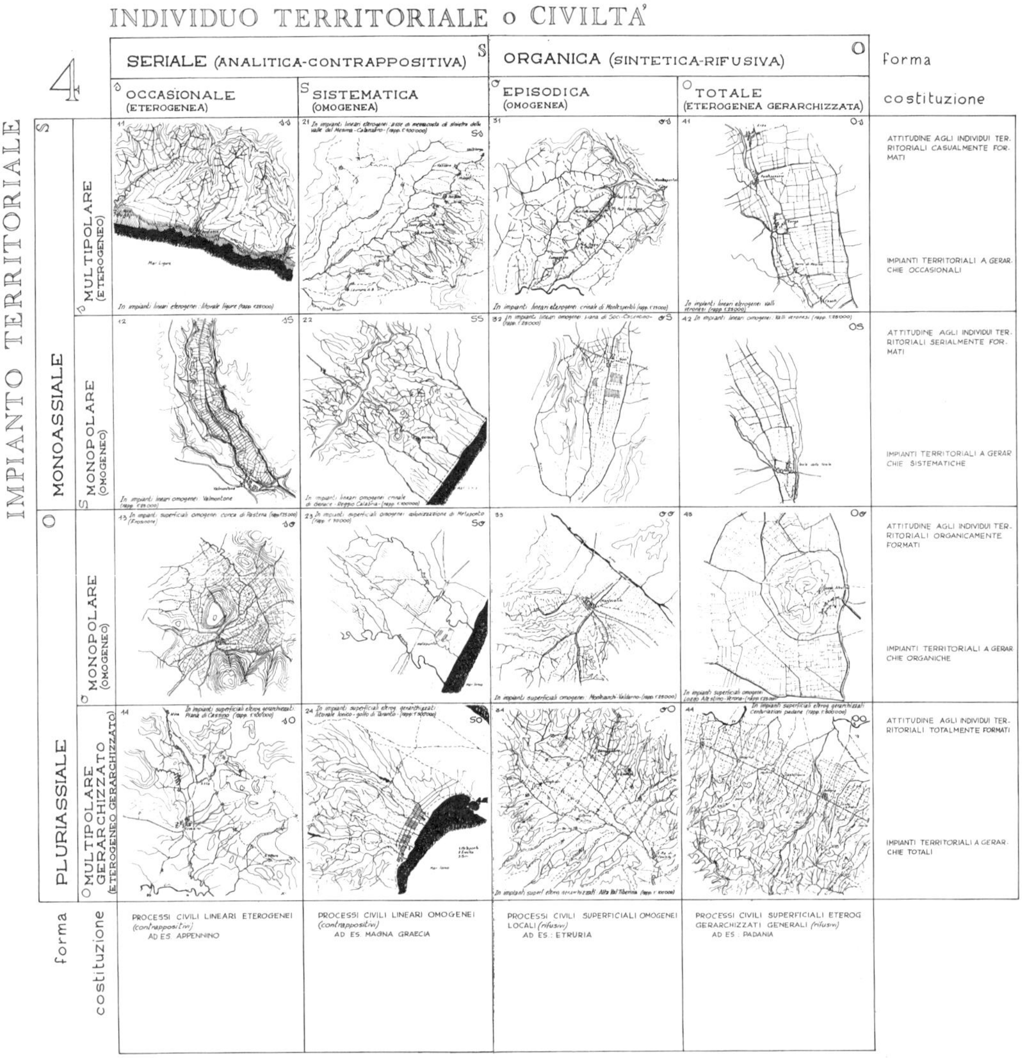


**Figure 1.** *Tabellone*. Territorial Individuals or Civilization. R. Bollati, S. Bollati, A. Giannini. 1978.

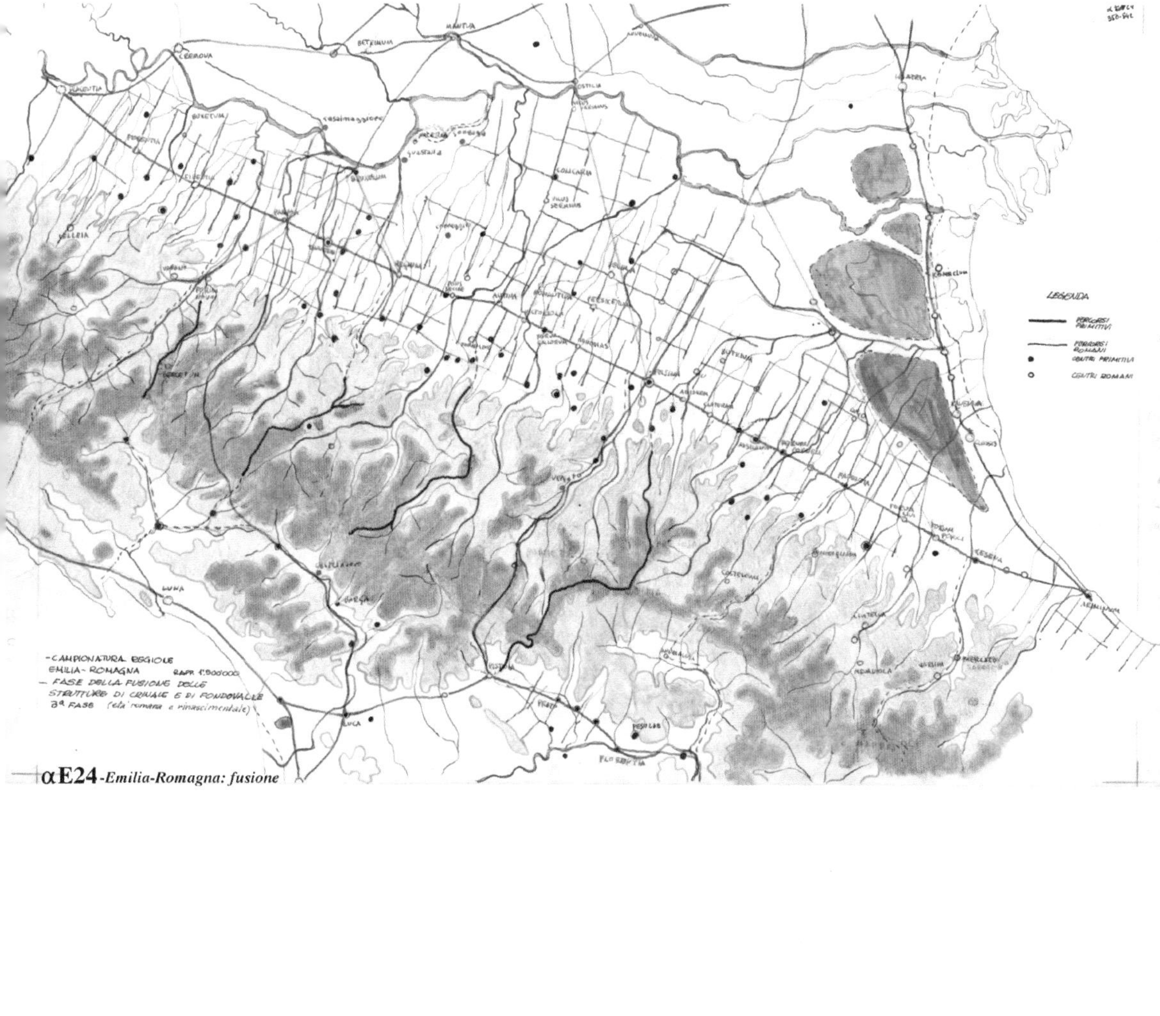


**Figure 2.** Sample of the Emilia-Romagna region. Phase of fusion of the ridge and valley structures. Undated.
**Figure 3 (Following pages).** Civilization of serial structure. Chinese ecumene II. Undated.

CENTRO STUDI DI STORIA URBANISTICA

# STUDI PER UNA OPERANTE STORIA DEL TERRITORIO

SAVERIO MURATORI RENATO BOLLATI SERGIO BOLLATI GUIDO MARINUCCI

SCALA 1 : 10.000.000

S16

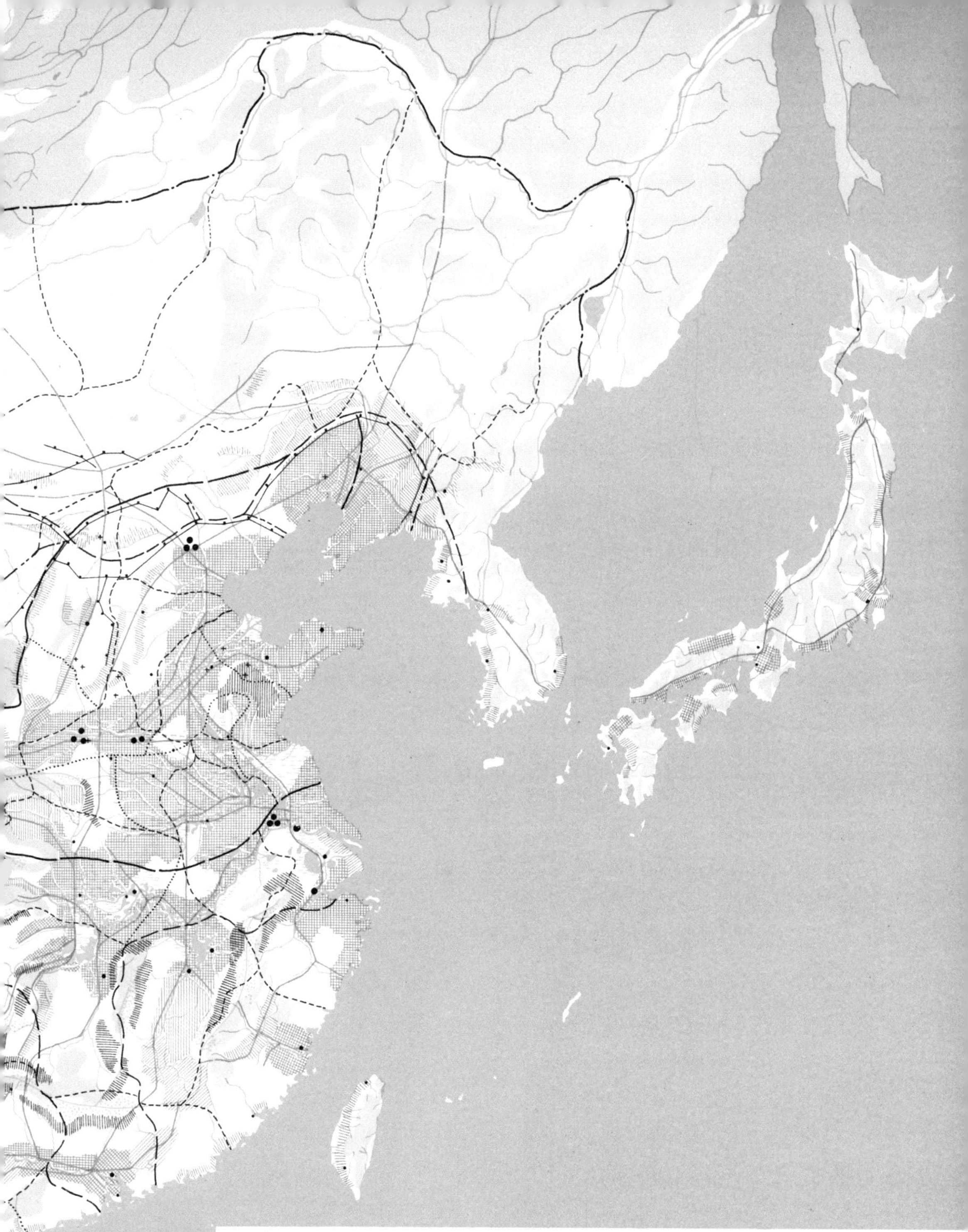

# CIVILTA' DI IMPIANTO SERIALE-ECUMENSE CINESE: II

**S/o :** STADIO DI SVILUPPO SERIALE TIPICO

| O/s | Fase di frazionamento/sovrapposizione | : | costitutiva | età Chan-kuo e Ch'in | −481−206 | e successive | dinastia Sui | +589+ 618 | — disgregaz. da Yüan a Ming | +1351+13... |
| S | Fase di espansione tecnico-sistematica | : | costitutiva | dinastia Han occ. | −206+ 23 | » » | dinastia T'ang anteriori | +618+ 759 | — dinastia Ming | +1368+16... |
| o | Fase di pianificazione economico-politica | : | costitutiva | dinastia Han orient. | + 23+220 | » » | dinastia T'ang posteriori | +759+ 907 | — Manchu anteriori | +1644+18... |
| O/s | Fase di saturazione etico-sociale | : | costitutiva | « Tre regni » e Chin | +220+316 | » » | disgr. T'ang. Sung sett. e Kitan | +907+1127 | — declino Manchu | +1859+19... |

| | PERCORSI DI USO TERRITORIALE | TESSUTI MODULARI TIPICI | | | | S, o, O ABBANDONATI | | NODI STATALI/LOCALI | CONFINI-ORGANI TERRITORIALI INDIVID... |
|---|---|---|---|---|---|---|---|---|---|
| | | s | S | o | O | | | • • • ◉ | |
| CIVILTA' PRIMITIVE | | | | | | | | • | MURA |
| CIVILTA' SERIALI (culture di monte/valle) | | | | | | | | • | HAN 206... ma... |
| CIVILTA' SERIALI (culture di piano) | | | | | | | | ● | ETA' ... 221... |
| | | | | | | | | + templi buddisti | T'AN... |

# **Beitrag zur Planetarisierung der Erde**
## Contribution to the Planetarization of the Earth

**Project:** 32. **Author:** Volker Sayn (1937). **Date:** 1968. **Themes:** Abstraction. Circulation. Linearity. Megastructure.

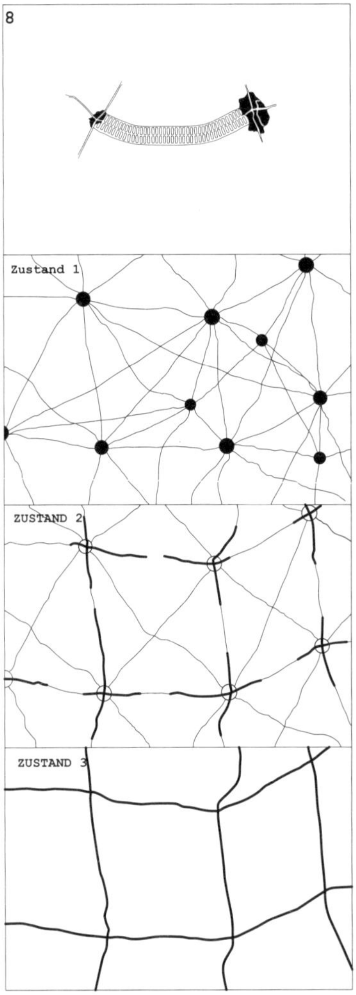


**Figure 0.** Soria y Mata's Linear City as model, and evolution from existing distribution of cities to proposed scheme. After Volker Sayn. 1968.

A victim of the geopolitical conflicts that follow World War II, West Berlin is a walled-in city in 1968, a segment of a historic capital divided between two antagonist political regimes. The city's landscape displays all too well the consequences of the war and of its aftermath. Since 1961 the Berlin Wall encircles the city, impeding free circulation between East and West Berlin. A broad area of urban wastelands surrounds this huge concrete frontier, and multiple, vast, empty spaces remain where the many buildings destroyed by the war previously stood.[1]

Contribution to the Planetarization of the Earth directly faces this physical and geopolitical context. The project is Volker Sayn's entry into the 1968 Schinkel competition. As West Berlin could not expand physically to house its new inhabitants, the competition brief proposed to densify the city by designing a building over a clover-leaf highway intersection in Berlin Zehlendorf. Sayn's response to the brief cannot be more provocative. A recent graduate from Technical University Berlin, where he was a disciple of Oswald Mathias Ungers, Sayn defies the type of piecemeal intervention that the competition promotes, which he decries as "purely futile attempts (Sisyphus attempts) to solve the contradiction by perfecting the existing system."[2] Instead of a building for the intersection, he proposes a hybrid between transportation infrastructure and building that circumscribes the whole globe **[fig. 1]**. Oblivious to all political frontiers, the building grows following the lines of parallels and meridians, creating a gridded graticule system that Sayn names the Hassloch system **[fig. 2]**.

The name Hassloch suggests a drastic, but also humorous, alteration of existing territorial logics. Hassloch is a minuscule German rural village whose houses form built ribbons along the roads, preserving big areas of landscape between them **[fig. 3]**. Sayn's proposal is an augmented version of this system. The design superimposes ribbons of buildings over the highway system, creating huge, highly technical, built complexes. Between them, however, the natural space remains unaltered by any form of construction. The upscaling of Hassloch's spatial logic seeks the coexistence of dense metropolitan conditions and natural systems. It contests the forms of dispersion and sprawl that characterize metropolitan systems as well as their environmental externalities of degradation and pollution. At the same time, the design avoids any form of rural nostalgia by fostering an ambitious project of modernization and population redistribution. One of the rationales of the project is to concentrate all the economic

**1.** André Bideau, "Elusive Ungers," *AA Files* 64 (2012): 3–16. According to the author, the urban landscape resulting from the war, "dominated by voids rather than by buildings, will be the mark of the city for another three decades."

**2.** Volker Sayn, *Modifiziertes Bewertungssystem (hier Hassloch System gennant) für den bewohnbaren Himmelskörper von Enine, dargestellt am Beispiel der Erde als Beitrag zur 'Planetarisierung,* Oswald Mathias Ungers's studio booklet 13 (May 1968): 1.

investments dedicated to building in the world to the construction of these vast architectural and infrastructural lines, which would progressively substitute all the world's pre-existing settlements—including, in an ironic act of self-cancelation of the design, Hassloch itself.

Despite being a response to the problems of urbanization, Sayn considers that his work exceeds the limits of terrestrial application. For him, the project is a prototype that shows how to create an "inhabitable orb, using the example of the Earth, as a contribution to its 'planetarization.'"[3] The neologism planetarization—coined before the notion of "globalization" emerged—indicates a process still to be initiated or fulfilled.[4] The term suggests that in order to truly become a planet, the earth requires social and architectural intervention. As the term "contribution" indicates, Sayn's project, more than being a finished solution, is an attempt to envision one of the possible ways toward a final planetary stage, one that challenges the conditions of the divided global context of the Cold War. Reacting against the proliferation of impassable national and geopolitical barriers that Berlin epitomized, the project suggests the abolition of frontiers. It counters the realities of uneven social and economic development with a radically equalitarian alternative, in which South, East, and West of the planet are built in the same way.[5] Against urban sprawl and environmental degradation, Sayn defines a form of order to rationalize the consumption of space, energy, and resources. Against the fantasies of freedom without repercussions of the capitalist, liberal state, he suggests the construction of a common form, which also impugns the position architects maintain toward the world: "Do you think this construction is 'inhuman'? Remember: the so present 'freedom' of today is the freedom of those who build their fenced-in houses on lakesides and south-facing hills, those who erect 'no entry' signs and who buy sleazy replicas of L.C., Mies and Scharoun."[6]

The primary trigger of the project is, thus, the consideration of existing global, social, political, and environmental conditions. In this regard, the design provides an architectural response to some of the most positive tendencies that Sayn perceives. He sees the creation of the United Nations Organization (UNO) as a platform for international discussion shortly after the war "caused by Germany" as a "project of hope" that needs to be continued.[7] The student revolts of the late 1960s and the generational feeling that the capitalist system needs to be overcome, compel him to think that it is possible to propose a "world improvement project."[8] These optimistic, social considerations provide the content and goals of his project. But, to address them, Sayn relies on the

3. Sayn, *Modifiziertes Bewertungssystem*, cover.

4. Roi Salgueiro Barrio and Benjamin Albrecht, interview with Volker Sayn (April 2018). The term globalization starts being widely used to refer to processes of political or economic integration in the early 1980s.

5. With the paradoxical result, noted by Sayn, that the network is denser in the poles.

6. Sayn, *Modifiziertes Bewertungssystem*, 16.

7. Salgueiro Barrio and Albrecht, interview with Volker Sayn.

8. Salgueiro Barrio and Albrecht, interview with Volker Sayn.

project's second trigger, namely: the design methodology that he had learned from Oswald Mathias Ungers (OMU).[9] In attention to both influences, the project has a dual dedicatory: to OMU, and to UNO.

Unger's relation to a world-scale proposal is in many ways paradoxical. Ungers starts teaching at Berlin Technical University in 1963 with a research agenda focused on the consideration of the city as an architectural artifact, and he limits his students' work quite strictly to the study of Berlin. Additionally, the clear articulation of his intellectual positions from the 1970s on favors the open-ended character of urban processes. As he states in the 1976 manifesto "Planning Criteria": "the projects are better characterized as fragments and partial solutions, than as ideal realizations of a platonic idea. They can be seen as an attempt to get away from the myth of the perfect plan."[10] The bases of this position, critical to any form of overdeterministic, global planning, are laid during his teaching at Berlin. Yet, his teaching method there also encourages the type of exploration that Sayn pursued. In fact, Contribution to the Planetarization of the Earth is the object and title of the issue 13 of the journal Ungers publishes to compile his academic activity.

As Pier Vittorio Aureli explains, Ungers asked his students to rigorously face the real conditions of Berlin and to confront systematically the infrastructural elements that make the city: "the *Autobahn*, the parks, the canals, the river Spree, the *U-bahn* network."[11] This interest in the infrastructural dimension of the city is at the core of the notion of *Grossform*, or big form, that Ungers coins in 1967 to explain his design agenda.[12] Although the notion itself does not imply necessarily a large size but a big urban impact, it brings to the discourse of architecture a clear infrastructural component. In Ungers's words: "The large form creates the framework, the order and the planned space for an unforeseeable, unpredictable, living process, for a parasitic architecture."[13] In this sense, *Grossform* is, above all, a project for the collective. It creates a common, unified framework that individuals can modify later.

The first image that Ungers uses to justify the notion of *Grossform* is taken from a paper project he had previously designed that year. It consists of a huge, one-hundred-floor-high, linear building, running along the 500 kilometer-highway that connects Hamburg and Frankfurt. The project offers an alternative way of distributing the eight million houses that were built in West Germany between 1950 and 1966, revealing with a single gesture how the postwar housing

**9.** Salgueiro Barrio and Albrecht, interview with Volker Sayn.

**10.** Oswald Mathias Ungers, "Planning Criteria," *Lotus International* 11 (1976): 13

**11.** Pier Vittorio Aureli, *The Possibility of an Absolute Architecture* (Cambridge, MA: MIT Press, 2011), 190.

**12.** Oswald Mathias Ungers, "Grossform," *Architecture d'Aujourd'hui* 56–57 (1967): 108–113.

**13.** Ungers, "Grossform," 88

boom, despite its size, had not been able to create a legible, territorial form. From a formal standpoint, the project reflects Ungers's fascination at that time with Soviet proposals made in the 1920s for linear cities **[project 10]**.[14] More importantly, the project represents the highly rationalistic and objective design attitude that Ungers and his assistant Michael Wegener demanded of their students.[15] The *Grossform* that Ungers proposes is the direct, unfiltered outcome of relating quantitative demographic data to the realities of industrialization and mass-production, and it points to how that clash questions conventional forms of urban production. Using Aureli's words again: "Rather than trying to 'solve' the crises of the city, the projects proposed with this [teaching] method sought to exploit them as the thematic form of the project itself."[16] For Ungers it was more important to reveal the contradiction, than to actually solve it.

Contribution to the Planetarization of the Earth is a radical expression of that design methodology. The project consists of a series of vignettes combining an aseptic, analytical text and extremely diagrammatic drawings. The sequence begins with an analysis of the current system of concentric cities and of its global distribution, and it follows with the definition of three possible alternatives for urban distribution at the world scale **[figs. 0 and 4]**. The text succinctly analyzes the strengths and weaknesses of these three models—namely the Hassloch graticule, a pentagonal "Zeiss Dywidag" network, and a system of extreme decentralization—in order to defend the selected one. The rest of the project explains the possible evolution toward the final stage, quantifies its demographic impact, and defines how the design rationalizes systems of aerial and terrestrial transportation, areas of agricultural production, and urban services.

The proposal's graphic restraint and objective tone deliberately contrasts with other forms of world-making. Sayn is fascinated with Archigram and knows some of the works of Werner Ruhnau and Eckhard Schulze-Fielitz (whom Ungers invites to teach a seminar), even if he does not associate their projects to the world scale **[projects 22, 24 and 25]**.[17] In particular, Sayn's rejection of Archigram's graphic exuberance emphasizes the technical character of his project and its status as a guide for later development. "The project," Sayn writes, "was less of an architectural design but more a planned, scientific approach to be carried by an interdisciplinary collective of specialists."[18]

The project's main interest lies, however, in the strong contrast between this technical drive and the schematic character of Sayn's arguments and representations. Contribution Towards the Planetarization of the Earth does not rely

**14.** Salgueiro Barrio and Albrecht, interview with Volker Sayn.

**15.** For Sayn, Wegener played a crucial teaching and intellectual role in Ungers's studios. Salgueiro Barrio and Albrecht, interview with Volker Sayn. For an analysis of the studios both architects taught together see *ARCH+: Lernen von O. M. Ungers* 181/182 (2006).

**16.** Aureli, *The Possibility of an Absolute Architecture,* 190.

**17.** Salgueiro Barrio and Albrecht, interview with Volker Sayn.

**18.** Salgueiro Barrio and Albrecht, interview with Volker Sayn.

19. Sayn, *Modifiziertes Bewertungssystem*, 16.

on complex technical knowledge. On the contrary, the project uses almost amateurish means to visualize and debate different forms of spatially organizing the planet. From this point of view, rather than an unchangeable, technocratic vision, the project acts as a tool to claim that the preoccupation with global matters should be a general social concern, accepting individual initiatives. Its semiscientific tone serves to question the status and procedures of architecture when the discipline confronts the scale of the world.[19] Sayn's overly confident, optimistic, and partly humorous elaboration of this project without a solid understanding of other world-scale proposals and in the absence of any overarching theoretical framework points to the consolidation of a historical moment in which it had become a pressing necessity to respond to geopolitical, economic, and environmental global challenges, no matter how tentative the means or how particular the point of view—even the spatiality of a small German village could be used as a model for the world. His project addresses these questions with an extremely equalitarian solution that reiterates many traits of previous world proposals, such as linearity, absolute continuity, and formal repetition. Following Ungers these spatial strategies create a *Grossform*, a collective construction ordering space at the scale of the world.

12

Lokalkolorit in der Zeichnung wurde vermieden; man stelle sich dazu nacheinander vor z.B.: Argolis, das Butjadinger-Land, die Cordilleren, die Wüste Gobi, Island, Masuren, die Pampa, die Pripjetsümpfe, Toskana u.a.

Eine suggestive Wirkung wie bei St. Elia wurde nicht beabsichtigt. Fertigkeit vortäuschende Details wie bei Archigram wurden nicht angegeben, da das Projekt von einem sehr großen Team von Experten aller Fachrichtungen jahrelang vorzuplanen wäre.

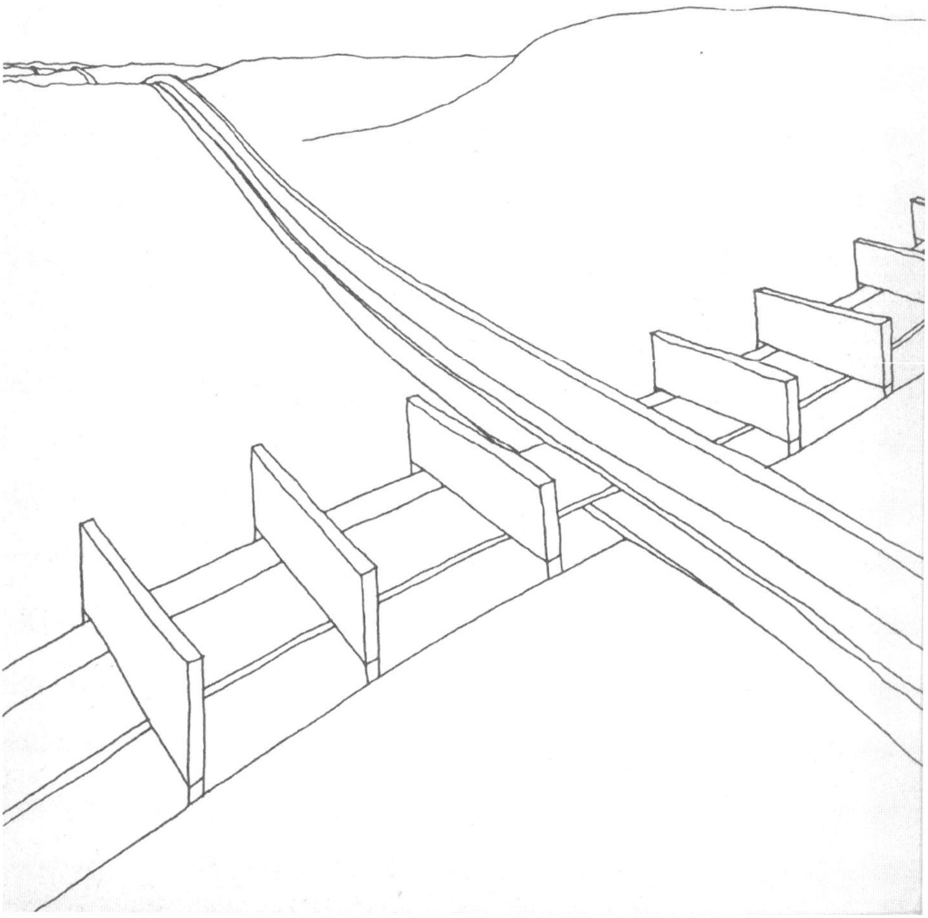

**Figure 1.** Perspective of proposed continuous building. Accompanying legend: "The drawing avoids showing local context." 1968.

VORSCHLAG EINER BEBAUUNG IM MODIFIZIERTEN GRADNETZSYSTEM (HIER HASSLOCH-SYSTEM GENANNT) FÜR EINEN BEWOHNBAREN HIMMELSKÖRPER, DARGESTELLT AM BEISPIEL DER ERDE, ALS BEITRAG ZU DEREN "PLANETARISIERUNG".

Gewidmet:
OMU und der UNO

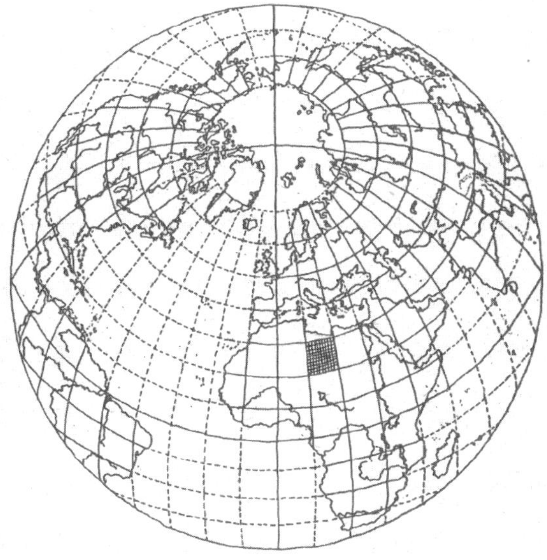

Eingereicht am 2.1.1968 zum Schinkelwettbewerb des A.J.V. Berlin (dessen Ausschreibung die Überbauung des Schöneberger-Autobahnkleeblattes vorsah).

von Volker Sayn

**Figure 2.** Terrestrial distribution of the building following the order of meridians and parallels. 1968.

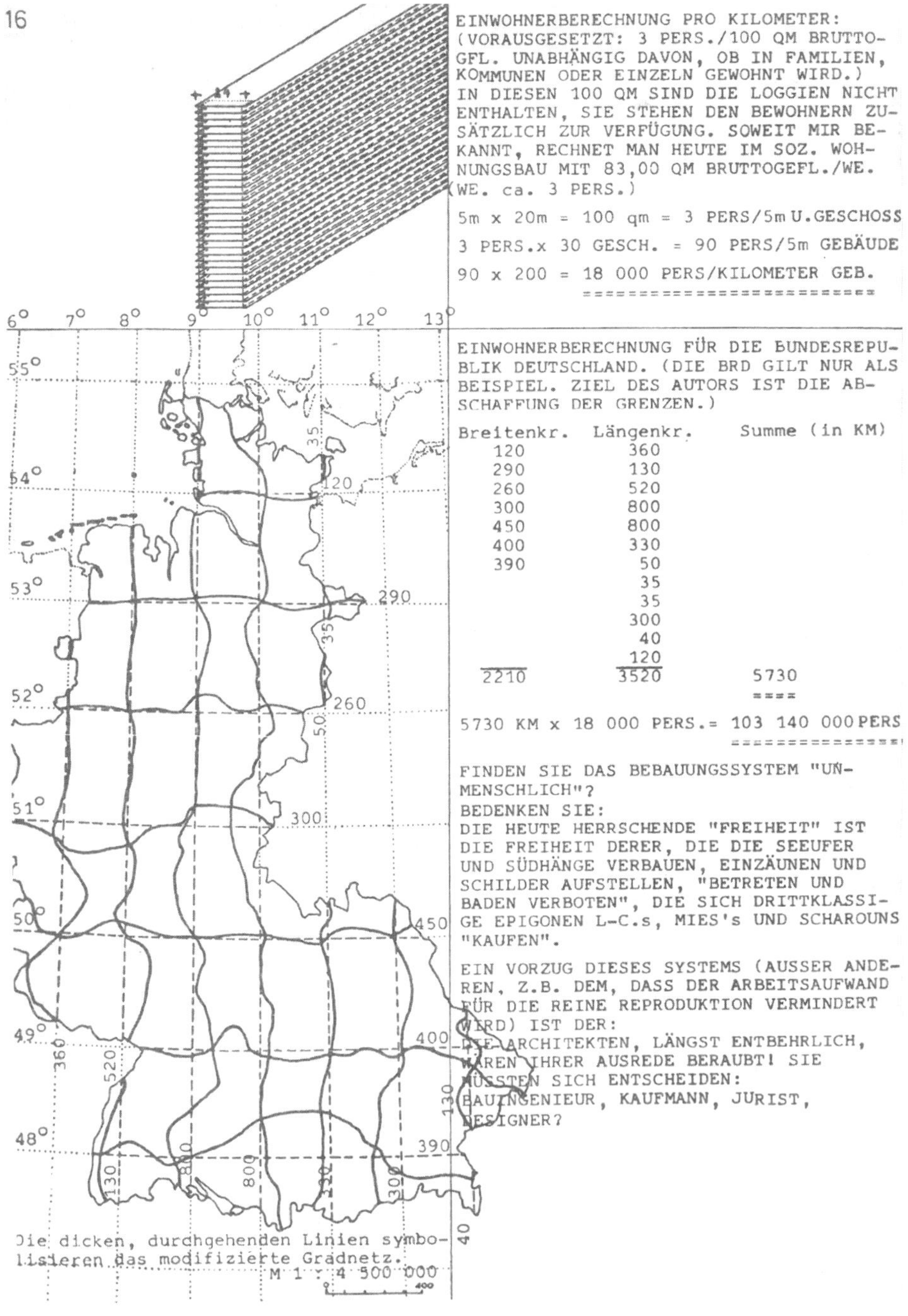
16
EINWOHNERBERECHNUNG PRO KILOMETER:
(VORAUSGESETZT: 3 PERS./100 QM BRUTTO-
GFL. UNABHÄNGIG DAVON, OB IN FAMILIEN,
KOMMUNEN ODER EINZELN GEWOHNT WIRD.)
IN DIESEN 100 QM SIND DIE LOGGIEN NICHT
ENTHALTEN, SIE STEHEN DEN BEWOHNERN ZU-
SÄTZLICH ZUR VERFÜGUNG. SOWEIT MIR BE-
KANNT, RECHNET MAN HEUTE IM SOZ. WOH-
NUNGSBAU MIT 83,00 QM BRUTTOGEFL./WE.
(WE. ca. 3 PERS.)
5m x 20m = 100 qm = 3 PERS/5m U.GESCHOSS
3 PERS.x 30 GESCH. = 90 PERS/5m GEBÄUDE
90 x 200 = 18 000 PERS/KILOMETER GEB.
6° 7° 8° 9° 10° 11° 12° 13°
55°
54°
53°
52°
51°
50°
49°
48°
EINWOHNERBERECHNUNG FÜR DIE BUNDESREPU-
BLIK DEUTSCHLAND. (DIE BRD GILT NUR ALS
BEISPIEL. ZIEL DES AUTORS IST DIE AB-
SCHAFFUNG DER GRENZEN.)
Breitenkr. Längenkr. Summe (in KM)
120 360
290 130
260 520
300 800
450 800
400 330
390 50
35
35
300
40
120
2210 3520 5730
5730 KM x 18 000 PERS.= 103 140 000 PERS
FINDEN SIE DAS BEBAUUNGSSYSTEM "UN-
MENSCHLICH"?
BEDENKEN SIE:
DIE HEUTE HERRSCHENDE "FREIHEIT" IST
DIE FREIHEIT DERER, DIE DIE SEEUFER
UND SÜDHÄNGE VERBAUEN, EINZÄUNEN UND
SCHILDER AUFSTELLEN, "BETRETEN UND
BADEN VERBOTEN", DIE SICH DRITTKLASSI-
GE EPIGONEN L-C.s, MIES's UND SCHAROUNS
"KAUFEN".
EIN VORZUG DIESES SYSTEMS (AUSSER ANDE-
REN, Z.B. DEM, DASS DER ARBEITSAUFWAND
FÜR DIE REINE REPRODUKTION VERMINDERT
WIRD) IST DER:
DIE ARCHITEKTEN, LÄNGST ENTBEHRLICH,
WAREN IHRER AUSREDE BERAUBT! SIE
MÜSSTEN SICH ENTSCHEIDEN:
BAUINGENIEUR, KAUFMANN, JURIST,
DESIGNER?
35
120
290
35
260
50
300
450
400
360
520
130
390
130
800
800
300
40
Die dicken, durchgehenden Linien symbo-
lisieren das modifizierte Gradnetz.
M 1 : 4 500 000

**Figure 3.** Plan and population calculation per kilometer, applied to West Germany. 1968.

Schema der Verteilung der heutigen Groß-
städte auf der Erde:
Wenige dichtbesiedelte Zentren an weit
auseinanderliegenden Punkten der Erd-
oberfläche sind durch ein üppiges Ver-
kehrsnetz, welches durch unbesiedeltes
oder dünn besiedeltes Gebiet führt,
miteinander verbunden.

SCHEMA DER VOM VERFASSER VORGESCHLAGE-
NEN BEBAUUNG DER ERDE:
EIN DEM GRADNETZ ENTSPRECHENDES NETZ,
BEI DEM SICH WOHNUNG, PRODUKTION,
KONSUMTION, VERSORGUNG UND VERKEHR
ÜBER DERSELBEN FLÄCHE ABSPIELEN.
DAS NETZ KANN DURCH KLIMATISCHE TOPO-
GRAFISCHE, GEOLOGISCHE, ÖKOLOGISCHE,
SOZIOLOGISCHE, PSYCHOLOGISCHE U.A.
VERHÄLTNISSE MODIFIZIERT WERDEN.

SCHWÄCHE DES SYSTEMS: DIE DICHTE NIMMT
MIT ENTFERNUNG VOM ÄQUARTOR ZU.

Schema einer möglichen Bebauung in
einem "Zeiss-Dywidag" Netz.

Das hätte den Vorteil der gleich-
mäßigen Dichte.

Schwäche des Systems: Schwierige
Orientierung.

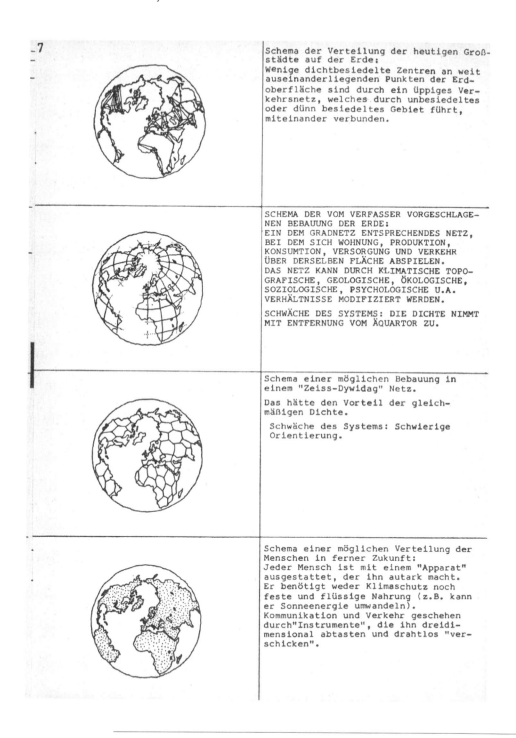

Schema einer möglichen Verteilung der
Menschen in ferner Zukunft:
Jeder Mensch ist mit einem "Apparat"
ausgestattet, der ihn autark macht.
Er benötigt weder Klimaschutz noch
feste und flüssige Nahrung (z.B. kann
er Sonneenergie umwandeln).
Kommunikation und Verkehr geschehen
durch"Instrumente", die ihn dreidi-
mensional abtasten und drahtlos "ver-
schicken".

**Figure 4.** Alternative planetary models of settlement distribution. 1968.

# The Continuous City

**Project:** 33. **Authors:** Alan Boutwell and Michael Mitchell. **Date:** 1968–1971. **Themes:** Circulation. Interiorization. Megastructure. Parallelism.

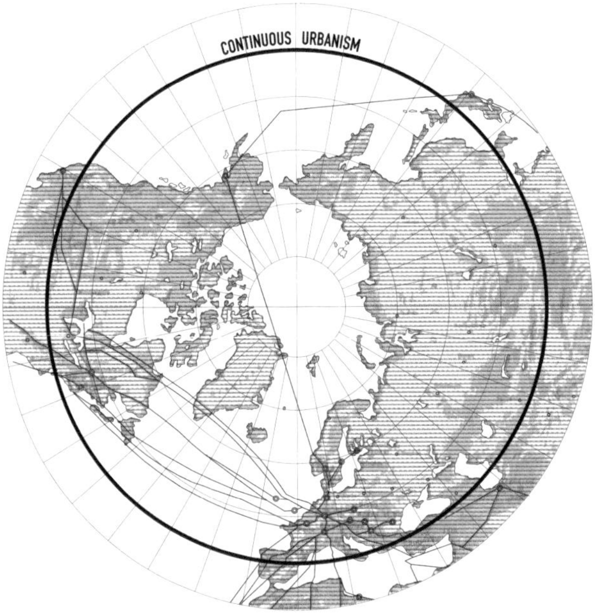


**Figure 0.** Continuous Urbanism. A City around the world. After Alan Boutwell. 1971.

When English architects Alan Boutwell and Michael Mitchell publish their project for a Continuous City in *Domus*, they present themselves as "comprehensive designers."[1] This ambitious, overarching self-identification reflects its authors' attempt to conceive a project that can exceed the conceptual and dimensional limits of architecture—their design is as much a large building as it is a city and a way to reorganize geography—and that considers integrally all the aspects human existence may require. The more detailed drawings of the Continuous City **[figs. 1 and 2]** show a vast, multilevel building, measuring roughly ten kilometers in length, standing around one hundred meters above the ground. Its organization and form of construction are approached from a highly technical perspective.[2] The elevated city is halved by a bridge. One half comprises residential, cultural, administrative, and leisure functions, and the other one half comprises industries and research and educational centers. Together with these conventional functions of an urban plan, the proposal integrates infrastructures for energy production (a nuclear plant), water treatment, and vertical and horizontal circulation (heliports, elevators, escalators, monorails) in order to ensure that the building is able to carry out every necessary function. At ground level, connected to the city through elevators, there are enormous parking areas from which a new road structure emerges. It segregates means of transportation according to their speed, and geometrically orders the territory in a systematic triangular pattern.

The technical rationality of the Continuous City thus operates at both the scale of the city itself and of the territory it aims to reorganize. One of the project's plans shows how the design might be placed in Germany, in the Ruhr region **[fig. 3]**. Beyond biographical reasons (Boutwell lived in Dusseldorf) the selection of this area is highly significant. The Ruhr's coal mining economy and industrial production generated a booming urban system, where original settlements spread into a quasi-continuous, sprawling, one-hundred-kilometer city. Acknowledging the importance and novelty of these conditions, in the mid-1960s the Ruhr starts being analyzed as a megalopolis, as a conglomeration of cities whose relations are creating a unified urban region—notably, by the English geographer Peter Hall, for whom the Ruhr operates at the world scale and represents a global trend of urbanization.[3] Boutwell and Mitchell address some of the spatial consequences of this process with technical rigor. For the designers of the Continuous City, housing population growth in the air serves as an antidote to the uncontrolled consumption of land urban expansion

1. Alan Boutwell and Michael Mitchell, "Planning on a National Scale," *Domus* 470 (January 1969): 2. The authors had previously elaborated the notion of comprehensive design in Alan Boutwell and Michael Mitchell, "Das umfassende Bausystem," *Bauen + Wohnen* 2 (1965): 71–76; and in Alan Boutwell and Mike Mitchell, "Das umfassende Bausystem," *Werk* 53 (April 1966): 143.

2. See in this respect Cornelia Escher, "Alan Boutwell: From the Modular Housing System to the *Continuous City*," in *Megastructure Reloaded: Visionäre Stadtentwürfe der Sechzigerjahre Reflektiert von Zeitgenössischen Künstlern = Visionary Architecture and Urban Design of the Sixties Reflected by Contemporary Artists*, ed. Sabrina Van Der Ley and Markus Richter (Ostfildern: Hatje Cantz, 2008), 165–167. Escher traces the relation of Boutwell's work to the investigations on the rationalization and systematization of construction techniques carried out in Germany by Konrad Wachsmann, Eckhard Schultze-Fielitz (see project 24), and, especially, Max Mengeringhausen.

3. Peter Hall, *The World Cities* (New York: McGraw-Hill, 1966), 3–4 and 15.

causes.[4] Despite the obvious difficulties of implementing such a proposal, they believe their project is realistic. The original plan for the Ruhr shows how the Continuous City overlaps with the existing nuclei but without replacing them. Not only are the settlements preserved, but, unlike most of the projects that propose to create a built layer in the air, the Continuous City preserves existing functions, social relations, and systems of production, both in the elevated city and on the ground.[5] When applied in the Ruhr, the project seeks their rationalization, not their substitution.

4. Boutwell and Mitchell, "Planning on a National Scale," 6.

5. Boutwell and Mitchell, "Planning on a National Scale," 5.

6. Boutwell and Mitchell, "Planning on a National Scale," 2.

7. Alan Boutwell, "Una città intorno al mondo," *Domus* 502 (September 1971): 4.

This is not, nevertheless, the only way in which the project operates. The level of detail that the Ruhr plan and the plans and sections of the ten-kilometer city represent is introduced in a second moment of the authors' discourse, as an exemplification of a broader argument. The Continuous City is first published in an article titled "La Città-Nazione. Planning on a National Scale," in which Boutwell and Mitchell argue that it is necessary to substitute parochial, regional approaches to planning with a comprehensive national plan.[6] Their representation of this statement is, however, not only national, but also continental. In this article, the first image of the project represents the North American subcontinent traversed by a colossal Continuous City spanning from New York to San Francisco **[fig. 4]**. Anticipating explosive demographic growth, the structure is meant to house one billion people in a scaled-up version of the ten-kilometer plans. The drawing shows exactly the same formal features of the Ruhr proposal but now in a linear structure that occupies three terrestrial parallels. Two years later, and again in *Domus*, Boutwell extends the schema to cover the whole world. In this version, the Continuous City, rebranded as Continuous Urbanism, crosses continents and oceans, linking major cities of the Northern Hemisphere through a single built band **[fig. 0]**. Through small, diagrammatic details, the author shows how this band is actually a grid of the buildings proposed for the Ruhr—a fact reiterated in a series of vignettes that depicts the project crossing New York and a natural space in a manner similar to Superstudio's Continuous Monument (1969). Although the article now recognizes the fantastic character of the proposition, Continuous Urbanism is nonetheless justified as a means of enabling "human survival on earth, menaced by super-population and natural decay."[7]

For Boutwell and Mitchell, the Continuous City oscillates, thus, between being a feasible design at a minor scale, and a utopian but nonetheless necessary proposition at a superior one. In it, the world scale acts both as the conceptual support of the project, the justification of its necessity, and the dimensional limit that reveals its implausibility. Similar oscillations appear at a formal level.[8] The project represents an architectural approach to world-making consisting of the inflation of an architectural form that can move seamlessly across scales. And yet, the three versions of the project reveal the difficulties of such an attitude. In the drawings for the Ruhr the buildings are separated from each other, distributed in a series of parallel bands. When representing the proposal for North America, the ten-kilometer Ruhr building is directly scaled up. At the scale of the world, the linear band is broken down into a grid. Rather than being a fully consistent proposal, to be imposed in a single form, the Continuous City appears as a series of essays about the difficulties of designing an architecture on a terrestrial scale.

The Continuous City enters architectural historiography through Reyner Banham's extremely critical analysis of the proposal. For the English critic, the gigantism and global aspirations of the project represent the logical and historical conclusion of the megastructural movement and by extension of modernity.[9] Between the mid-1950s and the mid-1960s architects throughout the world, from South America to Europe, from the United States to Japan, investigate how architecture can be reconfigured as a fixed infrastructural framework to house smaller, interchangeable units.[10] The term megastructure, coined by Japanese architect Fumihiko Maki in 1964, serves to conceptually group these various experiments, while clarifying that they also suggest an exploration of the big scale.[11] Megastructures are, at their origins, investigations pertaining to the architectural object, but they always tend to the urban and territorial scales. As Boutwell and Mitchell understood, a megastructure's latent logic is to produce comprehensive designs which, conflating architecture, infrastructure, and urbanism in a single built piece, can address all functions and scales.

For Banham, such a megastructural approach to architecture is the ultimate representation of the "modern claim for 'the design of the whole human environment,'" as it was expressed in demiurgic notions such as Walter Gropius's "total design."[12] Architectural historian Sarah Deyong has reinforced Banham's thesis, by explaining how megastructures were actually supported by international organisms such as the UN, by global corporations, and by architectural organizations, which saw in them viable solutions to pressing, global problems.[13] In these readings, the terrestrial extent of the Continuous City constitutes the final expression of an ambition to shape the world scale that the megastructural movement inherits directly from modern architecture.

8. See in this respect Antoine Picon's observations on the procedures of utopian design in Antoine Picon, "Notes on Utopia, the City, and Architecture," *Grey Room* 68 (2017): 97.

9. Reyner Banham, *Megastructure: Urban Futures of the Recent Past* (London: Thames and Hudson, 1976), 9–11.

10. Banham emphasizes the multiple geographies of the megastructural movement, which for him reaches from Horacio Caminos's project for the Universidad de Tucuman (Argentina) to the works of the Japanese Metabolist group, Yona Friedman, Paolo Soleri, Constant and, punctually, Oswald Mathias Ungers.

11. Fumihiko Maki, *Investigations in Collective Form* (Saint Louis, MO: Washington University School of Architecture, 1964), 8–14.

12. Banham, *Megastructure*, 9.

13. Sarah Deyong, "Planetary Habitat: The Origins of a Phantom Movement," *Journal of Architecture* 6, no. 2 (2001): 113–119.

For Banham, the absurdity of Boutwell and Mitchell's proposition is then the clear evidence that a radical break with the totalizing logics of modernity is required. The historic role of the Continuous City is, for him, to act as the final stage of the long century of planetary proposal that this book explores.[14] In fact, contemporaneous projects such as Superstudio Continuous Monument or Archizoom's No-Stop City are already critically exposing the politico-economic conditions of possibility of such a global project and the ideological agendas embedded in it **[projects 36 and 38]**. From now on, world projects will often serve as instruments to critique the processes of global structuring and their social or environmental consequences.

The Continuous City is not, however, an example of a single, unitary project of the world, but of a specific way of conceiving it. In Maki's early definition, the megastructure is conceived as a human-made equivalent of landscape, and thus as the instrument toward the substitution of the natural one.[15] To construct megastructures implies for him, developing a series of techniques that imply "environmental engineering," and a consequent development of new technical figures that operate at the intersection of architecture, and structural and civil engineering. The convergence of "earth-forming," "large scale climatic control," and "highway aesthetics," will lead to the emergence of a new type of physical structure, which he calls "environmental building," and that Banham appropriately perceives as a tool for "extreme environmental insulation."[16] The megastructural ideal is that of a complete interior, an architectural world without an outside. Boutwell and Mitchell's project certainly constitutes one of the most radical explorations of this possibility. Especially in the version for the North American continent, the Continuous City represents a project for the world that, at the same time, supplants the world. It is a seemingly uninhabited project that requires, only, technical representations: plans, diagrams, sections. Despite the authors' words, and the small vignettes that, in 1971, contextualize the project, it abstracts natural geography and existing cities and reduces them to mere background, while the Continuous City houses all the new demographic and technical development of humanity. Consequently, the project does not address the relationship between existing ground and elevated city; and the geometric grid acts simply as a tool to rationalize the surface of the planet.

Overcoming its initial aspirations to negotiate with the existing world, the Continuous City ceases to be humanity's second nature in order to become its primary one. As such, the City is subject to processes of natural degradation,

**14.** Banham, *Megastructure,* 199 and 216.

**15.** Maki, *Investigations in Collective Form,* 8. For Maki, the megastructure is "a man-made feature of the landscape. It is like the great hill on which Italian towns were built."

**16.** Maki, *Investigations in Collective Form,* 13; and Banham, *Megastructure,* 42–43.

evolutionary obsolescence, and decay. This is the topic of the more pessimistic drawings that conclude the project, drafted by Alan Boutwell during the 1980s **[fig. 5]**. In them, vegetation and organic life take over the hovering structure, negating the artificiality of the construction. The conditions and processes characteristic of nature's metabolism now dominate and engulf the Continuous City, finally bringing it back to the natural world. A repressed nature seizes the project, anticipating the coming decline and collapse of technical fantasies of ordering the world.

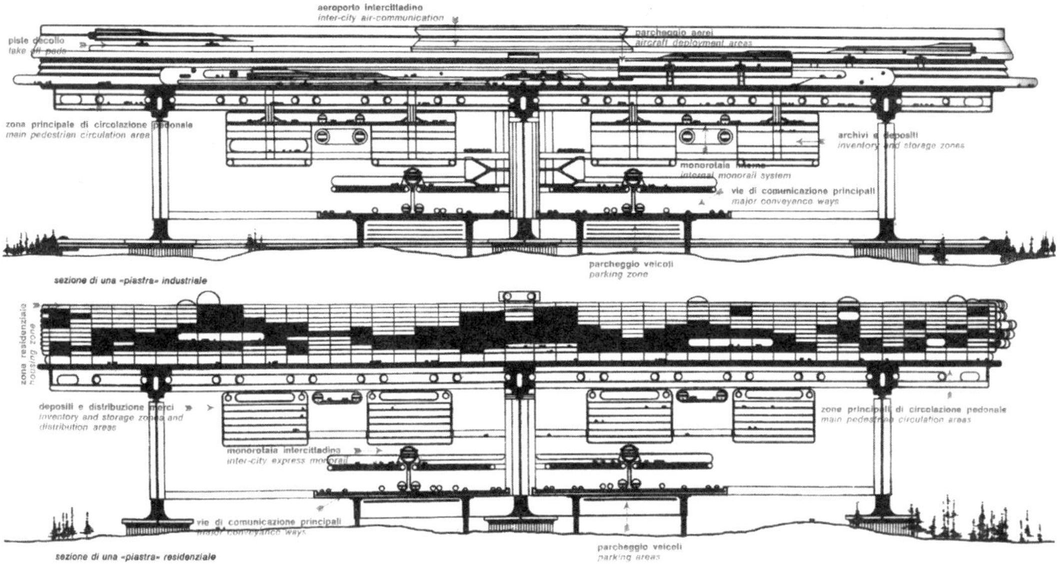


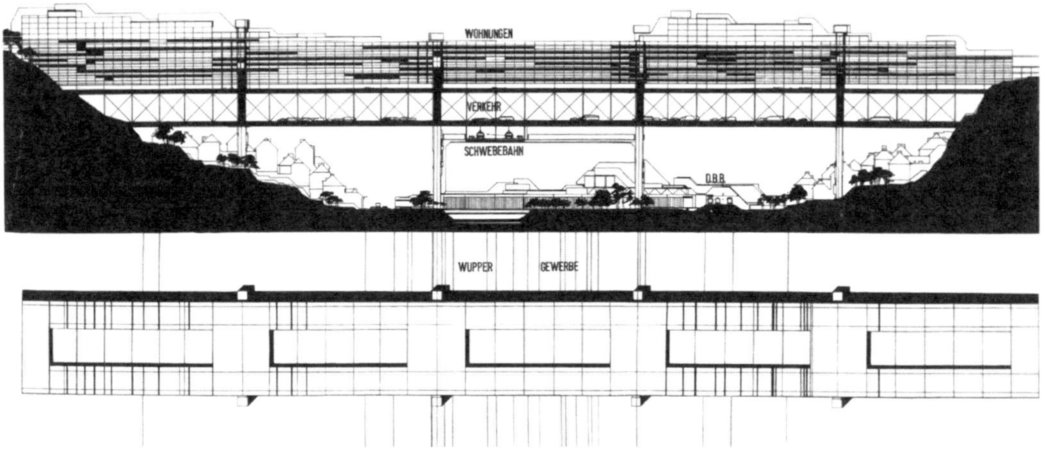


**Figure 1 (Top).** Section of a residential plate. 1969.
**Figure 2 (Bottom).** Bridge City. 1970.

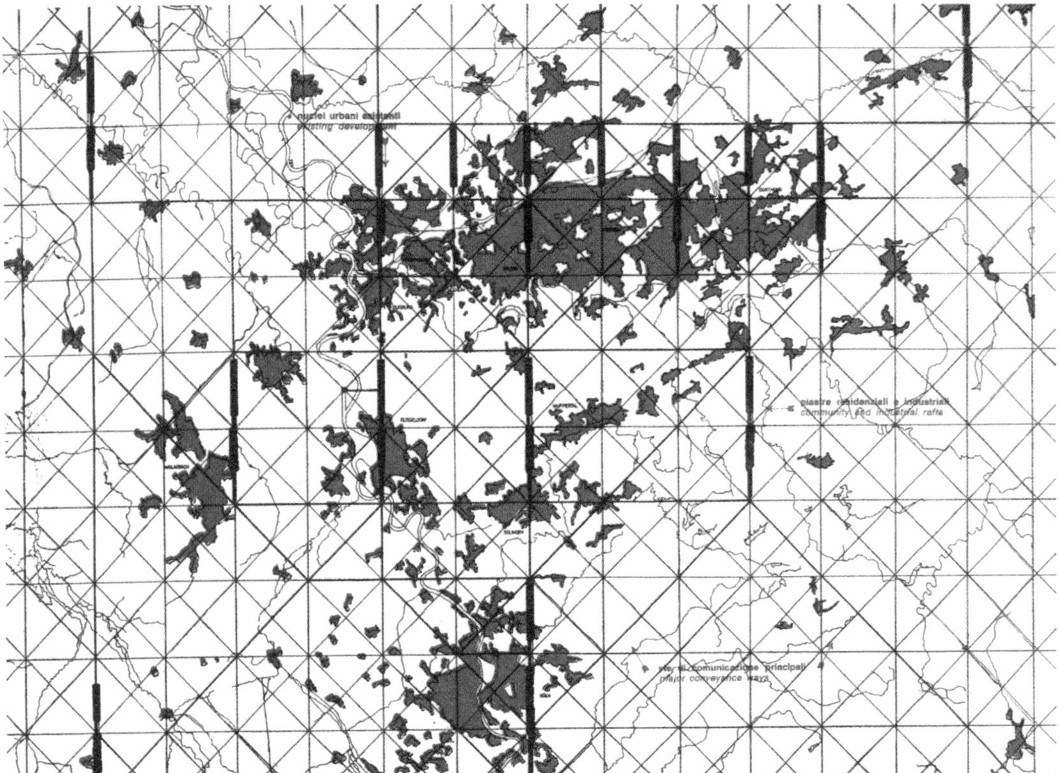


**Figure 3.** Continuous city in Ruhr Valley, Germany. 1969.

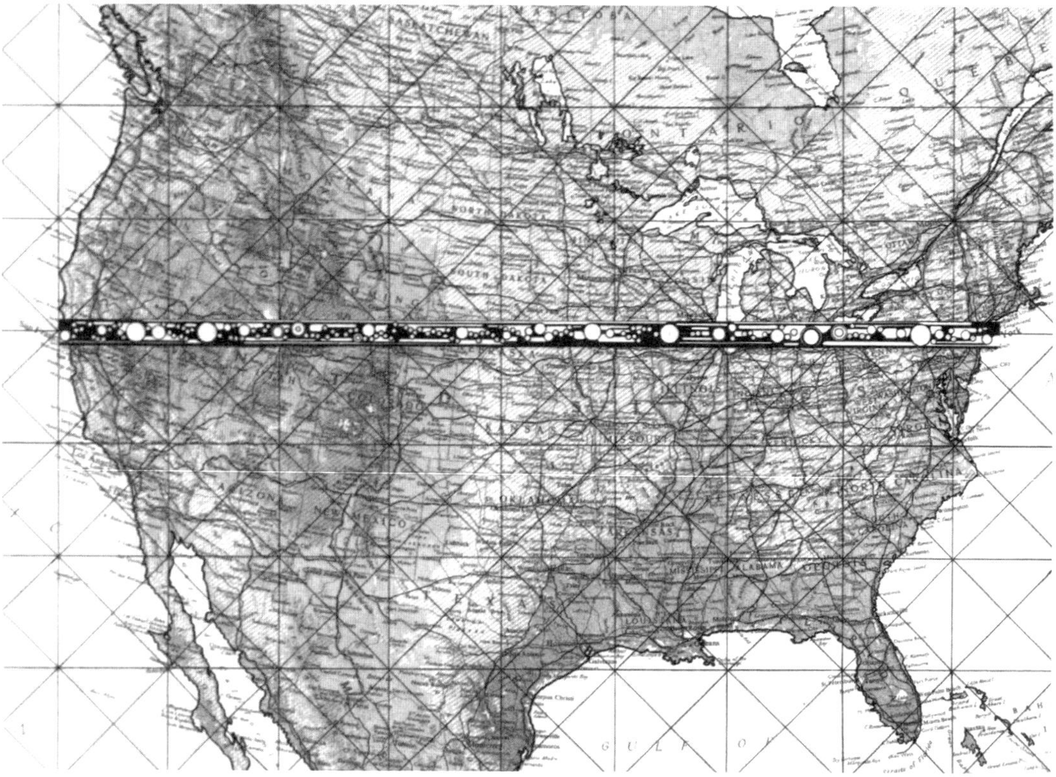

**Figure 4.** Continuous city for 1,000,000,000 human beings. 1969.

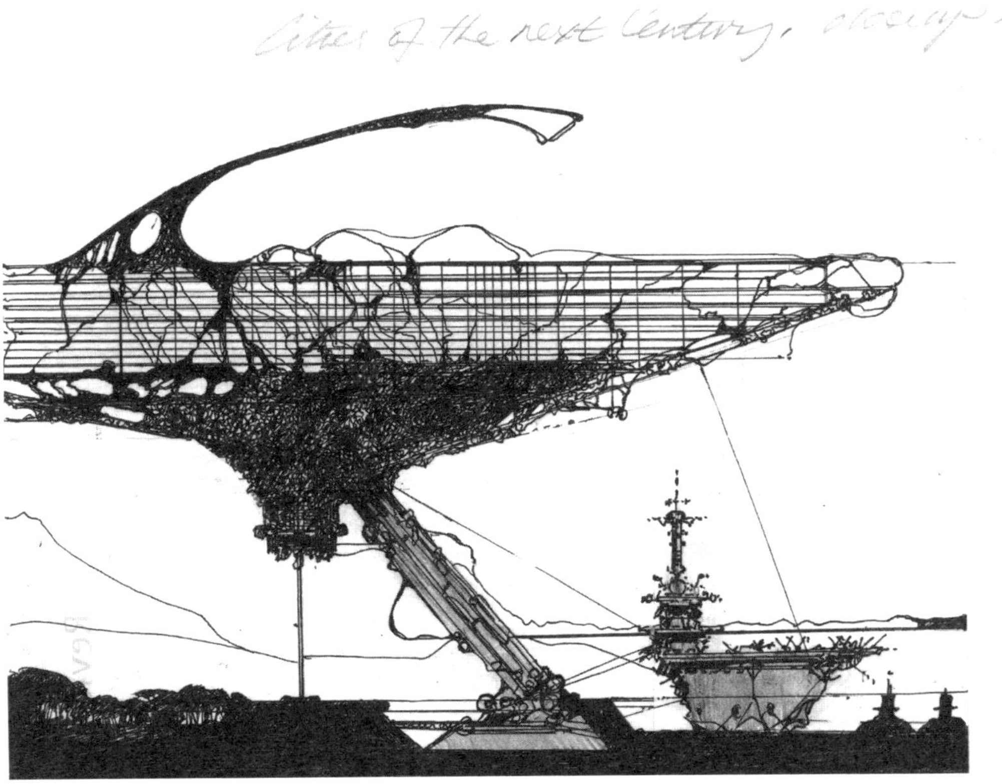


**Figure 5.** Cities of the Next Century, Close Up. ca. 1980.

# totale stadt, ein globales modell

## integral urban, a global model

**Project:** 34. **Author:** Fritz Haller (1924–2012). **Date:** 1968–1975. **Themes:** Abstraction. Typology. Automation. World Urbanization.

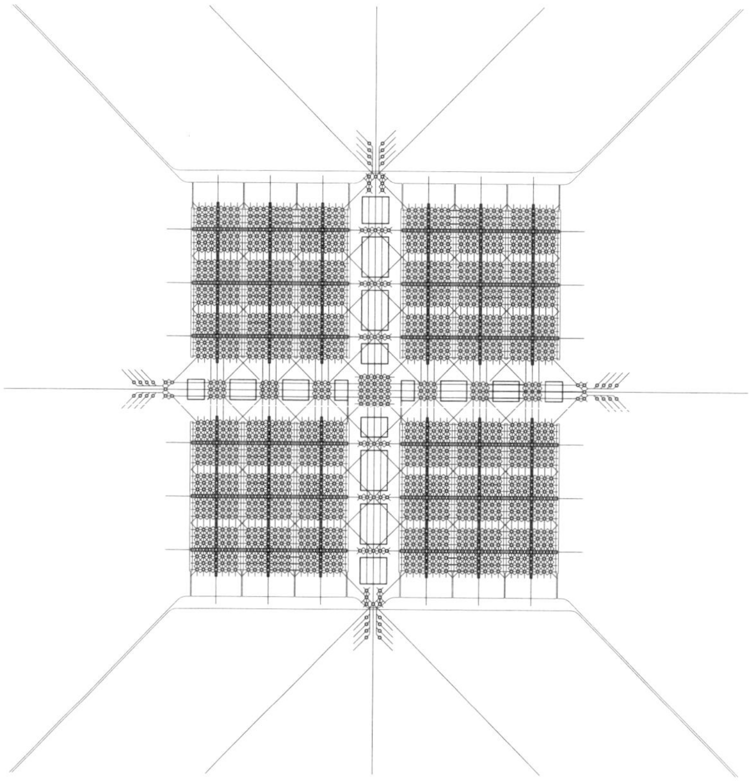

**Figure 0.** Third Order Unit. After Fritz Haller. 1975.

*integral urban, a global model* (1975) is the second volume amid Fritz Haller's trilogy of projects about the future of settlements and the world scale. In his first exploration of the theme, *integral urban, a model* (1968), the idea of integration supports an urban project of nested scales where architecture, technical systems, and means of transportation are designed to operate coordinately. A first order unit of settlement—a single building for 3,200 people—is progressively assembled within a second order unit for 120,000 inhabitants, a third order unit for 4,500,000, and a fourth order unit for 61,000,0000, but without reaching the definition of a fifth unit for the world scale.[1] In turn, the third piece of the trilogy, s*pace colony* (1987), abandons Earth in order to explore the utmost case of integrated, self-sufficient settlement: the space station. The *space colony* defines an absolute interior that considers and reconciles every social and material necessity, be it the negotiation between collective life and individual freedom, the ratio of energy production and consumption, or the processes of recycling waste.[2] Sitting between the 1968 and the 1987 designs, *integral urban, a global model* synthesizes the ambitions of both projects. It extends the system of progressive scalar articulation of the first work to the world scale. The fifth order unit of "integral urban is a system of resting and moving objects and energies covering the entire world." It constitutes a possible "global model" **[fig. 1]**. At the same time, Haller conceives the internal conditions of the design through the same lens as the project of the space capsule.[3] The most important element of *integral urban, a global model*—the second order unit for 80,000 inhabitants—is a totally interior environment, coordinated in all its aspects through cybernetics and automation, as is the rest of the project **[fig. 4]**.[4] The grouping of these units into vaster complexes apportions the spaces required for the production and supply of food, materials, and energy, thus granting the self-sustainability of the ensemble. Haller's is a world without mismatches, working always in optimal, efficient coordination.

Haller describes *integral urban, a global model* in a book that combines extremely precise technical drawings—always abstract and diagrammatic plans and sections—with an explanatory, rhetorically quasiscientific, textual apparatus. The book's format and size, the order and techniques of argumentation, and the means of representation rigorously continue those employed in Haller's previous *integral urban, a model*, in order to emphasize that both books constitute a continuous experiment. There is, however, a significant novelty in the second work. The sequential representation of increasingly bigger scales of urban orga-

**1.** Fritz Haller, *totale stadt, ein modell. integral urban, a model* (Olten: Walter-Verlag, 1968), 60.

**2.** Nils Röller, "Architekturen der Bodenlosigkeit. Haller und Flusser im Dialog," in *Fritz Haller: Architekt und Forscher*, ed. Laurent Stalder and Georg Vrachliotis (Zurich: GTA Verlag, 2015), 169.

**3.** Haller, *totale stadt, ein globales modell*, 9.

**4.** Already in the first *integral urban* project, Haller states: "it would seem that the step into the cosmos, which so often appears foolish to us, will give us the necessary experience and methods which are indispensable to the creation of a world worth living in." See Haller, *totale stadt, ein globales modell*, 8.

nization that made up the core of the first version occupies now only one section of the book, titled "specific model." Haller describes this specific model as a possible example of particularization of a previously defined "general model," and asserts that others can be conceived to register "the specific requirements of an ethnic group, a climatic region, an economic area." Following this logic, he shows the specific model's different implementation in two "concrete" groundings of the project in the Po Valley and the environs of Lake Geneva **[fig. 2]**.[5] But these are just possible, variable examples of the "general model," which is the inalterable piece of Haller's second iteration; the central core from which the rest of the project emanates.

The general model corresponds to *integral urban*'s second order unit, and it adopts a radio-concentric pattern of geometric organization based on the optimal connection between units. On one hand, the general model operates in a manner similar to the blocks of an urban grid. It is a pattern (not a building) that establishes an overall spatial framework that can be occupied in different ways, so that even if the continuous repetition of this model makes subsequent, bigger *integral urban* units, they also allow infinite internal variation. At the same time, the general model serves as a joint, much in the same way as Haller's celebrated USM system (the metallic form of connection that makes it possible to construct either different types of furniture or buildings).[6] Finally, the general model conflates an emphasis on external connectivity with the definition of an inward-looking and fixed, unitary, spatial element that is always perceived as a whole. The circular form of the general model bounds an autonomous, self-sustaining cell and expresses a form of collective living environment. Despite Haller's aseptic tone and vocabulary, the reiteration of the term *unit* in his discourse constantly emphasizes the value of convergence and association. At every scale of the project, Haller defines the spaces for unified social groups.

The central piece of *integral urban, a global model* is thus an autonomous but connected cell—certainly an alteration of the model envisaged in the late 1920s by the German architect Erich Gloeden.[7] From this original cell, the project advances always by creating increasingly bigger units, bodies, and collectives, until arriving at the unit world. The ascension toward the scale of the world and, conversely, the descent from the scale of the world to the individual units correspond to the different moments of a global unitary organism. One moves between these different scalar units as one does when seeing an organic tissue through a microscope. The smooth transition among the different scales shows a continuous process of composition and recomposition of units into bodies of

5. Haller, *totale stadt, ein globales modell*, 10.

6. Laurent Stalder, "No Limits to Growth: The Global and Interplanetary Urban Models of Fritz Haller," *AA Files* 66 (2013): 146.

7. Erich Gloeden, *Die Inflation der Gross-städte und ihre Heilungsmöglichkeit* (Berlin: "Der Zirkel" architektur-verlag, 1923). For an analysis of Gloeden's project, see Paola Vigano, *Territories of Urbanism. The Project as Knowledge Producer* (Lausanne: EPFL, 2016), 64–76. Laurent Stalder, "Raster, Netzwerk, Register. Fritz Hallers Totale Stadt," in Stalder and Vrachliotis *Fritz Haller: Architekt und Forscher*, 198–199.

different complexity **[figs. 0 and 3]**. Haller's world is made of repetition and differences. It seeks the ceaseless variation of a singular logic that is inflected by external factors—it can be adapted to geographical conditions and modified by the multitude of internal requirements of the cells.

What this system of scalar transitions rejects, in any case, are gaps, obstacles, and breaks. Enabling smooth passage from one unit to the next effectively renders the world scale as the accessible environment of the citizens of *integral urban, a global model.* By treating the general model, second order units as transportation hubs, by designing the overall schema guided by transportation considerations, and by considering how novel modes of automated transport can be integrated in the system, Haller details the movements within and among units down to minutes. Within the fourth order unit for 120,000,000 people, for example, the average time to get from the most peripheral dwelling to places of work and command in the center of the city is just 46 minutes. The arrival to any of the four airports that surround the complex and connect this local unit to the broader world system takes fewer than 34 minutes.[8]

In unit five, the last stage of *integral urban, a global model*, almost the entire population of the earth has been relocated to eighty units of the fourth order. Outside these units, there are only historical settlements preserved for their cultural interests and tourist locations that make it easier to visit a nature that, around the world, has returned to a primeval state.[9] Despite the radically systematic character of the schema and its ambitions of global restructuring, Haller gives the project the fragile and provisional character of an experiment. Not only does *integral urban, a global model* substantially modify the original, 1968 version of the project, but Haller himself calls for ulterior versions that interdisciplinary scientific teams capable of creating "super-complex" inventions ought to produce.[10] In this sense, Haller understands that the validity of *integral urban* does not derive from its condition as a fixed project, but from being a methodological model of architectural work. He addresses the incapacity of existing metropolises to efficiently manage huge transportation flows and to create a cohesive collective sphere, and thus questions the viability of this model in a future characterized by dramatic demographic growth and increased global relations. His aim is to look for an alternative through a rigorous technical examination of the possible alliance between extremely efficient transportation systems and autonomous settlement units. The result is at once radically disruptive of existing conditions and technically feasible. The global model can be produced incrementally starting with the construction of singular cells that progressively replace the existing settlements of the world.[11]

**8.** Haller, *totale stadt, ein globales modell,* 82.

**9.** See the intervention in the Po valley in Haller, *totale stadt, ein globales modell,* 101–103.

**10.** Haller, *totale stadt, ein globales modell,* 7 and 9.

**11.** The intention is explicit in the example of Berlin in the first version of integral urban. See Haller, *totale stadt, ein globales modell,* 67–70. The same logic applies to the second version.

Haller's rigorous technical rationality aims to distance the project from the unrealistic tendencies of utopian imagination. In *integral urban*, the notion of "ideal" is present from the book cover on, while the word "utopia" is absent in a project that avoids ideological intentions. Yet, in Haller's search for an ideal global urban system, there is an attitude that is not unlike the utopian aspirations Ernst Bloch's *The Principle of Hope* had previously put forward.[12] For both authors, the future offers the possibility of a radical departure from what exists.[13] Conceived when the Club of Rome reports are becoming globally influential, *integral urban* denies the possibility of facing global demographic and environmental threads by merely relying on the conservationist notions of "protection," which the Club of Rome reports promote.[14] To the conception of the future only as an improved ordering of the present, Haller counterpoises the necessity of new forms and scales of imagination, which can carry humanity to even more distant futures: "very few speak of a new era with a new environment, of new relationships that change our existence. the landing on the moon apparently frightened people instead of inspiring them to multiply their efforts to achieve a world with new standards and possibilities."[15] This interest in imagination leads the architect to envisage the spatial solutions that can address ongoing social and environmental problems, but also those that can reflect the emergence of new scales of political organization. A future "world-planning" will emerge for Haller "primarily because communal action is becoming indispensable due to the enormous rise in the living requirements of all people, in order to satisfy the demands of each individual."[16]

Designed in a decade abundant in explorations about the world scale, *integral urban* barely responds to the work of any of Haller's contemporary peers—his main interlocutors seem to have been the German architect Konrad Wachsmann, and, only in the 1980s, Gerard K. O'Neill, the American physicist and author of *The High Frontier: Human Colonies in Space* (1977).[17] It is possible to see in the original German title of *integral urban*, *totale stadt* a recuperation of Walter Gropius's earlier vocabulary in *Scope of Total Architecture,* and of his claims to consider the whole natural and artificial environment as the realm of architectural intervention as well as to abandon the "morbid hunt for 'styles.'"[18] Haller's response to the idea of totality concentrates on challenging the scale, form, and content of the notion of settlement. ". . . by 'urban' we do not mean a confined, overcrowded settlement, but a living space, in the broadest sense, built for people. living space is the area where people live or move about and by means of which they can dispose of goods and information."[19] As a space

12. Ernst Bloch, *The Principle of Hope* (Cambridge, MA: MIT Press, 1986 [1954–1959]).

13. Fredric Jameson, "Ernst Bloch and the Future," in *Marxism and Form: Twentieth-century Dialectical Theories of Literature* (Princeton: Princeton University Press, 1974), 116–159.

14. Stalder, "No Limits to Growth," 147.

15. Haller, *totale stadt, ein globales modell*, 7–8.

16. Haller, *totale stadt, ein globales modell*, 60.

17. Röller, "Architekturen der Bodenlosigkeit," 169.

18. Walter Gropius, *Scope of Total Architecture* (New York: Collier Books, 1962), 143–153.

19. Haller, *totale stadt, ein globales modell*, 9.

of flows, the urban lacks specific dimensions; or better, such dimensions are ultimately functions of relations: "the foreign minister of a great nation lives in the city 'earth' and the small child in the city 'dwelling.' in between there is whole chain of personal city sizes. therefore, the discussion about the optimal size of a city is pointless. there are no definite sizes anymore because the city is of a different dimension for everybody."[20] What matters then, and what *integral urban, a global model* ensures, is the smoothness, almost the abolishment, of the scalar transitions.

**20.** Haller, *totale stadt, ein globales modell*, 9.

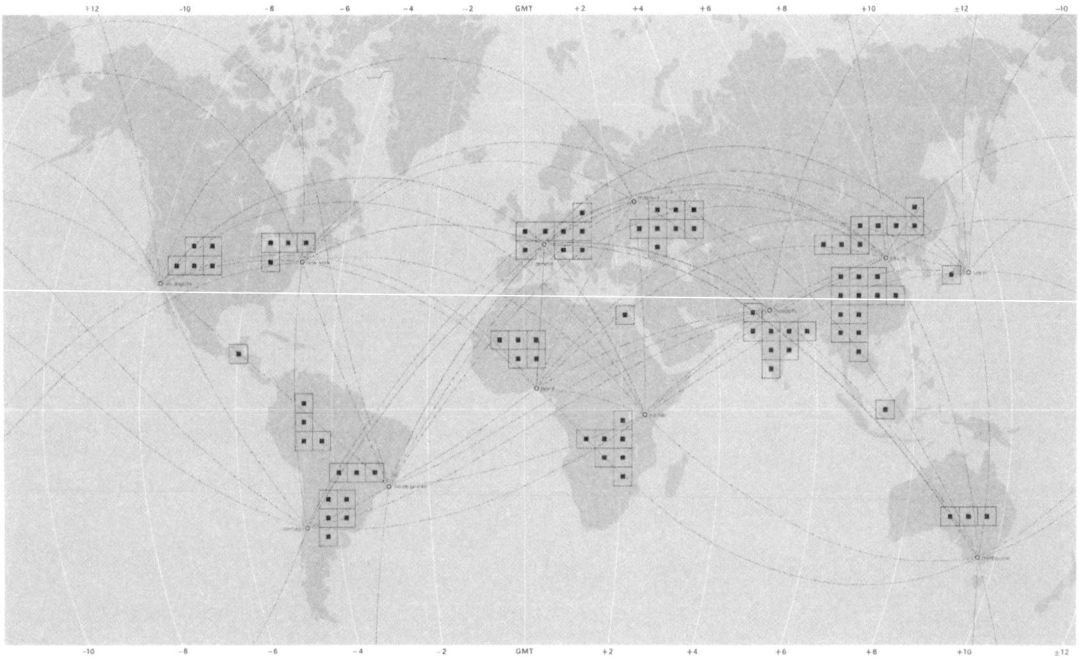


**Figure 1.** Fifth Order Unit. 1975.

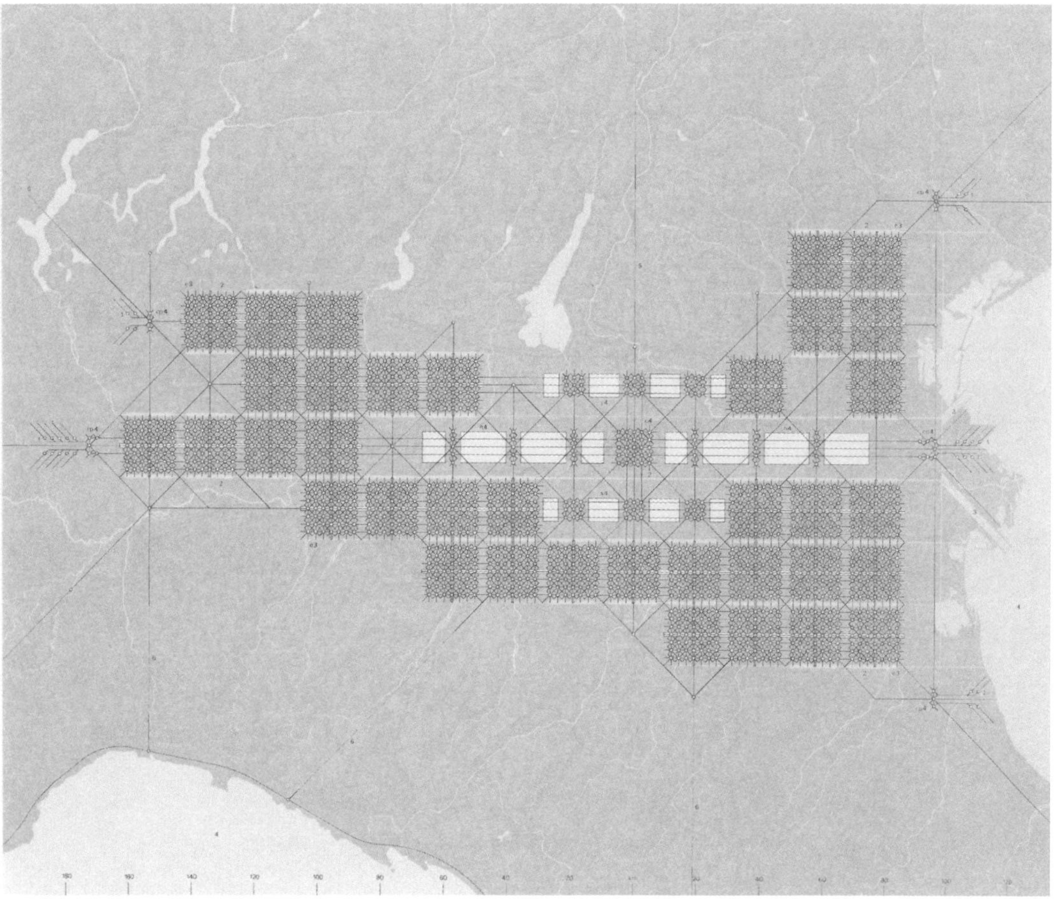

**Figure 2.** Fourth Order Unit . Po Valley, Italy. 1975.

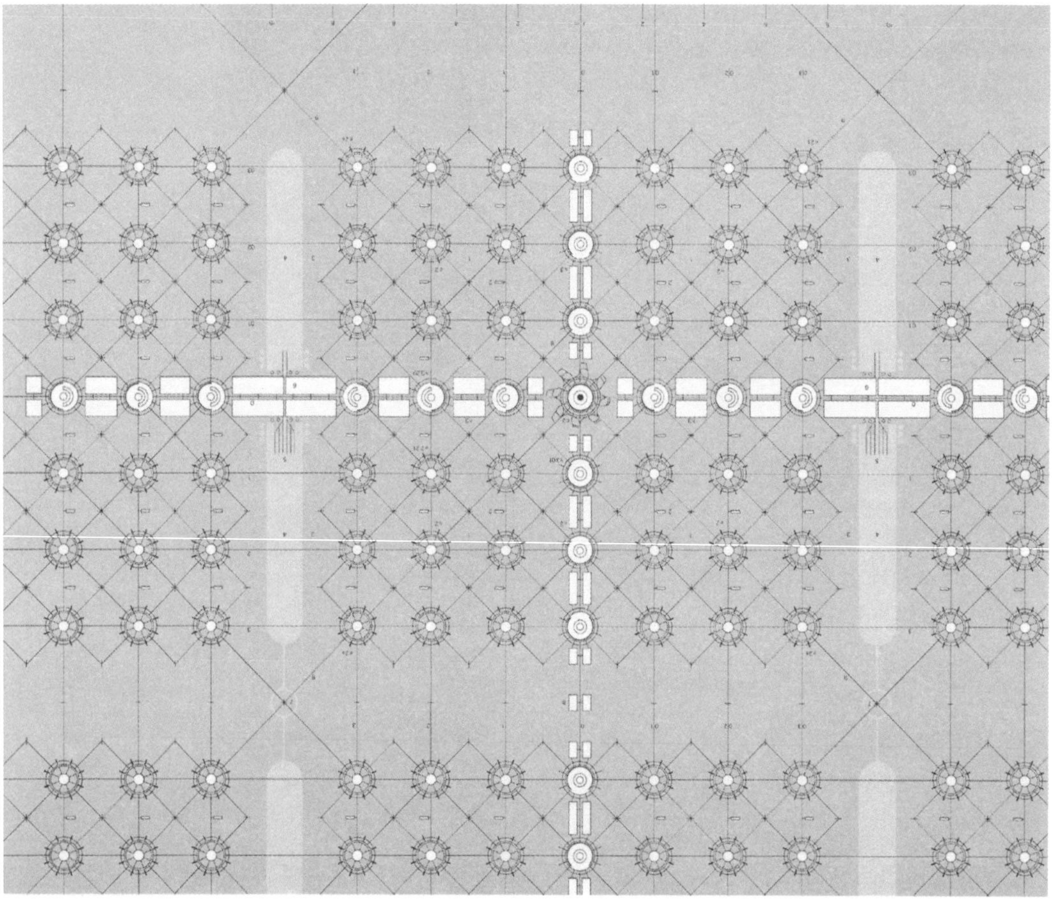

**Figure 3.** Third Order Unit. Fragment. 1975.

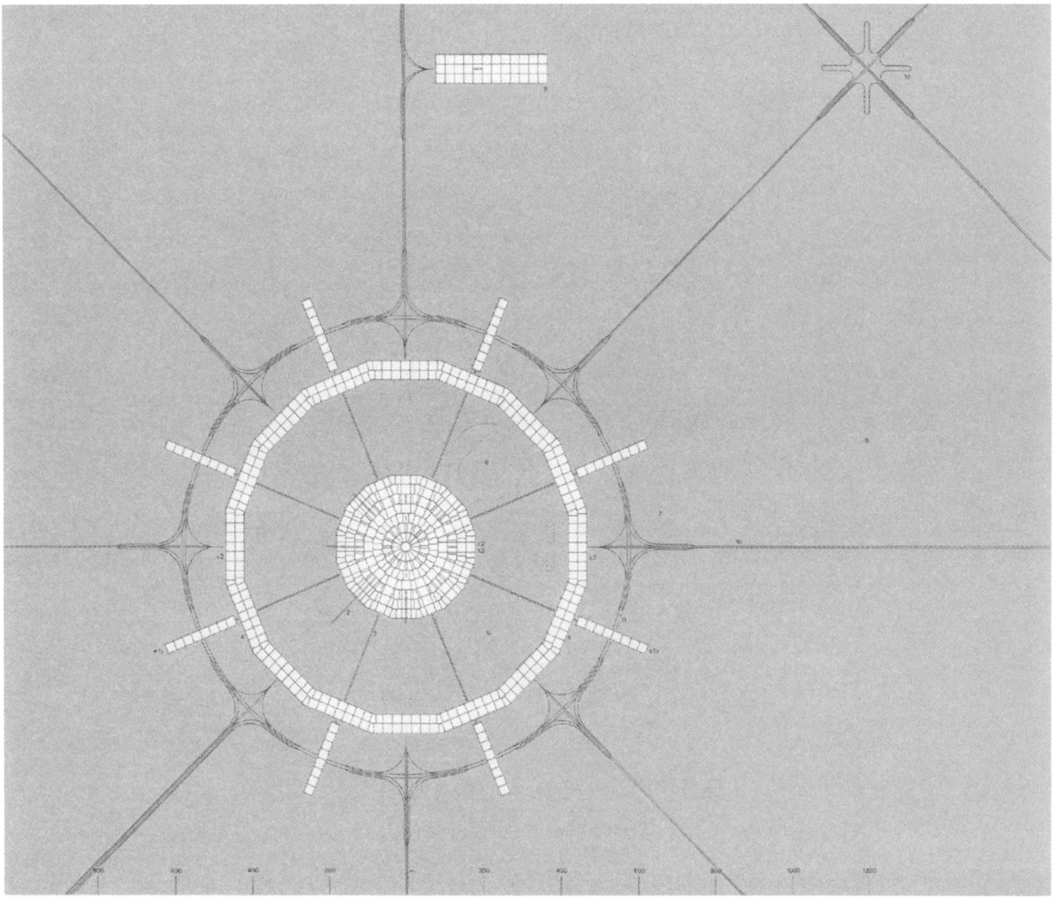

Figure 4. Second Order Unit. 1975.

# Arcology

**Project:** 35. **Author:** Paolo Soleri (1919–2013) **Date:** 1969–2013. **Themes:** Autonomy. Ecology. Human-Earth System. Monumentality.

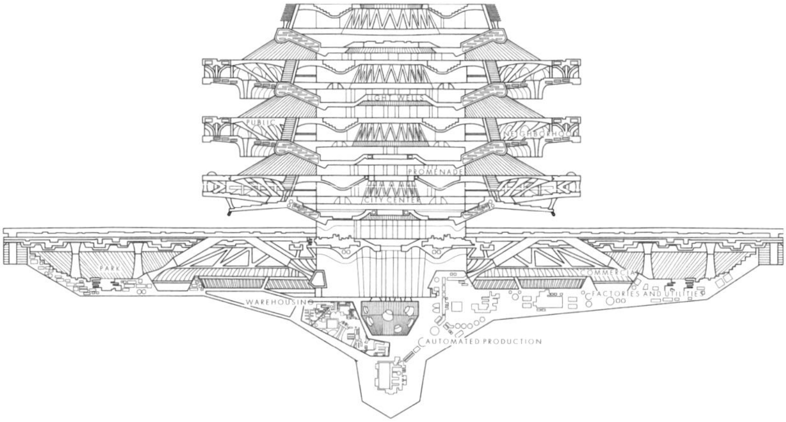


**Figure 0.** Babel IIB, a city for 550,000 people. Section. After Paolo Soleri. 1969.

Arcology, a neologism contracting "architecture" and "ecology," is both the concept through which Paolo Soleri expresses his ideals on the relationship between human-made and natural ecosystems, as well as the architectural and urban forms necessary to bring this relation to life. It is a worldview whose very beginnings can be found in Soleri's first contact with the Arizona desert and Frank Lloyd Wright, while he was a Taliesin Fellow in 1947. His contact with Wright helped Soleri define his architectural language, either by affinity—admiring the master's manipulation of light, forms, and materials, for example—or by opposition—such as rejecting Wright's city–territory ideas.[1] The harshness of the desert, in turn, imprinted on Soleri notions of frugality and the cosmic interconnectedness among humans, landscape, and nature.

Soleri leaves Taliesin within less than two years to start building a community based on his ecological thinking. In 1956, after concluding a couple of architectural projects, he and some followers begin the construction of Cosanti on a 5-acre plot in Paradise Valley, on the outskirts of Phoenix. Initially conceived as an openly experimental research center for binding nature and architecture, Cosanti later becomes a nonprofit foundation to extend Soleri's ecological vision. Preceding Arcology, but in similar fashion, the name Cosanti is a combination of two words: *cosa* ("thing" in Italian), and *anti*, celebrating the antimaterialistic attitude that guides the philosophy of the group.[2]

In 1969, the year that marks the publication of Arcology, Soleri takes a big step to "urbanize the (Cosanti) foundation" and to broaden its scope by preparing the construction of Arcosanti. Conceived as a prototype of Arcology and envisioned to house 5,000 people, construction on Arcosanti starts a year later in the middle of the Arizona desert.[3] It is organized as an urban laboratory, a real-time building site for empirical workshops, where students will test new types of habitats. Knowledge will be generated through "doing" and, as such, it will be unashamedly connected to failure. Everything will be a living process without the pretense of finality. Therefore, according to Soleri, it is the antithesis of utopia.[4]

The most comprehensive view of Arcology becomes available to the broader public with two tandem events. First, in 1969, MIT Press publishes *Arcology: The City in the Image of Man*. Then, in 1970, the Corcoran Gallery of Art in Washington, DC, opens Soleri's landmark exhibit *The Architectural Vision of Paolo Soleri*, which by the end of the following year had traveled to the Whit-

**1.** Antonietta Iolanda Lima, *Soleri: Architecture as Human Ecology* (New York: Monacelli Press, 2003), 22.

**2.** Lima, *Soleri: Architecture as Human Ecology*, 160.

**3.** Lima, *Soleri: Architecture as Human Ecology*, 231.

**4.** Paolo Soleri, *Arcosanti: An Urban Laboratory?* (San Diego, CA: Avant Books, 1984), 59.

ney Museum, the Chicago Museum of Contemporary Art, the Berkeley Art Museum, the Canadian Government Conference Center, and the Phoenix Art Museum. Those two events put that "little known architect from Arizona," as some articles characterized Soleri, onto the world stage.[5]

*Arcology: The City in the Image of Man* is a large, 223-page book depicting thirty models of Arcologies, which housed communities ranging from 1,500 to 6,000,000 people **[figs. 0 and 5]**. Opening with a critique of Constantinos Doxiadis's Ecumenopolis notion of total urbanization, the book presents the philosophical and technical aspects of Arcologies through meticulously crafted elevations, sections, and plans, complemented by diagrams and numbers to ground the visions in reality **[fig. 1; and project 23]**. Despite the publication's heft, the amount of content and the enormous architectural–urban configurations it provides, the epigraph reads "this book is about miniaturization" **[fig. 2]**.[6] Similarly grand, the exhibit showcases drawings as large as 1 × 48 meters and models that occupy entire double-height rooms in a display setting as large as ten big galleries.[7]

Arcology is a response to the bidimensional organization of cities, which for Soleri is not suitable for society's complexity to flourish. Instead, humans should shape their living environments according to their own condition of three-dimensional, compact organisms.[8] In Arcology cities fold inward to create highly condensed urban structures where all systems—from the circulation of people and resources to the way waste and water are managed and energy is harvested from the sun—are integrated and optimized. The pieces are anthropomorphically conceived: people are equated to cells, transportation networks to veins and arteries, food supply and waste removal to internal delivery and retrieval systems, and the artificial environment to a living body.[9] The urban phenomenon and the architectural object collapse, and cities appear as individual buildings of humongous scale, reaching as high as 400 stories. Countering sprawl, Arcology thus suggests a world made of diverse, hyperconcentrated typologies of buildings-cities, each of them particularized to respond to singular geographic conditions. There are Arcologies for rivers and seas, for valleys and farmlands, for canyons and deserts. Each is exhaustively, meticulously depicted. Formally and programmatically.

Based on Soleri's anthropomorphic thinking and on Arcology's formal language, which is very much indebted to the works of Antoni Gaudí, Bruno Taut, Erich Mendelsohn, and Wright, this work is often labeled "organic."[10] Soleri

5. "Exhibition History–Corcoran," *Arcosanti*. Accessed online July 8, 2016: https://arcosanti.org/arconews-blog-15160/.

6. Lissa McCullough, *Conversations with Paolo Soleri* (New York: Princeton Architectural Press, 2012), 11.

7. Dana White, "The Apocalyptic Vision of Paolo Soleri," *Technology and Culture* 12, no. 1 (1971): 75–76.

8. Paolo Soleri quoted in Lima, *Soleri: Architecture as Human Ecology*, 211.

9. Paolo Soleri, "The Concept of Arcology," in McCullough, *Conversations with Paolo Soleri*, 46.

10. White, "The Apocalyptic Vision of Paolo Soleri," 78; and Paolo Soleri, *The Bridge Between Matter & Spirit Is Matter Becoming Spirit; the Arcology of Paolo Soleri* (Garden City, NY: Anchor Books, 1973), 46. In addition to these influences, Soleri's work also follows functionalist procedures, especially when functions are streamlined along the building, such as with "living" placed upwards and "automated services and production" on the lower or underground levels of Arcology.

11. Paolo Soleri, "The City as Hyperorganism," in McCullough, *Conversations with Paolo Soleri*, 37.

12. Soleri, "The City as Hyperorganism," 37.

13. Paolo Soleri, "Responsibility of the Architectural Profession," in McCullough, *Conversations with Paolo Soleri*, 33.

14. Soleri, "The Concept of Arcology," 45.

15. White, "The Apocalyptic Vision of Paolo Soleri," 79.

16. Soleri, *Arcosanti*, 14.

finds this appreciation misleading. He believes architecture is nonorganic by nature as is any human creation. If any instance is to result from the discrimination of the mind and, therefore, be intellectualized, it can never be organic.[11]

Architecture and the city, belonging to what he called "homosphere," should be formally and aesthetically conceived to offset society's damage to the real organic world, the biosphere.[12] Soleri believes that materialism and gigantism cause such impact, with suburbanization being their most acute physical outcome **[figs. 3 and 4]**. Suburbanism for him is a metastasis of the city, "a pathology of performance" pursued on a planetary scale, deprecating aquifers, fertile land, forests, etc.[13] It is a model of development that impedes the scale of relations necessary for human life. Urban sprawl follows the logic of explosion, and the way to counteract this gigantism is through its reverse: implosion.[14] The concentration from a dispersed state into a single mass becomes Arcology's core goal and the tool to fight the threats of the unlimited consumption of the world that Doxiadis's Ecumenopolis epitomizes.[15] "Miniaturize or die" becomes the project's response for society's growth dilemma.

Soleri develops his ideas of miniaturization and compactness through the concepts of "urban effect" and MCD. The MCD—Miniaturization, Complexity and Duration—describes the natural processes of evolution any cell and organism undergo, from the scale of a molecule to the scale of the universe. Over an extended temporal stretch (duration) particles necessarily cluster to form extremely complex and advanced life forms (complexity), which can only exist in a regime of economy of mass, energy, and space (miniaturization).[16] The idea of "urban effect" reflects just such process of intensification and efficient aggregation. Here, the term "urban" precedes any social construct, as it is displaced toward the biological realm and is independent of human actions. What is usually understood as the urban environment, then, becomes the imperfect artificial mirror of a natural evolutionary state, which leads Soleri to argue for the necessity of developing extremely concentrated cities in accordance with the natural MCD principle. Soleri's argument is ecological. And yet it leads to designing interiorized worlds. Even if the different Arcologies get shaped in response to their specific contexts, their highly defined interiors resonate with the controlled environments that captured, in different ways, the architectural imaginary at the time **[projects 33 and 34]**.

Miniaturization, however, does not presuppose a reduction in size. What is shortened is the area where the same activity takes place. Miniatuarization is the resizing of space to allow for faster and more dynamic exchanges.[17] Compressing space dramatically increases the bonding of all the units in the system, leading to what Soleri defines as "religion." The architect rejects the usual meaning associated with this word and argues for an understanding of the term more closely related to its etymological root, *religare*: to bond, to pull together.[18] This return to root-meaning allows a more precise explanation of the self-organization process innate to all organisms and, by extension, human awareness of it. Awareness is the path to transcending the mundane, ultimately differentiating humans' creations from those of other beings. "The termite hill is a non-self-aware hyperorganism. The city is, or could be, a self-aware hyperorganism."[19]

The elimination of the theological connotations of *religare* marks for Soleri the path toward moral–aesthetic fulfillment, a goal which he thinks should be pursued at the scale of civilization.[20] In this sense, the aesthetic value of architecture and its capacity for bonding ecology and individuals into a new form of collective body become a way to build a "planetary ethics," which turns the "idiosyncratic into the universal."[21] Soleri argues for the capacity of architecture to weave a thread tying biology, nature, cosmos, and humanity. The discipline then assumes its responsibility of co-creating reality.[22] Anything less than that situates architecture as an isolated, atomistic phenomenon, disfiguring its planetary and cosmic potential, and ultimately contributing to destroying our species.

These formulations set the basis for Soleri's understanding of architecture in temporally long terms. He considers his work as just an individual and partial contribution to the imagination of a mode of living that would fully blossom in the future. Arcology was never meant to be achieved in Soleri's lifetime. It is the vision of a process where architecture takes on increasingly large scales. His exploration starts in the sphere of the individual habitat, and soon becomes a vision for entire cities and for their interconnection across the globe. Ultimately, the idea of Arcology takes off, reaching for outer space. Soleri foresees the need to think about an architecture serving continental migrations that are displacing millions of people for political, environmental, or racial reasons as well as considering universal, planetary migrations.[23] Coinciding with the imagery of space conquest—as seen in Stanley Kubrick's *2001: A Space Odyssey* (1968), the Cold War's space race (1957–1975), or the moon landing in 1969—Soleri's

**17.** Paolo Soleri, "A Conversation with Paolo Soleri," in McCullough, *Conversations with Paolo Soleri*, 68.

**18.** Paolo Soleri, "The Urban Effect," in McCullough, *Conversations with Paolo Soleri*, 42.

**19.** Soleri, "The City as Hyperorganism," 39.

**20.** McCullough, *Conversations with Paolo Soleri*, 19.

**21.** Paolo Soleri, "Esthetogenesis," in McCullough, *Conversations with Paolo Soleri*, 56.

**22.** Soleri, "A Conversation with Paolo Soleri," 74.

**23.** Soleri, *Arcosanti*, 26.

publication in 1969 includes the vision of "Astronomo" **[fig. 6]**, a seventy-thousand-people Arcology in space, on a revolving ring around an infrastructural cylinder, which is further elaborated throughout the next twenty years in different versions (Space for Peace, 1988; Ovum, 1985; Euclidean, 1987; The Bite, 1987; Ovum 2, 1985; Urbis et orbis, 1985–1986).

Soleri's vision of the way society is part of and should interact with its natural environment was steadily coherent throughout his whole life. His notions of "urban effect," MCD, religion, or moral-aesthetics are only a part of a series of concepts he used to describe an ecological form of life. Many of his followers continue his project, allowing Arcosanti, and its sister entity, the Cosanti Foundation, to continue to operate today, although not without controversy.[24] The community is, for Soleri, in any case, just the germ of a new form of collective living in the world, the first step toward the reconciling of humans and their environment, which, in his view, had to determine any society yet to come.

**24.** Lima, *Soleri: Architecture as Human Ecology*, 249. Recently, Soleri's figure is being revised after his daughter Daniela Soleri accused the architect of sexual abuse when she was a teenager.

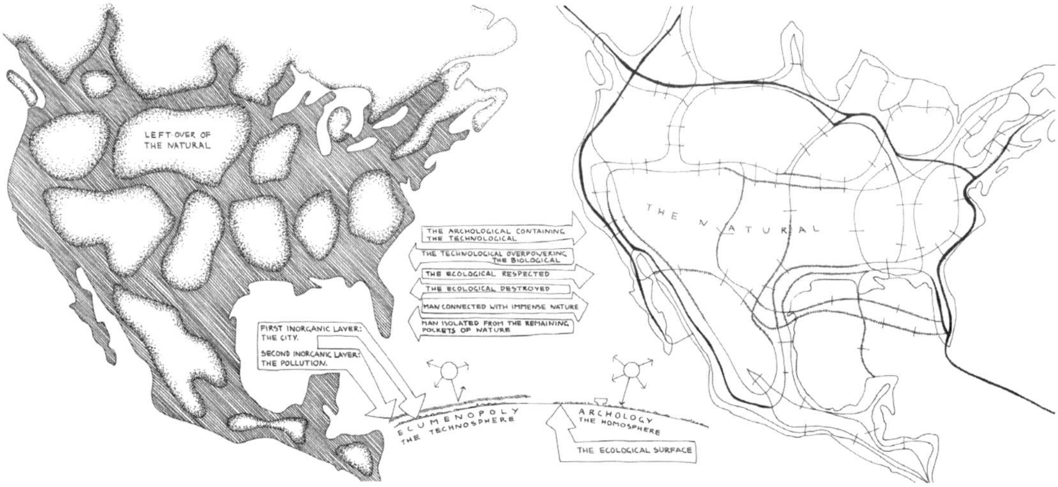


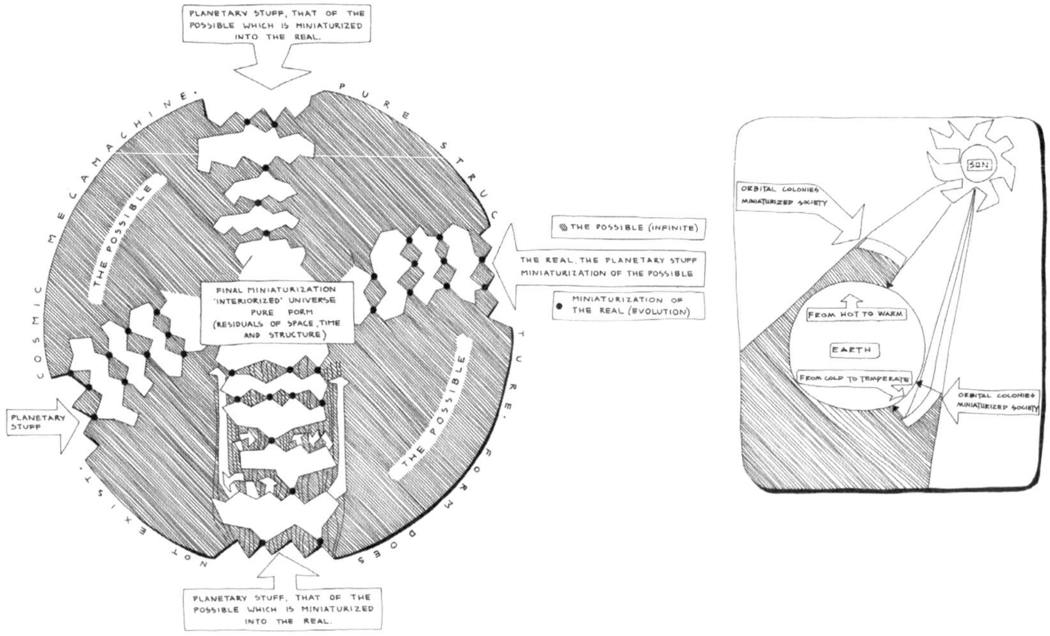


**Figure 1 (Top).** Ecumemopoly vs. Arcology. 1969.
**Figure 2 (Bottom).** Universal Miniaturization and Miniaturization of Space. 1969.

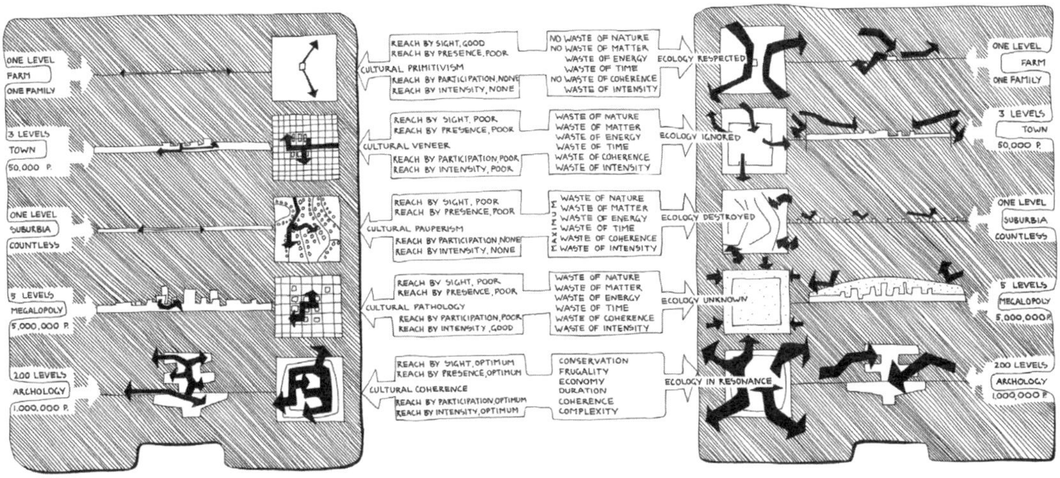


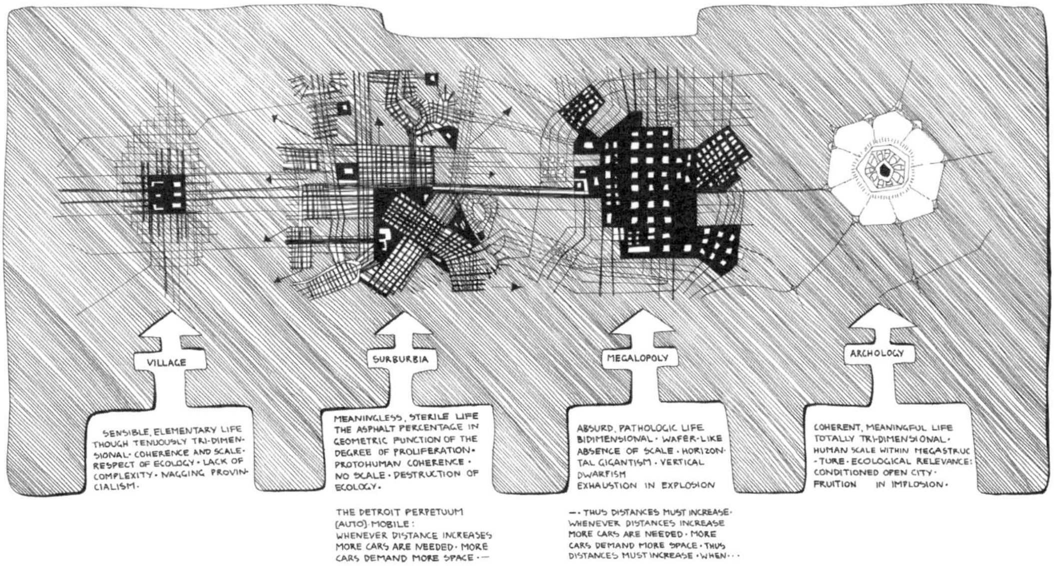


**Figure 3 (Top).** The Reach and The Waste. 1969.
**Figure 4 (Bottom).** Evolution to Arcology. 1969.

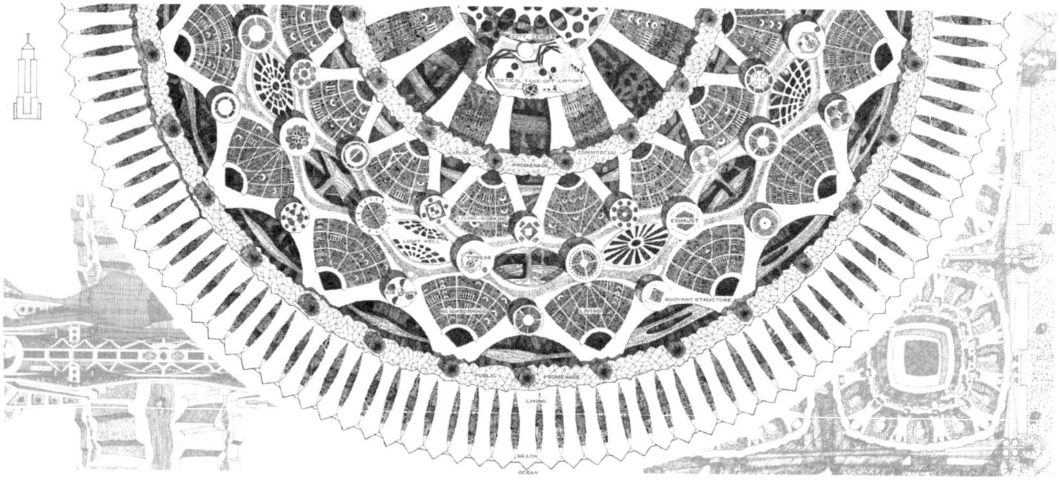


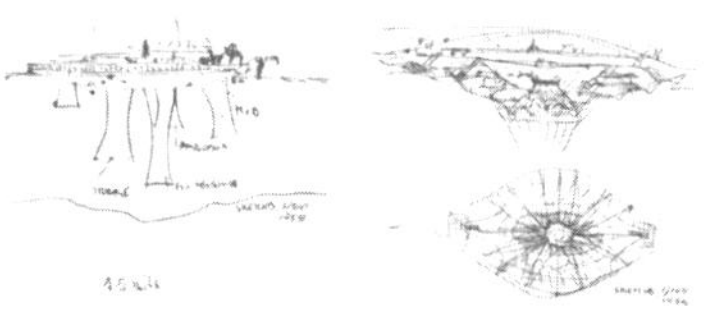

Figure 5. Novanoah I, a city for 400,000 people. Plan. 1969.

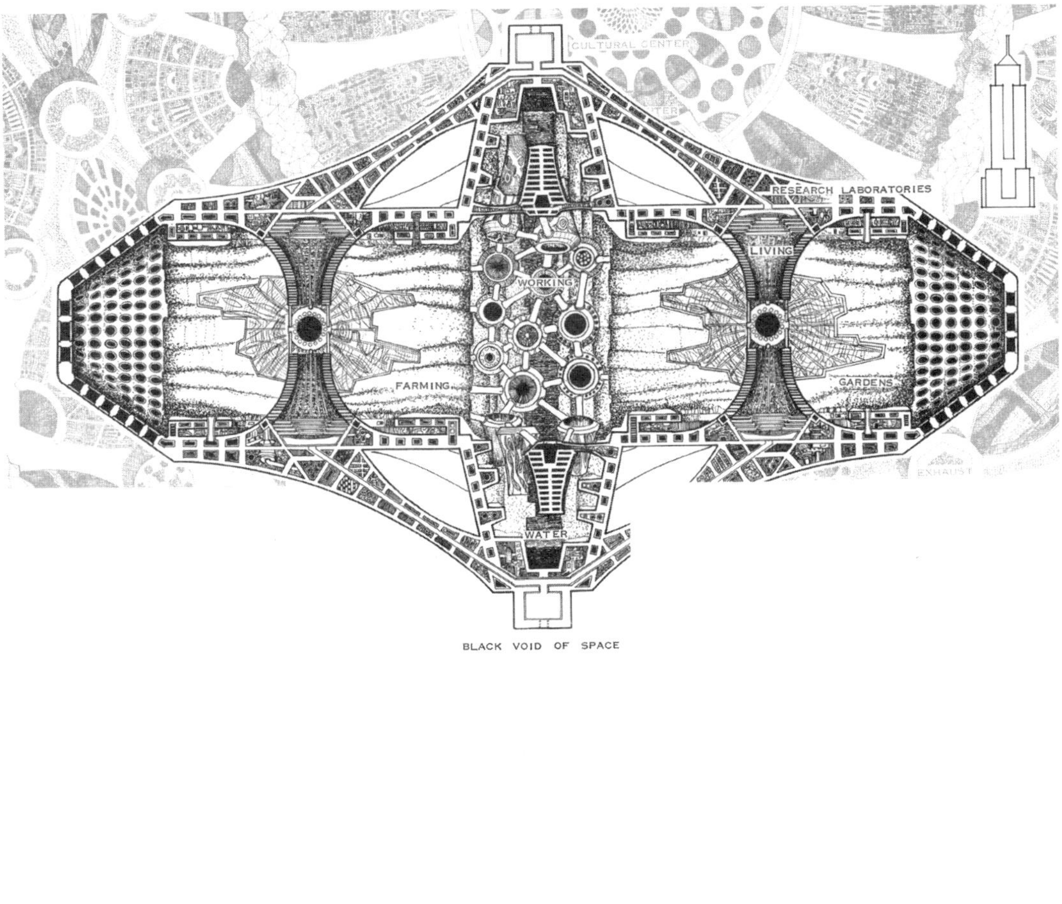


**Figure 6.** Asteromo, a city in space for 70,000 people. 1969.

# No-Stop City

**Project:** 36. **Author:** Archizoom Associates: Andrea Branzi (1938), Gilberto Corretti, Paolo Deganello, and Massimo Morozzi. **Date:** 1971. **Themes:** Abstraction. Infrastructure. Interiorization. Total Urbanization.

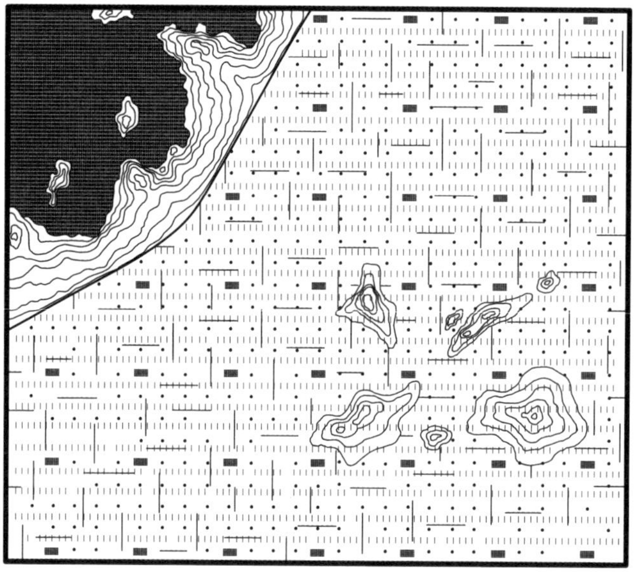

**Figure 0.** Example of a Continuous Plan for Inhabitation. After Archizoom. 1971.

The publication of Manfredo Tafuri's article "Toward a Critique of Architectural Ideology" in 1969 epitomizes the consolidation in Italy of a highly critical vision of the discipline's social and political role during the twentieth century. Tafuri reads the evolution of modern architecture in political–economic terms. In this light, the role of the discipline has been to show how "planning" can be an effective technique of control, affecting increasingly large scales of the social system. Contrary to the confidence that conventional historiography places in the progressive character of modernity, Tafuri believes that architecture is dominated by an "ideology of planning" whose ultimate effect is to support the necessities of capital.[1] In so doing, the discipline has interiorized the necessity of addressing world processes, but only with the purpose of redressing the imbalances capitalism creates, not challenging them:

"We must realize one thing: that the entire course of modern architecture and the new systems of visual communication was born, developed and brought into crisis in a grandiose attempt—the last of bourgeois culture—to resolve on the level of an ideology all the more insidious because it lies entirely within concrete activities and real production cycles, the imbalances, contradictions and delays typical of the capitalistic reorganization of the world market."[2]

The work of Italian collective Archizoom has to be read against this critical background. As the most politically committed members of the Architettura Radicale movement, a loosely organized group of architects that Tafuri severely condemns, Archizoom investigates through its projects how architecture can critically operate under post-Fordist social conditions **[project 38]**.[3] The team shares the Tafurian preoccupation with how architecture addresses productive processes and the urge to respond to their global dimension. Similarly, Archizoom assumes Tafuri's skepticism toward the capacity of architecture to actually transform the *status quo*—an incapacity that post-Fordism has nothing but reinforced.

For Archizoom's members, architecture can only become a positive social force after a change of political settings.[4] Consequently, their capacity to foster that change does not derive from the activity of building—a possibility that was also extremely difficult in the Italian economic context—but through a refor-

**1.** Manfredo Tafuri, "Toward a Critique of Architectural Ideology," in *Architecture Theory Since 1968*, ed. K. Michael Hays (Cambridge, MA: MIT Press, 1998 [1969]), 20 and 29.

**2.** Tafuri, "Toward a Critique of Architecture Ideology," 32.

**3.** The term "Architettura Radicale" is credited to have been coined *post festum* by art historian Germano Celant. The coinage referred, with Archizoom, to the collectives Superstudio, U.F.O., Zziggurat, and 9999, and individuals Gianni Pettena and Remo Buti, in Florence; Ugo La Pietra, Alessandro Mendini, Gaetano Pesce, Franco Raggi, and Ettore Sottsass, in Milan; Riccardo Dalisi, in Naples; and the groups Libidarch and Strum, in Turin. See Marie Theres Stauffer, "Utopian Reflections, Reflected Utopias: Urban Designs by Archizoom and Superstudio," *AA Files* 47 (2002): 25. Archizoom begins its activities in a shared exhibition with Superstudio initially displayed in Pistoia in 1966 and later in Modena in 1967 and entitled "Superarchitettura." For Tafuri's critique of radical architecture, see Tafuri, "Toward a Critique of Architectural Ideology," 30–31. See also Pier Vittorio Aureli, "Manfredo Tafuri, Archizoom, Superstudio, and the Critique of Architectural Ideology," in *Architecture and Capitalism: 1845 to the Present*, ed. Peggy Deamer (New York: Routledge, 2014), 132–150.

**4.** Emilio Ambasz, "Email 09," *Domus* 943 (2011): 34.

mulation of architecture as critical intellectual labor.[5] Theoretically formulated as a "refusal to work," Archizoom's position leads to seeing design as a critical activity whose purpose is both to reveal and to question existing sociospatial configurations by using media as diverse as texts, paper-projects, art-pieces, or exhibitions.[6] No-Stop City, a paper project first presented in the journal *Domus* in 1971, represents the most accomplished example of this position **[fig. 1]**.

Archizoom's project—a vision of a city of unlimited growth—questions the status of architecture and urbanism as well as the conditions of subjectivity under post-Fordism. Principally, Archizoom detects the overcoming of the city as the spatial and cultural expression of capital accumulation and its transformation into "the most backward and confused sector of Capital."[7] The emergence of new, "electronic" forms of production and consumption turned the city into a weak, obsolete, element for channeling information.[8] In order to adapt life to this transformation, Archizoom believes that it is necessary to definitely abandon the existing concept of city and to recognize that "the metropolis ceases to be a 'place,' to become a 'condition.'"[9] No longer a concentrated, physical settlement, the metropolis is now a potentially worldwide phenomenon. "The future dimension of the metropolis coincides with that of the market itself."[10] That is, with the world.

No-Stop City thus literally equates the scale of the city to that of the world market. In it, the city and the system entirely coincide.[11] This effect of planetary totality is paradoxically achieved through quite minimal visual means. The representations of No-Stop City amount to some photomontages showing the project in different geographic locations; to a small number of detailed plans and vistas of the urban interior **[figs. 2 and 3]**; and, above all, to a multitude of small vignettes showing in plan fragments of the system **[figs. 0 and 4]**. The latter produce an uncanny effect of unlimited expansion. In them, we see mere sections of the city, urban patterns seemingly made of meaningless dots and lines that engulf every possible geography; parts of an infinite city whose edges always exceed the picture frame. Resembling the repetitive patterns of suburban developments, they prefigure and explain the phenomena of urban expansion and land consumption that will transform vast areas of the planet from the 1970s on.[12]

5. During that period, Italy is passing through a tough economic situation. Recovering from the war, the rapid growth fueled by international aid, the low wages, and the drastic devaluation of the Italian lira trigger a massive industrialization process and internal migration from countryside to urban agglomerations that leave two million people unemployed by the late 1950s.

6. Felicity D. Scott, "Involuntary Prisoners of Architecture," *October* 106 (2003): 84.

7. Archizoom, "No-Stop City," *Domus* 496 (March 1971): 53.

8. Archizoom, "No-Stop City," 53.

9. Archizoom, "No-Stop City," 53.

10. Archizoom, "No-Stop City," 53.

11. Archizoom, "No-Stop City," 55.

12. Alan Berger, Joek Kotkin, and Celina Balderas Guzmán, *Infinite Suburbia* (New York: Princeton Architectural Press, 2017).

13. Archizoom, "No-Stop City," 55.

14. Archizoom, "No-Stop City," 55.

15. Archizoom, "No-Stop City," 53.

16. Andrea Branzi, *The Hot House: Italian New Wave Design* (London: Thames and Hudson, 1984), 55.

In addition to expressing the spatial dimension of the urban, the absence of limits reflects its economic rationality and ideological content. The orientation of capitalist economy after World War II toward the hyperproduction of all imaginable types of consumer goods created the illusion of a "quantitative utopia" sustained by the presumed possibility of always producing or obtaining more.[13] The infinitude of No-Stop City is thus not only a reflection of capitalism's world operations, but also of its drive to produce in excess. The maps of No-Stop City—unending variations of the same—do not exhaust the project. They are produced through a combinatorial and isotropic logic that reveals the actual lack of meaning or special validity of any of the configurations, and suggests the existence of other iterations; of more and more similar urban forms. For Archizoom these generic urban forms represent the ideology underlying production and consumption; namely, "programming."[14] By modeling No-Stop City simultaneously as a "supermarket" and a "factory," the architects express the transition from the production-oriented "ideology of the plan" that Tafuri denounces, to the post-Fordist ideology of the program. The conditions of the latter are both an exacerbation of the spatial connotations of the notion of plan and a rejection of the structuring, regulating character it used to have. Almost all the images of No-Stop City are planar representations. They represent the flattening of geography and its absolute interiorization within the urban in order to allow the "complete penetrability and accessibility of the territory."[15] Through this operation, it is the urban which becomes now a sort of landscape—flat, isotropic, ahierarchical—at once a field and a digital circuit. The resulting plans lack any formal or cultural meaning, becoming thus open, indeterminate diagrams whose value only emerges when activated by the connections among the subjects and objects that inhabit it—in other words, by changing necessities of programming.

No-Stop City's limitless expansion reveals that the megastructural interior was a hysteric reaction to reality under late capitalism, an anachronistic residue of an irrelevant, defunct form of spatial production **[project 33]**. The world interior of capital exceeds any conceivable architectural gigantism. The project's infinitude implies the utter lack of an outside, the absolute incorporation of every possible externality into the urban.[16] As the only existing residential space for humanity, No-Stop City indistinctly incorporates all the necessities of consumption society. The images of its artificially-lit interior bring together consumer goods and debris, the spaces of leisure and those of work, the mechanical instruments of circulation, and the domestic sphere **[figs. 5]**. The ultimate expression of this lack of an outside is the absolute self-identity of the proposal across every scale. The same organizational logics presides over every aspect of the project. The distribution of objects in the interior—"a bath every 100 meters, or a computer every 40 . . ."—coincides with the purely quantitative organization of the territorial scale.[17] The continuous, frictionless, self-perpetuating condition of the system goes from the domestic to the globe.

Seen as an architectural expression of the logics supporting the social reproduction of the system, No-Stop City seems a radical dystopia. Its critical value is to reveal that under the apparent capacity of capital to produce an infinite number of different commodities lies the endless repetition of the same and the consideration of human life only as the necessary, mediating agent between consumption and production. The project, though, does not only operate at this critical level. For Archizoom, only after accepting the real conditions of existence within contemporary capitalism can a different form of life emerge. No-Stop City is a critique of architecture's role in perpetuating the hegemonic, humanistic, and bourgeois vision of society and housing. Reacting against such use of the discipline, Archizoom's project has no urban design, and architecture stops being a singular, distinct element of the city. The team establishes the basis for a "non-figurative design" that reduces architecture to an equally distributed organizational device.[18] To abolish architecture's spatial singularity is, for Archizoom, the necessary step to freeing mankind from the formal and social structures architecture historically supported.[19]

Tafuri's "Critique" builds a historical narrative in which modern architecture always serves to support the system's needs. Archizoom's interest in the disappearance of architecture brings forward a different vision of modernity. Speaking about the absence of architecture, Archizoom's founder Andrea Branzi argues that "all the most vital aspects of modern culture run directly toward that void, to regenerate themselves in another dimension, to free themselves of their disciplinary chains. When I look at a canvas by Mark Rothko, I see a picture

**17.** Sander Woertman, "The Distant Winking of a Star, or The Horror of the Real," in *Exit Utopia: Architectural Provocations 1956–76*, ed. Martin Van Schaik and Otakar Máčel (Munich: Prestel Verlag, 2005), 153.

**18.** Pier Vittorio Aureli and Martino Tattara, "Stop City," *Perspecta* 43 (2010): 51.

**19.** Archizoom, "No-Stop City," 55.

dissolving into a single color. When I read Joyce's *Ulysses*, I see writing disappearing into thought. When I listen to John Cage, I hear music dissipating into noise. All that is part of me. But architecture has never confronted the theme of managing its own death while still remaining alive, as all the other twentieth-century disciplines have. This is why it has lagged behind."[20] To embrace the totalizing, planetary logics of the system is thus paradoxically to support a radical project of disciplinary critique, in which architecture first has to die in order to reclaim its place in society.

**20.** François Burkhardt and Cristina Morozzi, *Andrea Branzi* (Paris: Editions Dis-Voir, 1997), 51. Quoted in Kazys Varnelis, "Programming After Program: Archizoom's No-Stop City," *PRAXIS: Journal of Writing + Building* 8 (2006): 89.

**Figure 1.** Cover of No-Stop City. *Domus*. 1971.

**Figure 2 (Top and center).** Interior Landscape. 1971.
**Figure 3 (Bottom).** No-Stop Theatre. 1971.

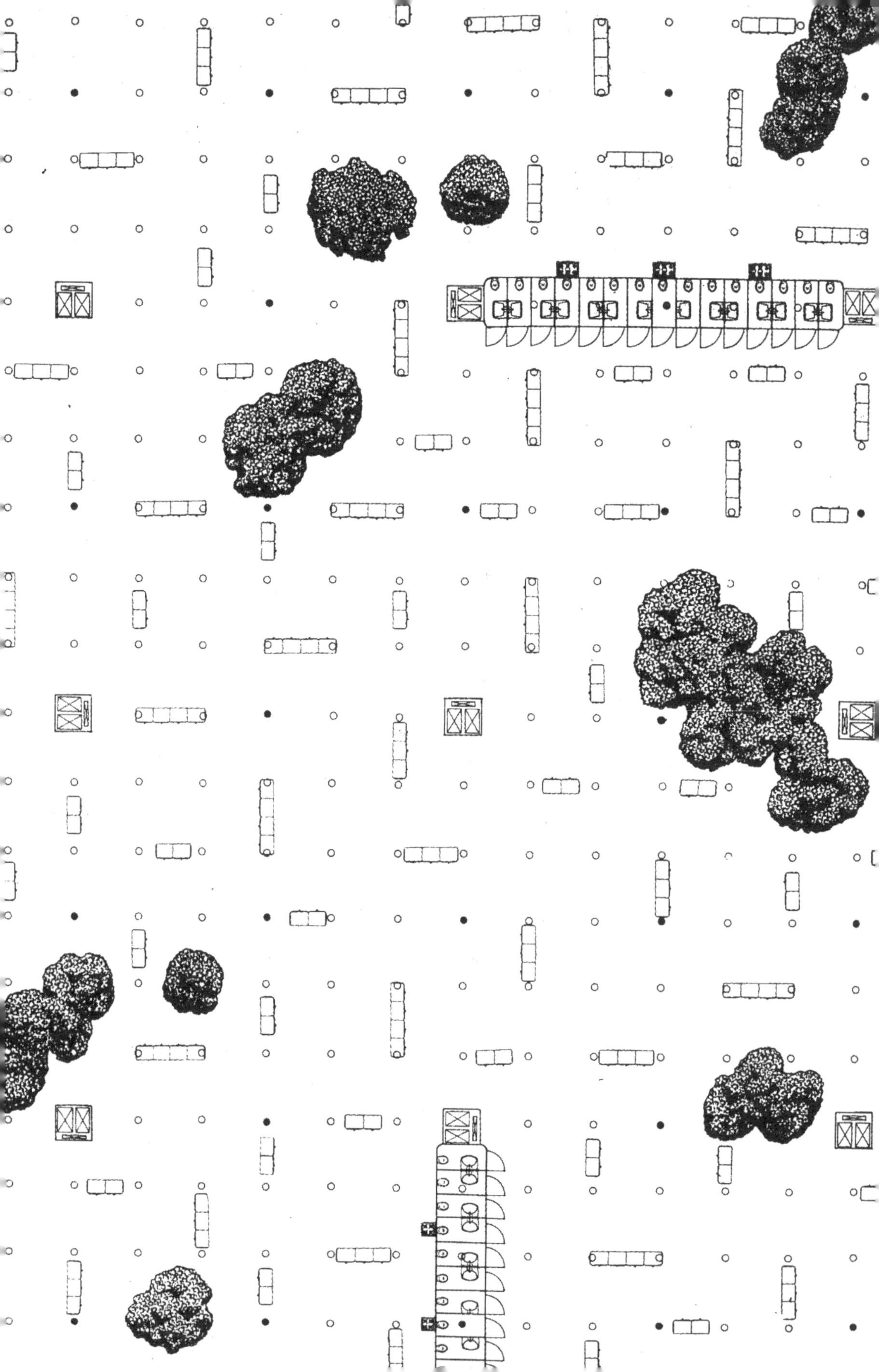

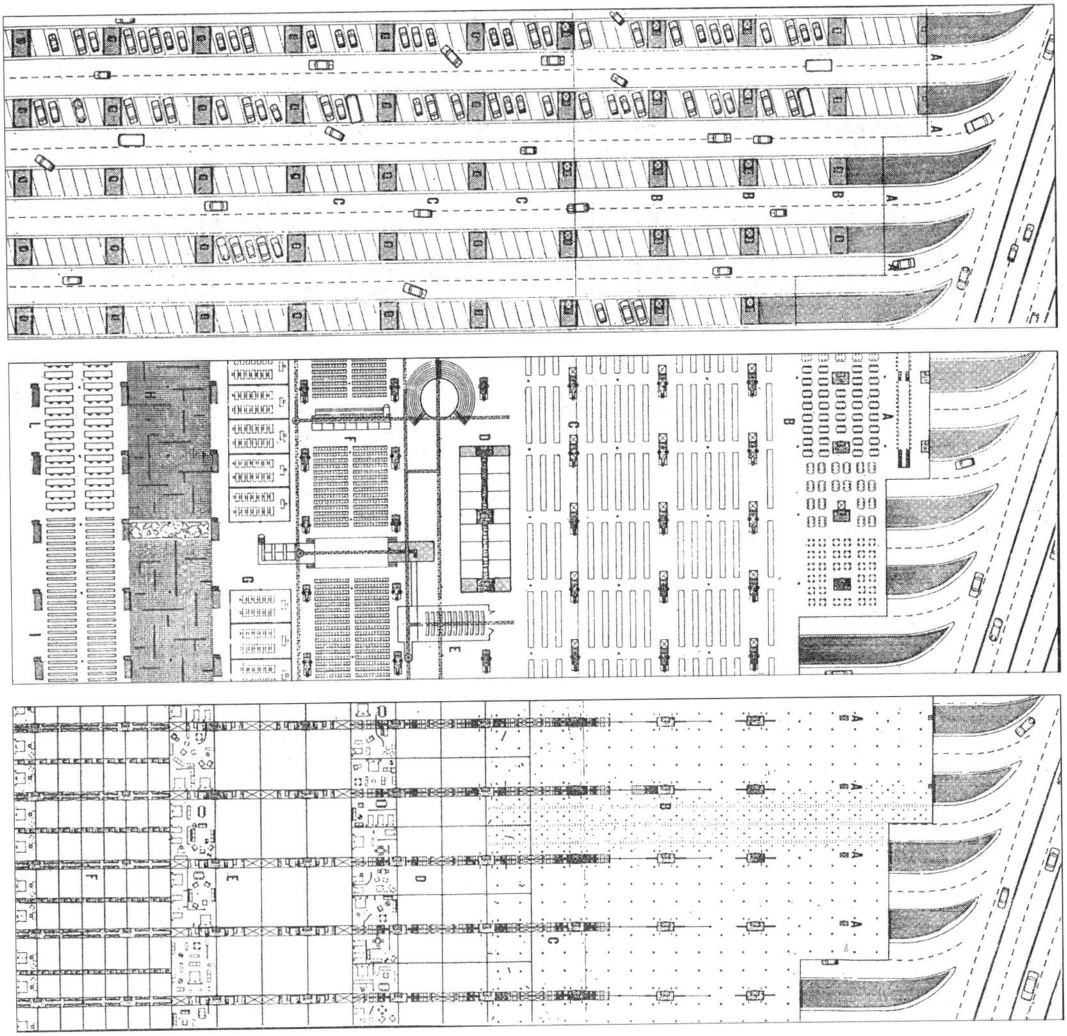

**Figure 4 (Opposite page).** Example of a Residential Wood. Fragment. 1971.
**Figure 5.** Top: Continuous Plan of Traffic Penetration. Middle: Continuous Plan of Services. Bottom: Continuous Plan of Residential Parking. 1971.

# Puertas
Gates

**Project:** 37. **Author:** Juan Navarro Baldeweg (1939). **Date:** 1971–1975. **Themes:** Cybernetics. Decentralization. Telecommunication. Typology.

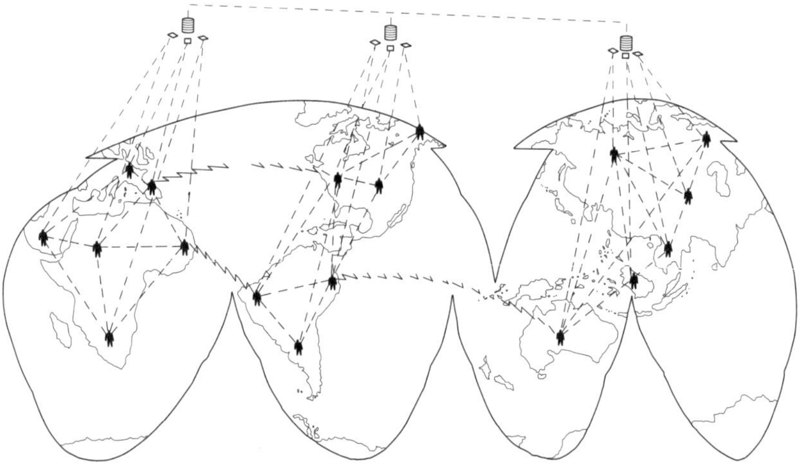

**Figure 0.** Global interactions between users of ISOFO transducers. After Juan Navarro Baldeweg. 1970.

Since the mid-1970s the goal of architect and visual artist Juan Navarro has been to express the universal constituents of the natural environment, such as light, atmospheric effects, and gravity. By dealing with intangible and variable forces that belong to the realm of energy and not to solid materiality, Navarro's work aims to overcome the fixed, static, and isolated character of matter and location. In his buildings, this ambition implies challenging the specific conditions of the site. The forms of plan and section are often disassociated from the geometries of the context, or they combine these geometries in such a way that they negate each other. The use of skylights creates different light effects, but these are zenithal and thus avoid visual links to the particular location. The selection of colors and surface materials multiplies the temporal variations light produces.[1] The interaction of these elements favors a sense of dematerialization, as if the buildings were merged with the energies that traverse them.

To describe this work, Navarro has developed a conceptual vocabulary that connects architecture to the phenomena that lie beyond it. The architect presents his buildings as "resonance chambers" or as "complementary geometries" of the universal energies that surround us.[2] Denying the notion of isolated objects, his buildings are segments or "sections" of an "infinite tapestry" of natural forces.[3] Yet, Navarro's interest in revealing those natural, universal constituents of space that grant "our participation in the world that surround us" is born of a seemingly opposite understanding of human engagement with the world.[4] His early work from 1967 to 1975 addresses the artificial and technological organization of the planet. It focuses on the global emergence of what he terms "artificial systems," and uses systems theory, cybernetics, and theories of proxemics and information to explore the role of architecture in this new context.[5]

This research employs a variety of means. In 1969, Navarro completes his PhD dissertation, titled "Sistemas urbanos: Exploraciones para la elaboración de modelos urbanos desde el punto de vista cibernético" (Urban systems: explorations to elaborate urban models from a cybernetic point of view), which is greatly influenced by his previous participation in London in the Joint Unit for Planning Research.[6] Between 1969 and 1971, he combines his teaching at the Madrid School of Architecture with design research at the Centro de Cálculo of Madrid University on the topic "Aplicaciones de la teoría de autómatas en arquitectura y urbanismo" (Uses of automatons theory on architecture and urbanism). Between 1971 and 1975, he is a Research Fellow at the MIT Center for Advanced Visual Studies (CAVS), after being invited by the center's

1. For the use of geometry see, for example, the Canal Theatre in Madrid (2000–2008) or the New Bibliotheca Hertziana (1995–2013). For the ways of manipulating light see, for example, the Salvador Allende Cultural Center (1993). For the uses of materials see the Salzburg Congress Hall (1992), the Bois Performance Centre (1991), or the Classrooms for the Pompeu Fabra University (1996–2004).

2. Juan Navarro Baldeweg, "La Geometría complementaria," in Navarro, *La Habitación Vacante*, ed. José Muñoz Millanes (Paterna, Spain: Editorial Pre-Textos, 1999), 13–21.

3. Juan Navarro Baldeweg, "Tapiz, Aire, Red," and "Un Objeto es una sección," in Navarro, *La Habitación Vacante*, 39–43 and 43–47. See also Luis Rojo de Castro, "Conversation with Juan Navarro Baldeweg," *El Croquis* 73 [II] (1995): 34–36.

4. Navarro, "La Geometría Complementaria," 37. Partial translation.

5. Among the intellectual references Navarro uses in the work of this period are the pioneer of cybernetics William Ross Ashby; the founder of systems theory Karl Ludwig von Bertalanffy; ecologist and systems theorist Howard T. Odum; anthropologist Edward T. Hall, who developed the concept of proxemics to understand the human use of space; and mathematicians Claude Elwood Shannon and Warren Weaver, authors of *The Mathematical Theory of Communication* (1948).

6. The research unit, directed by Peter Cowan, was a joint program created by the Bartlett School of Architecture and London School of Economics. See Ignacio Moreno, *Dibujos Mentales. Principios del universo creativo de Juan Navarro Baldeweg* (Madrid: Ediciones Asimétricas, 2017), 86 and 326, note 18.

director, György Kepes, to collaborate with him and Nicholas Negroponte.[7] It is at CAVS that Navarro finishes his earlier investigations. As he explains, CAVS was at the time the only academic arena in which to pursue work that crossed disciplinary boundaries, from planning theory, to architecture, to art, to research. Working in all these realms, Navarro explores how to create forms of architecture and artificial systems that can contribute to the creation of a world-system. He groups the clearest examples of this preoccupation with the world scale under the concept of "gates," and explains them in "The City as a Meaningful Environment," included in the summary of his activities at MIT.[8]

Navarro's doctoral dissertation already advances a preliminary conceptualization of the world system. Abandoning the understanding of the city as form, the dissertation uses systems theory to define the concept of urban systems as the evolving output of changing inputs, such as social processes, energy flows, or means of communication.[9] Because of the broad scalar spectrum of these processes, which can range from direct human interaction, to forms of global communication, Navarro posits that the urban is no longer a geographically bounded unit. Urban systems are a part of an ongoing process of terrestrial transformation; an element of the totality that he calls "city-world."[10]

Conceptually, Navarro concludes from this that urban planning has to be rethought as an "architecture of the earth," and that the notion of urban system has to be subsumed within the spatially open and technologically complex idea of "artificial systems."[11] The latter concept substitutes nature entirely, as he expresses in a diagram that translates all the factors that Patrick Geddes assigned to different geographic locations in the "Valley Section" to a generic urban section **[project 2]**. This diagram constitutes a preliminary synthetic image, an emblem, of the artificial system. It shows how nature has been entirely subsumed within the artificial realm, making it indispensable to find artificial equivalents to natural phenomena.[12] Yet, it still correlates this artificial realm uniquely to the built form of the city.

Navarro's next step will be to understand how artificial systems go beyond previous organizations of the built environment. The key element for this spatial transformation is information, which he believes is substituting physical infrastructures as the main organizer of artificial systems and global relations.[13] To intervene in this condition it is necessary to conceive a new disciplinary figure. One who can design the spaces and means for new forms of intersubjective communication, in order to challenge the sociospatial attributes of dominance

**7.** Covadonga Lorenzo Cueva, "La Noción de ciudad como ambiente significante. Las Primeras propuestas teóricas urbanas de Juan Navarro Baldeweg | The Notion of City as a Significant Environment. Juan Navarro Baldeweg's First Theoretical Urban Proposals," *ZARCH* 8 (2017): 170,

**8.** Juan Navarro Baldeweg, *El Medio ambiente como espacio de significación* (Cambridge, MA: Center for Advanced Visual Studies, 1975), n.p. A partial version of the memoir was published in Juan Navarro Baldeweg, "La ciudad como ambiente significante," *Nueva Forma* 94 (1973): 12–15.

**9.** Moreno, *Dibujos Mentales*, 93.

**10.** Moreno, *Dibujos Mentales*, 90.

**11.** Moreno, *Dibujos Mentales*, 98. In Thesis 6.1 of his dissertation, Navarro defines artificial systems as: "all that is intentionally shaped by humans. [Artificial systems] comprise the physical effect of the reorganization of the natural, and the modes and forms in which humans structure in productive systems their individual and social actions." Our translation.

**12.** Moreno, *Dibujos Mentales*, 119.

**13.** Juan Navarro Baldeweg, "Arquitectura Informática," *Arquitectura* 161 (1972): 16.

or subordination, of richness or scarcity that the capacity to possess, transmit, or access information is starting to define.[14] Navarro names this figure the "computational architect" and summarizes his agenda in two points: to avoid that existing spatial hierarchies constrain the emergence of new relations of communication—and thus of new ideological and political possibilities—and to impede the appropriation of the spaces of communication by private interests.[15] Both will determine Navarro's design approach to the spatial articulation of the world scale, and his attempt to produce new forms and concepts of "territoriality."[16] What interests Navarro at this point is to resituate the architect as an enabler of new forms of communication, pushing her toward the establishment of new social and scalar relations.

Sounding Mirror (1969) explores this agenda by breaking the power structures embedded in hegemonic, monodirectional information flows, such as those provided by radio or television. The project consists of a personal gadget, the ISOFO, which can emit light and transform light impressions into sound **[fig. 1]**.[17] Its manipulation by several users enables them to engage in nonverbal conversation, and to produce a shared territory. The movement of one user produces light. The reception of this light by other ISOFOs and its conversion into sound in turn motivates the movement of the other users, the emission of more light, and the consequent creation of feedback loops of communication. Navarro sees the experiment as an exploration "of the phenomena of social coordination . . . and of the ways to discover and organize goals and subgoals."[18] What is important from a global perspective is that the project is an instrument for creating global collectives: the use of Sounding Mirror can be individual, mutual, or in groups; the latter "organizing games or happenings at the global scale" **[fig. 0]**.[19] The user's actions are preserved in a sort of external memory, the "cloud," represented as an information field hovering above citizens **[fig. 2]**. The cloud expresses Navarro's understanding of the "artificial universe of information as a human environment," as it collects the results of the participants' interactions and the territorial relations they create.[20]

Sounding Mirror becomes the first of the four schemes of Gates that Navarro finalizes at CAVS. All of them propose mechanisms and spaces to produce and receive information and explore the trans-scalar collective relations that they generate. The second scheme proposes to use light textures to make visible, at the environmental scale, trivial gestures of human behavior such as greetings, handshakes, and hugs. The goal is to reveal the "social atmosphere" and to create a responsive environment for human action. More interestingly, the third

**14.** Navarro, "Arquitectura Informática," 16. In the article, the author states: "Associated to, and in correspondence with, the nature and modalities of participation in the processes of information, there will be attributes of richness, plenitude, integrity, or, on the contrary, poverty, scarcity, and partiality of life." Our translation.

**15.** Navarro, "La ciudad como ambiente significante," 12. See in particular the affirmation: "There are two different problems or needs. First, to avoid having the physical environment establish and determine the poles and links of the semiological triangle, thus serving ideological perpetuation and ossification. Second, to avoid the appropriation of spaces of communication by particular interests." Our translation.

**16.** Navarro, "Arquitectura Informática," 16.

**17.** There is a clear relation between Juan Navarro's proposal and contemporary pieces of performance art using technological media. Navarro links these approaches to a possible system of global relations, for example, with Dan Graham, *Body Press*, 1970–1972.

**18.** Navarro, "Arquitectura Informática," 19. Our translation.

**19.** Navarro, "Arquitectura Informática," 18 and 19. Our translation.

**20.** Navarro, "Arquitectura Informática," 19. Our translation. The idea of cloud is described in Navarro, "La ciudad como ambiente significante," 13. In the article, Navarro explains: "The evolution of the sound, which works as a feedback mechanism between the individuals, or between the individuals and the groups, appears in the drawing through an omnipresent cloud that acts as a global indicator for the individual decisions." Our translation.

scheme is an urban service that allows users to obtain and transmit information, to vote, and to express themselves. These actions would then be projected as symbols in the environment, adding new layers of information over the built fabric. The result of all the user's operations will generate, once again, a cloud of information. As a nonphysical entity, this cloud can be accessed from abroad, becoming then an external representation or mental image of the city. In Navarro's words: "This urban service is a perceptual mechanism: urban ecology can be made manifest and intelligible in a manner similar to the image of Patrick Geddes (as a projection of the region in the city), through the projection of the city itself, once its image has been processed by the community 'mind,' into a cybernetic reality deposited in a new physical texture."[21] If, in his doctoral dissertation he had provisionally translated Geddes's Valley Section to the built fabric of the artificial, urban system, with the third scheme he suggests that this whole system can be transferred to the informational sphere. The global system of cities then becomes a system of cybernetic representations **[fig. 3]**. What remains from the dissertation is the attempt to create the mechanisms that translate social totality into cognitive, mental emblems.

The fourth scheme (1973) takes these propositions to an actual, physical location. The proposal suggests the construction of four gates in a historical city **[fig. 4]**. The "Gate to the world" projects the relationship of the city to the external world. The "Gate to the social and cultural life" consists of an urban service of communications designed for the third schema. The "Gate to the city" translates the sound of intraurban communications by telephone into light projections. The "Gate to the earth" acts as a sun clock, channeling sun rays through optic fibers in order to show the changes of the relative position of the earth to the sun.

In all four schemas, information becomes a layer that counters and dissolves the limitations and the fixity of physical built space. Instead, information privileges inhabitants' actions and the changing spatial relations they can create. Navarro's world is, *a la* McLuhan, a conglomerate of variable social relations, rather than a specific spatial form. Consequently, he designs the tools that can contribute to the production, symbolization, and visualization of global relations, without determining a fixed world image. At CAVS, Navarro also designs projects that associate Kepes's notion of environmental art to the world scale: capsules that transport ecological systems around the world, and devices that react to light variations and create figures that can be seen when traveling by plane **[fig. 5]**.[22] Through them, he begins to address the interrelation between architecture and

**21.** Navarro, "La ciudad como ambiente significante," 14. Our translation.

**22.** See György Kepes, *Arts of the Environment* (New York: G. Braziller, Vision Value Series, 1972), 192–193. Kepes includes in the book Navarro's Buckminster Fuller-inspired proposal of ecological capsules. Navarro explains all his environmental projects under the label Fifth Schema in Juan Navarro Baldeweg, *El Medio ambiente como espacio de significación*, 17–20.

natural forces that will characterize his later designs. His stay at the CAVS is thus determinant for reorienting his work.[23] Between the initial focus on the artificial and the later attention to omnipresent energies, however, Navarro's central preoccupations remain. His holistic thinking always questions the individuality and isolation of the place. He systematically conceives of objects as part of scalar relations that exceed them. He designs buildings as frameworks to produce and perceive these relations; as cognitive models to comprehend a broader totality. Through these buildings, the goal is to question the status of the object itself and to draw our attention to the phenomena in which they are immersed, phenomena that are immaterial, trans-scalar, and global.

**23.** Moreno, *Dibujos Mentales,* 326, note 27. Moreno indicates that Navarro's interest in the global networks of communication will lead him to investigate less obvious means of globalization in the CAVS. See also: Covadonga Lorenzo Cueva, "La influencia de György Kepes en la obra temprana de Juan Navarro Baldeweg realizada en el Center for Advanced Visual Studies del MIT (1971–1975)," *Revista de Arquitectura* 19 (2017): 67–78.

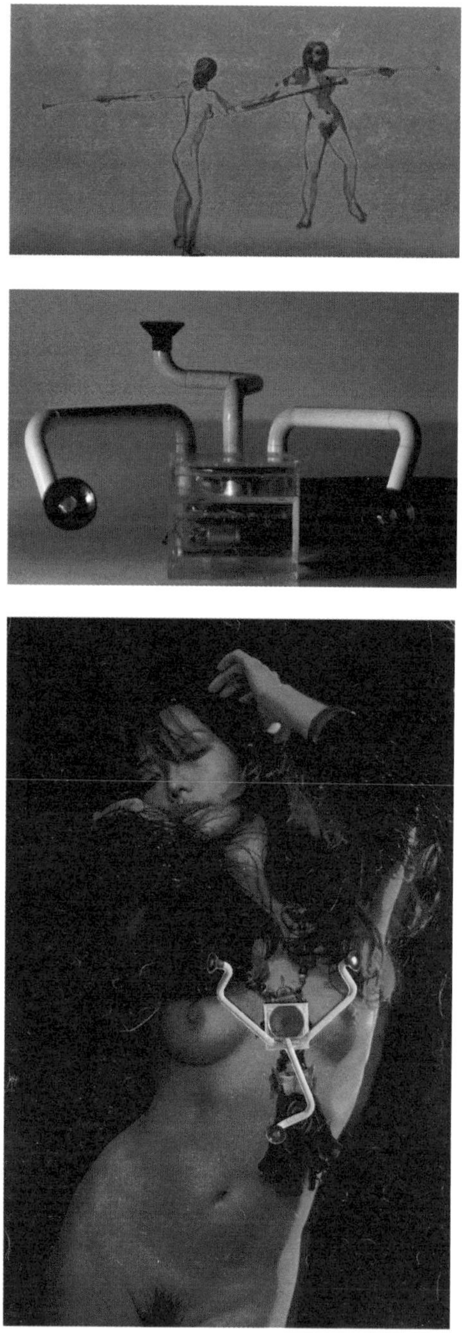

Figure 1. Sounding Mirror. 1970.

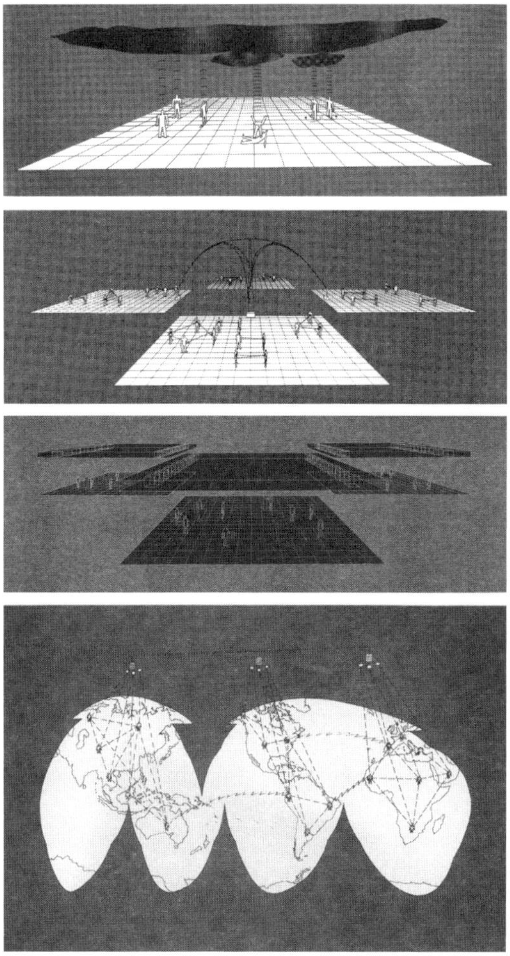

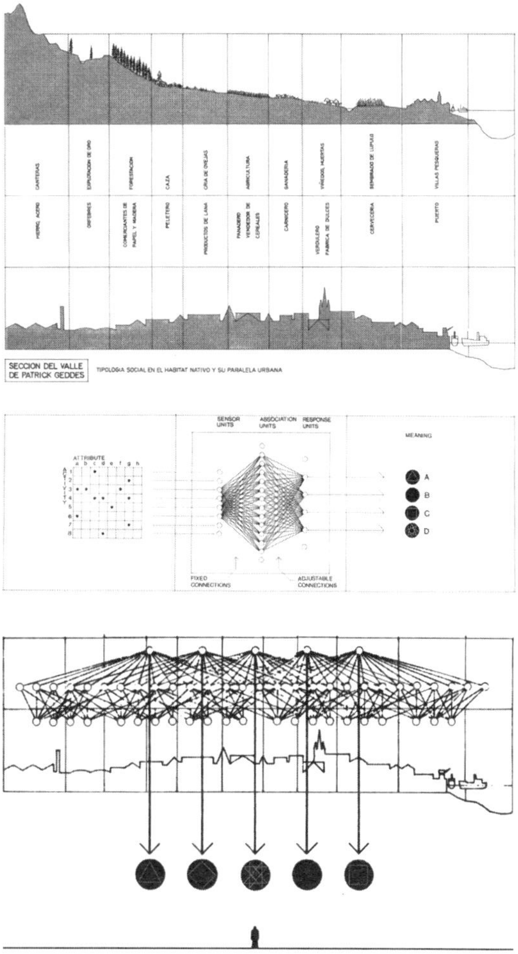


**Figure 2 (Left).** First Scheme: diagram of possible uses of transducers to establish interpersonal relationships or to establish telemetric links with other places. 1970.
**Figure 3 (Right).** Third scheme: proposal for new urban service to open channels of information between individuals and community with gates, or information inputs. 1970.

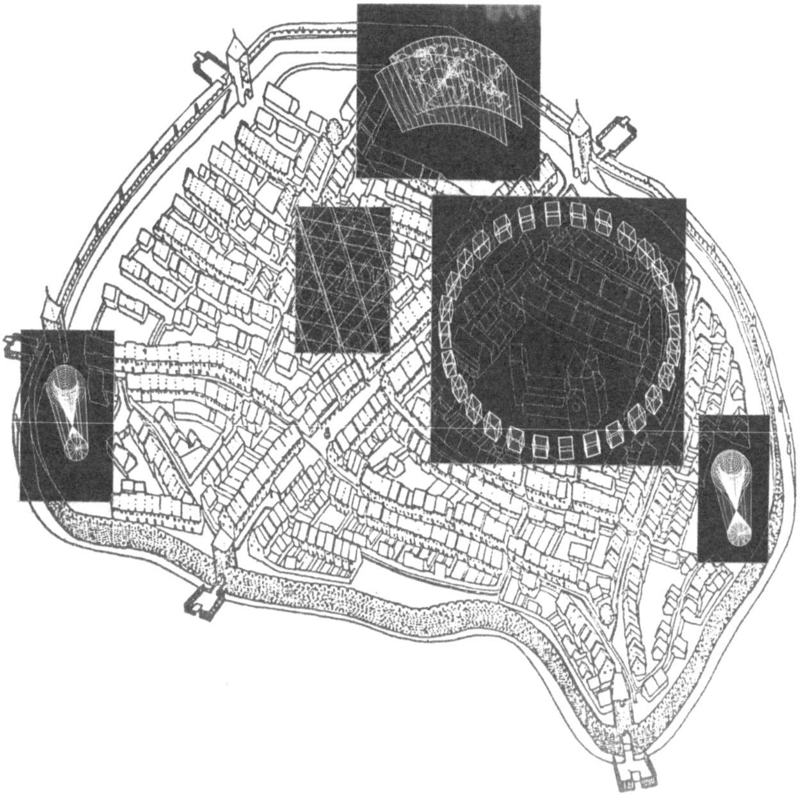

**Figure 4.** Fourth Scheme. The Gate. 1973.

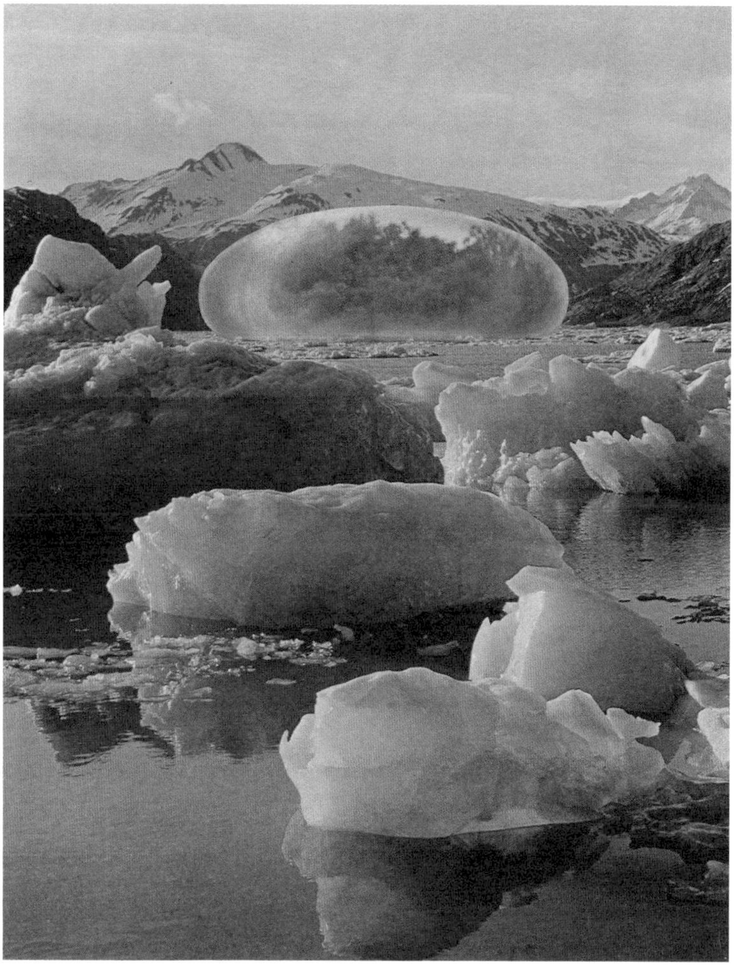

**Figure 5.** Proposal for the Increasing of Ecological Experiences. Transferring ecosystems. 1972.

# Atti Fundamentale

## Fundamental Acts

**Project:** 38. **Author:** Superstudio: Adolfo Natalini (1941), Cristiano Toraldo di Francia (1941), Roberto Magris (1935), Alessandro Poli (1941), Alessandro Magris (1941), Gian Piero Frassinelli (1939). **Date:** 1972–1973. **Themes:** Abstraction. Environmental Control. Monumentality. Telecommunications.

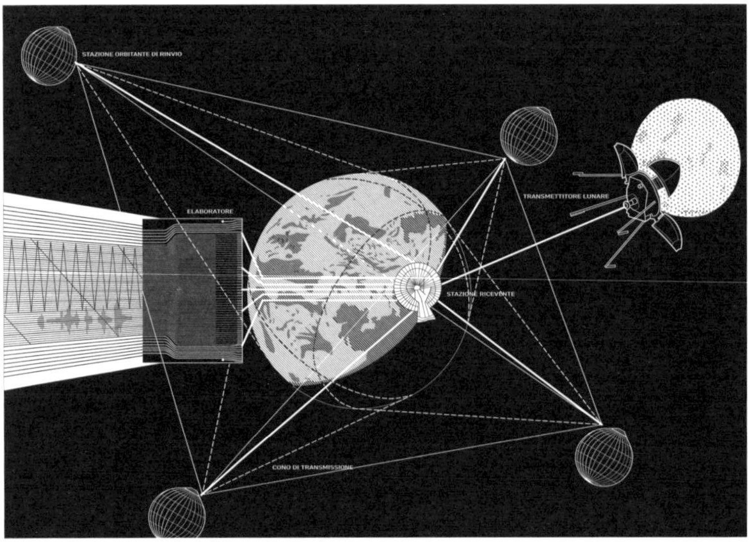


**Figure 0.** Five Fundamental Acts: Education. After Superstudio. 1972.

1. Cristiano Toraldo di Francia, "Memories of Superstudio," in *Fxit Utopia: Architectural Provocations, 1956–1976*, ed. Martin Van Schaik and Otakar Máčel (Munich: Prestel, 2005), 70.

One of the most powerful representations of Superstudio's Continuous Monument (1969) depicts a fish-eye view of the project stretching from East River to Manhattan to the extremely curved horizon. By occupying both foreground and background with the Monument, the image represents the unstoppable continuity of the project around the planet, and offers a seemingly impossible scalar reconciliation between the monument, the skyscrapers of the transformed New York City—renamed as New New York—and the globe. Cristiano Toraldo di Francia, a founding member with Adolfo Natalini of Superstudio, notes yet another of the central propositions contained in the image.[1] In Manhattan, the Continuous Monument frames and contains a fragment of the city, the downtown skyscrapers preserved within a rectangle. Toraldo di Francia argues that the tradition of modern urbanism conceived the metropolis as the way to transform an original nature, which was preserved as a vestige within the urban fabric—paradigmatically in Le Corbusier's voids and, to the case, in New York's Central Park **[project 15]**. By preserving skyscrapers as relics, the Continuous Monument emphasizes that it represents a new stage and a new scale of civilization, one for which the modern metropolis is only an archaeological remain. At this stage, the planet is the only possible scale of reference. The first sketches Superstudio does for the project—titled Viaduct of Architecture as a competition entry for the 1969 Tri-national Biennial Trigon, in Graz, Austria—depict the thesis even more dramatically. All the metropolises of the world explode. The dispersed elements of their urban fabric at first orbit above the earth and then progressively coalesce to form a single built structure around the world.

Superstudio's whole production in the period 1968–1972 constitutes a constant investigation of this postmetropolitan world scale. In the Continuous Monument, a built infrastructure circumvents the world as a new parallel. Interplanetary Architecture (1970–1971) envisages a single Earth-Moon entity, bringing the satellite closer to our planet and linking both by building a connective infrastructure. Three Projects for the Planet (1971) suggests three planetary alternatives: to contain the earth within a cube, to dig a gigantic cube in it—from the earth's crust to its core—and to create an equatorial, built ring. During the same years, Twelve Ideal Cities proposes to reconfigure the settlement structure of the planet with new urban models. They occupy rivers, deserts, prairies, the atmosphere, and the interplanetary space. Five Fundamental Acts (1972) addresses "the relationship between architecture (as the conscious formalization of the planet) and human life" **[fig. 0]**.[2] The earth for Superstudio is no longer a possible project among others, but the very scale from which to interrogate the role of architecture and the conditions of human existence.

In this exploration of the planetary scale, the Fundamental Acts constitutes a singular and conclusive moment. With the Continuous Monument, Superstudio initiates its activity by developing a critique of urbanization under capitalism.[3] Conceived of as an "Architectural Model for Total Urbanization," the project is "a form of architecture all equally emerging from a single continuous environment: the world rendered uniform by technology, culture and all the other inevitable forms of imperialism."[4] In this context, Superstudio argues in favor of a Single Design—a unique way to build around the world—which on one hand exaggerates the ongoing tendency toward urbanizing the planet, and on the other reverses its effects by recapturing the disappeared monumental, symbolic, and structuring power of architecture. In Fundamental Acts, the proposition is entirely different. The project no longer focuses on critique, but on suggestions of alternatives. Instead of exaggerating architecture, it proposes its disappearance in favor of a direct, non-three-dimensional mediation between subject and world through networks of infrastructure, environmental control, and information.

Fundamental Acts consists of five sections: Life, Education, Ceremony, Love, and Death. As most of Superstudio's production, the project is conceived for its publication in magazines, in this case for the Italian journal *Casabella*, where the project appears between 1972 and 1973. The section "Life," however, was developed earlier, in the Supersurface project, Superstudio's contribution to the 1972 exhibition *The New Domestic Environment: Achievements and Problems in Italian Design*, at New York's Museum of Modern Art **[fig. 1]**. The incorporation of their work into this institutional context is important, as it reinforces Superstudio's transition from critique to positive proposition. Argentinian architect Emilio Ambasz, MoMA's curator of design between 1968 and 1976, makes their participation in the exhibit possible.[5] Ambasz has a clear agenda, in which design is a field with vague disciplinary boundaries. It includes a range of things: object production, architecture, the creation of networks, and pure intellectual production, all of them oriented toward broader goals of environmental and territorial organization.[6] As he states in a 1970 MoMA *Interim Report*, his curatorial goal is "to explore alternative solutions to the problem of the man-made environment through environmental design projects."[7] The

**2.** Superstudio, "Fragments of a Personal Museum," quoted in Adolfo Natalini, "How Great Architecture Still Was in 1966," in Van Schaik and Máčel, *Exit Utopia*, 187; originally published in Superstudio, *Fragmente aus einem persönlichen Museum / Fragments from a personal museum / Frammenti da un museo personale* (Graz: Neue Galerie am Landesmuseum Joanneum, 1973).

**3.** Pier Vittorio Aureli, "Manfredo Tafuri, Archizoom, Superstudio, and the Critique of Architectural Ideology," in *Architecture and Capitalism: 1845 to the Present*, ed. Peggy Deamer (New York: Routledge, 2013), 140–144; and Fernando Quesada, "Superstudio 1966–73: From the World without Objects to the Universal Grid," *Footprint* 5, no. 1 (2011): 23–34.

**4.** Superstudio, "Discorsi per immagini / Speaking through Images," *Domus* 481 (December 1969): 44. English translation in Van Schaik and Máčel, *Exit Utopia*, 126.

**5.** See in this respect: Ross K. Elfline, "Superstudio and the Staging of Architecture's Disappearance" (PhD diss., University of California, Los Angeles, 2009), 179–196; Sander Woertman, "The Distant Winking of a Star, or the Horror of the Real," in Van Schaik and Máčel, *Exit Utopia*, 150–152.

**6.** Felicity D. Scott, *Architecture or Techno-utopia: Politics after Modernism* (Cambridge, MA: MIT Press, 2007), 89–117.

**7.** Emilio Ambasz, "The Museum of Modern Art and the Man-Made Environment: An Interim Report," in *Members Newsletter* (Spring 1970), quoted in Scott, *Architecture or Techno-utopia*, 91.

8. Sander Woertman, "The Distant Winking of a Star, or the Horror of the Real," 152.

9. Superstudio, "Distruzione, metamorfosi e ricostruzione degli oggetti," in *Argomenti e immagini di design* 2, no. 2–3 (March-June 1971): 14–25; quoted in Natalini, "How Great Architecture Still Was in 1966," 186.

10. On this occasion, Superstudio takes images for their photomontages from Anders Holmquist, *The Free People* (New York: Outerbridge & Dienstfrey, 1969).

11. Superstudio, "Life," *Casabella* 367 (July 1972): 194. English translation in Van Schaik and Máčel, *Exit Utopia*, 194.

12. Superstudio had developed a similar attempt to deprive education of its physical dimension in their competition entry for the University of Florence.

tone of Ambasz's report and its confidence in advancing alternative scenarios of environmental organization through technical solutions are entirely assumed in Superstudio's MoMA project; as is his request to not design objects, but environments.[8]

In fact, in 1971, Superstudio had already contributed to the Italian avant-garde journal *IN* with a text devoted to "the destruction of the object; the elimination of the city; the disappearance of work."[9] Supersurface at MoMA creates a global environment that literally translates those three propositions. Peeping into the interior of a small cube made up entirely of mirrors except on one side, visitors see a horizontal surface extending ad infinitum. A film explains the conditions of operation of this surface: Supersurface is a gridded, reflective plane that supports a technical system of climate control, infrastructures, and communications. Extending relentlessly throughout the earth, Supersurface provides a fully equipped system that makes all other constructions unnecessary. Cities vanish, as do objects. For Superstudio—who populate the images with hippies—the design makes possible "An Alternative Model for Life on Earth," the means for a life without objects and work.[10] The project links personal liberation to the development of technical systems, and associates the recuperation of the earth from urbanization with the technical administration of all nature: the planet is "rendered homogeneous through an energy and information grid."[11] The film shows how Supersurface is a tool to continuously incorporate and render artificial geographical space. Its successive stages of development reveal an arbitrary artificiality: from the linear organization of the surface, to the 50% planar occupation of an area in a chessboard-like configuration, to the full construction of the Supersurface plane **[fig. 2]**.

Without architecture, Supersurface proposes a direct relation between individual and world through technological means of communication. The most elaborate propositions of the Fundamental Acts, "Education" and "Death," reiterate the thesis. In "Education" Superstudio returns to their Interplanetary Architecture and proposes the creation of a Universal Information-Exchange System, which would connect the whole planet **[fig. 3]**. Acting as a proto–World Wide Web, the system would allow global and direct access to education.[12] In "Death," a project partly illustrated through the studio's entry in the Modena Cemetery competition, the memory of the earth's inhabitants is kept in computers and made globally accessible after they pass away **[fig. 4]**.

With their suggestion of a global information system, the members of Superstudio know that they are exploring possibilities already considered by Archigram **[project 25]**.[13] They had also previously reacted to the megastructural approach to the construction of the world or to the propositions of Yona Friedman or Claude Parent **[projects 24 and 22]**. There is already in Superstudio an awareness about the different forms through which to address the project of planetarization, even a clear understanding that it does not constitute a novelty, but an inquiry initiated (in their view) with the Russian avant-garde **[projects 5 and 9 to 12]**.[14] Malevich is a constant reference point for the group. Victor Kalmykov's Saturn City prefigures one of the possibilities of Three Projects for the World **[project 12]**.[15] From this historical consciousness, Superstudio addresses the world as a scale that may not be directly built but must be architecturally thought.[16] Political economy, infrastructural systems, and mass media all develop techniques of world-production and generate a common global geographical imaginary. Superstudio's projects attempt to situate architecture as a counterforce to these other techniques of world-making. They thus inquire which nonconstructive means architecture can deploy to rethink the world.

When designing Fundamental Acts, Superstudio had already consolidated three main techniques to challenge the hegemonic global imaginary, which are present in the projects independently of their specific content. The first of these techniques is to abandon the design of conventional architectural projects in favor of producing images that can circulate globally through printed media. In fact, Superstudio's method is one of duplication: they appropriate images from magazines and advertisements and recirculate them, altered, through the same media. A consequence of this appropriation is that Superstudio's representations do not challenge the visual conventions which produce the image of the world, nor the techniques of representation on which architecture has historically relied. Despite the profusion of media the group explores—photomontages, storyboards, films—they always adhere to well-settled perspectival and narrative canons in order to ensure the intelligibility of the image as a medium of global communication.[17] Their attention to the world scale does not transform historic architectural codes either. What happens is the opposite. By adding their proposals to postcards, advertisements, and the like, Superstudio treats architecture as a defamiliarizing instrument that breaks with the understanding of geography as a commodity apt for global consumption in order to present it *ex novo*.[18] In the impenetrable Continuous Monument or the planar Supersurface, all the effort resides in the production of a new perception of the geographical exterior.

**13.** Roberto Gargiani and Beatrice Lampariello, *Superstudio* (Rome: Editori Laterza, 2010), 72.

**14.** Toraldo di Francia, "Memories of Superstudio," 69.

**15.** Gargiani and Lampariello, *Superstudio*, 68.

**16.** In this sense, Superstudio affirms that the Supersurface is not a model to be directly scaled. See Elfline, "Superstudio and the Staging of Architecture's Disappearance," 209.

**17.** See in this respect Peter Lang, "Suicidal Desires," in *Superstudio: Life Without Objects*, ed. Peter Lang and William Menking (Milan: Skira, 2003), 44. A contrasting approach is the one elaborated by the collective Archizoom, who experiment in their projects with an extremely abstract system of architectural notation.

**18.** Piero Frassinelli, "Journey to the End of Architecture," in Lang and Menking, *Superstudio: Life Without Objects*, 79–83.

The second technique derives from understanding that the relation between architecture and the world involves the creation of an imaginary, and thus a form of fiction or narration. Superstudio's projects propose stories, fables, and scenarios. Taken all together they emphasize the value of intellectual sedimentation. The reiterative representation of the world as a theme is already an instrument for its production. During its brief career, Superstudio constantly recapitulates its fictional scenarios, and recuperates or alters motifs from one world project to another.[19] Its members create multiple partial views of their projects, which appear to occupy different and distant locations. Images form sequences and projects are organized in series: Three Projects for the World, Twelve Cities, and Five Acts. Superstudio's work is structured as catalogues or inventories.[20] It mimics the Enlightenment's ideas about encyclopedic knowledge—now fictional knowledge—to the point that it occasionally adopts the visual codes of Diderot and D'Alembert's *Encyclopédie*.

The third method is the association between world-scale and formal reduction. Superstudio's sympathies for the Enlightenment informs their early embrace of Aldo Rossi's notion of "exalted rationalism," and of his praise of the formal purity sought by Étienne-Louis Boullée **[project 41]**.[21] For the group, the scale of the world serves to end, once and for all, the ever-ongoing search for new architectural languages; something that Natalini describes as a process of liberation from all "archimanias."[22] The group's formal resources, including elementary volumes, neutral surfaces, mirrors and grids, basic units for limitless repetition, take the logic of modern abstraction to its very limit, so as to emphasize that it constitutes the very logic of the world scale. They praise radical abstraction and neutrality as truly effective spatial techniques on a geographical scale, which beneficially reduce architecture into an instrument of terrestrial measurement and of "visualization of geographical reality."[23]

Defamiliarization, fiction, and abstraction are the means through which Superstudio offers its view of new forms of inhabiting and occupying the world. Throughout their work, from the Continuous Monument to the Fundamental Acts, the value of the nonarchitectural and nonurban increasingly prevails. Their critique of global urbanization progressively leads to searching the spaces that remain unaffected by it. Their last collaborative works, Global Tools and, especially, Extra-Urban Material Culture, do only concentrate on handcrafted artifacts, on small operations of cultural preservation, on techniques that reveal what is still possible outside the impositions of consumerist society.

**19.** Superstudio, "Fragments of a Personal Museum," quoted in Natalini, "How Great Architecture Still Was in 1966," 187.

**20.** Superstudio, "Fragments of a Personal Museum," quoted in Natalini, "How Great Architecture Still Was in 1966," 187.

**21.** About Superstudio's debt to Rossi, see Gargiani and Lampariello, *Superstudio,* 24.

**22.** Natalini, "How Great Architecture Still Was in 1966," 186.

**23.** Gargiani and Lampariello, *Superstudio,* 66.

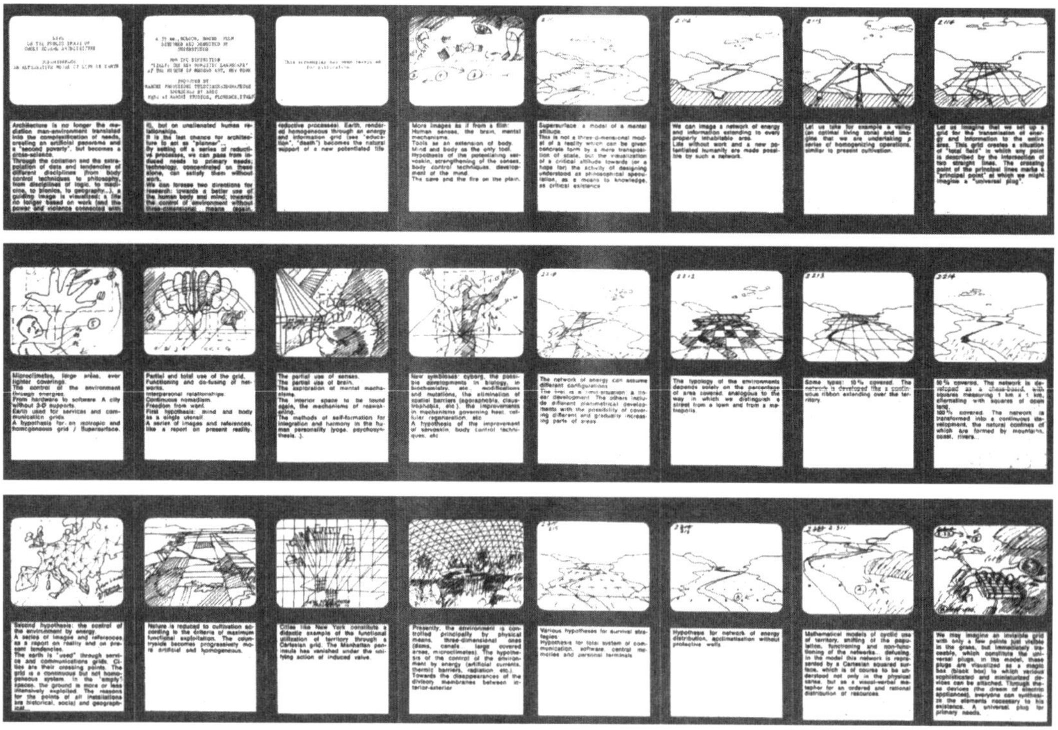

**Figure 1.** Five Fundamental Acts: Life. Supersurface. Storyboards for film. 1972.

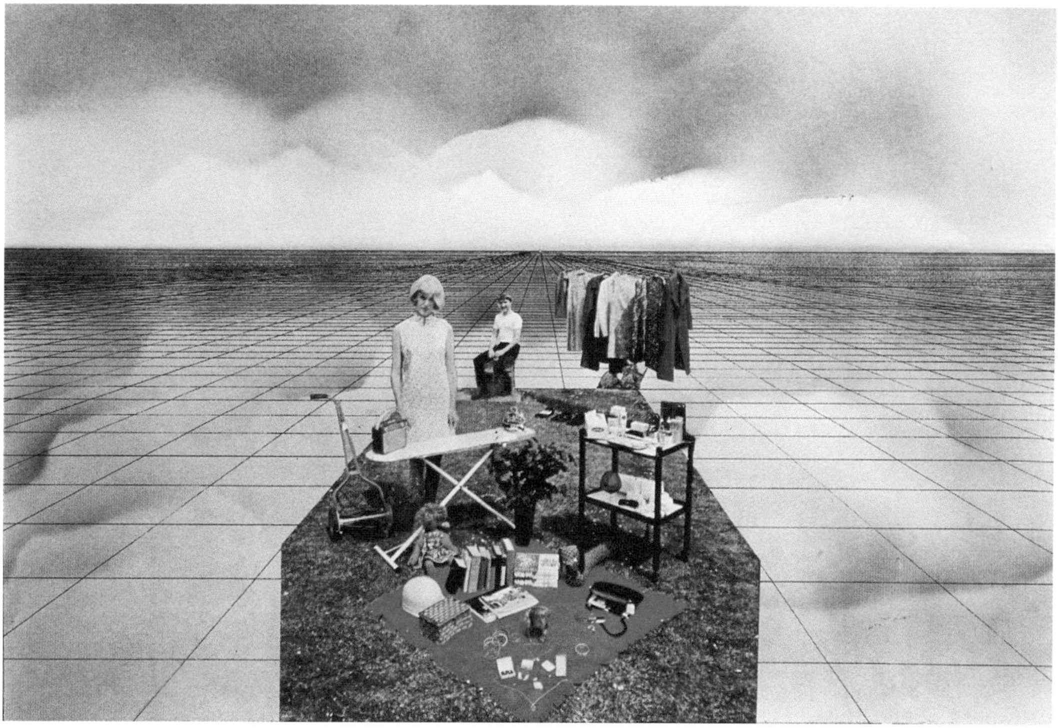

**Figure 2.** Five Fundamental Acts: Life. 1972.

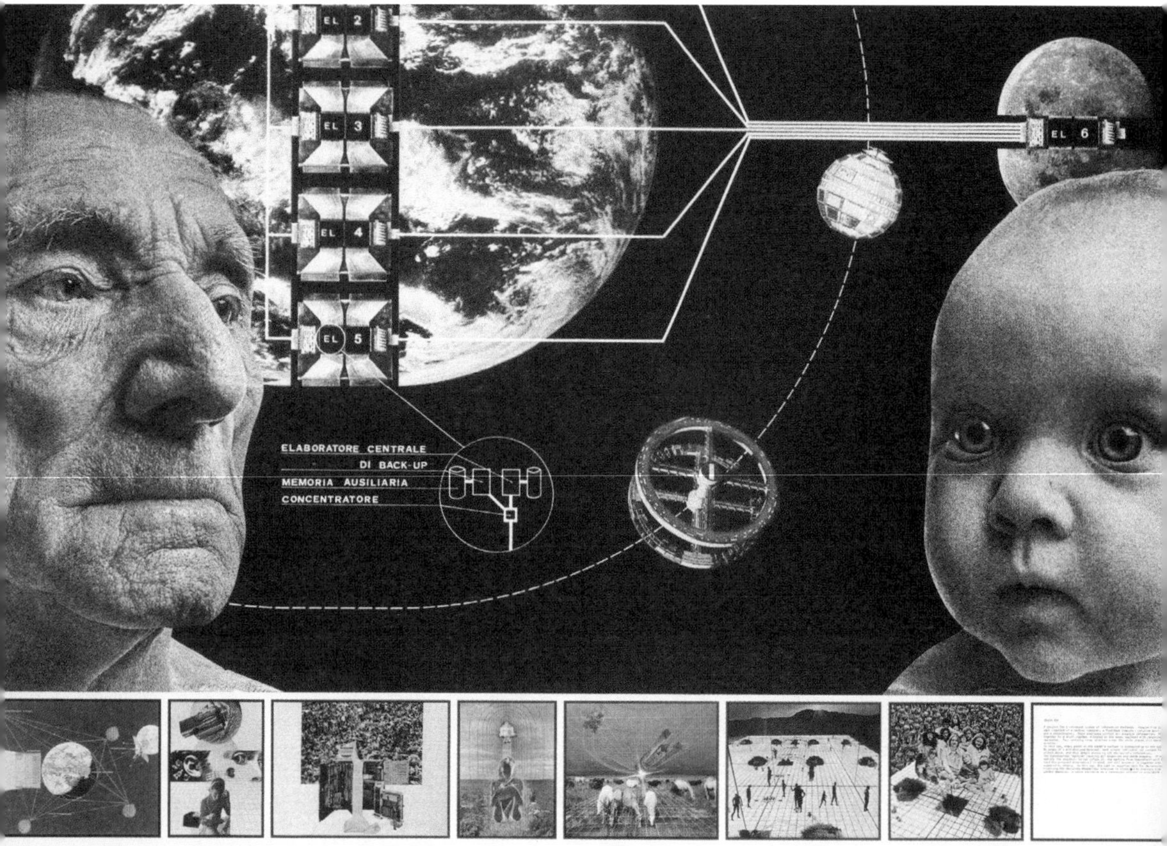


**Figure 3.** Five Fundamental Acts: Education. 1972.

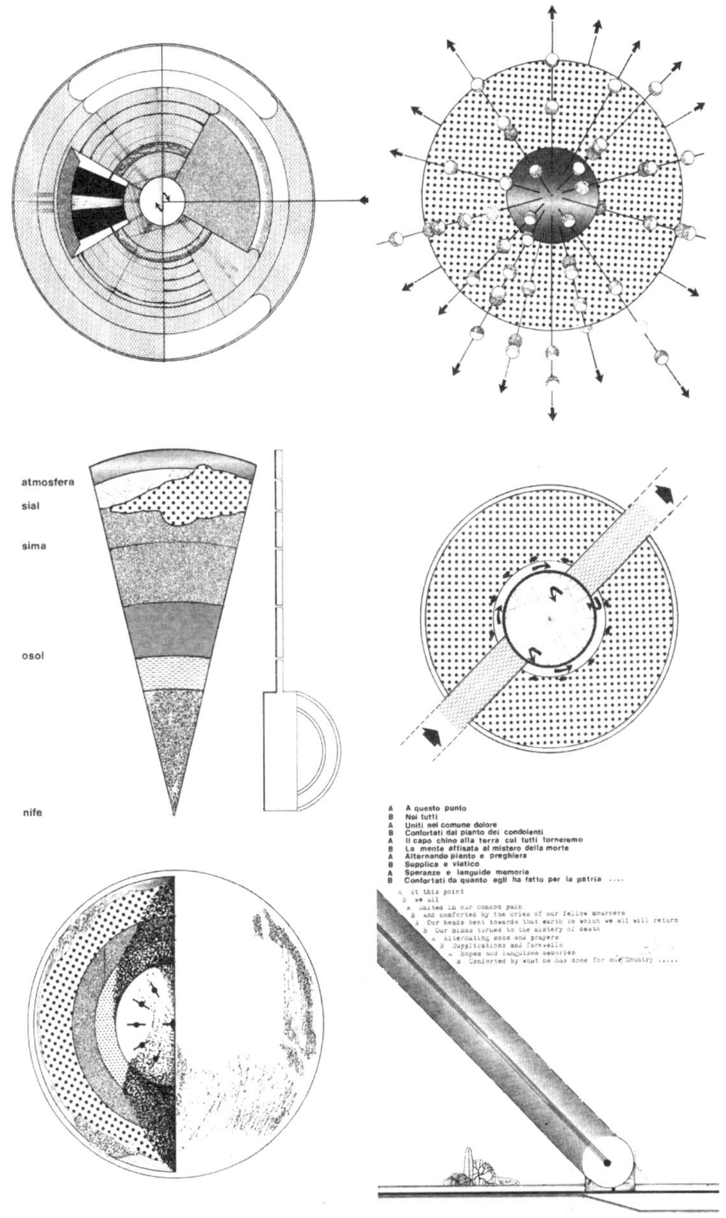


**Figure 4.** Five Fundamental Acts: Death.
Fragment of Superstudio's competition entry for the expansion of the San Cataldo cemetery, Modena. 1971–1973.

# The City of the Captive Globe

**Project:** 39. **Authors:** Rem Koolhaas (1944) with Madelon Vriesendorp (1945). **Date:** 1972–1973. **Themes:** Abstraction. Autonomy. Total Urbanization. Typology.

**Figure 0.** The City of the Captive Globe. Fragments. After Rem Koolhaas and Madelon Vriesendorp. 1978.

The axonometric view that represents The Square of the Captive Globe was originally designed in 1972 for Exodus, or The Voluntary Prisoners of Architecture—the project that Rem Koolhaas, Elia Zenghelis, Madelon Vriesendorp, and Zoe Zenghelis submitted to The City as a Meaningful Environment competition and that marks the beginning of activities for their Office for Metropolitan Architecture (OMA) **[figs. 0 and 1]**.[1] Their entry complements Koolhaas's recently finished diploma project at the Architectural Association (AA) with some texts and additional collages. Its argument begins with the division of London into two parts: the Good Half, a continuous rectangular band delimited by two gigantic walls that frame the space of new constructions, and the Bad Half, or London's existing urban fabric.[2] The Good Half is an area of voluntary seclusion, inhabited by the citizens who wish to live in it, permanently separated from those condemned to remain in the Bad Half. Dominated by the idea of voluntary confinement, the tone of Exodus is dystopian and cynical: it presents as a positive project the use of architecture as a means of spatial and social division that Koolhaas had discovered in his study of the Berlin Wall (1970–1972). For the authors, it is only by accepting Exodus's architectural constraints that the real fruition of the possibilities of life and imagination can take place. Each of the transversal sectors that form the central band allows for a radical exploration of a form of life, experience, or social relation. The one named The Square of the Captive Globe is the symbol of this vision of Exodus as an incubator of social and spatial possibilities. The drawing depicts the terrestrial globe, confined within a sunken square and surrounded by a field of contrasting architectural images.[3] This coexistence of architectural visions represents the very theme of the project: "This square is devoted to the artificial conception and accelerated birth of theories, interpretations, mental constructions and proposals, and their infliction on the World."[4] Later the text presents the different architectures of the square as: "an enormous incubator for the World itself. They are breeding on the globe, changing it, adding something to its contents."[5]

Exodus ends with an ironic negation of its status of unrealizable fiction: in the project's "Epilogue," the authors affirm that its construction only presupposes "a fundamental belief in cities." The second life of the Captive Globe emphasizes the urban nature of the project. The design, now retitled The City of the Captive Globe, reappears in the "Appendix" of *Delirious New York* (1978),

1. Rem Koolhaas, Elia Zenghelis, Madelon Vriesendorp, and Zoe Zenghelis, "Exodus," *Casabella* 378 (1973): 42–45. The OMA partnership includes Elia Zenghelis until 1987, when the Greek architect starts his own professional practice with Eleni Gigantes.

2. For complete information about the Exodus project see Rem Koolhaas, Bruce Mau, and Office for Metropolitan Architecture, *SMLXL* (New York: Monacelli Press, 1995), 2–21. See also Martin Van Schaik and Otakar Máčel, eds., *Exit Utopia: Architectural Provocations, 1956–1976* (Munich: Prestel, 2005), 236–253.

3. Importantly, the representation is similar to the cover of Aldous Huxley's *Brave New World Revisited*. See Ingrid Böck, *Six Canonical Projects by Rem Koolhaas* (Berlin: Jovis Verlag, 2015), 42.

4. Böck, *Six Canonical Projects by Rem Koolhaas*, 42.

5. Böck, *Six Canonical Projects by Rem Koolhaas*, 42.

Koolhaas's eulogy of the American metropolis. Here, Koolhaas presents the design as an intuitive prefiguration of the book's thesis. The drawing's main traits—the division of space into homogeneous blocks, the separation of the buildings from the ground, and their formal pluralism—correspond to the three mechanisms that, according to the architect, produce a metropolis, namely "grid, lobotomy, and schism."[6] The isotropy of the grid turns the city into a matrix of equally valid architectural islands, an archipelago of "cities within cities."[7] Lobotomy makes the interior of each piece independent of the urban exterior. Thanks to schism, each interior is a succession of autonomous installments. Koolhaas's early conception of a metropolitan architecture is a *mise en abyme* of independent entities, aimed at granting successive levels of enclosure, and relentless spatial differentiation. The metropolis is an architectural product. Architecture is a provider of urban instability.[8]

The mutation of the Captive Globe from its original position within Exodus's dystopian urbanism into a symbol of metropolitan dynamism is a sign of the strong polysemy that characterizes the image. The drawing also acts as a claim for the production of fictitious worlds and against the closure of the real promoted by a restrictive reading of modernity that limits architecture's goals to mere rationalization.[9] Moreover, it is a representation of an earth that lacks any inherent, natural value. The quotation from Italian philosopher Giambattista Vico that heads *Delirious New York*, in which the philosopher states the necessity of elaborating "a science not based on the external world, but in the very modifications of the mind that meditates on it," condenses the antinaturalist attitude that Koolhaas develops throughout the book.[10] Additionally, The Captive Globe represents a society in which the idea of utopia is limited to the production of finite and isolated scenarios; it negates the globalizing, universalist aspirations of the modern movement.[11] Finally, and maybe inadvertently, it represents a planet entirely captured by urbanization. Through all these meanings, the Captive Globe synthesizes a set of themes that will recur from the author's early work on: anti-naturalism and artificiality, the metropolis as aggregate of utopias, architecture as the incarnation of desire. It also points to a limit of such an understanding of architecture that Koolhaas will face only at a later stage of his career: the worldwide generalization of the urban condition.

Since the beginning of his architectural education, Koolhaas is in contact with a series of designers who confront the world scale. As a journalist for the magazine *Haagse Post*, he interviews the Dutch architect-artist Constant about

**6.** Rem Koolhaas, *Delirious New York: A Retroactive Manifesto for Manhattan* (New York: Monacelli Press, 1994 [1978]), 296. See also 100–101 and 105–107.

**7.** Koolhaas, *Delirious New York*, 296.

**8.** Koolhaas, *Delirious New York*, 296.

**9.** Koolhaas, *Delirious New York*, 294–296. In this book, Koolhaas also builds his thinking about the city on Salvador Dalí's Paranoid-Critical Method (PCM). The section of *Delirious New York* containing The City of the Captive Globe was also published in a special issue of *Architectural Design* dedicated to Surrealism. See: *AD Profiles* 48, no. 2–3, *Surrealism and Architecture* (1978).

**10.** Koolhaas, *Delirious New York*, 9.

**11.** Lynn Fitzpatrick and Doug Hofius, eds., *Rem Koolhaas: Conversations with Students* (Houston: Architecture at Rice University; 1991), 65. For a general discussion about the relation between Koolhaas's work and the ideas of universality and utopia see Nathaniel Coleman, "Koolhaas Utopianism," in *Utopias and Architecture* (London: Routledge, 2005), 83–88.

New Babylon **[project 19]**.[12] The critical position Koolhaas maintains toward this project (later reversed) also characterizes his judgment of the work of Archigram, some of whose members taught at the AA when Koolhaas studied there.[13] The rejection of these architects' work is not due to the attention they pay the world scale, but to their naive social and technological optimism. Koolhaas finds, in fact, an alternative position in the work of Superstudio, which since 1967 was constantly proposing ways of reimagining the planet **[project 38]**. On a purely formal level, the influence of the Italian group can be perceived in the many affinities between Exodus and the Continuous Monument (1969): from the imposition of a monumental structure, to the use of grids to create neutral surfaces, to a similar use of collage to represent the conflict between the existing environment and the new structure. Conceptually, Koolhaas detects in Superstudio a critical approach to architecture that matches his own and a similar attempt to use architecture to envisage radical alternatives to reality. The work of Superstudio also reinforces his fascination with the Soviet architectural avant-garde of the 1920s.[14] In *Delirious New York*, Koolhaas celebrates the ambition of this generation of Soviet architects, equally dedicated to "designing flying cities, spherical theaters, whole artificial planets" **[projects 5, 11, and 12]**.[15] He values their vision of architecture as an "activist profession with a capability, and indeed a responsibility, for redesigning the human environment," which was being imperiled by the emphatic historicism of an emerging postmodernity.[16] Their goal was nothing less than "to establish a world totally fabricated by man, to live inside fantasy."

"Otherworldliness," the section of *Delirious New York* in which Koolhaas confronts the figures of Le Corbusier and Salvador Dali, perfectly captures this understanding of architecture as a way to construct totally artificial alternatives to reality. For Koolhaas, architecture needs to fully admit that it acts on the world in a manner not unlike Surrealism. The equation of modernity to technical rationalization conceals the disruptive character that is intrinsic to architecture: "Architecture = the imposition on the world of structures it never asked for and that existed previously as clouds of conjectures in the minds of their creators." One extreme of this position is the extension of a singular vision to the global scale, which characterizes the works of Le Corbusier.[17] In opposition to that possibility, the revision of modernity that *Delirious New York* promotes favors limiting the idea of world-making to the construction of many singular artifacts. The grid-lobotomy-schism triad is, in this sense, a tool to turn the metropolis into a multiplicity of different worlds.

**12.** Bart Lootsma, "Now Switch Off the Sound and Reverse the Film . . . Koolhaas, Constant, and Dutch Culture in the 1960s," *Hunch: The Berlage Institute Report* 1 (1999): 154–157 and 171–173. Bart Lootsma, "Le film à l'envers: les années 60 de Rem Koolhaas," *Le Visiteur* 7 (2001): 90–94. The last stage of Koolhaas's changing relation to Constant is the mimicking of the artist's signature and name in the cover of Koolhaas's *Content*. Rem Koolhaas and Office for Metropolitan Architecture, *Content* (Cologne: Taschen, 2004).

**13.** Lieven De Cauter and Hilde Heynen, "The Exodus Machine," in Van Schaik and Máčel, *Exit Utopia*, 262–264.

**14.** Koolhaas is in direct contact with Superstudio's members. He invites Natalini to lecture at the AA and later suggests creating together a research center on the idea of metropolis. De Cauter and Heynen, "The Exodus Machine," 270.

**15.** Koolhaas, "The Story of the Pool," in *Delirious New York*, 307.

**16.** Rem Koolhaas, "The Future's Past," *Wilson Quarterly* 3, no. 1 (Winter 1979): 140.

**17.** Koolhaas describes Le Corbusier as an extreme case of PCM.

Koolhaas idealizes the "Manhattan Skyscraper" as the typology that enables this multiplication of worlds. The multiplication of the ground in each of the skyscraper's floors facilitates, he believes, the "reproduction of the world." The Manhattan skyscraper is also a "self-contained universe," merging the seemingly opposed ideas of a "needle" and a "globe" in a new hybrid, "with the needle wanting to become a globe and the globe trying to turn into a needle."[18] The first manifestation of this convergence is the unbuilt Globe Tower (1906), a project that for Koolhaas captures the essence of such hybridization **[fig. 2]**.[19] As such, it constitutes a formal motif that will constantly haunt the architect's imagination. In *Delirious New York* images of spherical globes abound that aim to encapsulate the world in their interiors. Later, Koolhaas's professional practice with OMA will return to the hybrid between tower and globe in many designs, from the De Bol in Rotterdam (1985)—a "sphere that houses an information center, theatre, restaurant and platform"—to the Zeebrugge Sea Trade Center (1989), to the master plan for Dubai's waterfront (2008) **[figs. 3 and 4]**.

OMA's early programmatic goal is to foster this understanding of architecture as the creation of artificial, *ex novo* environments. At this stage, for the office there is no world beyond its internalization in buildings. Nor is there any possible global project. In the following decades, Koolhaas will have to confront more severely the dimensions of planetarization that his early work neglected. While maintaining a quite strict focus on the design of buildings, the world scale comes to challenge his early postulates about architectural design. The formulation of the notion of "generic city" in 1995 reflects the architect's reading of the spatial repercussions of the post-1989 wave of liberal globalization as a form of spurious Hegelian infinity. The concept is a reaction to the transformation of the metropolis into an all-encompassing spatial formation—the generic city is "so pervasive that it has become the country"—and to the global expansion of a single type of urban space.[20] The generic city is a worldwide trend that manifests itself at continental scales and that intensifies the urban occupation of tropical geographies. Its elements are the same everywhere: its structure is the endless repetition of the same module, its style is "postmodern *and will always remain so.*"[21] In "Junkspace" (1999), Koolhaas's tone is even more pessimistic. Described as "what remains after modernization has run its course,"[22] Junkspace becomes our only physical perception of the universal.[23] In this context Koolhaas admits that the unpredictability of the metropolis that he praised no longer exists.[24] His response to Junkspace is to entirely question

**18.** Koolhaas, *Delirious New York*, 27 and 82.

**19.** Koolhaas, *Delirious New York*, 71.

**20.** Koolhaas, Mau, and Office for Metropolitan Architecture, *SMLXL*, 1249 and 1250.

**21.** Koolhaas, "The Generic City," in *SMLXL*, 1251–1252, and 1262.

**22.** Rem Koolhaas, "Junkspace," *October* 100 (2002): 175–190.

**23.** Koolhaas, "Junkspace," 184 and 190.

**24.** Koolhaas, "Junkspace," 185.

the exceptionalism his buildings had cherished, turning them now into standards and patents. In this sense, globalization motivated a self-reflexive attitude that gradually led Koolhaas to transcend his first architectural formulations, either by exploring a generic form of monumental architecture, either through the rehabilitation of alternative forms of modernity, such as the Team X and the Metabolists **[projects 18 and 21]**, that can influence a new type of global project, or through the exploration of spatial conditions—the generic city, the countryside, the infrastructural and energetic networks—that exceed the metropolitan paradigm.[25]

**25.** World Wide Forum, Ecofys, and OMA AMO, *The Energy Report, 100% Renewable Energy for 2050* (2011). Rem Koolhaas, "Countryside: Future of the World," exhibition at the New York Guggenheim Museum ( Spring 2020).

**Figure 1 (Previous page).** The City of the Captive Globe. 1978.
**Figure 2.** Coney Island Globe Tower. Samuel Friede. 1906.

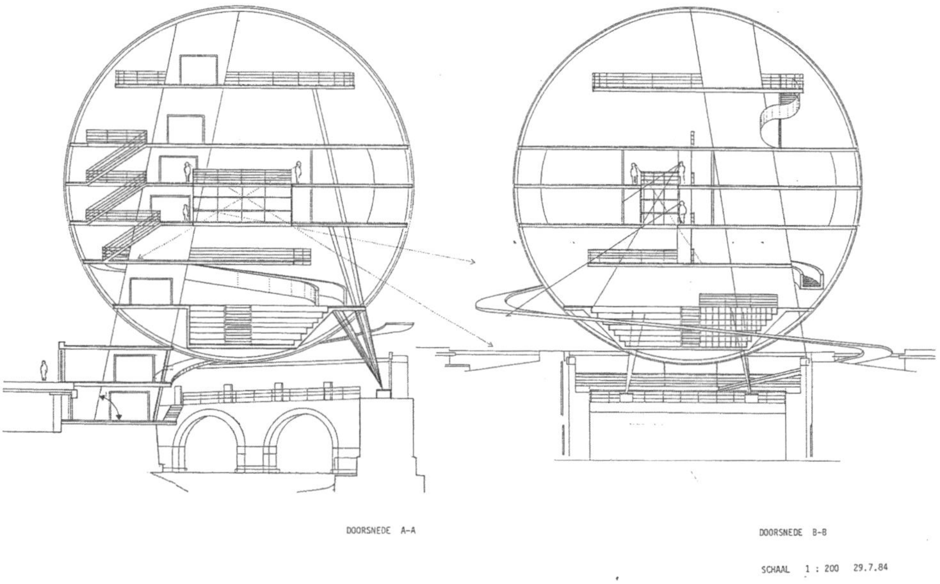

**Figure 3 (Top).** De Bol. Section. OMA. 1985.
**Figure 4 (Bottom).** De Bol. OMA. 1985.

# Planetary Architecture

**Project:** 40. **Author:** Zaha Hadid (1950–2016). **Date:** 1977–1983. **Themes:** Abstraction. Autonomy. Human-Nature Split. Immateriality.

**Figure 0.** The Peak. Fragment. After Zaha Hadid. 1983.

"Now she is a PLANET, in her own inimitable orbit."[1]

Zaha Hadid graduates from the Architectural Association (AA) in 1977 with a project that inquires into the possibility of expanding the architectural repertoire by borrowing from modern Soviet art. Hadid's interest in the Russian avant-garde, sparked by Elia Zenghelis's teachings, her readings of El Lissitzky's books and, more specifically, Anatole Kopp's *Town and Revolution: Soviet Architecture and City Planning 1917–1935*, culminates in a thesis project that appropriates Kazimir Malevich's *Alpha Architekton* (1920) while reprogramming his elemental monolith as a hotel.[2] Hadid docks the *Architekton* to London's Hungerford Bridge and, after a series of manipulations through drawing and painting, brings the configuration to a point of shedding new light on Malevich's heritage and its potential to reinvent architecture's vocabulary **[fig. 1]**.

In the six years that follow, Hadid vigorously develops the explorations she started at the AA, to the extent of creating her own architectural tools and language and moving a step further to investigate the application of her new techniques to real projects. Hadid continues following the thread of the Russian avant-garde she had investigated during her thesis year, however, evolving to release herself from the constraints of a repertoire of predefined forms. She extracts from those art movements operational concepts to free her practice from disciplinary constraints, thus distancing her work from the historicism and emphasis on popular culture, irony, and wit, characteristic of post-modernism. In fact, for Hadid, modernity itself is an incomplete project to be resumed: "I came to realize that architecture's role had yet to be fulfilled and that there were new territories which were yet to be explored . . . We, the authors of architecture, have to take on the task of reinvestigating Modernity."[3] This is a task already modernist in nature and clearly present in her early work, positive of architecture's role in reforming the world.[4]

Among Hadid's Russian references, suprematism's nonobjective world and its search for the substitution of "thing" and "concept" for feeling is especially influential.[5] Dispossessed of utilitarian aims, the forms generated under suprematism materialize this goal by a reduction toward their elementary geometries and the interaction between them. Malevich's art generates new elements that he concludes will eventually transition from canvas to architectural space **[project 5]**.[6] Hadid's early work ventures in this translation from the two- to

**1.** Rem Koolhaas, quoted in Alvin Boyarsky, "Alvin Boyarsky Interviews Zaha Hadid," in Zaha Hadid, *Planetary Architecture Two* (London: Architectural Association, 1983), 4.

**2.** Zaha Hadid, interviewed by Hans Ulrich Obrist, "The Russian Avant-Garde or Zaha Hadid's Influences," in *Zaha Hadid: Early Paintings and Drawings*, ed. Amira Gad and Agnes Gryczkowska (London: Serpentine Galleries, 2016), 91.

**3.** Hadid, *Planetary Architecture Two*, 1.

**4.** Lebbeus Woods, "Zaha Hadid's Drawings 1," *Lebbeus Woods* (blog), 2009. Accessed online March 2, 2019: https://lebbeuswoods.wordpress.com/2009/03/23/zaha-hadids-drawings-1/

**5.** Kazimir Malevich, *The Non-Objective World* (Chicago: P. Theobald, 1959), 68.

**6.** Malevich, *The Non-Objective World*, 100.

the three-dimensional expression of Malevich's forms, sharing with them their abstractness and the possibility of suspension in space, putting-off the need to respond to gravity.[7] Her immaterial geometrical configurations, released from the ground, hover over the planet as "random snapshots of an endless universe made of floating architectural planes."[8]

In 1983, Zaha Hadid presents a compilation of her early works with the exhibition and book *Planetary Architecture Two* organized by the Architectural Association. Featuring seven of her projects, an essay by Kenneth Frampton, and an interview with Alvin Boyarsky, the collection of works showcases meticulously crafted large-scale drawings and paintings. Usually rendered in gray scale with punctual single-color insertions, they emanate the technical complexity and bold distortions that characterize the uniqueness of Hadid's explorations during those years. Two of the works receive privileged position. The winning competition entry for the Peak Hotel in Hong Kong (1982–1983) fills twelve of the eighteen plates **[figs. 0 and 2]**. Consisting of all types of perspectives, axonometric and fragments of specific elements of the project, the set represents Hadid's grandest achievement to that date and the assertion that her visions have a real place in practice, the possibility of materialization. In turn, the painting *The World (89 degrees),* initially titled *The Earth*, is the largest displayed and first to open the book's plates **[fig. 3]**. Measuring 182 × 213 centimeters, the painting brings together all of Hadid's projects in one canvas—from Architekton to the Peak—and accompanies a text of the same name introducing the book. Together they epitomize Hadid's architectural preoccupations in a form of manifesto and worldview.

*The World (89 degrees)* is the culmination of her formative years in venturing into "architecture's uncharted territories" as a response to the speed at which technology evolved; and, with it, society's living habits changed. It is a response to the unfinished project of modernity in its latent capacity of further expanding architecture's field.[9] As Lebbeus Woods suggests, it offers new ways of mediating or structuring the interaction of opposites, "sky and earth, horizon and ground, the artificial and the natural," while simultaneously claiming a detachment from its built surroundings.[10]

In the world depicted in *The World (89 degrees)*, forms release themselves from their hosting context by registering on a different datum: the existing city is flattened into a two-dimensional reduction of its main features whereas the

**7.** Zaha Hadid, interviewed by Obrist, "The Russian Avant-Garde or Zaha Hadid's Influences," 94.

**8.** Hashim Sarkis, "Inscription: On the Surface of Exchange between Writing, Ornament, and Tectonic in Contemporary Architecture," in *Histories of Ornament: From Global to Local*, ed. Gülru Necipoğlu and Alina Payne (Princeton: Princeton University Press, 2016), 35.

**9.** Aaron Betsky, "Introduction: Beyond 89 Degrees," in *The Complete Zaha Hadid* (London: Thames & Hudson, 2017 [2009]), 24.

**10.** Woods, "Zaha Hadid's Drawings 1."

proposed buildings exist over it in volumetric form. This lack of interest in negotiating with the existing site conditions is reinforced by the symbolic gesture of allowing her buildings to escape the confines of the drawing area, represented by a framed ground plane. The buildings and their shadows subtly move beyond the drawing boundary. They reach to the outside not because they need to conquer more space but because the very operations that create them, such as explosion and fragmentation, imply a destructive force that shatters both Hadid's new forms and the preconditions that are supposed to define their limits. As if trying to emancipate themselves from the sight lines that rule the scene, each of her projects uncomfortably distorts the perspective in calculated increments, forcing the horizon to anticipatedly bend according to their presence. This unwillingness to conform to the world as given, and the tension it inflicts to transform such world, is the common ground among Hadid's architectural operations. *The World (89 degrees)* announces her project's will to ultimately reform the terrestrial surface.

Unsurprisingly, Hadid's propositions demand their own visual imagery. The same way the radicality of her projects requires new techniques of communication, the manipulation of architecture's representational tools unleashes new formal possibilities, a process that anticipates aspects of computational design. Drawing surpasses representation and acts as a research method to uncover previously unimaginable paths.[11] Either distorting images using a Xerox machine,[12] or painting with "color modulations, fading effects and Pointillist techniques," or experimenting with explosion, pixilation, warping, and bending through perspectival view, Hadid creates a "new ontology of blurred boundaries and soft transitions" emblematic of the emerging ways of living as a more connected society.[13] The resulting images both try to capture the experience of movement through those spaces and build the unique architectural world in which they can exist in 89 degrees instead of only in one, the 90°. Here, a method of world-building, communicated via painting, is established, one that sees the world as a site to be recreated out of new spatial forms.

The planetary thinking in Hadid, as it draws similarities with the suprematists, purposefully undervalues the existing urban and natural conditions in favor of a totally new occupation of Earth's surface. The same way *The World (89 degrees)* depicts a world inhabited only by Hadid's own buildings, Malevich had envisioned the Earth's ground transfigured into a suprematist formation, populated by his *Architektons* and *Planits*.[14] The world, as it exists, is not just insufficient,

**11.** Zaha Hadid, in Boyarsky, "Alvin Boyarsky Interviews Zaha Hadid," 5.

**12.** Hans Ulrich Obrist, "On Painting, Drawing, and the Digital," in Gad and Gryczkowska, *Zaha Hadid: Early Paintings and Drawings*, 75.

**13.** Patrik Schumacher, "Formalism and Formal Research," in Gad and Gryczkowska, *Zaha Hadid: Early Paintings and Drawings*, 23.

**14.** Kazimir Malevich, quoted in Alexander Lavrentiev, "Zaha Hadid and the Russian Avant Garde," in *Zaha Hadid and Suprematism* (Ostfildern: Hatje Cantz Verlag, 2012), 165.

it should be rectified. According to Malevich, "our Earth, the surface of the Earth is not organized. It is covered with seas and mountains. Some kind of Nature exists. I would like to create Suprematist Nature according to the laws of Suprematism instead of this Nature."[15] In suprematism this confrontation of new and old, of created and found, divided humans and nature as antithesis of each other, with the latter being merely a starting point for the creations of the former.[16] Coincidently, and caricatural to her disliking of nature, Hadid's projects can also be seen in that same light of the struggle to overcome innate principles, such as gravity, attraction, or time.[17] Uninterested in reality as given, Hadid would rather probe with "building as if on another planet, but on Earth," a statement that cannot help recall Malevich's painting title "Future Planits (Houses) For Earth Dwellers (People)" from 1924.[18]

Despite all the energy invested on the explosion of architecture, on the carving of unheard of territories for the discipline, or the way her designs register the act of inscription of foreign bodies into worldly grounds, which altogether prevent her forms from "really occupy[ing] just any kind of moment," in the early 1990s Hadid starts building and thus negotiating with real constraints of *de facto* spaces.[19] From then on, the site is not a blank canvas anymore. A floating beam or a dislodged column now has to be domesticated and set into place. A sliced landscape now has to remember it should comply with property laws. Tilted walls now are considered in light of a construction budget. Progressively, the audacity of her early work shifts in nature along with the urgencies of her architecture. Formal fragmentation turns into formal fluidity; flight turns into velocity. In order to keep pushing the boundaries of architectural practice, Hadid has to adapt her vocabulary. She continues the quest of building a unique formal reality, but now her forms cannot pretend they exist detached from contextual constraints. The world she now gradually constructs no longer aspires to totality. Later in her career, on the occasion of the Pritzker Prize, Hadid states that "what is new in our epoch is a new level of social complexity; and that there are no secret formulas anymore, *no global solutions*."[20]

Paradoxically, as her work gains in volume and pushes the industry to follow its evolution—from the emergence to the consolidation of techniques in digital design and fabrication—her formulas seem indeed to be globally applied. Progressively Zaha Hadid's work comes to represent the possibility of imagining and materializing a world formally and spatially richer than the one restricted to the modern orthogonality. Her projects fulfill a generalized desire for

**15.** Lavrentiev, "Zaha Hadid and the Russian Avant Garde," 164. This was a common position within the movement; El Lissitzky, for example, in his 1920s essay "Suprematism in World Reconstruction," advocated for the replacement of all existing forms belonging to established universal systems for a unique formal lexicon to build a world never experienced before.

**16.** Malevich, *The Non-Objective World*, 20 and 32.

**17.** Zaha Hadid, in Boyarsky, "Alvin Boyarsky Interviews Zaha Hadid," 10.

**18.** Hans Ulrich Obrist, "On Mobile Architecture," in Gad and Gryczkowska, *Zaha Hadid: Early Paintings and Drawings*, 81.

**19.** Hans Ulrich Obrist, "Lessons Learned from Fragmentation," in Gad and Gryczkowska, *Zaha Hadid: Early Paintings and Drawings*, 84.

**20.** Obrist, "Lessons Learned from Fragmentation," 84.

complexity as well as for a new image that can resonate with a possible future, bringing it closer to the present. The forms she created, so unique to her, are today found all over the world. Their initial reformist planetary aspirations, however, progressively wore off their pioneering radicality as they opened space for a global market of architectural consumption. In the end, perhaps as an ironic reflection of the cosmic aspirations of the Russians that so much helped build Hadid, her work has indeed conquered the universe, claiming their right to the "scintillating paradise of the world."[21]

**21.** Kenneth Frampton, "A Kufic Suprematist," in Hadid, *Planetary Architecture Two*, 4.

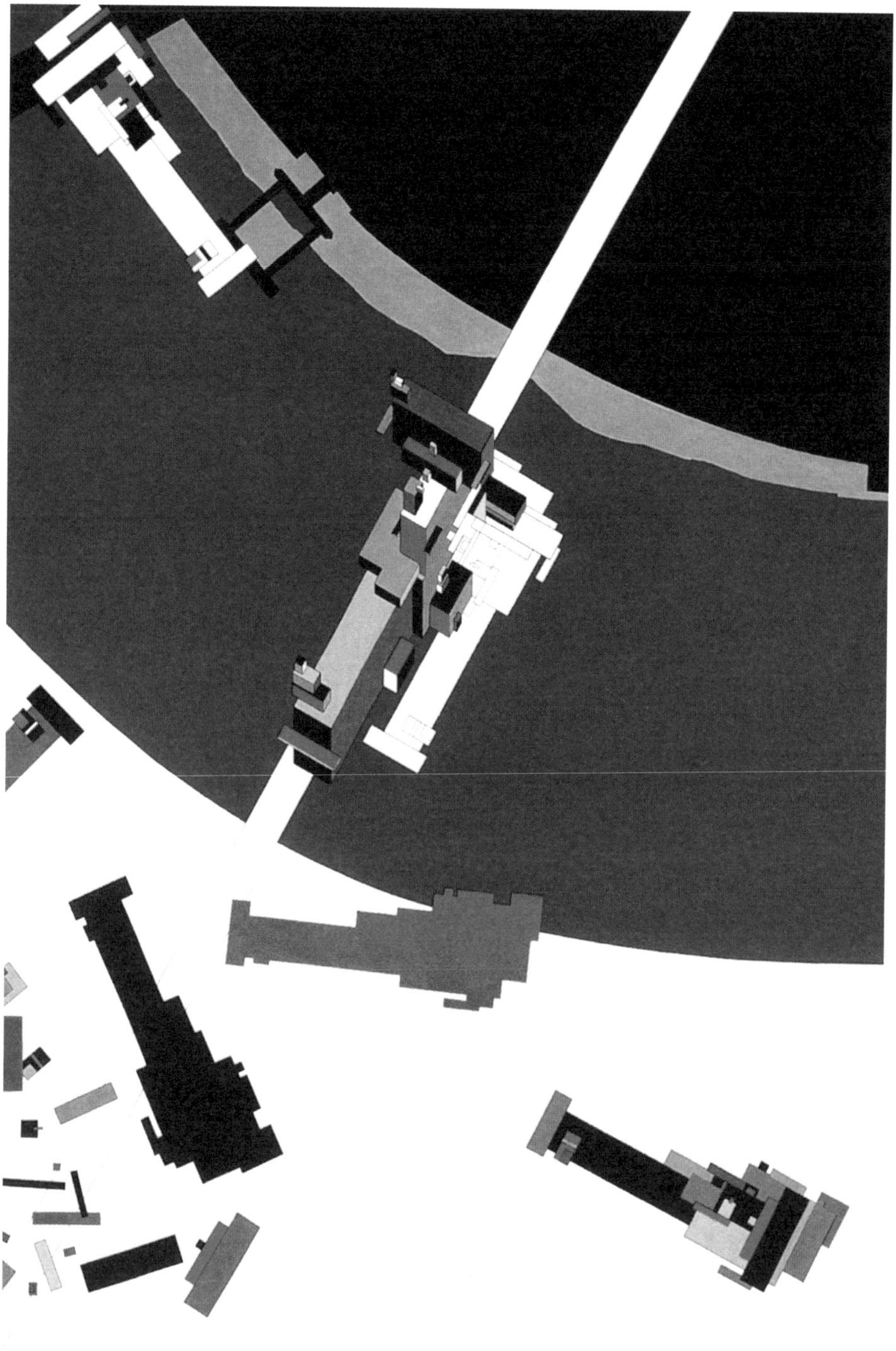

**Figure 1.** *Malevich's Tektonik.* 1976–1977.

**Figure 2.** The Peak. *Slabs*. 1983.

Zaha Hadid

Figure 3. *The World (89 Degrees)*. Originally titled *The Earth*. 1983.

# Teatro del Mondo

## Theater of the World

**Project:** 41. **Author:** Aldo Rossi (1931–1997). **Date:** 1979–1980. **Themes:** Autonomy. Monumentality. Place(lessness). Typology.

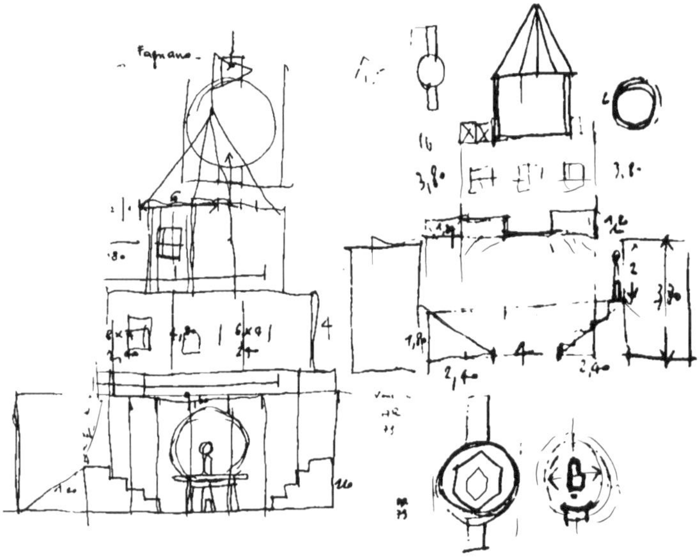

**Figure 0.** Teatro del Mondo. Study Sketches. After Aldo Rossi. 1979.

Autonomy. Limitation. Finitude. Singularity. Discreteness. History. Memory. The central topics of Aldo Rossi's work reflect his utter commitment to the value of the architectural object and to the formal and typological questions that affect its production, and a parallel disinclination toward the possible spatial articulation of the world scale. Notably, Manfredo Tafuri closes "Toward a Critique of Architectural Ideology" by stating that a radical alternative to modern architecture's connivance with the spatial articulation of the world market can be found primordially in the retreat to the architectural object that Rossi praises.[1] Rossi himself does not dissimulate his dissatisfaction with previous totalizing approaches to urbanism that are based on structural readings of the global spatial organization, such as Le Corbusier's *Three Human Establishments* or Erwin Anton Gutkind's decentralization theories.[2] And yet, in 1979 Rossi builds the Teatro del Mondo, a project that includes the world in its very name **[fig. 0]**. Certainly, the design's title is, first and foremost, an appropriation of the name given to some of the floating theaters built in Venice during the 1500s.[3] At the same time, supported by images of Noah's Ark, a construction that had to contain the world for its reproduction, it is pertinent to question if the Teatro is also a project that actually reflects upon the relations between architecture and world, and in what forms it allows us to discern how Rossi's work addresses the topic **[fig. 1]**.

Rossi builds the Teatro del Mondo for the 1980 Venice Biennale. The extremely simple form of its components—a square-plan, prismatic volume for the theater, surrounded by two regular volumes for the stairs that surround it—generates a building that is reminiscent of Italian baptisteries on the outside and of anatomic theaters inside **[fig. 2]**. Built in 1979, and dismantled in 1980, it was a brief, ephemeral structure. This temporal aspect has a spatial correlate: the project disregards permanence in place, too. During its short life the Teatro travels, always supported by a barge, from its site of construction in Fusina, to Venice and Dubrovnik; traversing Po Valley canals and the Adriatic Sea **[fig. 3]**. The building's engagement with the city of Venice is, in this sense, temporally and spatially limited. As Rossi indicates, in Venice the Teatro is placed in the threshold between land and sea, like a "lighthouse."[4] But even this liminal condition is only a momentary stage, a phase of the building's broader commitment through its travel to the geographic scale.

1. Manfredo Tafuri, "Toward a Critique of Architectural Ideology," in *Architecture Theory Since 1968*, ed. K. Michael Hays (Cambridge, MA: MIT Press, 1998 [1969]), 32–33.

2. Aldo Rossi and Silvano Tintori, "Aspetti urbanistici del problema delle zone arretrate in Italia e in Europa," in Giovanni Demaria et al., *Problemi sullo sviluppo delle aree arretrate* (Bologna: Il Mulino, 1960), 248–249. Aldo Rossi, "Nuovi Problemi," in Rossi, *Scritti scelti sull'architettura e la città 1956–1972*, ed. Rosado Bonicalzi (Milan: Clup, 1989 [1975]), 190.

3. Manlio Brusatin, "Theatrum Mundi Novissimi," in *Aldo Rossi: Teatro del Mondo*, ed. Manlio Brusatin and Alberto Prandi (Venice: Cluva, 1982), 41–43.

4. Aldo Rossi, *A Scientific Autobiography*, trans. Lawrence Venuti (Cambridge, MA: MIT Press, 2010 [1981]), 67.

Geographical theory plays a crucial part in Aldo Rossi's architectural thinking, especially at the beginning of his intellectual career. Among the many geographers who support his gradual elaboration of a theory of architecture during the 1960s, Rossi often references the Italian historian Carlo Cattaneo (1801–1869) in order to denounce the falseness of the division between city and countryside, and to posit an integrated understanding of both as constituents of a single process of transformation of geographical space by architectural means.[5] Cattaneo backs a structural line in Rossi's thinking, which can be traced from his first published text, "La Coscienza di potere 'dirigere la natura'" (The Consciousness of being able to direct nature, 1954), to the recognition in "Architettura per i museii" (Architecture for museums, 1966) that nothing affects him more "than the great manufactures that cross the countryside, than the architectures that appear as a concrete sign of the transformation of nature through the works of humankind."[6] For Rossi, the purpose of architectural form, "to reveal a process of transformation" of reality, is better captured beyond city confines.[7]

This privilege of the direct relation between architecture and territory pervades Rossi's thought. It explains *The Architecture of the City*'s insistence on the structuring power of the monument as emanating from a reading of territorial organization, not of urban structure.[8] It also supports a theory of the city that, as Peter Eisenman points out, entirely rejects the idea of scale.[9] Rossi's exploration of the role of architecture in the production of the city is an inquiry about a relation where the scale and conditions of architecture are fixed, while those of the city are not. The city is a space or a scale in a constant state of production, which appears thanks to the structuring and transformative power of monuments. Considering the Teatro's construction and travel as essential parts of the project clarify this aspect of Rossi's thought.[10] The construction process shows the conversion of matter into object as well as the transformation of the landscape by the architectural sign. All along its journey, the Teatro's displacements establish the geographical space *as* city.

The notion of *locus*, understood as the "relationship between a certain specific location and the buildings that are in it," is a crucial part of Rossi's theory, one that leads him to understand that the role of architecture is to invest the place it builds with singularity.[11] Throughout its travel, the Teatro elevates the different spaces it crosses to the condition of *locus*, and thus clarifies that *locus* is, precisely, produced architecturally. At the same time the Teatro constantly abandons

**5.** Aldo Rossi, *The Architecture of the City*, trans. Diane Ghirardo and Joan Ockman; revised for the American edition by Aldo Rossi and Peter Eisenman (Cambridge, MA: MIT Press, 1982 [1966]), 128. Rossi and Tintori, "Aspetti urbanistici del problema delle zone arretrate in Italia e in Europa," 252.

**6.** Aldo Rossi, "Architettura per i museii" [1975], in *Scritti scelti sull'architettura e la città 1956–1972*, 326. Our translation.

**7.** Rossi, "Architettura per i museii," 326.

**8.** Rossi maintains this position already in his first writings about territorial organization. See Rossi and Tintori, "Aspetti urbanistici del problema delle zone arretrate in Italia e in Europa," 263–268.

**9.** Peter Eisenman, "Introduction," in Rossi, *The Architecture of the City*, 9. Rossi, "Architettura per i museii," 326. See also Rossi's recognition that architectural theory still doesn't know what the city is in Rossi, *The Architecture of the City*, 49.

**10.** Manfredo Tafuri, "L'Éphémère est éternel," in Brusatin and Prandi, *Aldo Rossi: Teatro del Mondo*, 147–148.

**11.** Rossi, *The Architecture of the City*, 103.

and thereby negates any particular location. There is a strong relation between this dialectic of affirmation and negation of place and Rossi's elaboration of the notion of "type," which locates his attention to geographic space and his investigation of architectural language as the two parts of a single search.

In her effort to contextualize Rossi's thinking within the Italian urban and political debates of the 1960s, Mary Louise Lobsinger has shown how Rossi's interest in the notion of realism informs his first approach to the idea of type, and how neo-Marxist philosophers such as Theodor W. Adorno and, especially, György Lukács influence his thinking about this topic.[12] By establishing the concept of "typicality," Lukács defends the unique power of realist literature to reveal sociohistorical conditions because of its capacity to condense the complex of social relations or "worldviews" within a specific literary character.[13] Similarly, for Rossi the architectural type is the concrete material expression of a certain social reality, and an instrument that defines the architect's position *vis-à-vis* society.[14] To be involved in the production of types requires deep self-restraint on the designer's part and an acceptance of formal conventions that emanate from the collective social sphere. Instead of the free play of individual, artistic creation, the use of types promotes an investigative process into type itself. To inquire into a type's processes of generation and to distill its formal principles are the steps the architect has to follow in order to establish a shared formal language that can transmit a common form of socialization. Years later, in 1985, Rossi will still affirm: "In a more direct manner, typology is a way to express a mode of life to be transmitted to ordinary people."[15] His long-standing eulogy of the classicist architecture of Soviet Realism derives from this position.

The identification between typology and way of life is also present in the geographical literature that Rossi read, most notably in the works of French geographer Maximilien Sorre.[16] Yet, the design of the Teatro del Mondo belongs to a moment in which Rossi's investigation of the formal essentials of type leads him to take this original, contextualized understanding of relations type-society relations in a new direction. Rossi's attempt at the time to design an "analogue architecture" by using only the most primary formal traits is an explicit way of bringing together distant places through a potentially infinite chain of typological references.[17] In *Scientific Autobiography* Rossi praises the architectural interior as a space to perceive, distilled, the environmental conditions of territory.[18] Invoking analogy, Rossi takes that territorial vision further. The

**12.** Mary Louise Lobsinger, "Antinomies of Realism in Postwar Italian Architecture" (PhD diss., Harvard University, 2004), 175–179. See also in this respect Pier Vittorio Aureli, "The Difficult Whole: Typology and the Singularity of the Urban Project in Aldo Rossi's Early Theoretical Work, 1953–1964," *Log* 9 (Spring 2007): 39–61.

**13.** Lobsinger, "Antinomies of Realism in Postwar Italian Architecture," 26–27.

**14.** Lobsinger, "Antinomies of Realism in Postwar Italian Architecture," 175–179.

**15.** Aldo Rossi, "Interview," *Japan Architect* (JA) 1 (January 1985): 10.

**16.** Rossi, *The Architecture of the City*, 103.

**17.** Daniel Libeskind, "Deus ex Machina ex Deo," in Brusatin and Prandi, *Aldo Rossi: Teatro del Mondo*, 120. Rossi, *A Scientific Autobiography*, 67.

**18.** Rossi, *A Scientific Autobiography*, 54.

attempt to found an architectural language with an extremely reduced palette of classical compositional elements is a way of opening up geographic associations. The elementary composition of the Teatro del Mondo does not reference "real Venice," but the space of the Greek islands dominated by Venetian forces and, through it, the whole Byzantine world: Moscow and the towers of the Kremlin.[19] Moreover, in another referential jump, the latter bring with them the boundless plains of the Siberian steppe.[20]

While the global and the planetary are absent in Rossi's discourse, universality and totality are present as a constant aspiration. His original, analytical approach to type is a research "on the forces that are at play in a permanent and universal way in all urban artifacts."[21] The notion of locus joins location and universality.[22] Formal simplification and analogy create a universal language and trigger an unending process of transgeographic associations. His remarks about the organization of the ecumenical space of the Church in *The Architecture of the City* indicate that for him a form of universal space can appear through the construction of concrete, partial manifestations.[23] If his own practice adopts a more disenchanted approach to this possibility and expresses itself through objects and fragments, it is not due to an ideological rejection of a possible totality, but rather to a specific historical condition: "the question of the fragment in architecture is very important since it may be that only ruins express a fact completely . . . this ability to use pieces of mechanisms whose overall sense is partly lost has always interested me, even in formal terms. I am thinking of a unity, or a system, made solely of reassembled fragments. Perhaps only a great popular movement can give us the sense of an overall design; today we are forced to stop ourselves at certain things. I am convinced, however, that architecture as totality, as a comprehensive project, as an overall framework, is certainly more important and, in the final analysis, more beautiful."[24]

Rossi's confession is, once again, indebted to neo-Marxist thought. Both Walter Benjamin's and Adorno's poetics involve uniting parts to provide "a glimpse of a unified world, of a universe in which discontinuous realities are nonetheless somehow implicated with each other and intertwined, no matter how remote they may at first have seemed."[25] Yet, Rossi takes the neo-Marxist project in a personal direction. Whereas Benjamin and Adorno want to reveal an existing unity concealed by the appearance of fragmentation, Rossi ends up cultivating the fragment in order to draw our attention to a totality that has been lost and that can only be recreated poetically. In his hands, architectural typologies and

**19.** Rossi, "Interview," 11.

**20.** Rossi, *A Scientific Autobiography*, 67.

**21.** Rossi, *The Architecture of the City*, 23.

**22.** Rossi, *The Architecture of the City*, 103–106.

**23.** Rossi, *The Architecture of the City*, 104.

**24.** Rossi, *A Scientific Autobiography*, 8.

**25.** Fredric Jameson, *Marxism and Form: Twentieth-century Dialectical Theories of Literature* (Princeton: Princeton University Press, 1974), 3–59. Terry Eagleton, *The Ideology of the Aesthetic* (Oxford, UK: Blackwell, 1990), 325–327.

analogies become reminiscences of an abandoned shared language. Similarly, the Teatro's travel points to the disappeared capacity of the single architectural project to transform geography and create interrelated territories in a world that has been aggressively urbanized. Rem Koolhaas's City of the Captive Globe (1972) shows an Earth that is caged by urbanization **[project 39]**. Eight years later, the Teatro still seeks a space that has not been interiorized; an untouched geography where architecture can act as the foundation of territorial structures. This is a world that no longer exists but can still be evoked. The role of architecture is then not to persevere in the modern engagement with ongoing processes of territorial production, but to offer us an alternative vision of the world. In this sense, Rossi wants to recover a way to make compatible architectural autonomy with addressing the world at large, one which, without a doubt, epitomizes the ethos of a postmodern period in which the discipline of architecture seldom considers the world scale and only through the means of the architectural object.

**Figure 1.** *The Deluge*. Jan Sadeler I (after Maarten de Vos). 1586.
**Figure 2 (Opposite page).** Teatro del Mondo. 1980.
**Figure 3 (Following pages).** Teatro del Mondo in the Adriatic Sea. 1980.

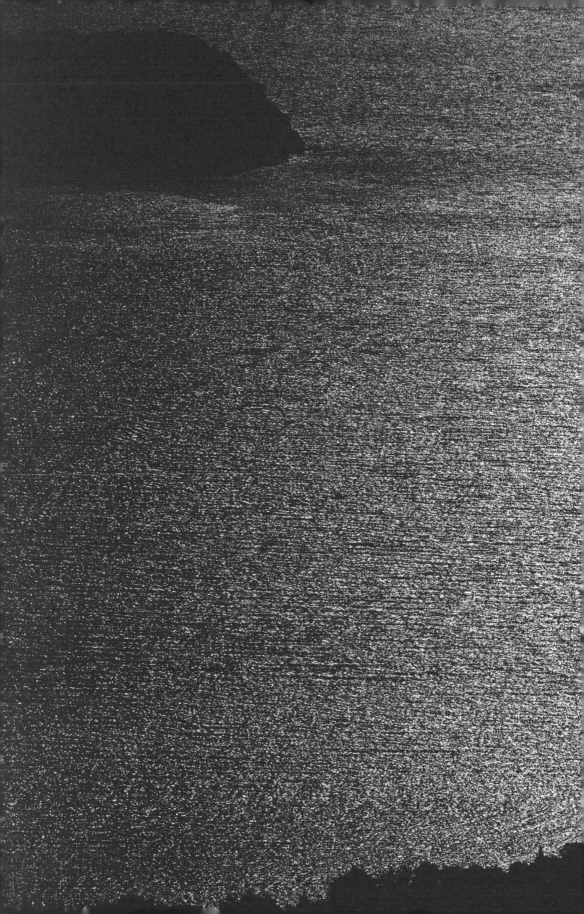

# Masques

**Project:** 42. **Author:** John Hejduk (1929–2000). **Date:** 1981–2000. **Themes:** Autonomy. Nomadism. Taxonomy. Typology.

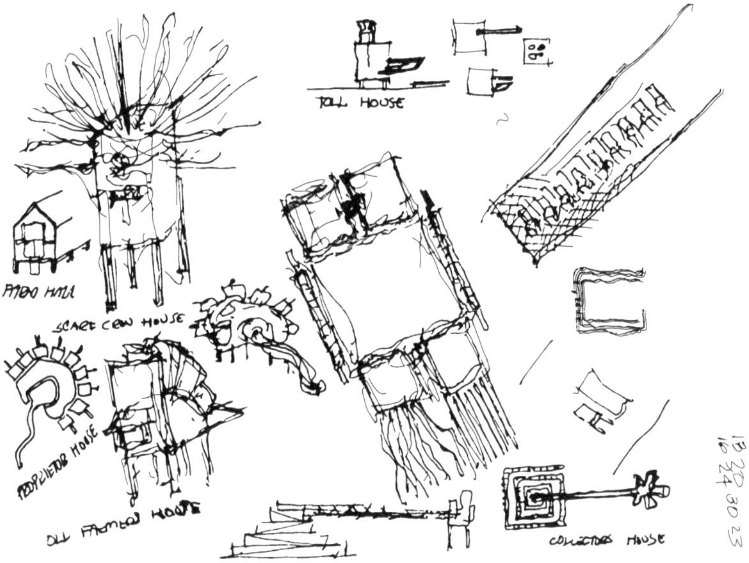


**Figure 0.** Lancaster/Hanover Masque. Objects. After John Hejduk. 1990.

"I cannot do buildings without building a new repertoire of characters of stories of language, and it's all parallel. It's not just building per se. It's building worlds," John Hejduk explains to poet David Shapiro.[1] In his Masques projects, architecture no longer consists of designing unique, self-sufficient buildings. Designs operate, rather, as the characters in a theatrical play. Even if they can exist individually, the final sense of the pieces results from their grouping together to generate a particular ensemble. Every piece references—and contains, *in nuce*—a broader whole, or world **[fig. 0]**.

The term "world" here is metaphorical. Its meaning is similar to the one American philosopher Nelson Goodman uses in his 1978 book *Ways of Worldmaking*: a world is a formal structure governed by an internally consistent logic.[2] In this sense Hejduk's definition of a multitude of architectural characters and of a cohesive formal system is a poetic act, which seeks to have an impact upon the physical world, but which disdains designing the planet as such. His position goes against modernity's globalizing, panoramic view and any pretensions of imposing a single form of universality.[3] In his conversation with Shapiro, Hejduk emphatically rejects the form of utopia that for him Le Corbusier's universalism represents. For Hejduk, instead of the utopian nonplace, only "places" exist.[4] "Building worlds" is, thus, a pluralistic project, seeking to substitute modernity's global ambitions for a multitude of distinct—and yet related—singularities.

To create worlds was not the initial object of Hejduk's work. Until the mid-1970s his designs focus on exploring the multiple possibilities of predefined architectural systems: the nine-square grid, walls, Le Corbusier's free plan. This way of producing forms through iterative variations of a settled architectural grammar, which Hejduk defines as the "Theory of Accumulation," also constitutes Masques's generative mechanism: they are always recombinations of a set of predetermined elements. To this formal procedure, Hejduk's world-building projects add two other key components. The first one recovers the symbolic and semantic dimensions that characterized architecture historically but that modernity diminished. Hejduk boosts the symbolism of Masques by treating them as literary artifacts. The form of each piece alludes to its role and meaning, which the architect explains with texts about the characteristics of each architectural "object," of the "subject" that inhabits it, and of the events that take place in it.[5] The result is a symbolic and figurative formal system, an inver-

**1.** John Hejduk and David Shapiro, "John Hejduk or the Architect Who Drew Angels," *Architecture and Urbanism* 471 (2009): 75. Transcript of the film *John Hejduk: Builder of Worlds*, commented by John Hejduk and David Shapiro (San Francisco: Kanopy Streaming, 2014), DVD.

**2.** Nelson Goodman, *Ways of Worldmaking* (Indianapolis: Hackett, 1978).

**3.** James McGregor, "The Architect as Storyteller: Making Places in John Hejduk's Masques," *Architectural Theory Review* 7, no. 2 (2009): 64.

**4.** Hejduk and Shapiro, "John Hejduk or the Architect Who Drew Angels," 76.

**5.** See in this respect John Hejduk, *The Lancaster/Hanover Masque = Le masque Lancaster/Hanover* (London: Architectural Association, 1992); John Hejduk and Kim Shkapich, *Riga, Vladivostok, Lake Baikal: A Work* (New York: Rizzoli, 1989); and John Hejduk, *Victims: A Work* (London: Architectural Association, 1986).

sion of modern architecture's abstraction. The second component is a precise relation to place. The overall formal system is site-less, but its implementation is always local. Each Masque is designed to intervene in a specific location: Berlin, Lancaster, Riga, Lake Baikal, and Vladivostok.

The architectural critic Robert Somol describes Hejduk's commitment to place as "choreography"; a Ptolemaic notion that refers to the "depiction of individual features" and that opposes the comprehensive view geography provides.[6] Masques's world-project consists, from this point of view, of the singularization and activation of the places they occupy. The critical dimension of this project appears enunciated, precisely, in one of the three projects that mark Hejduk's transition toward the construction of worlds: The Silent Witnesses (1976) **[fig. 1]**.[7] The project describes the transformation of a coastal location over five consecutive thirty-year periods starting—almost like this book—in 1878 and ending in 1998. The work links each of these periods to a literary figure and to a synthetic world-system constituted by geographical space, architecture, and transportation techniques. The centennial progression depicts an unstoppable approximation of technology to architecture, resulting in the transformation of location into an undifferentiated space. The immediate future (then 1998) represents this collapse in a series of gray, undifferentiated boxes that showcase the condition that Hejduk will seek to work against, first with the Thirteen Towers for Cannaregio, and then, from 1981 on, with the Masques **[fig. 2]**.

Hejduk's Masques develop a critique of the rationalization and homogenization of space. It is articulated primordially by subverting the instruments of epistemic totalization on which those two phenomena rely. The many objects that constitute Masques are not only the characters of a theatrical play. They also make up a type of world-system that contradicts any attempt to systematize and control. The Berlin Masque, the first project of this kind, already appropriates and subverts the classifying mechanisms of a dictionary. The following projects mimic the procedures of the Enlightenment encyclopedia: they present each of the design's parts in textual order, explain their content with aseptic descriptions, and depict them in catalogues with the necessary technical information **[project 2, 8 and 38]**. And yet, instead of the systematization of global knowledge that the encyclopedia represents, Masques subverts any form of categorization. As in the works of Jorge Luis Borges or Italo Calvino, which the architect quotes, taxonomies reflect multiplicities without particular order, organization, or universal validity.[8] In Masques, Hejduk uses the same word

6. Robert E. Somol, "One or Several Masters," in *Hejduk's Chronotope*, ed. K. Michael Hays (New York: Princeton Architectural Press, 1996), 104.

7. The other two are The Cemetery for the Ashes of Thought, and The Thirteen Watchtowers of Cannaregio. See in this regard Martin Søberg, "John Hejduk's Pursuit of an Architectural Ethos," *Footprint* 10/11 (2012): 113–127.

8. Italo Calvino, *Invisible Cities* (London: Vintage, 1997 [1972]). Jorge Luis Borges, "The Analytical Language of John Wilkins," in *Other Inquisitions, 1937–1952* (New York: Simon and Schuster, 1965 [1952]).

to denote different things and, conversely, different words for identical things. Categories disappear in favor of individual entities. The projects apply the same subversive tone to other forms of world categorization. Polar orientation becomes a combinatorial system—NEWS, NESW, WSEN—in the projects for houses.[9] The Clock Towers conceal time. The many institutions that populate the Masques do not promote any particular form of social organization. They change from location to location. Instead of facilitating social normalization, they provide the space for individual encounters among different and conflicting agents.

This neglect of rational forms of organization informs the representation and the design of each piece. Hejduk originally presents the Masques in books that combine technical drawings and a rich array of graphic and textual procedures. Sketches, collages, watercolors, and descriptions bear the same importance as the technical representations.[10] The design of individual pieces, on the other hand, results from the combination of a series of elements—spikes, pyramids, curved forms, cylinders, tunnels—without any predetermined logic. The result is often figurative, but also aberrant and disproportioned **[fig. 3]**. Finally, the implementation of Masques in different locations produces another combinatorial iteration: the pieces always appear in different configurations, revealing that they do not require any order. Hejduk's formal method is the contrary of a system of restriction and control. It fosters the proliferation of architectural possibilities, as if the system could always create more disparate forms.

For Hejduk, this proliferation and the availability of his architectural repertoire are the key components of Masques. There is implicit in it, he believes, a reconsideration of what an architectural practice means, a reconsideration that implies moving from the subjective to the collective, and from the initial location of the project to other places. "Now what's happening is that, in different places throughout the world, they are building each of these characters . . . So there is a time when the people come as a community and they build it. They draw it up, they detail it. They are part of the creation of the thing. Then they put it out into the public domain and it becomes some kind of strange, strange celebration of the art of building, of the structure of the social and political aspects of architecture which seem to have disappeared."[11] The many projects and their combinations are thus instrumental to the constitution of a local, and particular community, and to linking that community and its place to other locations throughout the world.

**9.** See in this regard the Silent Witness and North East South West House projects.

**10.** The use of very evocative representations makes the environmental phenomena represented in them (the color, the atmosphere, the character of the pieces) appear as integral to the projects, so that, when the Masques travel from one place to other, the associated structure of experiences also moves. See, for example Hejduk and Shkapich, *Riga, Vladivostok, Lake Baikal*; and John Hejduk and Gregory Palestry, *A Berlin Masque* (New York: Chelsea Associates, 1982).

**11.** Hejduk and Shapiro, "John Hejduk or the Architect Who Drew Angels," 75–76.

Such movement between location and totality is a crucial aspect among the diverse theoretical analyses Hejduk's work has motivated. Edward Mitchell opines that Hejduk is reacting to globalization by proposing a view of architecture and the urban as an "energized network."[12] Robert Somol treats the projects as an exploration of the dialectics of part to whole, and borrows Gilles Deleuze and Félix Guattari's philosophical vocabulary to interpret Masques as "war-machines" and "agents of deterritorialization" that are incompatible with the agenda of neoliberalism.[13] For him the projects move from place to place to subvert their social and physical conditions. For her part Catherine Ingraham thinks Masques's nomadism inflicts a degree of violence upon the places where they intervene, as symbolized by the bellicose aspect of most of the pieces. In her view, instead of accepting local conditions Hejduk imposes a new form of wilderness.[14] All told, Masques's policy of place-activation is a policy of place-questioning, which points to connecting to other territories and forming an alternative territorial system. The projects are always physically and socially unrelated to the cities where they are located. Moreover, their evolution shows a progressive abandonment of the possibility of delimitation. The Berlin Masque, for example, is confined to a sector of the city, whereas in Riga, Vladivostok, and at Lake Baikal, the projects are a mere collection of site-less elements **[fig. 4]**.[15]

Hejduk's writings do not contain philosophical references. Somol's Deleuzian reading, as other attempts to read Masques through a poststructuralist lens, is, in this sense, a valid effort to interpret and situate the architect's work as part of an epochal attempt to supersede some aspects of modernity's spatial project.[16] Hejduk's position also resonates with some of Martin Heidegger's postulates. Masques's critique of totalization and its proliferating, architectural pluralism parallel the German philosopher's critique of reducing the world to a unified "world-picture" that can be technically instrumentalized and his alternative understanding of the world as an "interconnected web of practices and objects that are public and shared but cannot be fully articulated or rationalized."[17] Hejduk's praise of the collective construction of Masques around the world approaches Heidegger's reconceptualization of artifacts as "things," as tools to assemble collectives and to visualize "shared modes of relating to each other and all the entities of the world."[18]

The resulting form of world-building is the contrary to a unified, overarching world-project. It postulates, instead, a form of architectural practice aimed at

**12.** Edward Mitchel, "The Nature Theater of John Hejduk," in Hays, *Hejduk's Chronotope*, 55.

**13.** Somol, "One or Several Masters," 109–111.

**14.** Catherine Ingraham, "Errand, Detour, and the Wilderness Urbanism of John Hejduk," in Hays, *Hejduk's Chronotope*, 130–132.

**15.** Wim Van Den Bergh, "Icarus' Amazement, or the Matrix of Crossed Destinies," in Hejduk, *The Lancaster / Hanover Masque*, 96. Van den Bergh points out, in relation to Hejduk's late projects: "With this transformation within the planning model from a spatial disposition in a static territory to a spatial disposition in a kind of dynamic field, the objects lose their topological positions and become places in a provisional and essentially mobile spatial 'articulation,' which consists of movements and charges with volatile static moments and markings."

**16.** Stan Allen, "Nothing but Architecture," in Hays, *Hejduk's Chronotope*, 87.

**17.** John Tresch, "Technological World-Pictures: Cosmic Things and Cosmograms," *Isis* 98, no. 1 (2007): 86. Accessed online July 1, 2018: http://dx.doi.org/10/1086/512833

**18.** Tresch, "Technological World-Pictures," 89.

19. Hejduk and Shapiro, "John Hejduk or the Architect Who Drew Angels," 75–76.

introducing poetic and political alternatives to the existing world.[19] Hejduk's projects point—just as his colleague Aldo Rossi's work does—to a strategic, postmodern recalibration of architecture's engagement with the world-scale. They propose that the constitution of a poetic vocabulary and of a system of interrelated objects are the only means to contradict the way the world is organized, and to present a vision of a possible alternative. Hejduk's use of Masques to intervene in diverse geographies reveals an interest in the world-space and a symmetrical aversion to its totalization. To combat it, Masques presents architecture as an inexhaustible formal machine that fosters the incessant invention of symbols, narrations, and collectives.

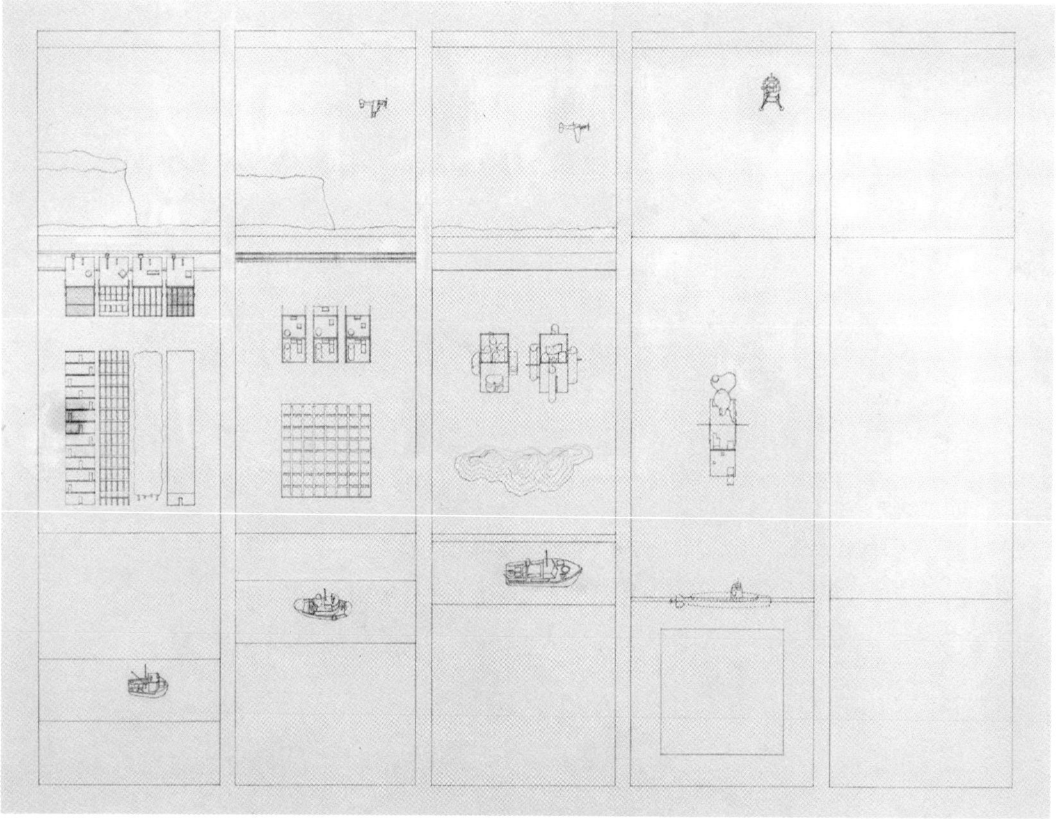

**Figure 1.** The Silent Witnesses. 1976.

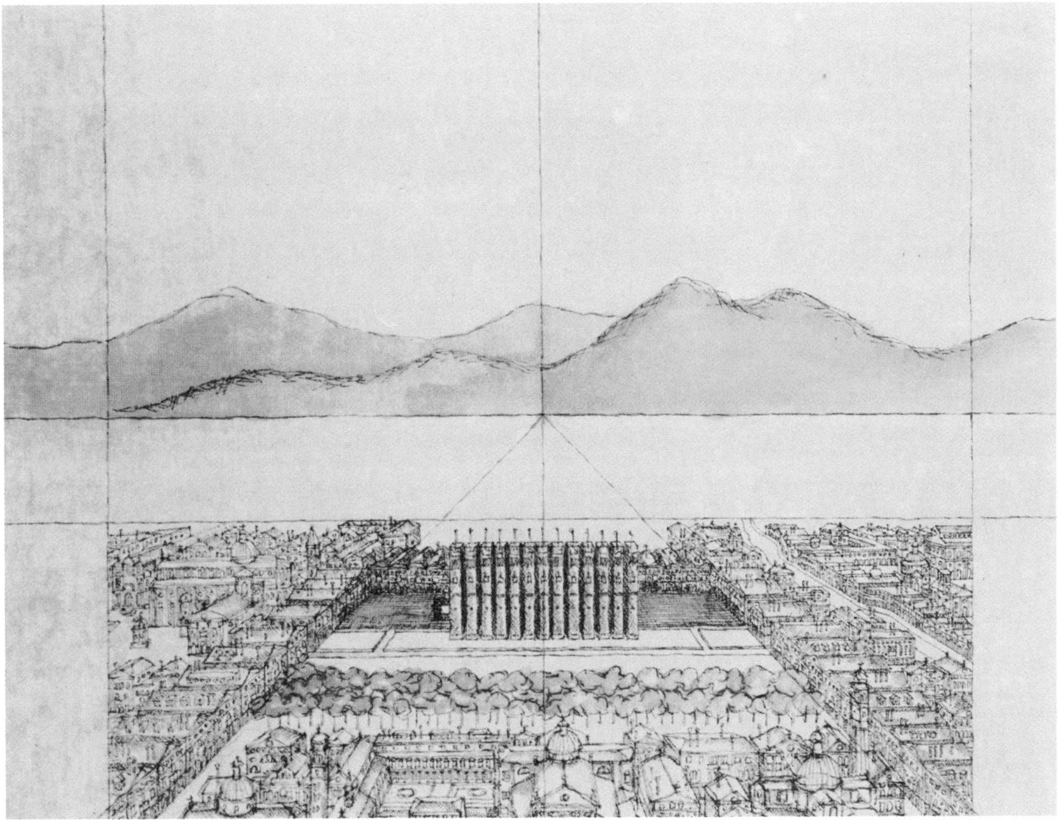

**Figure 2.** The 13 Watchtowers of Cannaregio. 1979.

**Figure 3.** The Hanover/Lancaster Masque. 1980–1982.

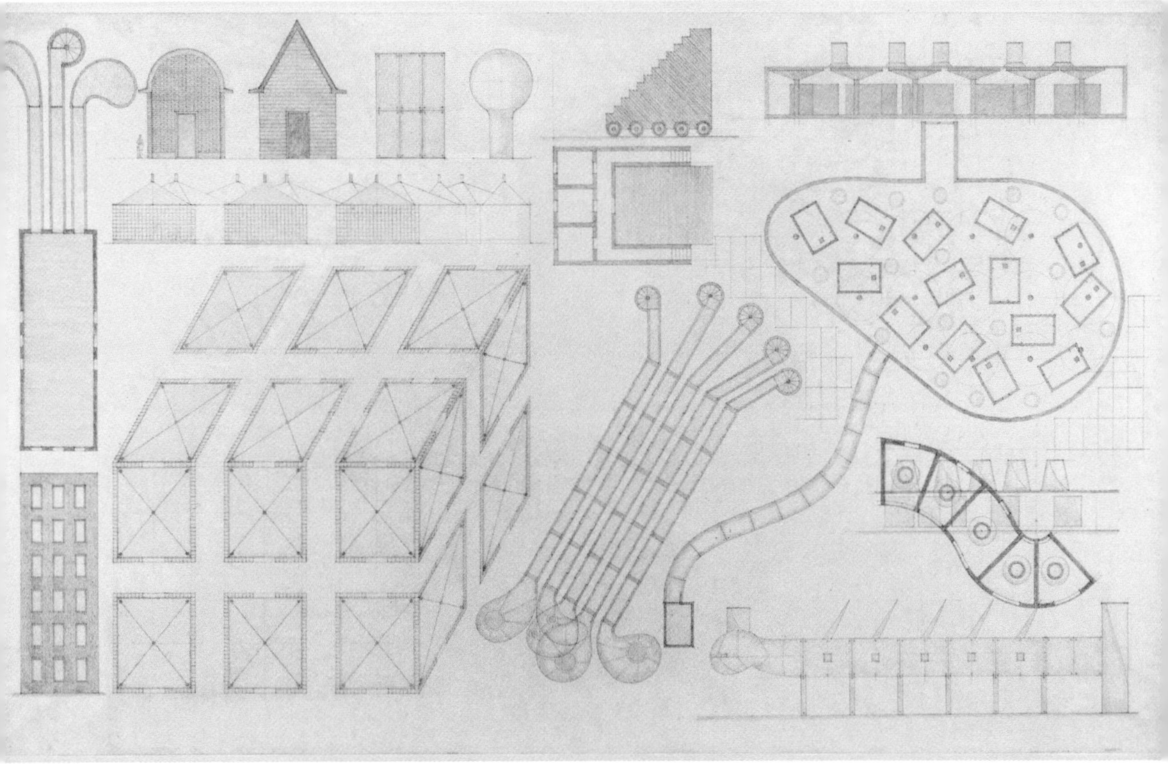

Figure 4. The Hanover/Lancaster Masque. 1980–1982.

# The Equal City

**Project:** 43. **Authors:** Franco Purini (1941) with Laura Thermes (1943). **Date:** 2000. **Themes:** Abstraction. Place(lessness). Telecommunications. Typology.

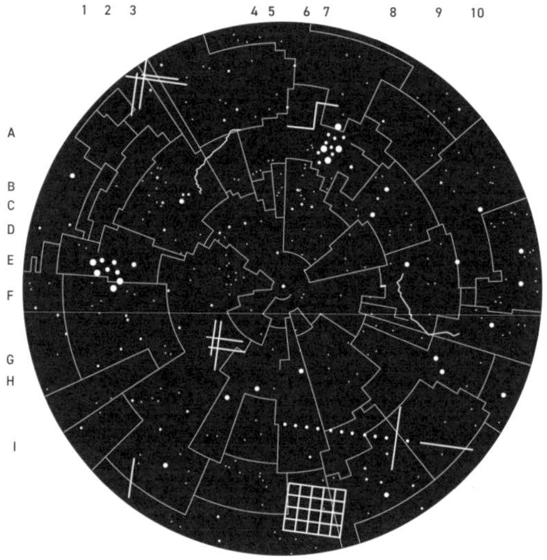


**Figure 0.** The Sky. Fragment. After Franco Purini. 2000.

In the most economically developed countries, in those most actively involved in globalization, architecture has become a superfluous activity.[1] Its role, thinks Franco Purini, no longer consists of fulfilling fundamental material needs. It has stopped being, in Marxist terms, a part of the social structure in order to become pure ideological superstructure—part of our systems of representing the social whole.[2] This reorientation of the discipline toward ideological production has evolved in parallel to two processes that are instrumental to globalization. The first is the increasing reduction of architecture to its image, which has served to transform buildings into cultural commodities circulating within worldwide networks of exchange. For Purini this transformation is a "negative utopia of communication," a bastardized form of universalism whose only message is to support the enclosure of public space by private interests.[3] The second is the "de-terriorialization of the world," the diminution of any traces of spatial identity in order to facilitate a process of "planetary homologation."[4]

Purini suggests two possible ways of operating critically in this context, each of which accepts and replies to one of the aforementioned conditions. The first is to resolutely acknowledge "universal atopism," or the absence of place, as a design leitmotif.[5] This means to promote a new type of linguistic commonality, in which architectural forms are entirely liberated from their original, local origins. The objective here is, in Edgar Morin's expression, to "recover the terrestrial identity of the world" by using architecture as a means to destabilize and transcend the local.[6] The second is to accept the ongoing transformation of design into a means of communication, but to carefully limit the "signals" each project emits to those who critically interrogate our reality.[7] Purini refers to this strategy as the "renaming of the existing" and suggests a three-tier process of design that goes from the "recognition" of a segment of reality to its intentional "appropriation" to the final creation of a "difference" with the current status quo through the configuration of spatial arrangements that suggest alternative forms of the future.[8] The use of design as a means of renaming the "existing" challenges the vision of reality as an inalterable given. It proposes, instead, that the existing is an arena subject to multiple, possible reconfigurations, each of which can become a different articulation of the social whole.

Most of these reflections appear in writings spanning from 1990 to the early 2000s. In historic terms they constitute an attempt to reconsider architectural practice at a time that witnesses the collapse of Eastern European commu-

1. Franco Purini and Laura Thermes, "Três caminhos," in *O que está feito está por fazer: Anonimato, fragmento, descontinuidade*, ed. Jorge Czajkowski (Rio de Janeiro: Centro de Arquitetura e Urbanismo, 1998), 10. Text originally dated 1997.

2. Purini and Thermes, "Três caminhos," 10.

3. Franco Purini, *Scrivere Architettura. Alcuni temi sui quali abbiamo dovuto cambiare idea* (Rome: Prospettive Edizioni, 2012), 41. Our translation.

4. Franco Purini, "Un disegno plurale," 59, and Franco Purini, "Il transito nel Simbolico," in *Dal Progetto: Scritti teorici di Franco Purini 1966–1991*, ed. Francesco Moschini and Gianfranco Neri (Rome: A.A.M., Architettura Arte Moderna, 1992), 169.

5. Purini, "Un disegno plurale," 59.

6. Purini, "Un disegno plurale," 59. Our translation.

7. Purini and Thermes, "Três caminhos," 10. Our translation.

8. Purini and Thermes, "Três caminhos," 13. Our translation.

nism and the rise of digital communications, and which Western, conservative ideologues were trying to advertise as the end of history. Purini's project of renaming the existing explicitly rejects this intention to stop history.[9] Its most explicit translation to design takes place in the installation Purini produces in the year 2000 for the 7th Biennale di Architettura di Venezia, which he titles The Equal City. The work, divided in five sections—The Sky, the World, The House of Man, The Equal City, and The City of 1966—uses the two previously outlined strategies in order to propose an alternative vision of globalization. On one hand, it proposes an extremely abstract, "grammatological" architecture that reduces form to its most elemental geometric attributes.[10] On the other, the project proceeds by individualizing some of the elements that in the late twentieth century are shaping the global—urban expansion, infrastructures, networks of information, satellite communications—in order to suggest how to possibly reconfigure them.

This reconfiguration begins at the cosmic scale. Purini's first proposal consists of a new image of the nocturnal firmament. In The Sky, extremely elemental geometric forms such as grids, lines, suprematist bars, and circles configure new, artificial constellations made of satellites **[figs. 0, 1, and 2]**. The proposal counters our incapacity to understand the sky as part of our lives by giving form to the still invisible networks of communication. Its final aspiration is to recover the capacity of architecture to express a universal totality: a cosmic order related to the terrestrial one.[11] Looking at the sky, we would see the requirements of planetary logistics, and we would connect the apparent fixity of the terrestrial to the fleeting networks that sustain world relations. Purini's piece turns an emerging, potentially pernicious phenomenon—the alteration of night sky by satellites—into a motive for symbolization.[12]

Purini's next section, The World, adopts a similar logic **[fig. 3]**. In this case, Purini proposes to provide "a new measurement of the planet" based on the social and spatial dynamics of globalization.[13] The project redistributes the meridians and parallels so that they emanate from the leading global cities. Similarly, it tilts the angle of the Equator and the Greenwich meridian, thus transforming the existing system of coordinates into a new "model of disequilibrium."[14] Both operations reject the uncritical assimilation of the human structuring of the world to the physical conditions of terrestrial space, and favor the creation of new geographical subdivisions grouping together otherwise unrelated areas. Through them, the division of the earth would no longer be based on naturalizing considerations, but on relational ones—a shift that Purini considers

**9.** Purini and Thermes, "Três caminhos," 12–13. Our translation.

**10.** Purini, "Un disegno plurale," 59. The term "grammatology" refers to Jacques Derrida's work.

**11.** Franco Purini, "The Equal City," *Compasses. Architecture and Design* (2001): 116. Our translation.

**12.** Only very recently, and in the light of current initiatives such as Elon Musk's Starlink, astronomers have raised concerns about the impact that satellites can have in the observation of night sky. See https://www.nationalgeographic.com/science/2019/05/elon-musk-starlink-internet-satellites-trouble-for-astronomy-light-pollution/. Accessed online June 17, 2019.

**13.** Franco Purini, *Le opere, gli scritti, la critica* (Rome: Electa, 2000), 207.

**14.** Purini, *Le opere, gli scritti, la critica*, 207. Our translation.

15. Purini, "The Equal City," 116.

16. Purini, *Le opere, gli scritti, la critica*, 205. Our translation.

necessary to create a new form of universality based on the relations among different and contrasting entities, and not on mere socioeconomic affinities or supposedly immutable natural factors.[15]

While these two proposals view globalization positively, the next one presents a more critical vision of its spatial consequences. Below the new parallels and meridians of The World lies an evenly distributed grid. This grid represents The Equal City, the urban model that accompanies Purini's planetary proposals **[fig. 4]**. In this case the term city is equivocal. What Purini defines is a "metropolitan infinitum," an unlimited urban field in which the spatial constituents of the former city are reduced to its most elemental conditions.[16] These are: individual private residences, huge spatial condensers for the collective facilities and the productive systems, infrastructures of transport, and voids. Among them float the vestiges of what used to be the city, fragments of a disappeared form of life—their geometric complexity contrasting with the absolute regularity and radical repetition of The Equal City, reflecting a dependence on local conditions that the new city has completely overcome.

Life in this city revolves around the relation between subject and planet. The fourth piece of the installation, The House of Man, is a housing unit for a single individual, which, repeated *ad infinitum* across the world, constitutes the basic piece of The Equal City. One of its walls is a large screen whose role is to create a dual dynamic of reception/emission of data. Toward the interior of the house, the screen receives every type of information and allows the inhabitant to connect to the entire world. Facing the outside, it retransmits what happens inside the house. This dual process already characterized the Club of a New Social Type designed by Ivan Leonidov, a major influence for Purini, who not only shares with the Soviet architect the use of a very abstract and elementary architectural grammar, but also the consideration of infrastructural and informational space as a fundamental enabler of world relations **[project 9]**. The last piece presented at the Biennale, Purini's and his professional partner Laura Therme's 1966 design of an ideal city, insists precisely on the importance that the architect always gave to infrastructures and information. This is a city that allows its inhabitants to manage television and radio flows and in which the urban form derives from the infrastructures of communication. Taken together, the diverse scales of the Biennale works emphasize that the world is increasingly pervaded by information, and the necessity of expressing architecturally that fact.

By presenting together his very first projects of 1966 and his new production, Purini situates the relations architecture-world as a recurrent thematic of his work. Certainly, already the most elaborate of his early writings, the 1973 article "Il progetto e il 'luogo'" (The project and the place), focuses on what should be the specificities of architectural design once designers acknowledge that the scope of architecture corresponds to the totality of the earth.[17] His answer to this question derives from evaluating the work of some international architects (the Japanese Metabolists, Yona Friedman, Archigram) and, especially, that of two salient Italian ones: Vittorio Gregotti and Aldo Rossi **[projects 21, 24, 25, 30, and 41]**. The central components of Purini's theoretical proposal are at this moment the notion of "culture of recovery of the existing"—a prefiguration of the later "renaming of the existing"—and the idea that the world should be addressed by acting at the smallest conceivable scale. The former implies revising Gregotti's theses in *The Territory of Architecture* and the latter elaborating a notion of "place" (*luogo*) that differs from the idea of "locus" that Rossi had influentially proposed.[18] For Purini, place is the "minimal portion of the physical world in which it is possible to perceive a process of transformation . . ."[19] It is an instrumental notion whose value is to define a spatial entity independent from the space of the city, thus enabling architecture to operate anywhere. It is, also, a tool to focus design on the confrontation between nature and construction.[20] Methodologically, Purini proposes to excavate the history of the place in order to recover a sense of the original landscape. His strategy is to create maximal tension between project and site in order to highlight that architecture is always a modification of the physical Earth. The transformation of the world is the horizon of architectural production, but it is always addressed by working at other, potentially minimal, scales. This is the possibility that his 1970s territorial interventions for Como, Fermo, Latina, Palermo, Firenze, and Calabria (the last three, significantly, with Gregotti) try to prove.

At first glance, the Venice Biennale installation rejects these early considerations. It substitutes the notion of place with universal atopism, the minimal intervention for the design of the cosmic and terrestrial scale. Yet, there are coincidences in the tools and goals of these two phases of Purini's work that show how strongly the attention Italian architects paid to territory in the 1960s and 1970s helped to support a broader consideration of the world scale. The two phases of Purini's work privilege the use of finite, geometrically severe, abstract architectural objects—autonomous artifacts in the Rossian sense. They also insist on the use of architecture as a means of reconfiguring our perception

17. Franco Purini, "Il progetto e il 'luogo'," in Moschini and Neri, *Dal Progetto: Scritti teorici di Franco Purini 1966–1991*, 11.

18. Aldo Rossi, *The Architecture of the City* (Cambridge, MA: MIT Press, 1982 [1966]), 103.

19. Purini, "Il progetto e il 'luogo'," 20. Our translation.

20. Franco Purini, *Luogo e Progetto* (Rome: Editrice Magma, 1976), 16–21.

of the existing without entirely substituting it, which has its roots in Gregotti's thought. More importantly, both emphasize the artificiality and regularity of architecture in order to radicalize the contrast between architecture and a primeval nature. Nowhere is Purini's aspiration to recover the original place more explicit than in his proposal to entirely reorganize the night sky and regain a sense of cosmic wonder. Nowhere is his early intention to "express the sense of human inhabitation of the earth as an original event" and to produce "radical alternatives to the existing" more ambitiously formulated than in his proposed modification of the coordinate system. The poetic and political impulses of the two phases of Purini's work are the same. The difference is that the awareness of the consolidation of a new global hegemon motivates, at the turn of the millennium, an equally vigorous scalar response. The conceptual and design arsenal elaborated in the 1960s is repurposed to imagine, now entirely, a different planet. Atopism and abstraction are not the negation of place, but the mark of a need to understand at what scale place now happens.

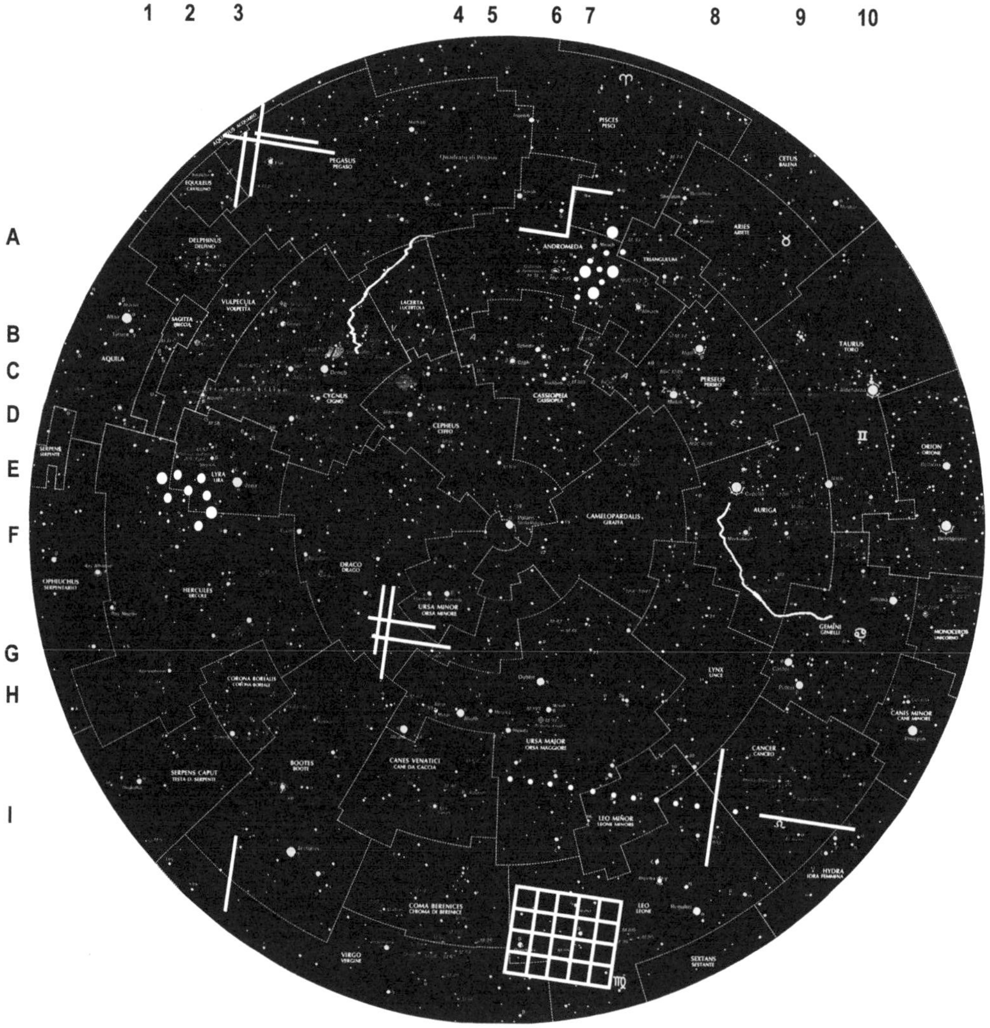


**Figure 1.** The Sky. 2000.

**Figure 2.** The Sky. 2000.

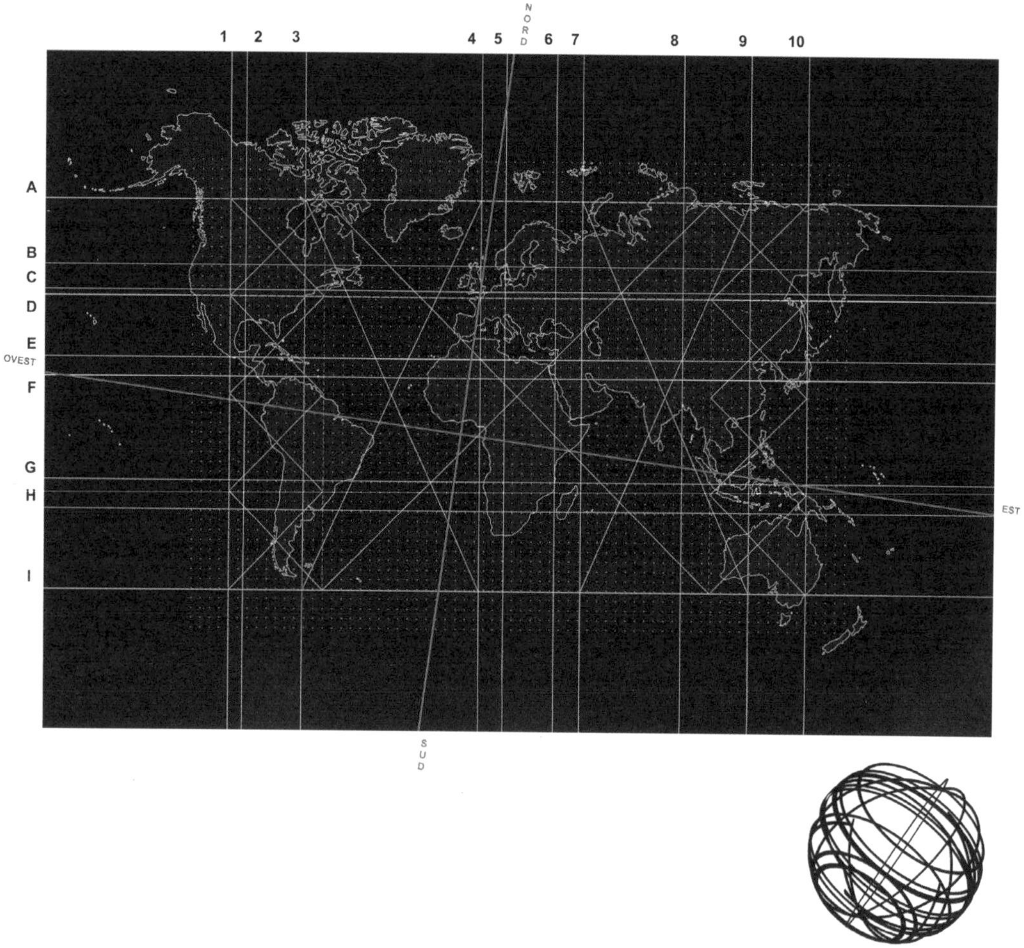


Figure 3. The World. 2000.

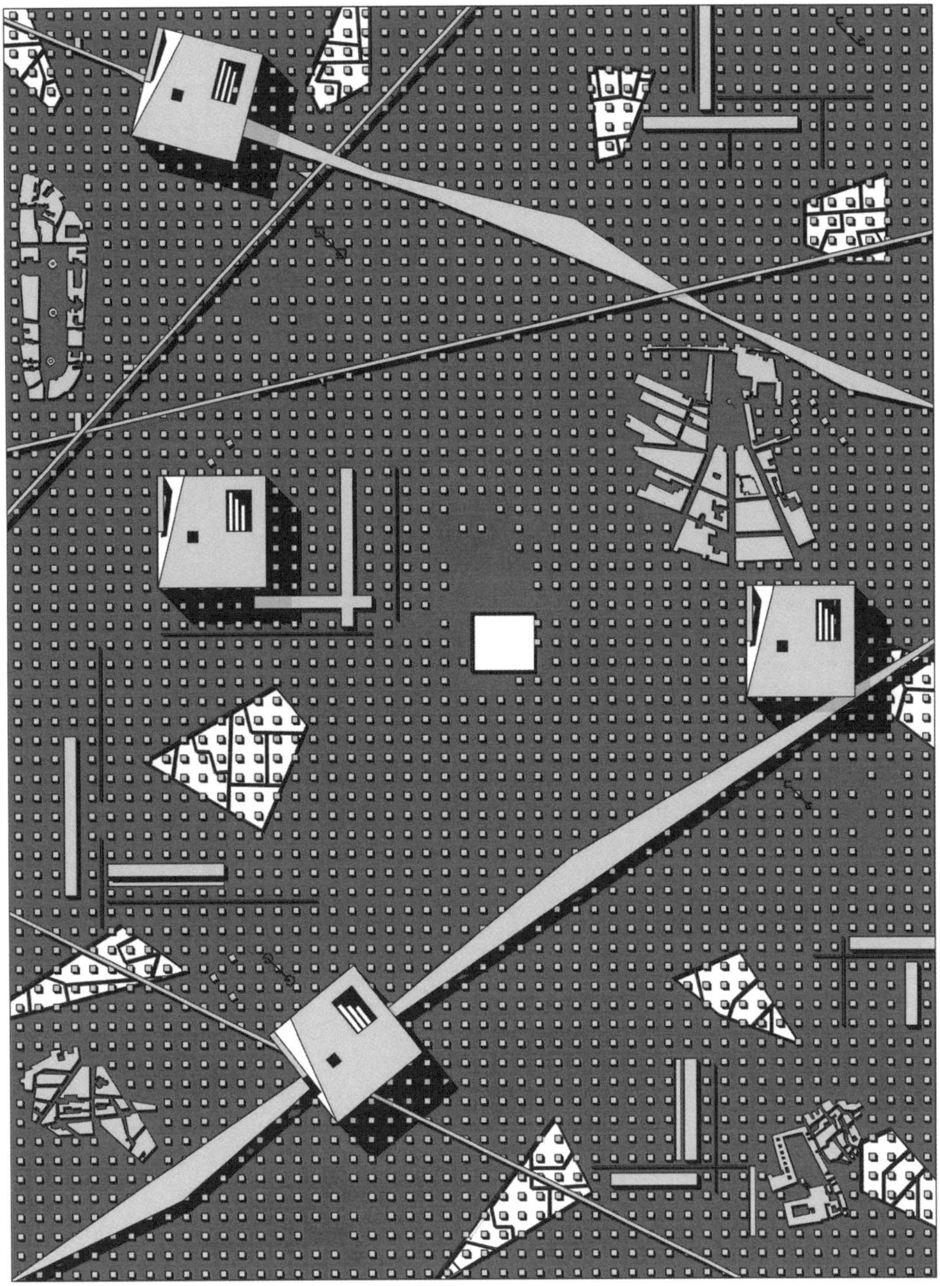

Figure 4. The Equal City. 2000.

# Orban Space

**Project:** 44. **Author:** T.O.P. Office: Luc Deleu (1944) with Isabelle De Smet and Steven Van den Bergh. **Date:** 2006–.
**Themes:** Colonialism. Geo-visualization. Geopolitics. Taxonomy.

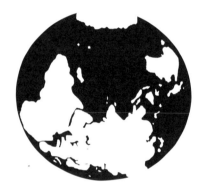

**Figure 0.** T.O.P Office logo. After Luc Deleu. 1970.

"Orbanism," affirms Luc Deleu, is the opposite of "Globalism."[1] The latter term stands only for capitalism and especially for the neoliberal order that has become dominant since the disappearance of the communist systems of Eastern Europe and the USSR. Orbanism—a term Deleu coins by merging the Latin word *orbis* with the term urbanism—represents, instead, a form of resistance that calls for the construction of a common public sphere and for the emergence of different forms of political and social organization. Nowhere is this ambition to change how we conceive and project the world more evident than in the logo Deleu designs in 1970 for T.O.P Office, the architectural firm that he founds that year with his wife Laurette Gillemont. The O in T.O.P, an acronym of Turn On Planning, is an upside-down globe. Antarctica sits on top. The positions of East and West are inverted. The Indian Ocean occupies the center of the earth **[fig. 0]**.

Deleu's critique of globalism is not, by any means, an attempt to reduce international social and economic integration. On the contrary, the intensification of the relations between countries is "not only evident but also indispensable."[2] His hope is the consolidation of "a world with global people and global institutions, in which there is a clearer view of our global rights, obligations, and responsibilities."[3] The many facets of Deleu's production since 1970 constitutes a series of architectural acts destined to create the circumstances for the emergence of such a world by revealing the conditions of contemporary globalization and the means through which society can change its course. These, the architect insists, do not imply the impossible task of designing the whole planet, but the situation of its scale as the horizon of every architectural production.[4] Urban space is a contribution to such a possible transformation; one that interrogates how we can articulate forms of public space that operate at the scale of the planet.

Deleu's interest in open, public space dates back to his first formulation of orbanism in the 1980 *Orbanism (Orban Planning) Manifesto*, where the architect states: "Free Space is his [the architect's] goal from now on."[5] This affirmation will acquire new relevance after the 1989 collapse of communism. In a historic situation in which, according to Deleu, architects are asked to design the ultimate image of capitalist society, it becomes increasingly important to reorient the discipline toward the construction of the public sphere **[project 43]**. It is through this commitment to the public that urban planning can create "an or-

1. Luc Deleu, *De Onaangepaste Stad: Werkdocumenten NAi96 = The Unadapted City: Work in Progress NAi96* (Rotterdam: NAi Publishers, 1996), 14.

2. Luc Deleu, *Urbi et Orbi: De Onaangepaste Stad* (Gent: Ludion, 2002), 22.

3. Deleu, *Urbi et Orbi*, 22.

4. Luc Deleu, *Éthique de l'architecture* (Saint-Benoît Du Sault: Tarabuste, 1989), 6.

5. Luc Deleu, *Orbanistic (Orban Planning) Manifesto.* Accessed online March 1, 2019: http://www.topoffice.to/Orban%20Planning%20Manifesto.html

ban framework and . . . become a part of a larger whole, global planning."[6] This interest in the public sphere, which progressively unfolds after 1980, will come together in the investigation for Orban Space.

Fundamentally, Orban Space is a research project about the many forms in which public spaces are built around the earth and about the possibility of creating a common analytical and design framework to study and design them. The work starts with the premise that open, unbuilt space constitutes a form of universal common, and with the recognition that these spaces are articulated at multiple scales, ranging from the urban to the regional, national, and planetary—like the oceans.[7] To understand the possible ways of interconnecting this diversity, Deleu suggests a "cataloging of [these] space types on a planetary scale" that can "raise spatial planning to a higher scale."[8] This taxonomical drive leads Deleu and his collaborators Isabelle De Smet and Steven Van den Bergh to search, through dictionaries and encyclopedias as well as in legal and administrative documents from several countries, for as many forms as possible of classification and definition of public space.[9] The first result of the work is a vast glossary of abstract terms compiled in the 1,000-page-long *Terminology* (2006–ongoing).[10] There they divide their findings into seven categories reflecting the many processes that inform the constitution of the world scale and the multitude of spaces affected by them. These categories are: 1. Scale; 2. From Virginity to Urbanization; 3. Water: Mother of Infrastructural Space; 4. Wake Up and Dream: the City; 5. Fora: Setting and Location; 6. Artificial and Cultured Landscapes; 7. Public Space: from Wild to Domesticated.[11]

The taxonomic procedure subjects the idea of public space to a strong process of abstraction. The accumulation of terminological data disregards materiality and differentiation. Its goal is simply to accumulate concepts. These operations of accumulation, abstraction, and generalization are a fundamental part of the proposal—as we will see, they enable the possibility of differentiating by understanding first what can become universal. The visual explorations of Orban Space thus emphasize the importance of abstraction. In the drawing Orban Space Analytics, the seven categories seem to occupy different sheets of paper, which are then overlaid on cosmic space, over the constellations **[fig. 1]**. What these different layers represent is only information: data, texts, flows of relations, numerical grids. Orban Space is, in this sense, an analytical, informational project establishing the conditions for possible, still undefined, forms of spatial intervention.

**6.** Luc Deleu, "Spaceship Earth" (unpublished), quoted in Felicity Scott, "Turn of Planning: Dreams of a New Mobility," in *Luc Deleu–T.O.P. Office: Orban Space*, ed. Wouter Davidts, Guy Châtel, and Stefaan Vervoort (Amsterdam: Valiz; Stroom, 2012), 189.

**7.** Deleu, *Urbi et Orbi*, 42.

**8.** Deleu, *Urbi et Orbi*, 42.

**9.** Wouter Davidts, "Architecture without Address," in Davidts, Châtel, and Vervoort, *Luc Deleu–T.O.P. Office: Orban Space*, 229.

**10.** Wouter Davidts and Stefaan Vervoort, *Orban Space: Luc Deleu–T.O.P. Office: Four Decades of Proposals and Recommendations for Public Space on the Scale of the Earth* (Antwerp: Extra City Kunsthal, 2013), 6. Accessed online March 1, 2019: https://wouterdavidts.files.wordpress.com/2010/02/orban-guide-en.pdf

**11.** Davidts, "Architecture without Address," 229.

The importance the textual register has in Orban Space characterizes Deleu's approach to architecture. The architect's preoccupation with the planetary scale begins directly after graduating in 1970. It is initially motivated by the perception of certain sociospatial trends that he perceives as problematic—mainly translating demographic growth to the expansion of urbanization and the consequent intensification of land consumption—and by illuminating intellectual discoveries such as the works of Buckminster Fuller, and Marshall McLuhan, and the photographs of Earth taken from Apollo 10 in 1969 **[projects 6 and 14]**. The direct consequence of Deleu's interest in this scale is a critique of the institution of architecture similar to the one initiated in art in the 1960s, as the title of his first exhibition, Farewell to Architecture (1970), attests. This process of institutional critique implies, on one hand, rejecting the participation of architects in some of the most settled parts of the process of construction. Deleu theorizes the world as if it is an ecological process where auto-regulated relations among individual agents are paramount. Because of this, he believes that those spatial operations that can be carried out at the individual scale should be executed by individual agents, without architectural intervention, while architecture and governmental action should be limited to creating the framework for large-scale forms of organization.[12] Correspondingly, for instance, housing should be built by citizens, as he suggests in his 1979 "Proposal for the abolishment of the law protecting the title and the profession of the architect."[13] The fact that this proposal consists initially just of its mere textual enunciation reflects the other side of Deleu's critique to conventional forms of architectural practice. To reduce architecture to building limits its scope. His is a multifaceted activity in which writing proposals, creating exhibitions and art pieces, building public space installations, producing images, researching, designing urban models or actual neighborhoods, have the same value. For Deleu, addressing the world requires taking advantage of every possible opportunity, intervening at every scale, using all possible design tactics. Once the planet is situated as a framework for design, it is possible to instrumentalize that framework in multiple ways and media.

For Deleu, the final result of all these activities is the production of theory. As he affirms, "the orbanist (orban planner) is now primarily a theoretician."[14] This theory can be produced by textual means, but they must always address the material and spatial realm. In this sense, the cataloging of the public spaces in Orban Space is nothing but the last episode of a series of attempts to create knowledge through the manipulation of the very materials and spaces that

**12.** Deleu, *Orbanistic (Orban Planning) Manifesto.*

**13.** Maarten Delbeke, "Being an Architect, Producing Theory, Making Architecture," in Davidts, Châtel, and Vervoort, *Luc Deleu–T.O.P. Office: Orban Space,* 78. In this case, the enunciation leads to action. Deleu decides to sign almost a hundred houses that he had not designed, a fact that causes a legal conflict with the Belgian association of architects.

**14.** Deleu, *Orbanistic (Orban Planning) Manifesto.*

structure globalization. Deleu's first important project, the 1972 competition entry for the University Institute Antwerp, which he titles Mobile Medium University, proposes a contemporary vision of the idea of "University" by placing the institution in three former aircraft carriers that would circumnavigate the planet, thus allowing the students to become "real world citizens."[15] Not only does the operation combine pedagogical purposes with geopolitical ones, as Felicity D. Scott has noted.[16] It also brings to light the importance of the aquatic medium as a fundamental enabler of international relations and the technologies that construct a particular form of world order—in this case, military technology structured around NATO. This type of operation, consisting of the appropriation and subversion of materials of hegemonic globalization, is a constant leitmotif in Deleu's work. The Proposal for a Worldwide Windmill Network (1981) suggests how to move toward sustainable forms of energy consumption by placing one windmill on every high-tension pylon of the ubiquitous electricity network **[fig. 3]**. The many works he executes using standardized shipping containers directly employ the technology that universalizes the exchange of commodities, which is now appropriated for civic purposes **[fig. 2]**. What all these pieces do is foreground the actual materiality, size, and scale of the artifacts that support the global. By placing high-tension pylons in public spaces, as he did in his dramatic intervention Scale & Perspective with Two Electricity Pylons (Ghent, 1986), or by creating monumental forms as triumphal arcs with containers, Deleu measures our quotidian environment against the fabric of globalization **[fig. 4]**. The final goal of these works is to contribute to the production of orban theory, but this process of construction of knowledge is generated by architecturally confronting the physical artifacts that structure the world.

15. Scott, "Turn of Planning," 178.

16. Scott, "Turn of Planning," 178.

The research for Orban Space lacks, still, this important physical dimension. What is more, the only glimpse of the material consequences of the work—the seven models of Orban Space Sector X—exacerbate the analytical, nonphysical character of Orban Space: these are objects of cardboard and plexiglass that subject a specific location in Antwerp to the analytical methods of Orban Space, resulting in the total abstraction of the particular place until it becomes a representation of a generic condition. Yet, it is precisely this operation of abstraction that may ultimately characterize Deleu's pursuit of a different social and spatial system. The urban model Deleu designs in the late 1990s, the Unadapted City, translates the planetary scale to the urban scale by reducing every aspect of the city to a matter of scale and metrics. It eliminates every socio-

17. Cesare Casarino, *Modernity at Sea: Melville, Marx, Conrad in Crisis* (Minneapolis: University of Minnesota Press, 2002), 1–17.

logical variable in order to connect humanity through our most basic common terrestrial patrimony: space itself. The Orban Space glossary is a design tool for similar operations of equivalence and relation. Its abstraction establishes what is common in order to bring into contact what is different and contrasting. Unsurprisingly, for the Orban Space research, Deleu returns to the sea—the medium the architect has continuously explored since Mobile Medium University—by traveling by boat to the Antipodes and by documenting the conditions in between. The sea is the abstract medium par excellence.[17] But it is also the one that has facilitated the encounter of distant geographies and cultures **[project 21]**. This idea—synthesized in the overlaying of Weber, New Zealand, and Madrid in the photomontage that concludes Deleu's first voyage to the Antipodes—is ultimately the purpose of Orban Space: to create the common, abstract, shared forms of public interchange that put what is singular into contact with what is different **[fig. 5]**.

**Figure 1.** Orban Space Analysis. 2006–.

Summer Solstice
Jun 15
Elnath
Aldebaran
Betelgeuse
Equator
Alnilam
Menka
ERID
COLUMBA
EASILY ACCESSIBLE, NOT RESTRICTED, NOT MONITORED, ALWAYS OPEN PUBLIC PROPERTY FOR EVERYBODY / NOT ACCESSIBLE, RESTRICTED, MONITORED, NEVER OPEN PRIVATE PROPERTY FOR NOBODY
URBANIZED PUBLIC SPACE
Infrastructural space
Forum
traditional public fora
urban open space
limited public fora
extension of urban open space
UNDER CONSTRUCTION

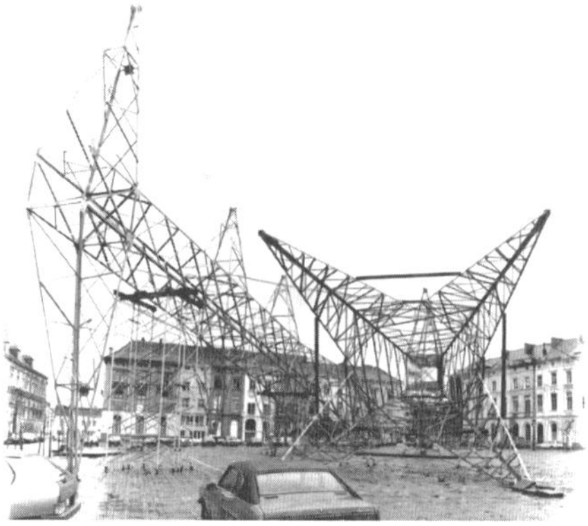

**Figure 2 (Top).** Big triumphal arch, Neuchâtel, Switzerland. 1983.
**Figure 3 (Left).** Proposal for a World Wide Windmill Network. 1981.
**Figure 4 (Right).** Scale and Perspective with Two Electricity Pylons, Ghent, Belgium. 1986.

**Figure 5.** Journey around the world.
Weber, Ernslaw One ltd. (40° 24′ 904 S – 176° 17′ 551 E) over
Madrid, Plaza Mayor (40° 24′ 904 N – 3° 42′ 449 W). 1999.

# Extreme Territories of Urbanization

**Project:** 45. **Authors:** Neil Brenner (1969) and Urban Theory Lab. **Date:** 2011–. **Themes:** Geo-visualization. Geopolitics. Territorial Intensification. Total Urbanization.

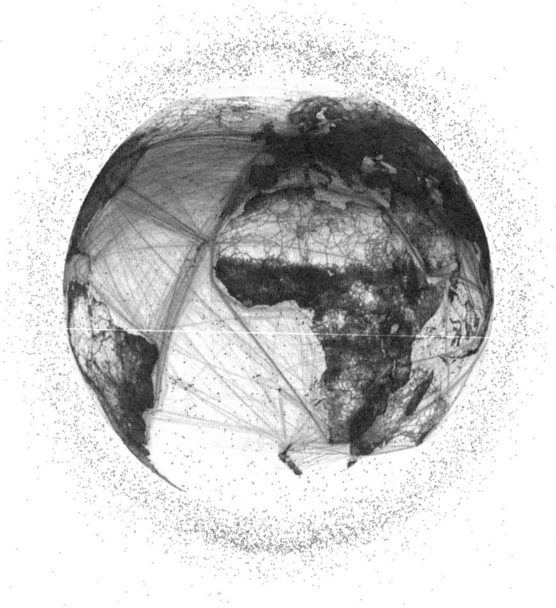

**Figure 0.** Planetary Urbanization. Daniel Ibáñez and Nikos Katsikis, Urban Theory Lab. 2014.

This book begins with Soria y Mata's intuition that cities will spread across the whole globe **[project 1]**. Throughout its pages it is possible to detect how architecture addressed territorial processes involving production and the exploitation of natural resources **[projects 15, 16, 17 and 30]**. It is also possible to see a recurrent interrogation about how urban expansion affects the scales of settlements, and, as a consequence, the very notion of what a settlement is **[projects 23, 34, and 36]**. The work of Neil Brenner with the Harvard University Urban Theory Lab (UTL) accumulates these multiple research interests about the urbanization of the globe as well as challenges some of the epistemological conventions through which urbanization has often been analyzed. Mostly produced after 2010, Brenner's work about the world scale coincides with the consolidation of the idea of "Urban Age," a notion the United Nations Settlement Program starts promoting in 1996 to describe the expected surpassing of the rural population by the urban one, and which gains new currency after 2005 when it was estimated that this demographic shift had already happened. Recognition of this fact immediately affects architectural discourse, leading to the organization of multiple academic and architectural events late in the first decade of the 2000s in which the notion of Urban Age serves to portray a planet dominated by cities.[1] Brenner's work directly addresses these assertions in order to contest the city centrism they entail. It questions: What does the notion of an urban world actually mean? What are its conditions? In which ways does this idea question and challenge the forms in which we have understood the urban? Are we using the right concepts to describe urbanization?

Brenner's definition of the urban world through the expression "planetary urbanization" originates in an article co-written in 2011 with Swiss geographer Christian Schmid, a frequent collaborator.[2] The core of the authors' argument is that urban studies originally define its analytical categories in the late nineteenth and early twentieth centuries and do so in response to the massive migrations from rural areas to cities that are then taking place. The necessity at that moment of defining the specificity of the city in contrast to other forms of settlement and spatial organization motivates the assimilation between the ideas of urbanization and city creation. The urban is, as a result, originally conceptualized in opposition to a non-city condition, often referred to as rural. This methodological lens persists in urban studies nowadays, supporting ideas of an "urban age," in which cities reign supreme.[3] Brenner and Schmid adopt a different perspective. For them, the urban is now an overarching, yet highly

1. Ricky Burdett and Deyan Sudjic, eds., *The Endless City: The Urban Age Project by the London School of Economics and Deutsche Bank's Alfred Herrhausen Society* (London: Phaidon Press, 2007).

2. Neil Brenner and Christian Schmid, "Planetary Urbanization," in *Urban Constellations*, ed. Matthew Gandy (Berlin: Jovis Verlag, 2011). The same year, Andy Merrifield presents a paper based on the notion of "planetary urbanization" at the 2011 meeting of the Association of American Geographers in Seattle. See Andy Merrifield, "The Urban Question Under Planetary Urbanization," *International Journal of Urban and Regional Research* 37, no. 2 (2013): 909–922.

3. Neil Brenner and Christian Schmid, "The 'Urban Age' in Question," *International Journal of Urban and Regional Research* 38, no. 3 (2014): 1.

uneven, sociospatial phenomenon. It is part of a process that has completely reorganized the spatiality of cities, altering their internal hierarchies and densities, and producing blurred "urban territories."[4] It is a condition that has also completely disintegrated the "hinterlands," breaking their original regional scale of connection in favor of new trans-scalar relations with different parts of the world.[5] The urban has engulfed the wilderness. It has incorporated every territory, from outer space, to the oceans, to the deserts, within urban networks. The urban, in sum, lacks an outside. Understanding this phenomenon requires, thus, expanding the focus on cities that historically characterized urban studies and practices in order to address the whole set of sociospatial transformations that urbanization produces worldwide.

Brenner's position builds upon Henri Lefebvre's thinking. The French philosopher suggests in *The Urban Revolution* (1970) that society is approaching a moment of complete urbanization, thus anticipating the condition that Brenner analyzes. The goal of Lefebvre's later book, *The Production of Space* (1974), is to address this condition by creating a theoretical framework that can supersede the existing segmentation of space by different forms of disciplinary knowledge and by their classification into predetermined and often segregated scales such as architecture, city, and territory. The result of this segmentation is the fragmentation of space into niches of specialization for particular disciplines and professions, fostering in turn a new iteration of the process of spatial and intellectual division.[6] Lefebvre counters this division of spaces produced and thought, claiming instead that space is produced *in toto* and therefore it must be conceptualized holistically, while acknowledging that the processes of spatial production are hierarchical, discontinuous, and fragmented. When, in *The Urban Revolution*, the author conceives of contemporary geography as approaching the moment of total urbanization, the term he uses to start describing the spatial conditions of that totality is "urban fabric."[7] Brenner makes an equivalent conceptual move and similarly aims to decipher what the urban fabric is. When explaining his position in relation to the classic procedure of urban studies—from the city toward increasingly large territorial constructs—he affirms: "We invert that intellectual starting point and the analytical frameworks, methodological tactics, and cartographic visions that flow from it, using a planetary (re)orientation as the impetus for a foundational reframing of the urban question as such."[8] Yet, this does not mean understanding urbanization as a single phenomenon with a unique axis of development, always going from the world down. On the contrary, Brenner's position emphasizes that urban-

4. Brenner and Schmid, "The 'Urban Age' in Question," 5.

5. Neil Brenner, "The Hinterland Urbanized?," *Architectural Design* 86, no. 4 (July/August 2016): 118–127.

6. Henri Lefebvre, *The Production of Space* (Oxford, UK: Blackwell, 1991 [1974]), 11.

7. Henri Lefebvre, *The Urban Revolution* (Minneapolis: University of Minnesota Press, 2003 [1970]), 3.

8. Neil Brenner, "Debating Planetary Urbanization: For an Engaged Pluralism," *Environment and Planning D: Society and Space* 36, no. 3 (2018): 6.

ization is an uneven and variegated process, articulated in many different, yet interconnected ways, which has to be fundamentally investigated through the multidirectional logics of open systems.[9]

To understand planetary urbanization, Brenner elaborates a series of epistemological propositions with Schmid. For our purposes, two of them are particularly important. The first implies accepting that the urban is "not a universal form, settlement type, or bounded unit," but a process.[10] Consequently, the analyses he and the UTL develop are mostly oriented toward understanding the dynamic restructuring of space urban processes produce. The second suggests dividing the process of urbanization into "three mutually constitutive moments: concentrated urbanization, extended urbanization, and differential urbanization."[11] As the term "moments" suggests, these are temporal situations, variable in time. The idea of concentration refers to the spatial clusters of population and infrastructure. It is the closest equivalent to the traditional idea of a city. Extended urbanization refers, in turn, to the operationalization of every possible territory as part of the urban networks, so that they productively support the concentrated areas. Finally, the notion of differential urbanization refers to the relentless processes of creative destruction that mediate between the previous two. It is a notion that allows for investigating uneven geographic development as the basis for the constant production of new forms of urbanization. The result of these interactions is, thus, an extremely dynamic vision of urbanization, populated by internal differences and uneven relations—the contrary, somehow, of the ordered vision of the evenly developed urban world Doxiadis's Ecumenopolis depicted **[project 23]**.

A crucial thesis of Brenner's work is that the process of planetary urbanization dramatically intensifies after the 1970s, in parallel to the consolidation of neoliberalism and globalization. Interestingly, the periodization coincides with the waning of the architectural concern with the world scale that we have treated throughout the book. At the very moment when a powerful wave of global spatial transformations is taking place, architecture focuses on its own internal conditions and privileges the space of the city. In this sense, the work that Brenner promotes and develops with the Urban Theory Lab is not only an analytical project designed to understand urbanization, but also an instrumental step toward repositioning design as a way of imagining new territorial possibilities.

**9.** Brenner, "Debating Planetary Urbanization: For an Engaged Pluralism," 8.

**10.** Neil Brenner and Christian Schmid, "Towards a New Epistemology of the Urban?," *CITY* 19, no. 2–3 (2015): 165–166.

**11.** Brenner and Schmid, "Towards a New Epistemology of the Urban?," 166–169.

The research of the Urban Theory Lab represents an example of such reorientation toward territory. The investigation "Extreme Territories of Urbanization," initiated in 2012, aims to understand what the urbanization of the planet means, by analyzing eight extreme cases of extended urbanization: the spatial transformations affecting the Pacific Ocean, the atmosphere, the Arctic, the Himalayas, the Gobi and Sahara deserts, Amazon, and Siberia **[figs. 0 to 4]**.[12] The resulting work studies the means by which these spaces of extended urbanization have become an indispensable part of the urban fabric. Its research focuses on the metabolic circuits of production, resource extraction, and labor, and the infrastructural operations that sustain them.

12. Urban Theory Lab, GSD Research Studio: "Extreme Territories of Urbanization: Regulatory Restructuring," Spring 2014. Accessed online March 20, 2019: http://urbantheorylab.net/news/gsd-research-studio-extreme-territories-of-urbanization-regulatory-restructuring-spring-2014/. See also Urban Theory Lab, "Operational Landscapes: Toward an Alternative Cartography of World Urbanization," 2013–2016. Accessed online March 20, 2019: http://urbantheorylab.net/news/gsd-research-studio-extreme-territories-of-urbanization-regulatory-restructuring-spring-2014/

Through an extremely exploratory use of techniques of geovisualization, ranging from almost anthropological forms of addressing the relation between local sociospatial conditions and planetary processes to the use of charts, diagrams, timetables, maps, and video animations, the work of the Urban Theory Lab unveils the link between spatial transformations and the power relations and institutional organizations that make them possible. What the Urban Theory Lab depicts is a world entirely shaped by trans-scalar relations of production, in which the existence and reproduction of what we usually define as urban—the agglomerations—is only possible by intensifying the operationalization of terrestrial, subterranean, oceanic, and atmospheric space. The collective research visualizes that the post-1970s wave of planetary urbanization increasingly subjects geographical space to multiple, and variable forms of exploitation. The integration of territories into transnational economic circuits motivates vast spatial modifications, including radical ecological modifications, huge infrastructural operations, and regulatory strategies facilitating the appropriation of space by transnational corporations. As a capital-driven process, planetary urbanization proceeds by dispossessing local communities from the use of resources, creating a world increasingly integrated, but also, in multiple ways, unjust.

The theoretical understanding of planetary urbanization and the involvement of design in deciphering its spatial conditions are, in this sense, a necessary step toward the development of a critical project seeking new, more just, forms of planetarization. In the same way that Lefebvre famously accompanied his analyses of the urban with the idea of the right to the city, and David Harvey's neo-Marxian analyses are committed to investigating possible postcapitalist urban worlds, Brenner's critical analyses of planetary urbanization establish the basis for investigating forms of alter-urbanization: "alternative pathways for the production, appropriation, and transformation of space, at once in the sphere of politics, law, social reproduction, ecology, infrastructure and everyday life," which are at once made possible and impeded by contemporary social and spatial conditions.[13] After more than a century of architectural explorations about the organization of the planet, Brenner and his collaborators at the Urban Theory Lab work to produce the concepts that allow us to understand the contemporary conditions of an urban world, to provide methodological tools that make possible its analysis, and to visualize its social and spatial effects. Their work contributes to revealing the ongoing processes of planetarization and, thus, the conditions that any possible critical project of social and spatial transformation should take into account.

**13.** Brenner, "Debating Planetary Urbanization: For an Engaged Pluralism," 15.

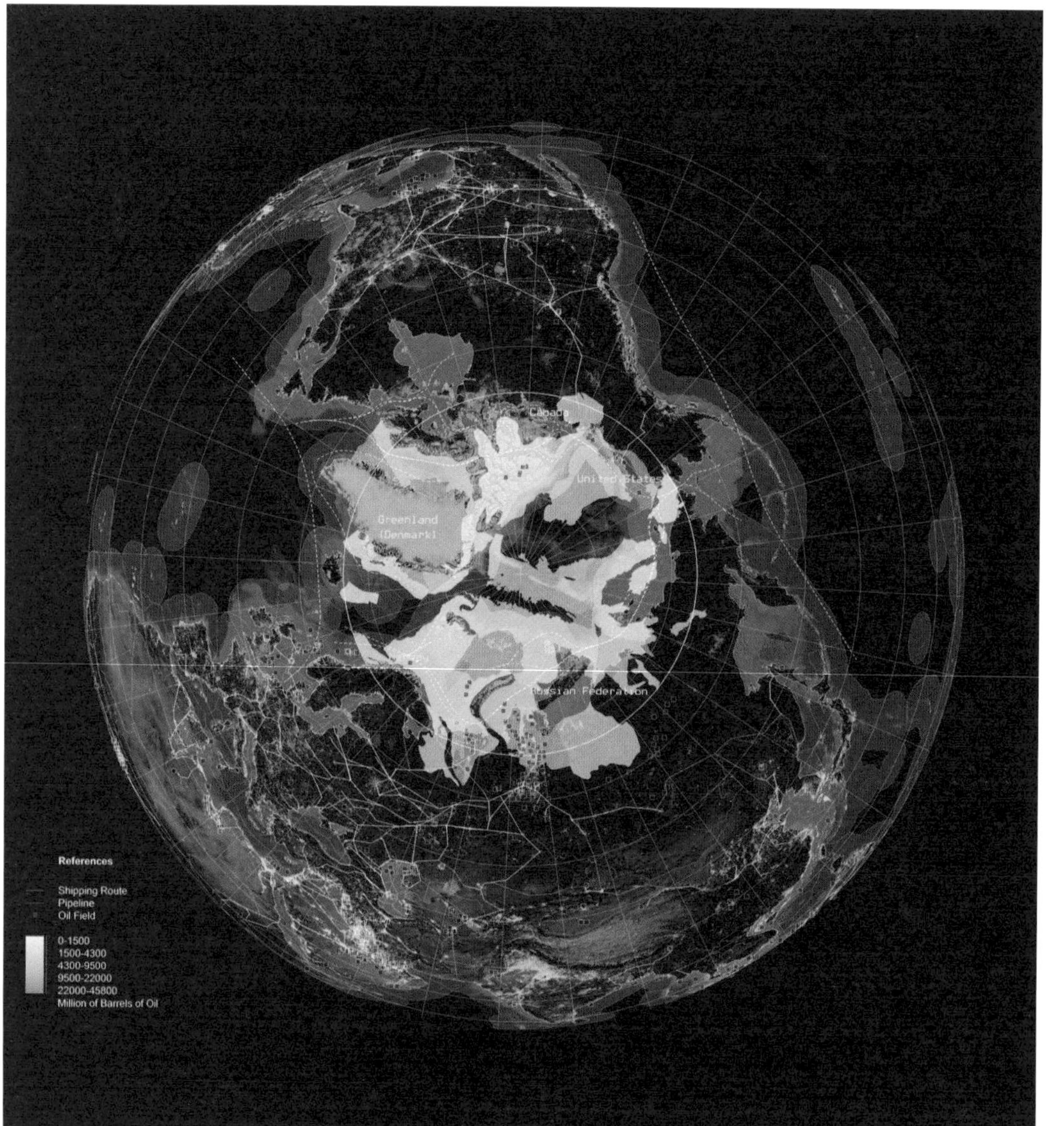


**Figure 1.** Extreme Territories of Urbanization: Arctic. The strategic/speculative space of the Arctic: oil fields, projected oil reserves, pipelines and shipping routes. Grga Basic, Urban Theory Lab. 2014.

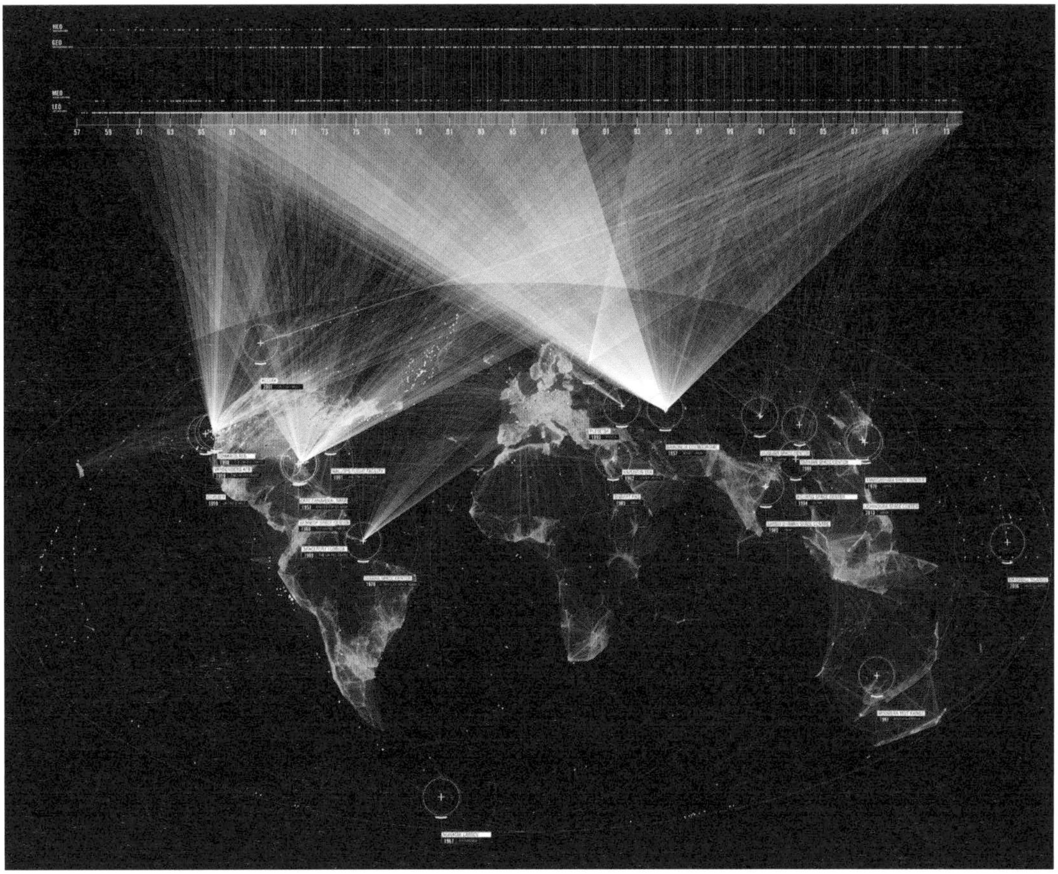

**Figure 2.** Extreme Territories of Urbanization: Atmosphere. Earth's atmosphere has been transformed into a field of logistical coordination in support of urban life. Chris Bennett, Urban Theory Lab. 2014.

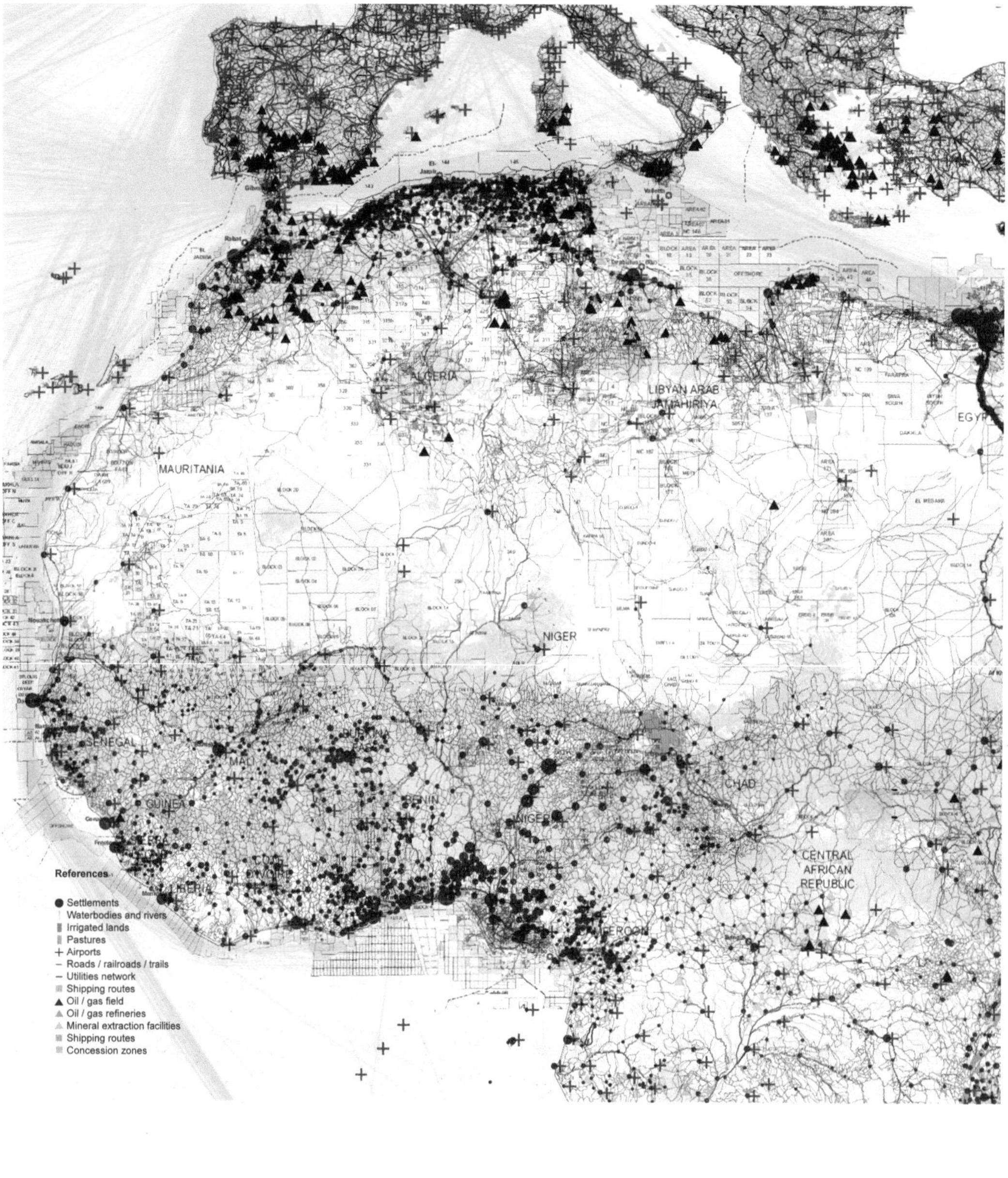


**Figure 3.** Extreme Territories of Urbanization: Sahara. The Sahara contains zones of intensive land use, resource extraction, and colossal industrial infrastructure that support city life elsewhere. Tamer Elshayal and Marianne Potvin, Urban Theory Lab. 2013.

**Figure 4.** Extreme Territories of Urbanization: Himalayas. The Himalayas are today being "infrastructuralized," transformed into a giant hydroelectric machine to support urban growth in India and China.
Vineet Diwadkar, Urban Theory Lab. 2014.

# Geodesign

**Project:** 46. **Author:** Carl Steinitz (1937). **Date:** 2012. **Themes:** Geo-visualization. Geopolitics. Taxonomy. World Urbanization.

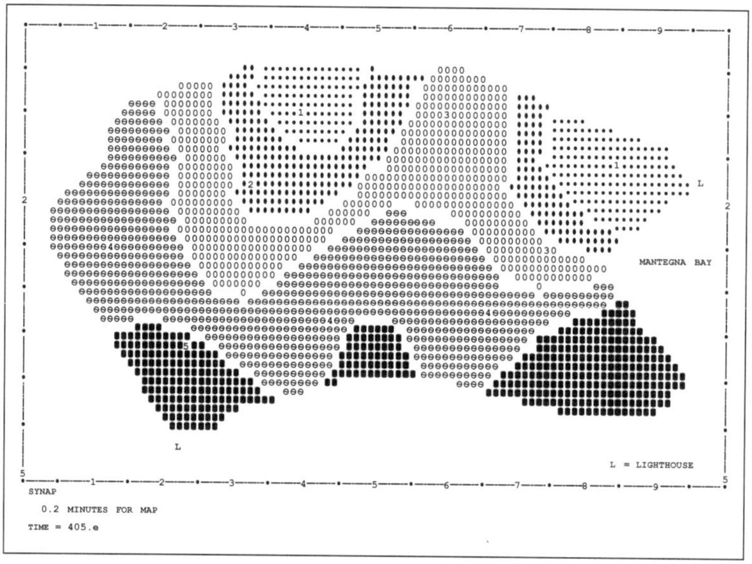


**Figure 0.** SYMAP contour map. After Howard Fischer. 1963.

1. Carl Steinitz, "Congruence and Meaning: The Influence of Consistency Between Urban Form and Activity Upon Environmental Knowledge" (PhD diss., Massachusetts Institute of Technology, 1967), v.

2. SYMAP is initially developed at the Northwestern Technological Institute in 1963 and later completed at the Harvard Graduate School of Design within Fisher's Lab.

3. The software packages developed at the time are systems such as CALFORM, SYMVU, GRID, POLYVRT, and ODYSSEY. Nigel Water, "GIS: History," in *The International Encyclopedia of Geography*, ed. Douglas Richardson (New York: John Wiley & Sons, 2017), 3.

4. Carl Steinitz, "Beginning of Geodesign: A Personal Historical Perspective," in *Geodesign: Past, Present and Future* (Redlands, CA: Esri, 2013), 12.

5. Water, "GIS: History," 3. "The Canada Land Inventory (CLI) was undertaken in the early 1960s as a cooperative, federal-provincial effort. This program resulted in the production of over 12,000 map sheets pertaining to the capability of Canada's lands to support various uses. The Canada Geographic Information System (CGIS) was designed to read, store, manipulate, and analyze thematic map information." Terry Fisher and Connie MacDonald, "An Overview of the Canada Geographic Information System (CGIS)," in *Canada Land Data Systems Selected Papers I, 1979–1980*, vol. 4, Ian Crain Collection, LAC, 610.

6. Water, "GIS: History," 2.

7. Water, "GIS: History," 3.

In 1965 Carl Steinitz finishes his doctoral dissertation in City and Regional Planning at MIT, "Congruence and Meaning: The Influence of Consistency Between Urban Form and Activity Upon Environmental Knowledge," supervised by Kevin Lynch. The dissertation uses a new methodological lens to study the perceptual geography of central Boston after Lynch's own *Image of the City* (1960). By acquiring, processing, mapping, and analyzing data the dissertation asks why certain parts of the city were either included or excluded from Lynch's book. Steinitz's develops his research methods also under the advice of Howard Fisher, the architect who had just invented the Synagraphic Mapping System (SYMAP) **[fig. 0]**.[1] Concluded in 1965 within his newly formed Harvard Laboratory for Computer Graphics and Spatial Analysis, this software is among the first computer programs applied to mapping that integrated functions for spatial analysis.[2] Fisher's Lab grows to become a powerhouse in the expansion of computer mapping, with a handful of other major packages coming from his Lab in the following years.[3] Steinitz's thesis is the first applied test of SYMAP and the very beginnings of processes used in Geographic Information System (GIS), among them: the acquisition of data and its digital encoding for the production of maps **[fig. 1]**.[4] These are processes that Steinitz will evolve to become the very basis of his method to potentially design at the scale of the world.

The 1960s are the formative years of GIS, and the Harvard Laboratory for Computer Graphics and Spatial Analysis, where Steinitz soon becomes an affiliate, spearheads the process within academic circles. Meanwhile, major advances are also taking place in the public and private sectors. Early in that decade, in collaboration with English geographer Roger Tomlinson (often acknowledged as the father of GIS) and the company Spartan Air Services of Ottawa, where Tomlinson works, the Canadian Government's Canada Land Inventory develops the first "fully functional vector-based GIS."[5] Around the same time, the US military also expands the field of analytical cartography with the "US CORONA program of reconnaissance satellites operated by the Central Intelligence Agency from 1959 to 1972 along with the associated SAGE program for processing the imagery."[6] These initiatives become consolidated during the 1970s, when government-supported GIS research starts having a broad applied use, one of the earliest instances being the first geocoded census produced by the US Census Bureau in 1970.[7]

At Harvard Steinitz engages in his first teaching assignment in 1966. It is a multidisciplinary studio that focuses on the future regional development and conservation of the Delmarva Peninsula.[8] Using SYMAP Steinitz involves students "to make and visualize a series of evaluation models for the future land uses under consideration," out of which they propose a design that probably represents "the first application of GIS-modeled evaluation to making a design for a large geographic region" **[figs. 2 and 3]**.[9] This is Steinitz's first regional-scale GIS base map. Even though experimental, it already contains advanced analytical methods that highlight the promise of GIS use in visualizing and setting the ground for design operations; among the methods implemented one would find "a gravity model; various terrain-related analyses; the effect of one map pattern on another; and overlain data maps combined via quantitatively weighted indexes."[10] Steinitz's Delmarva explorations are highly significant as many of the study's concepts are further carried into most of his later work, ultimately evolving into the broader rubric of "geodesign."

The term "geodesign" refers to the action of changing geography by design. It is a method that relies on the extraction of geographic data from a specific context and then processing it using digital technology to inform design operations while simulating possible outcomes and impacts. Steinitz regularly reiterates that geodesign is neither a science nor a profession. There is not such a thing as a "geodesigner"; rather, his position is that "all the relevant design professions and geographic sciences should adopt and adapt geodesign ideas and methods, and then collaborate as needed on the world's most serious geodesign challenges."[11]

Although humans have consciously manipulated geography by means of design for thousands of years, the specificities of geodesign and its intrinsic reliance on digital technology are not conceived until the last third of the twentieth century. The first use of the term seems later yet: "Not later than 1993, Kunzmann (1993) uses the term 'Geodesign' to discuss opportunities and threats related to illustrative sketches communicating ideas of spatial structures like the 'European Banana.'"[12] To this day, Jack Dangermond, who in 1969 founds the first successful commercial GIS company, Esri, and is a strong advocate of the term, credits Steinitz, his professor at Harvard, for introducing him to the methodology and laying the foundations for its widespread adoption.[13]

The most characteristic and fundamental process of geodesign builds upon previous forms of geographic visualization. The technique of layering spatial

8. The Delmarva Peninsula is situated between Delaware and Chesapeake bays, comprising the state of Delaware and parts of Maryland and Virginia.

9. Steinitz, "Beginning of Geodesign," 6.

10. Steinitz, "Beginning of Geodesign," 7.

11. Carl Steinitz, *A Framework for Geodesign: Changing Geography by Design* (Redlands, CA: Esri, 2012), 12.

12. Antje Stokman and Hans-Georg Schwarz-v. Raumer, "GeoDesign–Approximations of a Catchphrase," in *Peer Reviewed Proceedings, Digital Landscape Architecture 2011: Teaching & Learning with Digital Methods & Tools*, ed. E. Buhmann et al. (Dessau, Germany: Anhalt University of Applied Sciences, 2011), 106.

13. Steinitz, *A Framework for Geodesign*, vii.

data progressively evolves since the late Enlightenment on—in 1781 Jean-Alexandre Berthier creates an overlaid map of troop movements at the Siege of Yorktown; later John Snow maps the 1854 cholera outbreak in London.[14] At the beginning of the twentieth century, Warren Manning, who has previously worked for Frederick Law Olmsted, uses the recently invented light tables to combine land information and devise a plan for the development and conservation of the town of Billerica, Massachusetts. This is a time when the United States is producing country-scale maps of its national resources and making them publicly available.[15] Later Manning collects and redraws hundreds of them to the same scale—soil, rivers, forests, etc.—overlaying information. From the combined maps he designs a plan for the entirety of the country, resulting from the combination of a system of parks, urban, commercial, and recreational areas alongside transportation networks. His plan is published in *Landscape Architecture* in 1923 **[fig. 4]**.

These techniques expand after World War II. Town planner Jaqueline Tyrwhitt, who serves as secretary to CIAM and collaborates with Constantinos Doxiadis in the organization of the Delos Symposia, is recognized for her innovative work on British postwar reconstruction through cooperative and decentralized planning practices **[project 23]**.[16] In this work, Tyrwhitt devises techniques of geographic analysis based on the overlay of transparent thematic maps that support her proposals for the New Towns Act of 1947. In so doing, she anticipates the forms of cartographic superposition popularized by the Scottish landscape architect Ian McHarg in the 1960s and later adapted in computerized GIS.[17] In his seminal *Design with Nature* (1969), McHarg suggests organizing geospatial data as a "layer cake" in order to determine potential threats and opportunities in the structuring of land uses.[18] McHarg's superimposed maps resemble a "complex X-ray photograph with dark and light tones," a type of image that would become ubiquitous among landscape and planning circles.[19]

Steinitz is aware of these experiments. Manning's work, for instance, is for him a pure manifestation of geodesign and "one of the most important, bold, and creative designs in our professional history."[20] Yet, the development of the digital techniques of geographic and data visualization on which geodesign relies implies also a strong modification of the geovisualizations advanced by Tyrwhitt and McHarg. Not only does the use of digital technologies lead to the incorporation of incredibly superior amounts of data, it also means that understanding geography is mediated by bits of information. Since the early

**14.** Water, "GIS: History," 16.

**15.** Carl Steinitz, Paul Parker, and Lawrie Jordan, "Hand-Drawn Overlays–Their History and Prospective Uses," *Landscape Architecture* 66, no. 5 (1976): 444.

**16.** Tyrwhitt is also known as the woman behind-the-scenes of famous architectural personalities, ". . . disciple of Patrick Geddes, translator and editor of Sigfried Giedion, and collaborator of Constantinos Doxiadis." Ellen Shoshkes, "Jaqueline Tyrwhitt: A Founding Mother of Modern Urban Design," *Planning Perspectives* 21, no. 2 (2006): 179.

**17.** Shoshkes, "Jaqueline Tyrwhitt," 183.

**18.** Frederick Steiner, "Healing the Earth: The Relevance of Ian McHarg's Work for the Future," *Human Ecology Review* 23, no. 2 (2017): 147.

**19.** Ian L. McHarg, *Design with Nature* (Garden City, NY: Natural History Press, 1969), 35.

**20.** Steinitz, *A Framework for Geodesign*, 10.

1960s' mapping experiments to the contemporary satellite imagery, it is the pixel of information that determines what is possible to measure and see. It is this sort of interrelation between digital technology and geovisualization that Steinitz will promote from the 1960s on. The publication in 2012 of *A Framework for Geodesign* will place this approach to geography under the rubric of geodesign, while seeking to formulate an epistemological theory and a design methodology based on it.

Steinitz's book outlines organizational methods and includes practical examples for thinking about the strategies regarding how to implement geodesign and the possible steps to building a coherent flow of information among all of the stakeholders involved. The book does not offer fixed formulas, but it tries to build a methodological system based upon Steinitz's previous work *A Framework for Theory Applicable to the Education of Landscape Architects (and Other Environmental Design Professionals)* (1990), which facilitates thinking of and managing the multiple scenarios that involve designing with digital data at the geographical scale.[21] The framework revolves around a set of questions that Steinitz believes any geodesign study should ask in order to build consensus about the best design solutions and avoid mishandling the data during the process. Owing to the multiscalar aspect of GIS-oriented studies and the steady increase in the amount of available information at any given moment, Steinitz sees the process of geodesign as one that can only play out properly when it is collaborative and inclusive, especially by connecting the design professions to the geographic sciences. Furthermore, he believes the aspirations of geodesign are global in nature. The first step is the need to "understand our world (as best we can)," and from there individualize the solutions for particular projects.[22]

"Concepts relevant for geodesign extend along a scalar continuum . . . At the global level, we tend to think and perhaps act for all of humanity. We work with both general and singular principles, hoping to make global laws and treatises that nations and their people can agree upon.

These are based largely in the sciences, especially physics and chemistry, ecology, and biology, because the subjects of those disciplines span continuously across the earth. They ignore regional and local political boundaries (or they should). I think the general aim of global studies is to understand change in order to stabilize it, something consistent with the word 'sustainable.'"[23]

**21.** Carl Steinitz, "A Framework for Theory Applicable to the Education of Landscape Architects (and Other Environmental Design Professionals)," *Landscape Journal* 2 (1990): 136–143.

**22.** Steinitz, *A Framework for Geodesign*, x.

**23.** Steinitz, *A Framework for Geodesign*, x.

24. Water, "GIS: History," 5.

Steinitz's positivist, scientifically-driven approach reflects the predominant ways of using GIS. The global ambitions of geodesign have gone hand in hand with the evolution and universalization of this digital system, which in turn resonates with advances in computer science. In substantial ways, this evolution has been supported by State or administrative apparatuses. From the end of the 1980s, large initiatives, governmental grants, and symposiums have backed the expansion and dissemination of GIS. In the United States, this included the creation of the National Center of Geographic Information and Analysis, which, among other works, produced a compendium of seventy-five lectures and laboratory material in GIS that by 1995 had reached over seventy countries and had been translated into Chinese, French, Hungarian, Japanese, and many other languages.[24]

Yet, as new libraries of geospatial data open to the public and countries make their datasets available, open source applications are democratizing GIS tools. The unrestricted ingraining of geographical information into every individual alive is in itself inseparable from the contemporary condition. The software that operates in the background of some of the most common applications such as Google Maps or OpenStreetMap attests to the worldwide use of those georeferenced systems. The impact and applicability of design at the scale and amplitude at which these systems operate, however, is still to show its full potential and conclusively confirm the broader possibilities of geodesign. These possibilities are increasingly the object of social debate. They can be employed by the most technocratic approaches to spatial management and geoengineering, by grassroots social movements, and in multiple forms of critical cartography alike, motivating a necessary debate about how and who uses the data and information upon which we build our world.

**Figure 1.** SYMAP analyses of Boston's imageability. 1965.

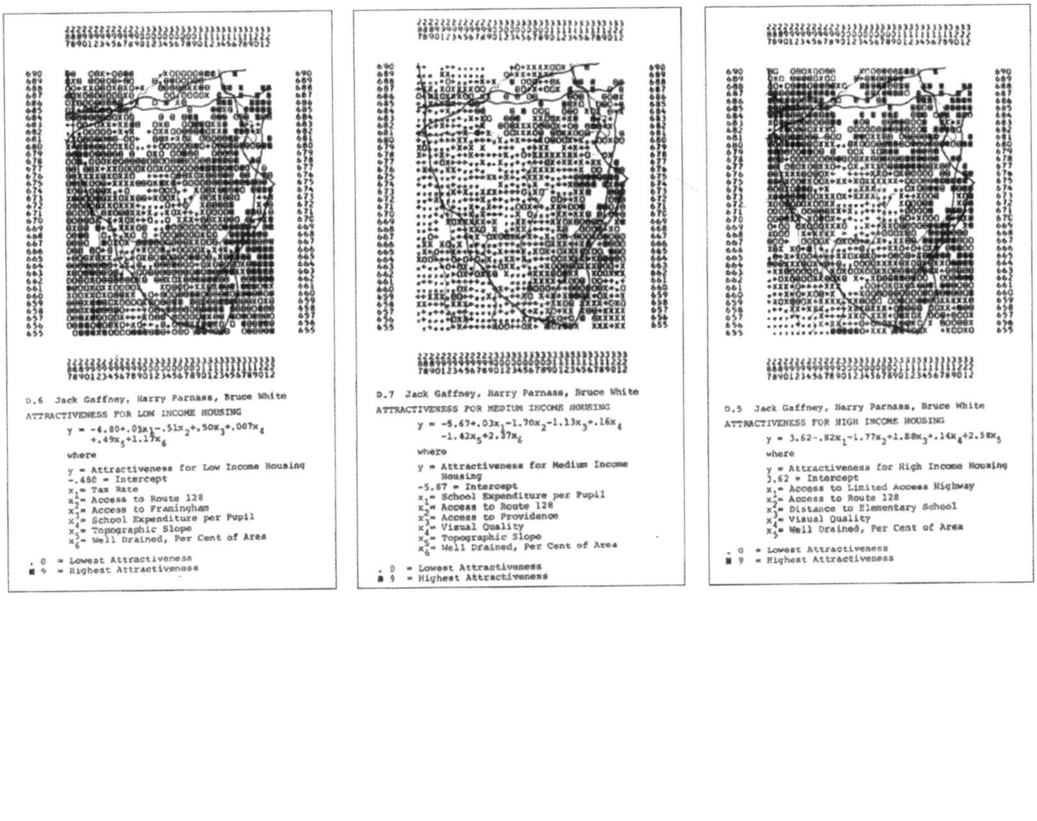


**Figure 2.** SYMAP analyses of attractiveness for new low-income housing. 1970.

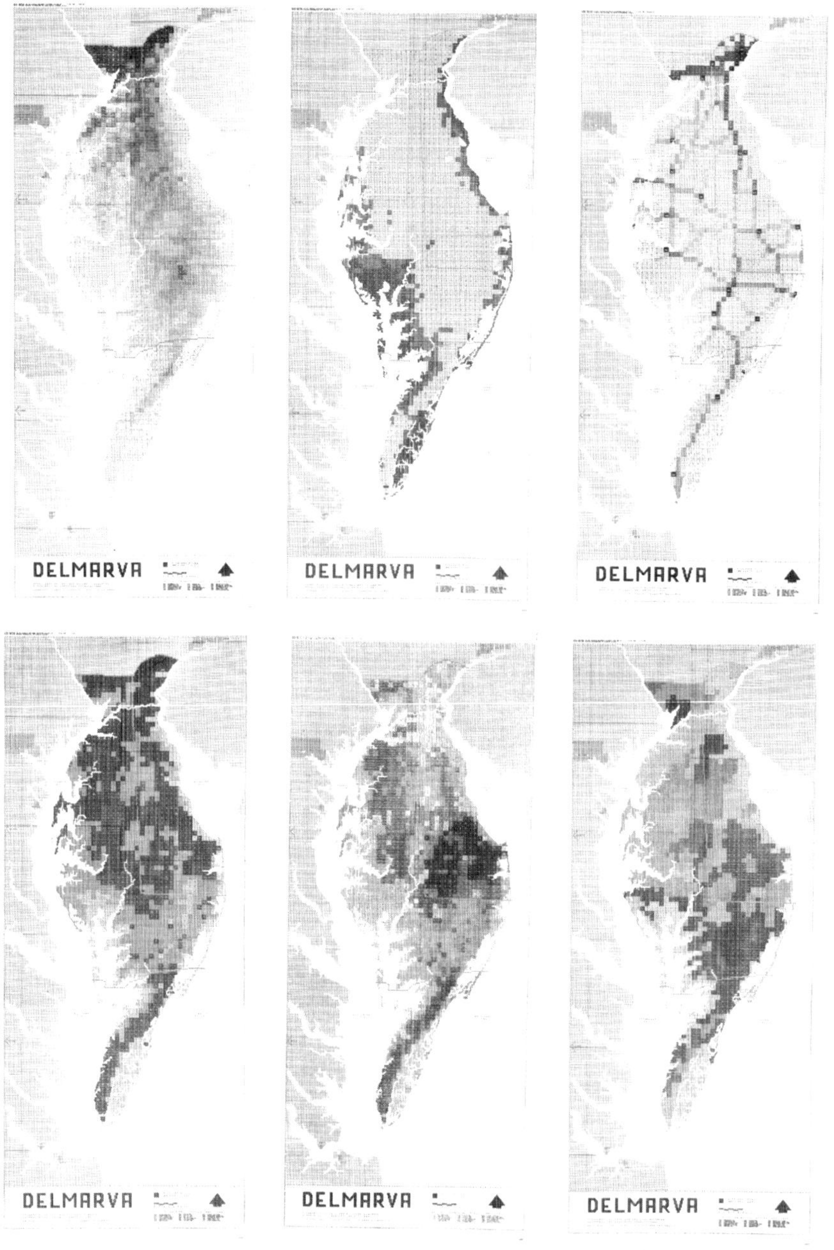


**Figure 3.** Delmarva peninsula study. Analyses of areas for ecological conservation. 1966.

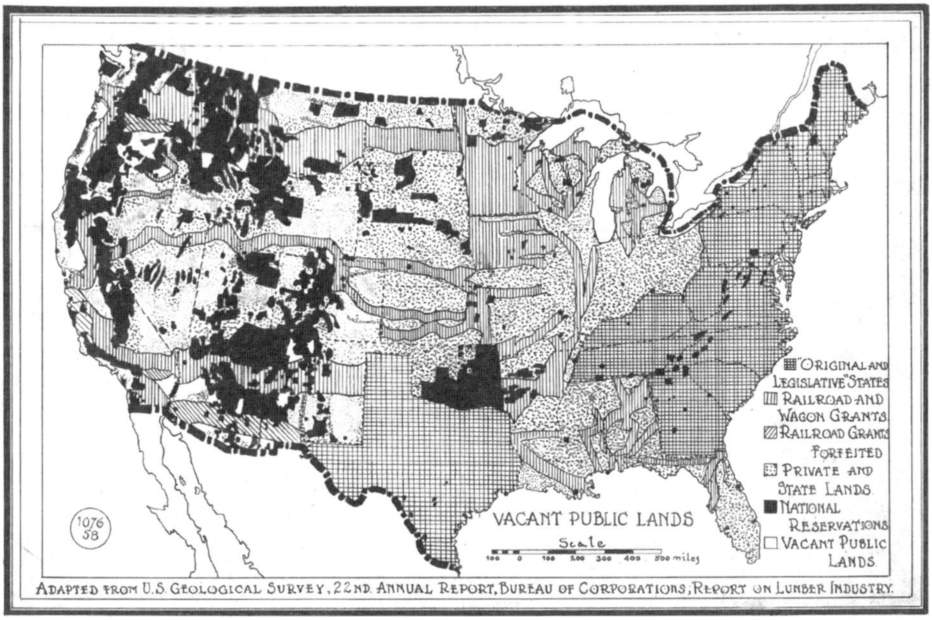

Figure 4 (Top). Overlays of vacant public lands. Warren Manning. 1923.
**Figure 5 (Bottom).** Proposal for new state boundaries. Warren Manning. 1923.

# World of Matter

**Project:** 47. **Authors:** World of Matter: Mabe Bethônico, Ursula Biemann, Lonnie von Brummelen, Siebren de Haan, Uwe H. Martin, Frauke Huber, Helge Mooshammer, Peter Mörtenböck, Emily Eliza Scott, Paulo Tavares. **Date:** 2014–. **Themes:** Ecology. Geopolitics. Human-Earth System. Territorial Intensification.

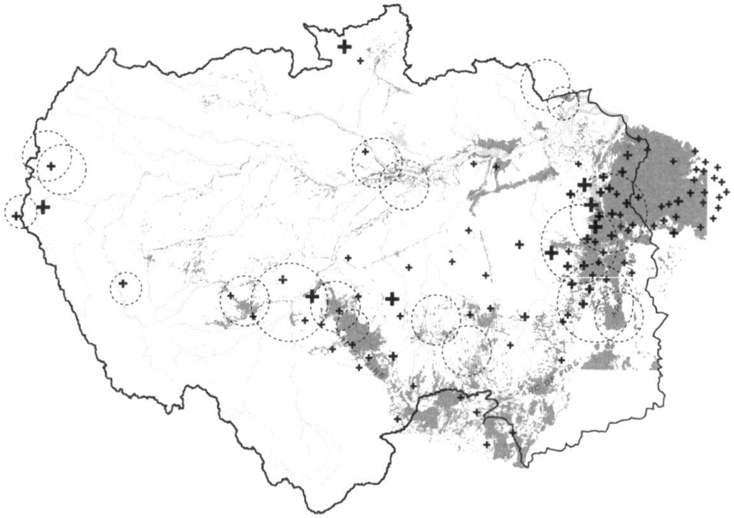

**Figure 0.** Deadly Environment. Politically motivated assassinations of nature rights defenders in Brazil. After Paulo Tavares. 2013.

Since its formulation in 2000, Paul Crutzen and Eugene Stoermer's Anthropocene hypothesis has become a dominant way of conceptualizing the planet, even if the hypothesis is still scientifically contested. Yet the questioning of the idea of the Anthropocene is not only a matter of scientific controversy. The concept is only one possible way of conceiving of Earth, one that focuses on the transformation of the planet's ecological conditions from a geological standpoint. The Anthropocene's methods of verification do not depend on analyzing social factors, but on data-gathering procedures and scientific discourse. They focus on conditions, while neglecting their causes. To this extent and despite its overarching ambition and influence, the idea of the Anthropocene remains a partial concept: other ways of thinking about the world need to complement and interrogate it. Ideas of globalization, *mondialisation* (world-forming), and planetary urbanization open up other ways of understanding our planet's processes of social and environmental transformation.[1] They thus offer other modes of intervening upon its conditions. Similarly, the idea of the Anthropocene has already motivated the emergence of alternative notions that question some of its main postulates. Donna Haraway proposes Plantationocene to describe the enclosure of vegetal life within economic circuits of production, and Chthulucene to refer to the possible emergence of a world of assemblages and to the coexistence between the human and the other-than-human.[2] She also supports Capitalocene, which geographer Andreas Malm and environmental historian and geographer Jason W. Moore first introduced to counter the idea of Anthropocene.[3]

While the Anthropocene hypothesis suggests a universal, "anthropic" responsibility for the environmental processes that are damaging the planet, Malm and Moore's Capitalocene points to the responsibility of a major agent of change: the capitalist system.[4] Not all humankind is causing environmental problems and transforming Earth. On the contrary, a good number of the world's inhabitants only suffer the consequences of ecological changes derived from the often-violent imposition across the globe of an economic system that is alien to their own social and productive structures. The world entirely modified by sociotechnical processes, which we currently inhabit, mostly arises from capitalism's profit-driven relation to nature and its relentless exploitation of natural resources no matter the environmental consequences. As Chilean poet Nicanor Parra critically expressed: "We will defeat nature / In the same way we defeated Marxism."[5] For the proponents of the Capitalocene idea, global warming

1. About these different terminological debates see "Prologue: Architecture and the World Scale" in this book.

2. Plantationocene is a term Haraway borrows. It was collectively generated during a recorded conversation for Ethnos at Aarhus University in 2014. See Donna Haraway, "Anthropocene, Capitalocene, Plantationocene, Chthulucene: Making Kin," *Environmental Humanities* 6 (2015): 160 and 162 footnote 5.

3. As credited by Haraway. See Haraway, "Anthropocene, Capitalocene, Plantationocene, Chthulucene: Making Kin," 160 and 162 footnote 6.

4. See in this respect T.J. Demos, *Against the Anthropocene: Visual Culture and the Environment Today* (Berlin: Sternberg Press, 2017), 39–57. Demos also focuses on the work of World of Matter. See also T.J. Demos, *Decolonizing Nature: Contemporary Art and the Politics of Ecology* (Berlin: Sternberg Press, 2016), 199–228.

5. Nicanor Parra, *Temporal* (Santiago, Chile: Ediciones Universidad Diego Portales, 2014). Our translation.

and similar phenomena of ecological degradation are intimately tied to social injustice. They are one of its salient facets. Correspondingly, to reverse environmental degradation it is not enough to change our technologies of production. We need to imagine new systems of social organization that help to re-establish relations between our species and other natures. We need not merely an ecology but a political ecology.

This political-ecological perspective characterizes the work of World of Matter, an international collective formed around 2014 by architects Peter Mörtenböck, Helge Mooshammer, Emily Eliza Scott, and Paulo Tavares; artists Mabe Bethônico, Ursula Biemann, Lonnie von Brummelen and Siebren de Haan; and visual storytellers Uwe H. Martin and Frauke Huber.[6] At one level their work leans toward the documentary. It exposes the sociospatial conditions of Capitalocene: the intermingling of global economic, social, and environmental processes; the creation of relational geographies linking disparate parts of the planet; the dispossession of local communities from their means of subsistence, and the transformation of the environments they inhabit. These documentary procedures support the collective's project. They help to construct a possible cosmopolitical and ecological project of social change by showing how new possibilities of collective organization and new ways of reimagining our relation to the planet emerge in the very same places that confront the most deleterious effects of the current system. In the classical Marxist perspective, the proletariat is the agent of social transformation. The work of World of Matter emphasizes the transformative role of an added agent: those who suffer the damaging environmental consequences of capitalism, including, importantly, nature itself.

The diversity of intellectual trajectories and forms of expertise of World of Matter's members finds a common space of interaction in the techniques of documentation and proposition the group employs. In their work some dominant visual practices like mapping, documenting in video-essays, and photographing coexist with the textual register of research activities and of theoretical and political reflection **[fig. 0]**. The World of Matter members value the writings of philosophers who work at defining solidarity, human–nonhuman alliances (mainly, Michel Serres, Vandana Shiva, Bruno Latour, Eduardo Viveiro de Castro, and Graham Harman), and insist on needing to translate their theoretical work to social and spatial practices.[7] Importantly, visual and textual production support social activism. Central to World of Matter's approach to world-making is engaging with the collectives and social processes they document and claiming their importance for reimagining how to inhabit the planet.

**6.** Inke Arns, Nabil Ahmed, Gavin Bridge, T.J. Demos, Timothy Morton, and Hartware MedienKunstVerein, Host Institution, *World of Matter* (Berlin: Sternberg Press, 2015), 60. The collective comes together in an exhibition at Hartware MedienKunstVerein (HMKV).

**7.** Arns et al., *World of Matter*, 10.

In this sense, World of Matter's very configuration as an international collective and its collaboration with multiple groups exemplify the cosmopolitical values they embrace. Despite the individual value of each of their projects, the significance of the work does not reside in any particular piece but in their cumulative effect. Similarly, the diversity of authors is a move toward the multiplication of research efforts, the cross-disciplinary intellectual dialogue, and the complexity of the analysis more than one toward the singularity of the contributions. The very formulation of the collective is the project itself. Its multiplicity favors open-ended and open-access archival work. Assembled on the eponymous web platform, the works add to one another until creating an atlas of the "global ecologies of resource exploitation and circulation," which is also a map of spaces that require transformation.[8]

In order to expose that the crudest exploitation of the world's matter lies behind the prevailing rhetoric of digital economies and knowledge society, the collective focuses on the transformations of nature. Its works intervene in the spaces that Neil Brenner and Christian Schmid call "extended urbanization," and reveal the phenomena of operationalization these two authors denounce **[project 45]**. Frauke Huber and Uwe H. Martin's project *LandRush* (2011–), for instance, brings to light the dramatic transformation of habitats produced by extensive monoculture. It documents imposing genetically-modified cotton in India; changing a surface equal to a large country from Savannah to agricultural land in Matto Grosso, Brazil; shrinking the Aral Sea due to the excessive irrigation of cotton fields; and transforming local agricultural production in Texas and Germany into economies of scale **[figs. 1 and 2]**. *LandRush* shows the vast spatial consequences of those transformations as well as their social impact. It brings to light contestations, such as those organized by the Landless Workers' Movement in Brazil (Movimento dos Trabalhadores Rurais Sem Terra) or by farmers who refuse to introduce genetically-modified crops. It shows the difficulties workers face when they see their traditions of production transformed, such as India's mass suicide of farmers.[9] Also, it illustrates how often farmers need to comply and collaborate with these transformations in order to ensure the economic viability of their work.[10]

Similar procedures of visualization characterize most of World of Matter's works. Ursula Biemann's *Deep Weather* (2013) connects the exploitation of tar sands in Alberta to the measures taken by indigenous populations in Bangladesh to protect themselves from global warming. Lonnie Van Brummelen and Siebren de Haan's *Episode of the Sea* (2014) shows how Dutch fishermen

**8.** For a complete recompilation of World of Matter's projects see https://www.worldofmatter.net/

**9.** Frauke Huber and Uwe H. Martin, "Of Seed and Land," in Arns et al., *World of Matter*, 136.

**10.** Huber and Martin, "Of Seed and Land," 140–145.

struggle to preserve their practices and forms of life **[fig. 3]**. Mabe Bethônico's *Mineral Invisibility* (2008–) reveals the hidden "occupation of indigenous lands for the illegal exploitation of natural resources" in Minas Gerais, Brazil, and how mining has negatively affected the lives of women workers.[11] All these works merge the investigation of the spatiality of Capitalocene with the voices of those who need to be considered in any possible project of social transformation, thus revealing the multiplicity of groups who insist on urgently reconsidering humanity's relation to nature in a nonexploitative manner.

Brazilian architect Paulo Tavares's work explicitly expresses this need to rearticulate human–nonhuman relations and, in the expression of art historian T.J. Demos, to decolonize nature.[12] In a series of research studies investigating the political ecology of Amazonia, Tavares analyzes the deep intermingling between corporations, financial institutions, South America's democratic deficits, and environmental modifications.[13] The most radical alternative to this complex political ecological array is also located in the region. In Non-human Rights (2012), Tavares uses different registers of video narration to explore how Ecuador introduced in its Constitution the notion of "rights of nature," thus considering for the first time nonhuman, natural entities as legal subjects with specific rights and allowing the world to actually matter. Non-human Rights presents the legislative innovation resulting from the 1990s protests of Ecuador's indigenous communities, as well as from contemporary developments in philosophy, represented by Serres's claim for a new "natural contract" (1990).[14] The coincidence of objectives among excluded communities, progressive ecological thinking, and legislative action points to the emergence of a shared, planetary political project. Even if the implementation of Ecuador's law has not been entirely successful, the country's intention to provide universal jurisdiction for the regulation of the rights of nature is a first, necessary step toward a new relation between the human and nonhuman.[15]

Collectivities, ecology, social justice. For World of Matter today's social struggles find their most crucial arena in the political-ecological discourse and in the hidden spaces of extended urbanization. That is where new movements of contestation and new desires for social and environmental imagination emerge. What happens there is, in any case, inseparable from a reconsideration of what cities are. As the collective's members Peter Mörtenböck and Helge Mooshammer remind us, cities are the prevailing destiny of resource exploitation **[fig. 4]**.[16] A change in our global ecologies cannot exist without a new understanding of how cities operate. The move that completes World of Mat-

**11.** Mabe Bethônico, "Conversations on Exploited Lands: Above the Grounds of Minas Gerais," in Arns et al., *World of Matter*, 77.

**12.** Demos, *Decolonizing Nature*, 199–228.

**13.** Paulo Tavares, "The Geological Imperative: On the Political Ecology of the Amazonia's Deep History," in *Architecture in the Anthropocene: Encounters Among Design, Deep Time, Science and Philosophy*, ed. Etienne Turpin (Ann Arbor, MI: Open Humanities Press, 2013), 209–239. Paulo Tavares, "In the Forest Ruins," *e-flux*. Accessed online April 20, 2019: https://www.e-flux.com/architecture/superhumanity/68688/in-the-forest-ruins/

**14.** Michel Serres, *The Natural Contract* (Ann Arbor: University of Michigan Press, 1995 [1990]).

**15.** Thomas F. Purcell and Estefania Martinez, "Post-neoliberal energy modernity and the political economy of the landlord state in Ecuador," *Energy Research and Social Science* (2018).

**16.** Peter Mörtenböck and Helge Mooshammer, "Demiurgic Worlds." Accessed online April 21, 2019: https://www.worldofmatter.net/geo-engineering-climates-control#path=geo-engineering-climates-control

ter's cosmopolitical call is precisely this reconsideration of the urban. Cities are historically paradigmatic examples of a positive value of social mix and interaction. They are also the spaces where the first planning technologies were implemented—just to be exported later to vaster, territorial scales. With the prospect of an expected collapse of normalcy caused by environmental changes, cities need to transform their habits of production and consumption, acknowledging and resolving their numerous material externalities. A new, scalable model of planning needs to emerge that favors the rise of alternative normalcies. For that, architecture's historical interest in spatial stability needs to be replaced by an open acceptance of change. A world of matter and time rather than space.[17]

17. Mörtenböck and Mooshammer, "Demiurgic Worlds."

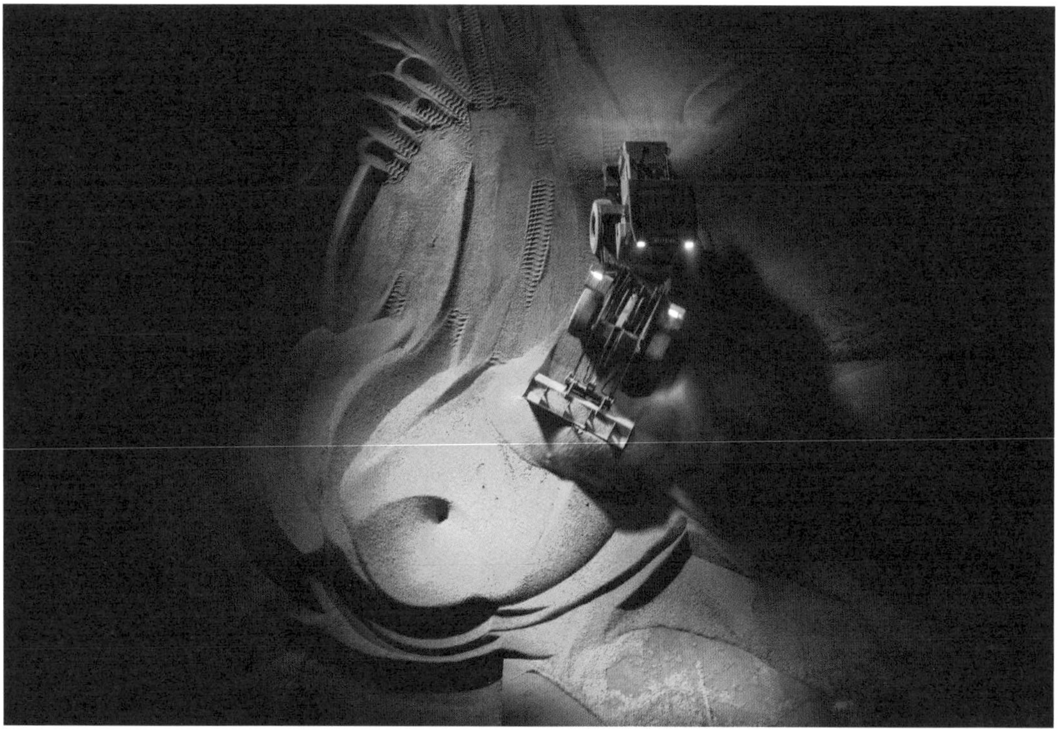

**Figure 1.** *LandRush*. Storage of soybeans in a warehouse of the Fiagril Agromercantil plant in Lucas do Rio Verde, Mato Grosso. Fiagril distributes its soybeans globally. Frauke Huber and Uwe H. Martin. 2011.

**Figure 2.** *LandRush.* Local Anuak guards watch over Karuturi's bulldozers. Frauke Huber and Uwe H. Martin. 2011.

**Figure 3.** *Episode of the Sea*. Lonnie van Brummelen and Siebren de Haan. Film still. 2014.

**Figure 4.** Helge Mooshammer and Peter Mörtenböck. *Demiurgic Worlds.* San Gorgonio Pass Wind Farm. California, USA. 2011.

# Geostories

**Project:** 48. **Author:** Design Earth: Rania Ghosn (1977) and El Hadi Jazairy (1970). **Date:** 2014–. **Themes:** Ecology. Geo-visualization. Human-Earth System. Monumentality.

**Figure 0**. Blue Marble Circus. Plan and section. After Design Earth. 2017.

One of the drawings of After Oil—Design Earth's speculation about a Persian Gulf no longer depending on fossil fuels—depicts two individuals on the top of a mountain, facing the Red Sea **[fig. 1]**.[1] Their situation is not unlike that of Caspar David Friedrich's *Wanderer above the Sea of Fog*. As in the romantic painting, the subjects occupy an elevated position on a mountain. In both cases, a vast and flat landscape surrounds them: two different types of sea, an atmospheric and an aquatic one. But here the similarities stop. Instead of the undoubtedly European figure of Friedrich's work, the subjects of Design Earth's drawings are two Arabs, correspondingly dressed with the clothes of the area. The mountain on which they stand is not a purely natural phenomenon, but an artificial crystalline structure; a replica of the Alpine peaks Bruno Taut conceived of **[project 4]**. The characters do not stand directly against the landscape. Instead, they survey it with the help of a telescope.

1. Originally presented at the Sharjah Biennial 13: Tamawuj (2017). For a full explanation of the project see Rania Ghosn and El Hadi Jazairy, *Geostories: Another Architecture for the Environment* (New York: Actar, 2018), 29–37.

It is difficult, at least initially, to assimilate what the two After Oil observers see to a sublime romantic landscape. The Red Sea of the image is populated by a multitude of cruise and cargo ships, their lines of movement traced above the surface of the water. The sea is a space of transit, occupied by technologies, humans, and animals alike: there are numerous birds flying above the water, clustered in the same areas as the ships; human figures stand on platforms placed above the water surface. Similarly, the horizon of this scene is a line of heterogeneous contacts: between the sea and the sky, and between them and the extremely dense group of skyscrapers that characterize the metropolises of the region.

It is the relation between the mountain, the skyscrapers, and the sea platforms that defines the drawing's main theme. The post-1973 boom in oil prices propelled the rise of entirely new cities around the Persian Gulf, crowned by some of the highest skyscrapers of the planet. Increasingly deep oil drilling wells, excavated to intensify the exploitation of underground conditions, and growing building heights mirror each other vertically above and below the surface. The platforms on the sea represent the relationship between the two processes by intervening at the Emirati oil and gas industrial facility Das Island. Design Earth's project there, rendered in section, intertwines the architectural and geological conditions of the area. It measures the huge vertical tunnels of all exploited reservoirs by placing inside them the biggest architectural landmarks of the region. The excavated material is used to create the artificial mountain where the two observers stand. The city in the background represents Design Earth's proposal for a floating city in the Strait of Hormuz. It extends the urban form that has recently proliferated in the Gulf in order to create a space of interstate cooperation based on real estate speculation, thus showing that, even in an after-oil scenario, the economy of the region would depend on forms of economic speculation that also have grave environmental consequences.

Design Earth's drawing shows how urbanization is tied to resource extraction, and how both cause deep environmental and ecological modifications. The drawing's claim is that the urban has no externalities. Interestingly, the proposal for the Strait of Hormuz city is a gridded scheme represented in axonometric projection **[fig. 2]**. The buildings are modern visionary projects such as Le Corbusier's Radiant City and Buckminster Fuller and Shoji Sadao's Tetrahedron City. The city's design and representation reference the logic of Rem Koolhaas's City of the Captive Globe **[project 39]**. And yet, the argument in After Oil is the opposite of Koolhaas's drawing. For the Dutch architect, modernity had been able to entirely substitute the earth. Design Earth's drawing reveals the illusory dimension of such a vision, by showing the complex and unavoidable interplay between urbanization, territory, and ecology: the return of a repressed Earth.

After Oil is one of Design Earth's Geostories; a series of projects framed as architectural contributions to discussions on climate change **[fig. 0]**. The projects do not address global warming directly, but rather through investigating the territorial impacts of urbanization and sociotechnical systems and through questioning the nature–society divide. The architects' approach to such questions is explicitly grounded in Bruno Latour's thinking, to which they make abundant reference. Especially relevant for their work is Latour's proposal to stop treating environmental questions as "matters of fact" and to start considering them as "matters of concern."[2] The former possibility promotes the instrumentalization of supposedly neutral, scientific forms of knowledge to promote the resolution of environmental questions by purely technical means. Matters of concern represent, in turn, a more contentious possibility, which acknowledges the complexity of the phenomena to be analyzed, the difficulty in fully understanding all the elements that affect them, and the resulting necessity of basing human action not on indisputable facts but on political debates. Instead of trying to build consensus about the alleged objectivity of technical actions, matters of concern try to produce them around common preoccupations.

**2.** Bruno Latour, "From Realpolitik to Dingpolitik or How to Make Things Public," in *Making Things Public: Atmospheres of Democracy*, ed. Bruno Latour and Peter Weibel (Cambridge, MA: MIT Press, 2005), 14–44.

A corollary of Latour's claim is the necessity of elaborating the mechanisms that allow social actors to understand the questions that affect them. The scale of climate change and similar environmental modifications is undetectable. It surpasses our individual capacity of perception. To understand them requires establishing forms of trans-scalar mediation. Another consequence is the necessity of finding ways to express the creation of social assemblies around those matters of concern; to elaborate a new cultural mythology that replaces the hegemonic, economically driven imaginary. It is precisely in these two realms that Design Earth seeks to intervene. By elaborating stories and "speculative fictions," the architects intend to create aesthetic syntheses of scientific epistemologies and sensible experience, of reason and imagination.[3] These syntheses are critical reactions to the aesthetics of matters of fact, which the architects consider as forms of "totalizing rationalization and scientific totalitarianism" that reduce ecological problems to data that is representable in charts, tables, and diagrams.[4] The aesthetic critique is epistemological and, ultimately, operational. It negates the claims of ecological thinking "to possess both a global reach and a universal authority," and the architectural approaches to ecology and sustainability derived from such assumption **[project 46]**.[5] Instead of the confidence in the resolution of ecological problems by merely technical means that characterizes architectural problem solving attitudes, Design Earth's Geostories seek to develop a political-ecological approach to reveal the problematics, actors, and relations associated with environmental questions **[project 47]**.

3. Ghosn and Jazairy, *Geostories*, 19–21.

4. Rania Ghosn and El Hadi Jazairy, "Airpocalypse: A Short Geostory," *San Rocco* 10: Ecology (2014): 149.

5. Ghosn and Jazairy, "Airpocalypse: A Short Geostory," 148.

Design Earth's political-ecological method proceeds by creating visual narratives about possible future conditions that are different, yet intrinsically related to the ones we currently witness. The classification of their body of work in the categories Terrarium, Aquarium, and Planetarium conceptually relates the designs to well-known heuristic devices, although the object is not to understand the natural state of the planet, but the broad spectrum of environmental modifications that affect the earth and extraterrestrial space **[fig. 3]**. The projects address processes of deforestation and trash accumulation, the paradoxical extraction of resources to mitigate the damaging consequences produced by extracting other resources, and the difficulty of reconciling the needs of conservation and production; the proliferation of space debris and the attempts to mine satellite and other cosmic bodies. The resulting collection is a world map of the multitude of spaces severely affected by economically-driven, sociotechnical processes. Their design interventions visualize the possible production of a new type of social imaginary that acknowledges that human actions are, ultimately, types of terrestrial production.

Design Earth's interest in the production of a new social and aesthetic imaginary seeks, in any case, to construct complicated, tense equilibriums between highly contrasting goals. On one hand, the projects continue, even exacerbate, existing trends of production and consumption, and acknowledge the profound environmental impacts they entail. On the other, they aim to recognize the importance of too often disregarded, nonhuman elements and to imagine spatial configurations in which their rights are granted. By bringing together the ecological, the technical, and the social, the projects portray the planet as a space of conflict, in which agents with extremely different purposes and necessities come up against each other. Their drawings do not seek to solve these tensions. Instead, they sublimate them into absurd, yet aesthetically powerful, syntheses of opposites that stand as symbols, or monuments, of possible configurations yet to come **[fig. 4]**.

Despite being speculations about our present and future, Design Earth projects present their architects' monumental visions in drawings that digitally emulate nineteenth-century forms of lithography, probably in an attempt to recreate the sense of awe that early geographic visualizations of the planet produced. This diachronic tension highlights that Design Earth's works are, substantially, reflections upon history and temporality, inquiries about architecture's participation in the definition of historical transformations. Design Earth's drawings are populated by an extensive catalogue of references that insist on architecture's commitment to modernity, avant-gardism, and utopia. With Taut, Fuller, and Le Corbusier, there are constant citations to Vladimir Shukhov's communication tower and to Vladimir Tatlin's Monument to the Third International; to William F. Lamb's Empire State Building and to the Enlightened sense of monumentality **[projects 4, 6, 8, 14, and 15]**. Their work also refers to more recent projects. Significantly, those of Superstudio, which are present in the drawings for Of Oil and Ice—a project dominated by a replica of the Italian architects' Continuous Monument and Supersurface—and in their Airpocalypse for Beijing **[project 38]**.[6]

6. Ghosn and Jazairy, *Geostories,* 76–86 and 132–135.

It is, in fact, this presence of Superstudio that reveals the last crucial contours of Design Earth's architectural and ideological project. Both groups of architects share an interest in the generation of a new monumentality. For both, design operates mostly at a discursive level, creating fictions in which the value of the projects derives from the debates and questions they can provoke. More importantly, in both cases, the central goal of the projects is to reflect upon modernity itself. Yet it is at this point that the two trajectories diverge. Superstudio's critical fascination with modern abstraction leads the Italian architects to imagine a world where the formal logics of modernity are utterly intensified. Working at a moment when the ethics of international style still dominate the profession, the Italian architects imagine how to radicalize the modern movement, and minimize figurative references to the past. Modernity still represents for them the spirit of the new. In Design Earth, the operation is more nostalgic. Their catalog of architectural references longs for the lost, transformative ambitions of modern architecture. It points to a capacity that has been lost and that can be only be evoked, thus highlighting the minor position contemporary architecture has in a global environment that is increasingly technologically produced. Their work is profoundly critical of the neglect of territoriality and geography in urban debates, of the lack of attention to the needs of nonhumans, of the serious ecological crises the hegemonic forms of production entail. Without a doubt, it presents modernity as the cause of our current environmental problems. And yet, Design Earth's projects oppose any naturalist or antimodern ideology. In turn, they suggest that, in its most utopian and ambitious propositions, a recovered modernity marks the only possible path for creating alternative environmental and planetary futures. If a new sublime cosmology is possible, it will have to be a technologically shaped one.

**Figure 1.** After Oil. Das Island. 2016.

Figure 2. After Oil. Strait of Hormuz city. 2016.

Figure 3. Trash Peaks. Installation for the Seoul Biennale of Architecture and Urbanism. 2017.

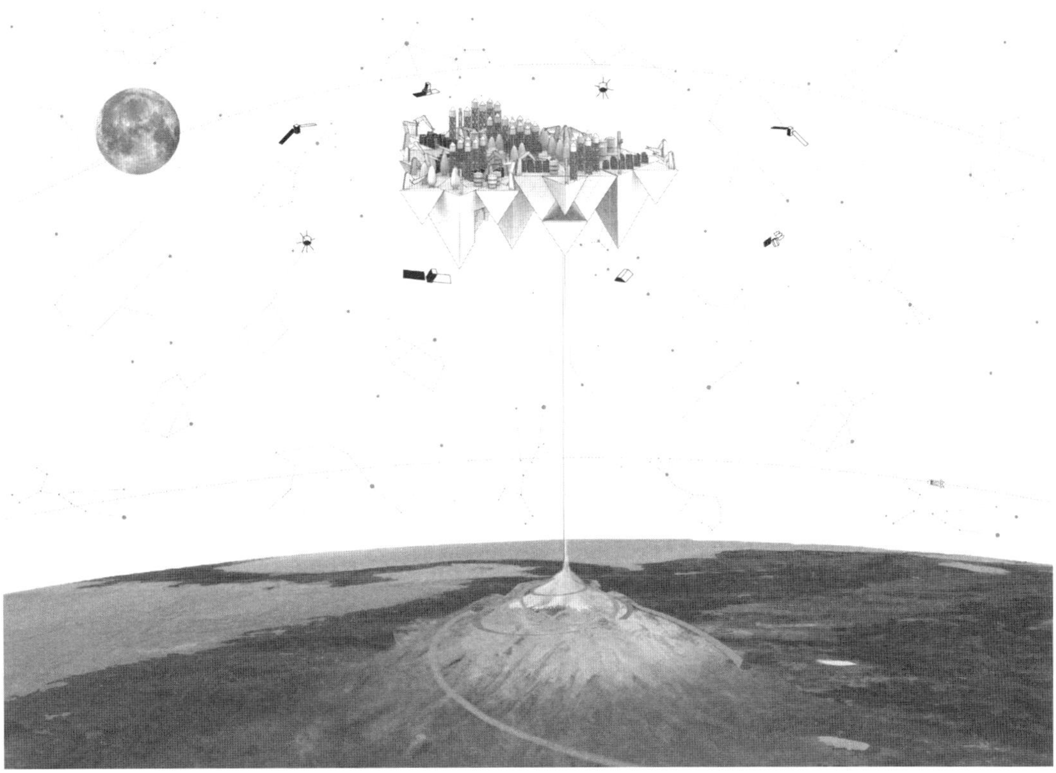

**Figure 4.** Neck of the Moon. Connection between Cotopaxi volcano and new satellite planet. 2015.

# Satellights

**Project:** 49. **Author:** Angelo Bucci (1963). **Date:** 2017. **Themes:** Abstraction. Geography. Monumentality. Remoteness.

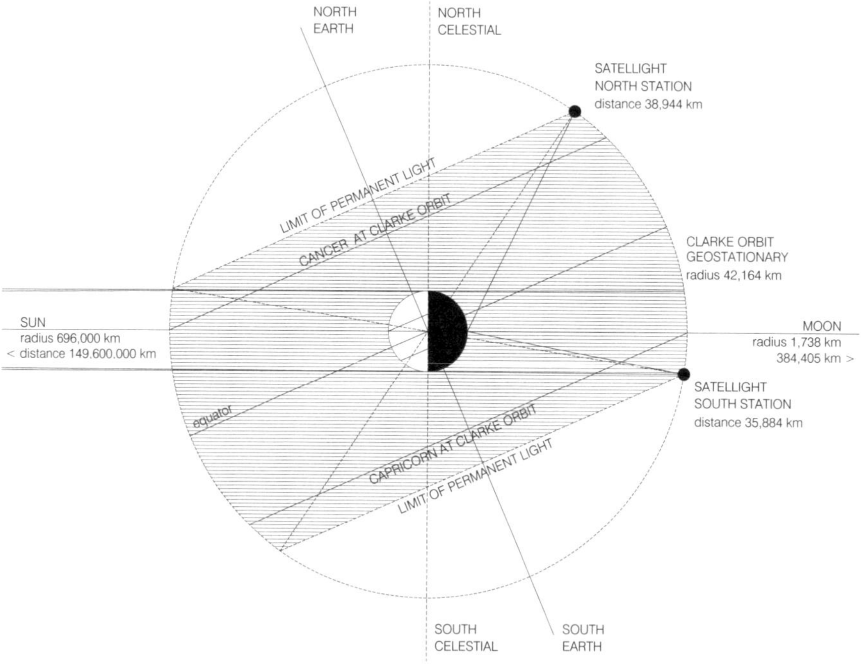


**Figure 0.** Satellights over São Paulo. After Angelo Bucci. 2017.

In the late nineteenth century, in the race for modernization and the frenzy to bring electric light to their streets, American cities start experimenting with alternatives to the grid of electric lamps, which had been mimicking the infrastructure of gas lamps but were too expensive and complicated to install. Instead cities sought to build artificial moons to light up their nights. This new public lighting, called "moonlight towers," consisted of four to six arc lamps suspended 50 meters above the ground by iron space truss towers, not much different from oil derricks but graceful and elegant.[1] In *The Age of Edison: Electric Light and the Invention of Modern America*, Ernest Freeberg characterizes those cities under their new man-made moons and the spectacle around the promise of replacing night for day.[2] One individual tower was powerful enough to illuminate a diameter of approximately 900 meters, or 60 hectares. Reflecting on the impact of such structures and delighted by the homage their name played to Earth's natural satellite, Brazilian architect Angelo Bucci calculated that, under a density of 500 people per hectare, the brightness generated from this single source of light could potentially reach thirty-thousand inhabitants. This became his starting point to rethink the way we light up the world while formulating a broader understanding of humanity's place in it.

Satellite-produced visualizations of Earth at night reminds one of a constellation of stars over a dark sky. "The boundaries between continents and oceans disappear and give way to another geography. In place of land and water there is darkness and light. Billions of points of light. It is the planet lit with small light bulbs that were, each single one, screwed into their sockets with the palm of a hand!"[3] The high-contrast image that emerges from the combination of light and no light falsely depicts the world's surface as an interplay of inhabited and vacant spaces. The same way it ignores fixed settlements in which electricity is not available, owing to development status, indigenous/natural conditions, or even size, it also fails to capture transient situations, such as the "100,000 people [who] at any given time of day or night are flying over the Atlantic Ocean."[4] This lack of nuance also contributes to the flattening of social and cultural differences, homogenizing the complexity of the built world in favor of the portrayal of one civilizational aspect only, the consumption of energy. Nevertheless, in the abstract, it does not fall short in beautifully representing "the most recent expression of our world: the shallowest archaeological layer in the construction of cities."[5] Bucci reminds us that this layer is not attached to the ground, but floats above it, carrying the thickness humanity built below it.

1. Megan Garber, "Tower of Light: When Electricity Was New, People Used It to Mimic the Moon," *The Atlantic*, March 6, 2013. Accessed online March 8, 2019, https://www.theatlantic.com/technology/archive/2013/03/tower-of-light-when-electricity-was-new-people-used-it-to-mimic-the-moon/273445/.

2. Ernest Freeberg, *The Age of Edison: Electric Light and the Invention of Modern America* (New York: Penguin Press, 2013).

3. Angelo Bucci, *São Paulo, Reasons for Architecture: The Dissolution of Buildings and How to Pass through Walls*, trans. Kristine Stiphany (Austin, TX: School of Architecture, the University of Texas at Austin, 2011), 55–56.

4. Bucci, *São Paulo, Reasons for Architecture*, 55–56.

5. Bucci, *São Paulo, Reasons for Architecture*, 55–56.

The combination of all the light spots together weaves a continuous mesh that varies in intensity according to the density of each city. This mesh reflects our horizontal plane of inhabitation, a plane of planetary scale "linked to the environment upon which all cities are sited and dependent for air, water and earth . . . This scale is present in the Roman aqueducts, in the cisterns of Istanbul and in every merchant ship ever launched into the sea. Each man walking on a path of compacted dirt has, potentially, this same planetary monumentality."[6]

Bucci is building on the formulations of geographer Milton Santos, known as the father of Critical Geography in Brazil, who conceptualized the relationship between "horizontalities" and "verticalities" as key elements in the formation of the territory and its functionality. On one hand, "verticalities" refers to a system of discontinuities of points imposed over a territory to establish its control and ensure a global functioning of capital and its reproduction. Although fragmented, these are interdependent and coordinated points for maintaining the hegemony of the current economic system while imposing a rationality to the functioning of society. They are hierarchical and disciplinarian forces. Horizontalities, on the other hand, are the extensions that aggregate points without discontinuities and create a nonhierarchical fabric that forms the basis for life in collectivity, as civil society. They build the fabric of everyday life where systems of rules are continuously formulated and reformulated. Horizontalities are the spaces of common existence and solidarity, the banal space where both compliance and rebellion take place.[7] Cities happen at the intersection between horizontalities and verticalities, but it is through the physicality of the horizontal stratum—the continuum of territorial occupation—that a layer of inhabitation can be seen as enveloping the Earth.

Thus, the horizontal plane is both metaphorical and physical. Its formal thickness, however, is not subject to speculation, as it is built out of given cultural parameters. In his doctoral dissertation, *São Paulo, Reasons for Architecture: The Dissolution of Buildings and How to Pass through Walls*, Bucci explains how the geographical features of the land that São Paulo was built on conditions the occupation of that territory. The combination of natural topography and man-made infrastructure, such as the bridges that span adjacent valleys, therefore establishes the total thickness of the possible inhabitable layer, which, according to him, is 30 meters high. Extracting this operation from the contextual specificity of that city and generalizing it to the world, Bucci argues that the thickness of humanity's layer should be measured by the height difference be-

**6.** Bucci, *São Paulo, Reasons for Architecture*, 30.

**7.** Milton Santos, *A Natureza do Espaço: Técnica e Tempo. Razão e Emoção* (São Paulo: Editora da Universidade de São Paulo, 2002), 191–194.

tween the lowest and highest human settlements. This range in altitude is defined, at one end, by La Rinconada in Peru, 5,098 meters above sea level with a population of 30,000 inhabitants, the highest permanent settlement in the world; and, at the other end, by Jericho, in Palestine, located 258 meters below sea level with a population around 19,000 inhabitants. Taking La Rinconada and Jericho as framing totems of human occupation of the earth's surface, it is possible to say that the thickness of this inhabited horizontal layer is about 5,350 meters **[fig. 1]**. This measure embodies the history of humanity's struggle to conquer space, to overcome both its own limitations as well as that of defying nature. Although this number may seem a long way to a human body, it is negligible at the scale of the world. When observed against the diameter of the planet, this thickness is reduced to a thin, faint skin. The whole of humanity lies on a single fragile line **[fig. 2]**.

This line carries the image of a perfect circle, the contour that binds the purest of forms. It represents the fundamental circumference without which it is impossible to draw a representation of the earth. It is also, nevertheless, "a limit; not a choice, it is the field we are able to live in . . . a beautiful project under construction for thousands of years."[8] From the inside, however, it lacks visual continuity, making it impossible to comprehend and leaving it subject to the imagination. Bucci's intention, as he puts it, is not to evidence this discontinuity as reasoning for design, or any plan of completing it. First and foremost, the intention is to emphasize that "the perfect circle is already completed." It is also to show that these interruptions just reinforce the beauty of a thought that otherwise would not be possible without the visualization of the world scale. The whole possibility of architecture exists in the delicacy of a line that can only be conceived through a planetary visualization of humanity's physical existence. If, following Bucci, "abstraction is a cultural achievement shaped in modern age," then the conception of this line is, in itself, the very confirmation of modernity.[9]

This grounded line bears a unique correspondence with another line orbiting the earth at 35,789 meters above sea level. This is a geostationary orbit where the orbital period matches the cycle of Earth's rotation. Referred to as the Clarke Orbit, after the 1945 observations of Arthur Charles Clarke, it maintains any object traveling at 3.07 kilometers per second stationary over a fixed location on Earth, regardless of its form, size, or weight. Communication satellites often occupy geostationary orbits so they can align with their counterparts

8. Angelo Bucci, "Satellights" (unpublished manuscript, 2017), 7.

9. Bucci, "Satellights," 1.

on the ground, namely satellite antennas. The Clarke Orbit's offset from the planet's ground generates a radius 6.61 times bigger than that of Earth, creating a mirror to the planet's surface in the sky where "a continent, a country, a city or any physical component at the surface of the planet can be somehow corresponded there."[10]

**10.** Bucci, "Satellights," 3.

**11.** Bucci, "Satellights," 4.

Recalling the moonlight towers, Bucci reflects on the possibility of illuminating Earth from that geostationary orbit. Taking São Paulo as an example, he infers that for a metropolitan area of 9,298 km$^2$ and a population of 21 million inhabitants there might exist around 1,039,686 light bulbs with a total capacity of generating 247 megawatts of power. "Imagine if we could replace those 1,039 million of light bulbs, thousands of kilometers of cables, hundreds of thousands of light poles with a pair of geostationary satellights. An equivalent to 250 megawatts power light, as installed on the metropolis of São Paulo, orbiting on Clarke **[figs. 0, 3, and 4]**." Those satellights would be placed on the orbit's regions with continuous exposure to sunlight, analogous to the winter and summer solstices, to harness energy directly from the Sun despite the inherent oscillation of the Earth's axis. The further organization of satellights in pairs is a solution to compensate, in most times, for bad weather conditions: if clouds blocked one of them, light emitted by the other would still reach the city because of its complementary, opposite angle. Beyond their functional role, Bucci also imagines the sublime effects weather might play over those lights, creating powerful aesthetic phenomena. Lastly, thanks to the precision of the space equipment, the beams of light are adjustable and either open their focus to cover the entire city or close it, effectively casting a multiplicity of laser-like points "imprint[ing] thousands of pixels on our cities' surface . . . Each person having their own dedicated light in each one of the satellight stations as their personal stars."[11]

Two satellights for each settlement add up to the close to 4,000 satellites (between active and inactive ones) that currently orbit the earth. Angelo Bucci sees in this image something resembling Kalmykov's orbiting city of Saturnia and its most approximate real materialization, the first modular space station *Mir* (literally meaning both *world* and *peace* in Russian), assembled between 1986 and 1996 and decommissioned in 2001 after being replaced by the International Space Station **[project 12]**. *Mir* was designed to be assembled in parts and expand limitlessly. "As stones in an arch," Bucci suggests, *Mir* could theoretically grow to complete an entire ring around the earth. Similarly, satel-

12. Bucci, "Satellights," 8.

lights, even if discontinuous, could ultimately form their own linear geography to encircle the planet. The configuration is a visual, symbolic reminder of our condition on Earth's surface: an offset in space of humanity's thin layer on the ground. Thus, every time we reach for the stars to contemplate the source of our lights, we would know that "a perfect circle is the drawing that best represents the entire human existence."[12]

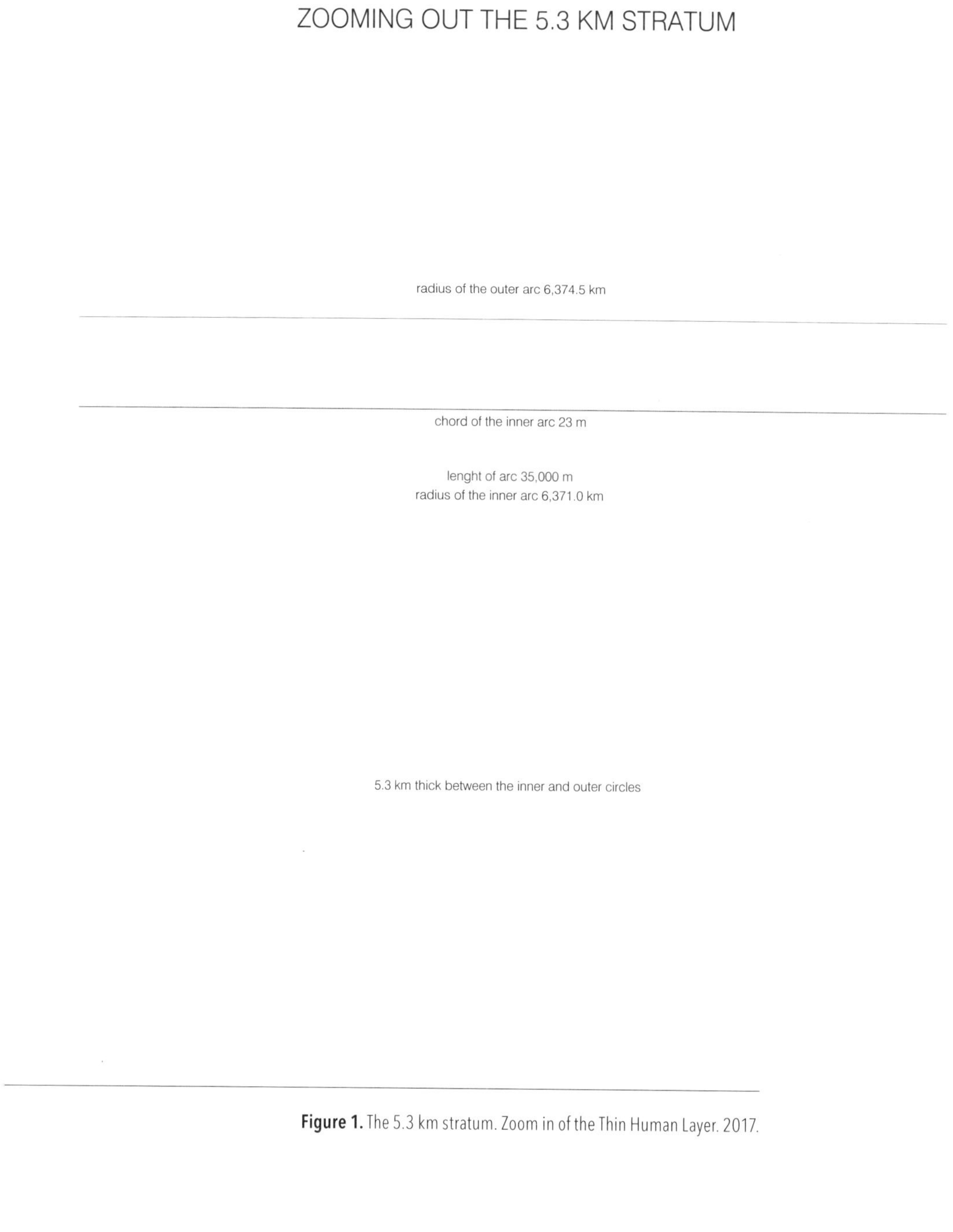


**Figure 1.** The 5.3 km stratum. Zoom in of the Thin Human Layer. 2017.

THE THIN HUMAN LAYER
5.3 km thick between the inner and outer circles

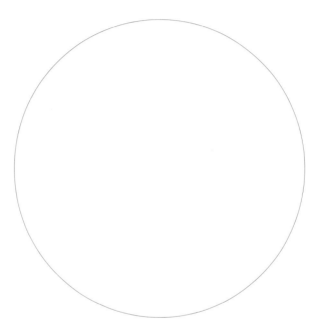

**Figure 2.** The Thin Human Layer. 2017.

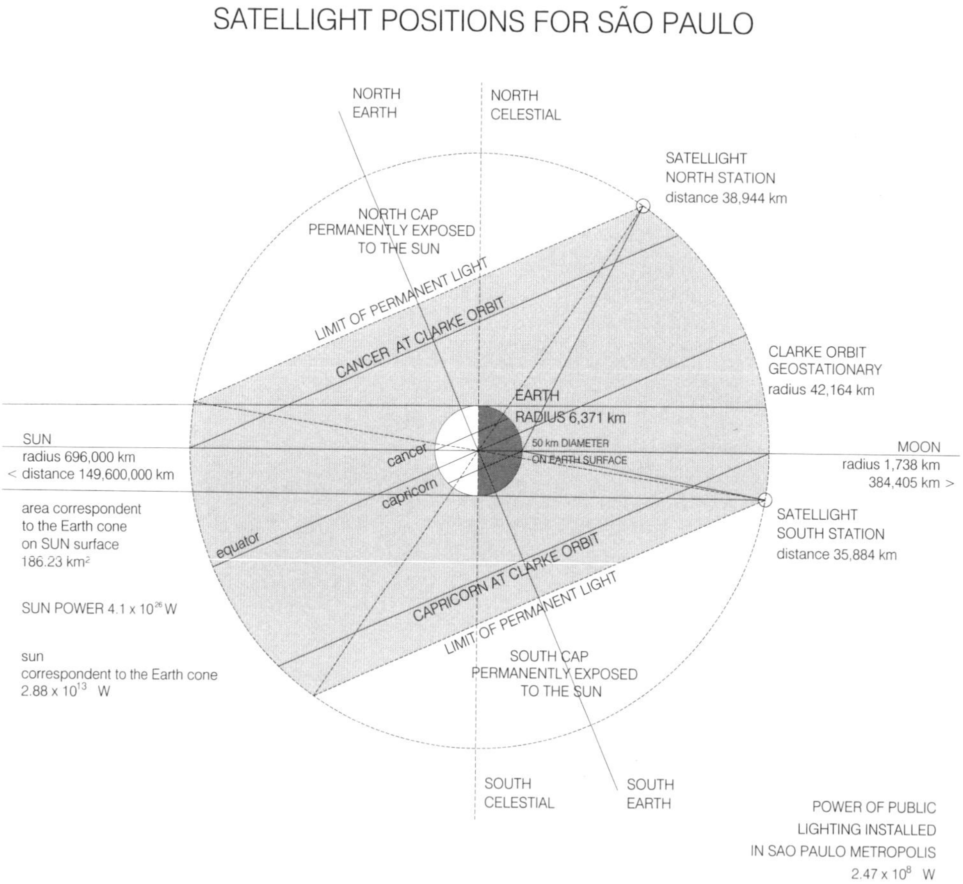


**Figure 3.** Satellights over São Paulo. 2017.

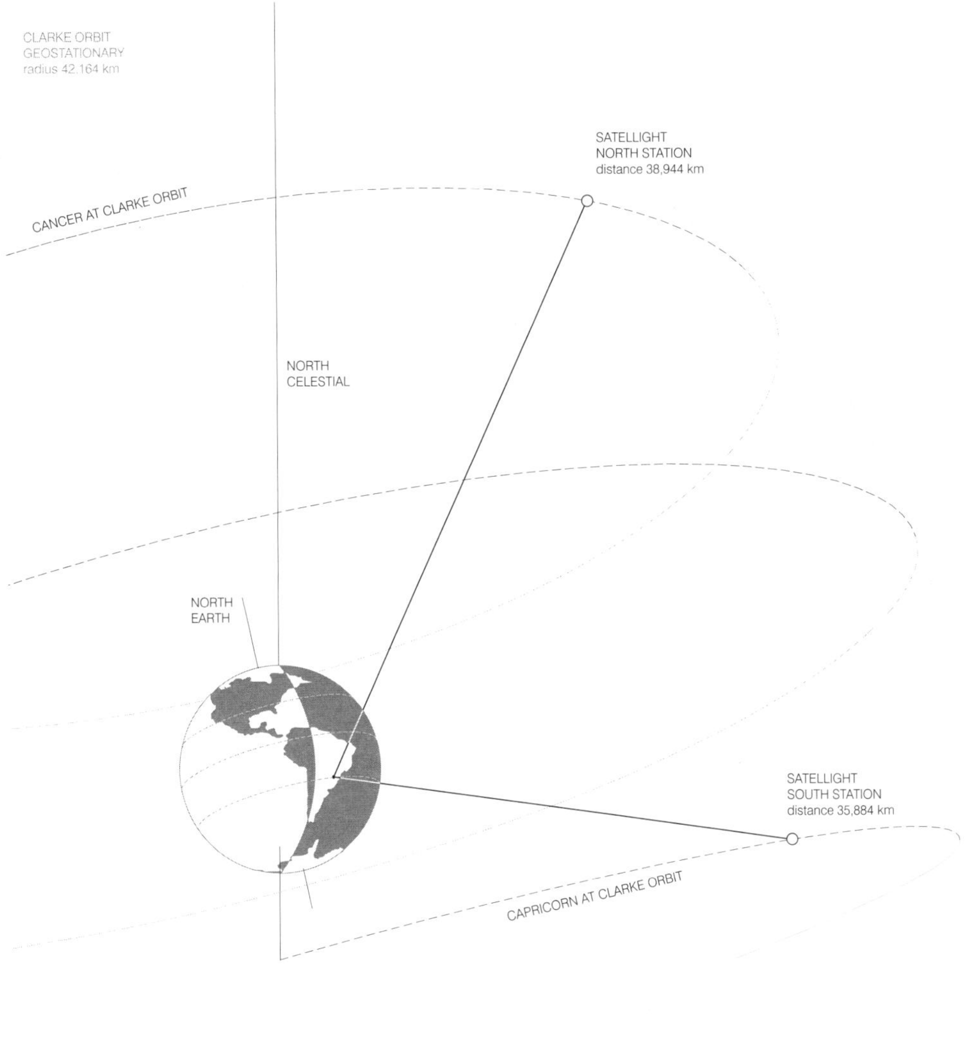


**Figure 4.** Satellights over São Paulo. 2019.

# City of 7 Billion

**Project:** 50. **Author:** Plan B: Joyce Hsiang (1977) and Bimal Mendis (1976). **Date:** 2015–2019. **Themes:** Geo-visualization. Infrastructure. Taxonomy. Total Urbanization.

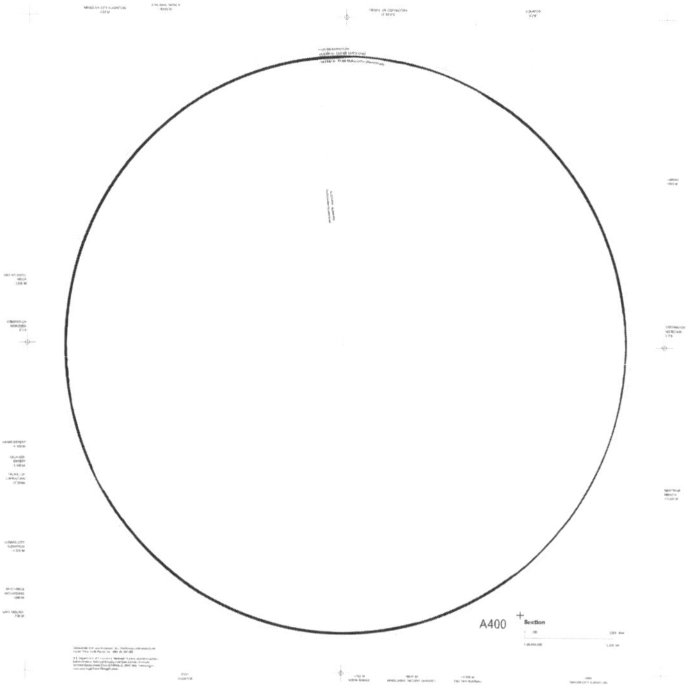


**Figure 0.** A400: Section. 2015.

1. Paul J. Crutzen and Eugene F. Stoermer, "The Anthropocene," *Global Change Newsletter* 41 (May 2000): 17–18.

Joyce Hsiang and Bimal Mendis's City of 7 Billion looks at the world as if it were a single urban entity: a city-world encompassing both occupied and uninhabited areas. City of 7 Billion is, in this sense, an architectural project that adopts a position not unlike Neil Brenner and Christian Schmid's notion of planetary urbanization **[project 45]**. The work rejects seeing Earth as a planet of discrete cities, and presents instead one where geography, infrastructure, and urbanization coalesce, tending to produce a deeply intermingled planetary space. The project's visualizations aim to elucidate how the world can be considered through this unitary vision and the implications this has for architectural discourse and practice.

The primary means of Hsiang and Mendis's work is a type of cartographic production intended to create a dialogue between urban theory and architectural speculation. On one hand, the project uses multiple cartographic means to elaborate a series of propositions regarding the status of urbanization today. These propositions address ongoing theories about the urban, its scales, and its interactions with nature, which have become prominent in relation to the notions of globalization and Anthropocene.[1] On the other hand, the project offers a projective image about the possible conditions of this planetary city. Its theoretical and speculative dimensions are not different parts of the work. On the contrary, they operate simultaneously and through the same cartographic tools. The type of cartography that City of 7 Billion explores is both descriptive and projective. It acknowledges that spatial propositions cannot exist without an initial conceptualization and visualization of their objects of intervention, without an initial act of framing, which, because it inevitably establishes the confines and possibilities of the project, is, often inadvertently, a project in itself. The exhaustive work of cartographic representation in City of 7 Billion insists upon this complex circularity between description and proposition as well as upon the breaches this relation contains. In dialogic terms, this makes the project interrogate not only urban theory, but also the forms of knowledge and data visualization that support contemporary considerations of the global scale.

The maps of City of 7 Billion are the assembly of a diversity; albeit a very structured one. The project's parts, namely Set of Drawings, Figures and Ground, The Sphere of the Unknown, Urban Core, and Scenes from the Horizon, systematically insist on four questions: 1) the variety of elements that constitute the city-world fabric; 2) the overlapping in this fabric of natural and man-made elements; 3) the different and contrasting points of view from which the city-world can be apprehended, and 4) the wide range of representational techniques required for comprehending it and intervening in it. In City of 7 Billion, many drawings use the graphic conventions of our discipline (plans, sections, axonometrics) to depict the earth as an architectural object **[figs. 1 and 2]**, but there are also huge panoramas of the planet as seen from the sky, vast models of the globe, and renderings showing the altitudes of urbanization **[fig. 3]**. Such a plurality of representations does not prevent the formulation of clear statements. It is, on the contrary, the medium through which City of 7 Billion seeks to construct a comprehensive and specific image of the city-world.

Among their contributions, a first one is that these images can be analyzed in relation to the postulates about world urbanization that derive from Henri Lefebvre's writings. One of the consequences contemporary urban theory has extracted from Lefebvre's thinking has been to abandon the analytic privilege of the discrete city in order to reveal the global circuits of production and communication in which cities are inscribed.[2] While the representations of City of 7 Billion share this approach, they emphasize another aspect of the French philosopher's thinking. For Lefebvre, the functional analysis of the processes of spatial production impedes neither the necessity of a structural and formal analysis of the space produced, nor the consequent understanding of the scales, forms, and textures the urban is acquiring. Hsiang and Mendis's work is particularly strong in this aspect, offering at least two key points to formally approach the city-world fabric. First, it presents agglomerations as a continuous system in three-dimensional interaction with geographic space, in contrast both to previous speculations about a global continuous urban system (such as Doxiadis's mostly planar representation of Ecumenopolis or the mere superposition of Richard Florida's Spiky World over the geographical space) and to the inverse segmentations of metropolitan areas from their surrounding geography, as it happened in Jean Gottmann's analyses of Megalopolis (1961) **[project 23]**.[3] Second, the work considers networks not as simply an immaterial space of flows but also as three-dimensional physical infrastructures, which help to constitute the urban realm. Combined, these points depict the urban fabric overlaying three-dimensional constructed flows, sectional geographical and geological conditions, and the volumes of agglomeration. This way, City of 7 Billion counters those visions of the urban that emphasize process rather than form, and stresses the relevance that formal and material analysis still have in architectural practice.

**2.** Neil Brenner and Christian Schmid, "Planetary Urbanization," in *Urban Constellations*, ed. Mathew Gandy (Berlin: Jovis Verlag, 2011), 10–13.

**3.** Richard Florida, Tim Gulden, and Charlotta Mellander, "The Rise of the Mega-region," *Cambridge Journal of Regions, Economy and Society* 1, no. 3 (2008): 459–476. Jean Gottmann, *Megalopolis: The Urbanized Northeastern Seaboard of the United States* (New York: Twentieth Century Fund, 1961).

A second and related contribution refers to the relation between Earth and World systems, emblems respectively of the natural and the human. Critically considered, this interaction is today characterized by the perverse forms of exploitation of the planet derived from its total integration in circuits of economic production and by the deleterious and neocolonial effects of urbanization. Both considerations support the concern for the dramatic alteration of natural and social ecosystems, for which mankind is responsible. They have informed the construction of politico-ecological discourses meant to critique this situation and develop instruments to counteract it **[projects 45, 47, and 48]**.

This lens structures the many drawings of City of 7 Billion reflecting the relation between agglomeration and hinterlands. These drawings complement the other argument about the Earth–World relations that Hsiang and Mendis's work unfolds. The paradigmatic representations of capitalist urbanization derived from the Global City theories present cities floating in an undetermined blank space, as if they uniquely existed in the networks of trans-scalar connections on which the operations of the market depend. The ubiquitous networks of City of 7 Billion acknowledge the importance of these connections. Yet the work shows that scalar jumps and related deterritorializing phenomena happen within a complex, and multidimensional, physical territoriality. The resulting vision of urbanization expands the geographic discourse of Le Corbusier, Vittorio Gregotti, and Saverio Muratori **[projects 15, 30, and 31]**. Complementing the works of these architects, City of 7 Billion presents urbanization as a geographic phenomenon that modifies the section and temporality of the earth, and it treats these dimensions as potential catalysts of architectural possibilities. The work therefore considers the interplay between Earth and World mostly through the design possibilities that this expanded territorial lens opens up. It presents the planetary agglomeration as an artificial geography merging natural topography and volumetric built form, thus opening up an exploration of the precise formal relations that can be constructed by relating these two aspects. The project explores the consequences of this sectional relation at different scales. Globally, one of the first drawings of the work is a section of the globe showing only the relation between its exterior topography, circular at the drawing's scale, and the varying depth of the Earth's crust **[fig. 0]**. This depth is then depicted in the cuts of the Urban Cores as a built and inhabited space, explicitly presenting the production of this zone as an object of architectural production. On the other direction of the vertical axis, the panorama of Scenes from the Horizon integrates the atmosphere within the set of themes architecture configures: the organization of material conglomerates, forms of relations, and visual experiences.

Hsiang and Mendis's arguments require using a massive amount of geospatial information. However, this data is carefully re-elaborated and questioned. Significantly, the first part of the work, the Drawing Set, opens with a blank map of the world, followed by a version of Lewis Carroll's Chart of the Ocean in *The Hunting of the Snark*. One of the centerpieces of the exhibition, the huge Sphere of the Unknown, represents the world at a scale of 1:3,000,000 and the material and immaterial infrastructures that connect it and survey it. It shows both the blank spaces between these nets and the intricacy that characterizes them, highlighting that the very complexity of these intermingled connections is what produces unknown, and therefore uncontrollable, realms. Yet, behind this questioning of the data employed and the processes and elements that attempt to facilitate an understanding of the world, there lies no epistemological incommensurability. What is at stake is the proposition of a different cognitive attitude toward data, in contrast both to geodesign's alleged objectivity and to the alternative tradition of critical cartography.[4] When City of 7 Billion employs geospatial information, its supposed objective condition is always rendered as manifestly insufficient: as a necessarily unaccomplished project of understanding reality **[project 46]**. The work shows that a big gap exists between the world and its supposedly neutral representations, not in order to denounce their inaccuracy but rather to highlight the positive value of this gap for spatial speculation.

Because spatial and aesthetic speculations are the crucial goal of City of 7 Billion. The systematic use of white and black renderings in most of the drawings decomposes every volume into its outlines and takes to the extreme the conceptual overlap between urban and nonurban realms. It equates the means of representation of the urban with the lines employed to represent the earth's meridians and parallels, its topography, the networks of communication that cross it, and even the messages contained in them. The proposed world is a matter of ethereal lines. Although entirely occupied, it can be, still, substantially hollow and essentially light—in the manner in which lightness is considered in Italo Calvino's *Six Memos for the Next Millennium* or in Michel Serres and Marcel Hénaff's Global City, to name some references close to the architect's discourse.[5] In that sense, the elevation of the epistemological abstraction of geospatial information to an aesthetic code legitimizes architectural sameness

**4.** See, for example, the work of William Rankin at http://www.radicalcartography.net/

**5.** Italo Calvino, *Six Memos for the Next Millennium* (Cambridge, MA: Harvard University Press, 1988); Michel Serres, *Atlas* (Paris: Editions Julliard, 1994); Marcel Hénaff and Anne-Marie Feenberg, "Of Stones, Angels and Humans: Michel Serres and the Global City," *SubStance* 26, no. 2 (1997): 59–80.

and, through it, the cross-geographic encounter of equivalent urban forms. Instead of a world of fragments and differences, we are confronted with a world of repetition and homogeneity. One where the global disguise of equivalent architectural and urban operations in particularized iconic or contextual dresses is substituted by the recognition of sameness as a fundamental and desirable constituent of its universal ethos.

City of 7 Billion thus moves from analysis to aesthetic proposition. It represents a possible object: the city-world, a type of *polis* and thus of political space, attuned to the scale of globalization. Its final goal can be read in these political terms, but Hsiang and Mendis's work underlines that the articulation of the political is also an architectural effect. City of 7 Billion shows that the planetary is an existing reality, although still substantially unstructured. Impossible to construct *ex novo*, this reality has to be configured rethinking, keeping in mind, the aesthetics, forms of vision, materials, and dimensions that architecture manages, and bringing to the forefront the relations created through those operations. It thus suggests a reorientation of architectural praxis in which metageographic analysis informs design positions, and it shows how and where to address the planetary by recognizing the multiple places, terrains, and scales at which it takes place **[fig. 4]**.

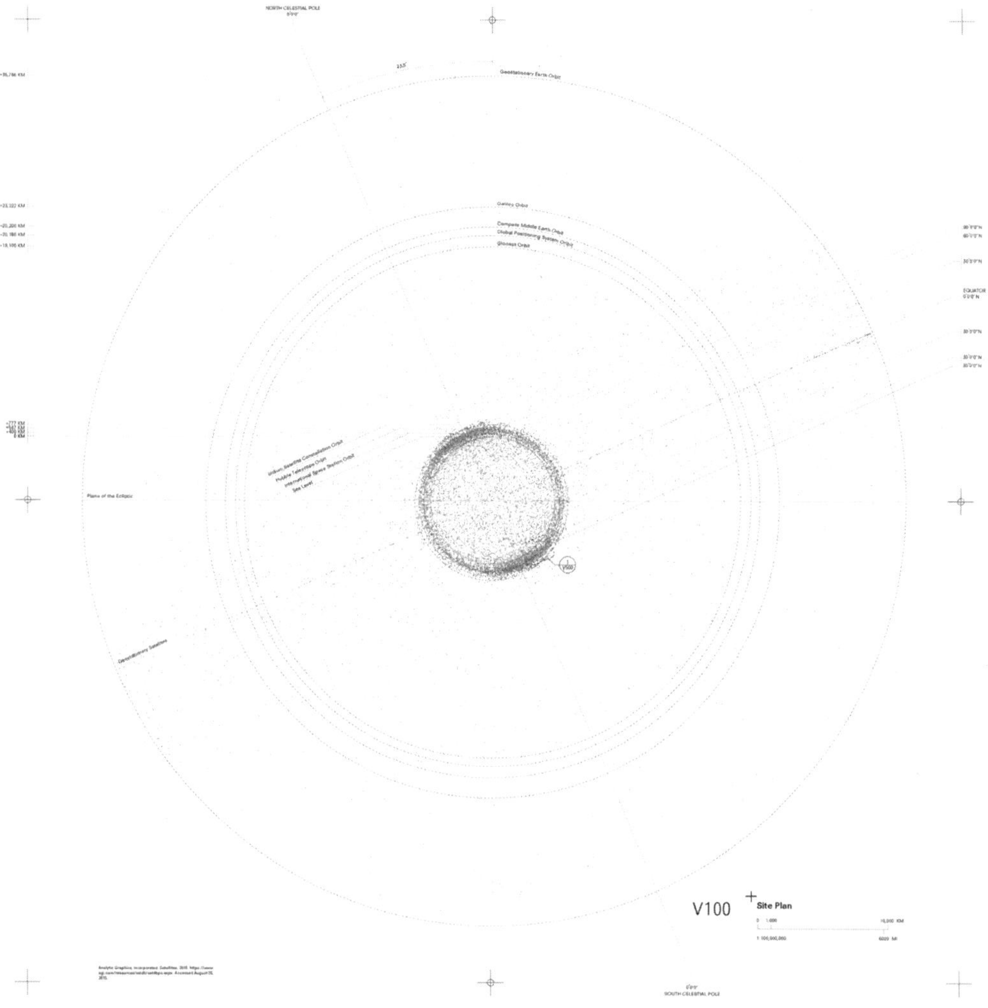


**Figure 1.** V100: Site Plan. 2015.

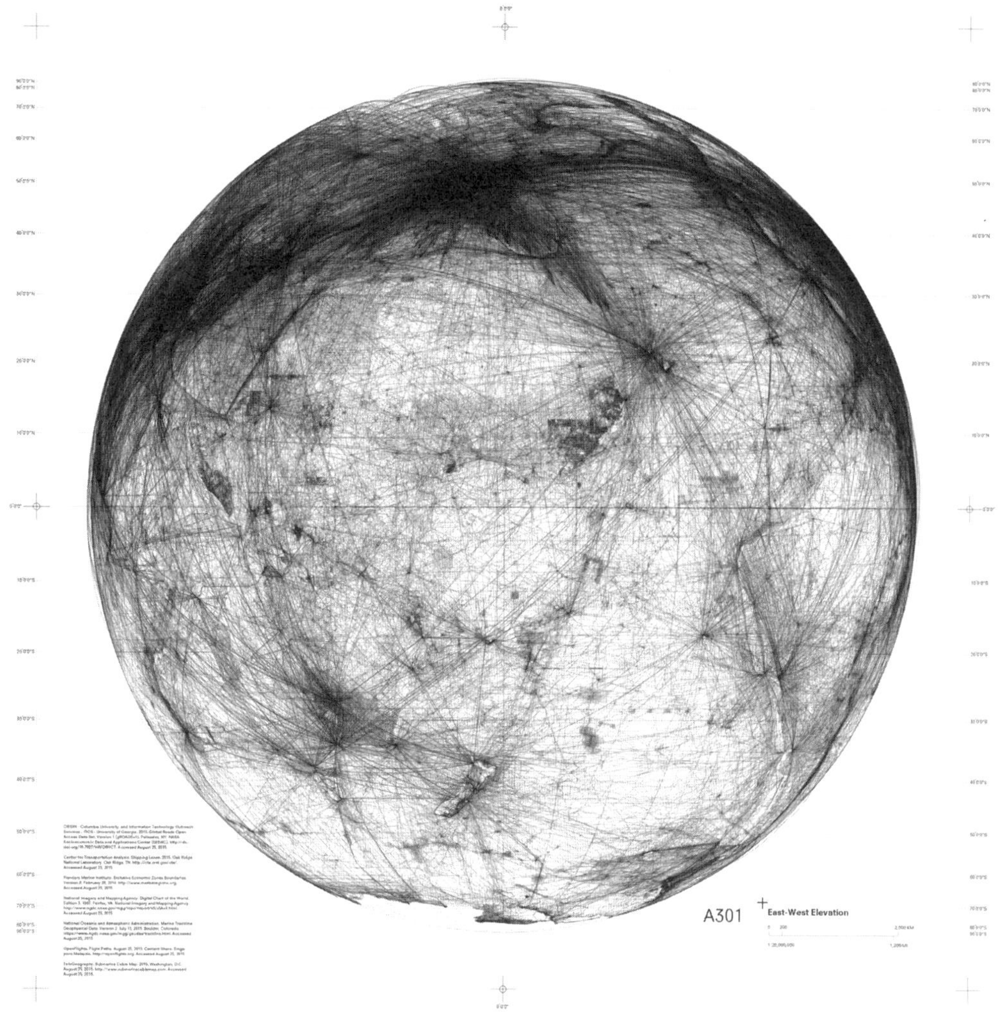


**Figure 2.** A301: East-West Elevation. 2015.

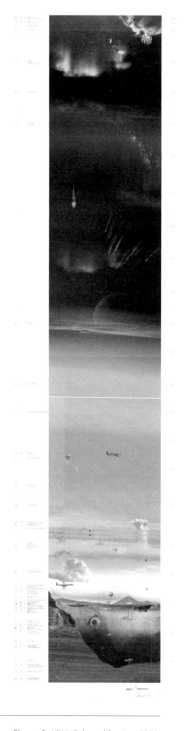

**Figure 3.** A811: Enlarged Section. 2015.

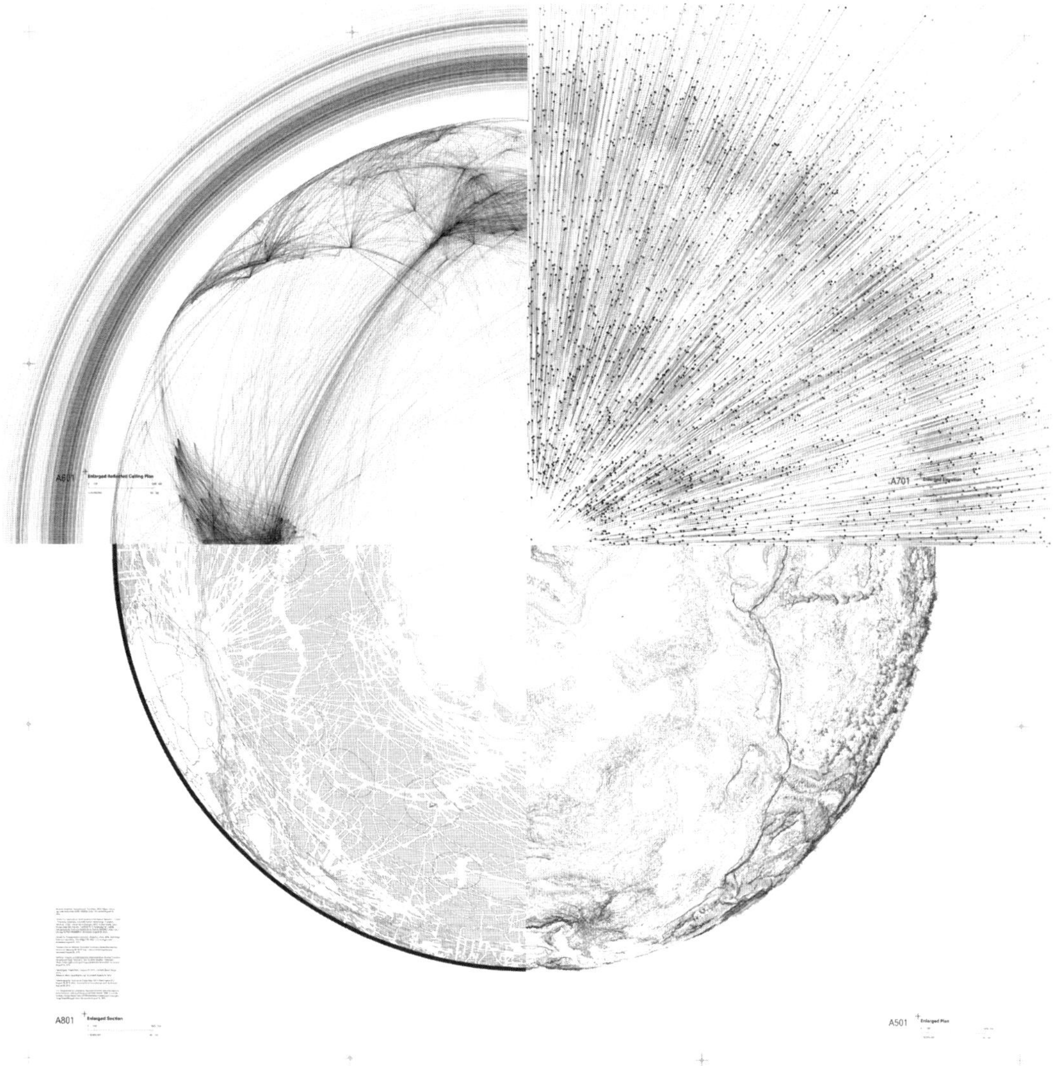


**Figure 4.** Clockwise from top left: A601: Enlarged Reflected Ceiling Plan; A701: Enlarged Elevation; A501: Enlarged Plan; A801: Enlarged Section. 2015.

# Five Wishes for the Next Fifty Worlds. Hashim Sarkis

A historical overview of speculative visions about architecture such as this book is bound to generate cross-historical associations, entanglements, and time warps. Some associations, however, are chronologically consecutive, the result of direct intragenerational dialogue. Think of the relation between Patrick Geddes, Élisée Reclus, Paul Otlet, Le Corbusier, and Rudolf Steiger. Reclus praises and supports Geddes's Outlook Tower. Later he develops with Louis Bonnier his own world-project: a colossal terrestrial globe. Paul Otlet, also in dialogue with Geddes, shares with these two authors the desire to create a building that can represent the planet, and asks Le Corbusier to design the Mundaneum in Geneva. Otto Neurath, after meeting Otlet, creates the Vienna Mundaneum. Rudolf Steiger, Wilhelm Hess, and Georg Schmidt collaborate with Neurath, adopting his symbols for graphic representation. Think also of the recurrence among Soviet architects of imagining how the more just society they are seeking can transform the world at large; of the often-polemical dialogue among Alison and Peter Smithson, Yona Friedman, and Constant.

The book also exhibits some family trees and strategies that straddle generations and continents. Linear urban forms, spatial structures elevated over the earth, new forms of cartography, and other techniques of geovisualization are recurrent approaches to world-making. Additionally, our research exposes time warps. Klein and Parent in the late 1950s, and Hadid two decades later, recover suprematist spatial strategies developed during the 1920s. In the year 2000 Purini adopts some of Leonidov's methods. Design Earth recovers now the techniques of visual argumentation Superstudio elaborated in the 1960s. Yet, even these warps, when examined carefully, resonate with the very times they escape. No matter how much architects aspire to being atemporal or aspatial, to suspend their time and context, their works are always bound by the moment they are trying to escape. After all, the exercise of imagining alternative worlds through architecture entails delegating to design the role of a time machine, a time machine of its time. As in Navarro Baldeweg's Gates, the memory of the city and the city's future are outcomes of a single operation.

The next fifty worlds may very well be produced with a different attitude about time and place, especially because of the sense of urgency we feel today to imagine a way out of global environmental and social challenges, and because we are increasingly realizing that alternative worlds have to be construed within this one. *There is not much time left and there is no other place to go.* Moreover, we will no doubt witness a proliferation of worlds in a much shorter period of time and with an intensity and resolve, but also sense of humility, that the last hundred years did not seem to necessitate. While we wait for these worlds to come, we can do more than anticipate or speculate. We can also wish architecture to bear more effectively on shaping the more pluralistic, equitable, non-anthropocentric, and temporally complex futures we choose to embrace. These directions acknowledge and reinforce the propositions of the past and recent projects that, for us, are more relevant for the social challenges ahead. The historical arc drawn underpins future architects' world-scale speculations.

## Confronting the Future World in the Present

The world is no longer the scale toward which architecture aspires. The scale of the world is now a given, as some 1960s projects, like Gregotti's or Muratori's, already intuited. In this context, the imagination of the world is no longer simply about apprehending the totality, although this remains an indispensable task. Imagining the planet is now increasingly coupled with a necessity to heal the world starting from the little architectural acts up. Through a myriad of small initiatives, architects are working together from different localities to address and change the planet. "The only politics is cosmo-politics," says Isabelle Stengers.[1] The only architecture is cosmo-architecture. The production of the world constitutes the horizon of every architectural action.

World-making is different today. The crucial challenge that stands before us is no longer the incomprehensibility of the scale, but rather the inhumanity of the global and how we need to imagine it otherwise, to question the boundaries that still divide it, and to reduce its pervasive inequalities. It is almost that the world is turning to architecture not to imagine its unity or its potential, but rather to imagine the means by which new and more just conceptions of the world can rise above today's.

Furthermore, it seems that not only the world is now given to us but the future as well, often in an almost dystopian way. The sense that the world is coming to an end is burdening and narrowing our imaginations, limiting our options to think the world otherwise. As Ulrich Beck observes in his seminal work on "risk society," humanity now faces annihilation propagated by its own devices.[2] Whether environmental, nuclear, or biogenetic, these threats have thrown society into a survival mode looking for solutions to save itself rather than possibilities for better futures.

1. Isabelle Stengers, *Cosmopolitics* (Minneapolis: University of Minnesota Press, 2010).

2. Ulrich Beck and Mark Ritter, *Risk Society: Towards a New Modernity* (London: Sage Publications, 1992).

3. Lauren Berlant, *Cruel Optimism* (Durham, NC: Duke University Press, 2011).

Fortunately, architecture can bypass the dystopias that have prevailed over the past decade. Architects seem to reject the closure of the future. Yet, while our discipline is condemned to optimism and seeks to construct positive worlds, our positivity may need adjusting to the constraints of global world-making realities. Our optimism no longer needs to envision futuristic scenarios; it needs to intervene critically upon the futures that are being deployed in the present.[3]

## Fostering Multiplicity within Worlds

A main premise for pluralism is that there should no longer be one source from which to seek guidance about how to live and how to organize the world. Multiple incomplete viewpoints are replacing the singularity and comprehensiveness of an ideological position. The main political questions are now located in a variety of arenas outside of politics, architecture included.

Driven by strong ideological constructs, many of the projects this book describes favor a deterministic approach to world-making, which may no longer be possible, let alone desirable. The profession of architecture may be better off not being bound to an illustrative, and therefore subservient role to political ideology. This does not mean that it should cease imagining worlds and new forms of social relation, but it needs to orient architectural projects toward a yet inexistent, pluralistic planet. The next fifty projects will need to imagine more pluralist ways of construing their work.

This combination of a pluralistic and constructionist logic rests on the premise of building internal consistencies to rehearse different forms of life without having them fully mapped in relation to external social configurations. The pluralistic project promotes the emergence of alternative worlds that maintain a critical distance from the world so that they suggest new models of shared life. Contrary to the immunological paradigm that sees in the return to bounded, protected forms of isolation the only response to all-too-present forms of hegemonic globalization, pluralism favors immanent critique and the imagination of new forms of open socialization and collectivity. Luc Deleu's investigation of a global public sphere, Neil Brenner's proposal of alter-urbanization, and World of Matter's "visibilization" of the disposed point in that direction. Through these and similar works, architecture contributes as a form of world-making to conceiving the diverse forms society may adopt. Such an overture is a precondition for the next worlds.

## Constructing a Non-Anthropocentric Vantage Point

Most world projects in this book emanate from an anthropocentric point of view. Even if some of the architects embrace ecological thinking, they ultimately imagine a fundamentally human planet, in which the complexity and diversity of the biome is organized from the perspective and for the benefit of our species. Now we inhabit a planet in which the predominance of the human is questioned from a variety of contrasting fronts. The recognition of the importance biological life has in shaping our planet is no less crucial than the acceptance of the power of our increasingly autonomous technologies to influence our social space and our forms of subjectivity.

A new cosmopolitical order thus requires a multiplicity of intelligences including animal and natural, as well as technological and artificial. Recognizing this favors the emergence of a human subject adopting a different vantage point, one offering a broader view of all beings living on the planet. To the dream of producing an even more human-mastered planet, where our species is in charge of regulating the whole environment through geoengineering technologies, it is necessary to counter a new spatial *ethics*—a prolegomenon to a new ecological contract across species. Similarly, the naïve vision of technology as a force entirely subjected to human will needs to be complemented with a more critical, dialogical vision that recognizes its positive as well as its deleterious—often unpredictable—effects on our biological and geophysical environment. In the time span of this book, architecture has regularly adopted a form of quasideterministic technological positivism in which social questions are reduced to technical problems. This sort of vision needs to be substituted by a more conscious interrogation of the social uses of technology in the production of a planet inhabited by humans and nonhumans alike. As Design Earth's Geostories suggest, the new worlds to come should derive from a form of architectural thinking that acknowledges our increasing role as mediators between the natural and the technological, as well as the responsibility that this mediation entails.

## Opening the Sources of Equity

The history of architectural world-making has often promoted forms of collaboration between architecture and other fields. Architects have also created institutions and engaged in international organizations, but these collaborative or institutional organizations have often relied on hierarchies of professional expertise and on systems of representation to the exclusion of multiple populations and alternative sources of knowledge. The next fifty worlds may very well continue to rely on individuals to author the projects or to orchestrate the collaborations around them, but the values that guide the world-making process will need to emerge from a more open and equitable approach.

The open source, the data cloud, the hacked, are all attributes of the new global which open new spaces for collaboration. These conditions challenge our current forms of professional organization, the means by which we produce architecture, and our criteria of evaluation. The ubiquity of digital technologies of communication produces a situation in which difficulties managing and navigating relentless flows of data hamper our possibilities of participating in society. This situation requires investigating how information transforms our ways of ordering and structuring knowledge. It requires contesting the forms in which information acts upon the world. Today the proliferation of data privileges a managerial approach to social organization that architecture as a discipline needs to critically address. In the next fifty worlds, data will be a constitutive part of society that needs to be harvested inclusively and openly, relying on architectural thinking and metaphors to be legible. Moreover, being propositional will require being both critical and creative toward data, an attitude that the works of the Urban Theory Lab and Plan B already bring forward. Importantly, data will need to support a project of social equity. Every piece of information matters in this new world. Every individual matters as a source and consumer of information. To build egalitarian and coherent worlds from this open source of information without compromising its specificity and diversity will be one of the most challenging and promising undertakings for architecture.

The assimilation of social equity with spatial equity that often characterizes this book's initial projects is increasingly edging toward a more diverse conception of equity, one that encourages the spatial representation of multiple voices. New communication and information tools are essential in that process, as Luc Deleu's and World of Matter's works investigate. These contemporary projects indicate a new trajectory in which equity is both the precondition and the outcome of world-making, and where social collectives are more present at the outset, shaping the design process all the way to the outcome. The next fifty worlds will therefore welcome the ways in which democratizing data will generate new forms of social engagement, increase public scrutiny of architecture, and produce new values for design to embrace.

## Anticipating Time

Finally, we need to highlight the importance of change as a constitutive dimension of world-making. The next fifty worlds will be deliberately open-ended, learning from their own self-generating powers and addressing them.

During the past one hundred years the spatial dimension dominated our world-making imagination. Now we need to acknowledge the increasing importance of the temporal dimension and the need to introduce time into our praxis. In the examples of *The World as an Architectural Project* there have been two predominant modes of temporality. One is a teleological, Hegelian mode of engaging time that sees evolution always moving in a certain direction, continuously pointing toward a unique horizon that—once achieved—will remain fixed and static. This is, for example, Constantinos Doxiadis's *modus operandi* in Ecumenopolis. There is also a more open vision of temporal progression, as in Yona Friedman's work, but it is one that sees the definition of a fixed, permanent spatial framework as the necessary precondition for the unfolding of future social processes. In the most extreme cases this spatial framework may be almost invisible and immaterial, but it is determined nonetheless. The works of Yves Klein and Claude Parent and of Superstudio pursue this approach in their Air Architecture and Supersurface, respectively.

Today these previous forms of spatial control of the temporal are at stake. We may need to approach architecture through a conception of time that is closer to the cosmology of Heraclitus's river. That is, to the idea that apprehending the world at its most essential implies accepting that we do not only live in a big unity of inhabitation but one that is always changing, dynamic.

To embrace the temporal is to support and promote an idea of open-ended *mondialisation*, or world-forming, as Jean-Luc Nancy has suggested, rather than the fixed and hierarchical image globalization too often seeks to produce, no matter how dynamic it may look.[4] It is also a way of recalibrating the actual capacities of architecture. The dynamism of contemporary processes of urbanization and environmental modification often challenges the mechanisms of spatial control on which architecture has relied for more than one century. A new engagement with temporality can help architects to think how to intervene in them in different, less physical ways.

4. Jean-Luc Nancy, *The Creation of the World, or, Globalization* (Albany: State University of New York Press, 2007).

5. Roberto Mangabeira Unger, *The Religion of the Future* (Cambridge, MA: Harvard University Press, 2014).

It may be increasingly difficult to define stable spatial conditions for social processes. Rather than pushing toward stabilization, it may be more beneficial to internalize the instability and uncertainty into the world-making process and to turn toward analyzing and imagining their temporal complexities. Architecture no longer works in a teleological fashion toward a single spatial horizon, nor toward the emergence of future conditions determined by spatial relations settled in our present. In the next fifty worlds, architecture will need to manipulate variegated forms of temporality: the almost geological consequences of some of our actions; the fast-paced, cyclical relations between production, consumption, and waste; the short life span of most of our buildings; the stabilized time of memory and preservation; the unstable, sometimes ephemeral, character of our present; the potentiality of our future.

***

The long century represented in this book corresponds to the project of social transformation associated with modernism. As Brazilian philosopher Roberto Mangabeira Unger observed, the beginning of modernism was triggered by the discovery that society is constructed by us and therefore transformable by us as well.[5] According to Unger what propels this transformation forward is our infinite capacity to reimagine society in order to emancipate individuals and groups, and strengthen their ability to reimagine society generation after generation. If we accept society as it currently is, we limit our infinite capacity and our originality. The architectural imagination, as this book shows, is a distinct part of the collective imaginary. Architecture at once constitutes this finite world and is an agent of its transformation. In the next fifty projects, this transformative practice has to reconcile the finitude of the world, its fragility and vulnerability, with the open nature of the future. We have no choice but to imagine the future, but for this future to be reflective of our humanity, it has to always remain incomplete, contested, and open to other possibilities. The next fifty worlds will have to rise to this ever-renewed challenge.

# Bibliography


Ábalos, Iñaki. *Atlas Pintoresco*, vol. 2: *Los Viajes*. Barcelona: Gili, 2008.

Abraham, Raimund. "Elementary Architecture." In *Raimund Abraham (Un)Built*, edited by Brigitte Groihofer, 133–136. New York: Springer, 1996.

———. "Essay by Raimund Abraham." *Design Quarterly* 122 (1983): 14–15.

———. "Negation and Reconciliation." *Perspecta* 19 (1982): 6–13.

Abraham, Raimund and George Ranall. *Raimund Abraham: Collisions*. New Haven: Yale School of Architecture, 1981.

Adams, Ross Exo. "Natura Urbans, Natura Urbanata: Ecological Urbanism, Circulation, and the Immunization of Nature." *Environment and Planning D: Society and Space* 32, no. 1 (2014): 12–29.

Alavoine-Muller, Soizic. "Un Globe terrestre pour l'exposition universelle de 1900. L'Utopie géographique d'Élisée Reclus." *L'Espace Géographique* 32, no. 2 (2003): 156–170.

Allen, Stan. "Nothing but Architecture." In *Hejduk's Chronotope,* edited by K. Michael Hays, 79–98. New York: Princeton Architectural Press, 1992.

Ambasz, Emilio. "Email 09." *Domus* 943 (2011): 32–35.

———. "The Museum of Modern Art and the Man-Made Environment: An Interim Report." *Members Newsletter (Museum of Modern Art)* 8 (Spring 1970): 10.

*Amereida: Volumen Primero*. Santiago, Chile: Editorial Cooperativa Lambda, 1967.

Anders, Peter. "The Lenin Institute: Leonidov's Icon of the Future." *Journal of Architectural Education* 37, no. 1 (1983): 20–26.

Anderson, Richard. "A Screen that Receives Images by Radio." *AA Files* 67 (2013): 3–15.

———. "Montage and the Mediation of Constructivist Architecture." In *Before Publication: Montage in Art, Architecture, and Book Design*, edited by Nanni Baltzer, Martino Stierli, and Richard Anderson, 24–43. Zurich: Park Books, 2016.

Arana, Luis Miguel Lus. "BUILDING A UTOPIE AUTRE [AMAZING ARCHIGRAM!—50 YEARS OF ZOOM!/ ZZZZRRTT!/ THUD!/ BLAAM." *Revista Proyecto, Progreso, Arquitectura* 11, (November 2014): 90–103.

Arango, Jorge. *The Urbanization of the Earth*. Boston: Beacon Press, 1970.

Archigram. *Archigram 3* (1963).

———. *Archigram 9* (1970).

———. *Archigram* 9½ (1970).

Archizoom. "No-Stop City." *Domus*, no. 496 (March 1971): 48–55.

Arns, Inke, Nabil Ahmed, Gavin Bridge, T. J. Demos, Timothy Morton, and Hartware MedienKunstVerein, eds. *World of Matter*. Berlin: Sternberg Press, 2015.

Arrighi, Giovanni. *The Long Twentieth Century: Money, Power, and the Origins of Our Times*. New York: Verso, 1994.

Aureli, Pier Vittorio. "Manfredo Tafuri, Archizoom, Superstudio, and the Critique of Architectural Ideology." In *Architecture and Capitalism: 1845 to the Present*, edited by Peggy Deamer, 132–147. Florence: Taylor and Francis, 2013.

———. "The Difficult Whole. Typology and the Singularity of the Urban Project in Aldo Rossi's Early Theoretical Work, 1953–1964." *Log*, no. 9 (Spring 2007): 39–61.

———. *The Possibility of an Absolute Architecture*. Cambridge, MA: MIT Press, 2011.

Aureli, Pier Vittorio, and Manuel Orazi. "The Solitude of the Project." *Log* 7 (2006): 21–32.

Aureli, Pier Vittorio, and Martino Tattara. *Dogma: 11 Projects*. London: Architectural Association, 2013.

Baird, George. "Architecture and Politics: A Polemical Dispute. A Critical Introduction to Karel Teige's 'Mundaneum,' 1929." *OPPOSITIONS* 4 (1974): 79–108.

———. "Karel Teige's Mundaneum, 1929 and Le Corbusier's 'In Defense of Architecture, 1933.'" In *Oppositions Reader: Selected Readings from a Journal for Ideas and Criticism in Architecture 1973–1984*, edited by K. Michael Hays, 585–615. New York: Princeton Architectural Press, 1999: 586–588.

Balladur, Jean, ed. *Les Visionnaires de l'Architecture*, vol. 3. Collection Construire Le Monde. Paris: R. Laffont, 1965.

Banham, Reyner. *Megastructure: Urban Futures of the Recent Past*. New York: Harper & Row, 1976.

Barbanova, Ekaterina A. "Igarka, la Construzione di una Città nell'Estremo Nord dell'Unione Sovietica." In *Ivan Leonidov, 1902–1959*, edited by Alessandro De Magistris, Irina Korob'ina, and Ivan I. Leonidov, 58–81. Milan: Electa architettura, 2009.

Beck, Ulrich. *Risk Society: Towards a New Modernity*. Translated by Mark Ritter. London: Sage Publications, 1992.

Berger, Alan, Joel Kotkin, and Celina Balderas Guzmán, eds. *Infinite Suburbia*. New York: Princeton Architectural Press, 2017.

Berlant, Lauren. *Cruel Optimism*. Durham: Duke University Press, 2011.

Bernardes, Sergio. *Cidade: A Sobrevivência do Poder*. Rio de Janeiro: Guavira Editores, 1975.

———. "Considerações de Base." In *Sergio Bernardes*, edited by Kykah Bernardes and Laura Pereira, 140–143. São Paolo: Artviva Editora, 2010.

———. "Entervista 1976." In *Sergio Bernardes*, edited by Kykah Bernardes and Laura Pereira, 202–211. São Paolo: Artviva Editora, 2010.

———. "Filosofia Urbana." In *Sergio Bernardes*, edited by Kykah Bernardes and Laura Pereira, 170–175. São Paolo: Artviva Editora, 2010.

———. "Letter to Clarice Bernardes," November 2, 1968.

———. "O Rio Do Futuro." *Manchete* 678 (April 17, 1965).

———. "(R)evolução." *Módulo Especial: Sergio Bernardes* (1983).

———. "Terrismo: Uma Ideologia." In *Sergio Bernardes*, edited by Kykah Bernardes and Laura Pereira, 214–215. São Paolo: Artviva Editora, 2010.

Besse, Jean-Marc. *Face au monde: Atlas, jardins, géoramas*. Paris: Desclée de Brouwer, 2003.

Betsky, Aaron. "Introduction: Beyond 89 Degrees." In *The Complete Zaha Hadid: Expanded and Updated*, 6–15. London: Thames & Hudson, 2009.

Bideau, André. "Elusive Ungers." *AA Files* 64 (2012): 3–14.

Binjaku, Xhulio. "The Issue of Geography." *Log* 43 (Summer 2018): 35–39.

Blistène, Bernard, Alison M. Gingeras, A. Guiheux, and Guggenheim Museum Soho, eds. *Premises: Invested Spaces in Visual Arts, Architecture, & Design from France, 1958–1998*. New York: Guggenheim Museum, 1998.

Bloch, Ernst. *The Principle of Hope*. Translated by Neville Plaice. Cambridge, MA: MIT Press, 1986.

Böck, Ingrid. *Six Canonical Projects by Rem Koolhaas: Essays on the History of Ideas*. Berlin: Jovis Verlag, 2015.

Bogdanov, Aleksaner. "Puti Proletarskogo Tvorchestva." In *O proletarskoi kul'ture 1904-1924*. Moscow: Kniga, 1924.

Bokov, Anna. "Space: The Pedagogy of Nikolay Ladovsky." *Walker Art Center*, What Is an Art School? n.d. https://walkerart.org/magazine/space-the-pedagogy-of-nikolay-ladovsky.

———. "Teaching Architecture to the Masses: Vkhutemas and the Pedagogy of Space, 1920–1930." PhD dissertation, Yale University, 2017.

Borges, Jorge Luis. "El Idioma Analítico de John Wilkins." In *Otras Inquisiciones (1937–1952)*. Buenos Aires: Sur, 1952.

Borges, Jorge Luis. *Otras Inquisiciones (1937–1952)*. Buenos Aires: Sur, 1952.

Borradori, Dario. "Parametri scalari e strutturazione formale negli insiemi a dimensione territoriale." *Edilizia Moderna* 87–88 (1966): 88–95.

Boutwell, Alan. "Una Città Intorno Al Mondo." *Domus* 502 (1971): 4–5.

Boutwell, Alan, and Michael Mitchell. "Das Umfassende Bausystem." *Bauen + Wohen* 2 (1965).

———. "Planning on a National Scale." *Domus* 470 (January 1969): 2–6.

———. "Das Umfassende Bausystem." *Werk* 53 (1965).

Bowlt, John E. *Russian Art of the Avant-Garde: Theory and Criticism: 1902–1934*. New York: Viking Press, 1976.

Boyarsky, Alvin. "Alvin Boyarsky Interviews Zaha Hadid." In Zaha Hadid, *Planetary Architecture Two*. London: Architectural Association, 1983.

Branch, Jordan. *The Cartographic State: Maps, Territory, and the Origins of Sovereignty*. Cambridge: Cambridge University Press, 2014.

Branzi, Andrea, and Arata Isozaki. *The Hot House: Italian New Wave Design*. London: Thames and Hudson, 1984.

Brenner, Neil. "Debating Planetary Urbanization: For an Engaged Pluralism." *Environment and Planning D: Society and Space* 36, no. 3 (2018): 570–590.

———. *Implosions / Explosions: Towards a Study of Planetary Urbanization*. Berlin: Jovis Verlag, 2014.

———. "The Hinterland Urbanised?" *Architectural Design* 86, no. 4 (July 2016): 118–127.

Brenner, Neil, and Christian Schmid. "Planetary Urbanization." In *Urban Constellations*, edited by Matthew Gandy. Berlin: Jovis, 2011.

———. "The 'Urban Age' in Question." *International Journal of Urban and Regional Research* 38, no. 3 (May 2014): 731–755.

———. "Towards a New Epistemology of the Urban?" *CITY* 19, no. 2–3 (2015): 151–182.

Brillembourg, Carlos, and Raimund Abraham. "Raimund Abraham." *BOMB* 77 (2001).

Brooks, H. Allen, ed. *Le Corbusier*. New York: Princeton University Press, 1987.

Brusatin, Manlio. "Theatrum Mundi Novissimi." In *Aldo Rossi: Teatro del Mondo*, edited by Manlio Brusatin and Alberto Prandi, 17–48. Venice: Cluva, 1982.

Brusatin, Manlio, and Alberto Prandi, eds. *Aldo Rossi: Teatro del Mondo*. Venice: Cluva, 1982.

Bucci, Angelo. *Sao Paulo, Reasons for Architecture: The Dissolution of Buildings and How to Pass Through Walls*, edited by Barbara Hoidn and Kevin Alter. Translated by Kristine Stiphany. Centerline 7. Austin: University of Texas at Austin Center for American Architecture, 2011.

———. "Satellights." Unpublished Manuscript, 2017.

Buchloh, Benjamin. "A Conversation with Constant." In *The Activist Drawing: Retracing Situationist Architectures from Constant's New Babylon to Beyond*, edited by M. Catherine de Zegher and Mark Wigley, 15–26. New York: Drawing Center, 2001.

———. "Plenty or Nothing: From Yves Klein's Le Vide to Arman's Le Plein." In *Premises: Invested Spaces in Visual Arts, Architecture, & Design from France, 1958–1998*, edited by Bernard Blistène, Alison M. Gingeras, A. Guiheux, 86–99. New York: Guggenheim Museum, 1998.

Buhmann, Ervin, Palmer, Tomlin, and Pietsch, eds. *Peer Reviewed Proceedings, Digital Landscape Architecture 2011: Teaching & Learning with Digital Methods & Tools*. Dessau, Germany: Anhalt University of Applied Sciences, 2011.

Burdett, Ricky, and Deyan Sudjic, eds. *The Endless City: The Urban Age Project by the London School of Economics and Deutsche Bank's Alfred Herrhausen Society*. London: Phaidon Press, 2010.

Burkhardt, François, and Cristina Morozzi. *Andrea Branzi*. Paris: Dis Voir, 1997.

Busbea, Larry. *Topologies: The Urban Utopia in France, 1960–1970*. Cambridge, MA: MIT Press, 2007.

Buttazzoni, Oscar, Manuel Casanueva, Alberto Cruz, Claudio Diaz, Godofredo Iommi, Jorge Sanchez, and Juan Verchueren. *Para una Situación de América Latina en el Pacífico*. Work presented to the Centro de Estudios del Pacifico for the Conferencia del Pacifico (September 27 to October 3, 1970). Santiago, Chile: Escuela de Arquitectura U.C.V., 1970.

Cabañas, Kaira M. "Yves Klein's Performative Realism." *Grey Room* 31 (Spring 2008): 6–31.

Calvino, Italo. *Invisible Cities*. New York: Harcourt Brace Jovanovich, 1978.

———. *Six Memos for the Next Millennium*. Cambridge, MA: Harvard University Press, 1988.

*Canada Land Data Systems Selected Papers I, 1979–1980*, vol. 4. LAC, n.d.

Caniggia, Gianfranco, and Gian Luigi Maffei. *Architectural Composition and Building Typology: Interpreting Basic Building*. Florence: Alinea, 2001.

Carlo, Giancarlo de. "Preface." In *The Ideal Communist City*, edited by Alexei Gutnov et al., ix. New York: George Braziller, 1971.

Cataldi, Giancarlo. "From Muratori to Caniggia: The Origins and Development of the Italian School of Design Typology." *Urban Morphology* 7, no. 1 (2003): 19–34.

———. *Per una scienza del territorio: Studi e note*. Florence: Uniedit, 1977.

Cataldi, Giancarlo, Gian Luigi Maffei, and Paola Vaccaro. "Saverio Muratori and the Italian School of Planning Typology." *Urban Morphology* 6, no. 1 (2002): 3–14.

Cerdà, Ildefons, Vicente Guallart, Angela Kay Bunning, Anne Ludlow, Graham Thomson, and Institut d'Arquitectura Avançada de Catalunya. *General Theory of Urbanization, 1867*. Barcelona: Institute for Advanced Architecture of Catalonia, 2018.

Chabard, Pierre. "L'Outlook Tower, anamorphose du monde." *Le Visiteur Ville Territoire Paysage* 7 (2001): 64–73.

———. "Towers and Globes: Architectural and Epistemological Differences between Patrick Geddes's Outlook Tower and Paul Otlet's Mundaneums." In *European Modernism and the Information Society: Informing the Present, Understanding the Past*, edited by William Boyd Rayward, 105–126. Aldershot, England: Ashgate, 2008.

Chalk, Warren. "Hardware of a New World." *Forum*, October 1966.

Chapel, Enrico. "Otto Neurath and the CIAM—The International Pictorial Language as a Notational System of Town Planning." In *Encyclopedia and Utopia: The Life and Work of Otto Neurath*, ed. E. Nemeth and F. Stadler, 167–182. Dordrecht: Kluweer Academic Publishers, 1996.

Chehonadskih, Maria. "The Stofflichkeit of the Universe: Alexander Bogdanov and the Soviet Avant-Garde." *e-flux* 88 (February 2018). Available at https://www.e-flux.com/journal/88/174279/the-stofflichkeit-of-the-universe-alexander-bogdanov-and-the-soviet-avant-garde/.

Chombart de Lauwe, Paul Henry. *La Découverte Aérienne du Monde*. Paris: Horizons de France, 1948.

Christaller, Walter, and Carlisle W. Baskin. *Central Places in Southern Germany*. Englewood Cliffs, NJ: Prentice-Hall, 1966.

Christensen, Peter. "Dam Nation: Imaging and Imagining the 'Middle East' in Herman Sörgel's Atlantropa." *International Journal of Islamic Architecture* 1, no. 2 (2012): 325–346.

Claramonte, Jordi. *La República de Los Fines. Contribución a Una Crítica de La Autonomía Del Arte*. Murcia, Spain: Cendeac, 2013.

Clarke, Bruce, and Linda Dalrymple Henderson, eds. *From Energy to Information: Representation in Science and Technology, Art, and Literature*. Stanford, CA: Stanford University Press, 2002.

Coleman, Nathaniel. *Utopias and Architecture*. London: Routledge, 2005.

Collins, George R., Carlos Flores, and Arturo Soria y Puig. *Arturo Soria y La Ciudad Lineal*. Madrid: Revista de Occidente, 1968.

Collins, George Rosenborough. "Introducción." In *Arturo Soria y La Ciudad Lineal*, edited by George Rosenborough Collins and Carlos Flores. Madrid: Revista de Occidente, 1968.

Colquhoun, Alan. "The Modern Movement in Architecture." *British Journal of Aesthetics* 2, no. 1 (1962): 59–65.

*The Complete Zaha Hadid: Expanded and Updated*. London: Thames & Hudson, 2017.

Constant. "Another City for Another Life (1959)." In Laura Stamps et al., *Constant: New Babylon. To Us, Liberty*, 206–209. Ostfildern: Hatje Cantz Verlag, 2016.

———. "Lecture at the Institute of Contemporary Arts, London (1963)." In Laura Stamps et al., *Constant: New Babylon. To Us, Liberty*, 210–215. Ostfildern: Hatje Cantz Verlag, 2016.

———. "New Babylon—Ten Years On (1980)." In Laura Stamps et al., *Constant: New Babylon. To Us, Liberty*, 216–225. Ostfildern: Hatje Cantz Verlag, 2016.

Cook, Peter. *Archigram*. Basel: Birkhäuser, 1991.

Cooke, Catherine. *Russian Avant-Garde: Theories of Art, Architecture and the City*. London: Academy Editions, 1995.

Cooke, Catherine, et al. *Architectural Drawings of the Russian Avant-Garde*. New York: Museum of Modern Art, 1990.

Costa, Lucio. "O Contrato Com a Doxiadis Internacional Associados." *Correio Da Manhã* (February 4, 1964).

Crary, Jonathan. *Techniques of the Observer: On Vision and Modernity in the Nineteenth Century*. Cambridge, MA: MIT Press, 1990.

Crinson, Mark, and Claire Zimmerman, eds. *Neo-Avant-Garde and Postmodern: Postwar Architecture in Britain and Beyond*. New Haven: Yale Center for British Art, 2010.

Crompton, Dennis, ed. *Concerning Archigram*. London: Archigram Archives, 2002.

Crutzen, Paul J., and Eugene F. Stoermer. "The Anthropocene." *Global Change Newsletter* 41 (2000): 17–18.

Cueva, Covadonga Lorenzo. "La Influencia de György Kepes en la Obra Temprana de Juan Navarro Baldeweg Realizada en el Center for Advanced Visual Studies del MIT (1971–1975)." *Revista de Arquitectura* 19 (2017): 67–77.

———. "La Noción de Ciudad Como Ambiente Significante. Las Primeras Propuestas Teóricas Urbanas de Juan Navarro Baldeweg = The Notion of City as a Significant Environment. Juan Navarro Baldeweg's First Theoretical Urban Proposals." *ZARCH* 8 (2017): 184–199.

Cupers, Kenny. "Géographie Volontaire and the Territorial Logic of Architecture." *Architectural Histories* 4, no. 1 (2016): 1–13.

Davidts, Wouter, Guy Châtel, and Stefaan Vervoort, eds. *Luc Deleu-T.O.P. Office: Orban Space*. Amsterdam: Valiz, 2012.

Davis, Kingsley. "The Origin and Growth of Urbanization in the World." *American Journal of Sociology* 5 (1955): 429–437.

De Cauter, Lieven, and Hilde Heynen. "The Exodus Machine." In *Exit Utopia: Architectural Provocations, 1956–76*, edited by Martin van Schaik and Otakar Máčel, 263–276. Munich: Prestel, 2005.

DeLanda, Manuel. *A Thousand Years of Nonlinear History*. New York: Zone Books, 1997.

De Magistris, Alessandro, Irina Korobina, and Ivan I. Leonidov. *Ivan Leonidov, 1902–1959*. Milan: Electa Architettura, 2009.

Deamer, Peggy, ed. *Architecture and Capitalism: 1845 to the Present*. Florence: Taylor and Francis, 2013.

Debord, Guy, and Gianfranco Sanguinetti. *I Situazionisti e la Loro Storia*. Rome: Manifestolibri, 2006.

———. "Sulla Scia Dei Surrealisti (1991)." In *I Situazionisti e la Loro Storia* by Guy Debord and Gianfranco Sanguinetti. Rome: Manifestolibri, 2006.

Deleu, Luc. *De Onaangepaste Stad: Werkdocumenten NAi96=The Unadopted City: Work in Progress NAi96*. Rotterdam: NAi Publishers, 1996.

———. *Ethique de l'Architecture*. Chagnon: Tarabuste, 1989.

———. "Orban Planning Manifesto." T.O.P. Office, March 18, 2019. Available at http://www.topoffice.to/Orban%20Planning%20Manifesto.html.

———. *Urbi et Orbi: De Onaangepaste Stad*. Gent: Ludion, 2002.

Demos, T. J. *Against the Anthropocene: Visual Culture and Environment Today*. Berlin: Sternberg Press, 2017.

Derrida, Jacques. *Negotiations: Interventions and Interviews, 1971–2001*. Translated by Elizabeth Rottenberg. Stanford, CA: Stanford University Press, 2002.

Deyong, Sarah. "Planetary Habitat: The Origins of a Phantom Movement." *Journal of Architecture* 6, no. 2 (2001): 113–128.

Difford, Richard J. "Proun: An Excercise in the Illusion of Four-Dimensional Space." *Journal of Architecture* 2, no. 2 (1997): 113–144.

Direk, Zeynep, and Leonard Lawler, eds. *A Companion to Derrida*. London: John Wiley & Sons, 2014.

Dix, Gerald. "Ekistics, Ecumenopolis and the Wilderness." *Land Use Policy* 2, no. 1 (1985): 41–53.

Douglas, Charlotte. "A Lost Paradigm of Abstraction: Alexander Bogdanov and the Russian Avant-Garde." In *The Russian Avant-Garde: Representation and Interpretation*, edited by Yevgenia Petrova, 203–212. St. Petersburg: Palace Editions, 2001.

———. "Aero-Art the Planetary View: Kazimir Malevich and Lazar Khidekel." In *Lazar Khidekel & Suprematism*, edited by Regina Khidekel and Tatiana V. Goriacheva, 27–34. Munich: Prestel, 2014.

———. "Energetic Abstraction: Ostwald, Bogdanov, and Russian Post-Revolutionary Art." In *From Energy to Information: Representation in Science and Technology, Art, and Literature*, edited by Bruce Clarke and Linda Dalrymple Henderson, 76–94. Stanford, CA: Stanford University Press, 2002.

Doxiadis, Constantinos A. "Anthropocosmos Model." *Ekistics* 72, no. 430–435 (2005): 70–76.

———. *Architecture in Transition*. New York: Oxford University Press, 1963.

———. *Ecology and Ekistics*, vol. 6, edited by Gerald Dix. Westview Environmental Studies. Boulder, CO: Westview Press, 1977.

———. "Ecumenopolis: Toward a Universal City." *Ekistics* 13, no. 75 (1962): 3–18.

———. *Ekistics: An Introduction to the Science of Human Settlements*. Oxford: Oxford University Press, 1968.

———. "On Linear Cities." *Town Planning Review* 38 (1967): 35–42.

Doxiadis, Constantinos A., John Papaioannou, and Athēnaïko Kentro Oikistikēs. *Ecumenopolis: The Inevitable City of the Future*. New York: Norton, 1974.

Drexler, Arthur, and Museum of Modern Art. "Visionary Architecture Press Release 108," September 29, 1960. Available at https://www.moma.org/documents/moma_press-release_326200.pdf.

Dunbar, Gary S. "Elisée Reclus and the Great Globe." *Scottish Geographical Magazine Scottish Geographical Magazine* 90, no. 1 (1974): 57–66.

Eagleton, Terry. *The Ideology of the Aesthetic*. Oxford: Blackwell, 1990.

Eco, Umberto. *The Open Work*. Cambridge, MA: Harvard University Press, 1962.

Eisenman, Peter. "Introduction." In *The Architecture of the City*, edited by Aldo Rossi. Cambridge, MA: MIT Press, 1966. 3–11.

Elden, Stuart. *Terror and Territory: The Spatial Extent of Sovereignty*. Minneapolis: University of Minnesota Press, 2009.

Elfline, Ross K. "Superstudio and the Staging of Architecture's Disappearance." PhD dissertation, University of California, Los Angeles, 2009.

———. "The Dematerialization of Architecture: Toward a Taxonomy of Conceptual Practice." *Journal of the Society of Architectural Historians* 75, no. 2 (June 2016): 201–223.

Escher, Cornelia. "Alan Boutwell: From the Modular Housing System to the Continuous City." In *Megastructure Reloaded: Visionäre Stadtentwürfe der Sechzigerjahre Reflektiert von Zeitgenössischen Künstlern = Visionary Architecture and Urban Design of the Sixties Reflected by Contemporary Artists*, edited by Sabrina van der Ley and Markus Richter, 153–168. Ostfildern: Hatje Cantz, 2008.

"Exhibition History—Corcoran." Archosanti (website), July 8, 2016. https://arcosanti.org/arconews-blog-15160/.

Faure, Bertrand. "Le professeur Geddes et son Outlook Tower." *Le Visiteur Ville Territoire Paysage* 7 (2001): 76–89.

Fedorov, Nikolai. "Astronomy and Architecture." In *Russian Cosmism*, edited by Boris Groys, 55–58. Cambridge, MA: MIT Press, 2018.

Fiel, Wolfgang, ed. *Eckhard Schulze-Fielitz: Metasprache des Raumes = Metalanguage of Space*. Vienna: Springer, 2010.

Fisher, Terry, and Connie MacDonald. "An Overview of the Canada Geographic Information System (CGIS)." In *Canada Land Data Systems Selected Papers I, 1979–1980*, vol. 4. LAC, n.d. 610–625.

Fitzpatrick, Lynn, and Doug Hofius, eds. *Rem Koolhaas: Conversations with Students*. Houston: Architecture at Rice University, 1991.

Florida, Richard, Tim Gulden, and Charlotta Mellander. "The Rise of the Mega-Region." *Cambridge Journal of Regions, Economy and Society* 1, no. 3 (2008): 459–476.

Folin, Marino. *La Città del Capitale: Per una Fondazione Materialistica dell'Architettura*. Bari: De Donato, 1976.

Foster, Hal. "1957a." In *Art Since 1900: Modernism, Antimodernism, Postmodernism*, edited by Hal Foster, Rosalind Krauss, Yve-Alain Bois, Benjamin Buchloh, and David Joselit, 453–459. London: Thames & Hudson, 2011.

Foster, Hal, Rosalind Krauss, Yve-Alain Bois, Benjamin Buchloh, and David Joselit. *Art Since 1900: Modernism, Antimodernism, Postmodernism*. London: Thames & Hudson, 2011.

Frampton, Kenneth. "A Kufic Suprematist: The World Culture of Zaha Hadid." *AA Files* 6 (1984): 101–105.

———. "Fragmentary Notes." In *Raimund Abraham (Un)Built*, edited by Brigitte Groihofer, 216–217. New York: Springer, 1996.

———. *Modern Architecture: A Critical History*. London; New York: Thames & Hudson, 2007.

Frassinelli, Piero. "Journey to the End of Architecture." In *Superstudio: Life Without Objects*, edited by Peter Lang and William Menking, 79–83. Milan: Skira, 2003.

Freeberg, Ernest. *The Age of Edison: Electric Light and the Invention of Modern America*. New York: Penguin Press, 2013.

Friedman, Yona. "Architecture and urban design from a particular point of view." In *Arquitectura Con la Gente, por la Gente, para la Gente = Architetcure with the People, by the People, for the People*, edited by María Inés Rodríguez, 55–63. León, Spain: Arte Arquitectura AA, 2011.

———. "Mobile Architecture: 10 Principles of Spatial Urbanism." In Yona Friedman and Manuel Orazi, *Yona Friedman: The Dilution of Architecture*, 216–217. Zurich: Park Books, 2015.

———. *Pour une Architecture Scientifique*. Paris: Pierre Belfond, 1971.

———. "Seen From Outside." In *Arquitectura Con la Gente, por la Gente, para la Gente = Architetcure with the People, by the People, for the People*, edited by María Inés Rodríguez, 93–106. León, Spain: Arte Arquitectura AA, 2011.

———. "Une Architecture pour des Milliards d'Hommes." In *Les Visionnaires de l'Architecture*, edited by Jean Balladur, 53–85. Paris: R. Laffont, 1965.

———. *Utopies Réalisables*. Paris: Union Générale d'Éditions, 1976.

Friedman, Yona, and Manuel Orazi. *Yona Friedman: The Dilution of Architecture*. Zurich: Park Books, 2015.

Fuller, R. Buckminster. *4D Time Lock*. Albuquerque, NM: Lama Foundation, 1972.

———. *Airocean Map*. March 1, 1943. Life.

———. *Airocean World-Town Plan*. 1927. Drawing.

———. *Critical Path*. New York: St. Martin's Press, 1981.

———. *Earth, Inc.* Garden City, NY: Anchor Press, 1973.

———. "Fluid Geography." In *The Buckminster Fuller Reader*, edited by James Meller, 128–147. London: Jonathan Cape, 1970.

———. "Foreword." In *Projections: Anti-Materialism*, edited by Lawrence Urrutia. La Jolla, CA: The La Jolla Museum of Art, 1970.

———. *Nine Chains to the Moon*. Philadelphia: J.B. Lippincott Company, 1938.

———. *Operating Manual for Spaceship Earth*. Carbondale, IL: Southern Illinois University Press, 1969.

———, ed. "Pan-Continental Service Systems." *Shelter* 2, no. 5 (1932).

———. *The World Game: Integrative Resource Utilization Planning Tool. World Game Series, Document One*. Carbondale, IL: World Resources Inventory, Southern Illinois University, 1971.

———, ed. "Universal Requirements of a Dwelling Advantage." *Shelter* 1 (1931).

———. *The Buckminster Fuller Reader*. Edited by James Meller. London: Jonathan Cape, 1970.

Furuhata, Yuriko. "Architecture as Atmospheric Media: Tange Lan and Cybernetics." In *Media Theory in Japan*, edited by Marc Steinberg and Alexander Zahlten, 52–79. Durham: Duke University Press, 2017.

Gad, Amira, and Agnes Gryczkowska, eds. *Zaha Hadid: Early Paintings and Drawings*. London: Koenig Books, 2017.

Gan, Alexander. *Constructivism*. Barcelona: Tenov, 2014.

Gandy, Matthew, ed. *Urban Constellations*. Berlin: Jovis, 2011.

Gannon, Todd. "Return of the Living Dead: Archigram and Architecture's Monstrous Media." *Log* 13/14 (2008): 171–180.

Garber, Megan. "Tower of Light: When Electricity Was New, People Used It to Mimic the Moon." *The Atlantic*, March 6, 2013. Available at https://www.theatlantic.com/technology/archive/2013/03/tower-of-light-when-electricity-was-new-people-used-it-to-mimic-the-moon/273445/

Gare, Arran. "Aleksandr Bogdanov and System Theory." *Democracy & Nature* 6, no. 3 (2000): 341–359.

Gargiani, Roberto, and Beatrice Lampariello. *Superstudio*. Rome: Editori Laterza, 2010.

Garrido, Ginés. "Cuidades Aéreas. Visions of Lazar Khidekel." *Arquitectura Viva* 153 (2013): 58–61.

Gassner, Gunter, Adam Kaasa, and Katherine Robinson, eds. *Writing Cities: Working Papers*, vol. 2. Cities Programme. London: London School of Economics and Political Science, 2012.

Gauthier, Pierre, and Jason Gilliland. "Mapping Urban Morphology: A Classification Scheme for Interpreting Contributions to the Study of Urban Form." *Urban Morphology* 10, no. 1 (2006): 41–50.

Geddes, Patrick. *Cities in Evolution: An Introduction to the Town Planning Movement and to the Study of Civics*. London: Williams & Norgate, 1915.
Ghosn, Rania, and El Hadi Jazairi. "Airpocalypse: A Short Geostory." *San Rocco* 10 (2014): 146–150.
———. *Geostories: Another Architecture for the Environment*. New York: Actar, 2018.
Gilpin, William. *The Cosmopolitan Railway: Compacting and Fusing Together All the World's Continents*. San Francisco: The History Company, 1890.
Gloeden, Erich. *Die Inflation der Gross-Städte und ihre Heilungsmöglichkeit.* Berlin: Der Zirkel Architektur Verlag, 1923.
Gohier, Jean. "Un cours a l'E.P.H.E., La géonomie de Maurice François Rouge." *Les Annales de La Recherche Urbaine* 37 (1988): 94–97.
Goodman, Nelson. *Ways of Worldmaking*. Indianapolis: Hackett, 1978.
Gorelik, George. "Bogdanov's Tektology: Its Nature, Development and Influence." *Studies in Soviet Thought* 26, no. 1 (1983): 39–57.
Goriacheva, Tatiana V. "Research in the Plane of the Suprematist Field." In *Lazar Khidekel & Suprematism*, edited by Regina Khidekel and Tatiana V. Goriacheva, 13–26. Munich: Prestel, 2014.
Gottmann, Jean. *Megalopolis: The Urbanized Northeastern Seaboard of the United States.* New York: Twentieth Century Fund, 1961.
Gowan, James, and Architectural Association London, eds. *A Continuing Experiment: Learning and Teaching at the Architectural Association*. London: Architectural Association, 1975.
Gozark, Andrei, Andrei Leonidov, Catherine Cooke, and Igor Palmin. *Ivan Leonidov: The Complete Works*. New York: Rizzoli, 1988.
Grabow, Stephen. "The Outsider in Retrospect: E.A. Gutkind." *Journal of the American Institute of Planners* 41, no. 3 (1975): 200–212.
Granö, Johannes Gabriel. *Pure Geography*, edited by Olavi Granö and Anssi Paasi. Translated by Malcolm Hicks. Baltimore: Johns Hopkins University Press, 1997.
Greene, David. "A Prologue Concerning Archigram." In *Concerning Archigram*, edited by Dennis Crompton, 1–4. London: Archigram Archives, 2002.
———. "C.S.8.634." *Archigram* 4 (1964). http://archigram.westminster.ac.uk/project.php?id=215.
———. "LAWUN. Project Number One: BOTTERY." In *Concerning Archigram*, edited by Dennis Crompton, 144. London: Archigram Archives, 2002.
———. "Popular Pak." *Archigram* 8 (1968).
Gregotti, Vittorio. "Form of the Territory." *OASE* 80 (2009): 7–22.
———. "Il Filo Rosso Del Razionalismo Italiano." *Casabella* 440–441 (November 1978): 31–35.
———. *Il Territorio dell'Architettura*. Milan: Giangiacomo Feltrinelli Editore, 1966.
———, ed. "La Forma Del Terriotio." *Edilizia Moderna* 87–88 (1966): 1–11.
Greimas, Algirdas Julien. *Sémantique Structurale: Recherche de Méthode*. Paris: Larousse, 1972.
Gropius, Walter. *Scope of Total Architecture*. World Perspectives 3. New York: Collier Books, 1962.
Groys, Boris. *Russian Cosmism*. Cambridge, MA; MIT Press, 2018.

Gutkind, Erwin Anton. *Creative Demobilisation*. International Library of Sociology and Social Reconstruction. London: Kegan Paul, Tench, Tubner & Co., 1943.
———. "Communità in Un Mondo Senza Stati." *Urbanistica* 6 (1950): 18–32.
———. "La Colonizzazoine Dell'Africa." *Urbanistica* 9 (1952): 4–34.
———. *Our World from the Air; An International Survey of Man and His Environment*. Garden City, NY: Doubleday, 1952.
———. "Pianificazione Nazionale in Un Mondo Che Si Restringe." *Urbanistica* 4 (1950): 5–19.
———. *The Expanding Environment: The End of Cities, The Rise of Communities*. London: Freedom Press, 1953.
———. "Universal Planning." *Building (UK)* 11, no. 2 (February 1936): 70.
Gutnov, Alexei, A. Baburov, V. Djumenton, S. Kharitonova, I. Lezeva, and S. Sadovskij. *Idee per la Città Communista*. Milan: Il Saggiatora, 1968.
———. *The Ideal Communist City*. Translated by Renee Neu Watkins. New York: George Braziller, 1971.
Guyou, George. *The Hollow Globe: A New Geographical Apparatus*. Edinburgh, 1902.
Haag Bletter, Rosemarie. "Global Earthworks." *Art Journal* 42, no. 3 (1982): 222–225.
———. "Paul Scheebart's Architectural Fantasies." *Journal of the Society of Architectural Historians* 34, no. 2 (1975): 83–97.
Hadid, Zaha. *Planetary Architecture Two*. London: Architectural Association, 1983.
Haffner, Jeanne. *The View from Above: The Science of Social Space*. Cambridge, MA: MIT Press, 2013.
Hall, Peter. *The World Cities*. New York: McGraw-Hill, 1966.
Haller, Fritz. *totale stadt, ein globales modell = integral urban, a global model*. Olten: Walter-Verlag, 1975.
———. *totale stadt, ein modell = integral urban, a model*. Olten: Walter-Verlag, 1968.
Haraway, Donna. "Anthropocene, Capitalocene, Plantationocene, Chthulucene: Making Kin." *Environmental Humanities* 6 (2015): 159–165.
Hays, K. Michael. *Architecture Theory Since 1968*. Cambridge, MA: MIT Press, 1998.
———. "Fuller's Geologic Engagements with Architecture." In *Buckminster Fuller: Starting with the Universe*, edited by K. Michael Hays and Dana A. Miller, 1–21. New York: Whitney Museum of American Art, in association with Yale University Press, 2008.
———, ed. *Hejduk's Chronotope*. New York: Princeton Architectural Press, 1996.
———. *Oppositions Reader: Selected Readings from a Journal for Ideas and Criticism in Architecture 1973–1984*. New York: Princeton Architectural Press, 1999.
Hays, K. Michael, and Dana A. Miller, eds. *Buckminster Fuller: Starting with the Universe*. New York: Whitney Museum of American Art, 2008.
Heidegger, Martin. *The Question Concerning Technology, and Other Essays*. New York: Harper & Row, 1977.
———. *What Is a Thing?* Translated by W.B. Barton and Vera Deutsch. Chicago: H. Regnery Co, 1967.
Hejduk, John. "Raimund Abraham, Architect." In *Raimund Abraham (Un)Built*, edited by Brigitte Groihofer. New York: Springer, 1996. 215–216.
Hejduk, John. *Victims: A Work*. London: Architectural Association, 1986.

Hejduk, John. *The Lancaster/Hanover Masque = Le Masque Lancaster/Hanover*. London: Architectural Association, 1992.
Hejduk, John, and Gregory Palestry. *A Berlin Masque*. New York: Chelsea Associates, Inc., 1982.
Hejduk, John, and David Shapiro. "John Hejduk or The Architect Who Drew Angels." *Architecture and Urbanism* 471 (2009): 73–79.
Hejduk, John, and David Sharpiro. *John Hejduk: Builder of Worlds*. DVD. Kanopy Streaming, 2014.
Hejduk, John, and Kim Shkapich. *Riga, Vladivostok, Lake Baikal*. New York: Rizzoli, 1989.
Hénaff, Marcel. "Of Stones, Angels and Humans: Michel Serres and the Global City." *Substance: A Review of Theory & Literary Criticism* 26, no. 2 (May 1997): 59–80.
Hendrix, John Shannon, and Lorens Eyan Holm. *Architecture and the Unconscious*. Farnham, England: Ashgate, 2016.
Highmore, Ben. "Streets in the Air: Alison and Peter Smithson's Doorstep Philosophy." In *Neo-Avant-Garde and Postmodern: Postwar Architecture in Britain and Beyond*, edited by Mark Crinson and Claire Zimmerman, 79–102. New Haven: Yale Center for British Art, 2010.
Holmquist, Anders. *The Free People*. New York: Outerbridge & Dienstfrey, 1969.
Hudson, Hugh D., Jr. *Blueprints and Blood: The Stalinization of Soviet Architecture, 1917–1937*. New York: Princeton University Press, 2015.
Huitzinga, Johan. *Homo Ludens: Proeve Ener Bepaling Van Het Spelelement Der Cultuur*. Groningen: Wolters-Noordhoff cop, 1938.
Huxley, Aldous. *Brave New World: Revisited*. New York: Harper & Brothers, 1932.
Ingraham, Catherine. "Errand, Detour, and the Wilderness Urbanism of John Hejduk." In *Hejduk's Chronotope*, edited by K. Michael Hays, 129–142. New York: Princeton Architectural Press, 1996.
Ivelic, Boris, and Escuela de Arquitectura y Diseño Pontificia Universidad Católica de Valparaiso. *Embarcación Amereida y la épica de Fundar el Mar Patagónico*. Valparaíso: Escuela de Arquitectura y Diseño Pontificia Universidad Católica de Valparaiso, 2005.
Ivelic, Ivan. "Claves de Amereida Son Presentadas en la 13 Bienal de Venecia." Escuela de Arquitectura y Diseño de la Pontificia Universidad Católica de Valparaíso, (September 5, 2012).
Jameson, Fredric. *Archaeologies of the Future: The Desire Called Utopia and Other Science Fictions*. London: Verso, 2005.
———. *Marxism and Form: Twentieth-Century Dialectical Theories of Literature*. New York: Princeton University Press, 1974.
Jencks, Charles. "Preface." In Kishō Kurokawa, *Metabolism in Architecture*, 1–22. London: Studio Vista, 1977.
Katsikis, Nikos. "Two Approaches to 'World Management': C. A. Doxiadis and R. B. Fuller." In *Implosions / Explosions: Towards a Study of Planetary Urbanization*, edited by Neil Brenner, 480–504. Berlin: Jovis Verlag, 2014.
Kawazoe, Noburu. *Metabolism: The Proposals for a New Urbanism*. Tokyo: Bitjutu Syuppan Sha, 1960.

Kepes, György. *Arts of the Environment*. Vision Value Series. New York: George Braziller, 1972.

Khan Mahsud, Ahmed Zaib. "Doxiadis' Legacy of Urban Design: Adjusting and Amending the Modern." *Ekistics* 73, no. 436–441 (2006): 241–263.

Khan Mahsud, Ahmed Zaib. "Rethinking Doxiadis' Ekistical Urbanism." *Positions* 1 (2010): 6–39.

Khan-Magomedov, S. O. *Viktor Kalmykov*. Moscow: Russkii Avangard, 2011.

———. *Georgii Krutikov: The Flying City and Beyond*. Translated by Christina Lodder. Barcelona: Tenov Books, 2015.

———. "Introduction." In Khan-Magomedov, *Pioneers of Soviet Architecture: The Search for New Solutions in the 1920s and 1930s*, 11–12. New York: Rizzoli, 1987.

———. "Ivan Leonidov, un Architetto Sovietico." In *Ivan Leonidov, 1902–1959*, edited by Alessandro De Magistris, Irina Korob'ina, and Ivan I. Leonidov, 10–45. Milan: Electa architettura, 2009.

———. *Mikhail Okhitovich*. Tvortsy Russkogo Klassicheskogo Khudozhestvennogo Avangarda. Moscow: Russkii Avangard, 2009.

———. *Pioneers of Soviet Architecture: The Search for New Solutions in the 1920s and 1930s*. Translated by Alexander Lieven. New York: Rizzoli, 1987.

Khidekel, Regina, and Tatiana V. Goriacheva, eds. *Lazar Khidekel & Suprematism*. Munich: Prestel, 2014.

Khiger, R. "Master of the Young Architecture." In *Ivan Leonidov: The Complete Works*, edited by Andrei Gozark, Andrei Leonidov, Catherine Cooke, and Igor Palmin, 104. New York: Rizzoli, 1988.

Kikutake, Kiyonori. "Marine City." In *Metabolism: The Proposals for a New Urbanism*, edited by Noburu Kawazoe, 10–47. Tokyo: Bitjutu Syuppan Sha, 1960.

———. "Marine City." In *Kiyonori Kikutake: Between Land and Sea*, by Ken Tadashi Oshima, 92–95. Cambridge, MA: Harvard University, Graduate School of Design, 2016.

Killer, Hermes. "The Tectonics of the Ruins: Rudolf Schwarz Von Der Bebauung Der Erde." Documents of the Università della Svizzera Italiana USI. Mendrisio: Accademia di Architettura di Mendrisio, 2014. Unpaged.

Klein, Yves. "Projekt einer Luft-Architektur." *ZERO* 3 (July 1961): n.p.

———. *Architecture de l'Air (ANT 102)*. 1961. Painting, 261 x 213 cm. Tokyo Metropolitan Art Museum. Available at http://www.yvesklein.com/fr/oeuvres/view/893/air-architecture/.

———. "Chelsea Hotel Manifesto." In *Overcoming the Problematics of Art: The Writings of Yves Klein*, edited by Klaus Ottman, 193–200. Putnam, CT: Spring Publications, 2007.

———. "Selections from Dimanche." In *Overcoming the Problematics of Art: The Writings of Yves Klein*, edited by Klaus Ottman, 99–137. Putnam, CT: Spring Publications, 2007.

———. "Je Raserai Tout à La Surface de La Terre Entière . . .," n.d. Div. sn. 613. Yves Klein's Archive, Paris.

———. "My Position in the Battle between Line and Color." In Otto Piene et al., *Zero*, 8. Cologne: DuMont Schauberg, 1973.

———. *Overcoming the Problematics of Art: The Writings of Yves Klein*. Edited by Klaus Ottman. Putnam, CT: Spring Publications, 2007.

Klotz, Heinrich. *Vision Der Moderne, Das Prinzip Konstruktion*. Munich: Prestel, 1986.

Knabb, Ken. *Situationist International Anthology*. Berkeley, CA: Bureau of Public Secrets, 1995.

Koolhaas, Rem. "Countryside: Future of the World." Forthcoming Exhibition at the New York Guggenheim Museum, February 20, 2020.

———. *Delirious New York: A Retroactive Manifesto for Manhattan*. New York: Monacelli Press, 1994.

———. "Exodus." *Casabella* 378 (1973): 42–45.

———. "Junkspace." *October* 100 (2002): 175–190.

———. "Dali and Le Corbusier: the Paranoid Critical Method." *Architectural Design*, AD Profiles: Surrealism and Architecture, 48, no. 2–3 (1978): 153–163.

———. "The City of the Captive Globe." *Architectural Design*, AD Profiles 5: 47, no. 2 (1977): 331–333.

———. "The Generic City." In *Small, Medium, Large, Extra-Large: Office for Metropolitan Architecture, Rem Koolhaas, and Bruce Mau*, edited by Bruce Mau and Office for Metropolitan Architecture, 1238–1269. New York: Monacelli Press, 1995.

———. "The Future's Past." *Wilson Quarterly* 3, no. 1 (Winter 1979): 135–140.

Koolhaas, Rem, Bruce Mau, and Office for Metropolitan Architecture. *Small, Medium, Large, Extra-Large: Office for Metropolitan Architecture, Rem Koolhaas, and Bruce Mau*. New York: Monacelli Press, 1995.

Koolhaas, Rem, Hans Ulrich Obrist, et al. *Project Japan: Metabolism Talks*. Cologne: Taschen, 2011.

Koolhaas, Rem, and Office for Metropolitan Architecture. *Content: Triumph of Realization*. Cologne: Taschen, 2004.

Kopp, Anatole. *Town and Revolution: Soviet Architecture and City Planning, 1917–1935*. New York: George Braziller, 1970.

Kurokawa, Kishō. *Metabolism in Architecture*. London: Studio Vista, 1977.

Laclau, Ernesto. "Universalism, Particularism, and the Question of Identity." *October* 61 (1992): 83–90.

Lacoste, Yves, Pierre George, Raymond Guglielmo, and Bernard Kayser. *La Géographie Active*. Paris: Presses Universitaires de France, 1964.

Ladovskii, Nikolai. "The Working Group of Architects in Inkhuk." In *The Avant-Garde: Russian Architecture in the Twenties*, edited by Andreas C. Papadakis, 24–25. London: Academy, 1991.

Lang, Peter. "Suicidal Desires." In *Superstudio: Life Without Objects*, edited by Peter Lang and William Menking, 31–51. Milan: Skira, 2003.

Lang, Peter, and William Menking, eds. *Superstudio: Life Without Objects*. Milan: Skira, 2003.

Lanzani, Arturo. *Immagini del Territorio e Idee di Piano: 1943–1963: Dagli approcci generalizzanti all'interpretazione dei contesti locali*. Milan: Angeli, 1996.

Latour, Bruno. "From Realpolitik to Dingpolitik or How to Make Things Public." In *Making Things Public: Atmospheres of Democracy*, edited by Bruno Latour and Peter Weibel, 14–43. Cambridge, MA: MIT Press, 2005.

———. *Reassembling the Social: An Introduction to Actor-Network-Theory*. Oxford: Oxford University Press, 2005.

Latour, Bruno, and Christophe Leclercq. *Reset Modernity!* Karlsruhe, Germany: Zentrum für Kunst und Medientechnologie: Center for Art and Media, 2016.

Latour, Bruno, and Peter Weibel. *Making Things Public: Atmospheres of Democracy.* Cambridge, MA: MIT Press, 2005.

Lavrentiev, Alexander. "Zaha Hadid and the Russian Avant Garde." In *Zaha Hadid and Suprematism*, 159–169. Ostfildern: Hatje Cantz Verlag, 2012.

Le Corbusier. *Concerning Town Planning.* New Haven: Yale University Press, 1948.

———. "In Defense of Architecture." *OPPOSITIONS* 4 (1974): 79–82.

———. *Looking at City Planning.* Translated by Elearnor Levieux. New York: Grossman Publishers, 1946.

———. *Precisions on the Present State of Architecture and City Planning: With an American Prologue, a Brazilian Corollary Followed by the Temperature of Paris and the Atmosphere of Moscow.* Cambridge, MA: MIT Press, 1991.

———. *The City of To-Morrow and Its Planning.* Translated by Frederick Etchells. London: Architectural Press, 1947.

———. *The Four Routes.* Translated by Dorothy Todd. London: D. Dobson, 1947.

———. *The Radiant City.* Translated by P. Knight, E. Leview, and D. Coltman. New York: Orion Press, 1933.

———. *The Three Human Establishments.* Chandigarh: Punjab Government Department of Town and Country Planning, 1945.

———. "Towards a Synthesis." In *Le Corbusier—Oeuvre Complète. Volume 4: 1938–46*, edited by Willy Boesiger, Oscar Stonorov, Pierre Jeanneret, and Max Bill. Zurich: Les Editions d'Architecture, 1991.

———. *Urbanisme.* Paris: Editions G. Crès, 1924.

Le Corbusier, Willy Boesiger, Oscar Stonorov, and Pierre Jeanneret. *Le Corbusier et Pierre Jeanneret, Oeuvre Complète de 1910–1929.* Zurich: H. Girsberger, 1937.

Le Corbusier, Willy Boesiger, Oscar Stonorov, Pierre Jeanneret, and Max Bill, eds. *Le Corbusier—Oeuvre Complète. Volume 4: 1938–46.* Zurich: Les Editions d'Architecture, 1991.

Le Corbusier, and Moisei Ginzburg. "Le Corbusier-Ginzburg Correspondence (1930)." In *Town and Revolution: Soviet Architecture and City Planning, 1917–1935*, edited by Anatole Kopp, 252–254. New York: George Braziller, 1970.

Le Corbusier, Pierre Jeanneret, Willy Boesiger, and Oscar Stonorov. *Le Corbusier et Pierre Jeanneret, Oeuvre Complète de 1910–1929.* Basel: Birkhäuser, 1995.

Lefebvre, Henri. *The Production of Space.* Translated by Donald Nicholas-Smith. Oxford: Blackwell, 1974.

———. *The Urban Revolution.* Translated by Robert Bononno. Minneapolis: University of Minnesota Press, 2003.

Lehmann, Philipp Nicolas. "Infinite Power to Change the World: Hydroelectricity and Engineered Climate Change in the Atlantropa Project." *American Historical Review* 121, no. 1 (February 2016): 70–100.

Leonidov, Ivan. "Extracts from Leonidov's Answers to Questions Put to Him about His Lecture Devoted to 'A Socially New Type of Club' at the First OSA Congress, 1929." In S. O. Khan-Magomedov, *Pioneers of Soviet Architecture: The Search for New Solutions in the 1920s and 1930s*, 554–555. New York: Rizzoli, 1987.

———. "Extracts from the lecture 'The Socially New Type of Club' given at the First Congress of Osa, 1929." In S. O. Khan-Magomedov, *Pioneers of Soviet Architecture: The Search for New Solutions in the 1920s and 1930s*, 554. New York: Rizzoli, 1987.

Leslie, Thomas W. "Energetic Geometries: The Dymaxion Map and the Skin/Structure Fusion of Buckminster Fuller's Geodesics." *Architectural Research Quarterly* 5, no. 2 (2001): 161–170.

Lewis, Simon L., and Mark A. Maslin. "Defining the Anthropocene." *Nature* 519, no. 7542 (March 2015): 171–80.

Ley, Sabrina van der, and Markus Richter. *Megastructure Reloaded: Visionäre Stadtentwürfe der Sechzigerjahre Reflektiert von Zeitgenössischen Künstlern = Visionary Architecture and Urban Design of the Sixties Reflected by Contemporary Artists*. Ostfildern: Hatje Cantz, 2008.

Libeskind, Daniel. "Deus ex Machina Machina ex Deo." In *Aldo Rossi: Teatro del Mondo*, edited by Manlio Brusatin and Alberto Prandi, 117–132. Venezia: Cluva, 1982.

Lightman, Bernard. "Spectacle in Leicester Square: James Wyld's Great Globe." In *Popular Exhibitions, Science and Showmanship, 1840–1910*, edited by Joe Kember, John Plunkett, and Jill A. Sullivan, 19. Pittsburgh, PA: University of Pittsburgh Press, 2012.

Lima, Antonietta Iolanda. *Soleri: Architecture as Human Ecology*. New York: Monacelli Press, 2003.

Lin, Zhongjie. *Kenzo Tange and the Metabolist Movement: Urban Utopias of Modern Japan*. London: Routledge, 2010.

———. "Metabolist Utopias and Their Global Influence: Three Paradigms of Urbanism." *Journal of Urban History* 42, no. 3 (2016): 604–622.

Lissitzky, El. *Russia: An Architecture for World Revolution*. Cambridge, MA: MIT Press, 1984.

———. "Suprematism in World Reconstruction" (1920). In *Russian Art of the Avant-Garde: Theory and Criticism: 1902–1934*, edited by John E. Bowlt, 151–160. New York: Viking Press, 1976.

Lobsinger, Mary Louise. "Antinomies of Realism in Postwar Italian Architecture." PhD dissertation, Harvard University, 2004.

Lodder, Christina. *Russian Constructivism*. New Haven: Yale University Press, 1983.

———. "Transfiguring Reality: Suprematism and the Aerial View." In *Seeing from Above: The Aerial View in Visual Culture*, edited by Stephen Bann, Mark Dorrian, and Frédéric Pousin, 95–117. London: I.B. Tauris, 2013.

Lootsma, Bart. "Le Film à l'Envers: Les Années 60 de Rem Koolhaas." *Le Visiteur*, no. 7 (2001): 90–111.

———. "Now Switch off the Sound and Reverse the Film" *Hunch: The Berlage Institute Report* 1 (1999): 153–173.

Lucan, Jacques, ed. *Le Corbusier, une encyclopédie*. Collection Monographie. Paris: Centre Georges Pompidou, 1987.

Maki, Fumihiko. *Investigations in Collective Form*. A Special Publication 2. St. Louis: Washington University School of Architecture, 1964.

Malevich, Kazimir. *The Non-Objective World*. Chicago: P. Theobald, 1959.

Mannheim, Karl. *Man and Society in an Age of Reconstruction*. London: Kegan Paul, Tench, Tubner & Co., 1940.

Mantziaras, Panos. "Rudolf Schwarz and the Concept of Stadtlandschaft." *Planning Perspectives* 2 (2003): 147–176.

Marx, Karl, and Frederick Engles. *The Communist Manifesto*. Marxist Internet Archives, 2010. Available at https://www.marxists.org/archive/marx/works/download/pdf/Manifesto.pdf.

Mason, Paul. *Postcapitalism: A Guide To Our Future*. Farrar, Straus & Giroux, 2017.

Massey, Anne. *The Independent Group: Modernism and Mass Culture in Britain, 1945–59*. Manchester, New York: Manchester University Press, 1995.

McCullough, Lissa. *Conversations with Paolo Soleri*. New York: Princeton University Press, 1900.

McGregor, James. "The Architect as Storyteller: Making Places in John Hejduk's Masques." *Architectural Theory Review* 7, no. 2 (2009): 59–70.

McHale, John, and R. Buckminster Fuller. *World Design Science Decade, 1965–1975*, Document 5. Carbondale: Southern Illinois University, World Resources Inventory, 1967.

McHarg, Ian L. *Design with Nature*. Garden City, NY: Natural History Press, 1969.

McLeod, Mary Caroline. "Urbanism and Utopia: Le Corbusier from Regional Syndicalism to Vichy." PhD dissertation, Princeton University, 1985.

Merrifield, Andy. "The Urban Question under Planetary Urbanization." *International Journal of Urban and Regional Research* 37, no. 3 (2013): 909–922.

Miller, Dana A. "Thought Patterns: Buckminster Fuller The Science-Artist." In *Buckminster Fuller: Starting with the Universe*, edited by K. Michael Hays and Dana A. Miller, 21–44. New York: Whitney Museum of American Art, 2008.

Miller, Norbert. "Imagination and the Calculus of Reality." In *Raimund Abaraham (Un)Built*, edited by Brigitte Groihofer, 7–14. New York: Springer, 1996.

Mitchell, Edward. "The Nature Theater of John Hejduk." In *Hejduk's Chronotope*, edited by K. Michael Hays, 53–64. New York: Princeton Architectural Press, 1996.

Monestiroli, Antonio. *L'Architettura della Realtà*. Turin: Umberto Allemandi & C., 1979.

Monteys, Xavier. *La Gran Máquina: La Ciudad En Le Corbusier*. Ediciones Del Serbal. Barcelona: Demarcación de Barcelona del Colegio de Arquitectos de Cataluña, 1996.

Moreno Rodríguez, Ignacio. *Dibujos Mentales: Principios del Universo Creativo de Juan Navarro Baldeweg*. Madrid: Ediciones Asimétricas, 2017.

Morris, William. *Hopes and Fears for Art: Five Lectures Delivered in Birmingham, London, and Nottingham, 1878–1881*. New York: Garland Publishing Inc., 1979.

Mörtenböck, Peter, and Helge Mooshammer. "Demiurgic Worlds." World of Matter, April 30, 2019. Available at https://www.worldofmatter.net/demiurgic-worlds.

Moss, Eric Owen. "Introduction." In *In the Absence of Raimund Abraham: Vienna Architecture Conference 2010*, edited by Peter Noever and Wolf Dieter Prix, 26–29. Vienna: MAK, 2011.

Mumford, Eric. *The CIAM Discourse on Urbanism, 1928–1960*. Cambridge, MA: MIT Press, 2000.

Muratori, Saverio. *Architettura e Civilta in Crise*. Rome: Centro Studi di Storia Urbanistica, 1963.

Mühlthaler, Erika, ed. *Lernen von O.M. Ungers*. Series 181/182. Berlin: ARCH+, 2006.

———. *Civiltà e Territorio*. Rome: Centro Studi di Storia Urbanistica, 1963.

Nairn, Ian, ed. "Outrage." *Architectural Review* 117 (1955).

———, ed. "Counter Attack Against Subtopia." *Architectural Review* 120 (1956).

Nancy, Jean-Luc. *The Creation of the World, or, Globalization*. Albany: State University of New York Press, 2007.

Natalini, Adolfo. "How Great Architecture Still Was in 1966." In *Exit Utopia: Architectural Provocations, 1956–76*, edited by Martin van Schaik and Otakar Máčel, 185–190. Munich: Prestel, 2005.

Navarro Baldeweg, Juan. "Arquitectura Informática." *Aquitectura* 161 (1972): 16–19.

———. *El Medio Ambiente Como Espacio de Significación*. Cambridge, MA: Center for Advanced Visual Studies, 1975.

———. "La Ciudad Como Ambiente Significante." *Nueva Forma* 94 (1973): 12–15.

———. "Le Geometría Complementaria." In Navarro, *La Habitación Vacante*, edited by José Muñoz Millanes, 37–38. Paterna, Spain: Editorial Pre-Textos, 1999.

———. *La Habitación Vacante*. Edited by José Muñoz Millanes. Paterna, Spain: Editorial Pre-Textos, 1999.

———. "Tapiz, Aire, Red." In *La Habitación Vacante*, edited by Juan Navarro Baldeweg and José Muñoz Millanes, 39–40. Paterna, Spain: Editorial Pre-Textos, 1999.

———. "Un Objeto es una Sección." In Navarro, *La Habitación Vacante*, edited by José Muñoz Millanes, 43–44. Paterna, Spain: Editorial Pre-Textos, 1999.

Necipoğlu, Gülru, and Alina Alexandra Payne, eds. *Histories of Ornament: From Global to Local*. New York: Princeton University Press, 2016.

Nemeth, E., and F. Stadler, eds. *Encyclopedia and Utopia: The Life and Work of Otto Neurath*. Dordrecht: Kluweer Academic Publishers, 1996.

Neurath, Otto. "L'Urbanisme et Le Lotissement Du Sol En Representation Optique d'après La Methode Viennoise." *Technika Chronika* (15 October-15 November 1933): 1036–1079.

Nikolow, Sybilla. "Gesellschaft Und Wirtschaft: An Encyclopedia in Otto Neurath's Pictorial Statistics from 1930." In *European Modernism and the Information Society: Informing the Present, Understanding the Past*, edited by William Boyd Rayward. Aldershot, England: Ashgate, 2008.

Nobre, Ana Luiza de Souza. "Fios Cortantes: Projeto e Produto, Arquitetura e Design No Rio de Janeiro (1950–70)." PhD dissertation, Pontificia Universidade Católica do Rio de Janeiro, 2008.

Noever, Peter, and Francois Perrin. *Air Architecture: Yves Klein*. Ostfildern: Hatje Cantz, 2004.

Noever, Peter, and Wolf Dieter Prix. *In the Absence of Raimund Abraham: Vienna Architecture Conference 2010*. Vienna: MAK, 2011.

Noviant, Patrice. "Les Trois Établissement Humains." In *Le Corbusier, une encyclopédie*, edited by Jacques Lucan, 414–417. Collection Monographie. Paris: Centre Georges Pompidou, 1987.

Nyby, Christian. *The Thing from Another World*. Winchester Pictures Corporation; RKO Pictures, 1951.

Nyilas, Agnes. "On the Formal Characteristics of Kiyonori Kikutake's 'Marine City' Projects Published at the Turn of the 50's and 60's." *Architectural Research* 6, no. 4 (2016): 98–106.

Obrist, Hans Ulrich. "Lessons Learned from Fragmentation." In *Zaha Hadid: Early Paintings and Drawings*, edited by Amira Gad and Agnes Gryczkowska, 84–90. London: Koenig Books, 2017.

———. "On Painting, Drawing, and the Digital." In *Zaha Hadid: Early Paintings and Drawings*, edited by Amira Gad and Agnes Gryczkowska, 74–80. London: Koenig Books, 2017.

Obrist, Hans Ulrich, and Zaha Hadid. "The Russian Avant-Garde or Zaha Hadid's Influences." In *Zaha Hadid: Early Paintings and Drawings*, edited by Amira Gad and Agnes Gryczkowska, 90–99. London: Serpentine Galleries, 2017.

O'Byrne, María Cecilia. "El Museo Del Mundaneum: Génesis de Un Prototipo." *Massilia: Anuario de Estudios Le Corbusierianos*, 2004.

O'Gorman, Edmundo. "Do the Americans Have a Common History." *Points of View* 3 (December 1941), Division of Intellectual Cooperation, Pan American Union (Washington, DC: 1941), n.p.

Okhitovich, Mikhail. "Editorial Favoring Deurbanization." In *Town and Revolution: Soviet Architecture and City Planning, 1917–1935*, edited by Anatole Kopp, 248–250. New York: George Braziller, 1970.

———. "Notes on the Theory of Resettlement." *Sovremennaia Arkhitektura* 1–2 (1930): 7–16.

———. "On the Problem of the City." *Sovremennaia Arkhitektura* 4 (1929): 130–134.

———. "On the Problem of the City." In *Russian Avant-Garde: Theories of Art, Architecture and the City*, edited by Catherine Cooke, 199. London: Academy Editions, 1995.

Orazi, Manuel. "Konrad Wachsmann's Technological Utopia." In Yona Friedman and Manuel Orazi, *Yona Friedman: The Dilution of Architecture*, 348–361. Zurich: Park Books, 2015.

———. "The Erratic Universe of Yona Friedman." In *Arquitectura con la Gente, por la Gente, para la Gente = Architetcure with the People, by the People, for the People*, edited by María Inés Rodríguez, 109–138. León, Spain: Arte Arquitectura AA, 2011.

Oshima, Ken Tadashi. *Kiyonori Kikutake: Between Land and Sea*. Cambridge, MA: Harvard University, Graduate School of Design, 2016.

Osterhammel, Jürgen. *The Transformation of the World: A Global History of the Nineteenth Century*. New York: Princeton University Press, 2014.

Ovsyannikova, Elena, and Vladimir Shukhov. "Phenomenon of the Russian Avant-Garde. Moscow Architectural School of the 1920s." *Docomomo Journal* 49 (2013).

Papadakis, Andreas C., ed. *The Avant-Garde: Russian Architecture in the Twenties*. London: Academy, 1991.

Papaioannou, John. "C.A. Doxiadis' Early Career and the Birth of Ekistics." *Ekistics* 72, no. 430–435 (2005): 13–17.

———. "Geography and the Future of Human Settlements." *Ekistics* 24, no. 145 (1967): 450–453.

Papalexopoulos, Dimitris, and Helene Kalaphate. *Takis Zenetos visioni digitali, architetture costruite*. Rome: Edilstampa, 2006.

Parent, Claude. *Colères, ou, La Nécessité de Détruire*. Marseille: M. Schefer Éditions, 1982.

———. *Demain, La Terre* . . .. Paris: Manuella Éditions, 2010.
Parnell, Steve. "The Collision of Scarcity and Expendability in Architectural Culture of the 1960s and 1970s." *Architectural Design* 82, no. 4 (2012): 130–135.
Penteleyeva, Masha. "Alexei Gutnov, the NER Group ('New Element of Settlement') and Giancarlo De Carlo." *Moscow Institute of Architecture MARKHI and Triennale Di Milano*, Radical Pedagogies, February 25, 2019. http://radical-pedagogies.com/search-cases/e06-moscow-institute-architecture-triennale-milano/.
Pérez de Arce, Rodrigo. "So Far Yet So Near: The Open City and the Travesías." In *Valparaíso School: Open City Group*, edited by Raúl Rispa, Rodrigo Pérez de Arce, and Fernando Pérez Oyarzún, 13–18. Montreal: McGill-Queen's University Press, 2003. Available at http://www.deslibris.ca/ID/420312.
Pérouse de Montclos, Jean-Marie. *Étienne-Louis Boullée: 1728–1799: De l'Architecture classique àl'architecture révolutionnaire*. Paris: Arts et Métier Graphiques, 1969.
Petrov, Antonio. "Rescaling Transnational Geographies." *Monu: Magazine on Urbanism* 22, Transnational Urbanism (2015), 16–23.
Petrova, Yevgenia, ed. *The Russian Avant-Garde: Representation and Interpretation*. St. Petersburg: Palace Editions, 2001.
Picon, Antoine. *French Architects and Engineers in the Age of Enlightenment*. Cambridge: Cambridge University Press, 1992.
———. "Fuller's Avatars: A View from the Present." In *Buckminster Fuller: Starting with the Universe*, edited by K. Michael Hays and Dana A. Miller, 45–60. New York: Whitney Museum of American Art, in association with Yale University Press, 2008.
———. *Les Saint-Simoniens: Raison, Imaginaire et Utopie*. Paris: Belin, 2002.
———. "Notes on Utopia, the City, and Architecture." *Grey Room* 68 (2017): 94–105.
Piene, Otto, et al. *Zero*. Cologne: DuMont Schauberg, 1973.
Piene, Otto, Heinz Mack, and Group Zero. *Zero 1, 2, 3*. Cambridge, MA: MIT Press, 1973.
Ponte, Alessandra, and Jessica Levine. "Building the Stair Spiral of Evolution: The Index Museum of Sir Patrick Geddes." *Assemblage* 10 (1989): 47–64.
Purcell, Thomas F., and Estefania Martinez. "Post-Neoliberal Energy Modernity and the Political Economy of the Landlord State in Ecuador." *Energy Research and Social Science*, 2018, 12–21.
Purini, Franco. *Dal progetto: Scritti teorici di Franco Purini 1966–1991*, edited by Francesco Moschini and Gianfranco Neri. Rome: Edizioni Kappa, 1992.
———. *Franco Purini: le opere, gli scritti, la critica*. Milan: Electa, 2000.
———. "Il progetto el il 'luogo'." In *Dal progetto: Scritti teorici di Franco Purini 1966–1991*, edited by Francesco Moschini and Gianfranco Neri, 11–31. Rome: Edizioni Kappa, 1992.
———. "Il transito nel Simbolico." In *Dal progetto: Scritti teorici di Franco Purini 1966–1991*, edited by Francesco Moschini and Gianfranco Neri, 168–169. Rome: Edizioni Kappa, 1992.
———. *Luogo e progetto*. Rome: Editrice Magma, 1976.
———. *Scrivere architettura: Alcuni temi sui quali abbiamo dovuto cambiare idea*. Rome: Prospettive Edizioni, 2012.

———. "The Equal City." *Compasses: Architecture and Design*, Sky Architecture 1 (2001): 116–125.
———. "Un disegno plurale." *Firenze Architettura* 1 & 2 (2003): 52–67.
Purini, Franco, and Laura Thermes. "Três caminhos." In *Franco Purini: O que está feito está por fazer: anonimato, fragmento, descontinuidade*, edited by Fernando Sendyk and Maria Pace Chiavari, 10–13. Rio de Janeiro: Centro de Arquitetura e Urbanismo do Rio de Janeiro, 1998.
Pyla, Panayiota Ioanni. "Ekistics, Architecture, and Environmental Politics, 1945–1976: A Prehistory of Sustainable Development." PhD dissertation, Massachusetts Institute of Technology, 2003.
———. "Planetary Home and Garden: Ekistics and Environmental-Developmental Politics." *Grey Room* 36 (2009): 6–35.
Quesada, Fernando. "Superstudio 1966–73: From the World without Objects to the Universal Grid." *Footprint:* 5, no. 1 (2011): 23–34.
Quilici, Vieri. "Introduction." In *Ivan Leonidov*, 3–14. New York: Institute for Architecture and Urban Studies, 1981.
Rancière, Jacques. *Aesthetics and Its Discontents*. Cambridge, UK: Polity Press, 2009.
———. *The Politics of Aesthetics: The Distribution of the Sensible.* London: Continuum, 2004.
Rankin, William. "Radical Cartography," April 24, 2019. http://radicalcartography.net/.
Ravagnati, Carlo. *L'Invenzione del Territorio: l'Atlante Inedito di Saverio Muratori.* Milan: F. Angeli, 2012.
Read, Herbert. "Preface." In *Creative Demobilisation*, edited by E. A Gutkind, ix–xii. International Library of Sociology and Social Reconstruction. London: Kegan Paul, Tench, Tubner & Co., 1943.
Reclus, Élisée. *Nouvelle Géographie Universelle,* vol. 2. Paris: Hachette, 1887.
———. "Projet de Construction d'un Globe Terrestre à l'échelle Du 100.000e." In *Report of the Sixth International Geographical Congress*, edited by the secretaries, 625–636. London: John Murray, 1896.
———. "The Evolution of Cities." *Contemporary Review* 67 (1895): 244–264.
Restany, Pierre. *Les Nouveaux Réalistes*. Paris: Editions Planète, 1968.
Ribeiro, Guilherme. "Regional Question, National Identity and the Emergence of Urban Industrial World: The Modernity in Paul Vidal's Work." *Annales de Géographie* 5 (2014): 1215–1238.
Richardson, Douglas, Noel Castree, Michael F. Goodchild, Audrey Kobayashi, Weidong Liu, and Richard A. Martson, eds. *The International Encyclopedia of Geography,* vol. 6. Hoboken, NJ: Wiley-Blackwell, 2017.
Rispa, Raúl, Rodrigo Pérez de Arce, and Fernando Pérez Oyarzún, eds. *Valparaíso School: Open City Group*. Montreal: McGill-Queen's University Press, 2003. Available at http://www.deslibris.ca/ID/420312.
Robic, Marie-Claire. "Elisée Reclus Visited and Revisited." Paper presented at the Axel Baudoin Homage, Trondheim, Norway, 2006.
Rodrigues, Gustavo Gama, and Paulo de Barros. *Bernardes*. 6D Filmes e Rinoceronte Produções, 2014.

Rodríguez, María Inés, ed. *Arquitectura con la Gente, por la Gente, para la Gente = Architetcure with the People, by the People, for the People*. León Spain: Arte Arquitectura AA, 2011.
Rojo de Castro, Luis. "Conversation with Juan Navarro Baldeweg." *El Croquis* 73, no. 2 (1995).
Röller, Nils. "Architekturen der Bodenlosigkeit. Haller und Flusser im Dialog." In *Fritz Haller: Architekt und Forscher*, edited by Laurent Stalder and Georg Vrachliotis, 202–204. Zurich: gta Verlag, 2015.
Romberg, Kristin. "Alexei Gan: Vvedenie v Tektoniky" (Alexei Gan: Introduction to Tectonics), in *Formal'nyi Metod: Antologiia Russkogo Modernizma*, edited by Sergei Oushakine, vol. 1: Systems, 845–858. Moscow: Kabinetnyi Uchenyi, 2016.
Rosenfeld, Allen. "Between Suprematist Utopia and Stalinist Reality." In *Lazar Khidekel & Suprematism*, edited by Regina Khidekel and Tatiana V. Goriacheva, 35–48. Munich: Prestel, 2014.
Rossi, Aldo. *A Scientific Autobiography*. Cambridge, MA: MIT Press, 2010.
———. "Architettura per i museii." In *Scritti scelti sull'architettura e la città 1956–1972*, edited by Rosaldo Bonicalzi, 323–339. Milan: Clup, 1975.
———. "Interview." *Japan Architect (JA)*, no. 1 (January 1985).
———. "Nuovi Problemi." In *Scritti scelti sull'architettura e la città 1956–1972*, edited by Rosaldo Bonicalzi, 175–192. Milan: Clup, 1975.
———. *The Architecture of the City*. Cambridge, MA: MIT Press, 1966.
———. *Scritti scelti sull'architettura e la città 1956–1972*. Edited by Rosaldo Bonicalzi. Milan: Clup, 1975.
Rossi, Aldo, and Silvano Tintori. "Aspetti urbanistici del problema delle zone arretrate in Italia e in Europa." In Giovanni Demaria et al., *Problemi sullo sviluppo delle aree arretrate*, n.p. Bologna: Il Mulino, 1960.
Rouge, Maurice François. *La Géonomie; Ou, l'Organisation de l'Espace*. Collection d'Études Économiques. Paris: Librairie Générale de Droit et de Jurisprudence, 1947.
Rouillard, Dominique. *Superarchitecture: le Futur de l'Architecture 1950–1970*. Paris: Éditions de la Villette, 2004.
Rozwenc, Edwin C. "Edmundo O'Gorman and the Idea of America." *American Quarterly* 10, no. 2 (1958): 99–115.
Sack, Robert David. *Human Territoriality: Its Theory and History*. Cambridge: Cambridge University Press, 1986.
Sadler, Simon. "The Living City: Pop Urbanism circa 1963." In Sadler, *Archigram: Architecture without Architecture*, 52–89. Cambridge, MA: MIT Press, 2005.
Sadler, Simon. *Archigram: Architecture without Architecture*. Cambridge, MA: MIT Press, 2005.
Salgueiro Barrio, Roi. "Birds Must Be Eliminated: Air Architecture and the Planetary Reenactment of the Modern Void." *Journal of Architectural Education* 70, no. 2 (2016): 311–323.
———. "Micro, Partial, Parallel, (In)Visible." *New Geographies* 8 (2016): 194–203.
Sambricio, Carlos. "Arturo Soria y La Ciuidad Lineal." *Q* 58 (1982): 22–30.
Samonà, Giuseppe. *L'Urbanistica e l'Avvenire Della Città Negli Stati Europei*. Bari: Editori Laterza, 1960.

Santos, Milton. *A Natureza Do Espaçao Técnica e Tempo: Razão e Emoçao*. 4th ed. São Paulo: Editora da Universidade de São Paulo, 2006.

Sarkis, Hashim. "Geo-Architecture: A Prehistory for an Emerging Aesthetic." *Harvard Design Magazine* 37 (2014): 124–151.

———. "Inscription: On the Surface of Exchange Between Writing, Ornament, and Tectonic in Contemporary Architecture." In *Histories of Ornament: From Global to Local*, edited by Gülru Necipoğlu and Alina Alexandra Payne, 34–45. New York: Princeton University Press, 2016.

Sarkis, Hashim, Roi Salgueiro Barrio, and Gabriel Kozlowski. "The World in the Architectural Imaginary." *New Geographies* 8 (2016): 176–193.

Sayn, Volker. *Modifiziertes Bewertungssystem (hier Hassloch System gennant) für den bewohnbaren Himmelskörper von Enine, dargestellt am Beispiel der Erde als Beitrag zur 'Planetarisierung'*. In Oswald Mathias Ungers's Studio Booklet 13 (May 1968).

Schaik, Martin van, and Otakar Máčel, eds. *Exit Utopia: Architectural Provocations, 1956–76*. Munich: Prestel, 2005.

Schalk, Meike. "The Architecture of Metabolism: Inventing a Culture of Resilience." *Arts* 3, no. 2 (2014): 279–297.

Schirren, Matthias. "Preface." In *Bruno Taut: Alpine Architecture: A Utopia*, edited by Bruno Taut and Matthias Schirren, 6–7. Munich: Prestel, 2004.

Schmied, Wieland. "Utopia Before One's Very Eyes." In *Raimund Abraham (Un)Built*, edited by Brigitte Groihofer, 226–227. New York: Springer, 1996.

Schmitt, Carl. *The Nomos of the Earth in the International Law of the Jus Publicum Europaeum*. Translated by Gary L. Ulmen. New York: Telos Press, 2003.

Schumacher, Patrik. "Formalism and Formal Research." In *Zaha Hadid: Early Paintings and Drawings*, edited by Amira Gad and Agnes Gryczkowska, 9–16. London: Koenig Books, 2017.

Schwarz, Rudolf. *Von der Bebauung der Erde*. Heidelberg: Verlag Lambert Schneider, 1949.

Schwarz-v. Raumer, Hans-Georg, and Antje Stokman. "GeoDesign-Approximations of a Catchphrase." In *Peer Reviewed Proceedings, Digital Landscape Architecture 2011: Teaching & Learning with Digital Methods & Tools*, edited by Buhmann, Ervin, Palmer, Tomlin, and Pietsch, 106–115. Dessau, Germany: Anhalt University of Applied Sciences, 2011.

Scott, Felicity D. "Involuntary Prisoners of Architecture." *October* 106 (2003): 75–101.

———. *Architecture or Techno-Utopia: Politics After Modernism*. Cambridge, MA: MIT Press, 2007.

Sendyk, Fernando, and Maria Pace Chiavari, eds. *Franco Purini: O que está feito está por fazer: anonimato, fragmento, descontinuidade*. Rio de Janeiro: Centro de Arquitetura e Urbanismo do Rio de Janeiro, 1998.

Senkevitch, Anatole. "Trends in Soviet Architectural Thought, 1917–1932: The Growth and Decline of the Constructivist and Rationalist Movements," PhD dissertation, Cornell University, 1974.

Serres, Michel. *Atlas*. Paris: Editions Julliard, 1994.

———. *The Natural Contract*. Translated by William R. Paulson and Elizabeth MacArthur. Ann Arbor: University of Michigan Press, 1995.

Shell, Marc. *Islandology: Geography, Rhetoric, Politics*. Stanford: Stanford University Press, 2014.

Shlapentokh, Vladimir. "The World Revolution as a Geopolitical Instrument of the Soviet Leadership." *Russian History/Histoire Russe* 26, no. 3 (1999): 315–334.

Shoshkes, Ellen. "Jaqueline Tyrwhitt: A Founding Mother of Modern Urban Design." *Planning Perspectives* 21, no. 2 (2006): 179–197.

Siracusa, Mariana. "Paul Otlet's Theory of Everything." *AA Files* 73 (2016): 48–57.

Sitney, Adams. "Dwelling-Place and Universe." In *Raimund Abraham (Un)Built*, edited by Brigitte Groihofer, 221–223. New York: Springer, 1996.

Sloterdijk, Peter. *In the World Interior of Capital: For a Philosophical Theory of Globalization*. Translated by Wieland Hoban. Cambridge, UK: Polity Press, 2014.

———. *Spheres 2: Globes: Macrospherology*. Translated by Wieland Hoban. Pasadena: Semiotext(e), 2014.

Smithson, Alison and Peter. *The Emergence of Team 10 out of C.I.A.M.: Documents*. AAGS Theory and History Papers. London: Architectural Association, 1983.

———. *Ordinariness and Light: Urban Theories 1952–1960 and Their Application in a Building Project 1963–1970*. London: Faber, 1970.

Smithson, Peter. "Conversation on Brutalism." *Zodiac* 4 (1959): 73–81.

———. "The Slow Growth of Another Sensibility. Architecture as Town Building," Lecture at Cornell University, 1972.

Søberg, Martin. "John Hejduk's Pursuit of an Architectural Ethos." *Footprint* 10/11 (2012): 113–128.

Solà-Morales i Rubió, Manuel de. *Las Formas de Crecimiento Urbano*. Barcelona: UPC, 1997.

Søberg, Martin. "The Culture of Description." *Perspecta* 25 (1989): 16–25.

Soleri, Paolo. "A Conversation with Paolo Soleri." In *Conversations with Paolo Soleri*, edited by Lissa McCullough, 67–80. New York: Princeton University Press, 1900.

———. *Arcosanti: An Urban Laboratory?* San Diego, CA: Avant Books, 1984.

———. "Esthetogenesis." In *Conversations with Paolo Soleri*, edited by Lissa McCullough, 56–61. New York: Princeton University Press, 1900.

———. "Responsibility of the Architectural Profession." In *Conversations with Paolo Soleri*, edited by Lissa McCullough, 33–36. New York: Princeton University Press, 1900.

———. *The Bridge Between Matter and Spirit Is Matter Becoming Spirit: The Arcology of Paolo Soleri*. Garden City, NY: Anchor Books, 1973.

———. "The City as Hyperorganism." In *Conversations with Paolo Soleri*, edited by Lissa McCullough, 37–40. New York: Princeton University Press, 1900.

———. "The Concept of Arcology." In *Conversations with Paolo Soleri*, edited by Lissa McCullough, 45–46. New York: Princeton University Press, 1900.

———. "The Urban Effect." In *Conversations with Paolo Soleri*, edited by Lissa McCullough, 41–44. New York: Princeton University Press, 1900.

Solomon R. Guggenheim Museum. *The Great Utopia: The Russian and Soviet Avant-Garde, 1915–1932*. New York: Guggenheim Museum, 1992.

Somol, Robert E. "One or Several Masters?" In *Hejduk's Chronotope*, edited by K. Michael Hays, 99–128. New York: Princeton Architectural Press, 1996.

Sörgel, Herman. *Atlantropa: Wesenszüge eines Projekts*. Künzelsau, Germany: Seemann, 1949.

Soria y Mata, Arturo. *La Cité Linéaire: Conception Nouvelle Pour l'Aménagement des Villes*. Translated by Georges Benoît-Lévy. Paris: Centre d'Études et de Recherches Architecturales, 1979.

———. "Comparación entre las Ciudades Jardines y las Ciudades Lineales." In *Arturo Soria y La Ciudad Lineal*, edited by George Rosenborough Collins and Carlos Flores. Madrid: Revista de Occidente, 1968.

———. "La Cuestión Social y la Cuidad Lineal (03/05/1883)." In *Arturo Soria y La Ciudad Lineal*, edited by George Rosenborough Collins and Carlos Flores, 189–193. Madrid: Revista de Occidente, 1968.

———. "La Cuidad Lineal (04/10/1882)." In *Arturo Soria y La Ciudad Lineal*, edited by George Rosenborough Collins and Carlos Flores, 170–173. Madrid: Revista de Occidente, 1968.

———. "La Cuidad Lineal en China." In *Arturo Soria y La Ciudad Lineal*, edited by George Rosenborough Collins and Carlos Flores, 307–311. Madrid: Revista de Occidente, 1968.

———. "La Línea Recta (02/27/1882)." In *Arturo Soria y La Ciudad Lineal*, edited by George Rosenborough Collins and Carlos Flores, 163–164. Madrid: Revista de Occidente, 1968.

———. "La Primera Ciudad Lineal Africana entre Ceuta y Tetuán. Carta abierta al Excmo. Sr. Conde de Romanones." In *Arturo Soria y La Ciudad Lineal*, edited by George Rosenborough Collins and Carlos Flores, 291–294. Madrid: Revista de Occidente, 1968.

———. "Nuevas Ideas para la Construcción de Ciudades." In *Arturo Soria y La Ciudad Lineal*, edited by George Rosenborough Collins and Carlos Flores, 299–311. Madrid: Revista de Occidente, 1968.

Soria y Puig, Arturo. *Hacia Una Teoría General de La Urbanización: Introducción a La Obra Teórica de Ildefons Cerdà (1815–1876)*. Madrid: Ediciones Turner, 1979.

Soulez, Antonia. "Otto Neurath or The Will to Plan." In *Encyclopedia and Utopia: The Life and Work of Otto Neurath*, edited by E. Nemeth and F. Stadler, 221–232. Dordrecht: Kluweer Academic Publishers, 1996.

Stalder, Laurent. "No Limits to Growth: The Global and Interplanetary Urban Models of Fritz Haller." *AA Files* 66 (2013): 145–152.

———. "Raster, Netzwerk, Register: Frit Hallers Totale Stadt." In *Fritz Haller: Architekt und Forscher*, edited by Laurent Stalder and Georg Vrachliotis, 92–107. Zurich: gta Verlag, 2015.

Stalder, Laurent, and Georg Vrachliotis, eds. *Fritz Haller: Architekt und Forscher*. Zurich: gta Verlag, 2015.

Stamps, Laura. "Constant's New Babylon: Pushing the Zeitgeist to Its Limits." In Laura Stamps et al., *Constant: New Babylon. To Us, Liberty*, 12–31. Ostfildern: Hatje Cantz Verlag, 2016.

———. "New Babylon—Destruction and Confusion." In Laura Stamps et al., *Constant: New Babylon. To Us, Liberty*, 190–205. Ostfildern: Hatje Cantz Verlag, 2016.

Stamps, Laura, et al. *Constant: New Babylon. To Us, Liberty*. Ostfildern: Hatje Cantz Verlag, 2016.

Starr, S. Frederick. "Visionary Town Planning During the Cultural Revolution." In *Cultural Revolution in Russia, 1928–1931*, edited by Sheila Fitzpatrick, 207–240. Bloomington: Indiana University Press, 1990.

Stauffer, Marie Theres. "Utopian Reflections, Reflected Utopias: Urban Designs by Archizoom and Superstudio." *AA Files* 47 (2002): 23–36.
Steele, James. *Contemporary Japanese Architecture: Tracing the Next Generation*. London: Routledge, 2017.
Steele, Tom. "Elisée Reclus and Patrick Geddes: Geographies of the Mind, the Regional Study in the Global Vision." *Refractions* 4 (1999). Available at http://www.haussite.net/haus.0/script/txt2000/04/reclus_geddes.html.
Steinberg, Marc, and Alexander Zahlten. *Media Theory in Japan*. Durham: Duke University Press, 2017.
Steiner, Frederick. "Healing the Earth: The Relevance of Ian McHarg's Work for the Future." *Human Ecology Review* 23, no. 2 (2017): 75–85.
Steiner, Hadas A. "Bathrooms, Bubbles and Systems: Archigram and the Landscapes of Transience." PhD dissertation, Massachusetts Institute of Technology, 2001.
Steinitz, Carl. *A Framework for Geodesign: Changing Geography by Design*. Redlands, CA: Esri, 2012.
———. "A Framework for Theory Applicable to the Education of Landscape Architects (and Other Environmental Design Professionals)." *Landscape Journal* 9, no. 2 (1990): 136–143.
———. "Beginning of Geodesign: A Personal Historical Perspective." In *Geodesign: Past, Present and* Future, edited by Esri, 4–14. Redlands, CA: Esri, 2013. Available at https://www.esri.com/library/ebooks/geodesign-past-present-future.pdf.
Steinitz, Carl, Paul Parker, and Lawrie Jordan. "Hand-Drawn Overlays—Their History and Prospective Uses." *Landscape Architecture* 66, no. 5 (1976): 444–455.
Steinmann, Martin, ed. *CIAM (Congrès Internationaux d'Architecture Moderne): Dokumente 1928–1939*. Basel: Birkhäuser, 1979.
Stengers, Isabelle. *Cosmopolitics*. Minneapolis: University of Minnesota Press, 2010.
Strum, Suzanne. *The Ideal of Total Environmental Control: Knud Lönberg-Holm, Buckminster Fuller, and the SSA*. Research in Architecture. London: Routledge, 2018.
Stuart, John A. "Unweaving Narrative Fabric: Bruno Taut, Walter Benjamin, and Paul Scheebart's *The Gray Cloth*." *Journal of Architectural Education* 53, no. 2 (1999): 61–73.
Superstudio. "Discorsi per Immagini / Speaking through Images." *Domus* 481 (December 1969): 44–48.
———. "Distruzione, Metamorfosi e Ricostruzione Degli Oggeti." *Argomenti e Immagini di Design* 2, no. 2–3 (June 1971): 115.
———. *Fragmente aus einem persönlichen Museum/ Fragments from a Personal Museum/ Frammenti da un Museum Personale*. Graz: Neue Galerie am Landemuseum Joanneum, 1973.
———. "Life." *Casabella* 367 (July 1972): 118–123.
Tafuri, Manfredo. *Architecture and Utopia: Design and Capitalist Development*. Cambridge MA: MIT Press, 1976.
———. *History of Italian Architecture: 1944–1985*. Cambridge, MA: MIT Press, 1989.
———. "L'Éphémère est éternel." In *Aldo Rossi: Teatro del Mondo*, edited by Manlio Brusatin and Alberto Prandi, 145–149. Venice: Cluva, 1982.
———. "Machine et Memoire: The City in the Work of Le Corbusier." In *Le Corbusier*, edited by H. Allen Brooks, 203–218. New York: Princeton University Press, 1989.

———. "Toward a Critique of Architectural Ideology." In *Architecture Theory Since 1968*, edited by K. Michael Hays, 2–35. Cambridge, MA: MIT Press, 1969.

Tafuri, Manfredo, and Francesco Dal Co. *Architettura Contemporanea*. Milan: Electa, 2009.

———. *Modern Architecture*. New York: Electa, 1986.

Tagliazucchi, Silvia. "Studi per una operante storia del territorio: Il libro incompiuto di Saverio Muratori." PhD dissertation, Università di Bologna, 2015.

Taut, Bruno. "Preface by the Editor." In *Bruno Taut: Alpine Architecture: A Utopia*, edited by Bruno Taut and Matthias Schirren, 118. Munich: Prestel, 2004.

Taut, Bruno, and Matthias Schirren, ed. *Bruno Taut: Alpine Architecture: A Utopia*. Munich: Prestel, 2004.

Taut, Bruno, and Ludovico Scarpa. "The Earth—A Good Home." Translated by Jane O. Newman and John H. Smith. *OPPOSITIONS* 14 (1978): 87–89.

Taut, Bruno, Paul Scheerbart, Erich Baron, and Adolf Behne. *Die Stadtkrone*. Jena: E. Diedrichs, 1919.

Tavares, Paulo. "In the Forest Ruins." *e-flux*, April 30, 2019. Available at https://www.e-flux.com/architecture/superhumanity/68688/in-the-forest-ruins/.

———. "The Geological Imperative: On the Political Ecology of the Amazonia's Deep History." In *Architecture in the Anthropocene: Encounters among Design, Deep Time, Science and Philosophy*, edited by Etienne Turpin, 209–240. Ann Arbor: Open Humanities Press, 2013.

Teige, Karel. "Mundaneum." *Stravba* 7, no. 10 (1929): n.p.

———. "Mundaneum." *OPPOSITIONS* 4 (1974): 589–598.

Tempel, Benno. "Preface." In Laura Stamps et al., *Constant: New Babylon. To Us, Liberty*, 6–11. Ostfildern: Hatje Cantz Verlag, 2016.

Todoli, Vicente, ed. *Richard Hamilton*. London: Tate Publishing, 2014.

Toraldo di Francia, Cristiano. "Memories of Superstudio." In *Superstudio: Life Without Objects*, edited by Peter Lang and William Menking, 65–72. Milan: Skira, 2003.

Torres-García, Joaquín. *Universalismo Constructivo: Contribución a la Unificación del Arte y la Cultura de América*. Buenos Aires: Poseidon, 1944.

Tresch, John. "Technological World-Pictures: Cosmic Things and Cosmograms." *Isis* 98, no. 1 (2007): 84–99.

Tret'iakov, Sergei. "Art in the Revolution and the Revolution in Art (Aesthetic Consumption and Production)." *October* 118, no. 17 and 18 (Fall 2006): 11–18.

Tsiambaos, Kostas. "Isotype Diagrams from Neurath to Doxiadis." *Architectural Research Quarterly* 16, no. 1 (2012): 49–57.

———. "The Creative Gaze: Doxiadis' Discovery." *Journal of Architecture* 14, no. 2 (2009): 255–275.

Unattributed. "Unitary Urbanism at the End of the 1950's." *Internationale Situationniste* 3 (December 1959). Available at http://www.notbored.org/uu.html

Unger, Roberto Mangabeira. *The Religion of the Future*. Cambridge, MA: Harvard University Press, 2014.

Ungers, Oswald Mathias. "Grossform." *Architecture d'Aujourd'Hui* 57–58 (1967): 108–119.

———. "Planning Criteria." *Lotus International* 11 (1976): 13.

Urban Theory Lab. "Operational Landscapes: Toward an Alternative Cartography of World Urbanization," 2013–2016. http://urbantheorylab.net/projects/operational-landscapes/.

———. "Urban Theory Lab, Extreme GSD Research Studio: 'Extreme Territories of Urbanization: Regulatory Restructuring,' Spring 2014." January 23, 2014. http://urbantheorylab.net/news/gsd-research-studio-extreme-territories-of-urbanization-regulatory-restructuring-spring-2014/.

Urrutia, Lawrence. *Projections: Anti-Materialism*. La Jolla, California: The La Jolla Museum of Art, 1970.

Van Acker, Wouter. "Internationalist Utopias of Visual Education: The Graphic and Scenographic Transformation of the Universal Encyclopaedia in the Work of Paul Otlet, Patrick Geddes, and Otto Neurath." *Perspectives on Science* 19, no. 1 (2011): 32–80.

Varnelis, Kazys. "Programming After Program: Archizoom's No-Stop City." *PRAXIS: Journal of Writing + Building* 8 (2006): 82–91.

Ven Eestern, Cornelis. "Prospekt für Die Funktionelle Stadt." Papers of Cornelis Van Eesteren, Netherlands Architecture Institute. n.d.

Vigano, Paola. *The Territories of Urbanism: The Project as Knowledge Producer*. Lausanne: EPFL Press, 2016.

Voigt, Wolfgang. *Atlantropa: Weltbauen am Mittelmeer: ein Architektentraum der Moderne*. Hamburg: Dölling und Galitz, 1998.

Vornskava, Alla. "Composing Form, Constructing the Unconscious: Empiriocriticism and Nikolai Ladovskii's 'Psychoanalytical Method' of Architecture at Vkhutemas." In *Architecture and the Unconscious*, edited by John Shannon Hendrix and Lorens Eyan Holm, 77–98. Farnham: Ashgate, 2016.

———. "Two Utopias of Georgii Krutikov's City of the Future." In *Writing Cities: Working Papers*, edited by Gunter Gassner, Adam Kaasa, and Katherine Robinson, 46–55. London: London School of Economics and Political Science, 2012.

Vossoughian, Nader. "Mapping the Modern City: Otto Neurath, the International Congress of Modern Architecture (CIAM), and the Politics of Information Design." *Design Issues* 22, no. 3 (Summer 2006): 48–65.

———. *Otto Neurath: The Language of the Global Polis*. Rotterdam: NAi Publishers, 2008.

Walsh, Victoria. "Seahorses, Grids and Calypso: Richard Hamilton's Exhibition Making in the 1950s." In *Richard Hamilton*, edited by Vicente Todoli, 61–92. London: Tate Publishing, 2014.

Water, Nigel. "GIS: History." In *the International Encyclopedia of Geography*, edited by Douglas Richardson, et al., vol. 6, 1–12. Hoboken, NJ: Wiley-Blackwell, 2017.

Welter, Volker. *Biopolis: Patrick Geddes and the City of Life*. Cambridge, MA: MIT Press, 2002.

Weststeijn, Willem G. "Aleksei Gan's Constructivism and Its Aftermath." *Avant Garde Critical Studies* 29 (2013): 373–387.

White, Dana. "The Apocalyptic Vision of Paolo Soleri." *Technology and Culture* 12, no. 1 (1971): 75–88.

Whyte, Iain Boyd. *Bruno Taut and the Architecture of Activism*. Cambridge Urban and Architectural Studies 6. Cambridge: Cambridge University Press, 1982.

———. "The Expressionist Utopia." *Mac Journal* 4 (1999): 256–270.

Whyte, William. *Ghent Planning Congress 1913: Premier Congrès International et Exposion Comparée des Villes*. Abingdon: Taylor and Francis, 2013.

Wigley, Mark. *Buckminster Fuller Inc.: Architecture in the Age of Radio*. Zurich: Lars Müller Publishers, 2015.

———. *Constant's New Babylon: The Hyper-Architecture of Desire*. Rotterdam: Witte de With, 1998.

———. "Extreme Hospitality." In Laura Stamps et al., *Constant: New Babylon. To Us, Liberty*, 38–49. Ostfildern: Hatje Cantz Verlag, 2016.

———. "Network Fever." *Grey Room* 4 (2001): 82–122.

———. "Paper, Scissors, Blur." In *the Activist Drawing: Retracing Situationist Architectures from Constant's New Babylon to Beyond*, edited by M. Catherine de Zegher, 27–56. New York: Drawing Center, 2001.

Wilkison, Gordon. *The Progress Report Austin: The Legends of Austin 2*. Texas Archive of the Moving Image, 1961.

Willkie, Wendell L. "Airways to Peace." *Bulletin of the Museum of Modern Art* 11, no. 1 (1943): 3–21.

Wisnik, Guilherme. "A Civilização Tropical e seu Contrário." In *Sergio Bernardes*, edited by Kykah Bernardes and Lauro Pereira Cavalcanti, 120–129. São Paolo: Artviva Editora, 2010.

Woertman, Sander. "The Distant Winking of a Star, or the Horror of the Real." In *Exit Utopia: Architectural Provocations, 1956–76*, edited by Martin van Schaik and Otakar Máčel, 146–155. Munich: Prestel, 2005.

Woods, Lebbeus. "Zaha Hadid's Drawings 1." *Lebbeus Woods* (blog), 2009. https://lebbeuswoods.wordpress.com/2009/03/23/zaha-hadids-drawings-1/.

World Wide Forum, Ecofys, and OMA AMO. "The Energy Report, 100% Renewable Energy for 2050," 2011, n.p.

*Zaha Hadid and Suprematism*. Ostfildern: Hatje Cantz Verlag, 2012.

Zegher, M. Catherine de. "Introduction." In *the Activist Drawing: Retracing Situationist Architectures from Constant's New Babylon to Beyond*, edited by M. Catherine de Zegher and Mark Wigley, 9–15. New York: Drawing Center, 2001.

Zegher, M. Catherine de, and Mark Wigley, eds. *The Activist Drawing: Retracing Situationist Architectures from Constant's New Babylon to Beyond*. New York: Drawing Center, 2001.

Zenetos, Takis Ch. *Electronic Urbanism—City Planning and Electronics Parallel Structures*. Athens: Architecture in Greece Press, 1969.

———. "Electronic Urbanism, City Planning and Electronics." *Architecture in Greece* 3 (1969): 114–125.

———. "Electronic Urbanism, Town Planning and Electronics." *Architecture in Greece* 7 (1973): 112–121.

———. "Electronic Urbanism, Town Planning and Electronics." *Architecture in Greece* 8 (1974): 122–127.

———. *Takis Ch. Zenetos, 1926–1977*. Athens: Architecture in Greece Press, 1978.

———. "Town and Dwelling in the Future. Town Planning in Space. A Study, 1962." *Architektonik* 42 (1963): 48–55.

# Image Credits

*Every effort has been made to contact the copyright holders of the materials used in this book. Any copyright holders we have been unable to reach or to whom inaccurate acknowledgment has been made are invited to contact the authors.*

*All other images not listed were drawn by our illustrators.*

**Akademie der Künste;**
Project 4; figures 1, 2, 3, 4.
**Angelo Bucci;**
Project 49; figures 1, 2, 3, 4.
**© Antonio Martinelli;**
Project 41; figure 3.
**The Archigram Archival Project, University of Westminster;**
Project 25; figures 1, 2, 3, 4.
**Archivo Histórico José Vial Armstrong, Escuela de Arquitectura y Diseño, Pontificia Universidad Católica de Valparaíso;**
Project 29; figures 1, 2, 3, 4, 5, 6.
**Arcosanti Archives;**
Project 34; figures 1, 2, 3, 4, 5, 6.
**Bibliothèque Nationale de France Département des Manuscrits;**
Project 3; figure 1.
**Biblioteca Civica d'Arte Luigi Poletti;**
Project 31; figures 1, 2, 3.
**Centre Pompidou, Paris. Courtesy of Marianne Homiridis;**
Project 24; figures 2, 3, 4, 5.
**© Constantinos and Emma Doxiadis Foundation;**
Project 23; figures 1, 2, 3, 4, 5.
**Courtesy of the Frances Loeb Library, Harvard University Graduate School of Design;**
Project 1; figures 1, 2, 3, 4, 5.
Project 18; figures 1, 4.
Project 46; figures 1, 2, 3, 4.
**Design Earth;**
Project 48; figures 1, 2, 3, 4.
**Deutsches Architekturmuseum;**
Project 6; figures 1, 2, 3, 4.
**© Eredi Aldo Rossi. Courtesy of Fondazione Aldo Rossi;**
Project 41; figure 1, 2.
**© Estate of John Hejduk / The Canadian Center for Architecture;**
Project 42; figures 1, 2, 3, 4.
**© The Estate of R. Buckminster Fuller, Courtesy of the Department of Special Collections, Stanford University Libraries;**
Project 6; figures 1, 2, 3, 4.
Project 14; figures 1, 2, 3, 4, 5.
**© The Estate of Yves Klein / ADAGP Paris;**
Project 22; figures 1, 2, 3, 4.
**Fondation Constant / © 2019 Artists Rights Society (ARS), New York / c/o Pictoright Amsterdam;**
Project 19; figure 1, 2, 3, 4.
**Fondation Le Corbusier / ADAGP Paris;**
Project 8; figures 3, 4, 5.
Project 15; figure 4.
**© Franco Purini;**
Project 43; figures 1, 2, 3, 4.
**Hatton Gallery Archive, Newcastle University;**
Project 18; figure 2.
**Courtesy of Kykah Bernardes;**
Project 28; figures 1, 2, 3, 4.
**Lazar Khidekel Family Archives;**
Project 5; figures 1, 2, 3, 4.
**Mundaneum, Brussels;**
Project 8; figures 1, 2.
Project 13; figure 2.
**© The Museum of Modern Art / Licensed by SCALA / Art Resource, NY;**
Project 27; figures 1, 2, 4.
Project 38; figures 1, 2.
Project 39; figure 1.
**Courtesy of Mutsuko Smith-Kikutake, Mitsunori Kikutake, and Yuki Kikutake;**
Project 21; figures 1, 2, 3, 4, 5.
**Nederlands Architectuurinstituut;**
Project 13; figure 1.

**Plan B Architecture & Urbanism;**
Project 50; figures 1, 2, 3, 4.
**Strathclyde University Archives;**
Project 2; figures 1, 2, 3, 4.
**SIAF/Cité de l'Architecture et du Patrimoine/Archives d'Architecture du XXe siècle;**
Project 3; figure 2, 3, 4.
**© Takis Ch. Zenetos Archive;**
Project 26; figure 1, 2, 3, 4, 5.
**T.O.P. Office. Courtesy of Luc Deleu;**
Project 44; figures 1, 2, 3.
**University of Pennsylvania;**
Project 17; figures 1, 2, 3, 4, 5, 6.
**Urban Theory Lab. Courtesy of Neil Brenner;**
Project 45; figures 1, 2, 3, 4.
**Volker Sayn;**
Project 32; figures 1, 2, 3, 4.
**Zaha Hadid Foundation;**
Project 40; figures 1, 2, 3.

*Digital scans have been made from the following books and reviews:*

**Arango, Jorge. *The Urbanization of the Earth*. Boston: Beacon Press, 1970. Reprinted by permission of Beacon Press, Boston;**
Project 20; figures 5, 6.
***Domus*, no. 470 (1969);**
Project 35; figures 1
***Domus*, no. 496 (1971);**
Project 36; figures 1, 2, 3, 4, 5.
***Edilizia Moderna* n.87-88;**
Project 30; figures 1, 2, 3, 4.
**Gilpin, William. *The Cosmopolitan Railway: Compacting and Fusing Together All the World's Continents*. San Francisco, CA: The History Company, 1890;**
Project 24; figure 1.
**Gozak, Andrei, and Andrei Leonidov. *Ivan Leonidov: The Complete Works*. New York: Rizzoli, 1988;**
Project 9; figures 1, 2.
**Gutnov, Alexei, A. Baburov, V. Djumenton, S. Kharitonova, I. Lezeva, and S. Sadovskij. *The Ideal Communist City*. New York: George Braziller, 1971;**
Project 20; figures 1, 2, 3, 4.
**Khan-Magomedov, S. O. *Viktor Kalmykov*. Moscow: Russkii Avangard, 2011;**
Project 12; figure 1, 2, 3, 4, 5.
**Khan-Magomedov, S. O. *Pioneers of Soviet Architecture: The Search for New Solutions in the 1920s and 1930s*. Translated by Alexander Lieven. New York: Rizzoli, 1987;**
Project 10; figures 1, 2, 3, 4.
**Khan-Magomedov, S. O. *Georgii Krutikov: The Flying City and Beyond*. Translated by Christina Lodder. Barcelona: Tenov Books, 2015;**
Project 11; figures 3, 4, 5, 6.
**Khan-Magomedov, S. O. *Georgii Krutikov*. Moscow: Russkii Avangard, 2008;**
Project 11; figures 1, 2.
**Ley, Sabrina van der, and Markus Richter. *Megastructure Reloaded: Visionäre Stadtentwürfe der Sechzigerjahre Reflektiert von Zeitgenössischen Künstlern = Visionary Architecture and Urban Design of the Sixties Reflected by Contemporary Artists*. Ostfildern: Hatje Cantz, 2008;**
Project 35; figures 2, 3, 4, 5
***Sovremennaia arkhitektura*, no. 3, 1929;**
Project 9; figures 3, 4.
**Schwarz, Rudolf. *Von der Bebauung der Erde*. Heidelberg: Verlag Lambert Schneider, 1949;**
Project 16; figures 1, 2, 3, 4.
**Vossoughian, Nader. Otto Neurath: *The Language of the Global Polis. Rotterdam*: NAi Publishers, 2008;**
Project 13; figure 3.

**Hashim Sarkis** is Dean of the School of Architecture and Planning (SA+P) at MIT and principal architect in Hashim Sarkis Studios. He is Curator of the 2020 Venice Architectural Biennale. **Roi Salgueiro Barrio**, an architect and urbanist and founder of RSAU, is an instructor and Research Scientist at the MIT SA+P. **Gabriel Kozlowski**, an architect and curator, is an instructor and Research Associate at the MIT SA+P and was cocurator of the Brazilian pavilion at the 2018 Venice Architectural Biennale.